KT-227-378

Brief Contents

Contents

CONSUMER BEHAVIOR: SCIENCE AND PRACTICE

Frank R. Kardes
University of Cincinnati

Thomas W. Cline
Saint Vincent College

Maria L. Cronley
Miami University

SOUTH-WESTERN
CENGAGE Learning™

Australia • Brazil • Japan • Korea • Mexico • Singapore • Spain • United Kingdom • United States

SOUTH-WESTERN
CENGAGE Learning™

Consumer Behavior: Science and Practice
Frank R. Kardes, Thomas W. Cline,
Maria L. Cronley

Executive Vice President and Publisher, Business
& Computers: Jonathan Hulbert

Vice President of Editorial, Business:
Jack W. Calhoun

Editor-in-Chief: Melissa Acuña

Executive Editor: Mike Roche

Developmental Editor: Julie Klooster

Vice President of Marketing, Business &
Computers: Bill Hendee

Marketing Coordinator: Shanna Shelton

Senior Content Project Manager:
Colleen A. Farmer

Media Editor: John Rich

Frontlist Buyer, Manufacturing:
Miranda Klapper

Production Service and Compositor:
S4Carlisle Publishing Services

Senior Art Director: Stacy Jenkins Shirley

Cover Image: Shutterstock

B/W Image: Getty Images/Hisham Ibrahim

Image Rights Acquisitions Account
Manager: John Hill

Photo Researcher: Darren Wright

Sr. Text Rights Acquisitions Account Manager:
Mardell Glinski Schultz

Text Permissions Researcher: Sarah D'Stair

For product information and technology assistance, contact us at
Cengage Learning Customer & Sales Support, 1-800-354-9706

For permission to use material from this text or product, submit all requests online at **www.cengage.com/permissions**
Further permissions questions can be emailed to
permissionrequest@cengage.com

Library of Congress Control Number: 2009939851

International Student Edition ISBN-13: 978-0-538-74686-1
International Student Edition ISBN-10: 0-538-74686-6

Cengage Learning International Offices

Asia
cengageasia.com
tel: (65) 6410 1200

Australia/New Zealand
cengage.com.au
tel: (61) 3 9685 4111

Brazil
cengage.com.br
tel: (011) 3665 9900

India
cengage.co.in
tel: (91) 11 30484837/38

Latin America
cengage.com.mx
tel: +52 (55) 1500 6000

UK/Europe/Middle East/Africa
cengage.co.uk
tel: (44) 207 067 2500

Represented in Canada by Nelson Education, Ltd.
nelson.com
tel: (416) 752 9100 / (800) 668 0671

For product information: **www.cengage.com/international**
Visit your local office: **www.cengage.com/global**
Visit our corporate website: **www.cengage.com**

Printed in China
2 3 4 5 6 7 16 15 14 13

**PART ❹   The Influence of the Social Environment
and Contemporary Strategies for Marketers 254**

Chapter   12 | The Role of Values and Cultures 259

CHEATERS PROSPER 259

Preface

Businesses spend enormous amounts of time, money, and other resources on monitoring, predicting, understanding, and influencing the behavior of consumers. Success depends on convincing consumers to use their products and services rather than competitors' offerings. Toward this end, consumers are inundated by marketing communications in the traditional media (e.g., television, radio, print advertising, and direct mail), the new media (e.g., Internet), and in retail stores (e.g., packaging and point-of-purchase displays). However, effective marketing requires an in-depth understanding of the variables that capture the attention and interest of consumers; that influence how consumers acquire, retain, and update product knowledge; and that influence how consumers use product knowledge as a basis for judgment and choice.

Consumer behavior encompasses all consumer activities associated with the purchase, use, and disposal of goods and services, including the consumer's emotional, mental, and behavioral responses that precede, determine, or follow these activities. The unwavering focus on the consumer is the unique contribution of marketing that distinguishes this activity from the other business functions (e.g., accounting, finance, production, management). An in-depth understanding of consumers is needed to develop better products and services, to market these products and services more effectively, and to achieve a sustainable competitive advantage.

This book provides in-depth, scientifically grounded explanations of consumer behavior without sacrificing breadth. We discuss a variety of "classic" consumer behavior topics, including consumer information processing, consumer decision making, persuasion, and the role of culture and society on consumer behavior. In addition, we address some novel topics that enhance the usefulness and impact of the text, including an emphasis on international and ethical perspectives, an examination of "contemporary" or "state-of-the-art" media, and a discussion of online tactics and branding strategies. In summary, we aim to strike a balance among theoretical concepts, research findings, and applied marketing examples to achieve a strong consumer-focused, strategy-oriented approach.

Organization of the Book

This book is organized in five main parts. Part One focuses on consumer behavior and marketing strategy. It explores what consumer behavior comprises, how it fits into the larger field of marketing, and how marketers study it. Part One also explains how marketing managers use their research-based knowledge about consumers to develop more effective segmentation and positioning strategies. Effective strategic decisions related to segmentation and positioning are essential for successful marketing practice.

Part Two focuses on consumer decision making, or how consumers use their knowledge about products and services to choose the brands they buy. The chapters in Part Two break down consumer decision making and examine each step in detail.

Part Three focuses on consumer information processing, or the steps or stages of thinking and reasoning that influence how consumers acquire, retain, and revise product knowledge. Here, we take an internal view of the consumer to examine how these fickle, stubborn, passionate, and fascinating creatures interact with the marketing world by processing information and making decisions.

Part Four focuses on consumer social influences and contemporary strategies for marketers. Part Four explains the external influences of culture, values, and referent others on consumers and their behaviors. It also explains how to reach consumers more effectively, how to develop more effective online tactics, and how to develop more effective branding strategies.

Part Five focuses on common biases and errors in managerial decision making and how to avoid them. Even experts are susceptible to a wide range of decision-making biases that can hurt business. A clearer understanding of managers' decision-making processes helps managers to avoid some common pitfalls.

Finally, it should be noted that although the chapters are presented in separate sections in this book, all chapters, topics, and themes are related to all the others.

Pedagogical Enhancements

We believe that students work best when they can see phenomena from all angles: when they can understand what theories and concepts mean, see how they integrate with other concepts, and see how they are applied to smart business practice. To help students understand, apply, and integrate the concepts of consumer behavior in terms of real companies and marketing situations, this book is filled with a variety of features, with a heavy emphasis on interesting examples, strong visuals, and applied exercises.

Part Features

Each of the first four parts of the book begins with an interview with one or two well-respected consumer researchers to stimulate student interest. This helps set the tone for each part, providing a "big picture" of its theme that helps students understand the relevance of the topics in the part.

At the end of the last chapter in each part is a link to a short video case study and set of applied questions to accompany the video. The videos are real-world examples that illustrate topics found in the parts. The accompanying questions are designed to apply chapter concepts. These videos can be found on the book companion site, http://www.cengage.com/international.

Chapter Features

Each chapter includes a variety of aids to enrich student interaction and learning, including:

- **Learning Objectives.** A list of key concepts and objectives for each chapter.

- **Opening Vignette.** A mini-case using a real company, product, or situation to bring the subject of the chapter alive.

- **Marketing in Action.** A feature that illustrates the use of various consumer behavior concepts in the practice of marketing for a real company, product, or situation.

- **Eye on International.** A feature that discusses the use of consumer behavior concepts in real companies, products, or situations in international contexts.

- **Ethics.** A feature to increase student sensitivity to ethical issues and to stimulate classroom discussion.

- **Advertisements, Websites, Photos, Charts, and Illustrations.** Specific examples to show students how companies attempt to persuade and influence consumers. Numerous photographs and illustrations of products, package designs, and consumers in action increase student interest and involvement in the material.

- **Chapter Summary.** An overview of key topics and concepts. Students can check their comprehension of the material by reviewing the summary.

- **Key Terms.** A list of the key concepts presented in the chapter, which can be used to reinforce students' comprehension.

- **Review and Discussion.** Questions to encourage students to think critically about what they have just read.

- **Short Application Exercises.** Questions help students apply the knowledge they have gained from reading the chapter.

- **Managerial Application.** A mini-case problem requiring the use of multiple concepts discussed in the chapter.

The *Consumer Behavior* Resource Package

Teaching consumer behavior is an exciting and challenging task. A comprehensive set of ancillary materials has been created to support instructors.

FOR THE INSTRUCTOR

Instructor's Manual

This teaching tool provides suggestions and additional assignments designed to supplement the textbook and help enhance the classroom experience. Each chapter includes the following materials:

- Learning objectives and teaching tips
- Lecture outlines
- Answers to review and discussion questions
- Suggested classroom activities and assignments

The Instructor's Manual can be downloaded from the book companion site, http://www.cengage.com/international.

Test Bank

A comprehensive test bank is available to assist instructors in assessing student learning. The test bank contains more than 1,200 questions, including a mix of:

- Definitional questions that test knowledge of concepts
- Conceptual questions that test the ability to recognize concepts and relate to situations
- Applied questions that test the ability to integrate and apply concepts

Question formats include multiple-choice, true/false, and essay questions for each chapter.

Recent pressure on faculty and institutions to implement and report on learning outcome requirements by the AACSB and other accreditation bodies is a challenge in higher education. The development of *Consumer Behavior* has given us the opportunity to help faculty meet these needs. We have tagged test items with general business and marketing discipline outcomes that allow you to more easily produce learning outcome reports for accreditation purposes. An electronic version of the test bank is available and allows instructors to add, delete, edit, and easily generate multiple forms of a test. The Test Bank can be downloaded from the book companion site.

ExamView

Available on the book companion site, ExamView contains all the questions in the Test Bank tagged as described above. This program is easy-to-use test creation software compatible with Microsoft® Windows®. Instructors can add or edit questions, instructions, and answers, and select questions (randomly or numerically) by previewing them on the screen. Instructors can also create and administer quizzes online over the Internet, a local-area network (LAN), or a wide-area network (WAN).

PowerPoint® Presentation

A comprehensive set of PowerPoint® slides is available to adopters of the textbook. These chapter-by-chapter slides include important figures, tables, and graphs taken directly from the text, as well as an overview of the key concepts of each chapter. User friendly, the PowerPoint® slides can be used "as is" or integrated with the instructor's own PowerPoint® presentations. Instructors can modify or delete any slide or add their own slides to the existing set. In addition, instructors may choose to share the slides with students by uploading them to the school's network. The PowerPoint® slides can be downloaded from the book companion site.

Instructor Book Companion Site

http://www.cengage.com/international.

Specially designed Web content provides additional information, guidance, videos, and activities for instructors. There is additional information for chapter 12 regarding demographics and subculture, along with student exercises for these topics to enhance learning on the site.

For the Student

http://www.cengage.com/international.

Specially designed Web content provides additional information, guidance, and activities for students. The student book companion site includes key terms, learning objectives, videos, interactive review quizzes, and a resource center providing useful links to other consumer behavior-related websites.

Acknowledgments

We would like to warmly acknowledge the many helpful comments and insights from David Ackerman, Ph.D. (California State University—Northridge), Ronald J. Adams, Ph.D. (University of North Florida), Jeri Mullins Beggs (Illinois State University),

Nivein A. Behairy, Ph.D. (University of California—Irvine), Drew Boyd (Ethicon EndoSurgery), Deborah L. Cowles, Ph.D. (Virginia Commonwealth University), Susan Emens (Kent State University), Vicki Blakney Eveland, DBA, (Mercer University), Annette D. Forti, DBA (SUNY College at Old Westbury), Dorothy Harpool (Wichita State University), Curtis Haugtvedt, Ph.D. (Ohio State University), Dale F. Kehr (University of Memphis), Michael Lynn, Ph.D. (Cornell University), Susan Powell Mantel, Ph.D. (Ball State University), Havva J. Meric, Ph.D. (East Carolina University), Bruce E. Pfeiffer, Ph.D. (University of New Hampshire), Andrew J. Rohm, Ph.D. (Northeastern University), Joel Saegert, Ph.D. (The University of Texas at San Antonio), and Eric Yorkston, Ph.D. (Texas Christian University). Finally, we would like to acknowledge the many undergraduate and graduate students we have taught over the years who have helped shape our thinking for this textbook.

About the Authors

Frank R. Kardes *Courtesy of Frank Kardes* Thomas W. Cline *Courtesy of Thomas Cline* Maria L. Cronley *Courtesy of Maria Cronley*

FRANK R. KARDES

Frank R. Kardes is the Donald E. Weston Professor of Marketing at the College of Business at the University of Cincinnati. He is a recipient of the Distinguished Scientific Achievement Award of the Society for Consumer Psychology, and a Fellow of the American Psychological Association, the American Psychological Society, the Society for Consumer Psychology, and the Society for Personality and Social Psychology. His research focuses on omission neglect, consumer judgment and inference processes, persuasion and advertising, and consumer and managerial decision making. He has published in many leading scientific journals and is frequently invited to present his research at leading universities throughout the world—including Wharton, Yale, Cornell, Chicago, Northwestern, Michigan, the Australian Graduate School of Management, the London Business School, the Hong Kong University of Science and Technology, and INSEAD (France). Dr. Kardes was an Editor of the *Journal of Consumer Psychology*, *Advances in Consumer Research*, and the *Handbook of Consumer Psychology*, and is currently an Associate Editor of the *Journal of Consumer Research* and the *Journal of Consumer Psychology*. He also serves on the editorial boards of *Behavioral Marketing Abstracts*, the *International Journal of Research in Marketing*, and *Marketing Letters*.

Thomas W. Cline

Thomas W. Cline is Professor of Marketing in the Alex G. McKenna School at Saint Vincent College, where he teaches courses in consumer behavior, marketing research, advertising and promotion, strategic marketing, and statistical methods. He is a recipient of the International Teaching Excellence Award from the Association of College Business Schools and Programs. Dr. Cline has twenty years experience as a marketing research consultant, specializing in surveys, experimental designs, and focus groups. He earned a Ph.D. at the University of Cincinnati and an MBA from the University of Virginia. Dr. Cline has published numerous articles in academic journals, including the *Journal of Advertising*, *Journal of Consumer Psychology*, and *Journal of Economic Psychology*, *Psychology and Marketing*, and *Journal of Marketing Communications*. Dr. Cline is widely cited in the popular press, including *USA Today*, *Psychology Today*, *CBS News*, *The LA Times*, *MSNBC*, and *The Washington Times*. Dr. Cline also serves as head coach for the men's and women's golf teams for Saint Vincent College, hosted at Arnold Palmer's Latrobe Country Club in Latrobe, PA.

Maria L. Cronley

Maria L. Cronley is an Associate Professor of Marketing in the Farmer School of Business at Miami University, where she teaches undergraduate and graduate courses in Consumer Behavior, Customer Acquisition, and Marketing Strategy. She earned her Ph.D. in Marketing from the University of Cincinnati and brings several years of industry experience to the field. Her primary research interests center on consumer judgment and decision processes, with specific emphasis in the areas of inference, biased processing, and persuasion. She sits on the *Journal of Consumer Psychology* Editorial Review Board and has published numerous articles in scholarly journals, including the *Journal of Consumer Psychology, Journal of Consumer Research, Journal of Business Research, Journal of Economic Psychology, Advances in Consumer Research,* and the *Journal of Experimental Psychology: Applied.* She has received over three dozen awards and grants for her scholarship and teaching. Dr. Cronley also serves on the Executive Board for the *Society for Consumer Psychology* and co-chairs the Training and Education Committee for the Society that oversees the prestigious national SCP Dissertation Proposal Competition.

CONSUMER BEHAVIOR: SCIENCE AND PRACTICE

Consumer Focused Strategy

CHAPTERS

Cheryl Stallworth: Navone Studios

Chief Executive Officer
GREENFIELD CONSULTING GROUP

Cheryl Stallworth is the Chief Executive Officer for the Greenfield Consulting Group, a global marketing research firm that specializes in qualitative research methodologies. The Greenfield Consulting Group is part of Millward Brown, one of the top ten global marketing research agencies. As a marketing generalist with expertise in qualitative research methodologies, Greenfield Consulting Group focuses on using insights to develop effective marketing strategies.

Why is it important for companies to acquire a deep understanding of their consumers?

Without a deep understanding of consumers it is impossible to meet their expectations. Going beyond the fundamental "functional" needs, e.g., the need for food and shelter, it is important to understand deeper needs like the need for social acceptance. These are the higher order needs that only surface when marketers dig deeper into brand relationships and how these relationships allow consumers to express themselves. For example, a consumer can tell me that they are purchasing a car because they need transportation. A deeper exploratory of their *real* need is to convey a certain image . . . so this consumer doesn't need just a *car* . ww. . they need a Toyota Prius because they want to be accepted within the tribe of people that are environmentally conscious opinion leaders.

What research techniques do you use to learn about your consumers?

Our company specializes in qualitative research, so these are tools that are not designed to be projectable to large populations. They are designed to allow us to probe deeply into motivations and desires. In addition to focus groups, we practice "qualographies" which are "ethnographic-like" tools that enable us to actively observe and interact with people in real life environments like their kitchens, or in-store in order to:

- Understand how people interact with categories and brands in a socio-cultural context
- Understand people's rituals, artifacts, and folklore to help de-codify the role and meaning of brands

We also use a number of digital tools that enable us to speak to creative consumers across broad geographies to understand trends, social development, and differences in attitudes based on geographic influencers.

Basic focus groups are a terrific way of letting consumers "play off of" perceptions relative to categories and brands. In order to understand the strengths and weaknesses of a brand's equity, we can create a "consumer brawl" in a focus group with consumers taking opposing sides to "argue" the benefits or drawbacks of a brand and highlight issues and opportunities for positioning enhancement.

These are just examples of the many tools that can be employed to "dig deeply."

How can knowledge about consumer behavior be used to develop more effective segmentation strategies?

Consumers can be clustered based on similar attitudes and behavior to determine which clusters are most similar. This then enables marketers to develop messages that appeal to specific clusters. The size of clusters is often quantified to determine if a viable business opportunity exists.

How can knowledge about consumer behavior be used to develop more effective positioning strategies?

Understanding consumer motivations, attitudes and ensuing behavior helps determine the role of a category or brand in the consumer's world. Uncovering the brand's role provides the context or language for talking about that brand in a way that makes sense and is useful for the consumer. So for example, understanding that a consumer feels better about the world that they are living in when they are doing something active to care for the environment, taps into a basic need for well-being (for them and their family). Not saying that Toyota has done this, but a brand like Toyota Pruis can become part of the consumer's "personal toolkit" of products that help them to achieve a personal sense of well-being. Thus, this can then be a position for Prius to play in, based on an insight that well-being is an important attribute/feeling/state-of-mind for environmentally conscious consumers.

How can knowledge about consumer behavior be used to help consumers make better choices?

This knowledge can help marketers develop products and shape messages that actually meet people's needs instead of creating products that "trick" consumers into buying them based on gimmickry. In other words, identifying and delivering against *real* needs allow marketers to develop sustainable long-term relationships with consumers, which is much more efficient and profitable in the long run.

THE STUDY OF CONSUMER BEHAVIOR

OBJECTIVES *After studying this chapter, you will be able to...*

1 | Define consumer behavior.

2 | Explain why it is important to understand consumer behavior.

3 | Describe how the study of consumer behavior has evolved as a scientific field of study.

4 | Discuss how consumer behavior is specifically examined and measured through marketing research.

5 | Provide examples of various methods for collecting consumer research data.

REALITY TELEVISION WORKS FOR CONSUMERS AND MARKETERS

Reality programming had its humble beginnings in MTV's *The Real World*, now the longest

running reality television drama with 22 seasons over 17 years, as of this book's writing. Today,

blockbuster challenge shows, such as CBS's *Survivor* and Fox's *American Idol*, underscore reality

programming as a legitimate and predominant genre of television entertainment that is not

going to go away, according to many.[1] Indeed, the most popular reality TV programs, such as

Survivor, American Idol, and *The Bachelorette*, have been among the top-rated shows over the last

several seasons. Every major American television network and cable network has produced at

least one reality show; there are well over 100 of them currently on the airwaves.[2] Even the Public

Broadcasting System has joined in with their *Colonial House* and *1900's House* series, where

participants don period costumes and try to live within the era. Furthermore, reality television isn't produced just for American viewers' tastes. *Trading Rooms* (like the American *Trading Spaces*) and *Bargain Hunt* (an antique purchasing contest) appear on UK television, and *Australian Idol* and *Big Brother Italy* (similar to their U.S. counterparts) are popular in those countries.

Reality TV programming is a product, just like t-shirts and coffee, and consumers can't seem to get enough of it. But why do consumers keep watching? This is one type of question that consumer behavior researchers are interested in answering: why are consumers continually and passionately tuning in to watch a woman in search of Mr. Right, dating a group of eligible bachelors and weeding them out one by one? According to consumer behavior researchers, reality TV programs offer several benefits to consumers, including satisfying their fundamental voyeuristic tendencies. "We all like to watch people in situations where we ourselves might be pressured or tense. . .It is a safe way of experiencing a socially traumatic event. . .We can vicariously feel what they are feeling but at a safe distance," says Professor Kip Williams of Macquarie University.[3] We also role-play with ourselves in the context of the show, imagining how we might react in a similar situation compared to the show participants, which researchers say, can teach us to be self-improving and improve feelings of self-worth, like learning how to decorate our space on a dime, stand up to our peers, or navigate the world of business.[4]

Reality TV also satisfies the notion that anyone can achieve fame—if only for "fifteen minutes," and provides the enjoyment of rooting for the underdogs of life, believing that the average guy really can get the beautiful girl, or the skinny redhead from nowhere can become a superstar, for instance.

Knowing that these shows satisfy consumers and keep them viewing is the biggest reason television producers keep churning them out. But there are also lots of reasons for marketing executives to love reality programming, the most obvious of which is that people are watching, and high ratings mean that the advertisements are also potentially viewed. Who is watching is also important. Reality television appeals most to older teenagers and young adults, highly desirable and sought-after groups of consumers.[5]

Another added benefit of reality programming is that marketers can place their products in the settings of the program, allowing consumers to view the products in the contexts of everyday living. These subtle product endorsements can't be tuned out like an advertisement; they appear to consumers as unsolicited. The judges on *American Idol* drink from Coca-Cola cups; the *Trading Spaces* crew cleans up with a Swiffer mop; and the kids on *The Real World* drink Starbucks coffee. In fact, *product placement* is so popular (thanks in large part to reality TV programming) that Nielsen Media Research began tracking products that appear in television programming in 2003.[6]

Finally, reality programs are often cheaper to produce than other forms of programming, such as dramas or situation comedies, so an advertiser can afford to sponsor a show, place products in the show, run 30-second commercials during the breaks, and block competitors from running advertisements. Coca-Cola is reported to have paid $35 million in one season for its role on Fox's *American Idol.*[7] And the profits don't end there. There are instant messaging and phone charges for voting, cross promotions on websites, and show gear for sale. Who doesn't want a buff from *Survivor?*

With the winning combination of consumer devotion and a surplus of revenue-generating opportunities, reality TV is a phenomenon that shows how consumers' behaviors can influence an entire industry.

People engage in behaviors as consumers on a daily (even hourly) basis. What purchases have you made in the last few days? Maybe you bought a cup of coffee or something more expensive and long-lasting, like a new cell phone or a new outfit. What were you thinking when you made the purchase? What were you feeling? Even if you didn't actually buy something, you were probably exposed to marketing information in the form of advertisements, product information on packages, opinions from friends or family, and brand symbols on almost everything. Simply being exposed to marketing information is a form of consumer behavior, albeit a passive one. Consumers devote a great deal of effort, time, and material wealth to evaluating products and services and purchasing and using products of all kinds. Thus, people's behavior as consumers is a critical component of their everyday lives. In our role as consumers, we define our world and our place in it; we interact with the world and collectively, we even shape and change that world, creating phenomena like reality TV.

(OBJECTIVE 1)

What Is Consumer Behavior?

Not many years ago, when students opened a textbook on consumer behavior, they read that consumer behavior (usually called buyer behavior) involves the study of how consumers decide to buy products. While this definition is accurate, it is an inadequate description of the full scope of activities in which consumers engage prior to purchase and during and after consumption. Contemporary definitions are much broader and try to capture the full range of consumer activities. **Consumer behavior** entails all consumer activities associated with the purchase, use, and disposal of goods and services, including the consumer's emotional, mental, and behavioral responses that precede, determine, or follow these activities (see Figure 1.1).

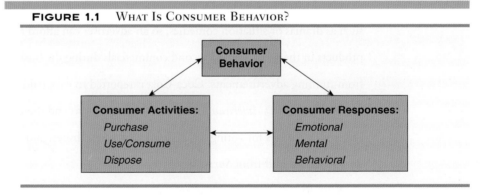

FIGURE 1.1   WHAT IS CONSUMER BEHAVIOR?

This definition covers a lot of ground. Let's break down the definition and examine consumers, consumer activities, and consumer responses more closely.

Consumers: Individual versus Organizational

The term "consumer" can describe either individual or organizational consumers. **Individual consumers** purchase goods and services to satisfy their own personal needs and wants or to satisfy the need and wants of others. Purchases for others include satisfying household uses, such as filling the family car with gasoline or paying the home's electric bill; gift purchases, such as buying a birthday gift for a brother; or charitable contributions, such as buying cookies from a Girl Scout or a raffle ticket at a school fundraiser. Individual consumers come in all ages, life stages, and social backgrounds;

they range from the six-year-old boy begging his mother for green ketchup in the grocery aisle to the 20-something college graduate renting her first apartment to the retired couple in their 70s browsing in antique shops while on vacation.

Organizational consumers purchase goods and services in order to:

- produce other goods or services
- resell them to other organizations or to individual consumers
- help manage and run their organization[8]

For example, Starbucks Coffee purchases coffee beans, brewing equipment, and paper cups in order to produce and offer its products. The company also purchases (and repackages) coffee beans to resell to individual consumers and other organizations, such as restaurants and grocery stores. Finally, Starbucks purchases office equipment, uniforms, and cleaning supplies, and may even hire a tax accounting firm, all to help keep the organization running smoothly.

Organizational consumers include for-profit firms, such as manufacturers, farmers, financial institutions, wholesalers, and retailers, and not-for-profit businesses, such as charities, political groups, and civic clubs. Local, state, and federal government agencies and other public institutions like schools, hospitals, and libraries are also organizational consumers. Although organizational consumer behavior is an important area of study, this book concentrates on individual consumer behavior.

Now that we understand who consumers are, let's examine consumer activities as they relate to our definition of consumer behavior.

Consumer Activities

Consumer behavior is broken down into purchase, use, and disposal activities. Categorizing consumer behavior by type of activity is useful because consumers' responses to stimuli may differ depending on whether they are purchasing, using, or disposing of a single product or service. For example, when leading up to purchase, a long line outside a night club is a positive factor in evaluating that club. Long lines imply that everyone wants to go there, and that the club is probably very good. But, after you have purchased your ticket, that long line is no longer a desirable factor, as you impatiently wait to get in. Furthermore, once you make it to the door, that long line ahead of you now means that the club is overly crowded, and therefore, a lot less appealing. So, from this example, categorizing activities by whether they occur prior to purchase versus during use shows how consumer responses can change significantly within a situation. Before we closely examine consumers' responses, let's first consider consumer purchase, use, and disposal activities in more detail.

Purchase activities are those through which consumers acquire goods and services. Purchase activities also include everything done leading up to the purchase, such as gathering and evaluating information about the product or service and choosing where to make the purchase. The purchase method and any additional services desired—home delivery and installation, and extended warranties, for instance—also influence purchase activities. So too are factors unique to the situation, such as the atmosphere of a store, the design of a website, the reason for the purchase, and the amount of time the consumer devotes to the buying decision.

Use activities describe where, when, and how consumption takes place. For example, do consumers immediately consume the product after purchase, like an ice cream cone or a haircut, or do they delay consumption, such as when they buy new clothing for a

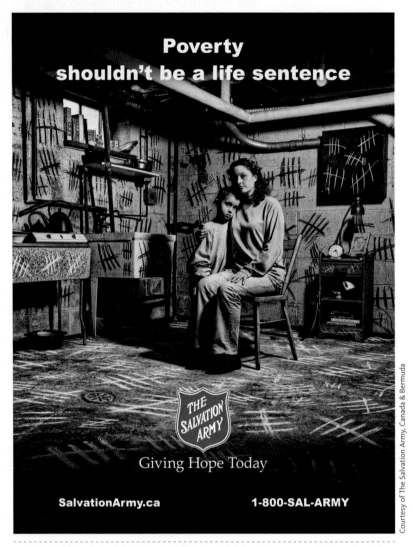

Courtesy of The Salvation Army, Canada & Bermuda

Donating gently used products to charitable organizations is one type of disposal activity.

future occasion or an airline ticket? Is the product consumed as part of a special event, such as going on vacation or attending a wedding, or as part of a special occasion, such as a holiday or birthday? Is the entire product consumed before disposal, such as a movie theater ticket or a battery, or is some left unconsumed, such as chewing gum or ink remaining in a toner cartridge?

Finally, *disposal activities* are the ways consumers get rid of products and/or packaging after consumption, and include discarding products, recycling, reuse, and resale. For example, sorting biodegradable trash, giving outgrown clothing to charity, and using paper grocery bags for book covers are recycling and reuse behaviors. Resale opportunities, like garage sales, classified ads, and flea markets have met their match in Internet auction sites like eBay.

Consumer Responses

Central to our definition of consumer behavior are consumers' emotional, mental, and behavioral responses to goods and their marketing.

Emotional responses (also called *affective responses*) reflect a consumer's emotions, feelings, and moods. For example, when a consumer buys his first car, both excitement and uncertainty are probably among his affective responses.

Mental responses (also referred to as *cognitive responses*) include a consumer's thought processes, opinions, beliefs, attitudes, and intentions about products and services. Weighing the pros and cons of financing a new car, making a mental list of attributes the car should have, and imagining oneself driving that car are some of the cognitive processes a consumer might experience in purchasing a new automobile. Mental responses can be evaluative, involving making a judgment that assigns value to something. They can also be non-evaluative, involving thinking about something without making a value judgment. Cognitive responses can be very specific and refer to one brand or even one attribute of that brand; they can also be very broad and deal with entire categories of products.

Finally, *behavioral responses* include a consumer's overt decisions and actions during the purchase, use, and disposal activities identified earlier. To continue the car purchase example, a consumer is likely to pay close attention to various car advertisements, read sales literature at the car dealership or on a manufacturer's website, test drive a car prior to purchase, discuss the decision with friends or family, and regularly maintain the car with oil changes after the purchase. Each of these actions exemplifies behavioral responses.

(OBJECTIVE 2) Why Study Consumer Behavior?

People study consumer behavior for a variety of reasons and in a variety of contexts, such as a student in a university class, a marketing executive working in an organization, an advertising designer working at a large agency, or a professor teaching and doing scholarly research. Let's examine a few of the benefits of studying consumer behavior, specifically, to improve business performance, to influence public policy, and to educate and help consumers make better decisions.

To Improve Business Performance

Organizations that market products and services often study consumer behavior—or use the results and recommendations of others' research—to improve business performance through customer-focused strategies. Marketers who understand their customers can create better products and services, promote their products and services more effectively, and develop marketing plans and strategies that foster sustainable competitive advantages. Their goal is to understand the general dynamics of consumer behavior that remain constant regardless of fads or trends. This understanding enables marketers to predict what motivates people to buy and then to deliver products that respond to those motivations, thereby successfully meeting and exceeding customer expectations over time.

For example, in 2001, global consumer goods producer Procter & Gamble (P&G) introduced Crest Whitestrips, the first product of its kind to offer over-the-counter tooth whitening affordably in a convenient delivery system. Crest had conducted extensive consumer behavior studies and drew upon everything it knew about consumers when developing and marketing this product. As a result, P&G gained a significant competitive advantage over its competitors in the home dental products market, an advantage it still enjoys today.

To Influence Public Policy

People working in government agencies or in non-profit organizations often are called to influence public policy and improve society's well-being. *Public policy* is the establishment of laws and regulations that govern business practice in order to protect

MARKETING IN ACTION
Crest Whitestrips Create Competitive Advantage with Consumer-Focused Strategy

When consumer packaged goods giant, Procter & Gamble, introduced Crest Whitestrips nationally in May, 2001, it was the first product of its kind to offer over-the-counter whitening at an affordable price in a convenient delivery system. The product comes in strips that are applied to upper and lower teeth for 30 minutes twice a day for 14 days. The clear, flexible strips contain a peroxide-based gel that bleaches the teeth. Most customers do notice a difference, and the company claims the product whitens teeth 10 times better than traditional whitening toothpaste.

Procter & Gamble also employed a strategically clever and unique marketing campaign for Whitestrips. Knowing that demand for this innovative technology would outpace production capabilities, Procter & Gamble introduced the product in a limited capacity, placing Whitestrips in dentists' offices, on home shopping television channels, and on the Internet and charging premium prices for kits, a pricing tactic referred to as *market skimming*. An added benefit of this marketing strategy was that the brand gained dentist approval and recommendation, because they were able to track the product's performance first-hand, and they also shared in early profits.

According to Procter & Gamble officials, a "consumer focus. . .is at the heart of everything we do. The consumer is boss, and the consumer demands the best value every day."[27] Part of offering better value is through unique, new-to-the-world products like Crest Whitestrips. In order to deliver this value to the customer, Crest conducts extensive consumer behavior studies and draws upon everything it knows about consumers when developing and marketing new products. The company has invested millions in consumer research in the United States and other countries, and even has several dedicated research facilities that watch, record, interview, and measure consumers in the laboratory. Recently, Procter & Gamble

has focused its consumer behavior research efforts out in the field, going into consumers' homes and studying consumers in "real life." Procter & Gambles's dedication to understanding consumers' needs and staying focused on the consumer appears to be well-founded. According to a research study examining products that consumers reported they were willing to buy, innovative products, such as Crest Whitestrips, that improve physical health or sense of well-being topped the list.[28]

Crest Whitestrips have become one of the most successful new products in Procter & Gamble's history. More than 10 million people have used Whitestrips, and the product was among the top 10 best-selling new non-food products in United States in 2001. Whitestrips continue to be one of the top-selling items in Crest's product line—now a $200 million plus business. More recently, Crest has introduced improved followup products, such as Premium Whitestrips and Advanced Seal. It seems there is no end in sight for our brighter, whiter smiles.[29]

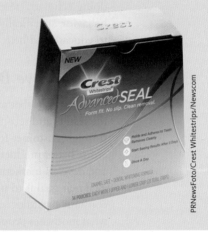

PRNewsFoto/Crest Whitestrips/Newscom

consumers. Those interested in shaping public policy study consumer behavior to understand the public needs and wants, and at the same time, to protect the public from unfair, unethical, or dangerous business practices. For example, in the packaged foods industry, the use of chemicals and preservatives has steadily increased as manufacturers have developed longer-lasting and more convenient forms of packaged food. In response, consumers have become increasingly concerned about the ingredients in processed food products because of their potential health risks and the nutritional consequences of synthetic additives. As a result, U.S. Food and Drug Administration (FDA) regulations now require marketers of food products to supply nutritional information on product packages in the form of "Nutritional Food Panels."

Nutrition Facts

Serving Size 1 cup (228g)
Servings Per Container 2

Amount Per Serving

Calories 250   Calories from Fat 110

	% Daily Value*
Total Fat 12g	**18%**
Saturated Fat 3g	**15%**
Trans Fat 3g	
Cholesterol 30mg	**10%**
Sodium 470mg	**20%**
Potassium 700mg	**20%**
Total Carbohydrate 31g	**10%**
Dietary Fiber 0g	**0%**
Sugars 5g	
Protein 5g	

Vitamin A	**4%**
Vitamin C	**2%**
Calcium	**20%**
Iron	**4%**

* Percent Daily Values are based on a 2,000 calorie diet.
Your Daily Values may be higher or lower depending on
your calorie needs.

	Calories:	2,000	2,500
Total Fat	Less than	65g	80g
Sat Fat	Less than	20g	25g
Cholesterol	Less than	300mg	300mg
Sodium	Less than	2,400mg	2,400mg
Total Carbohydrate		300g	375g
Dietary Fiber		25g	30g

www.fda.gov

Nutrition food panels are the result of consumer behavior research related to public policy."

To Educate and Help Consumers Make Better Decisions

Many people study consumer behavior because they want to educate consumers or help them act responsibly. For example, in addition to enacting labeling laws to protect consumers, the FDA provides detailed advice to consumers on how to interpret dietary information. You can visit the FDA's website on food and nutrition to learn more at http://www.fda.gov. How consumers gather, process and use information, and what motivates them, are important research topics for those interested in consumer education.

Finally, agencies and organizations involved in consumer education and assistance study consumer behaviors that are socially (or individually) destructive. These behaviors are often referred to as the "dark side of consumer behavior." This dark side includes consumer actions that are unhealthy, unethical, illegal, and potentially dangerous to individuals or society, such as misusing or overusing products, compulsive purchasing, shoplifting, and product tampering. Governments, businesses, and consumer interest groups want to curb these undesirable behaviors. Accordingly, these groups often study consumer behavior to best formulate strategies to promote positive behaviors (e.g., getting regular mammograms) or aid in the cessation of negative behaviors (e.g., quitting smoking).

Understanding the definition of consumer behavior and examining some of the benefits of studying consumer behavior provide a foundation for how research measures consumer behavior. First, let's look at how consumer behavior became a scientific field of study. This subject is useful in understanding how the current scientific discipline of consumer behavior evolved and suggests future directions for consumer research. In the next few pages, we also discuss how this text approaches the study of consumer behavior.

OBJECTIVE 3   Consumer Behavior as a Field of Study

Consumer behavior is an applied social science that draws on theories and concepts of psychology, sociology, anthropology, economics, and statistics. A fairly young science, the study of consumer behavior emerged in the late 1940s when many firms shifted from a *selling orientation* (selling consumers the excess inventory of what they produced) to producing goods that consumers actually needed and wanted. This change in focus was the beginning of the **marketing concept**, the idea that firms should discover and satisfy customer needs and wants in an efficient and profitable manner, while benefiting the long-term interests of society.

Today, the marketing concept is a core philosophy for many successful organizations. As for the future, the field of consumer behavior is likely to emphasize satisfying basic customer needs and wants. As a result, organizations are already focusing on delivering customer perceived value and customer delight. **Customer perceived value** "is the consumer's overall assessment of the utility of a product based on perceptions of what is received and what is given."[9] In other words, it is the estimated net gain customers receive from their sacrifice of time, money, and effort expended to purchase, use, and dispose of a product or service (i.e., benefits vs. costs). **Customer delight** goes a step beyond customer perceived value, suggesting customer benefits that not only meet, but also exceed expectations in unanticipated ways. Procter & Gamble executives state that offering customers better value when they purchase products and delighting customers during their usage experience with those products represent fundamental "moments of truth"

EYE ON INTERNATIONAL

L'Oréal: Delighting Customers with Beauty Inside and Out

L'Oréal, the French cosmetic company known worldwide for its cosmetics and hair-care products, is at the forefront of a new marketing concept designed to deliver customer delight and to "change the lives of women everywhere," according to Laurent Attal, Managing Director of L'Oréal's Active Cosmetic division.[30] The concept, called *Nutricosmetics*, combines cosmetics and nutrition to offer consumers nutritional supplements with beauty benefits that work from the inside out. The company's first product in its nutricosmetic line, launched in March, 2003, is called Innéov Firmness, an oral supplement that firms the skin, according to laboratory research. Of course, L'Oréal claims the supplements are even more effective when used in conjunction with the company's line of topical anti-aging creams. L'Oréal teamed up with Nestlé, a Swiss multinational company with expertise in nutrition, to create the product. The "beauty pill" contains lacto-lycopene, which is similar to

heather_mcgrath/iStockphoto.com

a natural molecules found in tomatoes and soy. The supplement is designed for women over 40 who are concerned about aging and want to improve skin tone and elasticity.

Known for the famous slogan, "Because I'm worth it," L'Oréal hopes its new slogan, "This pill could change women's lives forever," is also taken to heart by its consumers worldwide. So far, it seems to be working. L'Oréal's Active Cosmetic Division, Innéov's home in the company, enjoyed an 11.9 percent increase in sales in 2003. The company claims that the pill has conquered the market and is the leader in anti-aging nutritional cosmetics. In addition, according to a consumer research study done by the company in August, 2003, loyalty to the new product is very strong. Some 80 percent of women who had taken the supplements over a three-month treatment period reported that they would purchase the product again.

---

for the company.[10] In other words, generating value and delight for consumers is essential for long-term success. Likewise, L'Oréal, a French cosmetic company, attempts to create customer delight by creating a new market called *Nutricosmetics* that combines cosmetics and nutrition. The company has launched a "beauty pill" that reportedly firms the skin. While both cosmetics and vitamins satisfy customer needs and wants, the interconnection of the two creates *unanticipated* benefits for the consumer, and hence, customer delight.

Most competitors in a product category can satisfy customers' expectations about the functional benefits of a product or service, but firms gain competitive advantage by anticipating and providing benefits that customers are initially unaware of and/or will desire in the future. Identifying and satisfying consumers' latent demand is critical to providing customer delight.[11] Thus, the overarching goal of a consumer-centered firm is to maximize long-term customer value and delight, while also maximizing profits and doing so better than the competition.

The Evolution of Consumer Behavior Research

How researchers study consumer behavior has also evolved over the past several decades. Three prominent approaches are examined here: motivation research, behavioral science, and Interpretivism.

MOTIVATION RESEARCH One of the earliest approaches to studying consumer behavior, *motivation research* applied psychoanalytic therapy concepts from clinical psychology to consumer behavior research. The method was developed by Ernest Dichter, a Freudian psychoanalyst, shortly after World War II. He used in-depth interviewing techniques to uncover a person's hidden or unconscious motivations.[12] In consumer research, an *in-depth interview* (IDI) is a lengthy (sometimes several hours), probing interview, where a carefully trained interviewer extensively questions a subject about his or her purchase motivations. Depth interviews are more formally described later in this chapter under specific research methods.

During the peak of motivation research, Dichter performed in-depth interviews in more than 200 different product categories.[13] He applied Freudian interpretations to consumer actions and viewed consumers as largely immature, irrational, and driven by hidden erotic desires. For example, Dichter believed that an underlying reason for the popularity of canned soup was that women unconsciously associated it with breast milk—nutritious and warm—and so, didn't feel guilty about serving it in place of preparing a full meal. A man who lights a woman's cigarette represented a form of eroticism—the physical act of lighting a match or lighter created a tension-filled moment, peaking with pressure (as the match is struck) and followed by relaxation.[14]

Over the years, many advertisers have embraced motivation research because of its seeming ability to tap deep-rooted needs. For example, Dichter's contention that baking cakes fulfilled a woman's inner desire for children helped lead to Pillsbury's doughboy character and slogan, "Nothing says lovin' like something from the oven." Exxon's tiger mascot with the slogan, "Put a tiger in your tank!" was created in part based on the supposed masculine masculine symbolism conveyed by the animal.[15]

Motivation research fell out of fashion in the 1960s. Critics of the approach pointed out methodological limitations, such as the subjective nature of interview interpretations, as well as the strategic and practical limitations of applying sexual explanations to most consumer actions. However, motivation research left two important legacies to the field of consumer research: (1) a focus on consumer motivations, i.e., trying to answer the question of why people behave as they do, and (2) the technique of in-depth interviewing. Today, motivation research is still used occasionally, but usually in conjunction with other, more rigorous techniques; strong Freudian sexual interpretations are de-emphasized.

A BEHAVIORAL SCIENCE PERSPECTIVE Since the 1960s, a behavioral science perspective (also referred to as *Positivism* and *social science*) has dominated the field of consumer research. **Behavioral science** applies the scientific method, relying on systematic, rigorous procedures to explain, control, and predict consumer behavior. Thus, behavioral scientists study people and their behaviors in the same way that natural scientists study physical phenomena. Because behavioral scientists study people, however, research findings are more difficult to interpret. The primary methods of behavioral science include the *experimental approach*—conducting controlled experiments—and the *marketing science approach*—employing computer-based simulations and mathematical models to explain and predict consumer behavior.

Behavioral scientists who study consumer behavior tend to view consumers as largely rational; they seek causes for behavior, conduct research to be used for strategic marketing decision making, and primarily use quantitative research methods. In **quantitative research methods,** *empirical data* are collected. Empirical data are numerical, based on observation, experiment, or experience, rather than speculation or theory. This data is used to perform sophisticated statistical analyses. Because quantitative research methods typically use representative samples of a larger consumer group of

interest (also called a *population* of interest), these results can typically be generalized from the study group to the larger group.

This textbook uses a predominantly behavioral science perspective for studying consumer behavior, although alternative approaches are also discussed. The scientific approach is advantageous for those interested in developing consumer-focused strategies and provides a foundation for critical thinking, creative problem solving, and decision making. This approach is based on the *scientific method*, a collection of systematic activities that enables researchers to study problems and find answers to questions.[16] Like a roadmap, the scientific method leads scientists in the right direction, but different researchers may take different routes to arrive at the same destination. But they always follow the rules of the road. (See Figure 1.2.) The steps of the scientific method include:

1. *Observe and ask the question*: Observations we make of the world around us are the basis for formulating questions or problems we want to solve.

2. *Form a hypothesis and make a prediction*: When a question or problem emerges from observation, we generate a potential explanation called a hypothesis that may provide the answer. A prediction is what we expect to happen if our hypothesis is correct.

3. *Test the hypothesis*: We test our hypotheses under controlled conditions, including testing only one hypothesis at a time and limiting the circumstances/environment of the testing to see if our predictions are correct. Hypotheses that cannot be confirmed through testing must be rejected, and hypotheses must be tested and re-tested before they can be accepted as true. When behavioral scientists test a hypothesis, an *empirical confrontation* ensues, i.e., empirical data are collected, and the results are compared to those suggested by the hypothesis.

4. *Theory generation*: If a hypothesis is confirmed via testing and re-testing, we generate a *theory*, which is a general answer to our original question. Once a theory is established, it also guides future research.

A scientific foundation should serve you well as a student and in your chosen career. Depth of understanding is key to success in today's complex marketplace. Marketers and business practitioners who possess in-depth, scientific understanding of their customers are more likely to succeed where others fail.

FIGURE 1.2   THE SCIENTIFIC METHOD

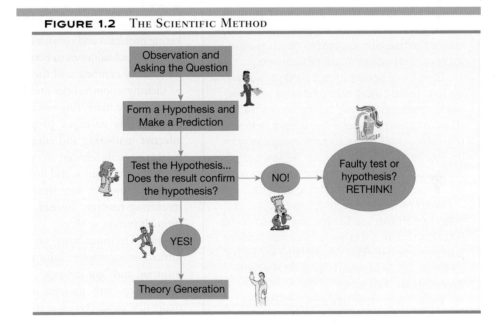

INTERPRETIVISM An alternative research approach to behavioral science that relies less on scientific and technological methodology is called **Interpretivism** (or *Postmodernism*). Researchers working from this perspective view consumers as non-rational beings and their reality as highly subjective. These researchers' goal is to collect data to describe and *interpret* this reality. Interpretivist consumer researchers are often especially interested in the consumption experience and stress understanding consumers from a broader societal perspective. They also tend to reject the quantitative approach of behavioral science in favor of qualitative research methods. In **qualitative research methods,** descriptive, non-empirical data are collected that describe an individual consumer's subjective experience with the product or service. Because qualitative research methods typically do not include

Tampering with research results is a serious ethical problem. A few years ago, The Coca-Cola Company and Burger King conducted an applied consumer research project in the form of a three-week promotional campaign in some Burger King restaurants in Richmond, Virginia. (Coke had been the main provider of fountain drinks for Burger King since 1999, after signing a 10-year deal with the chain.) The objective of the project was to test the appeal of Frozen Coke, a slushy drink. Coke wanted Burger King to offer the frozen drinks as a kids' snack. If the tests were successful, Burger King would make Frozen Coke a regular offering nationwide.

Apparently the initial research results of the campaign weren't pleasing to some people at Coke, and they decided to inflate their test results—without Burger King's knowledge, of course. It was reported this involved paying a man $10 thousand to get hundreds of kids to go to Burger King restaurants and ask for the Frozen Coke value meal. With the "rigged" results of the test market sales appearing to be quite positive, Burger King ramped up the Frozen Coke program. Burger King and its franchisees committed to a national promotion of Frozen Coke in more than 7,600 restaurants, and invested an estimated $65 million in advertising and the equipment and syrup to make the frozen drinks.

Then a finance executive in Coke's fountain-drink division was let go. He filed a lawsuit, claiming that he had been unfairly fired for complaining about these, and other, unethical practices at Coke. In his lawsuit, he accused Coke of rigging the Frozen Coke research project. This led to informal investigations by the U.S. Securities and Exchange Commission (SEC) and the U.S. Justice Department. Coke was subpoenaed by a federal grand jury. Eventually, Coke admitted that it had rigged the test.

Needless to say, Coke's customer, Burger King, was not thrilled. Sales of Frozen Coke have been about one-half of what Burger King expected, and for a while, the company threatened to discontinue the drink. Finally, Coke and Burger King reached a settlement, with Coke agreeing to pay up to $21 million to Burger King and its franchisees.

Wouldn't you hate to be in the shoes of the marketing managers who created this whole mess? Not surprisingly, the executive who approved the scam is no longer employed by Coke. Unfortunately, cases like this one have been too common in today's highly competitive business environment, with marketers on the front lines when it comes to producing positive results for their stakeholders. While finding the "right" results from the research may seem crucial, failing to maintain integrity and high ethical standards in research can be serious mistake that everyone typically pays for in the end.[32]

large, representative samples from the population of interest, their results cannot be generalized. But while these techniques typically lack generalizability, they provide in-depth, detail-rich descriptions of consumers' experiences that can be very useful in developing further questions and understanding consumers on an abstract level.

The field of consumer behavior has a rich heritage of diverse scientific disciplines on which to draw. And, regardless of the perspective or methods used, the primary goal is to advance the field of consumer behavior in order to benefit students, marketers, business, scholars, and society. The following sections of this chapter discuss how consumer behavior is examined and measured through marketing research.

Consumer Behavior Research   OBJECTIVE 4

Consumer researchers study consumer responses and activities by using marketing research methods. **Marketing research** is a systematic process of planning, collecting, analyzing, and interpreting data and information relevant to marketing problems and consumer behavior. Marketing research also enables businesses to better understand the market(s) in which they compete and the broader environment in order to identify opportunities and threats. Finally, consumer researchers use marketing research to analyze the effectiveness of marketing strategies, programs, and tactics. Ultimately, effective marketing and consumer research should provide marketers with relevant information for making decisions, reducing uncertainty, and improving profits.

Unfortunately, sometimes marketers forego conducting marketing research. Instead, they often rely on their intuition. Intuition is simply common sense, a guess, or "gut feeling." Decisions based on intuition are often made with limited or incomplete information. Relying too heavily on intuition and "gut feelings," rather than on sound research, can lead to costly business mistakes. This is one reason so many new products fail, as many as 95 percent by some estimates.[17] For example, not long ago, Heinz introduced a new clam chowder made with the finest ingredients, including expensive, very tender clams, working under the assumption that consumers would prefer high quality ingredients—a rather common sense assumption. The product was a failure. If the company had done systematic research on consumer preferences, it would have discovered that, counter to the common sense assumption, consumers actually prefer lower quality, tough, rubbery clams in their chowder.

Another area of concern in studying consumer behavior is the unethical and/or unintended manipulation of research data or results. Firms sometimes manipulate, alter, or misinterpret—intentionally or unintentionally—research results, often to their own advantage.

Now that we've broadly examined consumer behavior research, the remaining sections of this chapter review:

- major classifications of research: basic versus applied
- two special relationships, correlations and causal
- two main sources of research data: secondary and primary
- popular methods for collecting primary data

Basic versus Applied Research

Consumer research is divided into two broad categories based on the goals of the research: basic research and applied research. **Basic research** looks for general relationships between variables, regardless of the specific situation. For example, basic research has shown that using celebrity endorsers in advertising can increase consumers' positive attitudes toward a brand, especially when the celebrity is well liked and fits well with the product or the product's image. Examples include Tiger Woods endorsing Nike golf equipment and Mariah Carey endorsing Pepsi Cola.[18]

This photo shows Tiger Woods involved in applied research for the development of "Gatorade Tiger."

The key benefit of basic research is that conclusions drawn from it generally apply across a variety of situations, and researchers can use these generalizations to guide strategic planning and develop marketing tactics. Thus, basic research findings apply not only to Tiger's hitting Nike golf clubs and Mariah's singing about Pepsi, but to most celebrities and brands in general. This helps marketers make more informed decisions, such as whether to use a celebrity endorser in advertising.

Basic research variables studied can include those related to the consumer, such as personality or demographic variables; they can also relate to the *marketing mix* (product, price, place, and promotion). Examples include advertising tactics involving humor appeals or sex appeals and the consumer's environment or personal situation, such as music played in a retail store, or shopping when pressed for time, e.g., 5:00 P.M. on Christmas Eve.

Applied research examines many of these same variables, but within a specific context of interest to a marketer. Applied research is more common than basic research because consumer researchers want to solve particular business-related problems of immediate interest.

Let's revisit our celebrity endorser example. Given what researchers know about the influence of celebrity endorsers from basic research, a company, let's say Kraft, decides to use a celebrity endorser to advertise a new line of kids' yogurt. The company develops two or three advertisements, each with a different celebrity endorser. These celebrities are people who might fit with the product or convey an image desired by the company, such as Kelly Ripa, the famous mom and talk-show host, or Hillary Duff, a popular young actress. The company then conducts applied research to test which of the endorsers is most effective. In this case, the research is aimed at evaluating a specific brand and endorser combination, and the results would not apply to other situations.

Correlations and Causal Relationships

Consumer researchers are especially interested in uncovering two special types of relationships—correlations and causal (cause-and-effect). When a statistically testable and significant relationship exists between two variables, we say the variables are **correlated** (see Figure 1.3).[19] A *variable* is simply any factor that that can potentially change. For example, if researchers are studying the relationship between advertising and sales, those would be the variables of interest. There are three main types of correlations: positive, negative, and zero. In a positive correlation, the two variables increase or decrease together. A negative correlation means that as one variable increases, the related variable decreases. For example, research has shown that there is a positive correlation between advertising expenditures and level of sales.[20] As advertising increases, sales also increase. On the other hand, a negative correlation between product malfunctions and customer satisfaction exists—as product malfunctions increase, customer satisfaction tends to decrease.

A *zero correlation* means that there is no predictable relationship between two variables. For example, there is zero correlation between the quality of non-frozen, concentrated orange juice and the physical distance between the orange grove and the

FIGURE 1.3   GRAPHS SHOWING CORRELATIONS BETWEEN ADVERTISING AND SALES

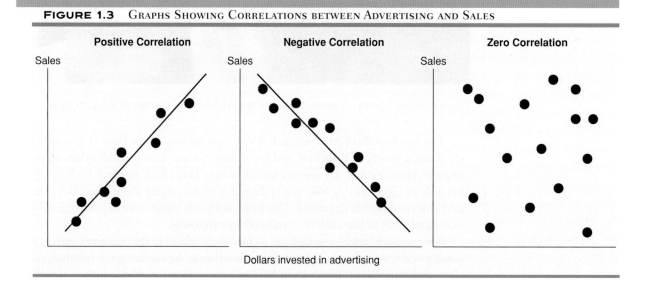

Positive Correlation   Negative Correlation   Zero Correlation

Sales   Sales   Sales

Dollars invested in advertising

processing facility. This may surprise you, because many consumers believe (and many orange juice marketers imply) that the closer the processing plant is to the field, the fresher and higher quality the orange juice. Believing there is a correlational relationship between variables where none actually exists is called an *illusory correlation*.

One limitation in identifying correlations is that they tell us nothing about which variable influences the other. This means that even if we know that two variables (A and B) are correlated, we still do not know whether variable A influences variable B; B influences A; or A and B influence each other. Applying the advertising and sales example, even though we know that sales and advertising are positively correlated, advertising may influence sales, sales may influence advertising, or both variables may influence each other simultaneously.

In contrast, causal relationships capture both correlation and direction of the relationship. A **causal relationship** between two variables means that the variables are correlated and that one variable influences the other, but not vice versa (see Figure 1.4). In other words, a causal relationship exists if the following requirements are met:

1. the two variables are correlated
2. the cause must precede the effect
3. other potential causes are ruled out[21]

Let's look again at the positive relationship between advertising and sales. Of course, marketers are interested in whether advertising actually drives sales. They know that the variables are correlated, and it seems logical to conclude that advertising is the cause and must precede sales, and not vice versa, but does this constitute a causal relationship? Does this relationship satisfy all the requirements for a causal relationship? While intuition may point marketers toward answering "yes" to these questions, they cannot truly establish a causal relationship between advertising and sales without some scientific evidence. Can they obtain such evidence? Yes, by employing the scientific method, they can conduct experiments to test causality. In fact, there is a causal relationship between advertising and sales. Experiments are discussed in more detail under "Research Methods."

Interestingly, marketers suspected the causal relationship between advertising and sales for centuries, and anecdotal evidence suggests that this relationship was tested systematically as long ago as the early 1800s in Boston. As the story goes, there was a lady, Lydia Pinkerton, who invented and marketed a tonic to women for "medicinal needs." To promote his mother's product, Mrs. Pinkerton's son created large banners advertising the tonic and placed them in neighborhoods and on bridges and buildings. Much to his amazement, he discovered that every time he moved the banners into a new neighborhood, sales increased in that area. So, he decided to specifically test the relationship. He went into several neighborhoods where sales were very high, and he removed all the banners. Not surprisingly, sales dropped in the neighborhoods that had been stripped

FIGURE 1.4   THE CAUSE AND EFFECT RELATIONSHIP

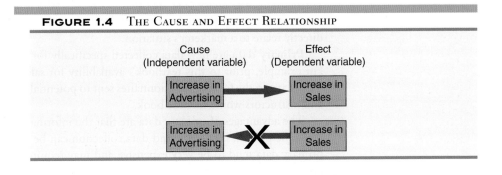

of the advertisements. Mr. Pinkerton concluded that advertising was related to sales and that the more he advertised in a given geographic area, the better were his sales. This is one of the first recorded marketing research studies examining this relationship.[22]

Systematic testing allows researchers to determine causal relationships with a high degree of certainty. However, whereas a scientific approach allows researchers to establish causality among variables in a controlled setting, variables seldom exist in isolation in the real world. Rather, confounding elements introduce uncertainty, making research difficult. Causal relationships also tend to overlap, with some effects—like increased sales—having many different causes that may work together or independently, such as amount of advertising, product quality, and price. Fortunately, although uncertainty can't be completely eliminated, scientific techniques described in this book allow consumer researchers to minimize it.

Up to this point in our discussion of consumer behavior research, we have seen that researchers conduct different broad types of research, namely basic and applied research, and that uncovering correlations and causal relationships are often of special interest. Now we turn our attention to specific types of data and methods for their collection.

Secondary versus Primary Data

Where do marketers collect data? There are two broad sources of data: secondary data and primary data. **Secondary data** is data that already exist and is readily accessible. One source could be internal organizational sources, such a company's sales history records, customer database, sales force observations, or even previous company research projects. Secondary data is also available from outside sources, including U.S. and foreign government agencies that offer a variety of reports, such as the *U.S. Census Population Report* and the *Vital Statistics Report*; academic and trade publications, such as *Moody's Manuals, Journal of Consumer Research*, and *Advertising Age*, that often publish the results of both basic and applied research; and finally, commercial syndicated data sources, such as Nielsen TV Ratings Reports and InfoScan data from supermarket scanners. *Syndicated data* are data that are periodically collected using standardized procedures and analyzed by a commercial firm, which then makes the results available for purchase. For example, Nielson Market Research Company monitors people's television viewing habits. Research participants are asked to keep journal information on their viewing habits and an electronic monitor attached to the television records channel selection and viewing time. Table 1.1 lists some examples of secondary data sources.

The advantages of secondary data are that it is usually readily available, rich in detail, and may not cost any more than the time and effort it takes to search the Internet or go to the library. The disadvantages of secondary data are that it may lack currency and relevancy. For example, the U.S. Census is done every 10 years, and eight- or nine-year-old information may not be timely enough to address our current problems. Furthermore, secondary data are often *aggregated*, which means they are reported as a whole, rather than broken down in detail. So, these data may not be specific enough to directly relate to a marketer's situation.

Primary data are new data collected specifically for the research purpose at hand. For example, prior to this textbook's availability for sale, the publisher collected primary data, in the form of questionnaires sent to potential users, to predict how students and instructors would like the book.

The advantages of primary data are that the information is specific and relevant to a specific project, is current, and data collection can be controlled. On the downside, primary data tend to be very expensive and may require considerable time to collect, organize, and analyze.

TABLE 1.1 SECONDARY DATA SOURCES

Internal Sources:
  a. Company customer records and databases
  b. Financial statement, such as annual reports, profit/loss statements, and balance sheets
  c. Sales Call Sheets and records
  d. Inventory records
  e. Prior research study reports

External Sources:
  a. Online Indexes and Databases
  • Business Source Complete
  • Business and Industry
  • Global Market Information Database
  • IBISWorld
  • Marketline (Datamonitor)
  • MRI + (Mediamark)
  • SRDS Media Solutions
  • Country Profiles and Country Commerce Online
  • Europa World Plus
  • Sports Business Research Network
  b. Specific Periodicals and Books
  • Standard and Poor's Industry
  • Moody's Manuals
  • *The Handbook of Consumer Psychology*
  • *The Advertising Age Encyclopedia of Advertising*
  • Marketing Journals, such as *Journal of Consumer Research, Journal of Consumer Psychology, Journal of Marketing, Journal of Marketing Research, Journal of Retailing, Journal of Advertising*
  • Trade Magazines such as *Advertising Age, Progressive Grocer, Sales and Marketing Management*
  • General Business Publication such as *Business Week, Forbes, The Wall Street Journal, Harvard Business Review, The Economist*
  c. Government Sources
  • U.S. Bureau of the Census (http://www.census.gov). The census includes reports not only on general population, but also on housing, the labor force, manufacturers, business, agriculture, and foreign aspects.
  • Integrated Public Use Microdata Series (http://www.ipums.umn.edu). This series of data includes samples of the U.S. census gathered for over 100 years and historical census files from other countries.
  • Bureau of Labor Statistics (http://stats.bls.gov). This source collects data on employment, industrial relations, prices, earnings, living conditions, occupational safety, technology, and productivity.

PRIMARY DATA COLLECTION METHODS A diverse set of methods enable researchers to "get inside the mind of the consumer" through primary data. There is no one perfect primary research method. Each has strengths and weaknesses, so the best methodology is the one that achieves the individual researcher's objectives. Let's examine four common primary research methods:

1. observation

2. direct questioning

3. experimentation

4. projective techniques

©Michael Greenlar/The Image Works

OBSERVATION By using *observational techniques*, researchers can record people's behavior, either with or without their knowledge. When a person is aware of the observation, the research is referred to as *obtrusive observation*. For example, toy manufacturers routinely invite children in for "playtime." In a research facility made to resemble a classroom, playground, or family room, children are encouraged to play with toys while researchers record all their behaviors and comments.

When a person is unaware of being observed, the research is *unobtrusive observation*. For example, in addition to monitoring security, cameras in retail stores can track traffic patterns, examining path and pace as customers move through the store and see where traffic jams occur. Consumer goods marketer Procter & Gamble sends employees into grocery stores to casually observe consumers shopping for its products. These observations yield valuable information about how much time customers spend at the store shelf, how many products they examine, where customers' attention is focused, and whether they seem confused.

A specialized form of observation called *participant observation* occurs when a researcher joins a family or group for an extended period and observes members' behaviors. Adapted from cultural anthropology, this type of research is also called *ethnographic research*. This type of research is growing in popularity, especially when the researcher needs an honest, behind-the-scenes peek into consumers' lives. For example, Whirlpool recently conducted an ethnographic research project for a new line of luxury jet-bathtubs by filming participants while they soaked in the tub. Innovations Focus, a firm that uses ethnographic research for new product development, was interested in understanding how women use lipstick. To that end, they observed Mary Kay in-home make-up parties run by a make-up consultant, participated in several in-home make-up application sessions, and even accompanied women while shopping for lipstick.[23]

Observational techniques are valuable because they can measure what consumers actually do, but observation alone cannot reveal a person's underlying motivations, attitudes, and preferences. In addition, observation may also raise ethical issues when it is used to collect data that consumers regard as private.

DIRECT QUESTIONING: SURVEYS, INTERVIEWS, AND FOCUS GROUPS Direct forms of questioning are probably the most popular types of consumer research methods because researchers can collect a wide variety of data, such as group versus individual, brief answers versus long answers, and qualitative versus quantitative. Researchers can also collect large amounts of data with direct questioning, and the variety of direct questioning methods adds flexibility to the data collection task. Questioning the consumer directly can take a number of forms, including written and oral surveys, which can be administered via mail, telephone, fax, e-mail, the Internet, or face-to-face.

A **survey** is simply a set of structured questions to which a person is asked to respond. For example, The Harris Poll, run by Harris Interactive, is one the country's largest Internet survey providers, with an active multi-million participant database covering 40 countries.[24] Mail and e-mail surveys are relatively inexpensive, but response rates are typically low—from 5 to 20 percent. Phone surveys achieve higher response rates but reduce the number of questions that can be asked because many answer options have to be repeated, and few people are willing to stay on the phone for more than 5 to 10 minutes. To talk to customers face-to-face, companies often recruit research participants in malls and shopping centers, a technique referred to as *mall-intercept*. Mall-intercepts are a convenient way to reach consumers, but respondents may be reluctant to discuss anything sensitive face-to-face with an interviewer.

Surveys are useful for collecting specific, often complex, information from a large number of individuals. They are typically easy to administer, and the general public is familiar and comfortable with this technique. However, as is true of all research techniques, surveys are vulnerable to bias. Wording questions correctly can be very difficult, and the language can influence a consumer's response. For example, consider the question, "In order to prevent terrorism, should airports be allowed to conduct passenger searches based on racial profiling and suspicious behavior?" This question has a number of potential problems. First, it is ambiguous. What behavior exactly is considered suspicious behavior in an airport? Second, the question is *double-barreled*, which means that it is really asking more than one question. What if the respondent approves of passenger searches on the basis of suspicious behavior but not on the basis of racial profiling—how should the respondent answer? Third, it is a leading question. Qualifying the question with, "In order to prevent terrorism. . ." clearly tips the respondent off to the fact that a "yes" answer is desired. This question may also suffer from what is referred to as *social desirability bias*. In this situation, respondents may not answer a question honestly or completely because they feel that the information is too personal or socially sensitive.

In face-to-face interviews, *interviewer bias* is an additional problem. Interviewer bias occurs when responses are influenced by variables such as the interviewer's age, gender, appearance, verbal or non-verbal reactions, or by a desire to please the interviewer. For example, male respondents may hesitate to give personal information to a female interviewer. Or, a respondent may fabricate answers in an attempt to not appear ignorant to an interviewer.

Another method of direct questioning is the **in-depth interview (IDI)**, a one-on-one, interview of at least one hour in length, but sometimes considerably longer. A highly trained interviewer establishes rapport with a respondent and then proceeds to lead him or her through a loosely structured discussion of the research topic. This method is particularly appropriate for sensitive or emotionally charged topics, or when the researcher is attempting to gather detailed information about very complicated behaviors. In an in-depth interview, the research can peel away layers of respondents' emotions, thoughts, or behaviors. The disadvantages of in-depth interviews are that they tend to be time-consuming and costly, because the interviewer must be highly trained. Furthermore, respondents are typically compensated for their time, and the data can be difficult to analyze and interpret.

Extending interviewing to the group level, a **focus group** consists of 6 to 12 current or potential customers run by a facilitator who monitors and guides the group discussion. Focus groups are conducted for a variety of reasons, including brainstorming for ideas, assessing new products, and evaluating promotional campaigns. With a skilled facilitator, focus groups are opportunities to generate energy and group synergies that can result in new ideas or unique insights. On the downside, like interviews, focus groups require a skilled facilitator and may yield unwieldy data. In addition, focus groups are vulnerable to problems associated with group dynamics. For example, *groupthink* is the tendency for groups to make poor quality decisions for the sake of unanimity.[25] Groupthink occurs when groups are highly cohesive, and when they are under considerable pressure to make a quality decision.

Focus group are a great way to initiate meaningful conversations with customers.

Digital Vision/Getty Images

EXPERIMENTS **Experiments** manipulate variables in a controlled setting to determine their relationship to one another. Researchers use experiments to rule out all but one explanation for a particular observation. In designing an experiment, researchers first identify any variables that can possibly change. There are three broad types of variables:

- *Independent variables* are the factors that are changed or manipulated.
- *Dependent variables* are factors that change in response to researchers' manipulations of the independent variables.
- *Constants* are factors that researchers do not allow to change, but instead control.

Recall our discussion of the potential causal relationship between advertising and sales. Experiments are the best methods for determining causality. For instance, a marketer could manipulate advertising (the independent variable) by showing an advertisement for a product to one group of participants and not showing the advertisement to a second, *control group*—a group that is not exposed to any independent variables and serves as a standard of comparison. The marketer could then examine the resulting influence of the advertisement on average sales (the dependent variable). If sales are significantly higher in the ad-group than in the no-ad-group, the marketer could conclude that changes in advertising are likely to cause changes in sales.

Participants in experiments should be *randomly assigned* to the conditions, which means the assignment is determined by chance, such as flipping a coin. Random assignment helps to rule out other possible causes for the results, such as different personalities among participants and varying levels of product knowledge and interest, among others. Random assignment forces these individual differences to cancel out. Ideally, researchers would replicate the experiment a number of times and in different settings to show additional support for their findings.

Experimentation is the most effective technique for determining causal relationships, but it does have a drawback in that consumers are removed from their natural surroundings. The contrived laboratory setting may prevent consumers from acting as they would in a real market setting.

PROJECTIVE TECHNIQUES Borrowed from psychology, **projective techniques** are an "unstructured, indirect form of questioning that encourages respondents to project their underlying beliefs, attitudes, feelings, and motivations in an apparently unrelated or ambiguous scenario."[26] In other words, projective techniques use seemingly meaningless exercises to uncover consumers' unconscious points of view. Projective techniques consist of a variety of tests that fall under four broad categories:

1. *Word-association tests*, which ask subjects to respond to a list of words with one or more associated words that come to mind

2. *Completion tests*, which ask subjects to fill in the blanks by finishing sentences or stories

FIGURE 1.5 EXAMPLE OF A CONSTRUCTION PROJECTIVE TECHNIQUE

3. *Construction tests*, including cartoon construction, which ask subjects fill in the word/thought "bubbles" in a cartoon; or picture construction, where subjects tell a story about a picture (see Figure 1.5)

4. *Expression tests*, including role-play activities and third-person techniques, which ask subjects to describe the actions of typical others

Projective techniques can often generate responses that participants would be unwilling or unable to give if questioned directly. For example, the makers of Old Spice High Endurance Antiperspirant-Deodorant use an expression-type projective technique, asking research participants to describe a "typical" user of their product and a "typical" user of a competing product. This technique helps paint a rich picture of how each brand is perceived and reveals subtle differences between brands that research participants are not able to articulate directly. On the negative side, projective techniques can be time-consuming and awkward to code (input as data) and analyze, and interpretation can be subjective.

Chapter Summary

Welcome to the exciting world of consumer behavior research! Now you have an idea of what consumer behavior entails, how it fits into the larger field of marketing, and how we study it. Consumer behavior comprises all consumer activities associated with the purchase, use, and disposal of goods and services, including the consumer's emotional, mental, and behavioral responses that precede, determine, or follow these activities. One dominant approach to studying consumer behavior is the behavioral science perspective, which relies on rigorous quantitative research methods and procedures to describe, explain,

control, and predict consumer behavior. An alternative approach, which relies less on scientific and technological methodology and more on the qualitative approach, is called Interpretivism.

Understanding, explaining, and predicting consumer behavior are complicated tasks. This textbook adopts a scientific approach to achieve a deeper understanding of consumer behavior. In this approach, researchers are especially interested in two special types of relationships between variables, namely, correlational and causal relationships. When a statistically testable and significant relationship exists between an event and a condition, we say that the event and the condition are correlated. A causal relationship between two variables means that the variables are correlated and that one variable influences the other, but not vice versa.

Consumer researchers conduct basic and applied research to identify important variables relevant to consumer behavior. Basic research aims at understanding relative relationships between variables, whereas applied research examines variables within a specific context of interest to the marketer. There are two broad sources of research data—secondary data and primary data. Secondary data are data that already exist and can be accessed within an organization or from external sources. Primary data are new data collected on a project-by-project basis.

Consumer researchers collect primary data by a number of methods, including observation, direct questioning, experimentation, and projective techniques. Observational techniques record people's behavior, with or without their knowledge. Questioning the consumer directly takes a variety of forms, including surveys, in-depth interviews, and focus groups. Experiments manipulate variables in a controlled setting to determine their relationship to one another and are the most effective technique for determining causal relationships. Projective techniques are indirect forms of questioning that uncover unspoken feelings and attitudes.

Researchers analyze consumer behavior research data in order to discover customer need and wants, deliver products and services that satisfy those needs and wants, and ensure that the customer remains satisfied over time. Ultimately, effective consumer behavior research provides marketers with relevant information for making better decisions and reducing uncertainty.

Key Terms

consumer behavior	interpretivism	secondary data
individual consumers	qualitative research methods	primary data
organizational consumers	marketing research	survey
marketing concept	basic research	in-depth interview
customer perceived value	applied research	focus group
customer delight	correlated	experiments
behavioral science	causal relationship	projective techniques
quantitative research methods		

Review and Discussion

1. Based on the definition of consumer behavior, identify some of the consumer behavior-related activities you have engaged in today.

2. What is/are the key difference(s) between customer perceived value and customer delight?

3. How do public policy makers use the results of consumer research?

4. How might an Interpretivist researcher attempt to examine why more men (versus women) have an emotional attachment to their automobiles? How would a behavioral science researcher approach the same question?

5. Define qualitative research and quantitative research and highlight the differences between them. Provide one example of each technique.

6. Discuss the advantages of conducting marketing research, rather than relying on intuition and common sense.

7. Give an example of a correlational relationship and a causal relationship that you have observed in daily life. Explain how each example illustrates the relationship.

8. Describe the major differences between secondary and primary data collection, as well as the advantages and disadvantages of each.

9. Discuss the advantages and disadvantages of using observational techniques of data collection.

10. Why is random assignment important in any experiment that seeks to determine causality?

Short Application Exercises

1. Find an advertisement that attempts to influence consumers' disposal activities and describe the disposal activity. Is the advertisement effective, in your opinion? Why or why not?

2. Design an experiment that tests the effect of using a celebrity endorser on consumers' brand attitudes. In addition, identify the independent and dependent variables and state the hypothesis.

3. Conduct a library search and find one article that describes either a basic or applied marketing research project. What were the goals of the project, the research method employed, and the major results of the project?

4. Using the Internet, conduct a secondary data collection to investigate aging trends in the United States. Hint: you may want to start at the U.S. Census Bureau website.

MANAGERIAL APPLICATION

The truths and power of consumer analysis become real when you observe consumers in real shopping situations. This is a common technique (sometimes called mystery shopping) used by many companies to better understand their customers. Your challenge is to use observational research to answer a behavioral research question.

Procedure:

Step 1: Choose one of the observational research tasks shown here to complete or make up a question/task of your own.

Possible Research Tasks:

1. Compare the behaviors of men shopping alone for groceries with those of women shopping alone for groceries.

2. Compare the behaviors of pre-adolescent boys shopping with an adult with those of pre-adolescent girls shopping with an adult.

3. Compare the shopping behaviors of senior citizen couples with those of young couples.

4. Observe the behaviors of teenage boys and girls shopping without a parent.

5. Compare the purchase of a specific food or beverage item in a supermarket versus a restaurant/bar.

6. Observe the purchase of impulse items at the point of check-out.

Step 2: Plan to go on at least two data-gathering trips.

Step 3: Collect your observations. You should collect at least five (5) observations of each type of subject (for example, five men and five women for a total of 10). You will definitely want to take notes on each observation and know what types of information you are looking for before you start. (And while you are observing, make sure that you do not distract or disrupt your subjects. You should make sure that you are inconspicuous as possible.)

Step 4: Summarize the information you collected and see if there are differences among the groups you selected. What are your findings? What are the potential implications for a company who wants to market to those groups?

CONSUMER SEGMENTATION AND POSITIONING

OBJECTIVES   *After studying this chapter, you will be able to...*

1 | Define segmentation, target markets, and positioning, and understand why this process is important to marketers.

2 | Explain how society benefits from market segmentation.

3 | Describe the factors that influence the determination of a segmentation strategy.

4 | Discuss various bases of segmentation.

5 | Provide examples of strategies marketers use to position brands after segmentation.

SEGMENTATION ACROSS CULTURES IS GAINING IMPORTANCE

While several market segmentation models are available for the U.S. market, they don't necessarily translate into foreign markets. To address this need, market researchers have attempted to create more global segments based on psychographics. One example of a cross-cultural lifestyle market segmentation system is called the *Cross Cultural Consumer Characterization*, or the 4C's for short. This model was developed by leading advertising agency, Young and Rubican. It is considered cross-cultural because its developers believe that the target values upon which the segments are based are universal and found in all cultures. The model was developed based on data from seven European countries: the UK, France, Italy, Spain, Germany, Switzerland, and the Netherlands, but it now includes a worldwide database.

Using a method that adapts values to local cultural norms, 4Cs has been constructed in over 50 countries including places as various as Iceland, Lithuania, Thailand, El Salvador, and Kazakhstan.

The model is based on seven *enduring human values,* a set of accepted personal principles and standards that emerged in the data, namely the need for status, security, control, discovery, enlightenment, survival, and escape. 4Cs is constructed using only values statements, nonetheless, values do connect with demographic circumstances. Based on these core values and data, seven relatively stable lifestyle segments were constructed:

Resigned: Tends to be older; is rigid, strict, authoritarian, and oriented to the past and to the value of survival. Brand choices stress economy, familiarity and communication with the segment is best centered on expert opinion and simple messages. (About 10% of the population)

Struggler: Limited resources and capabilities; disorganized and alienated from mainstream society. Brand choices are centered on sensation and escape. (About 8% of the population)

Mainstreamer: The largest segment; members are conventional, conforming, passive and above all avoid risk; represents the majority view. Focus is on well-known brands and value-oriented brands, and communication with the segment should be emotionally warm and reassuring. (About 30% of the population)

Aspirer: Tends to be younger; may be in entry-level white-collar profession; oriented to status value and the external—material possessions, appearance, image, and fashion. Brand choices are trendy, fun, and unique. (About 13% of the population)

Succeeder: Confident and accomplished but is all about control; may be an executive or in top management; oriented to confidence, work ethic, goals, and leadership. Brand choices are based on prestige, reward, and caring for oneself, and communication with the segment should focus on evidence of claims. (About 16% of the population)

Explorer: Based in discovery, explorers are adrenalin junkies who love breaking rules, seeking out the unconventional, and being impulsive. Brands for this segment are innovative and daring. (About 9% of the population;)

Reformer: Focused on enlightenment, freedom, and personal growth; typically higher

education and higher income; oriented to healthy debate and is not impressed

by status. Brand choices tend to innovative and practical. (About 14% of the

population)[1]

Mordin, C., May 2005, Connecting with consumers, 4Cs Overview, www.4cs.yr.com. Reprinted by permission.

A Divide and Conquer Strategy

OBJECTIVE 1

A primary aim of organizations operating from a marketing perspective is anticipating and satisfying customer needs and wants. One of the most important ways in which marketers do this efficiently and profitably is through the strategic use of market segmentation and positioning.

Market segmentation is the process of dividing the large and diverse mass market into subsets of consumers who share common needs, characteristics, or behaviors, and then targeting one or more of those segments with a distinct marketing mix. By identifying groups of highly similar consumers, a marketer can develop products and services specifically tailored to that group's needs that also closely match the capabilities of the organization, thus maximizing the chances of profit and success. Specifically, market segmentation allows a company to efficiently focus resources and efforts by avoiding those parts of the market it cannot satisfy well, thereby avoiding unwieldy competition. Given the diverse preferences of consumers today and the myriad products and services available, it is difficult for most companies to be everything to everyone. In addition, when evaluating a market through the segmentation process, a company is able identify segments that are saturated with strong and powerful competitors, as well as underserved segments that may represent areas of opportunity.

Two key assumptions underlie market segmentation. First, consumer preferences vary. Some consumers prefer plain pizza with sauce and cheese, while others prefer their pizza "loaded." Some consumers prefer a car that gets good gas mileage, whereas others are more concerned about cargo space and towing features. Although this may seem obvious, if all consumer preferences were universal, there would be few advantages to market segmentation. Second, by tailoring a product or service to a segment's specific needs, marketers can make the offering so appealing that the members of the segment are willing to pay a price that offsets the costs associated with catering to the specialized needs of the segment. We will return to these assumptions when we examine the factors that influence whether a firm engages in market segmentation and to what extent.

After a marketer has segmented its market, the firm can select appropriate segment(s) to target. Thus, a **target market** is simply the segment(s) toward which a firm's marketing efforts are directed. Selection of the target market(s) should be based on a thorough strategic analysis of the organization's external environments (the mass market, competitors, and general technical, political, and socio-cultural environments) and internal

Given the number of choices available coupled with the diverse preferences of customers, effective segmentation and positioning is crucial for marketers today.

Stone+/Getty Images

situations (past performance analysis and determination of future options), ultimately matching organizational strengths with market opportunities.[2] Finally, a positioning strategy is developed. **Positioning** is the process of communicating with our target market(s) through the use of marketing mix variables—a specific product, price, distribution channel, and promotional appeal—in such a way as to help consumers differentiate a product from competitors and understand how a particular product best satisfies their needs.

Market segmentation and positioning are two of the most important concepts in the study of consumer behavior and in marketing, because consumers today have more product categories from which to choose and more choices within those categories. Marketers conduct a great deal of consumer research to identify appropriate bases for market segmentation, select appropriate target markets, and develop effective positioning and marketing mix execution strategies.

OBJECTIVE 2

How Consumers and Society Benefit from Market Segmentation

Through market segmentation a firm offers products and services specifically tailored to the needs and wants of consumers within a specific segment. While this implies an obvious benefit to consumers, namely having their specific needs catered to, other benefits to consumers and to society may not be so obvious.

First, by committing efforts and resources on market segmentation, consumers no longer have to receive and evaluate marketing information that is irrelevant or unwanted. This reduces consumers' time spent in search, evaluation, and purchase activities. For example, a married, suburban, stay-at-home mom doesn't need or desire to receive direct-mail containing an offer for an urban nightclub's rapid dating service any more than a young, urban, single, living in an apartment, needs or wants a telemarketer calling and offering lawn and landscaping services. While these marketing misfires occasionally happen, in general, consumers benefit by the efficiency that market segmentation offers in terms of appropriately directing marketing information.

Imagine for a moment that marketers never discovered the efficiencies of dividing consumers into segments and targeting those segments. Most consumers are so accustomed to this marketing practice that such a scenario is hard to imagine. But, if the process of market segmentation did not exist, consumers' lives would probably be very different. For instance, imagine getting pizza coupons in the mail from a pizza parlor in Rome, Italy. Or, imagine a telemarketer calling you and attempting to sell you industrial lubricant for your large industrial drill press—you don't have a large industrial drill press in your dorm room or apartment? Beyond being buried in paper and flooded with irrelevant telemarketing, chances are you would also never learn about the new products and services that actually would benefit you and make your life better—products like low-cost cellular phones, ergonomically correct backpacks that don't hurt your spine, and low-carb peanut butter. Many marketers would argue that the reason for our high standard of living is that marketers learned that for most products and services a single-product marketing strategy cannot efficiently or effectively reach and service everyone, and that markets must be broken into manageable segments. Then, companies can tailor offerings and messages to their benefit and the benefit of consumers and society.

ETHICS

Can market segmentation create market segregation? Although segmentation offers several important benefits that we discuss in this chapter, it is not a panacea. Namely, segmentation can reinforce societal prejudice.

While market segmentation may seem far removed from the serious social problem of prejudice, some marketing researchers and sociologists argue that market segmentation reinforces separatism between groups and members of society, minimizing exposures to others and reinforcing a "me" orientation— "I own certain products, have particular interests and activities, and belong in a group with others like me."

Formally, *prejudice* is defined an unfounded fear, hatred, or mistrust of a person or group of people, based on insufficient knowledge and typically centered on ethnicity, nationality, religion, or social class. If prejudice is based in based on insufficient knowledge and fear of others, it is possible and quite probable that market segmentation reinforces societal prejudice. After all, market segmentation certainly does not encourage the coming together of the diverse members. On the contrary, the explicit goal of market segmentation is to create homogenous subsets from the diverse marketplace. Once that is accomplished, marketers deliver—via the marketing mix and mass media— products, services, and promotional messages that feed consumer's most narcissistic tendencies. From personalized tennis shoes and exclusive customer reward programs to advertisements that speak directly to the customers and the customer's peers (and to no one else), marketers do encourage people to develop personal and distinctive styles, stress the uniqueness and "special-ness" of a person's own in-group, and highlight differences between their groups and others.

Although there are a number of ways that segmentation is beneficial to consumers, marketers, and society, consumers should also recognize the degree to which segmentation reinforces ignorance, stereotypes, and prejudice. We have yet to learn how harmful to society and its values this separatism or segregation is, but it is important for current and future marketers (that's you!) to consider potential hidden costs and ethical implications of our marketing strategies.[24]

Courtesy of BMW of North America

Mass customization allows marketers to cater to individual needs and wants.

Hulton Archive/Getty Images

The Ford Motor company is generally recognized as the first "mass marketer" in the United States.

OBJECTIVE 3

Factors Influencing Market Segmentation Strategies

Market segmentation is a multi-product strategy: different products are developed for different subcategories. For example, Pepsi Cola markets Pepsi, Diet Pepsi, Pepsi Max, Diet Pepsi Lime, and Caffeine Free Pepsi Wild Cherry Pepsi and Pepsi One to different market segments.[3] *Market aggregation* is the opposite of market segmentation—a single-product, one-size-fits-all strategy in which individual differences among consumers are ignored.

If a firm chooses not to target specific segments, but rather, pursues an aggregation strategy, offering the same product and marketing mix to all consumers, this is called *mass marketing.* The first generally recognized mass marketer in the United States was Henry Ford, founder of the Ford Motor Company, who offered the Model-T automobile to the market "in any color as long as it is black." Ford was also the first company to advertise on a national level.[4] Opposite of mass marketing, a firm may choose to market one-to-one with a customer, a strategy also called *micromarketing.* A special form of one-to-one marketing, called *mass customization*, is the targeting of large segments, or traditionally mass markets, with highly customized products.[5] For example, BMW's Build-a-Car website feature allows BMW customers to design their own BMW 3-Series car, mixing and matching exterior and interior colors, options, and accessories.[6]

When should a firm pursue a market segmentation strategy (instead of an aggregation strategy), and at what level of individual targeting? The best answer follows from four main considerations: consumer preference heterogeneity, the majority fallacy, the sales-cost trade-off, and the potential for cannibalization.

We've seen that perhaps the most important consideration related to market segmentation is the extent to which tastes and preferences differ among consumers. Formally, this assumption is called **consumer preference heterogeneity**. Some people prefer spicy food, whereas others prefer bland foods. As preference heterogeneity increases, the case for segmentation increases. Moreover, the greater the variability, the more potential profits provided by individual segments.

When consumers' preferences vary, it is important to analyze how these preferences are distributed. Let's return to our spicy food example. In terms of level of spiciness, the vast majority of consumers prefer foods that are average (not too bland and not too spicy), but there are also smaller segments of consumers who prefer very mild, bland tastes, and customers who prefer extremely hot and spicy foods. Because it is logical to assume that size of the potential market segment is positively correlated to profit, it is often easy for a company to focus exclusively on large average segments, where the majority of customer preferences lie, and neglect smaller less typical segments. This tendency is called the **majority fallacy**; pursuing the majority segment is considered a "fallacy" because the largest segment, where competition tends to be most intense, is not always the most profitable. Smaller segments can actually be more profitable when there is less competition. (Figure 2.1 illustrates the majority fallacy.) For example, Ragu spaghetti sauce and many other sauces are average in terms of spiciness and are very popular, but competition in this segment is intense. There are at least 10 different brands that would be considered an average spicy sauce. On the other hand, Hunt's Prima Sauce is a fairly spicy spaghetti sauce that appeals to a much smaller market segment. Although this segment is small, it is quite profitable because there is little competition.

Another influence on segmentation strategy is the **sales-cost trade-off.** This trade-off recognizes that, as market segmentation increases, sales increase because a firm's offerings align more closely to consumers' preferences. But at the same time, costs also increase because a multi-product strategy costs more to implement than a one-product strategy. Why? Manufacturing and marketing costs increase as the number of products offered increases due to additional equipment, skills, and resources needed to make and market a variety of products. Hidden marketing costs associated with multi-product strategies also exist. For example, retail shelf space is limited, and retailers may be unwilling to carry many different varieties of a product. For example, when Coca Cola introduced New Coke in the 1980's, Burger King switched from carrying Coke to Pepsi because it did not want to carry both New Coke and Coke Classic in its fountains.

FIGURE 2.1   THE MAJORITY FALLACY

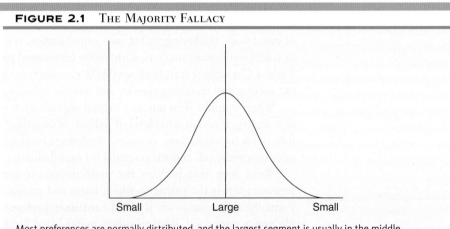

Small   Large   Small

Most preferences are normally distributed, and the largest segment is usually in the middle segment. However, competition is usually greatest for this segment.

Finally, the risk of cannibalization influences market segmentation decisions. **Cannibalization** occurs when products offered by the same firm are so similar that they compete among themselves, thus creating a case of *oversegmentation*. For example, if a consumer drinks Pepsi, she might also drink Pepsi One; thus Pepsi competes against itself for her drink purchase. At one time, Quaker State offered 1,500 different brands of motor oil. The company cut its product line in half and profits increased dramatically because cannibalization and other types of costs decreased. Sharing manufacturing and marketing costs across product offerings is important when cannibalization is a potential issue. Thus, a company must strike a delicate balance between effective market coverage and too many offerings.

Now that we have discussed what market segmentation is and some of the influences related to market segmentation and targeting strategies, we turn our attention to the various bases of market segmentation.

OBJECTIVE 4

Bases of Segmentation

There are many different ways to segment a market, and marketers should consider multiple approaches. Consumers differ on many dimensions, and each dimension suggests a potentially useful basis for dividing up the market. While we will discuss each base of segmentation as a single strategy, remember that firms typically use multiple methods in combination to divide and group consumers. A number of segmentation bases are listed in Table 2.1, along with possible segmentation variables and examples associated with that segmentation base. Let's consider some of them in detail.

Demographic Bases

Market segmentation is often based on customers' vital population statistics, called **demographic characteristics**. Popular demographic characteristics include age, gender, income, education, occupation, social class, marital status, household size, family life cycle, and culture or ethnicity. Demographics-based segmentation is the most popular segmentation base because demographic characteristics are visible, relatively easy and inexpensive to measure, and most secondary data, such as U.S. Census data, is described in terms of demographic characteristics.

Not surprisingly, our preferences, buying habits, and behaviors vary dramatically as a function of many different demographic characteristics. For example, males and females prefer different brands of clothes, health and beauty products, and many brands are targeted exclusively at a particular gender, such as Dove for women and Axe for men.

Geographic Bases

In **geographic based segmentation**, marketers split the market based on physical location of potential customers. An underlying assumption of this market segmentation base is that consumers located in geographic proximity share similar needs and preferences for products and services. Boundaries defined by zip code districts, towns, cities, states, regions, countries, and continents might indeed be useful to a company. For example, Heineken markets a non-alcoholic beer in several countries in the Middle East, where the sale of alcoholic beverages is forbidden. Procter & Gamble markets different formulations of Tide detergent throughout the world, depending on regional water quality and washing machine type. Geographic segmentation also includes climate or topographical characteristics of an area. Snow blowers are marketed in cold areas of the country, and surfboards sell better along warm, coastal regions.

TABLE 2.1   POSSIBLE MARKET SEGMENTATION BASES, CATEGORIES, AND ILLUSTRATIVE EXAMPLES

Possible Bases:	Possible Segmentation Variables:	Illustrative Examples:
Demographic		
Age	Under 6, 7–12, 13–21, 22–34, 35–50, 50+	Seeking to cater to the under-25 market,
	Pre-depression, Depression era, Baby boomers, Generation X, Generation Y, Millennials	Sprite sponsors rap concerts and MTV events.
Gender	Female, Male	In Japan, females are targeted as the
Income	Under $25,000, $25,000–$75,000, $75,000+	main coffee consumers by coffee companies like Starbucks, who operates
Education	Some H.S., H.S. graduate, Some college, College graduate, Postgraduate	over 500 outlets in that country.[7]
Occupation	Blue-collar, White-collar, Military, Craft	
Social Class	Lower, Middle, Upper	
Marital Status	Single, Married, Divorced, Co-habitating, Widowed	Carnival Cruises offers a line of special cruises aimed at couples.
Family Life Cycle	Single, Young married, Full nester, Empty Nester, Single elderly	
Culture/Ethnicity	White, African American, Hispanic, Asian, Pacific Islander, Middle Eastern, American Indian	Hallmark offers a line of cards specifically targeted to African Americans, called Mahogany.
Geographic		
Pop. Density	Urban, Suburb, Exurb, Penturbia, Rural	Gottschalks' clothing store chain targets small rural markets to avoid competing with large national clothiers (avoiding the majority fallacy).
Region	North, South, East, West Neighborhood, Town, City, State, Country Mountains, Plains, Deserts, Ocean, Jungle	Campbell's Soup markets a spicy nacho soup in Texas and California.
Climate	Temperate, Hot, Rainy, Dry	
Psychographic		
	VALS (see discussion) 4C's (see discussion)	Dyson vacuum cleaners, with its trendy and innovative design appeals to Aspirers in the 4C's group.
Behavioral		
Attribute/Benefit	Price, Convenience, Ease-of-use, Status	Snackwell's products are aimed at people that want sweet snacks but are also conscious of their health and weight.
Occasion	Morning, Evening Leisure, Work, Rush Holiday, Special day	Campbell's markets Soup-On-The-Go for those times when people don't have time to sit down and eat lunch.
Product Usage	Current user, Potential user, Lapsed user Light, Medium, Heavy	Subway offers frequent users rewards of free food after a certain number of purchases.

ESNI0223478   PENGZHOU, CHINA: A BAG OF TIDE WITH CHINESE CHARACTERS FOR SALE A SMALL STORE ON YAN XIU JIE. ©Lee Snider / The Image Works

Tide is marketed world-wide and adapted to local markets.

Community type is also a segmentation variable and includes urban environments, suburbs, *exurbs* (remote suburbs), and *penturbia* (small towns). In the United States, people continue an exodus out of the cities, which began in the 1920's, first to suburbs and then to the exurbs, and finally to small towns, called penturbia. This trend has strongly influenced the growth of the suburban "strip" mall and large regional shopping malls. Only recently have U.S. cities seen a resurgence in urban living. Worldwide, the trend is still a shift toward the urban, and by 2006, the majority of people will live in urban areas, with the number of mega cities, defined as urban areas of 10 million or more, projected to grow to 26 by 2010.[8]

Geo-demographic segmentation combines geography and demographic segmentation bases. Sometimes called *zip-code marketing*, this segmentation strategy relies on the common tendency for people who are similar along demographic dimensions to live in close proximity. In other words, we tend to live near people who are like us (i.e., "birds of a feather . . ."). For example, it is not surprising to drive into certain suburban neighborhoods in the U.S. and see swing-sets in almost every yard, minivans in the garages, and bicycles in the driveways. Sometimes we may make a conscious choice to live near others who are similar to us on certain dimension. For example, in San Francisco, there is a neighborhood called The Castro District, which is predominantly populated by gay and lesbian households. Alternatively, we may not consciously choose to live by those who are similar to us, but situational factors simply make a certain neighborhood or living situation a logical choice. Take our suburban neighborhood example. That neighborhood may attract young families more than other kinds of homebuyers or renters because it is near a school, or has houses in the price range of what a young family can afford, or simply because there are so many families with children already living there. Those who also have children find the presence of potential playmates for their kids an attractive social benefit of the neighborhood.

MARKETING IN ACTION

Hallmark Reaches African Americans in a Culturally-Relevant Way

African Americans account for approximately 13 percent of the population, according to the 2000 U.S. Census, and Hallmark, a leader in greeting cards since the early 1900's, has tapped into this market with their line of Mahogany greeting cards. Introduced as a limited 16-card promotion in 1987, the selection of seasonal and everyday cards became a permanent line in 1991, and is now the largest, most extensive brand of cards centered on the African American demographic and culture. According to the company website (www.hallmark.com), "Mahogany features more than 1,000 cards to help African Americans honor their relationships in innovative, compelling, and culturally relevant ways."

Hallmark conducts extensive research to maintain its understanding of this unique market segment, including working with African American artists and writers in card design, seeking out culturally relevant African American artwork to incorporate into Mahogany cards, and talking to consumers about their lifestyles. The goal is to truly understand African-American culture and heritage and reflect that understanding in the product line.

The top two retail markets for Mahogany cards are Washington D.C. and New York, which have high concentrations of African American populations. Other top markets include Chicago, Philadelphia, and Altanta. In 2005, Hallmark introduced two additional Mahogany card lines: *Sister to Sister* and *DaySpring® Inspired by Mahogany. Sister to Sister* targets female African-Americans with warm, conversational messages for women communicating with other women, while *DaySpring®* has an evangelical Christian theme. In addition to the full line of cards, consumers will find the Mahogany Cards With Sound and a new offering of humor cards. By effectively employing demographic segmentation, Hallmark is meeting the needs of this ethnic community.

Courtesy of Hallmark Cards, Inc.

Another interesting aspect of this phenomenon is that people who live near each other may become even more alike over time. Neighbors observe one another and may compare their actions, opinions, activities, and possessions as well as purchase products in order to gain social acceptance and fit in, or they may simply see the benefits of owning a product their neighbors enjoy. For example, suppose someone in a suburban neighborhood builds an outdoor patio. In order to fully enjoy the patio, the homeowner has frequent outdoor cookouts and parties, inviting friends and neighbors. It isn't long until one of the neighbors thinks, "This patio is great; I want one for myself." And, even better, the patio owner will probably recommend his own patio builder.

Claritas, a company specializing in geo-demographic based segmentation, markets a segmentation system called PRIZM® (recently updated and now called PRIZM$_{NE}$®) that incorporates geographic data down to the neighborhood and household levels, demographic data from the U.S. Census, and consumption and media usage information, resulting in segmentation of the U.S. market into 66 distinct segments, combined into 14 broad social groups. Any household or neighborhood in the U.S. can be profiled. Here is a sampling of some of the 66 segments:

#3 Movers and Shakers is the nation's group of upwardly mobile executives, who are highly educated, wealthy, and live in dual-income suburban households. Members of this group are the most likely to own a small business.

#4 Young Digerati are an affluent, well-educated, ethnically diverse group that is comfortable in this high-tech era. They are singles and couples living in high-end condos and apartments in trendy urban neighborhoods.

#13 Upward Bound represents the legendary soccer moms and dads and are a key market for child-centered products. Households in this group consist of dual-income earners with college degrees and white-collar jobs. These upper-class families live in newer suburban subdivision.

#21 Domestic Duos is a group that consists of middle-class empty-nesters living in older suburban neighborhoods. With their home paid off and their fixed-pension income, living is stable and enjoyable, although not extravagant.

#51 Shotguns and Pickups tend to be young, working-class couples with large families, and not surprisingly, are the most likely of all the segments to own a hunting rifle and a pickup truck. One third of this group also lives in mobile homes.

#61 City Roots is a segment of lower-income retirees living low-key lifestyles on fixed incomes. These folks – made up largely of African Americans and Hispanics—live in urban neighborhoods in condos and townhouses that they have owned for many years.[9]

Companies can use the PRIZM$_{NE}$® system to identify clusters in their markets and custom design marketing campaigns to penetrate into specific segments. For example, Cox Communications, a large cable provider, was able to identify segments nationwide that used its products. Armed with this information, the firm could target non-users in these segments in various markets, increasing sales and market penetration.

Psychographic Bases

Marketers also segment markets based on **psychographics,** which is the measurement of lifestyle, often combined with measures of attitudes, beliefs, and personalities. Lifestyle, which is simply how we live, is traditionally defined in terms of a person's activities (how they spend their time doing things such as volunteer work, vacationing, and exercising), interests (what they consider important or value in life such as home, recreation, and family), and opinions (how they feel about the world around them such political, religious, and social beliefs). Researchers use large batteries of questions (called *AIO Inventories*) to measure activities, interests, and opinions to develop consumer profiles, usually called *psychographic profiles* or *AIO's*. Psychographic information is more comprehensive than demographic information. Whereas demographic analysis focuses on who buys products, psychographic research focuses on why they buy.

THE VALS SYSTEM One widely used market segmentation tool that employs psychographics is the VALS™ System developed by SRI Consulting Business Intelligence (SRIC-BI). VALS originally stood for "values and lifestyles," and when it was first introduced in 1978, it segmented consumers based on social values and lifestyle variables. The system was significantly revised in 1989 social values were replaced with psychological motivators and personality variables in order to tap into the enduring attitudes and values that influence buyer behavior in the marketplace. An individual's VALS type is determined by their answers to 39 measured statements (35 psychological and

MARKETING IN ACTION

America's Most Entertaining Supermarket Destination

You know you're not visiting a traditional grocery store when you park your car in the shadow of the jungle animals standing in a watering hole outside the store, and you enter the building through doors flanked by traffic signals flashing "Start Your Carts" in red, yellow, and green, with a race car hanging above the entrance. You also know you're in for a unique experience when you see an olive display bigger than most salad bars, when you encounter the alligator meat, goat heads, and rattlesnake steaks in the meat section, and when you are directed to wine selection that rivals any selection anywhere.

The supermarket is Jungle Jim's International Market and this grocery store, which carries an amazing variety of food from around the world, is one of the most popular specialty supermarkets in the Midwest. Located in southwest Ohio, the 300,000 square foot store draws over 70,000 visitors a week, including many arriving in tour buses from neighboring states. From the animatronic Robin Hood that performs in the "Sherwood Forest" of foods from England section, to the yacht named for the "Gilligan's Island-ish SS Minnow" in the seafood section, Jungle Jim's is a marriage of two defining traits that make it completely unique in world of supermarkets: shopping as an entertainment destination and international specialty foods. While this dual emphasis seems like an unconventional combination, Jungle Jim's has managed to differentiate and insulate itself from the fiercely price-competitive grocery market and establish a unique position in consumers' minds.

The entertainment pleases the young and the young-at-heart, while the depth and variety of international products, in addition to standard supermarket fare, offer customers choices that aren't available other places. According to development director, Phil Adams, "We pride ourselves on getting items from every country in the world and not just a few items, but many items. A regular store may carry two or three items from India; we carry everything you would find in a typical store in India. That's the difference."[22] Sure enough, the store carries over 150,000 products from 75 different countries, including 1,300 varieties of hot sauce, 1,600 different kinds cheese from 40 countries, 65 different kinds of imported olive oil, 12,000 labels of wine, and a huge assortment of exotic produce, including Chinese okra, Indian bitter melons, and baby bananas from Mexico.[23]

By carving out a unique position in the Midwest grocery market and serving the specific needs of its customers, Jungle Jim's has managed to grow over the last 35 years from a roadside fruit stand to a sprawling six-and-a-half acre food experience.

Courtesy of Jungle Jim's

There is too much sex on television today.
I like the challenge of doing something I have never done before.
I would like to understand more about how the universe works.[10]

VALS classifies American adults into eight distinct consumer segments, as shown in Figure 2.2 and Table 2.2.

The segments are grouped along two dimensions: (1) primary motivation and (2) resources. An individual's *primary motivation* governs his or her activities. Consumers are inspired by one of three primary motivations—ideals, achievement, and self-expression. Consumers motivated by ideals are guided by ethical codes,

FIGURE 2.2 THE VALS SEGMENTS

Innovators	Thinkers	Achievers	Experiencers
Take-charge	Reflective	Goal oriented	Trend setting
Sophisticated	Informed	Brand conscious	Impulsive
Curious	Content	Conventional	Variety seeking
Survivors	**Believers**	**Strivers**	**Makers**
Nostalgic	Literal	Contemporary	Responsible
Constrained	Loyal	Imitative	Practical
Cautious	Moralistic	Style conscious	Self-sufficient

SOURCE: SRI Consulting Business Intelligence, www.sric-bi.com/VALS. Reprinted by permission.

TABLE 2.2   DESCRIPTION OF THE VALS SEGMENTS

Innovators

Innovators are successful, sophisticated, take-charge people with high self-esteem. Because they have such abundant resources, they exhibit all three primary motivations in varying degrees. They are change leaders and are the most receptive to new ideas and technologies. Their purchases reflect cultivated tastes for upscale, niche products and services.

Thinkers   *Motivated by ideals; high resources*

Thinkers are mature, satisfied, comfortable, and reflective. They tend to be well educated and actively seek out information in the decision-making process. They favor durability, functionality, and value in products.

Believers   *Motivated by ideals; low resources*

Believers are strongly traditional and respect rules and authority. Because they are fundamentally conservative, they are slow to change and technology averse. They choose familiar products and establish brands;

Achievers   *Motivated by achievement, high resources*

Achievers have goal-oriented lifestyles that center on family and career. They avoid situations that encourage a high degree of stimulation or change. They prefer premium products that demonstrate success to their peers.

Strivers   *Motivated by achievement; low resources*

Strivers are trendy and fun loving. They have little discretionary income and tend to have narrow interests. They favor stylish products that emulate the purchases of people with greater material wealth.

Experiencers   *Motivated by self-expression; high resources*

Experiencers appreciate the unconventional. They are active and impulsive, seeking stimulation from the new, offbeat, and risky. They spend a comparatively high proportion of their income on fashion, socializing, and entertainment.

Makers   *Motivated by self-expression; low resources*

Makers value practicality and self-sufficiency. They choose hands-on constructive activities and spend leisure time with family and close friends. Because they prefer value to luxury, they buy basic products.

Survivors

Survivors lead narrowly focused lives. Because they have the fewest resources, they are not active consumers and therefore do not exhibit a primary motivation. They tend to be brand loyal and buy discounted merchandise. While they make do with limited material goods they are often satisfied with their lives.

SOURCE: SRI Consulting Business Intelligence, www.sric-bi.com/VALS. Reprinted by permission.

WE LIVE IN A WIDE-ANGLED WORLD. GET A CAMERA THAT ACCOMMODATES IT.

Get more out of every picture. By getting more in. And the new EasyShare P880 zoom digital camera makes it easy. With a 24–140 mm wide-angle lens as standard, 8.0 MP, professional-quality 5.8x zoom, 2.5-inch high-res LCD screen, 30 fps VGA video, in-camera editing, stills from video, zoom during video, and RAW file formats. There's a whole wide world out there, just waiting to be shot. See more at kodak.com. **Kodak**

Always choose Kodak memory cards.

Courtesy of Kodak

Segmenting markets on core benefits is smart when your brand offers a distinctive attribute that is easy to communicate and remember.

religious beliefs or personal philosophies and a general quest for life knowledge and understanding. Those motivated by achievement seek social approval from society and base their behaviors on the reactions of their peer or *aspirational* (a group to which person desires to belong) groups. Consumers motivated by self-expression emphasize individuality and direct experience and seek out variety and risk.

Resources comprise psychological attributes, such as self-confidence, energy, vanity, and intellectualism, coupled with demographic characteristics that influence one's ability to act on his or her primary motivation such as income and education. Table 2.2 provides a description of each of the VALS segments.

National data about the VALS segments preferences for products, services, leisure activities and media is provided through a linkage with Mediamark Research

Intelligence, LLC. Financial behaviors are available from SRIC-BI's Consumer Financial Decisions survey. Custom services are regularly conducted for specific client needs. GeoVALS™ estimates the percentage of VALS segments by zip code. JapanVALS™ segments Japanese consumers.

Behavioral Bases

Behavioral-based segmentation groups consumers based on their preference for a particular product attribute or benefit, usage occasion, user status, rate of product usage, and loyalty status.

PRODUCT ATTRIBUTES OR BENEFITS Important product attributes like taste are useful segmentation tools because they are easy to identify. When segmenting the market for digital cameras, for example, companies have relied on product attributes such as resolution quality to define market segments and develop appropriate products. The Kodak Company offers cameras ranging from six megapixels to 14 megapixels for the non-professional camera buyer.

Which is among the most common product attributes used to segment consumers? *Price.* Consumers can be segmented based on price in many ways. One price segmentation model is presented here (see Figure 2.3). It divides segments based along two dimensions. One dimension, referred to as *perceived pain*, is the amount of anxiety and negative feelings a consumer experiences when paying what he or she believes is a high price for a product. The other dimension is called *perceived value*, the amount of product differentiation a consumer perceives among products, or the degree to which a consumer views brands within a product category as unique based on price. A consumer rated high on perceived value tends to view large differences among brands in terms of quality and other product benefits. A consumer rated low on perceived value tends to view brands as commodities with little brand differentiation.

Will a consumer always fall into one category for all products purchased? Of course not—the segment will depend on the product category and is influenced by situational variables.

FIGURE 2.3 MARKET SEGMENTATION BASED ON PRICE

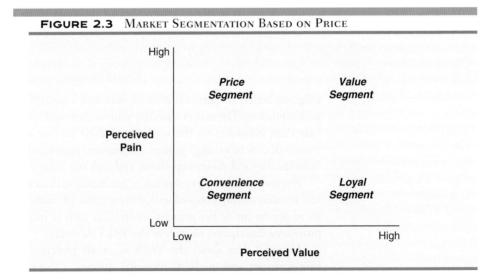

AP Photo / Al Behrman

These two dimensions form four price segments. Consumers who possess high levels of perceived pain and low levels of perceived value represent the *price segment*. These consumers reside in the upper-left quadrant of Figure 2.3. In other words, consumers in this segment feel that most brands are pretty much alike and don't want to pay a high price for a particular brand. These consumers tend to be the ultimate price shoppers and may sacrifice extra benefits and services in order to achieve the lowest price. For example, stores that carry discontinued or slightly damaged items (called *off-price discounters*) have become very popular and appeal to the price segment. Also, generic brands and store brands tend to appeal to this segment.

Those consumers with low levels of perceived pain and low levels of perceived value fall into the *convenience segment*. They reside in the lower-left quadrant of Figure 2.3. While these consumers also view brands as having little differentiation, unlike the price segment, these consumers are not particularly sensitive to price. These consumers are most sensitive to the time they have to spend shopping and want to minimize search and evaluation, and thus, they are willing to pay a higher price for the convenience of easy brand selection. Internet and catalog shopping appeal to these consumers. Although shipping costs associated with buying on the Internet or from a catalog tend to drive up product prices, the consumer can conveniently shop and compare several brands very quickly from the comfort of home.

Consumers residing in the lower-right quadrant of Figure 2.3 represent the *loyal segment*, a combination of low perceived pain and high perceived value. This segment is highly desirable to marketers who have invested to build meaning into their brand name and offer a premium product. This is the "choosy mom" who chooses Jif (whether she has a coupon for it or not), and she *always* buys Jif. If the brand is not available, then she won't purchase peanut butter that week because she is so brand loyal that substitutes are unacceptable.

The last segment is called the *value segment*. Consumers who reside in the upper-right quadrant of Figure 2.3 demonstrate a combination of high perceived pain and high perceived values. While these consumers view brands as highly differentiated, they also do not want to pay for that differentiation. In other words, these consumers want it all: the best brand names at the very lowest price. In many ways, this is the most difficult segment to satisfy. For example, outlet malls that carry overstocks of premium brands—Coach bags, Calvin Klein clothing, and Wedgwood china, for instance—are very popular and appeal to the value segment. Coupon usage is also high among this group because coupons allow shoppers to feel like they are getting a special, exclusive deal on a quality brand.

USAGE OCCASIONS AND PRODUCT USAGE Usage occasion segmentation describes purchasing and consuming products at different times of day, different times of year, and at different events or on different occasions. For example, people prefer to eat toast and drink hot tea at breakfast but prefer sandwiches and ice tea at lunch. Different seasons call for different types of products. Heavy coats and wool sweaters are necessary in winter in many parts of the U.S., whereas summer calls for t-shirts and shorts. Finally, products might be consumed every day or as part of a special event or occasion. For example, many people consume honey on a daily basis, using it as substitute for sugar or jam, but honey manufacturers have also identified a specific segment of users who consume the product while running or exercising. Clever marketers have designed special portable honey packets for this purpose. Many consumers also use specific products for specific events or on special occasions, such as pumpkins on Halloween and sparklers on the 4th of July. Marketers may rely exclusively on an event or occasion for product usage, such as a local mortuary service, or may simply adapt their all-occasion product to fit the occasion, such as M&M's in Christmas red and green.

Product usage segmentation is based on identifying light, medium, or heavy users of a product or identifying current, potential, or lapsed users. Different marketing tactics are required for different groups of consumers. For example, potential users may be unaware of the product category or unaware of the benefits of the product. Thus, marketing efforts targeted toward this group should work to increase awareness and educate potential consumers about the specific product benefits. Heavy users, on the other hand, already know about and like the product. Therefore, marketing efforts targeted toward this group should remind them to keep purchasing and maintaining their loyalty. For example, many firms now practice *customer loyalty programs*, marketing tactics and programs designed to reward and retain a company's most loyal customers. For years, airlines and hotels have offered special reward programs for frequent travelers. Frequent airline flyers can earn free tickets, class upgrades, and faster check-in service, while hotels offer free rooms or room upgrades to frequent guest. Now, a variety of firms offer customer loyalty programs, including bookstores, restaurants, movie theatres, and gas stations, just to name a few. The more purchases the customer makes, the more rewards and benefits he or she earns.

OBJECTIVE 5

Positioning

The previous sections have detailed the various segmentation bases by which consumers can be divided, clustered, and targeted. So far, we've explained why it's important for marketers to identify individual customer segments, i.e., the "divide" portion of the divide and conquer strategy. Next, we describe the "conquer" portion of the strategy, namely positioning. We've already seen that positioning is the process of communicating with target market(s) in such a way as to help consumers differentiate the firm's product from other products and understand how the product can specifically satisfy their needs and wants. Sometimes marketers use terms like *value proposition* or "*The Big Idea!*" to describe a brand, product, or company's specific positioning strategy within the market. For example, Dove's big idea is The Campaign for Real Beauty and is reflected in the brand's promotional efforts.

According to positioning experts Reis and Trout, the "position" of a product is the place the product occupies in the customers' minds, relative to the competitor's products.[11] What is important about this definition is: (1) a firm must always position in terms of the competition, and (2) positioning is not something a marketer does to a product, it's actually something that happens in the mind of the prospect as a result of the brand messages and communication that the marketer provides. Thus, marketers can't definitively position a product, although they talk about positioning strategy as if that is what they do. All marketers can do, however, is communicate the marketing mix to the target market in such a way that the consumer accurately

campaignforrealbeauty.com Dove

New Dove Firming. As tested on real curves.

Courtesy of Dove/Unilever

Marketers like Dove communicate their value proposition through advertising and other elements of the marketing mix.

positions the product in his or her own mind, hopefully in line with the intentions of the marketer.

All marketing activities influence positioning and vice versa. For example, Armani does not allow Walmart to carry its men's clothing line because this low-cost retailer would undermine Armani's high-end positioning strategy. Likewise, Walmart does not want to carry Armani suits because this would be inconsistent with its image as a low-cost retailer. Such inconsistent channel decisions would confuse customers of both firms.

Companies use several strategies to position their products; depending on the product's characteristics; market segmentation bases used; competitive environment; and goals of the company. We'll review some of them here.

Positioning a Leader

Some brands have the distinction of being the first brand to enter and define a market. These brands are referred to as *pioneering brands*. Research has shown that pioneering brands have an advantage in the market for a number of reasons. First, they are novel and interesting; thus, consumers tend to pay much more attention to them than to redundant, copycat brands.[12] Second, when a new product category is created, consumers are typically unsure of their preferences. When this is the case, the combination of features and benefits associated with the pioneering brand seems especially useful, so much so that the pioneer actually sets the ideal points for the category in terms of product features and benefits.[13] In addition, when follower brands are introduced, consumers tend to compare follower brands with the pioneer but not vice versa, and consequently, the pioneer seems unique and special while followers seem like pale imitations.[14]

All of these advantages lead to greater strategic opportunities for pioneering brands because they enable the pioneer to clearly positing itself as the leader of a category, and positioning as a leader means setting a *standard of comparison*, which means being the brand against which all the other brands in the category are judged. Consider the following classic positioning statements (communicated via Coke's advertising): "Coke is the real thing," "Coke is it!" and "Coke is the pause that refreshes." All these messages imply that everything else is a pale imitation. Coca-Cola invented the cola category and much of its marketing emphasizes this point. Similarly, advertising for many pioneering brands argues, "we invented the product," implying that the brand knows more about the product category than any other competitor. Some examples are Jeep – "There's Only One," and Xerox – "The document company" and "The knowledge company."

Positioning a Follower

How do firms market a product that isn't the pioneering brand? One strategy for positioning a follower brand is to separate the brand from the leader by creating what appears to the customer as a new product category.[15] For example, Pepsi has been very successful competing against Coca Cola by positioning itself as a hipper, trendier brand for a new generation. Several years ago, Anheuser-Busch held the domestic beer market. When Heineken entered the U.S. market, it was positioned under a new category—*premium imported beer*—and is still the leader in this category. Anheuser-Busch also wanted to expand in the premium category so it invented the *premium domestic beer* category with Michelob. Anheuser-Busch quickly followed with Michelob Ultra to serve the *diet beer category*.[16]

Pursuing a "doing the opposite" positioning strategy is also an option for a follower brand.[17] When following this approach, a brand positions itself opposite the leader. Take, for example, the battle between Mercedes-Benz and BMW. For many years, Mercedes-Benz was the most famous luxury car in the world. BMW decided to take an opposite strategy. While Mercedes was known for comfort and luxuriant roominess, BMW focused on nimble performance. Its big idea was "The Ultimate Driving Machine." BMW outsells Mercedes in most markets in the world, including the U.S.[18]

Another classic example of doing the opposite is the famous 7-Up uncola campaign, which began in the 1960's. A cola is opaque, sweet, and strong in aftertaste, and the opposite of a cola is uncola. Television advertising for 7-Up used a highly successful comparative theme in which dried-up, shriveled cola nuts (actually cocoa beans) were compared with juicy, colorful, lively "uncola nuts" (fresh lemons and limes). The company also created uncola drinking glasses, which were upside-down Coca-Cola hourglass design glasses. During the campaign in the late 1960's sales rose a whopping 20% per year. Prior to the campaign, consumers did not think of 7-Up when they purchased soft drinks. 7-Up was used primarily as a headache remedy and alcoholic mixer (it was promoted "for home and hospital use" when first introduced in 1929). Interestingly, despite 7-Up's growth in the soft drink market; its old reputation has persisted. Many older U.S. consumers still keep it in their liquor cabinet, and some people still drink it when they are sick, although there is no medicinal benefit to 7-Up because it is full of sugar.

Finally, turning disadvantages into advantages is a useful strategy for follower brands. Avis is the number two brand in car rentals so "we try harder." Often, smaller companies will also use the phrase "not the biggest, just the best" to convey that smaller can mean higher quality and more individualized service.

Positioning Linked to Segmentation Bases

Beyond broad strategies for positioning leaders and followers, some specific strategies apply to all types of brands. These strategies parallel bases of segmentation discussed earlier in the chapter.

POSITIONING BY CORE BENEFIT One popular strategy employs a **core benefit proposition**, which relies on a single attribute or benefit that differentiates the brand from competitors' offerings. When positioning with a core benefit, the proposition should be short and easy to remember, and should *sharply* differentiate the product from competing brands. In others words, the benefit should be exclusively associated with the brand and strongly held in the consumers' minds.[19] Volvo is safety; Federal Express is overnight; Brawny Paper Towels are strong; and Subway is fresh.

POSITIONING BY PRICE Sometimes it is difficult to focus on a core benefit. Perhaps a competitor already is known for a key benefit; or perhaps a firm's core benefit is complicated and difficult to communicate to the consumer. Price is an alternative attribute. It is easy to understand and communicate, and it is important to most consumers because they consistently use price as a gauge of quality— "You get what you pay for."[20] The assumption that there is a strong relationship between price and quality leads consumers to infer that high price signals high quality. This is called the *price-quality heuristic*. Communicating price differences among brands to consumers translates into perceived quality differences.

Positioning by price typically takes the form of using premium pricing or pricing below competitor brands. **Premium pricing**, sometimes called prestige pricing, is pricing the brand at the high end of product category's price range. It can be applied to any type of product, such as Piaget watches for $15,000, ST DuPont lighters for $7,000, Clive Christian #1 Perfume for $1,900 per ounce, and Ben and Jerry's Ice Cream for $5.00 a cone.

Pricing lower than competitors' brands is a strategy often used by store brands, such as Kmart brands, Kroger brands, and so on. These brands typically promote the store brand as being the same as the name brand, simply lower in price. Moreover, retailers can highlight price differences easily by placing store brands next to name brands on the store shelf. Walmart is the most well-known low-price positioned company in history. It sets prices up to 10% less than competitors in many areas.

POSITIONING BY PRODUCT USAGE SITUATION Product usage strategy focuses on when or how a product is purchased and consumed. Promotion that builds a strong association between a particular brand and a particular usage situation leads consumers to think of that brand whenever the situation arises. For example, Campbell's soup is predominantly positioned for use at lunchtime (this strategy dates back to days when schoolchildren came home for lunch). Gatorade is positioned as good for replacing bodily fluids lost during vigorous exercise and participation in sporting activities. Finally, Peeps candies are a must-have at Easter, although the marshmallow treats are now sold throughout the year during most holidays.

POSITIONING BY PRODUCT USER Sometimes it is useful for marketers to identify their brand with the user of the product. To do so, marketers use either "real-life" representations—Secret Deodorant is "strong enough for a man but made for a woman," for instance—or through characters that are *archetypes* (typical, ideal, or classic examples) of the user, such as the fictitious Betty Crocker or the Marlboro Man. Interestingly, Marlboro cigarettes were originally targeted to women; they had red-tipped filters to hide lipstick stains and were packaged in a pink box. When the brand failed to do well, the rugged Marlboro man helped reposition the brand toward men. We will discuss repositioning next.

Repositioning

Repositioning attempts to change the way consumers perceive a brand, either their own brand or a competitor's. One of the most famous examples of repositioning the competition's brand was a campaign for Tylenol.[21] Tylenol radio ads in the 1980s stated, "For the millions who should not take aspirin, if your stomach is easily upset, or if you have an ulcer, or if you suffer from asthma, allergies, or iron-deficiency anemia, it would make sense to check with your doctor before you take aspirin. Aspirin can irritate the stomach lining, trigger asthmatic or allergic reactions, and cause small amount of hidden gastrointestinal bleeding. Fortunately, there's Tylenol." Aspirin, especially the Bayer brand, was known as the "miracle drug," but Tylenol's campaign repositioned aspirin as potentially harmful to health. Today, aspirin is once again the miracle drug, through Bayer's and other brands' repositioning based on the core benefit of heart health.

In another classic case, Royal Doulton china changed consumers' perception of Lenox china by simply informing consumers that Lenox is made in Pomona, New Jersey, while Royal Doulton is made in Stoke-on-Trent, England and hence it is real English china. Moreover, New Jersey conjures up negative images of factories, black smoke and pollution for some consumers. Finally, Scope mouthwash used repositioning to combat the competition, Listerine, quite effectively. Scope's advertising campaign stated that Listerine "gives you medicine breath," but Scope delivers "fresh minty breath." This campaign was even more effective because Listerine's slogan at the time was, "The taste you hate twice a day."

In summary, there are many different positioning strategies. The best depends on the characteristics of the product, the competition, and the type of mental associations marketers want consumers to form about their brands. If a brand is the pioneer, the firm should emphasize this in their promotion, i.e., take credit for being first. If a brand is markedly different on a single easy-to-communicate and important dimension, a single core benefit proposition can succeed. If a brand is highly similar to competitors' offerings or difficult to differentiate, a firm may be able to differentiate via price, usage situation, or user. Finally, if competing brands have an exploitable weakness, repositioning is a tenable strategy.

Perceptual Mapping

Measuring consumer perceptions is an important part of positioning. Perceptual maps measure the way products are positioned in the minds of consumers and show these perceptions on a graph whose axes are formed by product attributes. The maps provide a research tool to assess how multiple products in a category are positioned, how the attributes relating to the product are seen in the customers' eyes, and whether there are any product "gaps" in the market.

Researchers create perceptual maps by surveying members of the target market, asking people to rate products across multiple product attributes. For example, if researchers were interested in soft drinks, likely attributes used in the analysis would include sweetness, carbonation, fruitiness, lightness, etc. Attribute ratings are then subjected to various statistical techniques and a perceptual map can be extracted. On the map, similar brands are plotted close together, and dissimilar brands are plotted far apart. Thus, one thing a perceptual map tells marketers is who their direct competitors are (those plotted near to one another) and what brands represent less vigorous competition. Blank spaces on perceptual maps indicate *gaps* in the market. Gaps typically indicate:

a. a true opportunity in the market that we might be able to pursue;

b. a combination of attributes that nobody actually needs or wants, which is why there is not competitor there;

c. a combination of attributes that is impossible to deliver to the consumer without the development of new technology. (There are many examples of products invented to fill these types of gaps, such as Air Pump athletic shoes and shoes with shocks, lightweight cell-phones, and mouse-pads on laptop computers.)

Figure 2.4 shows a hypothetical map for our soft drinks example. This map is based on two dimensions: (1) sweetness and (2) carbonation or "bubbliness."

FIGURE 2.4   PERCEPTUAL MAP

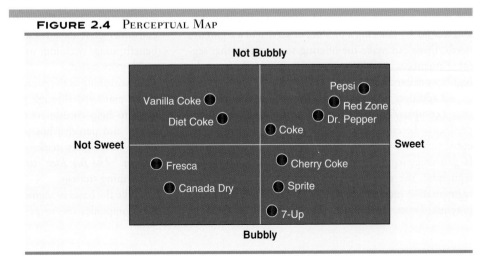

(Perceptual maps can have more than two dimensions but then they become more difficult to interpret.) What does this map show if we work for the 7-Up company? It shows that our closest direct competitors are Cherry Coke and Sprite; we are perceived as very fruity but not too sweet; and there is a gap in the market in the lower left quadrant. Additional research is required to determine the nature of the gap.

Finally, *ideal vectors* can also be plotted on perceptual maps, which show ideal combinations of attributes. The slope of the ideal vector indicates the ratio of the two dimensions preferred by consumers. We can generate ideal vectors for all consumers or by specific market segments.

Chapter Summary

One of the most important ways in which marketers discover and satisfy customer needs and wants efficiently is through the divide and conquer process of market segmentation and positioning.

Market Segmentation is the process of dividing the large and diverse mass market into subsets of consumers who share common needs, characteristics, or behaviors, and targeting one or more of those segments with a distinct marketing mix. By identifying groups of highly similar consumers, a marketer is able to develop products and services specifically tailored to that group's needs that also closely match the capabilities of the organization, thus maximizing the chances of profit and success.

Marketers make two underlying assumptions related to market segmentation: first, consumer preferences vary, and second, by tailoring a product or service to a segment's needs, firms can make the offering so appealing that segment members are willing to pay a price that offsets the higher associated costs.

In addition to these assumptions, four factors influence a company's market segmentation strategy: consumer preference heterogeneity (the idea that consumer preferences vary), the majority fallacy (the risk of focusing on large average segments and neglecting smaller, less typical segments), the sales-cost trade-off (the fact that market segmentation increases sales and cost simultaneously), and potential for cannibalization (the case in which different products offered by the same company are so similar they compete with each other).

Bases of segmentation include demographic, geographic, psychographic, attributes/benefits, and behavioral. Demographic based segmentation divides customers along vital population statistics. In geographic based segmentation, the market is divided based on physical location of potential customers. An underlying assumption of this market segmentation base is that consumers located in geographic proximity share similar needs and preferences for some products. Geo-demographic segmentation combines geography and demographic segmentation bases. Psychographic based segmentation centers on customers' lifestyles, and one of the leading lifestyle segmentation systems is the VALS System. Behavioral based segmentation includes segmenting consumers based on consumer preference for a particular product attribute or benefit, usage occasion, user status, rate of product usage, and loyalty status.

Positioning is the process of communicating with our target market(s) through the use of marketing mix variables to help consumers differentiate our product from others and perceive how our product best satisfies their needs. Sometimes marketers use terms like *value proposition* or "*The Big Idea*" to describe a brand, product, or positioning strategy.

Like the bases of segmentation, there are several strategies companies use to position their products. The best positioning strategy depends on the characteristics of our product, market segmentation bases used, the competition, and the type of mental associations we want consumers to form. If our brand is the pioneer, we should emphasize this in our promotion. If our brand is markedly different on a single easy-to-communicate and important dimension, a single core benefit proposition should be used. If our brand is highly similar to competitors' offerings or difficult to differentiate, we may by be able to differentiate anyway via price, usage situation, or user. If competing brands have an exploitable weakness, repositioning is a possible strategy. Finally, marketers use perceptual mapping to measure consumer preferences and develop competitive strategy.

Key Terms

market segmentation	sale-costs trade-off	psychographics
target market	cannibalization	behavior based segmentation
positioning	demographic characteristics	core benefit proposition
consumer preference heterogeneity	geographic based segmentation	premium pricing
majority fallacy	geo-demographic segmentation	repositioning

Review and Discussion

1. Clearly distinguish between the following terms, demographics, psychographic, lifestyle, and positioning.

2. What are the two underlying assumptions of market segmentation?

3. How do the majority fallacy and the potential for cannibalization influence market segmentation decisions?

4. According to the VALS technique, what type of consumer would probably buy a digital video camera? What type of consumer would take a fishing vacation trip? Justify your answer.

5. Describe how marketers of Tropicana orange juice could use usage situation to broaden the products segment.

6. Why might the pioneering advantage be even stronger for services than it is for physical products? Give one example.

7. How might a leading brand of personal music players, such as Apple's iPod, best position itself? Give specific examples.

8. What steps might a follower brand of personal music players, such as Sony, do in terms of positioning to increase its chances of success? Give specific examples.

9. Describe when it is best to position using a core benefit proposition. Why?

10. Describe the three situations that gaps in perceptual maps represent.

Short Application Exercises

1. Find print advertisements that reflect segmentation based on the following:

   a. Demographic based using ethnicity/culture

   b. Attribute/benefit based

   c. Behavioral based on usage occasion

2. Visit the PRIZM website and enter your own zip code to see your neighborhood profile. Do you feel it accurately reflects your household and neighborhood? Why or why not?

3. Visit the VALS website and complete the online questionnaire to find out the segment to which you belong. Take some time to read the segment descriptions. Do you feel your segment accurately portrays your lifestyle? Next, take the survey again, but answer the questions from the perspective of someone else: your crazy neighbor, you elderly uncle, or your conservative grandfather. (NOTE: Make sure to click the "yes" button that asks whether you have taken the survey before.) Again, are you satisfied with the profile? Why or why not?

4. Develop a questionnaire to measure some AIO's of your fellow college students. Administer the questionnaire to 20 students and generate lifestyle segments based on your results.

5. Identify one example in the marketplace of a company that has repositioned either itself or a competitor. Was the campaign successful? Justify your opinion.

MANAGERIAL APPLICATION

According to the U.S. Federal Research U.S. credit card debt per household was $8,475, making credit card debt a large portion of all consumer debt. The use of credit cards varies extensively. For some, a credit card is a convenient substitute for cash, while others like to "buy now"—even it they can't afford it.

Imagine you have been hired as a consumer behavior consultant for JP Morgan Chase, one of the country's largest issuers of consumer credit card products. The company has decided one of the highest growth potential market segments for their credit card products is a "young influentials" segment. In light of this potential market segment, consider the following questions:

1. How would you define this market segment?

2. How would this segment use (and/or potentially abuse) credit cards?

3. What major benefits of owning a credit card should be stressed to this target segment?

4. What do you think is the best way to get information about your credit cards to these consumers?

5. What would be the primary message of your advertisements?

6. JP Morgan Chase is also concerned about the ethics of marketing credit card products to consumers who might abuse them. U.S. consumers' filings for personal bankruptcy are at an all time high. Additionally, in every major city, many people are flocking to classes and consultations designed to help them get out of consumer debt—a process that begins by cutting up credit cards. Besides the ethical issues, many consumers who abuse credit cards will never pay their credit card bills entirely. How can the company modify the advertising message to attract ONLY responsible credit card users?

The part video is designed to expand and highlight the consumer behavior concepts in this part of the book. To view the videos, go to **http://www.cengage.com/international** and click on the student companion site link. After viewing the video, answer the following questions to test your knowledge on the part content and its application to the video case.

Segmentation at Lake, Snell, Perry, and Mermin Associates

Lake, Snell, Perry, and Mermin and Associates is a marketing research company that uses both research to profile and segment various groups in the U.S. population. The company helps its clients to understand and better appeal to these various groups. Clients are typically political candidates, non-profit foundations, and public interest groups.

1. Imagine you work for this company and are proposing a new research project to a prospective client, a political candidate. What are the advantages of segmenting potential voters? How will identifying and understanding potential segments help the candidate ultimately win?

2. Consider your own school. Develop a research methodology to segment and profile the population of your school. What specific questions would you pose? How would you collect this data? Speculate on what some potential segments might look like. Name the segments and provide a descriptive profile of these segments.

3. Engage in a secondary research project and gather information on one of the segments discussed in the video case. If a political candidate were trying to appeal to this group, what specific marketing tactics/messages might the candidate use?

How Consumers Make Decisions

CHAPTERS

AN INTERVIEW WITH BABA SHIV

Professor of Marketing
STANFORD UNIVERSITY

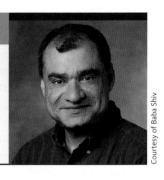

Courtesy of Baba Shiv

Baba Shiv is Professor of Marketing at Stanford University. He studies consumer decision making and decision neuroscience, with specific emphasis on the role of emotion in decision making, the neurological basis of emotion, and nonconscious mental processes in decision making.

Q Please describe the role of affect in consumer decision making.

All emerging evidence seems to suggest that by and large, affect is fundamental to and essential for making decisions that one can live with and be committed to. In several of my recent studies, I show that individuals with a more muted emotional circuitry have trouble making committed decisions, which manifests in a greater propensity to change one's mind following a decision. Affect seems to play its role in making committed decisions by promoting what is called pre-decisional distortion—distorting information in favor of the affect-laden option. The result is a clear dominance structure, where the affect-laden option clearly dominates the other options in the choice set.

Q Recently, you conducted some fascinating work on neuroimaging and the marketing placebo effect. Please describe this work and its implications for understanding the consumer.

For a number of years, I had been puzzled by the widespread use of the price-leadership strategy, wherein the marketer focuses on lowering prices to create a super customer value proposition. Given that price affects quality perceptions, I was puzzled with the ubiquity of the use of this strategy across different categories. When I would meet with marketers who use this strategy, I would ask them if this price-quality relationship is something that concerns them. The common response was that indeed lower prices can affect *perceptions* of quality, but then these perceptions would be corrected by the marketplace; once consumers use the product, they would realize that the product is of good quality, and the word will then spread around. In other words, what these marketers were assuming was that predicted

utility (predictions of the utility one would derive from a product) has no impact on experience utility (the actual utility one derives from a product). I embarked on this research topic essentially to question the validity of this assumption—that price affects not merely perceptions and thus predicted utility, but can shape experience utility as well.

One of the studies I conducted on this topic was with Hilke Plassmann, John O'Doherty, and Antonio Rangel. Test subjects were told that they would be consuming five different wines ranging in price from $5 to $90. The wines were delivered in random order through a mouthpiece while the test subjects were in an fMRI scanner. A trial would begin with the price of the wine being flashed on a monitor. The wine was then delivered and the test subject was told to swirl the wine in the mouth for five seconds and then swallow the wine when prompted. Water was then delivered through the mouthpiece to rinse the mouth, following which the next trial began. The activity in the entire brain was recorded across trials and across various phases within each trial. We then compared the brain activation across trials (different price levels), and what we found was that the activation of an area of the brain called the medial orbitofrontal cortex (mOFC) was greater when the wine was at a higher price than a lower price (the mOFC is the area of the brain that measures experienced pleasure). Now, here is the twist in the story: unbeknown to the test subjects, the same wine was delivered across trials!

The accumulated evidence across different studies suggests that the core assumption behind the price-leadership strategy—that predicted utility does not influence experience utility is invalid. In reality, from the consumer's point of view, Pro tali numismate tales merces [One gets what one pays for].

What type of advances do you predict with respect to neuroscience and consumer behavior? What should we expect to learn in the near future? What should we expect to learn in the distant future?

An obvious advantage of integrating research in neuroscience with that in consumer behavior is that neuroscientific methods such as fMRI offer the promise of localizing neural activity associated with various phenomena. These methods offer the advantage of providing direct tests for existing as well as new theories. This is particularly important for furnishing process-level evidence especially when the underlying processes are nonconscious and thus, difficult to tap using conventional psychological techniques. Apart from providing new methodologies for testing theories, neuroscience offers considerable promise in terms of

1. Providing confirmatory evidence about the existence of a phenomenon

2. Generating a more fundamental (i.e., a neural-level) conceptualization and understanding of underlying processes

3. Refining existing conceptualizations of various phenomena

AN INTERVIEW WITH GEORGE LOEWENSTEIN

Professor of Economics and Psychology
CARNEGIE MELLON UNIVERSITY

Courtesy of Anna Jekel

George Loewenstein is the Herbert A. Simon Professor of Economics and Psychology at Carnegie Mellon University. He studies intertemporal choice decisions involving trade-offs between costs and benefits occurring at different points in time, negotiation, and people's predictions of their own future feelings and behavior.

How does the field of behavioral economics enhance our understanding of consumer decision making?

Traditional economics assumes that people make rational, self-interested decisions. It doesn't shed much light on commonly observed self-destructive patterns of behavior, such as smoking and other forms of drug abuse, overeating, and overspending except to say that if people are doing them, they must be rational.

Behavioral economics attempts to provide a more realistic account of consumer behavior by recognizing that people make certain types of systematic mistakes. For example, people overweight immediate, relative to delayed, costs and benefits (a phenomenon known as "present-biased preferences"); they overweight small probabilities (which helps to explain the appeal of lottery tickets); and they tend to take the path of least resistance, going with the status quo or default options even when superior alternatives are available. By providing a more realistic account of human decision making,

behavioral economics can account for a much wider range of consumer behavior, including self-destructive patterns of behavior that traditional economics assumes don't exist.

What role does behavioral economics play in the administration of U.S. President Barack Obama?

By assuming that behavior is rational and self-interested, traditional economics doesn't provide many useful ideas for policies aimed at helping people overcome self-destructive patterns of behavior and is, in fact, generally hostile to such interventions. Recognizing these limitations of traditional economics, the Obama administration, which includes many behavioral economists, has incorporated insights from behavioral economics into the policies it has been promoting. For example, their proposal to require employees to make enrollment in tax-protected IRAs (individual retirement accounts) automatic, i.e., the default upon employment, plays on the default bias. Likewise, legislation to encourage employers to offer immediate incentives for employees to engage in healthy behaviors plays on present-biased preferences, because it introduces an immediate reward for self-beneficial behavior where the delayed rewards of better health seem insufficient to motivate behavior change. Yet a third example is the proposal to require credit card companies which specify a minimum payment in the monthly bill to also report how long it would take to pay off the credit card balance making payments of this magnitude.

How does the field of neuroeconomics enhance our understanding of consumer behavior?

Ultimately, knowing how the brain solves the problem of consumer decision making cannot fail to enhance our understanding not only of the triggers that lead to purchasing but also the ways that consumer behavior can go wrong. However, the field of neuroeconomics is still in its infancy. Despite the rise of firms offering to provide retailers and manufacturers with data from brain scans and other neuroscience measures, I believe that at present this type of information provides, at best, limited value to businesses.

What advances do you expect to see in the future of neuroeconomics and consumer behavior?

As neuroeconomics matures as a field, we are likely to see the emergence of theoretical models of behavior that are much more closely tied to what we know about how the brain processes information. Currently, behavioral economists tend to begin with the rational choice model, modifying it to incorporate the types of insights I mentioned above, e.g., present-biased preferences, overweighting of small probabilities, etc. As neuroeconomics advances, it is likely that we will see the emergence of new models of economic behavior that bear little resemblance to rational choice models and that are able to accommodate the full range of economic behavior in more comprehensive fashion, rather than as deviations from the rational choice model.

OVERVIEW OF CONSUMER DECISION MAKING

OBJECTIVES *After studying this chapter, you will be able to . . .*

1 │ Define the four primary types of consumer decisions

2 │ Describe the traditional model of consumer decision making

3 │ Explain the differences among consumers' wants, needs, and opportunities

4 │ Understand the nature of information search

5 │ Discuss the importance of consumer uncertainty in decision making

6 │ Provide examples of how marketers manage consumer satisfaction

KELLOGG'S COMPANY: CEREAL WITH DISCLOSURE

The marketplace is filled with information about brands—some useful, some superfluous. In fact, so much brand information exists today that consumers often feel overwhelmed and confused. Kellogg's Company, the Battle Creek, Michigan, breakfast cereal giant known for *Special K, Froot Loops,* and *Rice Krispies*, is trying to change all of that—for the better. Recently, Kellogg's unveiled new cereal boxes designed to make it easier for consumers to find nutritional information about the brands. All Kellogg's ready-to-eat cereals sold in the United States will feature "Nutrition at a Glance" banners on the front of its boxes. Kellogg's introduced similar packaging in Europe as early as 1986. The nutritional banners will display information

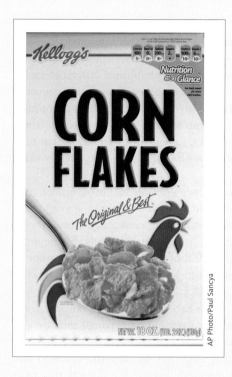

AP Photo/Paul Sancya

about fat, sugar, sodium, and calorie content. In addition, the banners will indicate whether the cereals contain ten percent of an adult's recommended daily allowance of magnesium, calcium, potassium, fiber, and vitamins A, C or E.

Kellogg's hopes to provide easy-to-read graphics of how their cereals satisfy requirements of consumers' daily diets. The new banners will accompany the traditional nutrition label found on the side panels of boxes. The new packaging follows Kellogg's effort to raise the nutritional value of the cereals and snacks it markets to children. Apparently, the Kellogg's Company is reformulating its products that currently contain high levels of sugar, such as *Apple Jacks, Corn Pops,* and *Pop-Tarts* toaster pastries. The firm expects to have products that meet the U.S. Department of Agriculture's 2,000-calories-a-day guidelines available by 2010. Perhaps just as important, if reduced-sugar versions of the products don't pass the taste test, Kellogg's will not market them to children.[1]

OBJECTIVE 1

The Consumer Decision Making Process

People make hundreds of decisions each day, from the mundane (e.g., choosing what clothes to wear) to the extremely important (e.g., selecting guardians for a child). As consumers, people constantly make decisions regarding the purchase of products and services. Some of these decisions are trivial, such as clicking a Web site for the daily news, and others are complex, like deciding on an anniversary gift. Thus, consumer decision making is a multifaceted process that ranges from automatic to highly structured problem solving. In this chapter, we discuss how consumers recognize problems, define markets of interest, gather information for consideration and purchase decisions, and measure their satisfaction.

Types of Consumer Decisions

One way to characterize consumer decision making is on an *effort continuum,* ranging from very low to very high. **Routine choice** is carried out automatically, with little conscious effort. As such, it involves no information search or deliberation. Frequently purchased, low-cost products, such as chewing gum and milk, generally involve habitual responses. These purchase decisions are highly familiar and relatively trivial because they involve little risk. **Intermediate problem solving** usually involves limited information search and deliberation. Consumers are not motivated to rigorously evaluate each alternative, so they engage simple decision rules or heuristics to aid their decision making. Products such as snack foods and soft drinks, for which consumers typically have established preferences, generally entail intermediate effort. Finally, **extensive problem solving** requires a deliberate and systematic effort from consumers. Here, consumers generally do not have well-established criteria to evaluate brands or may be unfamiliar with the product category. Consumers generally engage in extensive problem solving for infrequently purchased, expensive products such as automobiles, graduate schools, and home security systems. Because these decisions involve high levels of risk, consumers normally dedicate a great deal of time and effort in gathering information and evaluating alternatives prior to actually making a purchase.

A more complete way to think about consumer decision making considers two separate factors: processing effort and involvement.[2] The first factor, *processing effort,* represents a continuum from automatic to systematic processing. At one extreme, consumers may process no information and simply respond intuitively. At the other extreme, consumers gather and evaluate a great deal of product information prior to choice. Processing effort closely parallels the routine—intermediate—extensive continuum discussed above.

The second dimension, *involvement,* represents a continuum ranging from decisions that entail low levels of consumer involvement or personal relevance to decisions that elicit much higher levels of interest and concern. It may be helpful to think of processing effort as primarily cognitive or thinking-oriented and involvement as more affective or feeling-oriented. Figure 3.1 depicts this two-dimensional model of consumer decision making, with its quadrants of brand laziness, brand loyalty, variety seeking, and problem solving. Figure 3.2 provides product examples.

Involvement is the personal relevance or importance of an issue or situation. Accordingly, high involvement decisions are characterized as important to consumers. High involvement is often associated with emotional outcomes. Consumers seek not only functional benefits, such as the warmth of a new jacket, but also the social rewards of compliments on their good taste or fitting in with group norms.[3] Finally, if a decision involves a high level of **perceived risk**, i.e., the possibility of negative outcomes,

---

FIGURE 3.1   TYPES OF CONSUMER DECISION MAKING

		Involvement	
		Low	High
Information Processing — Low		**1. Brand Laziness** *Commodity Products*	**2. Brand Loyalty** *Self-Concept Enhancing Products*
Information Processing — High		**3. Variety Seeking** *Parity Products*	**4. Problem Solving** *Complicated big-Ticket Items*

SOURCE: Adapted from Assael, H. (1998). *Consumer Behavior and Marketing Action.* Cincinnati, OH: South-Western Publishing.

FIGURE 3.2 PRODUCT EXAMPLES BY DECISION TYPE

		Involvement	
		Low	High
Information Processing	Low	**1. Brand Laziness** butter, ammonia, salt, flour, cheese, toothpaste*	**2. Brand Loyalty** jeans, athletic shoes, TV programs, cigarettes, magazines, toothpaste*
	High	**3. Variety Seeking** beer, candy, sports drinks, chewing gum, breakfast cereal, toothpaste*	**4. Problem Solving** automobiles, appliances, furniture, airlines, consumer electronics, toothpaste*

*some products, such as toothpaste, can appear in multiple quadrants.

SOURCE: Adapted from Assael, H. (1998). *Consumer Behavior and Marketing Action.* Cincinnati, OH: South-Western Publishing.

then consumers are more likely to demonstrate higher levels of involvement.[4] Perceived risk comes in a variety of forms: financial, physical, performance, psychological, and social. Figure 3.3 provides definitions and examples of these five forms of risk. Next, the four quadrants shown in Figures 3.1 and 3.2 are examined in detail.

FIGURE 3.3 CATEGORIES OF PERCEIVED RISK

Risk Type	Risk Capital	Perceived Consequences	Risk Target	Examples
Financial	Time and money	The costs of the product or service will exceed the benefits	Consumers whose investment in time or money is large relative to their resources	1. Real estate 2. Automobile 3. Graduate school
Functional	Task performance	The product fails to provide the desired functional benefits	Consumers who are dependent on the product to do a job, especially technologically driven consumers	1. Laptop computer 2. Home security system 3. Automobile
Physical	Personal health and safety	Product failure causes physical harm	Unhealthy consumers or sensation-seeking	1. Pharmaceuticals 2. Food and beverages 3. Motorcycles
Psychological	Self-concept	Product will be inconsistent with a consumer's self-concept	Compulsive shoppers and consumers with low self-esteem	Privately consumer luxury items (e.g., HDTV)
Social	Self-esteem	Product will not meet the standards of the consumer's reference group	High self-monitors	Publicly consumed luxury items (e.g., fashion clothing)

SOURCE: Adapted from a variety of sources, including Assael, H. (1998). *Consumer Behavior and Marketing Action.* Cincinnati, OH: South-Western Publishing.

Brand Laziness

When both involvement and information processing are low (Figure 3.1, quadrant 1), consumers typically make choices as a matter of habit, requiring little effort. This is referred to as **brand laziness,** a consumer's natural inertial movement toward a product or service based on familiarity and convenience, rather than a fundamental commitment to the brand. Consumers sometimes stick with old, familiar brands for no apparent reason other than the fact that they purchased it before, and it seems fine. Most consumers' daily market decisions lack interest, risk, and emotion; brand laziness is quite pervasive.

Consumers have been described as *cognitive misers*; we rarely think about all the cogent arguments or rational claims surrounding a brand choice.[5] Furthermore, people are often pressed for time, distracted, or confused about brand information. Accordingly, consumers reduce their information processing to the bare minimum. Similarly, when a purchase decision is not particularly important or relevant, consumers' emotional involvement is low. Most of the time, they just don't care which brand of ammonia they buy. In short, consumers rarely have the motivation, ability, or opportunity to respond to marketing communication in a thoughtful manner.[6]

In fact, brand laziness is not necessarily irrational because carefully evaluating low-risk decisions could steal valuable time from the consideration of important issues and concerns. However, brand laziness is dangerous for marketers because consumers quickly shift their preferences when a better deal comes along. With no underlying commitment to a brand, competitors can disrupt consumers' inertia with promotional activities such as samples, rebates, by-one-get-one-free offers, price discounts, and end-of-aisle displays. The result is brand switching and a new cycle of brand laziness.

Although brand laziness varies from consumer to consumer (along with motivation, ability, and opportunity), commodity-type products such as flour, butter, and cheese are often associated with low involvement and minimal processing. It's important to point out, however, that one consumer may be highly involved with the purchase of cheese if s/he is a cheese aficionado. Similarly, another consumer may engage in detailed information processing of butters because of nutritional concerns. Notice that *toothpaste* is present in all four quadrants of Figure 3.2, because different consumers may exhibit each of the four decision types for this product category. For example, a college student may buy the brand offering the best deal (brand laziness), but a parent may be loyal to *Crest* on the basis of its historical association with cavity prevention (brand loyalty). A single professional may seek a variety of brands depending on her needs (variety seeking), and a senior citizen may carefully evaluate toothpaste brands if he needs something for sensitive teeth (problem solving).

Brand Loyalty

Brand laziness is often confused with brand loyalty. The former describes a habitual response that lacks underlying reasons or motivation. In contrast, **brand loyalty** involves intrinsic commitment to a brand based on the benefits or values it provides consumers. Both brand laziness and brand loyalty consist of minimal information processing. The difference between the two types of decisions can be explained by involvement.[7] Consumers who exhibit loyalty are more highly involved in a decision than those who display laziness. Faced with repetitive but relatively important decisions, loyal consumers may perceive that they already possess sufficient information to make quick decisions. Thus, limited information processing is likely to occur, and consumers rely on earlier experience to make decisions. But loyal consumers choose their brands because of previous experience with them, not because of deals or convenience.

For example, the purchase of dishwashing detergent and coffee may be highly involving as a result of perceived performance risk. If the dishwashing detergent doesn't function well, embarrassment could ensue (Have you ever served dishes with dried food stuck to the plate?). Likewise, coffee that disappoints can ruin a consumer's entire morning. Nevertheless, consumers make these purchases (dishwashing detergent and coffee) several times a year, and they don't need to think deeply about the decisions. Instead, they rely on prior brand evaluations. If those evaluations are positive, brand loyalty is likely to follow. Quadrant 2 of Figure 3.1 depicts brand loyalty as a combination of low information processing and high involvement. Brand loyalty consists of both attitudes and behaviors. Attitudes reflect consumers' overall feelings toward a brand, and behaviors deal with consumers' tendency to repeat purchase. Consumers often exhibit brand loyalty with products that enhance their self-concepts.

Variety Seeking

Thus far, we've discussed decisions that involve only low levels of information processing—brand laziness and brand loyalty. Sometimes consumers make low involvement decisions that require somewhat higher levels of information processing. At this level of decision making, consumers may understand the criteria for evaluating a product category, but they have yet to establish clear brand preferences. Thus, even with low levels of interest, consumers' limited past experience with brands requires moderate to high levels of information processing. We refer to this type of decision as **variety seeking,** typically defined as the desire to choose new alternatives over more familiar ones. It is represented as quadrant 3 in Figure 3.1. Variety seeking is the opposite of brand loyalty. Unlike brand loyalists—who have clearly developed preferences—variety seekers must gather additional information to discriminate among their choice alternatives. Also in contrast to brand loyalists, involvement is low for variety seekers, and they often switch brands to reduce boredom.[8]

Variety seeking has generated considerable attention from researchers. Let's examine two important types of variety seeking, derived varied behavior and intrinsic variety seeking.[9] Derived varied behavior describes situations where consumers' brand switching is either *externally imposed* or *extrinsically motivated.* In both cases, variety is not its own virtue. Instead, variety behavior is a by-product of other constraints or goals.[10] For example, a consumer may switch brands of candy because her most recently purchased brand is not available in the vending machine (out-of-stock conditions). Similarly, while enjoying a ball game at Bush Stadium, a consumer may switch from Samuel Adams beer to Budweiser

PRNewsFoto/Sara Lee Bakery Group/AP Photo

Variety seeking can be extrinsically motivated by situation-specific consumption goals, such as better health and nutrition.

because Anheuser-Bush maintains an exclusive contract with the St. Louis Cardinals. Both examples depict externally imposed switching behavior, i.e., the consumers had little choice in the matter. Consumers also switch brands as a result of situation-specific preferences. Perhaps a consumer generally buys white bread, but she purchases whole wheat to improve her health. Similarly, consumers may switch brands to obtain specific benefits or values not offered by their previous selection. For example, a new brand of toothpaste may offer long-term whitening benefits. The last two cases depict extrinsically motivated switching behavior because the incentive to switch derives not from an inherent need for variety, but to avoid or attain a specific consumption goal (better health and whiter teeth).[11]

In contrast, **intrinsic variety seeking** begins with the consumer who seeks variety for the inherent pleasure of change and the positive stimulation it brings.[12] Intrinsically motivated variety seeking can occur, out of curiosity,[13] because of a need for change to reduce boredom, or because consumers have become satiated with a particular attribute offered by a brand.[14] For example, a consumer may wonder what a new chewing gum tastes like, or switch to a brand of cereal that contains nuts or raisins. Variety seeking can be a powerful internal force for consumers. Fascinating research shows that individuals sometimes switch from their preferred brands to new ones, even though they predict that the new brands are likely to bring less enjoyment than their preferred brand.[15] These findings highlight the inherent value in variety; consumers actually forego the satisfaction of a highly predictable, favorable experience just for the sake of variety. Change is good, if you will.

Research also reveals that consumers' positive feelings can lead to increased variety seeking within safe, enjoyable product categories such as crackers, soup, and snack foods.[16] Also interesting, when people make multiple choices for future consumption, they seek more variety than if they make each choice in sequence—one at a time.[17] For example, consumers who buy a year's worth of canned soups are more likely to buy a variety of brands than if they buy the same quantity of soup, but shop weekly for it. A recent study provides evidence that consumers expect boredom associated with making the same choice to occur more quickly with others than with themselves. Therefore, consumers demonstrate more variety seeking when they buy products for others, especially when they are held accountable for their choices.[18]

Is there an upper boundary to variety seeking? Research demonstrates that when the degree of novelty and complexity in a purchase situation is extreme, consumers diminish these complexities by simplifying their buying decisions.[19] Ironically, by decreasing information processing, consumers reduce variety seeking and usher in brand laziness, i.e., choosing the same brand over and over, with little rationale except to reduce unwanted stimulation. Another stream of research argues that most consumers desire an intermediate level of stimulation.[20] Thus, clever marketers who provide variety on the premises, say in a retail environment, can encourage brand laziness within a product class.[21] For example, a retailer such as JCPenney may constantly change the store décor and limit the number of non-store brands offered. In this way, consumers' needs for stimulation may be satisfied by the shopping environment, and subsequently, routine buying behavior is encouraged, i.e., the JCPenney brand becomes the choice. Similarly, a restaurant might provide a wide variety of appetizers, but limit the entrée choices to high-margin items, such as steak and lobster. Variety seeking can also depend on individual differences. Those individuals who need a good deal of variety are more likely to engage in variety seeking behavior than in repeat purchasing.[21]

The introduction of low-involvement product categories and brands can elicit variety seeking behavior. For example, Gatorade's *powder packets*, a single-serving water beverage mix, may require more than minimal information processing because consumers have no prior exposure to the product. However, the category is low risk, so consumers are likely to exhibit low levels of emotional involvement. Here, consumers might examine the package and purchase the product on a trial basis as a substitute for a more familiar product (e.g., lemonade or other sports drinks), or as a complement to an existing product, like bottled water.

Variety seeking is also prevalent among products offering hedonic rewards, such as beer and candy,[21] particularly if the category is comprised of **parity products,** i.e., brands that possess functionally equivalent attributes, making one brand a satisfactory substitute for most others. Some researchers maintain that advertising and promotional messages are especially effective for this type of decision making (quadrant 3 in Figure 3.2). They reason that in low-involvement product categories, such as sports drinks and chewing gum, consumers either don't care which brand they buy, or their propensity to seek variety leaves them open to minimal processing. Put simply, consumers just look for interesting new items. Thus, repetitive advertising and promotional incentives can tip the balance in favor of a heavily exposed brand.[22]

Problem Solving

The fourth type of decision combines high involvement with high levels of information processing. Represented in quadrant 4 of Figures 3.1 and 3.2, this is referred to as **problem solving.** Decision making of this type typically involves unfamiliar, expensive products that are purchased infrequently. Consumers who shop for automobiles and electronics often exhibit problem solving. Because their emotional involvement is high and the search task is new, consumers try to collect as much information as possible and carefully evaluate each brand. At this level of decision making, consumers need extensive information to understand the various brand attributes as well as the relative performance of these attributes for each brand. For example, a consumer who shops for dining room furniture first needs to determine which attributes to include in the decision process. Does furniture construction make a difference—veneer or solid? Does the type of wood matter (cherry versus oak)? Is the warranty important? Is the source of the wood significant (domestic versus imported)? How critical is price? What about architecture, delivery, size, weight, and brand name? Clearly, consumers cannot consider all criteria, particularly if competing brands closely resemble one another. Consequently, consumers must identify one or more **determinant attributes,** characteristics of a product that are most likely to affect the buyer's final choice.[23] Determinant attributes can be described according to their *importance* and *uniqueness*. Important attributes matter deeply to consumers, often producing emotional responses. For instance, a consumer may insist, "I've always wanted oak," or "I'm not putting veneer in my new dining room." On the other hand, some attributes can be trivial. For example, a consumer may proclaim, "Money is no object," or "Color doesn't matter much to me." Uniqueness, on the other hand, embodies the perceived variation among alternatives on a particular attribute. If all brands offer a solid oak finish, then wood type is not a unique attribute. In contrast, if only one brand features Alaskan spruce and another firm exclusively offers wormy chestnut, then wood type is a unique attribute. Figure 3.4 provides an overview for assessing determinant attributes.[24]

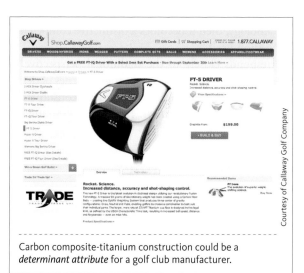

Courtesy of Callaway Golf Company

Carbon composite-titanium construction could be a *determinant attribute* for a golf club manufacturer.

FIGURE 3.4 ASSESSING DETERMINANT ATTRIBUTES

| | | Perceived Attribute Variation (Uniqueness) | |
		Low	High
Perceived Attribute Importance	Low	**1. Irrelevant Attribute** *Who cares?*	**2. Optional Feature** *That's nice.*
	High	**3. Defensive Attribute** *Keep up with the competition*	**4. Determinant Attribute** *A positioning opportunity*

SOURCE: Adapted from Guiltinan, J. P., Paul, G.W., and Madden, T. J. (1997). *Marketing Management: Strategies and Programs*, 6th ed.. New York: The McGraw-Hill Companies, Inc.

Consumers could, potentially, place any attribute in one of the four quadrants of this figure. For example, a consumer shopping for a set of golf clubs might consider spin-milled technology important to iron play; Titleist, Callaway, and other brands offer this important feature. Thus, a spin-milled iron surface is categorized as a defensive attribute, and brands not offering it would be at a disadvantage. Alternatively, a consumer may consider forged (versus cast iron) construction inconsequential with respect to the performance of an iron. All brands offer this feature. Thus, forged technology is labeled an irrelevant attribute. In other words, who cares? In contrast, when brands provide unique attributes that matter very little to consumers, they are known as optional features. For example, if a consumer doesn't care whether golf clubs feature a "blade" style (versus cavity back), then a firm that differentiates itself by offering this option may elicit a humdrum "that's nice" response. Finally, when a firm is fortunate enough to develop a unique attribute important to consumers, it has a potentially powerful positioning opportunity. Let's say that a firm develops a golf club with a carbon composite-titanium head that provides extraordinary ball velocity and minimal side spin. Most consumers care deeply about the distance and accuracy of their golf shots. Thus, if only one firm offers this technology, then it becomes a distinctive competency around which the firm is likely to position itself.

Consumer problem solving corresponds closely to the traditional perspective in consumer behavior, where consumers are thought to proceed through as series of deliberated steps prior to and after making a purchase.[25] This approach views consumers as highly involved information processors, i.e., *problem solvers*. Next, we'll examine the traditional model of consumer decision making.

OBJECTIVE 2

The Traditional Model of Consumer Decision Making

All consumer purchase decisions are not alike. Routine decisions involve little risk and low involvement. At the other extreme, emotionally involving decisions entail substantial risk and extensive problem solving. Figure 3.5 shows the five sequential stages of consumer problem solving:

FIGURE 3.5 THE TRADITIONAL MODEL OF CONSUMER DECISION MAKING

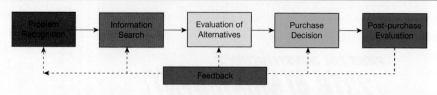

SOURCE: Adapted from Engel, J. Blackwell, R. D., and Miniard, P. W. (1995). *Consumer Behavior*, 8th ed. Hinsdale, IL: Dryden Press.

1. Problem recognition
2. Information search
3. Evaluation of alternatives
4. Purchase decision
5. Post-purchase evaluation.[26]

Problem recognition takes place when consumers experience a disparity between what they have and what they want. This inconsistency creates arousal and motivation to act, leading to information search, which involves both the active and passive processing of data aimed at solving the problem. Information search is closely linked to evaluation of alternatives, where consumers must determine which characteristics or attributes of a product are important and which brands to evaluate on the basis of these criteria. Eventually, consumers cease gathering information and comparing alternatives, and they make a purchase decision. Purchase decisions do not always result in actual purchases. Instead, they represent consumers' predispositions or intentions to buy a brand. Finally, post-purchase evaluation provides an opportunity for consumers to compare their perceptions of a brand with their expectations. This traditional model of consumer decision making flows in a linear fashion, one stage following the next. Before introducing a more recent model of consumer decision making, let's examine these stages in detail.

The Nature of Problem Recognition

The first step in the traditional model of consumer decision making is problem recognition. It occurs when a consumer acknowledges a significant difference between what is perceived as the desired state and what is perceived as the actual state. In short, a *discrepancy* exists between what the consumer wants the situation to be and what the situation really is. We call this discrepancy a **want-got gap.**[27] (See Figure 3.6.)

These gaps between consumers' acceptable and actual states do not always trigger problem recognition. First, the gap must be substantial. After all, consumers rarely

FIGURE 3.6 THE WANT-GOT GAP

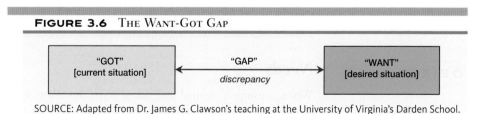

SOURCE: Adapted from Dr. James G. Clawson's teaching at the University of Virginia's Darden School.

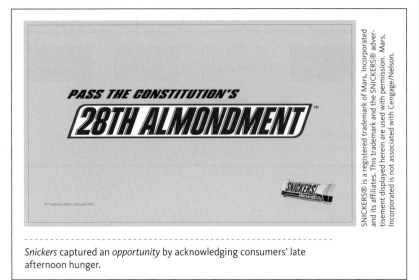

Snickers captured an *opportunity* by acknowledging consumers' late afternoon hunger.

SNICKERS® is a registered trademark of Mars, Incorporated and its affiliates. This trademark and the SNICKERS® advertisement displayed herein are used with permission. Mars, Incorporated is not associated with Cengage/Nelson.

attend to trivial differences between their desired and actual states. For example, a consumer may momentarily perceive a gap between her actual and desired states of hunger. But, it's just a small grumble in her stomach, and she doesn't give it a second thought. On the other hand, sometimes the psychological or physical discomfort derived from a discrepancy is of sufficient magnitude to compel us to action. For example, if the same consumer experiences the effects of low blood sugar (e.g., mild shaking, grouchiness), she may be motivated to reduce her hunger immediately. Not coincidentally, *Snickers* implemented a successful campaign targeting consumers' mild afternoon hunger. The strategy was simple but effective: remind consumers of their want-got gap.

Second, the discrepancy must relate to a problem that is readily solvable. In other words, dreams and fantasies do not constitute want-got gaps. As far as the psychological process of problem recognition is concerned, consumers must reasonably understand the desired state as one that s/he can attain. Let's say you perceive a want-got gap regarding your automobile. You've "got" a 1997 Ford, and you "want" a new Bentley. Assuming you're a typical college student, this discrepancy is not likely to be recognized as a problem, because college students rarely possess the means to obtain a Bentley. Alternatively, if you envision a more realistic trade-up to a 2005 Toyota Camry, true problem recognition is more likely to ensue.

Given that the want-got gap is substantial and attainable, problem recognition is triggered in three ways: the actual state changes, the desired state changes, or the actual and desired states change simultaneously.[28] All three situations are depicted in Figure 3.7.[29]

FIGURE 3.7   PROBLEM RECOGNITION: NEEDS, WANTS, AND OPPORTUNITIES

| Desired State |
| Actual State |

No Problem Recognition   Need   Want   Opportunity

SOURCE: Adapted from Bruner, G. C. and Pamazal, R. J. (1988). Problem Recognition: The Crucial First Stage of the Consumer Decision Process. *Journal of Consumer Marketing*, 5:53–63.

OBJECTIVE 3

Needs

When consumers' desired and actual states are relatively close together, *no problem* is recognized. However, when consumers' actual states fall below their desired states, *needs* emerge. A **need** is a fundamental physical or psychological state of felt deprivation. Thus, needs are not created by marketing efforts directly. This is consistent with the marketing concept, which describes marketing as an outside-in process designed to anticipate and satisfy consumer needs and wants—not create them. It may be helpful to think of needs as internal states that fall below a threshold of acceptability. Consumers possess a variety of needs, as described by Maslow's hierarchy of needs. Following Maslow's approach for understanding human motivation, physiological needs, such as hunger and thirst, manifest a basic level of adequacy. When you feel hungry or dehydrated, you experience a basic physiological need. While marketing cannot make you hungry or thirsty, marketing activities can remind you of your deprivation. For example, Wendy's "Eat great—open late" campaign draws attention to consumers' potential late night hunger. Similarly, when you feel deprived of love or affection, you are experiencing a fundamental social need. Again, marketing activities cannot directly withhold love and affection from you. Those gifts come from people. But marketing activities can indirectly influence perceptions about your current state of belonging. Not surprisingly, eHarmony.com advertises its patented compatibility matching system designed to reduce loneliness among singles. If you perceive personal neglect in your attitude toward conserving the environment, then you are experiencing a psychological need, i.e., a gap between a current and desired way of thinking. Marketing is not capable of dictating your thoughts, but marketing activities often trigger latent psychological problem recognition. For example, BP boasts of developing biofuels and new carbon storage "gasification" technologies. Given that most consumers consider gasoline brands at parity, BP appears a good choice for environmentally conscious consumers. In the same way, Honda advertises, "Accord drivability with a hybrid heart" for those concerned about global warming.

A "need" depicted in Figure 3.7 shows an actual state that has dropped below the threshold of acceptability, a baseline ideal state. Given that the need is substantial, problem recognition occurs, and consumers are motivated to reduce this gap. Some researchers describe needs as *informational* or *negative-oriented motives* because when a consumer's actual state drops below the ideal, it creates a negative condition and a desire for information.[30] **Motives** are internal drives that push people to resolve a problem or reduce a need. The greater the disparity between a consumer's actual and ideal state, the stronger the motive is to satisfy the need. Informational motives come in a variety of forms, including problem removal, problem avoidance, incomplete satisfaction, and normal depletion.

Although marketing activities cannot create needs directly, marketers are eager to identify and satisfy needs. For example, if your car's transmission breaks down, your actual state of affairs will fall dramatically below the acceptable level, and you will follow a problem removal motive. Fortunately, the market stands ready to offer services (automobile repair), products (automobiles), and substitutes (public transportation) to help bring into equilibrium your ideal and actual states. Similarly, problem avoidance motives occur when consumers proactively avoid negative outcomes such as burglary (*ADT Systems*), heartburn (*Prevacid*), or fatigue (*Red Bull*). Here, consumers take action to prevent their actual states from declining. In contrast, incomplete satisfaction motives arise when products fail to live up to our expectations. Perhaps a consumer's laundromat has become too busy, or her hairdresser now keeps odd hours. Maybe a consumer's favorite restaurant recently increased prices, or a new brand of shampoo makes her hair too dry. Each of these examples creates a need on the basis of dissatisfaction. Consequently, a consumer's motive is to reverse this condition, i.e., to bring her actual state back to an acceptable level. Consumers also experience normal depletion when they exhaust supplies of products such as aspirin, orange juice, and frozen vegetables. Marketers are eager to replenish those supplies through well-established distribution systems.

In some cases marketers come very close to creating consumer needs. For example, producers of personal hygiene products, such as mouthwash, antiperspirants, and beauty aids, sometimes enlist marketing programs to create insecurities that consumers

"Made in China," once synonymous for cost-effective, high-quality products, has suddenly become synonymous with "hazardous to your health" to many of China's global trading partners. During 2007, China was accused of producing faulty, dangerous, and potentially lethal consumer goods almost on a daily basis. A series of Chinese ethical meltdowns began with contaminated pet food, containing poisoned wheat gluten, followed by counterfeit toothpaste, falsely packaged as "Colgate," containing an antifreeze agent that can poison the liver and kidneys and depresses the central nervous system. Within two weeks, nearly 450,000 Chinese-made tires sold in the United States were recalled after federal regulators claimed the tires lacked an important safety feature designed to make them durable. Following this, Chinese shrimp, catfish, and eel were found to contain illegal antibiotics and chemicals and were subsequently banned by the FDA. During the same month, American consumer-protection authorities recalled Chinese-made children's necklaces and earrings because they contained dangerously high levels of lead. And most recently, Mattel Inc. issued recalls for 9.6 million toys, finding magnets that can be swallowed by children and hazardous levels of lead paint. Prior to 2007, there were claims of excessively flammable candles, weakly structured hammocks, bad wiring on fake palm trees, poorly made saws, and weak bicycle frames.[71] These alarming series of health scares eventually led to the execution of China's former head of the State Food and Drug Administration on July 10, 2007.

Truth be told, deadly products are not news in China. As early as 2004, for example, bad baby formula killed at least a dozen infants and sickened many others. According to reports by the Asian Development Bank and World Health Organization, approximately 300 million Chinese citizens suffer from food-borne diseases annually. That number is equivalent to the total U.S. population. And accidents in China's infamous coal mines took thousands of lives in 2006.

Why would so many people in China be willing to cut corners to make an extra dollar, even at the cost of human lives? According to the *Wall Street Journal*, one former Chinese diplomat described the national ideology of China as an "anything-for-a-profit attitude."[72] There seems to be widespread agreement among ordinary Chinese and Western business people that, in China, ethical considerations become lost in the race to get rich. China's remarkable economic output (GDP) catapulted from 7th in 2004 to 4th largest in the world by 2007. Unfortunately, unethical business practices have accompanied this growth.

Some experts argue that China's "ethical crisis" is simply a function of the country's meteoric economic development. Xiaobo Lu, a political science professor at Columbia University, predicts that once the proper institutions are in place, the Chinese will gradually understand certain "ethical rules of the game." Other experts claim that the Chinese lack an ethical framework. The communists destroyed traditional values and beliefs, replacing them with nothing sustainable. Now that many Chinese have lost faith in communist ideology, getting rich has become the national religion. But until China addresses the root causes of these widespread unethical practices, the lives of its people—and those of its trading partners—remain at risk.

can resolve by purchasing these products.[26] Sports franchises regularly alter their logos to encourage the sales of new licensed products. Fashion clothiers also change styles in order to draw attention to consumers' outdated wardrobes. Nevertheless, assuming that marketers obey the regulatory system and follow ethical guidelines set forth by their appropriate trade associations, consumers ultimately determine whether their actual state has dropped below the threshold of adequacy.

Wants

When consumers' ideal states rise above their actual states, *wants* occur. **Wants** are *need satisfiers* that are shaped by a consumer's personality, experiences, and culture—including marketing. In fact, marketing activities deliberately create wants. The distinction between needs and wants is important. Needs occur when consumers' real conditions decline while their desired conditions remain stable. On the other hand, wants occur when consumers perceive an increase in their desired states while their actual states remain constant. As depicted in Figure 3.7, wants represent a consumer's perceptions that they can improve their current situations by obtaining better. Earlier, needs were depicted as *informational* motives, because they are negatively reinforcing, i.e., the motive is to remove something negative. In contrast, wants can be thought of as *transformational motives* and positively reinforcing. Here, consumers are driven to purchase products and services that will produce benefits beyond their normal states.[31]

Marketing activities famously influence consumers' perceptions as to what their ideal states should be via advertising, promotion, endorsements, product placements, buzz marketing, and the like. For example, Dell tells us how much more productive we can be with *Bluetooth*, Wi-Fi, and mobile broadband options; Verizon elevates our expectations regarding mobile communication with unlimited nationwide calling; and Toyota raises our perceptions of automobile reliability via exceptional service history.

By exposing consumers to new and better products, marketers induce problem recognition and provide a means for consumers to attain their ideal states, or wants. But want creation also has a dark side. Targeting vulnerable audiences such as children, the elderly, and disadvantaged consumers can produce a wide range of deleterious effects on society. Likewise, a plethora of ethical concerns such as puffery and stereotyping surround the advertising business. Unscrupulous practices such as spamming, spyware, adware, pyramid schemes, planned obsolescence, telemarketing fraud, and infomercial schemes also dot the marketing landscape with unsightly blemishes. Each of these unethical practices, though beyond the scope of this text, has generated considerable research in marketing.[32]

Some researchers have linked marketing to various problems in society, including pollution, materialism, alcohol and nicotine addictions, obesity and poor nutrition, and the denigration of cultural values.[33] Others argue that marketing has positively contributed to consumers' quality of life by reducing search costs, fostering innovation and broad product choices, facilitating product acquisition (e.g., e-commerce), and reducing prices via increased competition. The overarching philosophy of this text maintains that individuals, businesses, and public policy can benefit from the study of consumer behavior. Following this perspective, the reader is encouraged to evaluate both sides of this complicated, global debate.[34]

Marketers are not alone in creating wants. Life changes also influence consumers' perceptions of their actual and ideal states. By virtue of time and circumstance, consumers lives do not stand still. Human bodies and minds mature with age; people's relationships change; and consumer preferences shift accordingly. When you were in high school, you probably desired less autonomy and independence than you do today. If so, your ideal state has increased over time, creating a "want" for independence. Also, when you graduate from college, your lifestyle, financial situation, and employment status will change, altering perceptions of both your ideal and actual states. A steady job may trigger a desire for more expensive clothing, a sporty automobile, and a wider range of food choices (wants). In short, your standards of comparison will change, and firms such as Brooks Brothers, BMW, and Foods of All Nations will be eager to provide products and services to help you attain your wants. Marketers are also keenly aware of major life changes in the family life cycle, such as marriage, having children, and divorce. For example, Procter & Gamble dedicates an entire Web site to *Pampers,* which includes advice on pregnancy and preparing for the arrival of new babies. Life insurance firms encourage customers to consider increasing their levels of coverage as family size increases. Taken together, both marketing activities and various aspects of consumers' lives trigger problem recognition in the form of wants.

Opportunities

When a consumer's ideal and actual states simultaneously move in opposite directions, **opportunities** emerge. Depicted in Figure 3.7, this combination creates a sizable want-got gap. Perhaps disenchantment with a current job is accompanied by a desire to experience a more promising future. Many non-traditional students describe their motivation to attend college in these terms. Alternatively, if a personal relationship begins to feel stifling at a time when a person's need for autonomy increases, she is likely to perceive a significant want-got gap and the motivation to close it. In a market context, if a consumer's favorite running shoes split and separate (a reduced actual state), and at the same time, Nike introduces shoes with more advanced features and improved durability (an elevated ideal state), the consumer may feel motivated to pursue the new product offer. In this sense, an opportunity can be viewed as a chance to dramatically shift a consumer's actual state to an elevated, ideal state.

Firms spend considerable time and effort creating opportunities in the marketplace. For example, Americans have repeatedly indicated their interest in fitness and health and at the same time, have reported feeling time-impoverished. As a consequence, clever marketers now offer time-saving, low-calorie foods (e.g., *Lean Cuisine* and *Weight Watchers*) and home fitness equipment (e.g., *Nordictrack* and *Bowflex*). Opportunities to close want-got gaps are emerging also in markets like China, whose 800 million rural citizens both need and want access to personal computing. In sum, opportunity creation represents the joint interplay of needs and wants because consumers' actual and ideal states diverge concurrently.

Researching consumers' discomforts and desires enables marketers to design and implement strategies that satisfy needs, wants, and opportunities, which is the essence of target marketing. Whether our want-got gaps are physiological, safety, social, or psychological in nature, marketers attempt to communicate benefits that shrink the gap between our ideal and actual states. But marketers are not always successful at closing these gaps completely. Consumers must perceive the benefits to be real (not just fluff), better than what they currently possess, and affordable. Furthermore, marketers must be able to articulate the benefits of their products. For example, despite millions of dollars aimed at educating consumers about its benefits, Tivo's digital video recorders (DVRs) initially generated disappointing market share because consumers did not understand what problems it would solve. Is the benefit of digital recording really worth the extra cost? How does "time shifting" work? Can consumers watch other programs while recording their favorite shows? Furthermore, many consumers would rather walk on hot coals than program a VCR, and *Tivo* was perceived

AP Photo/Paul Sakuma

Tivo failed to capitalize on an *opportunity* by inadequately communicating its benefits to consumers.

EYE ON INTERNATIONAL

SPECIAL DELIVERY: COMPUTERS FOR CHINESE FARMERS

Incorporated in Hong Kong, and headquartered in Raleigh, North Carolina, Lenovo Group Ltd. has a personal computer for China's 800 million rural inhabitants. Lenovo Group is the world's third-largest computer company by shipments and wants to increase global market share. Enter the bare-bones, low-cost PC aimed at China's farmers. The PC will sell for between $199 and $399, and include only a keyboard and processor. Televisions will have to substitute as monitors. Software designed to help farmers gather information about agricultural products is included.

As PC sales reach the maturity phase of the product life cycle in the United States, computer manufacturers are beginning to develop simple, lower-cost products aimed at first-time buyers in emerging markets, such as rural areas of China and India. China is the world's second-largest PC market after the United

AP Photo/Ng Han Guan

States; PC sales in China exceeded $14 billion in 2008. But less than ten percent of Chinese people own a computer.

Lenovo's marketing plan is not without challenges. Although a $199 PC may appear to be a bargain to Westerners, it may be a difficult sell in rural China, where the average annual income is less than $600. However, Lenovo hopes to establish a dominant presence in China, despite new competition from Hewlett-Packard Co. and Dell. Currently, about one-third of all computers sold in China are made by Lenovo. Some experts claim that the PC may not be the triumphant technology in the developing world. For instance, in India, the rapid adoption of cell phones in rural areas suggests that high-tech handheld mobile devices could surpass the personal computer as the primary method for gaining access the Internet.[70]

to be *more* complicated that traditional recording devices. By the time consumers understood the benefits of DVRs, cable companies began offering similar features to their current customers—a captive audience.

The Nature of Information Search

Once a problem is recognized, consumers often gather information to inform their purchase decisions. Researchers refer to this activity as **prepurchase search** because the information gathered relates directly to a consumption problem at hand.[35] Prepurchase search follows the linear pattern of decision making outlined by the traditional model, where consumers first recognize a want-got gap and subsequently perform search activities to help close it. During prepurchase search efforts, consumers may access information from their long-term memories to recall past experiences with brands, potential options, and relevant evaluative criteria.[36] This deliberate retrieval of information, known as **internal search,** is common with low involvement decisions that comprise much of consumers' day-to-day activities. When internal search fails to provide adequate problem-solving information, consumers actively seek external sources of information. **External search** can engage personal sources (e.g., friends and relatives), market sources such as advertisements and brochures, public sources (e.g., *Consumer Reports*), and product trial, i.e., examining or testing the product on a limited basis.

Consumers also obtain product information *without* recognizing a consumption problem. In these situations, consumers are not yet in the market for the products they examine and consider. Instead, they simply browse through catalogs, window shop, surf the Internet, or read specialty magazines without the intent of making a purchase. This type of information gathering, known as **ongoing search,** involves external search activities independent of solving an immediate purchase problem.[37]

Influences on Search

The extent of information processing is determined by consumer involvement, the marketing environment, situational influences, and individual differences. Researchers have identified two distinct types of consumer involvement: enduring and situational.[38] **Enduring involvement** describes a consumer's long-term and continuous interest in a brand or product category. Here, personal relevancy resides in the product itself and the inherent satisfaction that consumption or use brings to a consumer.[39] Most of us maintain enduring involvement with certain products. Fashion-conscious consumers enjoy clothes and jewelry, so they sustain long-term relationships with these products. Golf professionals are drawn to new golf clubs, training aids, and apparel, and they relish the opportunity to play new golf courses. Wine connoisseurs seek out new varieties, build wine cellars, collect rare specimens, and visit vineyards. They are deeply and permanently involved with their avocation.

In contrast, **situational involvement** reflects a consumer's relatively temporary and context-dependent interest in a product or category. For example, an infrequent flyer who decides to visit a foreign country may suddenly find airline services and luggage products personally relevant. However, the level of involvement is related only to this specific context. After returning from her trip, her involvement with travel-related products and services all but disappears—until the next journey. Search in a prepurchase situation generally derives from situational involvement with the product or consumption problem. To a large extent, consumers enlist prepurchase search strategies to reduce perceptions of risk.[40] Quite the reverse, ongoing search necessitates enduring involvement.

This reflects more permanent interest and enthusiasm for a product or category on the part of the consumer, and not just a temporary concern triggered by immediate needs.

The marketing environment influences both prepurchase and ongoing search. Product information from advertising, salespeople, promotions, and the Internet can increase consumers' search efforts, along with highly accessible distribution channels (e.g., stores, retail catalogues, and e-commerce). Research shows that the location, availability, and distance between retail stores in a given geographic area can affect the number of visits consumers make prior to purchase. Thus, close proximity among stores can increases consumers' external search efforts.[41] Consumers' perceptions of wide price ranges can also increase external search. A recent study shows that consumers reduce information search when retailers offer *price-matching refunds*, because such policies are seen as a signal of low store prices. These findings are intuitive.

External information search is not free—it takes time and effort. Traveling, parking, and dealing with crowds extract both monetary and psychological costs. Thus, consumers weigh the benefits of additional search against the costs of conducting it. Not surprising, the Internet can be an effective tool at reducing search costs, especially for those who are relatively young and well educated.[42] As a general rule, the greater the number of products in a category, the greater the external search is. More brands require more information processing. Too many choices, however, can cause psychological distress for consumers, causing them to end their search and select the most recognizable brand, a special case of brand laziness. Have you ever felt overwhelmed by the sheer number of available brands and as a result quickly grabbed the one most familiar to you? This type of information overload is known as **brand chaos,** a condition brought on by the proliferation of brands that offer few distinctive attributes or benefits.

Situational variables (separate from the market environment) can affect consumers' information search. For example, *time constraints* can pressure consumers into reducing their information processing. A recent study demonstrates that, under time constraints, consumers evaluate fewer alternatives and tend to ignore moderately important attributes.[43] Perceptions of crowding also cause people to reduce external search. As more people enter a store or restaurant, or as the store becomes packed with displays and merchandise, consumers are likely to experience discomfort. As a result, they process less information, make quicker decisions, and spend less time in the store. In addition, satisfaction with their shopping experience declines.[44] Other research reveals that consumers increase external search efforts when the purchase is important, information is highly accessible, and perceived risk is high.[35]

Individual differences influence both prepurchase and ongoing search activities. In general, younger, better-educated consumers expend more effort searching than those who are older and less educated. Also, middle-income consumers engage in more external search than both lower- and upper-income groups. For some individuals, gathering information about products and services is a full-time hobby. If you need to replace your cell phone or want a new car, to whom would you turn for product information? You might seek out **market mavens,** people who search, accumulate, and share product knowledge with others. In some circles, market mavens are known as "price vigilantes" because they keep the marketplace honest through their vigilant watch over marketers' pricing tactics and trends. They are also regarded as product data banks. Market mavens are not just passive collectors of information; they also initiate discussions with other consumers and eagerly respond to requests for information. They read more magazines and newspapers than the average consumer; they examine junk mail; and they regularly scrutinize *Consumer Reports*.[45] Because market mavens collect information for future use, they are experts at conducting ongoing search.

In contrast, some consumers enjoy shopping just for the sake of shopping. For them, it's the journey that counts. Research reveals that women are more likely to indicate that shopping is relaxing and enjoyable than are men. Specifically, only 29 percent of men say they enjoy shopping for clothes, compared with 48 percent of women. Stores with a wide selection appeal less to men. For men, it's convenience that counts. Also, stores that are easy to browse, that are close to one's home or office, or have knowledgeable salespeople, appeal more to men than to women.[46] It follows that women typically conduct more external search than men.

Prior knowledge and experience also affect the extent to which consumers conduct external search. Intuitively, one might expect those with low levels of expertise to spend the most time gathering product information. After all, they have the most to learn. On the other hand, consumers who possess product expertise might find external search easy to process and so, search the most. Research supports neither of these views. In fact, moderately knowledgeable consumers process more product information than either the low or high knowledge groups.[47] These counterintuitive results can be explained as a function of two determinants of information processing: motivation and ability. Those low in product knowledge and experience are likely to be motivated to gather information, but without requisite knowledge, they couldn't make sense of the data even if they gathered them. Thus, because they view the task as too difficult, they give up searching and seek a simple solution. In contrast, those high in experience and knowledge—although perfectly capable of understanding the information—are not motivated to search. Instead, they rely on their past experiences and memory to guide their decisions. The moderately experienced consumer, on the other hand, may possess just enough motivation and ability to devote substantial search effort to the decision task. Figure 3.8 depicts search effort as a joint function of motivation and ability. The inverse U function illustrates that consumers who are both low and high with respect to product knowledge are less likely to conduct extensive search than those with moderate levels of product knowledge. This is consistent with classic personality research, which demonstrates that the greatest attitude change occurs at an intermediate level of a personality trait (e.g., knowledge).[48]

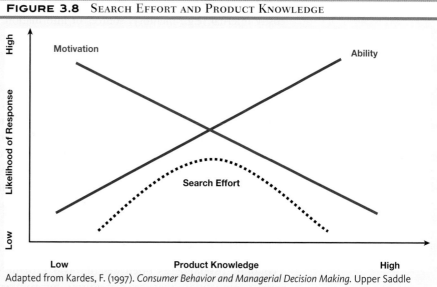

FIGURE 3.8 SEARCH EFFORT AND PRODUCT KNOWLEDGE

Adapted from Kardes, F. (1997). *Consumer Behavior and Managerial Decision Making.* Upper Saddle River, NJ: Prentice Hall.

Motivation to Search

Regarding prepurchase search, consumers' motive is straightforward—to make a better purchase decision. For ongoing search, however, two separate motives emerge: to acquire a data bank of product information for future use [49] and pleasure or recreation. The first motive centers on consumers' desire for product knowledge, while the second motive derives from consumers' consumption experience.[50] Building a warehouse of product knowledge involves increasing product expertise for reasons other than optimizing an immediate decision. It can make consumers feel well informed, improve future choices, and enhance self-actualization.[51] Ongoing search activities can also be fun. Many consumers simply enjoy seeking information about products, whether by surfing the Internet or browsing through a bricks-and-mortar store. For these consumers, shopping doesn't need to be purposeful. Shopping represents a leisure pursuit in and of itself, similar to attending a concert or movie or participating in a softball game. As the weekend approaches, listen to your friends discuss their alternatives plans. They are likely to include shopping—in terms of ongoing search—in the same consideration set as watching a movie, taking a road trip, or going to a sporting event. Similar to these activities that compete for consumers' time, shopping, literally, is considered an *event.*

Results of Search

The outcomes or results of information search differ for prepurchase versus ongoing search. When consumers search for product information explicitly to solve a problem, prepurchase search can increase knowledge, optimize brand choice, and heighten satisfaction. For example, a consumer dedicates considerable prepurchase search effort to finding a brand of moisture-rich cosmetics to keep her delicate skin comfortable during a grueling business conference. If successful, she will have attained important information to reduce her search the next time she's in the market for cosmetics (e.g., *Elizabeth Arden's Flawless Finish Radiant Moisture Makeup SPF 8* works well for her skin type). Perhaps most important, this consumer will have made a good choice, giving rise to satisfaction, i.e., comfortable skin.

Ongoing search can increase consumers' efficiency by allowing them to rely on less costly internal (e.g., memory) sources of information. For example, most consumers realize that they will eventually need to replace their automobile tires. Ongoing searchers keep their "antennas" active long before the decision is necessary. They may read blogs on the Internet, pay attention to magazine and newspaper ads, and query friends who enthusiastically relay their experiences with various brands. Thus, when the decision is imminent (the tires won't pass the penny test!), ongoing searchers may be prepared to make a wise choice, without costly external search. Ongoing searchers also like to disseminate their stored knowledge to friends and family. Perhaps this is how market mavens are born. Being regarded as a product expert or opinion leader can enhance self-esteem. Finally, ongoing search engenders **impulse buying**, i.e., purchases made without prior planning. The more frequently consumers surf the Web and browse through stores, the higher the probability is that they will eventually purchase on impulse.[52]

Economics of Search

Economic psychologists often describe two extreme cases of industry structure. In perfect competition, there are many firms, but competition among them is so intense that anytime one of them achieves a market advantage, the others quickly duplicate it.

As a result, the firms end up producing identical products. In perfect competition, brands do not have identities because the "sameness" of the products makes the concept meaningless. For example, while you are likely to recall the brand of cereal you ate for breakfast this morning, you probably do not know the brand of the milk you poured on the cereal. Milk comes close to satisfying the requirements of a perfectly competitive product; a gallon of milk from one producer is virtually identical to a gallon of milk from any other producer. At the other extreme of industry structure is monopoly, in which case, there is only one producer. For example, almost everyone who owns a PC needs a copy of the *Windows* operating system, and that is offered by only one producer, Microsoft Corp.

What do these two extremes of industry structure have in common? In both cases, the consumer decision making process is simple, and information search is virtually eliminated. In the case of perfect competition, while there are many competing brands (e.g., gasoline), the fact that the products are virtually identical means that consumers need not compare brands. Instead, consumers only need to answer the question, "Do I want this product at the going price?" In the case of monopoly (e.g., cable TV), there is only one brand and so again, the only relevant question is, "Do I want this product?"

Most consumer choices take place in the intermediate case of industry structure known as monopolistic competition. In a monopolistically competitive industry, consumers are faced with many competing brands, each of which is different from the other in one or several attributes. Monopolistic competition creates a unique problem for consumers: It is nearly impossible to obtain full information about all competing brands prior to making a purchase decision. In fact, fully aware that they may choose the wrong brand, consumers try to make the *best* choice, given limited information search. In general, researchers refer to this concept as **bounded rationality,** the idea that consumers can only make rational decisions within the limits of time and cognitive capability.[53] Economic psychologist Antony Davies has developed a theoretical model for understanding how consumers interpret the marketplace, given their bounded rationality.[54] The model provides a framework for examining alternative evaluation and choice.

Alternative Evaluation and Choice: An Uncertainty-Reduction Model

We have discussed why consumers conduct information search. But exactly what information do consumers need? There are three pieces of information necessary to conduct prepurchase and ongoing search: the number of available brands, the determinant attributes for the product category, and how an individual reacts to a brand after it is purchased. In practice, consumers almost never know even one of these three pieces of information. For example, how many brands of beer can the average consumer recall? Beer connoisseurs (product experts) might recall as many as 20 or more brands. Nevertheless, 500 brands of beer exist in U.S. markets alone. Even the most avid beer expert would not be aware of all these! Next, suppose that a consumer considers six important attributes for the product category, beer: color, aroma, taste, alcohol content, carbonation, and price. Can this consumer rate each brand on these six attributes? Probably not (unless the consumer's list was very short). Lastly, this consumer probably does not know exactly how well he would like these brands, even if he could rate them all. For example, he may claim not to like dark beer, but it's possible that he might like a dark beer brewed with a lot of hops, or a dark beer with heavy carbonation. Thus, consumers' inability to perfectly predict how much they will like a brand is another source of uncertainty.

Given enough search effort, consumers could, potentially, acquire all the information necessary to make a rational purchase decision. The term *rational* means that, with complete information, consumers would make decisions that maximize their satisfaction. However, the cost of acquiring information often exceeds the benefits of making the best decision.[55] For example, no one is willing to spend five years of research just to find the single best cereal. Instead, we settle for the good-though-perhaps-not-best cereal. The consumer decision process, given incomplete information, is referred to as an **uncertainty-reduction process.** This approach to decision making involves four stages:

1. Product-market perception
2. Consideration of a single subset of brands within the perceived product-market
3. Choice of one brand from among the consideration set
4. Consumption experiences relating to the chosen brand

Through this repetitive, back-and-forth process, consumers adjust their perceptions of product-markets. Figure 3.9 illustrates this decision model.

FIGURE 3.9   Uncertainty-Reduction Model of Decision Making[53]

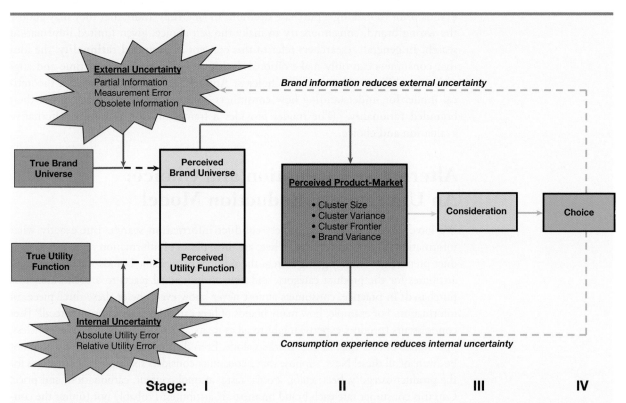

SOURCE: Adapted from Davies, A., and Cline T. W. (2005). A Consumer Behavior Approach to Modeling Monopolistic Competition. *Journal of Economic Psychology*, 26:797–826.

OBJECTIVE 5

Consumer Uncertainty

Like the traditional model of consumer decision making, the uncertainty-reduction model views consumers as relatively involved problem solvers. Accordingly, consumers must come to terms with the *true brand universe*. The **true brand universe** is the set of all brands that exist along with measures of each of their attributes. The true brand universe is an objective reality. Because it is prohibitively costly to gather complete and fully accurate information about all existing brands and their attributes, what is in a consumer's head is not the true brand universe but a **perceived brand universe**. The perceived brand universe includes only those brands that a consumer acknowledges—whether real or not. Three sources of **external uncertainty** cause a consumer's perceived brand universe to differ from the true brand universe. The sources of external uncertainty are: incomplete information, measurement error, and obsolete information. *Incomplete information* suggests that consumers may be unaware of all the brands in the true universe. For example, if you have never heard of *Castle Rock* beer, then your perceived brand universe suffers from incomplete information. Quite the reverse, if you mistakenly perceive a brand that doesn't exist, your perceived brand universe also contains incomplete information. *Measurement error* describes a condition in which consumers may measure brands' attributes inaccurately or may be unaware of a particular attribute. For example, you may believe that all dark beers are sour tasting. However, because some are actually sweet, your perceived brand universe suffers from measurement error. Finally, *obsolete information* describes a situation such that consumers fail to update their perception of the true brand universe as quickly as the true brand universe evolves. Perhaps the last time you purchased an Apple laptop computer, the price was double that of other brands. Since then, Apple has lowered its prices to be more competitive with Dell and other brands. If you do not revise your perception of Apple's price to match the changed reality, your perceived brand universe suffers from obsolete information.

Consumers must also come to understand their *true utility functions*. Economic psychologists use the term *utility* to describe the relative happiness, pleasure, or satisfaction a consumer gains by using or consuming a product. Every consumer also has a *utility function*, which describes how much pleasure s/he will obtain by using various combinations of brands or brand attributes. For example, some consumers obtain more utility from coffee than tea. In the same way, a consumer may gain more utility from a dark roast Columbian variety versus a decaffeinated coffee. A consumer's **true utility function** is the *actual* satisfaction s/he will obtain from consuming a brand, i.e., another objective reality. However, consumers don't know as much about their own preferences as they think they do. It is time-consuming and expensive to sample every existing brand. So, even when consumers fully understand a brand's attributes, their reactions to those attributes may be different from what they anticipated. Thus, a consumer's **perceived utility function,** what a consumer believes his/her reaction will be to a brand with certain attributes, differs from his/her true utility function.

Two sources of **internal uncertainty**—uncertainty about the consumer him/herself—cause a consumer's perceived utility function to differ from his/her true utility function: absolute utility error and relative utility error. *Absolute utility error* describes a consumer's uncertainty regarding satisfaction that a particular

Through experience, consumers learn how much pleasure they will gain by using or consuming various products.

sjlocke/iStockphoto.com

attribute will deliver. For example, a consumer may have full information about a car's safety features, but she may incorrectly believe that safety is less important than it truly is. It may not be until she has driven the car for a while that she realizes side airbags are very satisfying. In contrast, *relative utility error* describes situations where consumers are uncertain about the relative influence or weight of *each* attribute on his/her utility functions. For example, a consumer may be fully aware of a car's gas mileage and engine power. However, he may incorrectly gauge his willingness to reduce mileage to increase performance. It may not be until he has purchased the car and filled it up a few times that he realizes he would have preferred to give up some engine power in exchange for more miles per gallon.[56] In sum, because consumers cannot know every brand in the market or how much they will like those brands, they cannot know either the true brand universe or their true utility functions. Accordingly, consumers construct a mental picture of their reactions (a perceived utility function) and the world around them (a perceived brand universe). Bounded by our rationality, consumers then organize that mental picture to form their notion of the overall market.

The Perceived Product-Market

Regardless of whether consumers conduct prepurchase or ongoing search, their perceptions of the brand universe, along with their perceived utility functions, influence how they construe the marketplace. The **perceived product-market** represents a patterned organization of brands in a consumer's mind. Consider the market for ice cream. Suppose a consumer views the product-market as possessing two determinant attributes: taste and calories. Furthermore, let's assume she is aware of six brands: Weight Watchers, Carnival, Edys, Haagen-Dazs, Ben & Jerry's, and Breyers. These brands and the consumer's belief about their attributes constitute the consumer's perceived brand universe. Although limited by internal uncertainty, this consumer is also aware how she "feels" about ice-cream taste and ice-cream calories. These feelings constitute the consumer's perceived utility function. When the consumer weighs her perceived brand universe against her perceived utility function, she forms an intuitive image of the perceived product-market. The perceived product-market for ice cream is represented in Figure 3.10. Each dot represents the consumer's perception as to the utility (pleasure) she will obtain from the attributes she perceives each brand to have. The further up and to the right a dot is located, the more (perceived) utility the consumer obtains from the brand's attributes.

Notice that in the consumer's mind, the brands naturally fall into two *clusters*. The three brands at the top left (Weight Watchers, Carnival, and Edys) score high on utility from calories but low on utility from taste. Together, these brands comprise the *low-calorie cluster*. The other three brands (Haagen-Dazs, Ben & Jerry's, and Breyers) score high on utility from taste but low on utility from calories. Together, these brands comprise the *high taste cluster*. This clustering of brands is the first step the consumer takes in looking, either consciously or subconsciously, for patterns among brands. By clustering, the consumer simplifies the task of choosing a brand by thinking not of many individual brands, but of a few clusters of brands. Consumers naturally think of brands this way. People talk about domestic versus imported beer, vans versus SUVs, houses versus apartments, city versus suburb, etc.

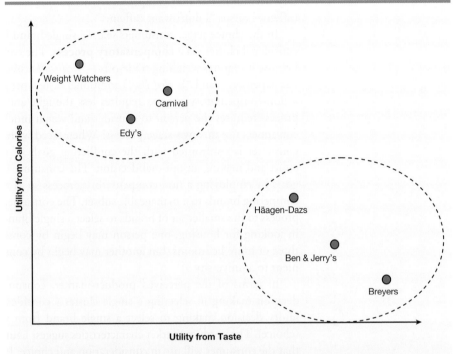

FIGURE 3.10 TWO-DIMENSIONAL PERCEIVED PRODUCT-MARKET FOR ICE CREAM

SOURCE: Adapted from Davies, A., and Cline T. W. (2005). A Consumer Behavior Approach to Modeling Monopolistic Competition. *Journal of Economic Psychology*, 26:797–826.

Four important characteristics of the consumer's perceived product-market describe something about the product-market that is relevant to the consumer's subsequent choice:

1. **Cluster size,** measured by the number of brands the consumer places in the cluster

2. **Cluster variance,** the degree to which brands within a single cluster are dissimilar from each other

3. **Cluster frontier,** the best possible combination of attributes observed within a cluster

4. **Brand variance,** a consumer's awareness of uncertainty as to a brand's attributes

In the consideration stage, consumers first identify a cluster of brands with similar attributes.

Consideration and Choice

After constructing perceptions of the product-market, consumers follow a two-stage choice process of *consideration* and *choice*. In the consideration stage, consumers often select a single cluster of brands via a non-compensatory process.[57] A **non-compensatory process** is a simple, although error-prone, way to make a decision in which the person does not consider trade-offs. For example, it is easier to decide whether to drink a caffeinated drink or a caffeine-free drink (a non-compensatory decision) than it is to decide *which* caffeinated drink or *which* caffeine-free drink to drink (a compensatory decision). The non-compensatory decision is easy because it is binary—"I want caffeine" versus "I don't want caffeine."

In the choice stage, consumers select a single brand from among the brands in the considered cluster via a **compensatory process**. The compensatory process is difficult because it requires weighing trade-offs—"*Red Bull* tastes better than *Hype*, but *Hype* is less expensive," and "Is *Red Bull's* additional taste worth the additional price?" While a non-compensatory process requires less thought and fewer facts, a compensatory process requires the person to consider and weigh much more information. Why do consumers use this two-stage process? When faced with many competing brands, the consumer is confronted with the conflicting goals of making a decision with little effort and making an optimal decision. The consumer balances these two conflicting goals by employing a non-compensatory process so as to "whittle down" the field of competing brands to a manageable subset. The consumer then applies a compensatory process to the smaller set of brands to select a single brand for purchase.[47] For example, in looking for housing, one person may begin by considering only apartments with three or more bedrooms, but another may begin by considering only locations convenient to a university.

In terms of the perceived product-market, consumers apply non-compensatory decision making in selecting a single cluster ("consideration") followed by compensatory decision making to select a single brand from within the considered cluster (choice). The product-market characteristics suggest heuristics—or "rules of thumb"—that the consumer will use in consideration and choice. Let's focus on a set of heuristics that derive from consumers' perceptions of a product-market.

CLUSTER SIZE Consumers may interpret larger cluster size as an indication of lesser *external uncertainty* because:

1. Observing more brands can imply that a greater proportion of the true universe is observed (reducing partial information).

2. Observing more brands with similar attributes (i.e., brands in the same cluster) can provide confirmation that the consumer has correctly observed attribute levels (reducing measurement error).

3. Observing more brands in a specific cluster can imply a lesser probability of a brand having altered its attributes; the cluster may be stable over time (reducing obsolete information).

For example, suppose a consumer observes ten cars all with reported gas mileage in the 25 to 30 mpg range and one car with a reported gas mileage of 50 mpg. All else being equal, this consumer is more likely to question the 50 mpg because all the other cars she has seen are in the 25 to 30 mpg range. Observing more brands with similar attributes provides confirmation that the consumer has correctly observed the attributes. Interestingly, during the 1970s, consumers may have believed that the VHS format would supplant the Betamax format because there were a greater number of brands using the VHS format. Similarly, despite being more user-friendly and employing a more powerful microprocessor, the Apple *Macintosh* brand lost substantial market share to IBM clones during the 1980s. One possible explanation is that there were a large number of brands in the IBM clone cluster and so, consumers interpreted this as a signal of greater survival probability for the PC cluster.

Consumers may also interpret the number of brands in a cluster as a proxy for the demand for brands in that cluster.[58] Thus, a larger cluster size can signal less *internal uncertainty* because observing more brands implies that consumers' preferences are being satisfied. This is consistent with evidence that consumers make use of other people's experience when making purchase decisions.[59] For example, suppose a consumer investigates ten cell phone plans, nine of which come with free texting, with one plan charging for texting. All else being equal, the consumer is likely to judge that other consumers like free texting and that, consequently, he will also like free texting. Additionally, people have inherent motives to justify their decisions to others and to themselves,[60] i.e., to bolster self-esteem,[61] to alleviate cognitive dissonance,[62] and to reduce anticipation of regret.[63] A larger set of brands in a cluster can help consumers justify their behavior to others and confirm their behavior to themselves. In sum, because a large cluster size decreases both perceived internal and external uncertainties, as the size of a cluster increases, the likelihood that a consumer will consider that cluster increases.

CLUSTER VARIANCE Consumers may interpret larger cluster variance as an indication of greater *external uncertainty* because observing large differences among brands within a cluster could indicate that

1. There are brands within the cluster of which the consumer is unaware.
2. Consumers have incorrectly grouped dissimilar brands into the same cluster.
3. Consumers have erroneously measured some of the attributes.
4. The brands' attributes are changing as firms search for improved brand positions.

Consumers may also interpret larger cluster variance as an indication of greater *internal uncertainty* because

1. Observing a large difference among brand attributes within a cluster implies greater uncertainty regarding the consequences of a purchase from this cluster.
2. High cluster variance may send confusing signals about the importance of the various attributes.

For example, suppose a consumer observes four brands of hair coloring. The brands require that the coloring treatment be left in for 1 minute, 5 minutes, 10 minutes, and 20 minutes, respectively. The large variation among the treatment times can make the consumer less certain as to the benefit of treatment time, increasing internal uncertainty. In sum, cluster variance increases the likelihood of a consumer making a bad purchase decision. Therefore, as cluster variance increases, the likelihood of the consumer considering that cluster decreases.

CLUSTER FRONTIER (THE IDEAL BRAND) Once the consumer has selected a single cluster for consideration, the consumer then employs compensatory decision making to select a single brand from within the considered cluster. The cluster frontier represents a hypothetical brand that contains the best attributes of all brands within the cluster. It may be helpful to think of the cluster frontier as the perceived ideal brand in a given cluster. For example, suppose John is selecting a marriage partner. He has already selected a cluster of potential mates. The consideration cluster contains people who: have decent-paying jobs and are attractive.

Within this cluster, John observes three people whom he perceives to have the following attributes. Anna has a salary of $75,000/year and ranks 7 (out of 10) on John's attractiveness scale; Brittany has a job that pays her $100,000/year and ranks 5 on the attractiveness scale; and Claire's job pays $50,000/year, and she ranks 9 on the attractiveness scale. John looks at these three people and imagines the ideal partner as being someone who contains the best of the attributes he has observed. In this case, it would be someone who earns $100,000 and ranks 9 on the attractiveness scale. John knows that such a person could exist because he has independently observed a $100,000 salary and a 9 on the attractiveness scale, but he hasn't observed this particular combination in the same person. Thus, John will select a partner who is closest to that ideal combination. In general, the likelihood of the consumer selecting a particular brand increases as the brand comes closer to the cluster frontier.

BRAND VARIANCE Consumers are rarely certain about a brand's true attributes. For example, a consumer can see that a water heater is rated to use $400 in electricity annually. But the consumer knows that this figure is only an estimate; differences in electric rates, in hot water usage, and a unit's efficiency cause the actual electricity usage to vary. The greater the brand variance, the less able the consumer is to infer the cluster frontier, or ideal brand. For example, suppose a consumer sees two water heaters within a cluster. One has an annual electricity usage of $400 and a 40-gallon capacity. The second has an annual electricity usage of $500 and a 60-gallon capacity. If brand variance were zero (i.e., if there was no uncertainty in the consumer's mind as to these attributes), then the consumer would know for certain that the perceived ideal water heater would have a 60-gallon capacity and cost $400 annually to operate.

Now, suppose that the consumer is unsure about the attributes. What if the consumer perceives that the operating cost could be off by as much as $200 per year, and that the capacity could be off by as much as five gallons? This means that the perceived ideal water heater in the best-case scenario could have a 65-gallon capacity and cost $200 per year, or, in the worst-case scenario, could have a 35-gallon capacity and a cost of $600 per year. Because the consumer is less certain as to the cluster frontier, the consumer is less certain as to how far from the cluster frontier these two brands are. Thus, the greater the brand variance, the less useful the cluster frontier as a benchmark for making a choice.

In summary, consumers, faced with incomplete information, construct perceptions of a product-market. After consuming the chosen product, consumers revise information about both the product's attributes and the utility gleaned from the attributes in an attempt to reduce uncertainty. Consumers then adapt their perception of the product-market via mentally repositioning the consumed brand and, possibly, reforming clusters. The consumer bases the next purchase decision on this revised mental mapping of the product-market.

Post-Purchase Evaluation

The uncertainty-reduction model emphasizes that consumers continuously process information about brands and their attributes *after* purchase and consumption. This feedback is depicted with dashed lines returning from "choice" to external and internal uncertainty in Figure 3.9. By potentially reducing uncertainties, consumers allow for updated product-market perceptions and, potentially, better future decisions. The traditional model also acknowledges consumers' feedback loop. Figure 3.5 shows that,

MARKETING IN ACTION

Ben and Jerry's and Miller Brewing: Changing Consumer Perceptions

At the height of the weight-conscious 1990s, Ben and Jerry's launched an ad campaign highlighting the fact that their brand was *not* low in calories. The ad went on to claim that Ben and Jerry's great taste was worth the higher calories. Perhaps unwittingly, the campaign altered consumers' perceptions of the cluster frontier among premium ice creams. Let's take a look at Figure 3.11, which shows a hypothetical consumer's perceived product-market for ice cream.

Among the high taste cluster, the consumer is aware of Haagen-Dazs, Ben and Jerry's, and Breyers. The consumer also perceives that the "ideal" premium ice cream is one that has the flavor of Breyers, but the calories of Haagen-Dazs. This point is labeled *original cluster frontier*. The point of the Ben and Jerry's ad campaign was to convince consumers that there is a trade-off between taste and calories, such that it is impossible for a brand to possess the taste of Breyers and the calories of Häagen-Dazs.

As a result, Ben and Jerry's hoped that consumers would shift their perceptions of the cluster frontier to the point labeled *new cluster frontier*. Why? Given that Ben and Jerry's is positioned between Haagen-Dazs and Breyers, moving the cluster frontier in this way puts Ben and Jerry's closer to this ideal point, resulting in an increase in market share for Ben and Jerry's at the expense of Haagen-Dazs and Breyers.

Similarly, in the early 1990s, the Miller Brewing Company introduced a new brand, Red Dog. With respect to taste and price, two of the most salient attributes for beer, Miller positioned Red Dog to be similar, although inferior, to its flagship brand, Miller Genuine Draft (MGD). Market analysts warned that, by introducing a new brand so similar to its flagship brand, Miller risked siphoning off market share from the flagship brand, a phenomenon known as *cannibalization*. What happened, however, was the reverse—Red Dog attained market presence

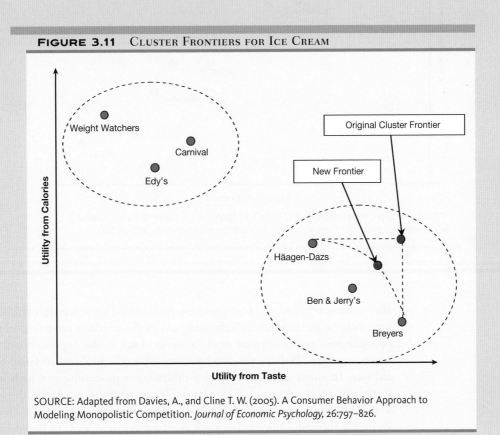

FIGURE 3.11   CLUSTER FRONTIERS FOR ICE CREAM

SOURCE: Adapted from Davies, A., and Cline T. W. (2005). A Consumer Behavior Approach to Modeling Monopolistic Competition. *Journal of Economic Psychology*, 26:797–826.

while increasing MGD's market share. The uncertainty-reduction model offers an explanation for these unexpected results.

Figure 3.12 shows a hypothetical consumer's perceived product-market following the introduction of Red Dog beer.

By positioning Red Dog as it did, Miller achieved two effects: (1) it increased the size of the "affordability" cluster, and (2) it did not alter the affordability cluster's frontier. The first effect increased the probability of consideration for the brands in the affordability cluster—a larger cluster attracts more consumer interest. Second, because the cluster frontier remained the same, the probability of choice,

given consideration, did not change for MGD. Miller Genuine Draft remained the same distance from the ideal point as it was prior to the introduction of Red Dog. Using probability notation, the overall impact on the probability of choice for MGD is:

Pr (consideration) × Pr (choice | consideration) = Pr (choice)
   [Increase]   [No Change]   [Increase]

Thus, the introduction of Red Dog, an objectively inferior beer, resulted in an increase in market share for MGD. This is known as the *attraction effect*: an inferior brand positioned closely to an existing brand makes the existing brand more "attractive."

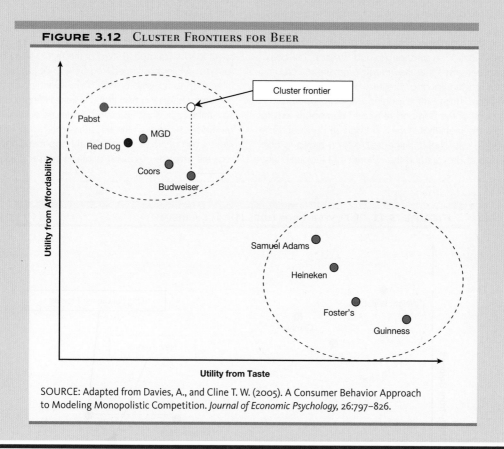

FIGURE 3.12   CLUSTER FRONTIERS FOR BEER

SOURCE: Adapted from Davies, A., and Cline T. W. (2005). A Consumer Behavior Approach to Modeling Monopolistic Competition. *Journal of Economic Psychology*, 26:797–826.

after consumers conduct "post-purchase evaluation," they integrate this information into their future decisions by informing any of the previous processes. In some cases, post-purchase evaluation may send consumers back to the drawing board with problem recognition. Perhaps the purchase created a new problem or failed to solve the old one. In either case, the extensive information processing and high levels of involvement necessitate an entirely new problem-solving process. On the other hand, a successful choice may require only that consumers loop back to the "choice" phase. Perhaps a successful low involvement purchase decision leads to brand laziness, or a higher involvement purchase encourages brand loyalty. In any event, consumers are not likely to conduct new search or re-evaluate alternatives. The intermediate case of variety seeking suggests that, even with a moderately successful post-purchase evaluation, consumers may return to the "evaluation of alternatives" or "information search" phases of decision making, seeking and processing new information that will lead to a different choice. How do consumers decide if the purchase was successful? In a word—*satisfaction.*

Consumer Satisfaction

High levels of consumer satisfaction can translate into brand loyalty.

Consumer satisfaction is determined by consumers' post-purchase evaluation of a product or service. Consumers constantly evaluate the efficacy of their choices as they integrate products into their daily lives.[64] Satisfaction is important to marketers because it influences future purchases. The marketing concept suggests that consumer satisfaction should be the focal point of marketing activities. Research shows that satisfaction positively influences consumers' repeat purchase intentions and leads to higher spending. However, these effects can be offset by competitive intensity, i.e., the number of available alternatives.[65] Another study demonstrates that satisfied customers are willing to spend more on a brand that they like.[66] Recent research reveals that extremely high levels of satisfaction can translate into brand loyalty, the most important strategic objective of marketing managers worldwide. Moreover, consumers who have a longstanding relationship with a brand demonstrate a high risk of switching when their loyalty is weakly held.[67]

DISSONANCE-REDUCTION Consumers ask themselves a number of questions after purchasing a brand. Was this brand the right choice? Is it better than alternative choices? One of the strategies consumers use to assess their satisfaction is to compare the chosen brand with a rejected alternative. The chosen brand is the product the consumer actually purchased, while the rejected alternative is a brand considered, but not chosen. If the chosen brand seems superior to the rejected alternative, then consumers experience satisfaction and minimal cognitive dissonance. The converse is also true: if the chosen product appears inferior to a rejected alternative, then cognitive dissonance sets in, leading to dissatisfaction. Evidence of post-purchase dissonance may include comments such as, "Gee, I wish I had purchased the other brand," and, "I paid too much. I should have searched more stores." Cognitive dissonance involves behavior-attitude inconsistency and produces an unpleasant tension referred to as dissonance arousal. When it occurs, people are motivated to reduce dissonance arousal by changing their attitude to match their behavior. Making almost any decision can set the stage for dissonance effects. Consumers employ four strategies to reduce post-purchase dissonance:

1. Increasing the perceived attractiveness of the chosen alternative
2. Decreasing the perceived attractiveness of the rejected alternative
3. Increasing the perceived similarity among alternatives
4. Revoking the decision

The first strategy, known as *sweet lemons,* involves attempts to raise the positive qualities of the chosen alternative. The second strategy, called *sour grapes,* entails disparaging the qualities of rejected alternatives. The third strategy attempts to level the playing field by interpreting all alternatives as similar. The final strategy involves reversing the choice. For example, you might attempt to return the chosen brand in exchange for one of the alternatives.

In a classic study of post-purchase dissonance, consumers were asked to rate the attractiveness of several products, including a stopwatch, silk screen print, portable radio, and fluorescent lamp.[68] They were also told that, at the end of the study, they would receive one of these products as a gift. In the high-dissonance condition, consumers were asked to choose between two products they rated nearly equal in desirability. In the low-dissonance condition, consumers were asked to choose between a product they rated highly and a product they rated much lower in desirability. After receiving their gifts, consumers were asked again to rate all the products. Large shifts in attitude occurred in the high-dissonance condition. The chosen product was rated slightly higher and the rejected product was rated much lower after the decision was made. In contrast, smaller shifts in attitude occurred for the low-dissonance condition. Only the chosen product was rated slightly higher after the choice occurred.

EXPECTANCY DISCONFIRMATION MODEL
In assessing their satisfaction, consumers may also want to know the extent to which their chosen product lived up to its expectations. The **expectancy disconfirmation model** suggests that consumers form expectations about product performance prior to purchasing a brand.[69] After buying a product, people compare their perceptions of its performance in various determinant attributes against the level of performance that was expected on those same attributes. If consumers' perceptions of the brand's performance are in line with their expectations, they are satisfied. If the brand performs more poorly than expected, dissatisfaction sets in, but if performance exceeds expectations, consumers may experience supra-satisfaction, or *customer delight*. Note that consumers' prior expectancies are confirmed if the product performs as anticipated, while expectancies are disconfirmed if the brand performs more poorly or better than expected. This model can be expressed statistically as:

$S = \Sigma w(p\text{-}e)$, where satisfaction (S) is a function of the importance weight that consumers assign to each attribute (w) and the difference between perceptions and expectations ($p\text{-}e$).

When the sum of all the perceptions minus expectations equals zero, consumers are perfectly satisfied. When this sum dips below zero, consumers become dissatisfied, and when the function returns a value greater than zero, consumers are supra-satisfied. The expectancy disconfirmation model suggests that consumers will be dissatisfied with excellent products if their expectations are too high. Conversely, consumers can be delighted with poor products that exceed expectations. So, whatever expectations exist in the minds of consumers prior to purchase are as important as their perceptions of a brand's performance. This line of thinking creates a potential *satisfaction paradox,* a conundrum in which marketers must create sufficiently high expectations to induce brand trial, but not so high as to engender disappointment. In other words, brands that generate extremely low expectations will experience difficulty in getting consumers to try them. Conversely, when marketers build unrealistic expectations for brands, they are destined to disappoint.

Chapter Summary

This chapter focused on how consumers recognize problems, define their markets, gather information related to their consideration and purchase decisions, and determine their satisfaction. Consumer decision making can be defined by the amount of effort people exert to solve a problem. Routine response behavior involves minimal effort, intermediate problem solving entails mid-level effort, and extensive problem solving requires a great deal of effort. Consumer decision making can also be characterized as a joint function of processing effort and involvement, which creates four distinct types of decisions. When both involvement and information processing are low, consumers typically make choices as a matter of habit, or exhibit brand laziness, as opposed to a fundamental commitment to the brand. When consumer involvement is high and information processing is low, consumers exhibit brand loyalty, an intrinsic commitment to a brand based on the benefits or values it provides consumers. When consumers experience low involvement and high information processing, they exhibit variety seeking behavior, the desire to choose new alternatives over more familiar ones—just for the sake of change. Finally, when both involvement and information processing are high, consumers engage in genuine problem-solving strategies. Because consumers cannot consider all the features of a brand, they must identify one or more determinant attributes, characteristics of a product that are both important and unique, and thus, most likely to affect the buyer's choice. Problem solving is the focus of the traditional model of consumer decision making because the decision involves relatively high levels of risk.

The traditional model of consumer decision making involves five stages of consumer problem solving. Problem recognition takes place when consumers experience a disparity between what they have and what they want. This is known as a want-got gap. Needs, wants, and opportunities trigger problem solving. Information search involves both the active and passive processing of data aimed at solving the problem. The level of search is determined by consumer involvement, the marketing environment, situational influences, and individual differences. Evaluation of alternatives requires consumers to determine which product attributes are important and which brands to evaluate on the basis of these attributes. Purchase decisions represent consumers' predispositions or intentions to buy a brand. Finally, during post-purchase evaluation, consumers compare their perceptions of a brand with their expectations and determine their satisfaction.

The uncertainty-reduction model of Consumer Decision Making recognizes that consumers can only make rational decisions within the limits of time and cognitive capability. This approach to decision making involves four stages that specifically deal with consumers' bounded rationality. First, consumers develop perceptions of what the product-market looks like. Next, they whittle down the vast number of brands into a single subset of brands for consideration. Then, consumers choose one brand from the consideration set. Finally, based on their consumption experiences, consumers adjust their perceptions of product-markets in an attempt to make better future decisions. This model emphasizes that consumers continuously sort out and manage information about their chosen brands in an attempt to reduce uncertainty. One of the ways that consumers evaluate their purchases is by assessing their satisfaction. A popular strategy that consumers use to assess their satisfaction is to compare the chosen brand with a rejected alternative. This strategy is known as dissonance-reduction. Another way consumers determine satisfaction is by comparing a brand's performance against expectations of that performance. If the performance equals expectations, then consumers are satisfied. If it exceeds expectations, consumers are delighted. And if the brand fails to live up to expectations, people become dissatisfied.

Key Terms

routine choice	opportunities	external uncertainty
intermediate problem solving	prepurchase search	true utility function
extensive problem solving	internal search	perceived utility function
perceived risk	external search	internal uncertainty
brand laziness	ongoing search	perceived product-market
brand loyalty	enduring involvement	cluster size
variety seeking	situational involvement	cluster variance
intrinsic variety seeking	brand chaos	brand frontier
parity products	market mavens	brand variance
problem solving	impulse buying	non-compensatory process
determinant attributes	bounded rationality	compensatory process
want-got gap	uncertainty-reduction process	expectancy disconfirmation model
needs	true brand universe	
wants	perceived brand universe	

Review and Discussion

1. What distinguishes *brand loyalty* from *brand laziness*? Which of the two is more likely to result in long-term repeat purchase behavior?

2. How are consumers' perceptions of *risk* related to their level of product *involvement*?

3. Which categories of risk do you think have the greatest influence on the purchase of: (a) fashion clothing, (b) a laptop, (c) real estate, (d) sushi, and (e) a cell phone?

4. Why is variety seeking prevalent among parity product categories?

5. What's the difference between a *defensive* and *determinant* attribute? Both types of attributes are important to consumers.

6. Under what conditions are consumers likely to follow the five stages of the traditional model of Consumer Decision Making?

7. What are the two conditions necessary for problem recognition to occur?

8. Discuss the differences among *needs, wants,* and *opportunities.*

9. Predict the level of search for
   a. A beginning skier interested in new skis
   b. A frequent flyer looking for a flight to New York
   c. A stay-at-home-dad who has moderate knowledge regarding baby foods

10. How do *external* and *internal* uncertainties cloud consumers' perceptions of the true brand universe and their true utility functions, respectively?

11. Review the two types of satisfaction models: dissonance-reduction versus expectancy confirmation. Which model would a consumer most likely use if she recently switched to a new brand after years of loyalty to one brand? Which model would a consumer use if he were processing information from advertisements and opinion leaders' word-of-mouth?

Short Application Exercises

1. Use Figure 3.4 (Assessing Determinant Attributes) to identify attributes in each of the four quadrants for *blue jeans.* On the basis of your analysis, what are the determinant attributes?

2. Identify three want-got gaps that you are currently experiencing. Characterize one as a *need,* the second as a *want,* and the third as an *opportunity.* To illustrate these three problems, sketch a figure similar to Figure 3.7.

3. Identify a product category for which you feel *enduring involvement* and a product category for which you show only *situational involvement.* Explain why these product categories affect you differently.

4. Interview a friend regarding his/her search activities in a recently purchased, high involvement product (e.g., automobile, computer, graduate school). Identify whether s/he relied primarily on *prepurchase* or *ongoing* search to make his/her choice.

MANAGERIAL APPLICATION

Imagine that you work for a well-known marketing research firm. Your supervisor has asked you to use the expectancy disconfirmation model to evaluate a consumer's post-hoc satisfaction level for a recent purchase of running shoes.

YOUR CHALLENGE:

1. Identify three determinant attributes for this consumer (e.g., comfort, style, durability).

2. Determine the consumer's importance weights for each attribute, such that they total 100 percent. For example, comfort = thirty percent, style = ten percent, and durability = sixty percent.

3. On a 1 to 7 scale, ask the consumer to rate how s/he expected the brand to perform on each of these attributes, *prior* to purchase (for example, comfort = 6, style = 4, and durability = 6).

4. Also on a 1 to 7 scale, ask the consumer to rate his/her actual perceptions of how the shoe has performed on each of these attributes.

5. Plug in the weights, expectations, and perceptions into the formula: $S = \Sigma w(p\text{-}e)$. Does the outcome of the function suggest that this consumer is satisfied, delighted, or dissatisfied? Ask the consumer if s/he is satisfied to see if the model is consistent with the consumer's response.

Consumer Evaluation and Choice

OBJECTIVES *After studying this chapter, you will be able to . . .*

1 | Explain the stages of consumer choice.

2 | Describe several marketing techniques for influencing consumers' consideration sets.

3 | Define stimulus-based, memory-based, and mixed choice.

4 | Explain the MODE model.

5 | Explain how many different heuristics or shortcuts are used to simplify prediction and choice.

SONY HAS A TELEVISION FOR EVERY CONSUMER TASTE

Consumers often are faced with an overwhelming sea of choices in thousands of product categories. Consider the television market. Each year, consumers in the United States buy about 32 million television sets, and they have plenty of options.[1] For example, typical Internet shopping site BizRate.com offers 125 different television brands and more than 3,200 models![2] The Sony Company, one of the world's leading television manufacturers, offers 248 different models of televisions.

Imagine that a consumer wants to purchase a new television. Even if she has narrowed her choice to a Sony brand of TV, would she choose a Sony 20-inch, a Sony 27-inch, a Sony 35-inch, a Sony 42-inch, a Sony 50-inch, a Sony 57-inch, or an even larger screen? Does she want standard definition, enhanced definition, or high definition? Does she want a conventional, direct view, cathode-ray tube (CRT) TV, a liquid-crystal display (LCD) TV, a plasma TV, a rear projection CRT TV, or a rear projection LCD or DLP (digital light processing) TV? For relatively small screens, CRT TVs are less expensive than the other options, but for big screens, rear projection models are less expensive. Plasma screens offer remarkable brightness and contrast, but static images can burn into the screen. Burn-in does not occur on LCD screens, but the image may dim as the consumer angles away from the center of the screen. This problem also occurs in many rear projection models.

With so many options to consider, it is easy to see how someone could become overwhelmed trying to choose just one. Sometimes when consumers are faced with too many choices, they try to simplify by using a shortcut or "rule of thumb." We'll see in this chapter that many different shortcuts are possible, such as the price-quality shortcut—the idea that you get what you pay for. Consumers often try to simplify, but if choosing a product is still too difficult or confusing, they may just postpone decision making or avoid making a choice altogether.[3] Of course, a purchase like a new television may not be a decision consumers want to put off, especially if their old set has stopped working. But you can live without television, right?

This chapter discusses how consumers evaluate brands and make purchase-related decisions. Extensive research on consumer decision making has examined how consumers combine and evaluate the information gathered from internal and external searches to make a purchase decision, and some of those concepts and processes are discussed here. It is important to remember that consumers employ a variety of decision-making processes, depending on the nature of the task and other factors that include motivation, ability, and opportunity to process the information, the information available, and the timing of the decision, to name just a few.

OBJECTIVE 1

The Consideration Set: Determining Choice Alternatives

Before a person can make a purchase, or even make evaluations of various alternative brands, they generate a set of brands to consider and evaluate—even if it's just one. A **consideration set** is the group of brands that consumers think about buying when they need to make a purchase. The brands included in the consideration set can come from the *evoked set* of brands, from brands discovered during external information search, and from point-of-purchase. This is discussed further when we examine consumer choice later in the chapter.

Because consumers can't select a brand unless it is included their consideration sets, the first job of a marketer is to encourage the consumer to consider buying his or her brand. This is often difficult because the consideration set for many products is quite small. Although consideration set size can range from one (a very brand loyal customer may consider only one brand) to as many brands as are available in the market—dozens or even hundreds for some products—consumers rarely consider more than seven brands (see Figure 4.1). Besides the fact that consumers just don't have the time or the desire in many cases (given the limited utility of evaluating 15 different brands of toilet paper, for instance) to carefully consider dozens of brands, limited information processing capacity also prevents people from considering more than Miller's magic number of seven plus or minus two.[4] Although there are always exceptions to every rule, this tendency to have small consideration

FIGURE 4.1   CONSIDERATION SETS

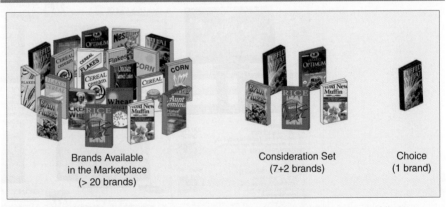

Brands Available
in the Marketplace
(> 20 brands)

Consideration Set
(7+2 brands)

Choice
(1 brand)

Source: Kardes, F. (1997). *Consumer Behavior and Managerial Decision Making.* Upper Saddle River, NJ: Prentice Hall.

sets exists across product categories, from toothpaste and breakfast cereal to cars and computers.

Because people consider so few brands, marketers have to be creative to encourage consumers to consider their brands, rather than competitors' offerings. One way marketers get consumers to consider brands is by drawing attention to the brand and making it memorable. When a marketer uses the principles of attention, learning, and memory to increase the likelihood that a brand is included in a consumer's consideration set, the marketer is one step closer to a potential sale.

Ensuring that a brand is simply included in consumers' consideration sets is an important first step to influencing brand evaluation and ultimate choice, but how many and what other brands are also included in the consideration set are also important factors. As the number of brands in the consumer's consideration set increases, the likelihood of a brand being chosen decreases. Thus, the next step should be to control the number of competitors' brands in the consideration set. Three techniques for influencing consumers' consideration sets are part-list cuing, the attraction effect, and the compromise effect.

(OBJECTIVE 2)

Influencing the Consideration Set

PART-LIST CUING One way marketers influence the consideration set is to decrease its overall size while at the same time maintaining their brand presence in the set. Marketers can reduce the number of brands considered for a purchase through **part-list cuing,** which involves presenting the names of just some brands when consumers are trying to recall as many brands as possible.[5] This technique is designed to make some brands more prominent than others by using a competitive advertisement or by listing the names of only a few competing brands in a promotional campaign or selling situation. As the partial list of brands becomes more conspicuous and more strongly connected with the product category, it becomes more difficult for the consumer to think of other brands. For example, let's imagine that a consumer want to purchase a new car. The consumer knows she wants a small, sporty car, but she doesn't know what brand of car she wants, and she knows that at least a dozen brands in the market fit her general purchase criteria. The consumer heads to a nearby new car dealer to "browse around." Of course, a salesperson quickly approaches her. After a few minutes of discussing the features available in a new car, the sales associate directs the consumer to a brand model that best fits her needs. The salesperson may then proceed to compare his brand to one or two other brands in the market. Of course, the salesperson will likely focus on competing brands that are inferior in some way to his brand. As the consumer focuses on these three brands—the one on the lot and the other two mentioned by the salesperson— it becomes more difficult for her to recall other brands that might also fit her needs. Suddenly, her consideration set has been reduced to three brands. The comparative advertisement for ID Patrol on page 218 works in a similar fashion. The ad tries to create a consideration set of just four, one in which ID Patrol is the only brand to offer all five, key attributes.

The part-list cuing effect is important because it can help consumers quickly and efficiently come to a decision, plus it can also lead them to focus on some brands while ignoring others that are potentially better. As a result, consumers may make choices they later regret.[6]

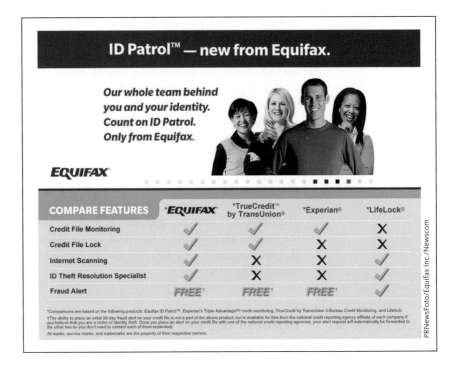

THE ATTRACTION EFFECT Marketers also attempt to influence which specific brands consumers are likely to compare and evaluate. A target brand seems more attractive when it is compared to inferior brands and less attractive when compared to superior brands. This is called the **attraction effect**.[7] Marketers want consumers to compare their brands to inferior brands—remember the car salesperson? Again, this can be done in a selling situation or by using comparative advertising and promotion that show the target brand as superior to other brands on some dimension. Alternatively, the attraction effect can unintentionally occur when a firm has multiple brands in its product line (see Figure 4.2). For example, Williams-Sonoma sold a home bread-baking machine for $275 and at first, sales were poor. Later, Williams-Sonoma added a much more expensive home bread-baking machine to its product line. When consumers compared the $275 machine to the much more expensive machine, the $275 machine seemed very attractive because of the price, and sales of this machine almost doubled! This occurred because $275 seemed like a more reasonable price when it was compared to an even higher price, and consumers like to save money.

THE COMPROMISE EFFECT Another way to improve the evaluation of a particular brand is to make the brand appear as an average (or a good compromise) brand against other brands in the consideration set. A compromise brand seems average on all important attributes or features. While other brands often have some really good and some really bad features, a compromise brand does appears to not have any very bad features and is at least acceptable on all features. Thus, a compromise brand seems like a safe choice. This **compromise effect**, or the increased probability of buying a compromise brand, is especially likely to occur when consumers are concerned about making a bad decision (see Figure 4.2).[8] For example, consider a consumer who wants to purchase a camera and is deciding between an inexpensive model and a moderately priced model. If a third camera, a high-priced model, is added to the consideration set, then the moderately priced model seems like a reasonable compromise. Brands that are

FIGURE 4.2 THE ATTRACTION EFFECT AND THE COMPROMISE EFFECT

Two Equally Preferred Brands	Attraction Effect	Compromise Effect
Dimension A	Dimension A	Dimension A
• Brand A	• Brand A	• Brand A
		• Brand B
• Brand B	• Brand B • Decoy	• Brand C
Dimension B	Dimension B	Dimension B
Brand A is better on dimension A (one attribute or one cluster of attributes). Brand B is better on dimension B. The dimensions are equally important.	Adding a decoy similar but inferior to Brand B increases preference for Brand B.	Adding a Brand C, which is excellent on dimension B but poor on dimension A, increases preference for Brand B.

Source: Kardes, F. (1997). *Consumer Behavior and Managerial Decision Making.* Upper Saddle River, NJ: Prentice Hall.

intermediate or "average" in terms of price, quality, and number of features are frequently chosen from the consideration set. They are chosen even more frequently when consumers need to justify their choice to others, such as a spouse, boss, or friends. It is often easier to justify the purchase of intermediate rather than extreme brands.

Of course, nearly any brand can appear to be a compromise brand depending on the brands to which it is compared. Advertising and promotion campaigns that encourage consumers to compare a seemingly average brand to more extreme brands increase the influence of the compromise effect.

The choices that consumers make follow their evaluations and judgments of the brands in their considerations sets (see Figure 4.1). Now that we have examined how consumers establish consideration sets and how marketers attempt to influence brand evaluations within these considerations sets, we turn our attention to the desired outcome of the consumer decision-making process: *consumer choice.*

Constructing Evaluations to Make Choices

Consumer choice involves selecting one product or brand from a set of possibilities. Marketers who want to influence consumers must understand three critical issues:

1. The brands in the consideration set
2. The types of information used to detect and evaluate the differences among the considered alternatives
3. How this information is ultimately used in the choice process[9]

The first point has already been discussed. The other two issues are discussed throughout the rest of the chapter. First, three types of consumer choice based on the physical presence or absence of the brand during choice are reviewed: stimulus-based, memory-based, and mixed choice.

OBJECTIVE 3

Consumer Choice: Stimulus-Based, Memory-Based, and Mixed Choice

After the consideration set has been determined, consumers need to evaluate the differences in the attributes among the considered brands to make a choice. When consumers can directly and physically observe all relevant brands in the consideration set and their brand attributes, they make a **stimulus-based choice**.[10] For example, in a grocery store, it is easy to compare brands and attributes simply by examining the different packages on a shelf.

When none of the relevant brands and attributes is directly and physically observable, however, consumers make a **memory-based choice.** Here, consumers must retrieve brand and attribute information from memory. An example is a consumer at home trying to decide what restaurant to go to for dinner. Finally, in **mixed choice**, consumers can see some brands but must remember others. This is the most common type of choice scenario. When this occurs, *stimulus brands*—the brands that are physically observed—usually have an advantage over *memory brands*—the brands not observed but drawn from memory—because consumers tend to forget specific details about memory brands.[11] For example, when shopping for a new car, a consumer is likely to visit an automobile dealership. While on the premises, the consumer may attempt to compare model brands on the dealership lot (stimulus brands) to model brands that she examined earlier at a different dealership (memory brands). If all the brands are similar in quality, the consumer

100nights/iStockphoto.com

Car shopping typically involves a mixed choice situation.

In 1985, John Schnatter founded a small pizza company named Papa John's. Part of the company's growth was fueled by its now famous advertising slogan, "Better Ingredients. Better Pizza." A few years after introducing the slogan, Papa John's began an advertising campaign centered around the slogan that specifically compared Papa John's to Pizza Hut pizza, with the aim of "proving" that Papa John's had better ingredients (on an ingredient-by-ingredient basis) than its competitors. For example, in one television commercial, Papa John's claimed that its dough was "better" than Pizza Hut's because Papa John's dough was made with filtered water, rather than tap water—depicted in the ad as less-than-clean and suitable only for washing dishes.

Faced with what they perceived as an attack on their brand, Pizza Hut sued Papa John's claiming that Papa John's claims of better pizza than Pizza Hut's were false, and that the slogan itself had become a comparative statement of superiority.[38] What was Papa John's defense? The company claimed the element of puffery. Puffery is an advertising element allowing a company to use general, non-provable, superlative claims—like "better," "faster," or "larger"—about their products and services because the general public understands that these claims are not necessarily true. Initially, the court ruled in favor of Pizza Hut, finding that the advertising was false, and the slogan had been tainted by the advertising campaign, taking it beyond harmless puffery. The finding did not hold up under appeal, however. A higher court ruled that, while the campaign may have indeed been misleading, Pizza Hut did not prove that the campaign had any "material" influence, i.e., it did not have an actual influence on consumers' purchase decisions.[39]

This case underscores the legal and ethical issues of using puffery in advertising. In general, the use of puffery is legal, but often only a thin line exists between puffery and deception—which is illegal. Papa John's claimed that using puffery is acceptable and that consumers expect it. Many critics agree, claiming that puffery is harmless.[40] Others claim that while puffery is not unethical, marketers still should not use it because it is a waste of advertising dollars.[41] In other words, consumers have become so accustomed to outrageous claims, such as, "We have the best selection," "The Real Thing," and " the ultimate in clean," that they have become immune to them. However, even when puffery is found to be legal, as in the Papa John's case, how ethical is the use of puffery when it accompanies comparative claims against competitors?

is more likely to choose the stimulus brand because she might not be able to remember the exact price or the exact level of performance on an important attribute of the memory brands.

Although consumers usually choose stimulus brands over memory brands, marketers can reverse this effect when memory brands have a very large number of favorable attributes. Consumers are likely to remember that these brands are very good even if they can't remember specific details about the brands.[12] "Puffery" or exaggerated advertising claims about a memory brand such as, "This brand is rated number 1 in its class," can also increase the likelihood that consumers will choose it. Thus, stimulus brands are preferred over memory brands except in special cases where memory brands seem too good to be ignored.

Now that we have looked at the differences in stimulus versus memory brands, let's examine some common ways consumers evaluate brand information and how the amount of effort expended on the decision-making process influences choice.

Attitude versus Attribute-Based Choice Strategies

Sometimes, consumers make choices based on general impressions about a brand and sometimes on specific brand attribute information. In **attitude-based choice**, they form overall evaluations and general impressions of brands in the consideration set based on a combination of everything they know about all the brands, and then select the one with the highest evaluation. Formally, an *attitude* is an evaluative judgment that a person forms of people, objects, and issues. In contrast to attitude-based choice, when consumers make **attribute-based choices**, they compare the specific attributes or features of each brand and select the one that performs best on key attributes.

When do consumers use attitude-based versus attribute-based choice strategies? One determinant is *accessibility*, or ease of retrieving either attitude or attribute information from memory. Research shows that, when drawing information from memory, a person usually finds it easier to use attitude-based choice because attitudes are easier to retrieve from memory than are specific brand attributes.[13] For example, it is easier for consumers to recall that they generally like the Skippy brand of peanut butter more than Jiff than it is to recall attributes of both brands (e.g., price, nutty taste, smoothness) and individual preferences for each attribute. Of course, attitude-based choice can occur only if the attitudes exist; a person must have a previously formed attitude toward a brand to pull it from memory.

On the other hand, usefulness of information is important too. When brands are very similar overall, small differences among them are easier to detect when comparing them along specific attributes. In this case, attribute-based choice may be preferable because the attribute information is more *diagnostic*, which means it is more relevant for distinguishing among brands. Therefore, while attitudes are often more *accessible*, attributes are often more *diagnostic*. In general, the information that is most accessible *and* diagnostic is the information that is used in a consumer's choice decision.

The accessibility and diagnosticity of information are not the only factors that influence the type of information that consumers use in their choices. The more important the product choice, the more consumers want to think about it, and this too, influences the type of information they use. For example, purchasing an engagement ring, selecting a university, or even choosing a new cologne are probably more important than purchasing a bottle of ketchup or selecting a movie rental. According

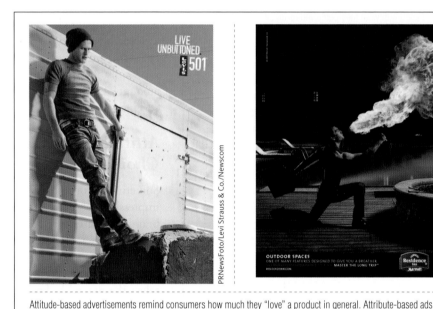

Attitude-based advertisements remind consumers how much they "love" a product in general. Attribute-based ads encourage consumers to choose a brand that performs best on key features.

to a theory called the **MODE model**, **M**otivation and **O**pportunity to **DE**liberate are key **DE**terminants of the processes that influence consumer choice.[14] Motivation is high when the decision is more personally relevant (motivation is synonymous with high involvement). Opportunity is high when people can take time and have the ability to think carefully and to deliberate about the decision. When both motivation and opportunity are high, consumers are likely to deliberate about the decision. This careful deliberation is more consistent with attribute-based choice because brands are carefully evaluated along every relevant product attribute. Recall that small differences among brands are easier to detect when comparing them along specific attributes, and even small differences between brands may be crucial when the purchase choice is very important. If either motivation or opportunity is low, attitude-based choice is more likely. See Figure 4.3.

FIGURE 4.3 The MODE Model

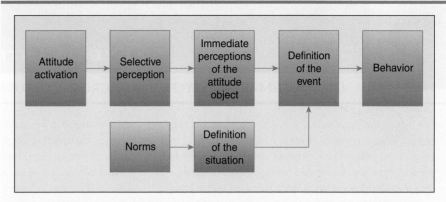

Source: Adapted from Fazio, R. H. (1990). Multiple processes by which attitudes guide behavior: The MODE model as an integrative framework. In M. P. Zanna (Ed.), *Advances in experimental social psychology* (vol. 23, pp. 75-109). New York: Academic Press. Reprinted by permission of Elsevier.

OBJECTIVE 4

Choice Based on Heuristic Processing

The MODE model is an example of a *dual process model*. This model suggests that sometimes consumers think carefully about decisions and sometimes they don't. As we saw in the discussion of the MODE model, motivation and opportunity are important determinants as to how much careful thinking people do when making a product choice. Also important are processing factors related to involvement and ability and situational factors. In general, when consumers think carefully about decisions, using all relevant information and considering all implications, they are engaging in **systematic processing**. In contrast, sometimes people are unwilling or unable to use careful and effortful decision-making strategies, such as when motivation or opportunity—according to the MODE model—are low. Instead, consumers use simple **heuristics** that enable them to make decisions quickly and easily. This is known as **heuristic processing**.[15] Heuristics are mental shortcuts that help consumers simplify their decision-making tasks. There are three types of heuristics—persuasion, prediction, and influence. All heuristics aid in simplifying cognitive tasks, but the type of heuristic consumers use depends on the specific task at hand.

Persuasion heuristics influence consumers' beliefs and attitudes. They come in three forms.[16] The *length-implies-strength heuristic* suggests "size matters." For example, advertisements and sales pitches filled with facts and figures appear more compelling than just a few claims. So consumers tend to evaluate the quality of the brand according to the number of favorable attributes it possesses. The *liking-agreement heuristic* is based on the assumption that consumers usually agree with people they like. This heuristic is embodied in balance theory. Finally, the *consensus-implies-correctness heuristic* is synonymous with "the bandwagon effect." It implies that if everyone is doing it, then it must be good, i.e., it offers social validation.

EYE ON INTERNATIONAL

DECISION-MAKING STYLES VARY ACROSS CULTURES

When making decisions, many North Americans are said to be analytical, relying on factual information, and individualistic, making one choice independently of others. Similarly, the French tend to consider many alternatives, and are highly rational and thorough in their decision making, while Russians are said to place more emphasis on values and appearance than facts. Germans are said to be deductive, and the Danes tend to be pragmatic when making decisions. In contrast, in Japan and other Asian cultures, logic and rationality seem less important; instead, one's "gut feeling" needs to be right, and the collective consensus is more important than the individual's opinion. Similarly, many Saudi Arabians are more intuitive in their decision making and avoid persuasion in favor of empirical evidence.[36]

In recent years, researchers have extensively examined cultural differences in decision making. While cross-cultural research related to decision making covers a broad range of topics, the overall results show that cultural differences are pervasive, not just along Eastern and Western philosophies, but also between countries and cultures within those countries. Additionally, within individuals, cultural influences are thought to influence consumers at all stages of the decision process.[37]

Developing a fuller understanding of how people from different cultures make decisions is essential for marketers as they expand globally. As our world becomes smaller as a result of information technology and the political opening of borders and economies, understanding cross-cultural difference in consumer behavior, decision making, and choice will become essential. Only by understanding cross-cultural differences can marketers effectively craft products and messages to satisfy global consumers.

Prediction heuristics are used to form likelihood judgments (e.g., representativeness, availability, simulation, and anchoring-and-adjustment). The third heuristic type, **influence or choice heuristics,** affects consumers' decisions directly (e.g., lexicographic, additive-difference, conjunctive, disjunctive, frequency of good-bad features). Prediction and choice heuristics are discussed in detail later in this chapter.

Heuristic processing occurs most often when a decision is perceived as unimportant—which ketchup brand to buy, for instance—or when decision making is stressful or difficult as a result of time pressure or information overload. Consumers' use of heuristics becomes even more prevalent as the amount of information available to them increases, as potential choice alternatives increase, and as the pace of life increases.

There are many ways consumers use heuristics when evaluating brands. Consumers often use heuristics to predict what will happen if they buy or don't buy a particular product or brand. For example, "If I buy the most expensive laundry detergent, my clothes will be extra clean." Heuristics also influence what and how much choice-related information consumers use to make a decision and how they use that information. For example, many consumers assume that price and quality are strongly related; that is where the idea that "you get what you pay for" comes from. This assumption leads consumers to predict that expensive products are high in quality, and inexpensive products are low in quality. When consumers use price as a heuristic cue for predicting quality, they base their judgment of quality on price alone. However, many other variables also influence quality, such as product reliability, durability, appearance, ease of use, cost of use, and the number of different uses of a product. Price is just one variable. Here lies a potential pitfall of using heuristic processing. Although it simplifies decision making and enables consumers to make choices quickly and easily, heuristic thinking often oversimplifies choice and leads consumers to overlook important information. Consequently, when consumers focus only on price, they over-simplify prediction and make poor decisions. For example, for many different products, price is only weakly related to quality.[17] This means that some brands are high in price but low in quality, and some brands are low in price but high in quality. Relying too heavily on the price-quality heuristic can lead consumers to buy a high-priced brand that is low in quality. Of course, price is not the only cue that consumers use to predict the quality of a product. People also rely on brand name, store reputation, warranty, the Good Housekeeping seal of approval, and company membership in the Better Business Bureau, among other heuristic cues.

In addition to using the specific heuristic cues noted above, people also use *general* heuristic cues. In their path-breaking research on the use of general heuristics, Tversky and Kahneman researched four important general cues that people use for simplifying predictions related to decision making: the representativeness heuristic, the availability heuristic, the simulation heuristic, and the anchoring-and-adjustment heuristic (see Figure 4.4).[18] Each of these heuristics can lead all people, including consumers and marketers, to make bad predictions and, thus, bad decisions.

FIGURE 4.4 PREDICTION HEURISTICS

Representativeness Heuristic	
Concept	Example
Assessing the likelihood that a particular target belongs to a category based on the degree to which the target and category appear similar.	If a consumer believes that Honda automobiles are high quality, he may conclude that Honda motorbikes are similarly high in quality.

Availability Heuristic	
Concept	Example
Searching memory for relevant examples of a particular event and basing one's prediction of that event on how easily these examples come to mind.	If a consumer recalls many floods, then he or she will predict that future floods are likely. As a result, this consumer may be inclined to buy flood insurance.

Simulation Heuristic	
Concept	Example
An event or sequence of events that is easy to imagine also seems very likely to occur.	Consumers who imagine a brand performing well are more likely to believe that this brand will actually satisfy their needs.

Anchor-and-Adjustment Heuristic	
Concept	Example
Random anchors or "starting points" influence probability estimates.	Real estate agents' estimates of the value of a property are very close to the prior observed list price (anchor).

OBJECTIVE 5

Prediction Heuristics

Good consumer decision making often requires accurate probability or likelihood judgments about events, such as accurate predictions about future product performance (will the product do what I need it to do?), about when a product needs replacement (should I buy a new car now or risk future repair bills?), about the behavior of others (will my sister like this gift? Will this salesperson try to trick me?), and about one's own future behavior (will I still like this color of paint two years from now?). However, although the ability to make predictions is very important, research suggests that people are not very good at making them, largely because they often unknowingly use heuristics to generate those predictions.

REPRESENTATIVENESS HEURISTIC Predictions are sometimes based on similarity or representativeness. People using the **representativeness heuristic** make predictions based on perceived similarities between a specific target and a general category. For example, if a new product has a similar name, package, or appearance to another product we like a lot, we usually predict that we will like the new product, too. If a person we just met reminds us of another person that we do not like—perhaps because the two people have similar glasses, clothing, gestures, or mannerisms—we often predict that we will dislike the new person, as well. Because whales have many traits and characteristics similar to those possessed by fish—such as fins, tails, the ability to swim and live in water—children often believe that whales are fish. Consumers make similar mistakes when they focus on superficial similarities between an object and a category. In the same way, marketers can use the representativeness heuristic to their advantage. For example, a private store brand often packages products in boxes with sizes, colors, and graphics similar to that of leading national brands, hoping that the superficial package similarities will lead consumers to predict that the store brands are similar to leading national brands on more important dimensions. Unfortunately,

Private labels, such as Kroger, can appear to be similar to or *representative* of national brands.

consumers often focus on these irrelevant similarities—package color and graphics—so their predictions may suffer.

Important information often overlooked because of the representativeness heuristic is the *base rate*, which is the incidence rate of an event. If consumers know that 10 percent of the products in a particular industry fail or need repair, then they can predict a 10 percent chance of a randomly selected product from this industry failing. In the absence of other information, that prediction should be based entirely on the base rate. However, Tversky and Kahneman have shown that even a small amount of marginally useful information can lead people to rely too heavily on the representativeness heuristic and subsequently neglect, overlook, or ignore the base rate.[19] For example, in a classic study, Tversky and Kahneman told research participants that a panel of psychologists administered personality tests to 30 engineers and 70 lawyers. Participants were asked to predict the likelihood that a randomly selected person from this sample was an engineer. When no other information was provided, most participants predicted correctly that there was a 30 percent chance that the randomly selected person was an engineer. However, in another experimental condition, participants received a brief, marginally informative description of the randomly selected person:

> Jack shows no interest in political and social issues and spends most of his free time on hobbies, which include home carpentry, sailing, and mathematical puzzles,

When participants received this brief description, they categorized Jack as an engineer, and they predicted that it was highly likely that Jack was an engineer. Even marginally relevant descriptive information can lead people to ignore highly relevant base rate information.

Sweepstakes can appeal to the *gambler's fallacy*.

PRNewsFoto/Continental Tire North America, Inc./AP Photo

Another bias related to the representativeness heuristic deals with the *law of large numbers*, which states that the larger the sample size, the more likely it is that statistics estimated from a sub-sample apply to the larger population from which the sub-sample was drawn. Unfortunately, people expect even very small samples to be representative of larger populations, but this may not be the case. For example, a small group of friends may tell you that a new movie is really good or a particular new restaurant is bad. It is very likely that you will rely on this information received from a small group and ignore that fact that the opinion of such a small group may not be representative of what the majority of people think.

The representativeness heuristic also encourages people to commit the *gambler's fallacy*. Gamblers often foolishly believe that events alternate frequently in random sequences and that long streaks of the same event must be nonrandom. Consequently, if a basketball player makes several baskets in a row, gamblers believe the player is more likely to make the next basket.[20] The streak seems nonrandom because it does not correlate with people's conceptions of chance. Similarly, when betting on whether a coin will turn up heads or tails, gamblers often believe that tails is more likely after a string of heads (e.g., four heads in a row). However, the actual likelihood of tails after four heads in a row is still the base rate: 50 percent. In the long run, the number of times tails turns up is 50 percent, but in small samples, random streaks are highly likely to be observed. Marketers use the gambler's fallacy to convince people to buy lottery tickets, enter sweepstakes, and look for winning game tokens, based on the idea that if consumers purchase enough tickets, etc. they will eventually win.

In business, a string of successes seems nonrandom, and lucky marketing managers often conclude that they have beaten the odds. Consequently, they predict that they will continue to beat the odds. This is another example of the gambler's fallacy. After a string of failures, unlucky marketing managers often predict that the odds will even out and, therefore, they are due for a success. Again however, marketing managers can get lucky or unlucky as a result of chance, and the laws of chance never change. Fortunately, many business outcomes are influenced by both skill and by chance. What marketers should hope is that the skill component is great enough to increase the probability of success, regardless of chance. But whenever chance exists, no matter how small, the probability of success cannot be 100 percent.

Finally, the representativeness heuristic influences how consumers might use information prematurely to make decisions. The likelihood of one specific extreme or unusual event is very low, by definition. Usually, extreme or unusual events are followed by less extreme or less unusual events. This is known as *regression to the mean*. In the long run, the average or typical level of a variable is observed. For example, many top athletes have remarkable rookie years, and much less remarkable second years (the so-called sophomore slump). Many restaurants seem to serve outstanding meals once, but less exciting meals over subsequent visits. Regression to the mean occurs for extreme negative events, also. A store where you received terrible customer service when you visited it the first time, may offer better service over the long term. In each of these examples, an initial extreme or unusual performance is followed by a more moderate, typical, or average performance. This is because the initial extreme performance was influenced by random factors (e.g., the rookie's style of play just happened to click well with the other players; the chef had especially fresh and delicious ingredients). However, in the long run, individuals, groups of people, and organizations perform at an average or typical level.

The representativeness heuristic makes it difficult to fully appreciate the statistical concept of regression to the mean. Good performances seem to come from skill, and skill seems to ensure continued success. Poor performances seem to stem from mediocrity, and mediocrity seems to ensure continued failure. However, chance factors can lead consumers to jump to conclusions. Prematurely categorizing customer service, products, or organizations on the basis of their initial performance can lead to poor predictions. Thus, it is important for marketers to limit the number of unusual events that can happen when dealing with customers, and strive for consistently good performance from their products and services.

To summarize, the representativeness heuristic encourages people to focus on simple similarities and to ignore complex but highly relevant statistical concepts, such as base rates, gambler's fallacy, and regression to the mean.

AVAILABILITY HEURISTIC   People use the **availability heuristic** to make predictions based on how easily they can retrieve information from memory.[21] Events that are highly memorable because of media exposure, frequent exposure, or recent exposure are easily recalled. Easily recalled events tend to be overestimated. For example, let's suppose a consumer is booking a flight reservation and is trying to determine the likelihood that his flight will be delayed. If the last time the consumer flew with a particular airline, his flight was delayed, then that event will be easily recalled. As a result, this consumer will be more likely to predict that his upcoming flight will be delayed, also. Likewise, events that are unmemorable tend to be underestimated. For example, is it more likely to be killed by a shark or by falling airplane parts? Most people believe that shark attacks are more likely because of movies featuring giant sharks and media reports of shark attacks. Deaths resulting from falling airplane parts, however, receive much less media attention. In reality, a person is 30 times more likely to die from falling airplane parts than from a shark attack.[22]

It is also important to distinguish between the *ease* with which examples of a to-be-predicted event can be retrieved from memory and the *number* of examples of a to-be-predicted event that can be retrieved from memory.[23] If it is easy to retrieve examples, the event seems likely. If it is possible to retrieve many examples, the event also seems likely. In many situations, ease of retrieval and the number of examples that can be retrieved are confounded. That is, ease and number are either both high or both low. When this is the case, it is impossible to determine whether ease of retrieval or the number of examples that can be retrieved has a stronger influence on predictive judgment.

In some circumstances, however, ease and number are *inversely related* (i.e., as one variable increases, the other variable decreases). In an important experiment that separates the effects on prediction of ease of retrieval versus number of examples retrieved, participants were asked to generate either ten (difficult task) or one (easy task) reason that a BMW is better than a Mercedes-Benz.[24] The results revealed that the BMW was more strongly preferred over the Mercedes-Benz when one reason was generated than when

MARKETING IN ACTION

All-in-One Products Offer Consumers a Good Reason to Buy

Historically, *Business Week's* best new products offer multipurpose all-in-one brands that build several different products into one unit. For example, the palmOne Treo 600 is a PDA with a cellular phone, speakerphone, digital camera, and a music player all-in-one. Similarly, the LGE cell phone is not just a cell phone, but also a digital camera. The Schick Intuition women's shaver is not just a shaver; it also provides a rich lather so that you can lather, shave, and moisturize in one easy step. The razor is built into the skin moisturizing solid and this makes it simple, easy, and more convenient for women to shave their legs while in the shower. Similarly, the Aquafresh Floss 'N' Cap is a tube of Aquafresh toothpaste with a floss dispenser built into the cap. This makes it easier for consumers to remember to floss after brushing. Finally, General Electric's Profile and Monogram oven with Trifection technology is a conventional oven, convection oven, and microwave oven all-in-one. This technology greatly reduces cooking times for a wide variety of foods.

Why are all-in-one products so popular? One reason is that choice is often *reason-based*.[35] This means that consumers often attempt to think of reasons why one product is better than all of the others. An all-in-one product has many different uses, and this often provides a

compelling reason for choosing an all-in-one product over a product with just one use or purpose. Also, buying one all-in-one product often seems more efficient than buying many different single-use products that, collectively, perform the same functions.

participants offered ten reasons. These results are surprising because ten reasons are better than one. However, one reason is easier to retrieve, and ease of retrieval is more important than the number of items retrieved when the availability heuristic is used as a basis for prediction.[25]

SIMULATION HEURISTIC   People use the **simulation heuristic** to make predictions based on how easily an event or a sequence of events can be imagined or visualized.[26] If an event or sequence of events is easy to imagine, it tends to be overestimated. If an event or sequence of events is difficult to imagine, it tends to be underestimated. In one study of this phenomenon, participants were asked to imagine how likely they were to contract a disease called Hyposcenia-B.[27] In the easy-to-imagine condition, participants were told that the symptoms of the disease were headaches, muscle aches, and low energy. Most of us have experienced these symptoms sometime in our lives, and consequently, it is easy to imagine suffering from them. By contrast, in the difficult-to-imagine condition, participants were told that the symptoms of the disease were disorientation, a malfunctioning nervous system, and an inflamed liver. Most of us have not experienced these symptoms, so they are difficult to imagine. The results indicated that people believed they were personally more likely to contract Hyposcenia-B when the symptoms of the disease were easy to imagine as opposed to difficult to imagine. These effects disappeared, however, when participants did not attempt to imagine experiencing any of the symptoms.

These findings have important implications to marketers. For example, the simulation heuristic affects healthcare marketing. Consumers with high blood pressure often forget to take their medicine because the symptoms usually aren't that bad, so it is difficult to imagine that their condition is serious. Consequently, their health deteriorates, and marketers at pharmaceutical firms sell fewer pills. Similarly, consumers suffering from infections often take antibiotics for a few days and then stop when they feel better because it is difficult for them to imagine that they are still sick. Consequently, antibiotic-resistant infections develop, and pharmaceutical firms have to spend millions on the development of new antibiotics.

ANCHORING-AND-ADJUSTMENT HEURISTIC   People using the **anchoring-and-adjustment heuristic** make predictions based on a first impression or an initial judgment (or anchor) and then shift (adjust or fine-tune) this judgment upward or downward depending on the implications of the imagined possibilities.[28] Unfortunately, people often do not adjust enough, and as a result, final judgments tend to be too close to initial judgments. For example, thinking about big numbers leads to big judgments, and thinking about small numbers leads to small judgments. Consequently, if you are asked to think of a big number first, such as 975, you would be more likely to overestimate the price of an inexpensive product that you don't buy frequently. If you are asked to think of a small number, such as 1, you would be more likely to underestimate the price of the same product. Similarly, expert real estate agents who receive a high list price (or high anchor value) for a house overestimate the value of a house, while agents who receive a low list price (or low anchor value) underestimate the value of the same house.[29]

The anchoring-and-adjustment heuristic can be used to trick consumers into buying more at a grocery store. In many cases, consumers intend to buy only one unit of a product when they enter the store (e.g., one container of milk); obviously the number one is a relatively low anchor. However, merely mentioning larger numbers can encourage consumers to consider higher anchors.[30] For example, multiple-unit pricing such as

3 for $1.99, or 12 for the price of 10, encourages consumers to buy more than one unit for two reasons: first, to obtain the volume discount, and second, multiple units suggest an anchor value that is higher than one. Ironically, purchase quantity limits (e.g., limit of 10 per customer) can also encourage consumers to think about higher anchors and buy more than one unit, even if they do not come close to purchasing the amount implied by the limit. Suggestive selling (grab six for studying, buy eight and save a trip, buy 12 for your freezer) and expansion anchors (101 uses around the house) also encourage consumers to consider larger anchors and to purchase multiple units.

Consumers and marketers could make better predictions and better decisions if they relied more heavily on statistics and less on perceptions of similarity, ease of retrieval, ease of imagination, and first impressions. However, statistical knowledge requires training and effort, while heuristic thinking does not. Consequently, heuristic thinking is common despite the fact that it usually leads to poor predictions and poor decisions. The next section examines heuristics further in how consumers use them when selecting products.

Choice Heuristics

THE LEXICOGRAPHIC HEURISTIC Consumers using the **lexicographic heuristic** (or single-attribute heuristic) compare all brands on one *key* attribute, such as price, size, weight, reliability, durability, calories, sugar, etc., and choose the brand that performs the best on that single attribute, while generally ignoring the other attributes.[31] If there is a tie, consumers examine the next most important attribute to break the tie. Assume that a particular consumer views style as the most important attribute for a new pair of blue jeans and comfort as the second most important attribute. This consumer will select the brand that appears to be most stylish, ignoring price, durability, colorfastness, and other attributes. Style is the key attribute; it is all that matters. If two brands appear equally desirable with respect to style, then this consumer chooses the brand from these two that performs best on comfort.

The lexicographic heuristic is a *non-compensatory choice strategy* because a high score on one attribute cannot compensate for a low score on another attribute. In this particular case, no other attribute can compensate for inadequacy on the key attribute. In fact, most choice heuristics are non-compensatory because attributes are evaluated one at a time. Unfortunately, this leads consumers to sometimes choose brands that are not the best choice because trade-offs are ignored. Consumers typically don't like making trade-offs because it is difficult to determine how much they should give up on one attribute to gain on another. For example, it is difficult for a consumer to express how much he would pay for a 10 percent improvement in the speed of his computer? But ignoring trade-offs can lead to bad decisions. Nevertheless, consumers assume this risk when they use quick-and-dirty heuristics that oversimplify the choice process.

THE ELIMINATION-BY-ASPECTS HEURISTIC
Another non-compensatory choice heuristic is the elimination-by-aspects heuristic. Consumers using the **elimination-by-aspects heuristic** reject all brands that do not have a key feature they want.[32] For example, if a consumer wants to buy a hybrid automobile, she might reject all non-hybrid cars. Next, she would

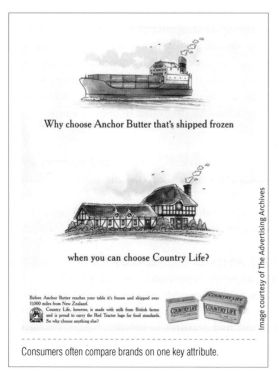

Why choose Anchor Butter that's shipped frozen

when you can choose Country Life?

Before Anchor Butter reaches your table it's frozen and shipped over 11,000 miles from New Zealand.
Country Life, however, is made with milk from British farms and is proud to carry the Red Tractor logo for food standards. So why choose anything else?

Image courtesy of The Advertising Archives

Consumers often compare brands on one key attribute.

focus on a different attribute and reject all brands that did not meet her requirements on that particular feature. For example, if the consumer prefers front-wheel drive, she might reject all hybrid automobiles that are rear-wheel drive. The process continues until only one brand remains. Rejecting brands is often easier than accepting multiple brands and then choosing among them. Consumers rarely need to examine a large set of attributes when using this choice heuristic. Furthermore, thinking about the attributes you do not want (a rejection frame of mind) often leads to different choices than thinking about the attributes you want (an acceptance frame of mind). The former focuses on avoiding negative outcomes from the purchase, while the latter emphasizes attaining positive outcomes.

THE ADDITIVE-DIFFERENCE HEURISTIC Consumers using the **additive-difference heuristic** compare two brands at a time, one attribute at a time, and subtract the evaluative differences.[33] Subtraction is performed on all relevant attributes, and each attribute is weighted for importance, i.e., each difference is multiplied by the importance of the attribute. Each weighted score is then summed to arrive at an overall score for each brand. The brand that performs the best on the most important attributes is selected. For example, if a consumer is evaluating automobiles and Brand A gets 35 miles per gallon, but Brand B gets 30 miles per gallon, the difference is 5 miles per gallon. If fuel economy is judged to be very important for this consumer (e.g., 5 on a scale of 1 to 5), then the weighted difference between Brand A and $B = 25$ (5×5). This method of multiplying the weights times the differences continues for all relevant attributes, and the differences are summed for a total score. This heuristic requires more effort because math (subtraction, multiplication, and addition) is used. However, more effort can lead to better decisions.

THE CONJUNCTIVE AND DISJUNCTIVE HEURISTICS Choice heuristics do not always involve making comparisons among brands. Sometimes consumers focus on one brand at a time, and no brand comparisons are performed. Examining one brand at a time is easy, and if the first brand seems satisfactory, a consumer might buy it without examining any other brands. Consumers using the **conjunctive heuristic** set a minimum value for all relevant attributes and select the first brand that meets this value for each attribute.[34] With this approach, all the attributes are considered together, and one poor attribute can eliminate the brand. In other words, if a brand performs unsatisfactorily on one or more attributes, it is rejected, and another brand is considered. Typically, however, the first brand considered has a large advantage over other brands; consumers often choose the first brand they consider.

Consumers using the **disjunctive heuristic** set an acceptable value, rather than a minimum value, for all relevant attributes and select the first brand that meets this value on one particular attribute—which is not necessarily the most important attribute. In contrast to the conjunctive heuristic, this approach focuses on each attribute separately, and one good attribute can save the alternative. Again, the first brand has a large advantage and is likely to be chosen unless it is clearly unsatisfactory.

THE FREQUENCY OF GOOD AND BAD FEATURES HEURISTIC While all the heuristic choice strategies we've considered thus far have been noncompensatory choice strategies, consumers also use *compensatory choice strategies*. With a compensatory choice strategy, good attributes can compensate for bad attributes. When using the **frequency of good and bad features heuristic,** consumers form a simple attitude toward each brand alternative by counting the number of good and bad product features and choosing the brand with the greatest difference between good product features and bad product features. For example, if Brand *A* appears to have six good attributes and three bad attributes (6 – 3 = 3), and Product *B* has nine good features and seven bad features (9 – 7 = 2), then Product *A* is chosen. This heuristic is easy to apply because counting is easy and relatively little information is needed. Consumers are concerned only with the number of attributes, not the importance of each attribute. In other words, all attributes are treated equally.

As we've seen, choice heuristics help consumers make purchase decisions quickly and easily. Unfortunately, these approaches also often reduce the likelihood of making the best possible decision because they oversimplify and minimize the amount of information involved in the choice task. See Figure 4.5 for a summary of choice heuristics.

FIGURE 4.5 CHOICE HEURISTICS

Lexicographic Heuristic
A consumer chooses the brand that appears best on the most important feature, ignoring all other attributes. If two or more brands are viewed as equal on this important feature, then the consumer chooses the brand that appears best on the second most important feature, and so on.
Elimination by Aspects Heuristic
A consumer rejects all brands that lack a key feature or possess an undesirable feature. Then, the remaining brands are evaluated on another important dimension in a similar manner. Eventually, only one brand remains.
Additive-Difference Heuristic
A consumer assigns important weights to all relevant attributes for a product and then compares brands, two at a time. Values for each attribute are then assigned to each brand. Next, the importance weights are multiplied by the differences in the values of the two brands' attributes and summed. More formally, $P = \Sigma w_i(A_i - B_i)$, where P = preference w_i = importance weight for attribute *i*, A_i = value of attribute *i* for brand *A* B_i = value of attribute *i* for brand *B* A positive score for *P* indicates a preference for Brand *A*, a negative score for *P* indicates a preference for Brand *B*, and a score of zero for *P* indicates no preference.
Conjunctive Heuristic
A consumer sets a minimum value for all relevant attributes and selects the first brand that meets these values for each attribute.
Disjunctive Heuristic
A consumer sets an acceptable value (usually higher than minimum) for all relevant attributes and selects the first brand that meets this value on one particular attribute (not necessarily the most important attribute).
Frequency of Good-Bad Features Heuristic
A consumer counts both the number of good product features and bad product features for each brand. The brand with the largest difference between its number of good and bad product features is chosen.

Chapter Summary

Consumer choice involves choosing one brand from a set of products. The set of products that consumers think about and evaluate—the consideration set—usually consists of fewer than seven brands, and the best brand is not always included in the consideration set. The more consumers think about some brands, the more difficult it is to think about other brands (the part-list cuing effect). Moreover, a given brand can seem attractive (the attraction effect) or unattractive depending on what other brands are included in the consideration set. Compromise brands, or brands that are average on multiple dimensions, often have an advantage over brands that are good on some dimensions and bad on others (the compromise effect). Attraction and compromise effects are often more pronounced when consumers feel the need to justify or explain their decisions to themselves or others.

After the consideration set has been determined, consumers need to evaluate the differences in features and attributes between the considered brands in order to make a choice. When consumers can directly and physically observe all relevant brands in the consideration set and the brand attributes, they make a stimulus-based choice, but when brand alternatives are drawn from memory, choice is memory-based. Mixed choice combines both stimulus-based and memory-based choices. Additionally, choice often involves focusing on differences among brands and using these differences as reasons or justifications for making decisions. These differences may be general (attitude-based choice) or specific (attribute-based choice), depending on the accessibility (salience in memory) and the diagnosticity (relevance) of the information used as a basis for choice.

Choice heuristics are mental shortcuts that simplify difficult decisions. Consumers use many different choice heuristics. Sometimes consumers focus on only one attribute (the lexicographic heuristic), and sometimes consumers eliminate brands that do not have a desired feature (the elimination-by-aspects heuristic). On other occasions, consumers compare two brands at a time and subtract the difference in the values of the attributes (the additive-difference heuristic). In other circumstances, consumers can focus on only one brand and choose the brand if it is satisfactory on all attributes (the conjunctive heuristic) or satisfactory on one attribute (the disjunctive heuristic). Finally, consumers may simply add up a product's good and bad features and choose the best overall brand (the frequency of good and bad features heuristic). Choice heuristics can lead to bad decisions when consumers overlook important information. Nevertheless, consumers are often forced to use choice heuristics when information overload, time pressure, or other stresses make decision making difficult.

Key Terms

consideration set	MODE model	simulation heuristic
part-list cuing	systematic processing	anchoring-and-adjustment heuristic
attraction effect	heuristics	lexicographic heuristic
compromise effect	heuristic processing	elimination-by-aspects heuristic
stimulus-based choice	persuasion heuristics	additive-difference heuristic
memory-based choice	prediction heuristics	conjunctive heuristic
mixed choice	influence or choice heuristics	disjunctive heuristic
attitude-based choice	representativeness heuristic	frequency of good and bad features heuristic
attribute-based choices	availability heuristic	

Review and Discussion

1. How can marketers increase the likelihood that their brands are included in consumers' consideration sets?

2. How can marketers use the part-list cuing effect to decrease the likelihood that competitors' brands are included in consumers' consideration sets?

3. Why does the trade-off contrast occur?

4. Describe a situation in which you purchased a compromise brand. Why does compromise seem like such a compelling reason on which to base a choice?

5. How does the availability heuristic influence how consumers make predictions about products?

6. How might the law of large numbers be related to word-of-mouth marketing? (*Word-of-mouth* marketing occurs when marketing messages, product information, and/or people's opinions of the product are passed from person to person through informal conversation).

7. When are consumers likely to use a choice heuristic? When are they unlikely to do so?

8. Choice heuristics are often non-compensatory. Explain what this means and how it can lead to bad choices.

9. Some choice heuristics involve comparing several brands on the same attribute or set of attributes. Describe a situation in which you used one of these choice heuristics.

10. Some choice heuristics involve focusing on one brand at a time rather than making comparisons across brands. Describe a situation in which you used one of these choice heuristics.

Short Application Exercises

1. Find three advertisements that use puffery. Do you think that puffery or exaggeration is an effective advertising tactic? Do you think the use of puffery is ethical? Why or why not?

2. Choose three products you purchased recently. Identify whether your choice of the product was stimulus-based, memory-based, or the result of mixed choice. How could a marketer use package information to better appeal to you for any of the products under conditions of stimulus-based choice?

3. Find two advertisements, one that appeals to consumers using attitude-based choice and one that focuses on attribute-based choice.

4. Identify a product for which you think people generally use price as a prediction of quality. Design an experiment to test this idea. Can you find evidence from the Internet that supports or refutes the price-quality relationship for this product?

MANAGERIAL APPLICATION

In the early 1980s, a format war took place between VHS and Betamax videotapes for video storage. VHS ultimately won. History always repeats itself. Between 2000 and 2008, another format war took place between Sony's Blu-Ray and Toshiba's HD DVD (high density optical disc for video storage). Blu-Ray ultimately won. But why? HD DVD had several advantages over Blu-Ray. HD DVD was the pioneering brand, or the first brand to enter the market, plus it was less expensive than Blu-Ray. Initially, almost as many movie titles appeared in HD DVD as did in Blu-Ray. Using the concepts in Chapter 4, how would you compare and evaluate these differences?

In January 2008, an important event tipped the scale in favor of Blu-Ray when Warner Brothers Studios decided to support Blu-Ray exclusively. Because Sony Blu-Ray already had the exclusive support of Sony Pictures (including MGM/Columbia Tristar), Disney (including Touchstone and Miramax), Fox, and Lions Gate, the Warner decision gave Blu-Ray the support of 70 percent of the movie studios. Toshiba was unable to overcome this advantage. In addition, Blu-Ray discs hold more data than HD DVD discs (50 GB versus 30 GB). The Sony PlayStation 3 can also play PS3 games, Blu-Ray discs, and standard DVDs. Using the concepts in Chapter 4, how would you compare and evaluate these differences?

YOUR CHALLENGE:

1. Using the concepts in Chapter 4, what strategies could HD DVD have used to beat Blu-Ray?

2. Using the concepts in Chapter 4, what strategies could Blu-Ray have used to beat HD DVD more quickly?

3. After Warner Brothers decided to support only Blu-Ray in January 2008, Toshiba reduced the price of HD DVD players to $150. Explain why this was too little too late. In February 2008, Net Flix, BestBuy, and Walmart announced that they would phase out HD DVD. After these announcements, Toshiba announced that they would stop producing HD DVD players. Explain why Toshiba needed the support of Warner Brothers, Net Flix, BestBuy, and Walmart.

4. In what other product categories do you currently see a format war? What steps can competing companies take to try to avoid format wars?

RISK AND CONSUMER DECISION MAKING

OBJECTIVES *After studying this chapter, you will be able to...*

1 | Explain expected value theory and how the framing effect violates this theory.

2 | Develop marketing strategies for segregating gains and aggregating losses.

3 | Explain several different ways preference reversals can occur.

4 | Define singular evaluation and comparative evaluation.

5 | Analyze the pros and cons of selective thinking.

CULTURE AND OVERCONFIDENCE

A great deal of research on behavioral decision making shows that decision makers are often overconfident. Imagine you were asked trivia questions, such as "Which contains more calories per unit of weight: (a) bread or (b) rice?" After selecting an answer, imagine you were asked to indicate how confident you were that your answer was correct on a scale from 50 percent confident to 100 percent confident.

When the average percentage of correct answers is compared to the average percent confidence ratings, the confidence ratings are typically higher than the percentage of correct answers. Thus, people are typically overconfident about the accuracy of their answers to trivia questions. Although overconfidence is very common, even among experts, research shows that Asian consumers are typically even more overconfident than American consumers.[17] This pattern was found even when participants were given the opportunity to win a gift certificate for $2.20 at their university's bookstore if they could provide confidence ratings that matched their percentage of correctly answered questions.

©zhu difeng, 2009/Used under license from Shutterstock.com

OBJECTIVE 1 # Expected Utility Theory

How should people think about risk? According to expected utility theory, people should think about uncertain events in terms of "gambles," and all gambles have two components: a probability component called p, and a value component called v.[1] The predicted or expected value of a gamble is simply p times v. For example, the expected value of a gamble that offers a 25 percent chance of winning $100 is $0.25 \times 100 = \$25$. This means that people should be willing to pay up to $25 to play this gamble, but no more than $25. Expected utility theory also shows how people should rank different gambles. For example, should a person play a gamble that offers a 25 percent chance of winning $100 or a gamble that offers a 20 percent chance of winning $130? As $0.25 \times \$100 = \$25$, and $0.20 \times \$130 = \$26$, the second gamble is the better deal.

People face similar decisions in the marketplace daily. Considering only the durability of a product, would a consumer rather purchase a $100 brand with a 50 percent probability of failure after two years or a $300 brand with a 20 percent probability of failure in two years? Perhaps surprisingly, the cheaper product is the better choice. The expected replacement cost of the first product is $\$100 \times 0.50 = \$50$, but the expected replacement cost of the second product is $\$300 \times 0.20 = \$60$.

MARKETING IN ACTION

Fear Appeals and Insurance

Many insurance companies run ads that increase risk perceptions. As risk perceptions increase, fear appeals become more effective. This is especially true when fear-appeal ads also provide a useful way for dealing with a threatening problem. Buying insurance is one way to cope effectively with risk. For example, Nationwide Insurance ran several different television ads showing that

"life comes at you fast." Each of these ads is designed to increase risk perceptions. Similarly, Travelers Insurance runs several different television ads showing that "your risks can change." These ads are also designed to increase risk perceptions. As risk perceptions increase, consumers are more likely to buy insurance products to protect themselves.

LIFE COMES AT YOU FAST™

1-877-On Your Side™

Expected utility theory suggests that all alternatives can be ranked from worst to best. It also suggests that alternatives with higher expected values **dominate** or are better choices than alternatives with lower expected values. In gambles with different stages, such as a game show in which you need to win in stage one in order to advance to stage two, stage one should cancel out, or be ignored, if it is identical for two different gambling games. This is called **cancellation.** Also, preferences should be **transitive;** in other words, if you prefer A to B, and B to C, then you must prefer A to C. Finally, according to the **invariance principle,** preferences should remain the same no matter how preferences are measured or no matter how decision alternatives are described.

Framing Effects

In direct violation of the invariance principle, extensive research shows that preferences change when decision alternatives are described in terms of different **frames** or perspectives.[2] For example, imagine you are a manager for a hospital preparing for a flu epidemic that is expected to kill 600 people. Your staff has developed two programs to combat the flu but because of cost constraints, you can implement only one of these two programs. If program A is selected, 200 people will be *saved*. If program B is selected, there is a 33 percent chance that all 600 people will be saved and a 67 percent chance that no one will be saved. Which program would you choose?

Now consider the very same problem with a slight change of wording. A flu epidemic is expected to kill 600 people. If program A is selected, 400 people will *die*. If program B is selected, there is a 33 percent chance that no one will die and a 67 percent chance that all 600 will die. Now which program would you choose? To be consistent, if you chose program A for the first version of the problem you must choose program A for the second version because the outcomes are identical. And if you chose program B for the first version of the problem, you must choose program B for the second version. However, most people are inconsistent. Most people choose program A when the problem is worded in terms of lives *saved,* and most people choose program B when the problem is worded in terms of *deaths*. Program A is the sure-thing alternative: 200 will be saved for sure and 400 will die for sure. Program B is the risky alternative: There is a 33 percent chance all 600 will be saved, and no one will die, and a 67 percent chance that no one will be saved, and all 600 will die.

When people think about a choice problem in terms of positive outcomes, such as lives saved or money gained, people typically prefer the sure thing. This is known as **risk aversion;** people typically prefer to avoid risky alternatives when outcomes are framed positively. However, when people think about a choice in terms of negative outcomes, such as deaths or money lost, people typically prefer the risky alternative. This is known as **risk seeking;** people are more likely to accept risk when outcomes are framed negatively. When people are inconsistent, i.e., sometimes risk averse and sometimes risk seeking, **preference reversals** occur. A preference reversal means that people prefer option A over option B at one point in time but can prefer option B over option A at another point in time.

FRAMING INFLUENCES MARKETING DECISIONS   Consider a marketing manager who has experienced a run of product failures in a difficult economy. For strategic reasons, the firm continues to maintain one of two poorly performing brands in the market. When considering which of these poorly performing brands to support, the manager may be evaluating the decision with a negative frame (i.e., the firm has already lost money on several products, and the economy is in recession). Given a negative frame, would this manager choose to support Brand A, a brand that is certain to lose $1 million, or Brand B, a brand that has a 40 percent probability of losing $2.5 million and a 60 percent probability of breaking even or losing nothing? Framing theory suggest that the marketing manager would choose to support Brand B. The manager will choose the riskier option because the decision has been framed negatively.

What if the frame were reversed? Consider a marketing manager who has had a string of successes with product introductions, and the economy has become robust. Given a choice between two brands, would this manager provide additional marketing support for Brand A, which is guaranteed to produce $1 million in profits, or Brand B, which offers a 40 percent probability of generating $2.5 million and a 60 percent probability of breaking even or generating no profits? Given the positive frame, this manager is likely to support Brand A and avoid unnecessary risks.

REFERENCE DEPENDENCE AND LOSS AVERSION Expected utility theory cannot explain the framing effect or preference reversals. According to expected utility theory, people should be consistent and choose the same alternative regardless of how the outcomes are framed or described. Expected utility theory also suggests that the pleasure experienced from winning $100 should be just as intense as the pain experienced from losing $100. However, prospect theory suggests that all outcomes are evaluated with respect to a neutral reference point, and that preferences change as reference points change. This is known as **reference dependence.** For example, $100 seems like a lot of money to poor people who use low reference points (e.g., $5). However, $100 seems like little money to rich people who use high reference points (e.g., $1 million). In Figure 5.1, the reference point is in the middle. Outcomes above the reference point are perceived as gains or positive outcomes. Outcomes below the reference point are perceived as losses or negative outcomes. As Figure 5.1 shows, the value function is much steeper for losses than for gains. This means that losses have a bigger impact on people, relative to equivalent gains. This is called **loss aversion.** For example, losing $100 has a bigger impact on people's feelings, relative to winning $100. Finally, Figure 5.1 shows that outcomes have weaker effects on people as distance from the reference point increases. This is called **diminishing sensitivity.** For example, the difference between $100 and $0 seems larger than the difference between $1,100 and $1,000.

Loss aversion is so powerful that it can lead people to violate the dominance principle.[3] For example, when asked to choose between A and B below, most people recognize that B dominates A:

   A. 25 percent chance to win $240 and 75 percent chance to lose $760
   B. 25 percent chance to win $250 and 75 percent chance to lose $750

FIGURE 5.1   REFERENCE DEPENDENCE AND LOSS AVERSION

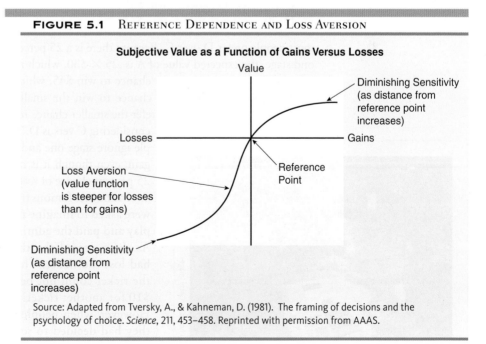

Subjective Value as a Function of Gains Versus Losses

Source: Adapted from Tversky, A., & Kahneman, D. (1981). The framing of decisions and the psychology of choice. *Science*, 211, 453–458. Reprinted with permission from AAAS.

B is better than A because you could win more or lose less with B than with A, so B dominates A. However, imagine you were asked to choose among the following back-to-back options:

C. a sure gain of $240

D. 25 percent chance to gain $1,000, and 75 percent chance to gain nothing
   versus the following back-to-back options:

E. a sure loss of $750

F. 75 percent chance to lose $1,000, and 25 percent chance to lose nothing

Now, most people prefer C over D because focusing on the sure gain makes people risk averse. Furthermore, most people prefer F over E because focusing on the sure loss makes people risk seeking. This violates the dominance principle because combining C and F gives you A in the previous choice problem, and combining D and E gives you B in the previous choice problem. But in the previous choice problem, it was obvious that B was better than A.

Research on framing also shows that people overestimate the likelihood of very small probabilities, which is what makes lotteries seem more attractive than they really are. People also underestimate the likelihood of moderate and large probabilities. This also leads to violations of the invariance principle, as shown in the following choice problem.

Consider the following two-stage game. In the first stage, there is a 75 percent chance to end the game without winning anything and a 25 percent chance to move into the second stage. If you reach the second stage you have a choice between:

A. A sure win of $30

B. 80 percent chance to win $45

Most people prefer A over B. However, when the gamble is changed to a one-stage choice between:

C. 25 percent chance to win $30

D. 20 percent chance to win $45

most people prefer D over C. Because there is a 25 percent chance to move to the second stage, the expected value of A is .25 × $30, which is the same as C. The expected value of B is .25 × .80 = .20 chance to win $45, which is the same as D. However, most people prefer the larger chance to win the smaller amount when considering A versus B, and most people prefer the smaller chance to win the larger amount when considering C versus D. This occurs because most people ignore stage one and this makes A look like a sure gain, even though it is not a sure gain; there is only a 25 percent chance of reaching stage two.

In another famous framing problem, participants were asked to imagine that they had decided to see a play and paid the admission price of $10 per ticket. As they entered the theater, they discovered they had lost the ticket. The seat was not marked, and the ticket could not be recovered. Would they pay $10 for another ticket? Only 46 percent said "yes." However, when people were asked to imagine that they had decided to see a play where admission is $10 per ticket, but as they entered the theater, they

Photodisc/Getty Images

discovered they had lost a $10 bill. Would they pay $10 for a ticket? Some 88 percent said "yes." In both versions of this problem, people lost the same amount ($10), but this loss seems like part of the price of the ticket in the first case but not in the second. The difference between the response to losing the ticket and losing $10 can be explained by *psychological accounting*. The purchase of another $10 ticket is entered into the "ticket account," and thus, the cost of seeing the play is interpreted as $20. In contrast, the loss of $10 was not specifically linked to the "ticket account," so the cost of seeing the show is interpreted as only $10.

THE ENDOWMENT EFFECT, THE SUNK COST EFFECT, AND CHOICE DEFERRAL   Even slight variations in the framing or wording of choice problems can change people's preferences dramatically, resulting in surprisingly inconsistent choices. Loss aversion and the framing effect also contribute to the **endowment effect**, the **sunk cost effect**, and **choice deferral**.[4] The endowment effect refers to the tendency to view a product as more valuable if one owns it than if one does not own it. Obviously, the value of an object should stay the same, but after buying a product or receiving it as a gift, consumers are surprisingly reluctant to sell the product or the gift. Selling the object is equivalent to losing it, and people are reluctant to give up what they have now. Consider the following examples:

- Example 1. Mr. Jones bought a case of good wine in the late 1950s for about $5 a bottle. A few years later his wine merchant offered to buy the wine back for $100 a bottle. Mr. Jones refused, although he has never paid more than $35 for a bottle of wine.
- Example 2. A neighbor's son offers to mow Mr. Smith's lawn for $8. Mr. Smith refuses and mows his own lawn, despite the fact that he wouldn't mow his neighbor's same-sized lawn for less than $20.

In these examples, consumers are reluctant to sell what they currently own or to pay much less for a service than their perceived value of the service. In both cases, consumers underestimate the importance of **opportunity costs.** Selling the wine would provide Mr. Jones with the opportunity of buying many bottles of wine in his usual price range, and paying the neighbor's son would provide Mr. Smith with the opportunity of doing something more enjoyable or productive than mowing his lawn.

The sunk cost effect also results from insensitivity to opportunity costs because as the amount of time or money invested in a product or a service increases, people are more reluctant to give up the product or service. Consider the following examples:

- Example 1. A family pays $40 for tickets to a basketball game to be played 60 miles from their home. On the day of the game, there is a snowstorm. They decide to go anyway, but note in passing that had the tickets been given to them, they would have stayed home.
- Example 2. A consumer joins a tennis club and pays a $300 yearly membership fee. After two weeks of playing, he develops tennis elbow. He continues to play (in pain) saying, "I don't want to waste the $300!"

In poker, there's a famous saying, "don't throw good money after bad money." At some point, people should cut their losses and avoid doing what they don't want to do even though they already paid for this activity. By performing a less preferred activity, people give up the opportunity to do something they enjoy more. Once again, opportunity costs are undervalued or neglected.

Choice deferral refers to the reluctance to make any decision even though the decision could benefit both parties. For example, Israeli Army soldiers are reluctant to trade patrol assignments, even when it would be convenient for both individuals to do so. They realize that if they traded assignments and their partner were killed, they would feel tremendous guilt and regret. These feelings can be avoided by simply refusing to trade patrol assignments. Similarly, when attribute trade-offs make it difficult to determine which brand is the best brand in a set of brands, consumers often decide not to decide and go home empty-handed.[5] Excessive concern about possible future feelings of regret can make consumers reluctant to make any choice.

OBJECTIVE 2

Loss aversion also implies that marketers should segregate gains and aggregate losses.[6] Many small gains are more pleasant than one large gain, even when the small gains add up to the same value as the large gain. The opposite is true for losses; many small losses are more unpleasant than one large loss, even when the small losses add up to the same value as the large loss. For example, most people are happier if they win $10 five times than if they win $50 once. The opposite is true for losses. So, based on these factors, marketers should aggregate losses because asking consumers to pay one large payment is less painful to consumers than asking them to pay several small payments. For example, based on this information, hotels would likely have better guest relations if they charged one fee covering several services, such as HBO, breakfast, and the use of the hotel's exercise equipment. Asking consumers to pay for each service individually is irritating. Most consumers would rather pay one lump sum. This one-fee-for-all approach is used by cruise lines, Club Med, and Tire Discounters. On the other hand, airlines have become infamous for tacking on separate, annoying surcharges for luggage checking, food, and beverages.

Price bundling is used by some firms to aggregate losses.[7] For example, instead of charging $40 per day for four days on ski-lift tickets, a resort could charge one lump sum of $160 for a four-day ski pass. If the weather is poor on the fourth day, consumers are likely to exhibit the sunk cost effect and go skiing anyway. However, the sunk cost effect is perceived as smaller to the consumer who paid one lump sum than to the consumer who bought four separate tickets. Price bundling is also used for complementary products, such as razors and razor blades and electronic products and batteries.

Although it is usually beneficial to aggregate losses, this is not true when the individual losses are extremely small.[8] For example, in a public service announcement for a children's charity, Sally Struthers tells us that we can feed a starving child for "only 72 cents per day," and a mattress retailer tells us that we can sleep comfortably for "only 10 cents a night." This is known as the pennies-a-day approach. Segregating losses makes sense, when the individual losses are so small, they are trivial. Of course even trivial expenses can add up.

ETHICS

The drug Ephedra was used to increase energy and reduce weight. Ephedra was taken off the market when some studies suggested that taking it resulted in health risks. Recently, Ephedra was once again allowed on the market. Ephedra ran an Internet ad stating that "Ephedra is back" and that "the ultimate energy and weight loss herb once banned for being too effective . . . is back." The ad also states that Ephedra provides smooth and confident energy, serious weight loss, and enhanced moods and motivation. At the bottom of the ad, the text states, "Get your Ephedra now . . . while you can. Click here now." The ad implies that Ephedra might be banned again, so consumers should act now and buy Ephedra. This is known as a scarcity appeal because it suggests that product availability is limited. Is it ethical to use scarcity to promote products that may or may not be safe? What type of research and how much research is needed to convincingly demonstrate that a product is safe?

Photodisc/Getty Images

OBJECTIVE 3

Preference Reversals

The framing effect is a type of preference reversal. Consumers prefer the safe alternative when options are framed in terms of gains. However, consumers prefer the risky alternative when options are framed in terms of losses. Thus, preferences reverse or switch when consumers think about a choice problem differently. One option looks better at one point in time, and the other option looks better at another point in time. Framing is not the only way to produce preference reversals, however. Preference reversals can occur anytime that consumers weigh information inconsistently.

For example, when evaluating gambles, people sometimes weigh the probability of winning higher than the value of the amount of money they can win.[9] This is called a p-bet, or a probability-based bet. At other times, however, consumers weigh value more heavily than probability. This is called a v-bet, or a value-based bet. Of course, there is typically a negative correlation between p and v: As p increases, v decreases. Consumers prefer a p-bet, or a bet that offers a high probability of winning a small amount of money, when they are asked to choose among gambles. However, consumers prefer a v-bet, or a bet that offers a low probability of winning a large amount of money, when they are asked to indicate a minimum selling price for each bet. Interestingly, this preference reversal has been documented for gamblers using their own money in Las Vegas. Different procedures for measuring preferences can change consumers' preferences, which violates the invariance principle discussed earlier. This pattern of results suggests that marketing managers prefer a p-bet when deciding whether to launch a new product or service and a v-bet when assessing the value or cost of a new product concept.

How serious is preference reversal? Consider the decision faced regularly by oil company executives. Any given drilling site has some probability of success (p) and some level of profit potential (v). Research shows that oil companies paid over $1 billion for the privilege of drilling in the Baltimore Canyon (in the Atlantic Ocean), even though leading oil geochemists determined that the probability of finding oil there was extremely low. This suggests that oil company executives often focus on the extremely large size of potential profits (v) and neglect the probabilities provided by the geochemists.[20] Ideally, of course, billion-dollar decisions should be based on both probabilities and potential earnings.

Why do different measurement techniques lead to different preferences? One reason is the **compatibility principle.**[10] According to this principle, different measurement techniques highlight different aspects of the choice options. For example, any measure that emphasizes money or value increases the importance of v and the likelihood that consumers will make a v-bet. Research also shows that the most important attribute seems even more important when a choice measure is used (e.g., choose or select the best bet) than when a judgment measure is used (e.g., rate the attractiveness of each bet). A choice task encourages consumers to focus on the most important attribute, but a judgment task requires them to think about all the attributes.

For many consumers, price is the most important attribute, and consequently, consumers are more likely to choose lower-price/lower-quality products (e.g., a $139 Goldstar microwave oven) when choosing one brand from a set of brands than when rating purchase intentions for each brand.[11] Purchase intention ratings or judgments encourage consumers to consider all the attributes of all the brands—which leads them to prefer a higher-price/higher-quality product (e.g., a $179 Panasonic microwave oven). This preference reversal occurs even when price range information (e.g., microwave ovens range from $99 to $299) is provided to consumers.

OBJECTIVE 4

Consumers often evaluate products one at a time, a process known as **singular evaluation,** or singular judgment. Sometimes, however, consumers compare two or more products concurrently, which is known as **comparative evaluation,** or comparative judgment. Surprisingly, consumers' preferences frequently change depending on whether they are forming a singular judgment or a comparative judgment. In singular judgment, familiar attributes that are easy to evaluate have a greater impact on preference.[12] Conversely, in comparative judgment, unfamiliar attributes that are difficult to evaluate carry more weight. This leads to a preference reversal when easy-to-evaluate attributes favor one brand and difficult-to-evaluate attributes favor a different brand.

For example, in one study, consumers were asked to evaluate two compact disc (CD) players:

	CD capacity	THD
CD player C:	Holds 5 CDs	0.003 percent
CD player S:	Holds 20 CDs	0.01 percent

The consumers were told that THD refers to total harmonic distortion, a measure of sound quality (smaller numbers are better). However, THD is difficult to evaluate because most consumers are unfamiliar with this attribute and do not know if a THD of 0.01 percent is good or bad. Consequently, in singular evaluation, most consumers ignored THD. Thus, when consumers evaluated each CD player separately, most consumers preferred CD player S. Conversely, in comparative evaluation consumers were less likely to ignore THD because they could see that 0.003 percent was better than 0.01 percent. Consequently, when consumers compared the two CD players, most consumers preferred CD player C.

In another study of singular evaluation versus comparative evaluation, consumers rated two dictionaries:

	Number of entries	Any defects?
Dictionary C:	20,000	Yes, the cover is torn
Dictionary S:	10,000	No, it's like new

Ladida/iStockphoto.com

In singular evaluation, consumers preferred Dictionary S because the presence or absence of defects is easy to evaluate. In comparative evaluation, however, consumers preferred Dictionary C because the number of entries is difficult to evaluate. However, when comparisons are performed, it is easy to see that 20,000 entries are better than 10,000 entries.

In another study, consumers saw a picture of an overfilled cup of ice cream (i.e., 7 oz. of ice cream in a 5-oz. cup) or a picture of an underfilled cup of ice cream (i.e., 8 oz. of ice cream in a 10-oz. cup):

	Amount	Filling
Serving C:	8 oz.	Under-filled
Serving S:	7 oz.	Overfilled

In singular evaluation, consumers preferred Serving S because an overfilled cup looks really good, but an under-filled cup seems stingy. In comparative evaluation, however, consumers preferred Serving C because directly comparing the brands made it clear that 8 oz. was better than 7 oz.

To summarize, consumers are remarkably inconsistent in the way they use different pieces of information. Inconsistency leads to preference reversals when consumers weigh one piece of information heavily at one point in time and weigh another piece of information heavily at another point in time. Different frames, different measures, and different judgment tasks (singular versus comparative judgment tasks) also lead to different preferences. Consumers are likely to make choices that they regret later when they prefer one brand initially and later prefer a different brand.

OBJECTIVE 5

Selective Thinking

Singular versus comparative judgment tasks change the way consumers evaluate products, and these different judgment tasks can lead to different preferences. Singular evaluation is easier, so it is therefore more common than comparative evaluation.[13] It is easier to focus selectively on one brand at a time than to compare two or more brands on many attribute dimensions concurrently. When consumers attempt to test the idea that a particular brand is a good brand, they focus selectively on information that confirms or supports this idea, and neglect information that disconfirms or fails to support it. Consumers also tend to interpret ambiguous information as supportive and to integrate information so a preferred brand is cast in a favorable light. This is known as **selective thinking,** or one-sided thinking, because singular evaluation often leads consumers to focus selectively on favorable information while neglecting unfavorable information.

In a classic study of selective thinking, people were asked to imagine they were serving on the jury of a child custody case following a divorce. Using the information below, which parent would you *choose*?

Parent A: average income
average health
average working hours
reasonable rapport with the child
relatively stable social life

Parent B: above-average income
very close relationship with the child
extremely active social life
lots of work-related travel
minor health problems

Most people chose parent B because the best way to choose an alternative is to focus on the most favorable information. When people focus selectively on favorable information, parent B has the advantage because of some very favorable attributes, while parent A has only moderately favorable attributes.

Another group of people were asked a slightly different question. Instead of asking which parent they would choose, they were asked which parent they would *reject*. The best way to reject an alternative is to focus selectively on unfavorable information. When people focus on unfavorable information, they are likely to notice that parent B has some very unfavorable attributes, but parent A has only moderately unfavorable attributes. Consequently, most people recommend rejecting parent B.

But wait a minute. Why did most people choose parent B when they performed a choice task, but reject parent B when they performed a rejection task? How can people both choose and reject the same alternative? The answer is selective thinking. Selective thinking makes parent B look very good when people focus on the positives, but makes parent B look very bad when people focus on the negatives. Thus, parent B is the best alternative *and* the worst alternative.

The same process occurs for products and services. Imagine that you had to choose between one of two different ice cream flavors. Flavor A is good, and flavor B is excellent, but high in cholesterol. When asked to choose a flavor, most consumers prefer B because it is excellent. When asked to reject a flavor, most consumers reject B because it is high in cholesterol. Consumers choose and reject the same alternative because it is the best and the worst alternative.

Imagine that you are planning a vacation and have to choose between two vacation spots:

Spot A: average weather
average beaches
medium-quality hotel
medium-temperature water
average nightlife

Spot B: lots of sunshine
gorgeous beaches and coral reefs
ultra-modern hotel
very cold water
very strong winds
no nightlife

Which spot would you *choose*? If you are like most people, you would choose B because B has some extremely favorable attributes. Which spot would you *reject*? If you are like most people, you would reject B because B has some extremely unfavorable attributes. Focusing selectively on mainly favorable information or on mainly unfavorable information leads to biased or lopsided decisions.

Asking consumers to reject alternatives is not the only way to encourage them to focus selectively on negative attributes. Whenever consumers attempt to reduce the size of their consideration sets, they are likely to focus on negatives. For example, the elimination-by-aspects heuristic reduces consideration sets by rejecting brands that do not have a particular feature of interest. Furthermore, recent research shows that when consumers expect to fill out a customer satisfaction survey, they focus on negatives to help firms improve their products and services.[14] Focusing on negatives leads consumers to form less favorable evaluations than they would have formed if they did not expect to fill out a customer satisfaction survey after using a product or service. This result was found for a wide range of products and services, including computers, electric utilities, supermarkets, drugstores, and magazines.

Selective thinking influences many other types of judgments as well. For example, selective thinking is much more likely in singular evaluation than in comparative evaluation. Furthermore, singular evaluation is very common. Non-comparative advertising encourages singular evaluation. End-of-aisle displays in grocery stores encourage singular evaluation. Exclusive dealerships, such as automobile dealerships that offer only one brand, also encourage singular evaluation. Even when it is painfully obvious that many different brands are available, consumers often focus singularly on one brand at a time when forming product evaluations.

Recent research on the **brand positivity effect** shows that consumers form unrealistically favorable evaluations of moderately favorable brands when they form singular evaluations, but not when they form comparative evaluations.[15] In one experiment, consumers were shown the brand names for four first-class hotels. They were told that they would be asked to evaluate one hotel, which would be selected randomly. Consumers formed unrealistically positive evaluations of the focal hotel no matter which hotel was selected. Furthermore, consumers acknowledged that the focal hotel was selected randomly. Similar results were found for laundry detergents. Follow-up studies showed that the brand positivity effect is reduced when consumers are encouraged to form comparative evaluations or when consumers happen to be very knowledgeable about a product category.

Selective thinking also influences the degree to which consumers rely on the **price-quality heuristic.**[16] Most consumers believe that as price increases, quality also increases. This belief becomes stronger when consumers are encouraged to test this belief, because the testing process encourages consumers to focus on information consistent with this line of thinking. For example, consumers often pay more attention to and have better memory for high price/high quality brands and low price/low quality brands than for exceptions (i.e., high price/low quality brands and low price/high quality brands). Thinking selectively about brands that support the price-quality heuristic is easier than thinking about exceptions that fail to support it. As a consequence, consumers often overestimate the magnitude of the correlation between price and quality by a factor of three! This result is reduced, however, when the amount of information presented is small, when time pressure is low, or when consumers are motivated or encouraged to consider exceptions.

Consumers often fall prey to the price-quality heuristic, assuming that higher priced brands offer superior quality and that lower priced brands offer inferior quality.

MARKETING IN ACTION

Vioxx

Merck, the second largest drug manufacturer in the United States, received FDA approval for Vioxx in 1999. Vioxx is a painkiller and anti-inflammatory drug used mainly to treat arthritis and menstrual cramps. In just a few years, Vioxx became an overwhelming success and was generating $2.5 billion in revenue annually. Then disaster struck. Vioxx patient Robert Ernst died from heart failure at age 59, and his wife won a $253 million lawsuit against Merck. More than 10,000 additional lawsuits followed, and Vioxx was withdrawn from the market in 2004 as a result of links to heart attack and stroke.

Behavioral decision research focuses mainly on **risky decision making,** or decision making under uncertainty. Decision makers frequently try to predict the future. What will happen if we launch Vioxx or another new product? However, the future is almost completely uncertain. The managers at Merck were unable to predict that Vioxx would be linked to heart disease. How should people think about risk? What level of risk is acceptable? What is the best way to manage risk? These are the types of questions addressed by behavioral decision research.

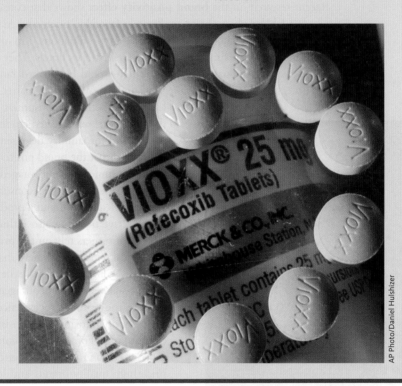

AP Photo/Daniel Hulshizer

Chapter Summary

Behavioral decision research focuses mainly on risky decision making, or decision making under uncertainty. To reduce uncertainty, consumers often attempt to predict the future. What will happen if I buy one brand instead of another? What will happen if I choose one course of action instead of another? Will I be satisfied with my decision one month from now, one year from now, or several years from now? Unfortunately, consumers' predictions are biased by framing effects and by selective thinking. Gain frames lead to risk aversion, but loss frames lead to risk seeking. The inconsistent weighting of information resulting from framing, measurement, or selective thinking leads to systematic preference reversals where consumers prefer one option initially and another option later. Consumers are remarkably inconsistent in their use of information, leading to inconsistent preferences and choices they later regret.

Key Terms

risky decision making	risk seeking	opportunity costs
expected utility theory	preference reversal	price bundling
dominance	reference dependence	compatibility principle
cancellation	loss aversion	singular evaluation
transitivity	diminishing sensitivity	comparative evaluation
invariance principle	endowment effect	selective thinking
frames	sunk cost effect	brand positivity effect
risk aversion	choice deferral	price-quality heuristic

Review and Discussion

1. What is risky decision making?
2. Why are consumers often unable to explain how they arrived at a prediction?
3. Why do consumers often fail to maximize expected value?
4. Give an example of a situation in which you chose a safe option.
5. Give an example of a situation in which you chose a risky option.
6. Why are consumers sometimes risk averse and sometimes risk seeking?
7. Why do different types of preference measures change preferences?
8. Describe the compatibility principle. How does this principle change people's preferences? Can you think of a situation in which this principle changed your preferences?
9. What is a preference reversal?
10. How do preference reversals lead to decisions that consumers later regret?

Short Application Exercises

1. Most consumers do not realize that information that initially seems really important may seem less important later. Think of some ways that marketers can influence the perceived importance of different types of information.
2. Think of some ways marketers can use preference reversals to their advantage.
3. Selective thinking occurs frequently. Think of some ways marketers can use selective thinking to their advantage.
4. Design an ad that gets consumers to think of the positive features of products while ignoring the negative features.

MANAGERIAL APPLICATION

The most recent recession is encouraging consumers to focus more on price in their decision making. One major consequence of this price focus is an increase in the market share of private labels at the expense of name brands.[18] The same thing happened in the U.K. and Canada in the 1970s. Tom Falk, CEO of Kimberly-Clark, says, "One thing you don't want to do is create a consumer who shifted to private label and then have to spend a lot to get them back." A. G. Lafley, CEO of Procter & Gamble, says, "Of course there's a shift to private label at this point, but it's not nicking us." In the past, P&G has fought against private labels by increasing promotions advertising, but in the current recession, consumers are buying private labels in categories that have been resistant to them in the past, such as feminine protection and skin care products. Furthermore, even relatively wealthier households with annual incomes greater than $100,000 have spent more on private labels. Across package-goods categories and retailers, private-label market share increased by 0.8 percent to 21.9 percent in 2008. This trend is likely to continue until the economy improves significantly.

YOUR CHALLENGE:

1. If you were a brand manager at P&G, what strategies would you pursue to encourage consumers to focus less heavily on price?

2. If you were a brand manager at P&G, what strategies would you use to protect product categories that are usually resistant to private labels?

3. If you were a manager at The Kroger Co., what strategies would you pursue to encourage consumers to focus more heavily on price?

4. If you were a manager at The Kroger Co., what strategies would you use to encourage consumers to buy private labels in more product categories? In what product categories do you see opportunities for private labels?

The part video is designed to expand and highlight the consumer behavior concepts in this part of the book. To view the videos, go to **http://www.cengage.com/international** and click on the student companion site link. After viewing the video, answer the following questions to test your knowledge on the part content and its application to the video case.

Marketing Jordan's Furniture

Jordan's Furniture is a family-run, regional, furniture retailer that sells mid-priced furniture. The company employs lovable spokespersons, humorous ads, and a shopping-as-entertainment mentality to attract potential customers.

1. Consumers are typically reluctant to buy furniture. What are the purchase obstacles (practical and psychological) to purchasing furniture? How has Jordan's Furniture tried to overcome these obstacles? Could they do more, and if so, what?

2. Using the consumer decision process model, describe the typical process of purchasing a piece of furniture. What type of consumer decision is this? How does understanding the decision process model influence Jordan's marketing strategy?

3. Jordan's Furniture's shopping-as-entertainment strategy has worked to make the company's business more successful. Would this strategy work for other product categories? Develop a campaign for another product category, employing some shopping-as-entertainment-style tactics.

PART

3

How Consumers Process Information

AN INTERVIEW WITH ROBERT S. WYER, JR

Courtesy of Norbert Schwarz

Professor of Marketing
UNIVERSITY OF ILLINOIS

Robert S. Wyer, Jr., is the J. M. Jones Professor of Marketing at the University of Illinois. He studies information processing; the representation of narrative information in memory and its use in judgment; priming effects on comprehension, judgment, and decisions; memory processes; and affect and cognition.

Q **Please describe the information processing paradigm and what this paradigm offers to the field of consumer behavior.**

Consumers' behavior is influenced to a large extent by the information they receive about the products they consider purchasing. It is therefore important to know how this information is used. An information processing approach to understanding consumer behavior breaks down the effects of information on judgments and decisions into a number of steps:

1. Attention to the information
2. Interpretation of its features in terms of preexisting concepts
3. Organization of these features into a representation of the referent as a whole
4. Storage of this representation in memory
5. Later retrieval of the representation, along with other knowledge acquired about the referent
6. Assessment of the implications of this knowledge for a subjective evaluation or behavioral decision
7. Translation of these implications into an overt response.

The effects of information about a product or responses to it and the way situational factors influence these effects can be mediated by its effects at any one or more of these stages.

Information processing researchers try to understand the cognitive processes that operate at each stage and the factors that affect them. In addition, they attempt to develop theoretical models that specify how the various stages of processing interface.

Most conceptualizations of information processing are metaphorical and do not pretend to describe the physiology of the brain. Thus, they should be evaluated on the basis of their utility and not their validity. The theories that have been proposed in cognitive and social psychology, many of which have been applied in the consumer area, have generally been very successful in explaining known phenomena and generating predictions of new ones.

Q **Please explain the priming effect and the different types of priming effects that you have studied.**

People normally do not use all the knowledge they have acquired about an object to evaluate it or decide how to respond to it. Rather, they only use a small subset of this knowledge that happens to be easily accessible in memory at the time. "Priming" refers to a procedure used in the laboratory to increase the accessibility of different subsets of knowledge and to investigate the effects of their use. Any number of procedures can be used, depending on the particular type of knowledge of concern. Single concepts can often be primed by having individuals construct sentences in which exemplars of the concepts are used. However, activating more general types of knowledge (stereotypes, affective reactions, procedures, and implicit theories) requires different techniques.

In many cases, concepts and knowledge can be primed subliminally. It is critical however, to ensure that individuals are unaware of the relationship between the priming task and the task that they are asked to perform subsequently. Individuals should not realize that the primed knowledge comes to mind for reasons that have anything to do with the judgments or decisions they are called upon to make. If individuals *are* aware, they often intentionally avoid using the concepts or knowledge to prevent bias, and this can lead the priming to have a contrast effect.

My own and others' work was initially designed to test various theoretical assumptions concerning the effects of priming *per se*. For example, we showed that the likelihood of using a trait concept to interpret a person's behavior increased with how recently and how frequently the concept had been primed in a prior, unrelated task. Once the person's behavior was interpreted in terms of this concept however, its effect on evaluations of the person described by the behavior increased over time.

The effects of priming are now well established. In our more recent work, we have used priming as a methodological tool to examine phenomena of interest for other reasons. Research with Catherine Yeung, for example, used priming techniques to examine the role of affect in product impression formation. We showed that priming positive or negative affect influenced consumers' initial impressions of a product formed on the basis of a picture. This impression, once formed, was used as a basis for later judgments of the product independent of the attribute information presented subsequently. A series of studies with Hao Shen has used priming techniques to demonstrate that cognitive procedures, if activated in one situation, can persist to influence the processing of information in a later, totally unrelated, situation. Thus, for example, individuals who have been induced to give the same answer to each of a series of questions about animals are less likely than other participants to choose a variety of different products in a later, multiple-choice decision task. Furthermore, the rate at which individuals are required to speak while shadowing a speech affects the speed with which they complete a marketing survey in an unrelated situation they encounter subsequently.

Of particular interest is a series of studies with Jing Xu. She finds that individuals who are induced to make comparative judgments in an initial situation develop a "which-to-choose" mindset that increases their likelihood of deciding which of two products to purchase in a later situation without considering the option of not buying anything at all. This is apparently true even when the comparative judgments are totally unrelated to purchase behavior. Thus, for example, comparing the physical attributes of wild animals or judging the similarity of foreign countries, can increase the likelihood of making a purchase in a product choice situation.

Q How does priming occur outside the laboratory? What is the role of television, advertising, and other types of marketing communication?

Although the concepts and knowledge that are primed in the laboratory are intentionally manipulated, the effects of knowledge accessibility generally occur without awareness. Consequently, numerous experiences that fortuitously occur in daily life can influence the concepts and procedures consumers apply in evaluating products and making purchase decisions a short time later. Perhaps more important, concepts and knowledge

that have been applied very frequently in the course of individuals' daily lives can become *chronically* accessible in memory and therefore, can have effects that generalize over a number of situations.

L. J. Shrum and his colleagues provide a particularly interesting demonstration of these effects in their research on the impact of television on perceptions of social reality. They found that individuals tend to overestimate the incidence of persons, objects, and events in the real world that are overrepresented on television. Shrum also found that the degree of their overestimation increases with the amount of television individuals watch. Although other explanations of this effect have been suggested, Shrum provides convincing evidence that it results from the fact that objects and events seen on television are more accessible in memory and are used as a basis for frequency estimates without considering the context in which they were encountered. So, heavy television viewers, relative to light viewers, overestimate the number of policemen and doctors in the general population, the incidence of violent crime, and the number of households with swimming pools in the backyard.

The chronic accessibility of concepts and knowledge can also vary with individuals' cultural backgrounds. A series of studies by Donnel Briley, Michael Morris and Itamar Simonson show that Asians, who are more inclined than Westerners to think of themselves in relation to one another, exhibit a tendency to choose the "compromise" option in a multiple-alternative product decision task. Put another way, they are more inclined to choose options that minimize the negative consequences of their decision, independently of the positive outcomes that might accompany them. Interestingly, these differences are not evident unless cultural norms are made more accessible in memory, either by asking participants to give reasons for their choices or, in the case of bilingual consumers, by varying the language in which the product decision task is administered.

Q How do consumers get into a buying mindset? Can marketers trick consumers into buying more than should?

Jing Xu's research provides one possible answer. It suggests that consumers who are asked by a salesperson to make comparative judgments before considering a purchase are more likely to make a purchase than they otherwise would. I'm reminded of my personal experiences with Oriental rug salesmen. After displaying a number of rugs, they frequently ask you to indicate which one you prefer, thus attempting to induce a "which to buy" mindset that will stimulate a purchase without considering the option of buying nothing.

BJECTIVE 2

The steps in the perceptual process are shown in Figure 6.1. Although the process appears sequential from sensory exposure through comprehension, the entire process occurs almost instantaneously, and the steps of the process interact and overlap seamlessly.

FIGURE 6.1 THE PERCEPTUAL PROCESS

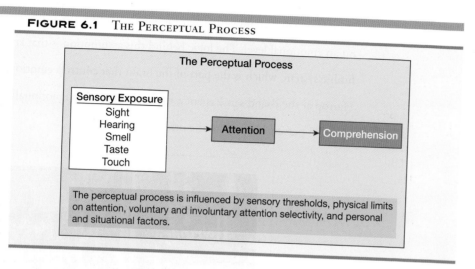

The Perceptual Process

Sensory Exposure
Sight
Hearing
Smell
Taste
Touch

Attention

Comprehension

The perceptual process is influenced by sensory thresholds, physical limits on attention, voluntary and involuntary attention selectivity, and personal and situational factors.

Perception of the environment requires consumers to use their physical senses. *Sensory exposure* occurs when a stimulus, like the smell of pretzels in the shopping mall or a print ad in the newspaper, is detected by the physical senses. Although the senses include dozens of secondary sensory systems, consumers' primary senses are sight, hearing, smell, taste, and touch. The body's first and immediate response to a stimulus is called **sensation**. Sensation involves gathering data from the sensory organs and nervous system and sending it to the brain for processing and interpretation. But not all stimuli receive attention. People perceive only a fraction of the stimuli to which they are exposed. In other words, consumers are not passive recipients of the world around them. To avoid being overwhelmed by the sheer volume of stimuli available in the marketplace, consumers are selective about stimuli. Thus, an important part of the perceptual process is discriminating among stimuli and selecting those to receive further processing. This step represents the act of attention.

Attention means focusing on one or more environmental stimuli while potentially ignoring others. Attention is highly selective in nature. If consumers didn't have *selective attention* (also called *perceptual selection*), they would be so overloaded with information in the marketplace that they couldn't function effectively. For example, in the United States are more than 1,100 television stations, more than 13,000 radio stations, and about 25,000 newspapers and magazines. The average U.S. consumer is exposed to about 3,000 ad messages per day.[2] In addition, the typical American watches about 4.3 hours of television per day, spends about 1.5 hours per day surfing the Web, 30 minutes each day talking on the phone, and reads a newspaper at least once per week.[3]

Adding to this state of media overload, American firms spend more than $45 billion a year on advertising and another $65 billion a year on promotions (e.g., coupons, sales, free samples, rebates, premiums, sweepstakes, sporting event sponsorships). Obviously, consumers cannot attend to all product information to which they are exposed. **Cognitive capacity,** or the ability to pay attention to and think about information, is limited. Consequently, marketers need to understand what guides consumers' allocation of cognitive capacity and their selective attention.

A more common situation may be exemplified by the shopping momentum effect identified by Dhar, Huber, and Kahn. Inducing individuals to make a small purchase early in the experiment increases their willingness to make a second purchase later on. They argue that the process of making the first purchase activates an "implemental" mindset that persists over time.

However, one could speculate about numerous other real-world priming phenomena that have implications for marketing strategy. Nunes and Boatright found that customers in a beachfront shopping area were more willing to pay a higher price for CDs being sold if the sweaters at an adjacent booth were priced relatively high than if they priced relatively low. Although the specific process underlying this effect is unclear, it provides yet another example of the effects of concept activation on purchase behavior outside the laboratory.

Having said this however, I personally believe that our objective as consumer behavior researchers is not to provide marketers with tools for tricking the public into buying more than they should, but to provide consumers with tools they can use to avoid being tricked. Because the effects of knowledge accessibility are largely unconscious, this is a challenging problem.

CHAPTER

6

CONSUMER PERCEPTION AND ATTENTION

OBJECTIVES *After studying this chapter, you will be able to...*

1 | Define perception, attention, cognitive capacity, and comprehension.

2 | Describe how the perceptual process works.

3 | Explain how sensory thresholds and physical influences affect perception.

4 | Discuss how selective attention is both voluntary and involuntary.

5 | Provide examples of how marketers appeal to the senses to obtain and maintain consumers' attention.

HARRODS SNIFFS OUT A NEW WAY TO APPEAL TO CUSTOMERS

Each year, *The Economist* publishes a collection of predictions for the coming year. Recently, the magazine predicted a boom in the business of marketing with scents. Harrods, a premier European retailer, has led this effort by injecting tailored aromas into its stores to try to extend the multi-sensory buying experience for its customers. The scent-marketing tactics were part of larger campaign called the "Senses" promotion, designed to encourage customers to look, touch, smell, taste, and listen more while they shopped.

The luxury retailer, working with The Aroma Company and the Brand sense agency, injected scents into several store areas. Vanilla and chocolate were featured in ladies shoes. The ladies swimwear department sported the scent of coconut oil. Basil and lime scents perfumed store entrances as well as the paper receipts that customers received after making a purchase (so they

took the scents home). The garden living department featured the fragrance of f grass. In one area, customers were able to sample all 12 different aromas from aro

Harrods' effort follows those of several U.S. retailers, including Macy's, Bloo and Saks Fifth Avenue, which all have adopted scent-marketing strategies. *Scent* associating your brand with a specific smell—supposedly helps brands connect wi on an emotional level. The logic behind this assumption is that smell directly ener limbic system, which is the part of the brain that controls emotion. According to th Harrop at the Brand sense agency, the sense of smell is emotionally powerful, affecti up to 75 percent more than the other senses.[1]

Stone/Getty Image

OBJECTIVE 1

Defining the Perceptual Process

Why do some product packages stick out on grocery store shelves, while others barely get noticed? Why do some television commercials generate attention, while others are ignored? This chapter describes how consumers physically acquire and interpret information about products, services, and the world around them through perceptual process.

Perception is a process of receiving, selecting, and interpreting environmental stimuli involving the five senses. Through perception, we define the world around us and create meaning from our environment. For example, consumers eat ice cream, and it feels cold and tastes sweet. People look upward, see blue, and know that they are viewing the sky. But, how cold or sweet or blue is different for every individual because each person's perceptual process is unique. This chapter demonstrates that myriad factors influence consumers' perceptions. That no two people perceive the world in the same way is a challenging concept because it's difficult for people to step outside their own physical senses, i.e., to try to see things as others see them. The erroneous assumption that everyone else perceives the world as we do is called **phenomenal absolutism**.

Consumers today are in a state of media overload but have limited cognitive capacity, which is why selective attentions is so important.

The last step in the perceptual process involves providing meaning to the sensory data that gets processed. **Comprehension** is the ability to interpret and assign meaning to the new information by relating it to knowledge already stored in memory. The ways new environmental stimuli are categorized, interpreted, and experienced are influenced by existing knowledge. Ask two people with radically different political opinions to interpret a political speech, and the answers will differ dramatically. To revisit the ice cream example from the opening of this discussion, when consumers taste chocolate ice cream, their senses take in sweetness, cold, chocolate flavor, the smell of chocolate, and wet stickiness. Consumers' ability to organize, categorize, and interpret these sensations help them recognize that, indeed, they are eating chocolate ice cream. After comprehension, preferences and choice follow.

Perception is important to marketers because it is the communication gateway to the consumer. Understanding perception and how it influences consumers' attention to the environment, their interpretation and comprehension of stimuli, and ultimately their behavior, is essential to developing successful products and marketing messages. The rest of the chapter explores the influences and limits of the perceptual process of importance to marketers, including sensory thresholds, physical limits on attention, and voluntary and involuntary attention selectivity.

OBJECTIVE 3

Sensory Thresholds

The Absolute Threshold

Have you ever watched a dog sniff the ground as he tracks some secret scent? Or listened to your cat move around the dark house at night, able to see every obstacle? There are some stimuli that people simply cannot perceive. Overall, however, the sensory limits or *thresholds* for animals—including humans—are relatively high. The minimum

MARKETING IN ACTION

Marketing to the Senses: The Ingenious Ways Marketers Use Color

Marketers have long realized the importance of perception and appealing to our physical senses, and perhaps our most important physical sense is sight. Through sight we perceive colors, sizes, and the position of objects in the environment. In fact, the majority of our sensual perception occurs through sight. Visual tools related to perception are used by marketers to increase attention to marketing messages.

An important tool for marketers related to sight is the use of color. According to color experts, color sells! Color catches attention, conveys meaning, and elicits emotions from consumers. Let's look at some common colors and how they are perceived:

- Red is typically associated with appetite and sexual arousal; it is attention-getting and exciting. Red can also convey a warning or a rescue from danger: think of the American Red Cross or a bright red fire engine.

- Orange is also a high-energy color associated with appetite and power. Tide laundry detergent uses an orange package to signify its strength.

- Blue is considered relaxing; it is associated with sky, water, trust, and the future. Blue is America's favorite color, according to the Crayola Crayon makers.

- Green is representative of health, refreshment, and the environment. The Healthy Choice packaged food brand uses green as its signature color to symbolize its low-fat content and health.

- Yellow sends a message of optimism, happiness, and nature. Yellow is symbolic of light, the sun, and cleanliness. Cleaning products are often packaged in yellow.

Marketers know that colors speak to people and give them messages about the product, making color an important part of the overall marketing message.

American Red Cross

PRNewsFoto/American Red Cross/Newscom

Marketers need to consider consumers absolute thresholds when designing marketing materials.

PRNewsFoto/Chick-fil-A, Inc./AP Photo

---

level of stimuli needed for an individual to experience a sensation is called the **absolute threshold**. It is the lowest point at which a person can detect "something" on a given sensory receptor. The smells that dogs can use for tracking are too slight to be detected by humans, so this stimulus is beyond our olfactory absolute threshold. Likewise, the farthest point at which a person can read a billboard advertisement from a moving car represents an absolute threshold.

In addition to the overall physical strengths and weaknesses of human senses, individual differences in sensory ability also exist. For example, children tend to experience lower absolute thresholds, which might explain why infants often react to startling noises and bright lights by crying or showing distress. Research demonstrates that women also tend to have lower absolute thresholds than men. Some people may have their senses impaired or altered because of disability or aging; some people often have one sense that they feel is particularly strong, such as a keen sense of smell or sharp vision. Two consumers riding together in a car may see a billboard advertisement at different times from different distances. Consequently, advertisers need to make sure that the type on the billboard is large enough and brief enough to maximize the number of people capable of reading it. As a general industry rule of thumb, because a billboard is read by the average person in six seconds or less, it should contain no more than six words in the primary message. Pharmaceutical companies and other industries that must include details and fine print in their advertisements must design the type large enough for the average person to read—particularly if the target market is seniors, who typically prefer 16 point font. So, as can be seen, the absolute threshold is an important consideration for marketers when designing marketing stimuli for targeted audiences.

The Just Noticeable Difference

Another important sensory threshold is the ability to detect changes in relative levels of stimuli. The **just noticeable difference (j.n.d.)**, also called the *differential threshold,* is the amount of incremental change required for a person to detect a difference between two similar stimuli. For example, the number of pounds you have to put on before your friends notice you've gained weight is the j.n.d., as is the amount you have to raise your voice in a crowded restaurant until you can be heard by your companions.

In the middle of the nineteenth century, German scientist Ernst Weber found that the magnitude of the j.n.d. between two stimuli was systematically related to the intensity of the first stimulus, rather than some absolute amount. In other words, Weber discovered that the ability to sense a change in stimulus level depends on the original magnitude of that stimulus. The greater or stronger the initial stimulus was, the greater was the amount of change required for it to be noticed. This is known as **Weber's Law**. For instance, consider a product just put on sale. A rule of thumb in retailing maintains that a price should be marked down at least 20 percent for consumers to notice the price change. So, if a grocer marks down a can of pineapple that normally costs \$1.00, the sales price should be \$0.80 cents (0.80 × \$1.00 or a \$0.20 discount). However, that same \$0.20 discount won't benefit a package of steaks that cost \$10.00; the steaks would have to be marked down to \$8.00 (a \$2.00 discount) to be noticed by consumers.

Consumers' abilities to detect change in stimuli and j.n.d. are critical to marketers, particularly when the goal is to ensure that negative product changes (e.g., increases in price or reductions in product quality) go unnoticed, falling below the j.n.d. Conversely, when positive product changes occur (e.g., sales discounts or updated product features), a marketer wants to ensure that the change is readily apparent, exceeding the j.n.d., without being excessive or wasteful.

Marketers also use j.n.d. in an attempt to increase the profit margin on a product by decreasing the amount of product offered in the package, rather than by increasing the price. Reducing the volume in a product's package reduces the firm's cost per unit. Here, understanding the amount of change that can be made to the product's volume, while remaining below consumers' j.n.d., can generate incremental profits. This practice is called *package-pricing*. It's a way for a company to enact an "invisible" price increase. In recent years, PepsiCo reduced the weight of its snack food bag from 14.5 ounces to 13.5 ounces while keeping the price constant; Dannon reduced the size of its yogurt cup from 8 ounces to 6 ounces—a 25 percent reduction, while only lowering the suggested retail price by 20 percent; Dreyer's and Edy's Grand Ice Cream cut package sizes from 1.89 liters (a half-gallon) to 1.66 liters.[4]

Courtesy of the General Mills Archives

But this tactic is not without risk. When Kimberly-Clark implemented a five percent package reduction while holding prices steady on its Huggies Diapers, rival Procter & Gamble flooded the market with coupons and price promotions on its Pampers and Luvs diaper brands. Consumers often feel cheated if they figure out that a brand has applied package-pricing. Nevertheless, research shows that while consumers prefer a straightforward price increase over reductions in package quantity, if a company can employ package-pricing and effectively fall below the j.n.d., most customers may never notice the change in price.[5]

Marketers also often use j.n.d. estimations to help update existing package designs or brand symbols without losing any brand recognition that has been cultivated through expensive marketing communication. When this is the case, small successive changes are made, each carefully designed to fall below the j.n.d. For example, Tony the Tiger, Betty Crocker, and Colonel Sanders (the Kentucky Fried Chicken Colonel) and Aunt Jemima have been subtly freshened up and modernized over the years.

Of course, sometimes the marketer's goal is to exceed the j.n.d. with package and message changes in order to generate attention and create "buzz." Pepsi has periodically introduced obvious and significant changes to its packaging as part of its marketing campaigns.

Adaptation

Another concept related to sensory thresholds is **adaptation**, the process of becoming desensitized to sensual stimuli. Over time, if a stimulus doesn't change, we adapt or orient to it and notice it less. This is important to marketers because as advertisements and other marketing stimuli become familiar, they are less likely to attract attention. The following conditions can increase adaptation:

- **High Repetition:** When an advertisement is overexposed, it loses the ability to attract attention and interest; this is also known as **advertising wear-out**.

- **Simplicity:** Simple stimuli tend to encourage adaptation because they don't require much cognitive capacity to process. A billboard with no words is easy to comprehend, but may quickly become part of the scenery.

- **Low Intensity:** Soft sounds, faint smells, and dull colors all produce quick adaptation because they require little input from human sensory systems.

MARKETING IN ACTION
Apple Paints the Market

Throughout the 1980s and 1990s—the first two decades of the home computer market—consumers had one choice when it came to computer color—beige. But when the Apple Computer Company launched its teal (officially, "Bondi Blue") iMac in August, 1998, the computer market changed forever. Surprised and dazzled by the new color, cool new design, and lower price, consumers stormed computer stores and bought more than 800,000 iMacs in less than five months.[6] By January, 1999, Apple had launched five more fruity flavors for its iMac and iBook lines—blueberry, grape, tangerine, lime, and strawberry. By 2000, other major computer manufacturers, including Dell Computer, Hewlett-Packard, and Compaq Computers, were considering offering colorful PCs.[7] Ironically, the Hewlett-Packard Company had received a proposal from Oregon industrial designer Ziba Design, Inc. to produce a teal-colored computer back in 1996, i.e., two years before Apple introduced its colorful model.

Ziba Design suggested teal as the color because it is not gender specific and, at the time, was not considered trendy, so, they reasoned, it would be seen as new and different. Hewlett-Packard rejected the recommendation, thinking that consumers would not want to buy outwardly colorful computers.[8]

Apple's success in daring to add a splash of color to computers changed the way computers were viewed and added a new attribute to those considered when consumers shop for personal computers. Apple's success also underscored the importance of color to consumers; it is a strong, distinguishing factor that can be used to grab consumers' attention and boost a company's reputation as an innovator.

Interestingly, while the rest of the computer industry appears to have finally found color, as shown by Dell's new line of Inspiron laptops, Apple has returned to monochromatic white, black, and silver as its signature colors, standing out once again.

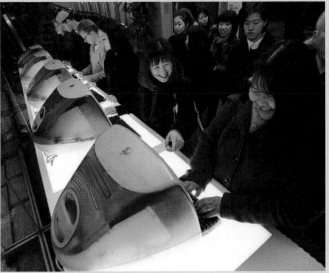

AP Photo/Chiaki Tsukumo

Marketers work hard to discourage adaptation. For example, how frequently an ad appears is typically monitored closely to avoid wear-out. In contrast, a marketer may try to increase the intensity of sensory input. Cadillac recently purchased all the ad time for the premier episode of A&E Channel's *Mad Men* to ensure that their message wouldn't get lost in advertising clutter. Additional information about how marketers design messages to rise above the clutter is provided later in the chapter.

Subliminal Perception and Advertising

In a typical college marketing class today, if a professor were to ask how many students believed that subliminal messages are effective in influencing people, the majority would answer in the affirmative.[9] That's because the public has been fascinated with the topic of subliminal perception for years. The popular press has taken advantage of this interest, perpetuating speculations and inaccuracies about the use of subliminal messaging in marketing. Many people believe in subliminal advertising. One older study reported that approximately 81 percent of the participants had heard of subliminal advertising, and 65 percent believed the practice was successfully used to sell products.[10] In response to public fears, even though no substantial body of research shows subliminal messaging has any practical behavioral influence on consumers, the practice is banned in Great Britain and Australia and can result in licensure penalties in the United States.

Subliminal perception is the unconscious awareness of a stimulus. Technically, "subliminal" means beneath the absolute threshold (*limen* is another word for threshold). Nevertheless, many subliminal messages are actually *supraliminal,* meaning they fall above the absolute threshold, but are consciously repressed by the recipient. In other words, consumers don't consciously engage these messages; they process them at a subconscious level.

Subliminal advertising has a notorious history. Although the basic terminology and concept of subliminal messaging has been around for more than a century, its close association to advertising emerged in the 1950s, and was brought to the public's attention by James Vicary.[11] In 1957, Vicary conducted a six-week subliminal message experiment in movie theatres in New Jersey during a showing of the movie *Picnic.* He flashed subliminal messages, "Drink Cola-Cola" and "Hungry? Eat Popcorn" during a movie, at 1/3000 of a second—far too quickly to be recognized via conscious awareness. Vicary claimed that popcorn sales increased by 57.7 percent, and Coke sales increased by 18.1 percent as a result of the subliminal embedded message. He coined the term, "subliminal advertising," to describe this form of messaging. His findings launched a flurry of research into subliminal marketing messages, a national debate on the ethics of subliminal messaging, and the perception among many consumers that subliminal messages are commonly (and successfully) employed by marketers. Regrettably, Vicary's results were fabricated to promote his business. After years of other researchers failing to replicate his experiments, Vicary finally admitted that he had done little research and did not have enough data to draw meaningful conclusions.

In the 1970s, Wilson Bryan Key reignited interest the topic.[12] His books focused on identifying supposed sexual symbols, pictures, and words embedded in advertising, so-called *subliminal embeds.* He claimed that marketers include the sexually themed subliminal embeds to physically arouse viewers to increase attention and persuasion.

Images courtesy of The Advertising Archives

Subliminal stimuli can be embedded in an image or symbolic, which means that subliminal content is actually visible but repressed by the viewer.

ETHICS

Learn Spanish while you sleep. Just pop in an audiotape or CD before you go to bed; listen to the soothing music as it lulls you to sleep; and within a few weeks, you will be speaking fluent Spanish. It sounds great, but like so many techniques that promise big results with little effort, subliminal self-help audiotapes are too good to be true. Here's how they claim to work: subliminal material is embedded into audiotapes that play soothing music or nature sounds. As you listen, your subconscious mind processes the subliminal information, resulting in the desired behavioral outcome. The audiotapes typically promise results with just a few weeks of listening. If listening to an audiotape doesn't suit your style, you can now have subliminal text messages flashed at you on your computer screen while you work. A variation on the audiotape theme, these messages work in basically the same way.

Subliminal self-help audiotapes have been around for more than 20 years, and have been used by large numbers of people. Even famous golfer Tiger Woods claims to have listened to subliminal self-help audiotapes as a child. These materials are still strong sellers on the Internet. A simple search of Amazon.com, a popular Web-based bookseller, reveals more than 250 different types of these materials for sale. They promise everything you can imagine, including learning a foreign language, curbing bad behaviors like smoking and overeating, improving self-esteem and self-confidence, curing phobias, and increasing happiness.

Unfortunately, like subliminal advertising techniques, there is no substantial body of credible research that shows that any of these materials yield real results. If a person wants to stop smoking, lose weight, or learn a foreign language, they are better served by doing it the old-fashioned way—through hard work and determination.

In 1989, a lawsuit was filed against the musical group, Judas Priest, for supposedly planting the hidden phrase "Do It" in their song "Better You Than Me." The subliminal phrase could be heard when the record album was played backward. The parents of two teenage boys brought the lawsuit and alleged that the phrase pushed their suicidal sons to act. The group argued they didn't intentionally place the message on the album and if they had, it should be protected by the First Amendment to the U.S. Constitution, which protects freedom of speech. However, the judge ruled that subliminal messages are not protected by the First Amendment because people can't avoid them, so they constituted an invasion of privacy. But the judge also ruled that actual persuasion via subliminal messaging had never been proven. As a result, the case was ruled in favor of Judas Priest.

Over the years, companies have tried to profit from the open use of subliminal messaging. The first recognized mass marketing use of subliminal advertising appeared in 1959 when Chevrolet aired a television commercial in which the announcers sang:

"Hey, have you heard about the crazy new way to send a message today?"

It's flashed on a screen too quick to see, but still you get it subliminally . . .

Ladies and gentlemen, the '59 Chevy.

The new car was then flashed on the screen subliminally. In the 1980s, a rash of companies selling self-help subliminal message audio tapes sprang up, promising everything from weight loss to a job promotion. In 2006, Kentucky Fried Chicken planted a hidden coupon in frames of television commercials. These were specifically designed for users of digital video recorders; when the commercials were played frame-by-frame, the coupon was revealed.

Recently, researchers have returned to the subject of the potential influence of subliminal stimuli. Some research has shown that under controlled circumstances, subliminal stimuli can influence attitudes and behaviors (we will return to this research when we discuss automatic information processing later in the text). Still, applications for subliminal messaging in a mass-marketing environment have not been demonstrated because the conditions needed to generate subliminal perception are very difficult to produce outside the laboratory. Unfortunately however, misconceptions about the use of subliminal messaging still persist today. In reality, the majority of marketers do not intentionally use subliminal messaging because it would be a waste of time and money. So, when subliminal words, symbols, or pictures do appear in marketing communications, they are typically accidental or the work of an unhappy, vindictive employee.

Now that we have examined the physical thresholds of the senses, let's look at two other physical influences on the perceptual process: cognitive limitations related to short-term memory and physical arousal.

<table>
<tr><td>OBJECTIVE 4</td></tr>
</table>

Physical Influences on Attention

Beyond the physical limitations of our senses, consumers possess limited cognitive capacity and mental resources for information processing, particularly with respect to attention. People are able to attend to and think about only a small amount of information at one time, and attention varies from person to person and from situation to situation. The next section examines two pervasive physical influences on attention: short-term memory limits and physical arousal.

Short-Term Memory

Short-term memory is the part of memory where small bits of information are stored for short periods of time. All information that is actively and consciously considered is processed in short-term memory. This is why short-term memory is sometimes called "*working memory*," "*active memory*," or "*conscious awareness*." Recently received sensory input utilizes short-term memory.

According to famous Harvard psychologist George Miller (1956), people are able to consider approximately five to nine (seven plus/minus two) units of information at one time. This is often referred to as "**Miller's Rule.**"[13] A unit of information can be very small, such as a single number, letter, or word, or very large, such as a string of numbers, letters, words, or ideas.[14] It is easy to test Miller's Rule. Quickly, off the top of your head, recall as many brands of breakfast cereal as you can. How many brands do you recall? For most, the number will fall between five and nine.

Because people can attend to only about seven units of information at a time, it is easy to overwhelm or overload consumers with too much information. For example, a grocery store may carry a dozen or more different brands of laundry detergent. In addition, detergents are often available in large (e.g., 150 ounces), medium (e.g., 100 ounces), and small (e.g., 50 ounces) containers. If 12 brands are available in each of these three sizes, consumers are faced with 36 different alternatives from which to choose. To compare all possible pairs of these 36 alternatives, consumers would have to make over 1,200 comparisons ($36!/(36 - 2)! = 1,260$). Few consumers are willing to commit the time and effort necessary to choose among a set of just 12 alternatives (resulting in $12!/(12 - 2)! = 132$ pairwise comparisons).

Interestingly, one factor that influences the amount of information people can attend to at one particular moment is prior knowledge or expertise.[15] People who are knowledgeable about a topic are able to attend to more pieces of information, and as knowledge increases, unit size increases. Consequently, compared with novices, experts attend to and think about larger units of information. Ultimately, this processing advantage enables experts to solve problems more effectively and efficiently compared to novices.

Arousal

Arousal, a state of physical wakefulness or alertness, also influences consumers' attention.[16] When arousal is extremely low, people are asleep. The level of wakefulness or alertness people experience during the normal course of a day is moderate. Viewing exciting events like action movies, rock concerts, basketball games, and football games (and, yes, even stimulating lectures) produce high levels of arousal. Consumption of caffeine products (e.g., coffee, tea, cola, energy drinks), as well as exposure to loud noises, flashing lights, and unexpected events, also produces high levels of arousal. Similarly, physical exertion from roller coaster rides, sports activities, and aerobic exercise produces high arousal.

An inverted-U-shaped relationship exists between arousal and consumers' ability to attend to information. Consumers' ability to pay attention to information is low when arousal is extreme (low or high). When arousal is too low, the amount of cognitive capacity and mental resources available for information processing is also low. It is difficult to attend to much information when people are tired, drowsy, or completely disinterested. Surprisingly, when arousal is high, cognitive capacity is also low. Under conditions of high arousal, consumers are over stimulated, and this arousal competes with their ability to attend to large amounts of information. On the other hand, when consumers are moderately aroused, they are alert but not over stimulated, freeing up cognitive capacity which can be used to attend to information (see Figure 6.2).

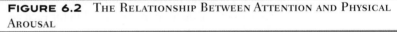

FIGURE 6.2 THE RELATIONSHIP BETWEEN ATTENTION AND PHYSICAL AROUSAL

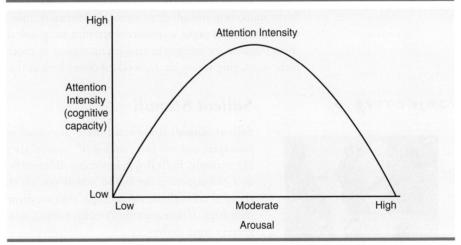

Consider the results of an interesting field experiment on attention and memory for television commercials aired during the Super Bowl.[17] Fans from the two cities represented in the Super Bowl were highly aroused and over stimulated, and as a consequence, attention and memory for the television commercials aired during the game were poor. In contrast, viewers from other cities across the country were only moderately aroused, and these viewers exhibited much better attention and memory for the same television commercials. Under moderate levels of arousal, attention and memory are at their best.

Voluntary and Involuntary Selective Attention

Consumers are exposed to so much marketplace information that they cannot possibly process and think about each and every product-related piece of data they encounter. If consumers had to think carefully about every ad, each package label, and every marketing communication they saw or heard, little time would be left for anything else. According to famous researcher Daniel Kahneman, the allocation of attention is influenced by both voluntary and involuntary factors.[18] People voluntarily attend to information consistent with their current knowledge and expertise and to information relevant to their plans, intentions, and goals. Specifically, we manage our perceptual exposure by focusing our attention to things in the environment that are meaningful and appealing. For example, people who dislike country music avoid tuning in to country-music radio stations. Likewise, consumers shopping for new laptops purposefully seek out marketing information about computers.

One real concern for marketers today is how to win the battle for broadcast advertising exposure in this age of the remote control. With the growing popularity of digital video recorders (DVRs), consumers can mute, fast-forward, and skip over commercials entirely. Some advertisers are trying to adapt to these technologies, similarly to the Kentucky Fried Chicken coupon example described earlier. Other practitioners are trying to make their advertisements more interesting and entertaining to discourage viewers from zapping past ads; still others are simply opting out of television advertising altogether. Some industry experts speculate that eventually cable providers and advertisers will be forced to provide incentives to encourage consumers to watch their messages. These incentives may come in the form of coupons, patronage rewards, or in extreme cases, a reduction in the cable bill for each ad watched.

Involuntary influences on attention are rooted in the very nature of the stimuli. Some marketing stimuli draw so much attention, they are difficult to tune out, even when consumers make a concerted attempt to ignore them. A clear understanding of these involuntary influences enables marketers to more effectively design and implement marketing strategies. Let's take a closer look at these influences.

<table><tr><td>(OBJECTIVE 5)</td></tr></table>

Salient stimuli are novel, intense, and complex.

Salient Stimuli

Salient stimuli draw consumers' attention involuntarily.[19] Some products, packages, and ads just "stick out" because they are different and interesting. For example, Rolls Royce is notably different from other types of automobiles; as a consequence, the brand stands out on the road. Pringles potato chips come in tall, cylindrical packages that are distinguishable from typical potato chip bags. Consequently, Pringles potato chip packages are conspicuous on grocery store shelves.

However, salience depends on context. In other words, stimuli that stand out in one context or situation may not stand out in another. For example, while a Rolls Royce automobile might be quite noticeable driving through most typical American college campuses, it would not be very salient in the parking lot of an exclusive country club in Beverly Hills, California, whose members all drive luxury automobiles. Stimuli are salient only when they are very different from other stimuli in a specific context. From a perception perspective, when a stimulus is salient, it is figural or focal, and everything else fades into the background. This is known as the **figure-ground principle** of perception. Marketers create salience through novelty, intensity, and complexity.

NOVELTY   A novel stimulus is one that is new, original, different, or unexpected. Sometimes the product itself is novel. Procter & Gamble is now offering flavor cartridges, called Pur Flavor Options, for the Pur Water Filtration System. Sumseeds are roasted sunflower seeds that are energized with caffeine.

Placing marketing messages in unexpected places also increases novelty. Charmin Toilet Tissue has opened a Charmin-themed public restroom in Times Square in New York. Other unexpected advertising venues are on eggs, airsickness bags, airplane tray tables, the sides of straws, and embedded in candy.[20]

AP Photo/Mary Altaffer

Advertisers constantly experiment with novel advertising and promotional executions. New characters, themes, and scenarios are constantly under development. For example, the Apple versus PC television commercials initially were novel, amusing, and attention-generating. They featured two actors playing the roles of an Apple brand computer and a PC, bantering about the flaws of the PC in humorous ways. Apple Computer Co.'s advertising agency was able to sustain the novelty for an extended period of time by developing many different variations on the theme.[21] One version of the ad showed the PC ill with a virus, while another version showed Apple giving PC a photo album for a gift. The ad campaign's novelty would have waned much more quickly if numerous variations of the theme had not been employed.

INTENSITY   The intensity of a stimulus, such as its loudness, brightness, or length, affects salience, and in turn, induces attention. Intensity can be influenced through several stimulus characteristics, including size, volume, color/brightness, odor, length, and position. Larger print ads, longer radio and television ads, and bigger retail displays tend to be more intense. Ever notice that sometimes a television ad is louder than the show you're watching? Bright colors are exciting, and warm colors (e.g., red, yellow, and brown) are more arousing than cool colors (e.g., blue, green, and grey). *Position* is the place an object occupies in space or time. A stimulus that is easy to see is more likely to be noticed,

© Spencer Grant/PhotoEdit

which is why suppliers jockey for the eye-level shelf or the displays at the end of aisles in stores. In magazines, ads placed either on the front or back covers or near the front of the magazine on the right hand page are more likely to be noticed than their counterparts.

While more intense stimuli generally draw more attention, the goal is to generate a level of intensity that results in that product or message standing out from surrounding stimuli. Thus, having a silent television ad among a series of loud ones or using a black and white print ad in a colorful magazine can also create intensity based on simple contrast.

COMPLEXITY   Stimuli that require substantial cognitive processing or that challenge consumers to make sense of them can be intriguing and draw attention. Dynamic stimuli—with constant change and movement—can be perceived as different and salient. Spokespersons in television commercials typically move or walk while they talk because presentations delivered by stationary speakers are much less engaging. Moving signs, like the famous Las Vegas cowboy sign with the arm that moves up and down, also draw more attention than stationary signs. Neon signs often display letters that light up one at a time and appear to move. Such stimuli are difficult to ignore.

Two perceptual concepts also related to complexity are closure and grouping. **Closure** is the tendency for a person to perceive an incomplete picture as complete, either consciously or subconsciously. People like to fill in missing pieces when a puzzle is incomplete (see Figure 6.3). Incomplete messages from marketers beg for completion, thus drawing the perceiver in, and messages where closure is required tend to elicit strong recall.

FIGURE 6.3   CLOSURE: THERE ARE NO COMPLETE SHAPES, BUT WE FILL IN THE MISSING PIECES.

Grouping is the tendency to arrange stimuli together to form well-organized units. Thus, objects viewed in close proximity tend to be grouped together, as do stimuli that move in the same direction together. Marketers can use grouping to create positive associations for their brands. For instance, placing an attractive, well-liked celebrity endorser in an advertisement with the brand can create a positive association to that brand. If marketers want an audience to associate the product with the presenter, they should place them close together; if marketers want consumers to perceive two ideas as associated, they should present them in close proximity.

Both closure and grouping help provide salient attention-drawing stimuli. Next, we examine another attribute of stimuli that draws attention involuntarily—vividness.

Vividness

Vivid stimuli, like salient stimuli, draw attention automatically and involuntarily.[22] However, unlike salient stimuli, vivid stimuli are attention-drawing across *all* contexts. Because vividness is context independent, it does not matter what other stimuli are present in a given situation. Vivid stimuli are:

- emotionally interesting
- concrete and imagery provoking
- proximate in a sensory, temporal, or spatial way[23]

Let's examine more closely these characteristics of vivid stimuli.

EMOTIONAL INTEREST Consumers' goals, hobbies, and interests determine what information is emotionally interesting and vivid. Stimuli that are interesting to one person may not be interesting to another, but a stimulus that is emotionally interesting tends to get noticed. Stamp collectors find stamps incredibly fascinating. They spend hours studying their collections, examining watermarks, postmarks, and even perforations. Stamp collectors have been known to dream about stamps and see stamps when looking at plaid shirts (the plaid squares turn into stamps). To these individuals, stamps are very vivid and emotionally interesting. By contrast, people who are not stamp collectors find stamps hopelessly boring.

Although both salient and vivid stimuli draw attention involuntarily, what is salient in one situation may not be salient in another, and what is vivid to one person may not be vivid to another. Salient stimuli capture the attention of all of the people some of time, while vivid stimuli grab the attention of some of the people all of the time. Unfortunately, marketers can't make their products interesting to everyone, just like stamp collectors can't make stamps interesting to everyone. Emotional interest is but one factor that influences the vividness of a product, ad, promotion, or package. Vividness is also affected by concreteness and proximity.

CONCRETENESS Concrete information is specific, easy to picture, imagine, and visualize, versus abstract information, which is conceptual or theoretical. For instance, the taste of a hot, juicy hamburger is more concrete than a picture the hamburger, but the picture is more concrete than a written description. Research demonstrates that making product attributes more concrete in a marketing message increasess the amount of attention paid to the attribute and subsequently increases the perceived importance of the attribute.[24]

Marketers try to make their advertisements as concrete, and thus vivid, as possible.

Face-to-face communications are typically more concrete and vivid than written communications, an important advantage of a field-based sales force. One research study investigated the effects of face-to-face versus written messages on judgment by presenting subjects with a description of a new personal computer.[25] The exact wording of the description was held constant. However, the description was presented either in a face-to-face format or in a written format. Even though the words presented in each situation were exactly the same, the face-to-face message had a much stronger impact on subjects' evaluations of the described product. However, results also showed that the vividness effect is weaker when subjects had a strong prior opinion about the described product and when a lot of negative information is available. When a product is described with many negative descriptions, strongly negative opinions are formed regardless of whether information is presented in a vivid or pallid manner.

PROXIMITY   Information that is proximal, or close to a consumer, is more vivid and has more impact than information that is distant or not immediately relevant. Three different kinds of proximities are important: sensory, temporal, and spatial. *Sensory proximity* refers to firsthand (proximal) versus secondhand (distant) information. Information that is perceived by consumers' own eyes and ears is more vivid than information perceived and relayed by another person. When consumers see for themselves that a product works, they are more convincing than if they receive secondhand, hearsay evidence. This is one reason marketers encourage consumers to sample products. *Temporal proximity* refers to how recently an event occurred. Events that occurred recently are much more vivid and draw more attention compared with events that occurred a long time ago. People are much more aware of and concerned about the awful flight they had the last time they flew on a particular airline than about the great flight they had five years ago. Finally, *spatial proximity* refers to the location of events. Events that occur near consumers' homes are much more vivid than events that occur far away in other countries.

To summarize, information can be made more vivid and draw more attention in many different ways. Vividness can be increased by making information more emotionally interesting, more concrete, or more proximal to the consumer. Obviously, information that grabs our attention has a stronger influence on judgment and choice relative to information that is virtually ignored.

Chapter Summary

This chapter looks at perception, the process through which we define the world and create meaning from our environment. Broken down, the perceptual process includes sensory exposure, attention, and comprehension. The process first relies on physical senses, such as sight, sound, smell, touch, and taste, to take in stimuli. Through attention and comprehension, those sensations are processed into meaningful and useful information and knowledge.

Not all stimuli to which consumers are exposed receive attention. People pay attention to a fraction of the stimuli to which they are exposed. In other words, attention is highly selective, and there are important limits and influences on attention and the perceptual process. The first of these influences deals with the thresholds of our sensory systems, including the absolute threshold, the just-noticeable-difference (j.n.d), and adaptation. Subliminal perception, the unconscious perception of stimuli, is an interesting topic related to these sensory thresholds.

Beyond the physical limitations of the senses, people also have limited cognitive capacity to devote to attention.

Because of short-term memory limitations, people are able to attend to and think about a relatively small amount of information at a time, usually between five and nine pieces of information. This ability varies from person to person and from situation to situation.

Finally, the allocation of attention is also voluntarily influenced by factors unique to each individual. Consumers voluntarily pay attention to stimuli consistent with their existing knowledge and expertise and their plans, intentions and goals. People involuntarily pay attention to stimuli that salient and/or vivid. Stimuli that are salient draw attention involuntarily but are context dependent. Novel, intense, and complex stimuli tend to be salient. Vivid stimuli are emotionally interesting, concrete, and proximal, and these stimuli are vivid, regardless of the physical context. Combined, the influences on attention and perception are pervasive, but these influences help us to function in an environment of information overload.

Key Terms

perception	just noticeable difference (j.n.d.)	arousal
phenomenal absolutism	weber's law	salient stimuli
sensation	adaptation	figure-and-ground principle
attention	advertisement wear-out	closure
cognitive capacity	subliminal perception	grouping
comprehension	short-term memory	vivid stimuli
absolute threshold	miller's rule	

Review and Discussion

1. Clearly distinguish among the following terms: perception, attention, cognitive capacity, and comprehension.

2. Why is sensation important in the perceptual process?

3. In what ways does selective attention differ for each person?

4. How does the absolute threshold influence the potential effectiveness of subliminal advertising?

5. What implications does the perceptual phenomenon of adaptation have for advertisers?

6. Do you think superstores that specialize in one type of product, such as office supplies, shoes, or electronics, run the risk of overloading consumers with too much information? Why or why not?

7. What is Miller's Rule?

8. What is the primary difference between salient and vivid stimuli?

9. How does closure in an advertisement increase salience?

10. How can marketers increase vividness for their advertisements?

Short Application Exercises

1. Ask five different friends to freely recall as many brands of hotel chains, pizza restaurants, and NFL teams as they can, and see if Miller's Rule regarding short-term memory applies. Do the results vary by level of knowledge or interest?

2. Find print advertisements that include salient stimuli and justify your choices.

3. Find a print advertisement that includes stimuli that are vivid (for you) and justify your choice.

4. Describe how marketers of Levi's Jeans could use sensory-based marketing messages to increase sales. Identify one technique for each of the five senses.

5. Read the Marketing In Action Box on the ways marketers use color and identify four brands that you feel effectively incorporate color into their marketing strategies. Explain why.

MANAGERIAL APPLICATION

Imagine you work in the marketing department for a mid-sized regional bakery that sells doughnuts, cookies, and snack cakes in retail grocery stores. Your company would like to increase sales of its doughnuts and is considering an in-store sampling campaign to generate more interest in the product. This campaign would involve offering retail customers free samples of doughnuts in stores, along with a coupon for a discount on a box of doughnuts. You know that taste is a powerful sense and would like to engage the consumer in as many ways as possible to entice them to buy the product.

For this campaign to be implemented, you need to convince your superiors in the company that giving away free doughnut samples, a sizable investment in product and labor, may actually increase sales. In addition, you suspect that retail grocery store managers are likely to be interested in how this in-store sampling campaign may influence overall store sales. You realize that some marketing research is needed. You decide to run an experiment in one local grocery store.

YOUR CHALLENGE:

1. Design an experiment to test whether in-store doughnut sampling influences sales of the doughnuts and/or the overall store sales. What should the independent and dependent variables be?

2. Given what we have studied in this chapter about sensory marketing, what experimental outcomes do you predict will occur?

3. How might a participant in your experiment who is very hungry affect the results?

4. Based on your answers above, is in-store food sampling a smart marketing technique for your company's product? Why or why not?

PERSUASION:
ATTITUDES AND JUDGEMENT

OBJECTIVES *After studying this chapter, you will be able to . . .*

1 | Define search, experience, and credence attributes.

2 | Define descriptive, informational, and inferential beliefs.

3 | Calculate numerical values for attitudes using expectancy-value models.

4 | Use dual-process models of persuasion to design more effective marketing communications.

5 | Use multiple strategies to develop more effective marketing communications.

ERRONEOUS BELIEFS ABOUT HOMEOPATHIC MEDICINES

People are capable of believing almost anything, and many beliefs are clearly not based on facts (e.g., superstitions). Some unethical companies take advantage of consumer gullibility by marketing completely ineffective homeopathic medicines.[1] Homeopathy is based on the "law of similars," which suggests that the effects of a substance on a healthy person provide clues regarding a potential cure for an unhealthy person. For example, if a substance causes a healthy person to experience slight nausea, very small amounts of the substance are presumed to cure an unhealthy person suffering from nausea. However, homeopathic medicines incorporate such small amounts of a given substance that the substance has no effect on anyone, healthy or unhealthy. Nevertheless, many gullible consumers continue to believe in the effectiveness of homeopathic medicines. Why?

Two psychological principles are involved here. First, the principle of similarity or "like goes with like" is surprisingly compelling, and judgments of similarity influence a wide variety of other judgments. The belief that "you are what you eat" is based on similarity. Many consumers believe that eating greasy foods gives you greasy skin, eating spicy foods gives you heartburn, and eating natural foods is healthy (despite the fact that arsenic and other poisons are "natural"). Second, placebo effects occur commonly in medicine. If a patient believes that a particular medicine will be effective, the patient often gets better even if the medicine had no effect. In summary, beliefs can be surprisingly powerful—even when they are not true!

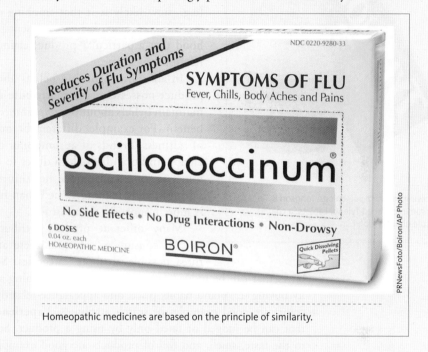

Homeopathic medicines are based on the principle of similarity.

PRNewsFoto/Boiron/AP Photo

Nonevaluative Judgments: Beliefs

Beliefs are nonevaluative **judgments**, or ratings about product attributes and benefits. Marketers define attributes as specific features or characteristics of a brand (e.g., size, price, style), and benefits as the outcomes or consequences that follow from each attribute (e.g., safety, exclusivity, trendy). Beliefs capture consumers' assessments about a specific relationship between a brand and an attribute or benefit. "Starbucks coffee is strong" describes a belief about the relationship between a brand and an attribute, without making judgments about whether strong coffee is good or bad. Similarly, "McDonald's hamburgers do not contain soy" describes a belief about how much of an attribute is present in a brand, also without placing a positive or negative value on soy in hamburgers. Some people like soy for health reasons; others find the taste objectionable.

More generally, beliefs entail assessments about probability or the likelihood of something occurring.[2] Because consumers often have imperfect information regarding products and brands, they sometimes think about the *likelihood* that a product contains a particular attribute or provides a specific benefit. For example, how likely is it that Bufferin has caffeine or that Tums relieves heartburn quickly? Likelihood judgments can also pertain to past events in the marketplace (e.g., how likely is it that competitors tampered with Tylenol capsules?), future events (e.g., what is the probability that a price reduction will occur?), or current events (e.g., how likely is it that aspirin therapy prevents heart attacks?). Likelihood judgments can also pertain to the probability of a cause-effect relationship (e.g., how likely is it that smoking cigarettes causes lung cancer?). In summary, beliefs represent judgments about the likelihood that a particular product claim, event, state of events, or relationship is true.

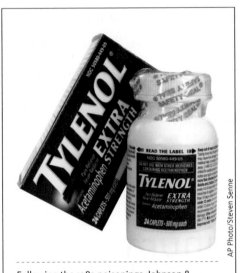

AP Photo/Steven Senne

Following the 1982 poisonings, Johnson & Johnson introduced Tylenol caplets, a coated, capsule-shaped tablet.

In addition to having beliefs about how likely it is that a product possesses a given attribute or benefit, consumers also maintain beliefs about the *importance* of a particular attribute or benefit. For example, different brands of snacks differ in terms of saltiness, brands of automobiles differ in terms of fuel efficiency, and brands of cloth differ in terms of softness and fashion. For some consumers, healthiness is more important than saltiness, style is more valued than fuel efficiency, and comfort is more important than fashion.

Many different product attributes are potentially important to consumers. Most of these attributes belong to one of three possible attribute categories. **Search attributes** are attributes that can be judged or rated simply by examining a product without necessarily buying it.[3] Brand name, price, and appearance-related attributes (e.g., design and color) are good examples of search attributes. **Experience attributes** are attributes that can be judged or rated only by using a product. Sensory attributes pertaining to the taste, smell, and feel of products are good examples of experience attributes. **Credence attributes**, a special case of experience attributes, are attributes that can be judged or rated only after *extended* use. Reliability, durability, and safety are good examples of credence attributes.

OBJECTIVE 2

Consumers establish beliefs on the basis of several different types of information. **Descriptive beliefs** are based on direct experience with a product or what we see with our own eyes or hear with our own ears.[4] Search attributes and experience attributes are used to form descriptive beliefs. Simply by examining the physical dimensions of a laptop, consumers can form descriptive beliefs about the laptop's size and weight. In the same vein, consumers who have experience with a plasma television develop descriptive beliefs about the TV's refresh rate or side-angle viewing.

In contrast, **informational beliefs** are based on indirect experience or on what other people tell us. Friends, relatives, acquaintances, spokespersons, and salespeople have beliefs about products, and they usually are eager to share their viewpoints. In addition, consumers often rely on word-of-mouth to form beliefs about the attributes and benefits of new or unfamiliar products and brands. For example, if a trusted friend describes a

Two consumers evaluate search attributes such as design, fabric, and color.

Blend Images/Jupiter Images

brand as durable, a consumer may adapt this belief. **Inferential beliefs** are beliefs that go beyond the information given.[5] Consumers often draw their own conclusions, or infer beliefs about attributes and benefits based on both direct and indirect experiences. For example, if a particular automobile is judged to be sturdy or durable, consumers might infer or assume that it is also safe, even though they were never told this specifically. If a product is expensive, consumers often infer that it is high in quality. Conversely, if a product is inexpensive, consumers often infer that it is low in quality. To the extent that two attributes, such as price and quality, are perceived or expected to be related (or correlated), information about one attribute permits consumers to draw inferences about the other.[6]

Correlation is not the only basis for inferential beliefs. Inferences can also be formed on the basis of overall evaluations about a product.[7] For example, if a consumer's overall evaluation of an Olympus digital camera is very favorable, the consumer may infer that the camera has a high quality zoom lens even if he or she never received any information about this camera's zoom lens specifically. Similarly, if a consumer's overall evaluation of the camera if unfavorable, the consumer may infer that this camera has a low quality zoom lens. The former is referred to as a "halo effect" (if a brand is judged favorably on one key attribute, it must be good on other attributes), while the latter is called the "devil effect" (if a brand is judged unfavorably on an important attribute, its other attributes must also be poor). Finally, inferences can be based on prior knowledge.[8] For example, consumers typically know a good deal about familiar product categories, such as cars. The typical car has four wheels, an engine, an exhaust system, and so on. Consequently, consumers do not need to be told that a brand new car model has four new wheels, a reliable engine, or a quiet exhaust system. Consumers infer or assume that the car has these features by default, even if they receive no information about them.

Overall, inferential beliefs basically involve some type of *evaluative judgment*, whereas descriptive and informational beliefs simply describe likelihoods or relationships between objects. Think of inferential beliefs as a bridge between beliefs and attitudes. In the next section, we discuss attitudes in greater depth.

Evaluative Judgment: Attitudes and Their Properties

Attitudes are evaluative judgments, or ratings of how good or bad, favorable or unfavorable, or pleasant or unpleasant consumers find a particular person (e.g., salesperson, spokesperson), place (e.g., retail outlet, Web site, vacation site), thing (e.g., product, package, advertisement), or issue (e.g., political platform, economic theory).[9] Evaluative judgments have two main components: *direction* (positive, negative, or neutral) and *extremity* (weak, moderate, or strong). Attitudes often follow from beliefs. When consumers believe that a new product has many features that match their needs, they are likely to form positive attitudes about the new product. For example, suppose consumers believe that Verizon offers a relatively simple service, and these consumers value simplicity. It follows that they will form favorable attitudes toward Verizon.

Marketers need to understand that all consumer attitudes are not created equally. Typically, consumers develop some attitudes that are strongly held or held with conviction and other attitudes that are weakly held or held with low confidence.[10] Strong attitudes tend to be highly accessible from memory, maintained with high confidence, held with little uncertainty, and highly correlated with beliefs. The last property is referred to as high **evaluative-cognitive consistency**. On the other hand, weak attitudes are relatively inaccessible from memory (or difficult to retrieve from memory), kept with low confidence, held with high uncertainty, and exhibit low evaluative-cognitive consistency. Attitude strength is important because strong attitudes are difficult to change and have a great deal of impact on other judgments and on behavior. In other words, strong attitudes guide consumers' thoughts and actions, while weak attitudes do not. So, it's no surprise that marketers strive to elicit strong, favorable attitudes from their target markets toward their brands and limit or reduce strong, negative attitudes.

In addition, marketing practitioners cannot simply assume that all favorable attitudes are the same. For example, two different consumers may express positive evaluations of the Verizon brand, and yet only the first consumer purchased a long-term service contract. This situation may occur because, even though both consumers indicated a liking for Verizon, the first consumer's attitudes were strongly held, whereas the second consumer felt only mildly positive about the brand.

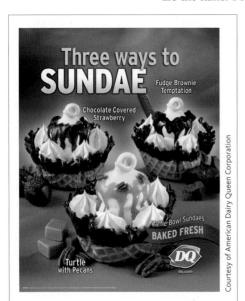

Courtesy of American Dairy Queen Corporation

Zanna and Rempel's Model

Research on evaluative-cognitive consistency shows that attitudes are often based on beliefs. However, attitudes can be based on other types of information as well. **Zanna and Rempel** developed a theory suggesting that attitudes can be based on cognition (beliefs), affect (feelings, moods, and emotions), or behavior.[11] Let's look at an example. A consumer's attitude toward a Dairy Queen hot fudge sundae is likely to be influenced by her cognitions, such as beliefs about the sundae's properties (e.g., features, taste, size), affect, or how she feels when she eats a Dairy Queen hot fudge sundae (e.g.,

MARKETING IN ACTION
Measuring Beliefs and Attitudes in Market Research

Marketers frequently conduct market surveys to learn about consumers' beliefs and attitudes. Consumers are typically asked to judge or rate several product attributes and to enumerate their overall attitudes toward the product. Beliefs about attributes and overall attitudes can be measured on **semantic differential scales**, also called bipolar adjective scales. For example, a new Nike running shoe can be rated on several attribute dimensions—comfort, price, and style—on rating scales ranging from 0 (not comfortable, not expensive, not stylish) to 10 (very comfortable, very expensive, very stylish). Similarly, overall attitudes can be measured on rating scales ranging from 0 (very bad, very unfavorable, very unsatisfactory) to 10 (very good, very favorable, very satisfactory).

Sometimes marketers use **Likert scales,** also called agree/disagree scales, instead of or in addition to semantic differential scales. To measure beliefs using Likert scales, marketers ask consumers to indicate how much they agree or disagree with several statements about a product's attributes. For example, consumers could be asked to rate their agreement with the statements, "Nikes are comfortable," "Nikes are expensive," and "Nikes are stylish" on scales ranging from 1 (strongly disagree) to 5 (strongly agree). Sometimes labels are provided for each scale point: 1 = strongly disagree, 2 = disagree, 3 = neither agree nor disagree, 4 = agree, and 5 = strongly agree. Similarly, attitudes toward the statements, "Nikes are very good," "My overall impression of Nikes is very favorable," and "I am very satisfied with Nike's

products" can be specified on rating scales ranging from 1 (strongly disagree) to 5 (strongly agree).

Obviously, data obtained from belief and attitude surveys are very useful. Firms use such data to determine the attributes of most importance to consumers. Firms can then use this information to develop better products and more effective promotion and advertising campaigns. Companies also use survey data to diagnose the weaknesses of existing products and to forecast demand.

AP Photo/Gene J. Puskar

good mood, refreshed, rewarded). In addition, her attitudes may be influenced by the very act of buying hot fudge sundaes. If a consumer buys a Dairy Queen hot fudge sundae as a reward for completing a difficult task, this *behavior* may encourage strong, favorable attitudes toward the brand. This is not unusual. After buying a product or service (behavior), consumers' attitudes toward brands are often more favorable than their attitudes prior to making the purchase.

In addition to being formed on the basis of cognition, affect, or behavior, attitudes can also *influence* or change cognition, affect, and behavior. In other words, there is a reciprocal relationship between attitudes and the bases of attitudes. Favorable attitudes lead consumers to focus on favorable beliefs (e.g., sundaes are made from milk and milk is healthy), rather than unfavorable beliefs (e.g., sundaes have a high fat content and are therefore unhealthy). Favorable attitudes also lead consumers to focus on positive feelings rather than on negative feelings. Finally, favorable attitudes toward sundaes increase the likelihood that consumers will buy and consume sundaes.

Attitudes can be based on one's own beliefs, especially if consumers consider themselves to be knowledgeable about a product category.[12] However, attitudes can also be based on the beliefs of other people, especially when consumers consider themselves to be less knowledgeable about a product category than other people. Television advertising often uses experts as spokespersons because experts are more knowledgeable about a topic than the typical person. The beliefs of experts can have a powerful influence on the attitudes of consumers, provided that consumers trust that experts are providing truthful and accurate information. On the other hand, consumers attempt to avoid expert influence when they suspect that an expert is lying to take advantage of them.

Mood can also influence attitudes, even if mood has nothing to do with the products or services that consumers evaluate.[13] For example, a sunny day might put people in a good mood, and this can lead people to evaluate products and services more favorably. However, when consumers suspect that their moods might be biasing their judgments, they attempt to avoid letting their moods influence them. So overall, attitudes can be influenced by many different variables—including cognition, affect, behavior, the opinions of others, and unrelated moods. Now that we've discussed attitudes, let's examine the importance of consumer involvement.

FIGURE 7.1   THE RECIPROCAL RELATIONSHIP BETWEEN ATTITUDES AND THEIR BASES

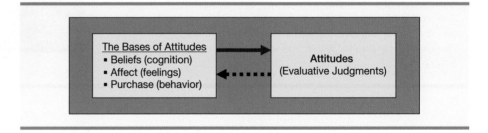

Overview of Involvement

Sometimes consumers think carefully about their beliefs and attitudes, and sometimes they reflect very little. One of the most important determinants of the amount or extent of thinking is the level of **involvement**, or the personal relevance and importance of an issue or situation.[14] When an issue or situation is relevant and important, higher levels of consumer involvement follow, and consumers think very carefully about the implications of the available information. When an issue or situation is not relevant or important, involvement is low, and consumers reflect very little. Involvement with a particular issue or topic is called *enduring involvement*. Here, consumers' levels of interest in the topic are fundamental—either high or low, and hence, their interest (or lack of interest) endures. For example, consumers who ski regularly become fundamentally involved with many aspects of skiing, including products, services, events, and weather conditions. As a result, their high levels of involvement with skiing endure through many winter seasons and over a variety of product life cycles. On the other hand, consumers who never ski demonstrate very low levels of involvement, which also endure, as even the newest, most interesting ski products and skiing events are likely to elicit only a passing glance.

A second type of involvement, based solely on special circumstances or specific conditions, is known as *situational involvement.* Here, any personal relevance that a consumer develops for a situation is ephemeral or short lived. When the situation goes away, the consumer's interest decreases correspondingly. For example, a consumer who travels infrequently is not likely to be concerned about luggage products in a serious or enduring manner. However, if an important travel opportunity suddenly arises, this same consumer may increase his situational involvement with luggage products. But, when this consumer returns from the trip, his interest in luggage will decrease to its prior, low level. His involvement with luggage is not enduring; it is strictly situational.

When a purchase decision is important or consequential, situational involvement is typically high and consumers are likely to think very carefully about the decision. For example, buying a car is consequential for most people, and they think carefully about what characteristics of a car are right for them. However, when a purchase decision is unimportant or inconsequential, situational involvement is low and consumers aren't likely to think carefully about the decision. For example, buying a candy bar is a fairly trivial exercise, and most consumers buy the brand they usually buy without thinking a lot about the purchase decision. Furthermore, when information is complex, inconsistent, or difficult to evaluate, a high degree of situational involvement is needed to appreciate the implications of the information for attitudes. However, when information is simple and easy to evaluate, a high level of situational involvement is not needed to determine its relevance or its implications.

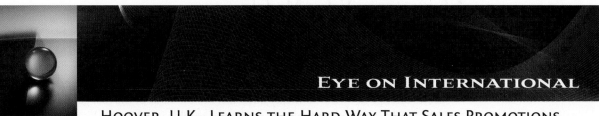

EYE ON INTERNATIONAL

HOOVER, U.K., LEARNS THE HARD WAY THAT SALES PROMOTIONS CAN BE TOO EXPENSIVE

Sometimes firms generate too much situational involvement for consumers. The U.K. division of Hoover, the famous vacuum cleaner manufacturer, ran a sales promotion in 1992 to stimulate growth.[24] Anyone who spent 100 pounds sterling or more on Hoover products received two free airline tickets for travel anywhere in Europe. Consumer response was so positive that Hoover, U.K., ran another sales promotion featuring two free airline tickets from the United Kingdom to the United States for anyone spending 250 pounds sterling or more on Hoover products. More than 200,000 consumers thought this was a good deal. As it turned out, it was a very good deal for consumers but bad deal for Hoover, U.K. The company ended up losing 48.8 million pounds sterling, and many senior managers were fired.

PRNewsFoto/Hoover/AP Photo

Attitude Models Based on High or Low Consumer Involvement

Several key models of attitude formation deal primarily with high involvement conditions. These models propose that consumers think a good deal about their evaluations of products and services, integrating a relatively large amount of information in a manner consistent with mathematical models. Examples include **expectancy-value models**, the **theory of reasoned action**, and **information integration theory**. Expectancy-value models suggest that attitudes toward a product depend on consumers' subjective evaluation of the product's attributes multiplied by the expectancy that the product possesses each attribute. The theory of reasoned action is one specific type of expectancy-value model that explains how beliefs are combined to influence attitudes and how social norms or rules and attitudes influence behavior. The information integration theory is another type of expectancy-value model that explains how beliefs are combined to influence attitudes. The two theories differ in at least one important way: the theory of reasoned action suggests that beliefs are *added* together, but information integration theory suggests that beliefs are *averaged* together.

Dual-process models of attitude formation assume that consumers think a great deal when involvement is high but they don't think much when involvement is low.[15] The **elaboration likelihood model** and the **heuristic/systematic model** are the most famous examples of dual-process models. Both models suggest that there are two different routes to persuasion: a high involvement route in which consumers think a lot (i.e., the central route of the elaboration likelihood model and the systematic route of the heuristic/systematic model), and a low involvement route in which consumers think very little (i.e., the peripheral route of the elaboration likelihood model and the heuristic route of the heuristic/systematic model). The next section of this chapter looks at the use of expectancy-value models to compute actual values for attitudes.

OBJECTIVE 3

Expectancy-Value Models

Early expectancy-value models were used to determine the value of gambles. For example, would you rather play a gamble that offers a 30 percent chance to win $100 or a gamble that offers a 25 percent chance to win $125? The answer is simple if you compute the expected values of each gamble. The expected value is the probability of success multiplied by the monetary outcome. So, the value of the first gamble is $0.30 \times \$100 = \$30$. The expected value of the second gamble is $0.25 \times \$125 = \$31.25$. Now it's obvious that the second gamble is the better deal.

Expectancy-value models can also be used to compute attitudes toward products. For example, would you rather buy car A, which offers low maintenance, good gas mileage, and reliability, or car B, which offers quick acceleration, excellent handling, and a quadraphonic sound system? First, you need to rate each attribute on a scale ranging from very bad (1) to very good (7). Next, you need to rate the likelihood that car A actually has the attributes of low maintenance, good gas mileage, and reliability, and the likelihood that car B actually offers quick acceleration, excellent handling, and a superior sound system. Finally, you multiply the attribute ratings by the likelihood ratings and add these ratings up separately for each car. The final calculations represent a specific consumer's attitudes toward each car.

The Theory of Reasoned Action

This type of expectancy-value model suggests that beliefs are added together to form attitudes and, as the number of favorable beliefs increases, the amount of favorable attitude also increases.[16] Specifically, $A = \Sigma be$, where A is the attitude toward a product or an attitude toward buying the product, b is the belief that the product has a given attribute considered important to consumers, and e is the evaluation or the extent to which consumers like each specific attribute. Beliefs (b) and evaluations (e) are measured for each important attribute. To compute an attitude, consumers multiply their b (beliefs) by their e (evaluations) for each attribute, and add these ratings.

For example, suppose a market researcher wanted to compute a group of consumers' attitudes toward Clark shoes. Consumers would rate the shoes on all important attributes, such as comfort, support, and style. Suppose the belief ratings for these attributes were 4, 3, and 5, respectively, on a scale from 1 (very low likelihood) to 7 (very high likelihood). Furthermore, suppose the evaluation ratings for these attributes were 5, 4, and 5, respectively, on a scale from 1 (very bad) to 7 (very good). $b \times e$ for each attribute is $4 \times 5 = 20$, $3 \times 4 = 12$, and $5 \times 5 = 25$, respectively. The overall attitude rating is $20 + 12 + 25 = 57$. If Clark shoes return a higher overall rating than other brands of shoes, a consumer develops more favorable attitudes toward Clark shoes than for other brands (see Figure 7.2). This model also suggests that marketers can change consumers' attitudes by changing beliefs (b) about the level of the attribute present in a brand, changing evaluations (e) about whether the attribute is important, or both. This particular model also informs marketing researchers about the specific attributes that perform well and perform poorly for their brands.

FIGURE 7.2 THEORY OF REASONED ACTION ATTITUDE FORMATION FOR CLARK SHOES

Attribute	Belief (b)		Evaluation (e)		Attitude (A)
Comfort	4	×	5	=	20
Support	3	×	4	=	12
Style	5	×	5	=	25
Overall Attitude					57

The theory of reasoned action is a simple *additive* model—as the number of favorable beliefs increases, overall attitudes increase. This theory also suggests that attitudes influence intentions, which subsequently influence behavior. This should be straightforward: as attitude favorableness toward a product increases, intentions to buy the product increase, and as a result, consumers are more likely to actually purchase the product.

However, variables other than attitudes also influence intentions. Specifically, subjective norms or social rules for behavior also influence consumer intentions. Specifically, $SN = \Sigma (NB \times MC)$, where SN refers to subjective norms, NB refers to normative beliefs or beliefs about what other people think of you if you use a product, and MC refers to the motivation to comply or how concerned you are about what other groups of people think of you if you use a product. For example,

Image courtesy of The Advertising Archives

Subjective norms influence consumers' intentions to purchase products and brands.

to measure normative beliefs about what other people think of you if you wear Clark shoes, you could rate how much you think your (1) friends, (2) parents, and (3) co-workers would like your Clark shoes on a scale from 1 (very bad) to 7 (very good). You could also rate your own motivation to comply with the wishes of your friends, parents, and co-workers on a scale from 1 (very low motivation) to 7 (very high motivation).

Suppose your ratings were 5, 7, and 6, respectively, for normative beliefs, and 7, 1, and 6, respectively, for the motivation to comply. Note that the motivation to comply is low (rating of 1) for your parents because you don't really care what they think of your shoes. However, your motivation to comply is high (a 7 rating) for your friends because you really care about what they think of your shoes. $NB \times SN = (5 \times 7) + (7 \times 1) + (6 \times 6) = 78$. The higher this number is, the more likely are normative beliefs to influence intentions. Attitudes plus normative beliefs influence intentions, and as intentions increase, consumers are more likely to buy a product (see Figure 7.3). Taken together, consumers use attitude formation and subjective norms to form their intentions to purchase, and purchase intentions often predict actual purchase. A flowchart for the theory of reasoned action is provided in Figure 7.4.

Information Integration Theory

The theory of reasoned action suggests that beliefs are *added* together to form attitudes. However, information integration theory suggests that beliefs are *averaged* together to form attitudes.[17] This distinction is important because an addition-based model implies

FIGURE 7.3 THEORY OF REASONED ACTION SUBJECTIVE NORMS
FOR CLARK SHOES

Source of Compliance	Normative Beliefs (NB)		Motivation to Comply (MC)		Subjective Norm (SN)
Friends	5	×	7	=	35
Parents	7	×	1	=	7
Co-workers	6	×	6	=	36
Overall Subjective Norms					78

FIGURE 7.4 THE THEORY OF REASONED ACTION

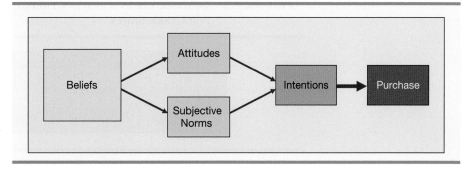

that more is better: as the number of favorable attributes increases, attitude favorableness increases. However, an averaging model implies that *less is more.* Here, advertisers should encourage consumers to focus only on the very best attributes of their products and services, because attributes with lower than average ratings pull the overall rating down. The theory of reasoned action and information integration theory differ in another important respect. The theory of reasoned action computes attitudes as a function of beliefs and evaluations. However, information integration theory estimates, or weights, how important an attribute is on the basis of overall attitude ratings and individual attribute ratings. Specifically,

$A = \sum ws$, with $\sum w = 1$, where A is the attitude toward the product, w is the importance weight of each attribute, and s is the evaluation of each attribute. The weights (w) must sum to one (1.00), and this makes the model an averaging model. The weights (w) are estimated using a statistical analysis—usually analysis of variance (ANOVA) or multiple regression. This procedure is useful because consumers can't always tell researchers how important a particular attribute really is to them. Consumers sometimes overestimate the importance of some attributes and underestimate the importance of others. Information integration theory suggests that marketers can change consumers' attitudes by changing w, s, or both. The model also informs marketers about which attributes perform well, which attributes perform poorly, and which attributes are most important.

Suppose you are forming attitudes toward Clark shoes by using information integration rather than the theory of reasoned action. You consider style to be most important, followed by comfort and support. Accordingly, you allocate style 50 percent of the total importance weights ($w = 0.50$), comfort 30 percent ($w = 0.30$), and support 20 percent ($w = 0.20$). Note that the weights total 1.00, or 100 percent. Next, you evaluate style, comfort, and support on a scale of -3 (very bad) to $+3$ (very good), 2, -1, and 3, respectively. By multiplying each importance weight (w) by each evaluation (s), you arrive at an overall attitude via information integration of $+1.3$ (see Figure 7.5).

Note that information integration theory suggests that overall values below zero indicate unfavorable attitudes, while overall values greater than zero indicate favorable attitudes. Unlike the theory of reasoned action (an additive model), in information integration (an averaging model), adding attributes doesn't guarantee higher overall attitudes. Consumers must rate any new attributes both important *and* positive for their overall attitudes to increase. Now, let's turn our attention to dual-process models, where high involvement is not always assumed.

FIGURE 7.5   INFORMATION INTEGRATION THEORY ATTITUDE FORMATION
FOR CLARK SHOES

Attribute	Weights (w)		Evaluation (s)		Attitude (A)
Comfort	0.50	×	2	=	1.0
Support	0.30	×	−1	=	−0.3
Style	0.20	×	3	=	0.6
Overall Attitude					1.3

OBJECTIVE 4

The Elaboration Likelihood Model

The name, elaboration likelihood, implies that consumers are sometimes likely to think about and elaborate on ads and other persuasive messages and are sometimes unlikely to do so. When consumers think a great deal, they are likely to consider supportive arguments if they agree with a message or counterarguments if they disagree with it. The elaboration likelihood model also suggests that there are two different routes to persuasion, the **central route** and the **peripheral route**.[18] When involvement is high, and when the ability to think about a marketing claim is high, consumers are likely to follow the central route to persuasion by focusing on information most central to or important for forming an accurate attitude. Strong arguments and reasons for forming a particular attitude are most persuasive when consumers follow the central route to persuasion.

On the other hand, when involvement is low or when the ability to think about a marketing claim is low because of distraction, a lack of relevant knowledge, time pressure, and so on, consumers are likely to follow the peripheral route to persuasion. They focus on peripheral cues or superficial information that makes it easy to form an opinion without much thought. Good examples of peripheral cues include attractive, likeable, and expert sources and positive moods and feelings. Attractive, likable, and expert sources seem trustworthy, so if these sources say that an advertised product is good, consumers often believe these sources rather than spend time thinking about the attributes and benefits of the product themselves. Furthermore, positive moods and feelings often transfer to the advertised brand when consumers follow the peripheral route to persuasion.

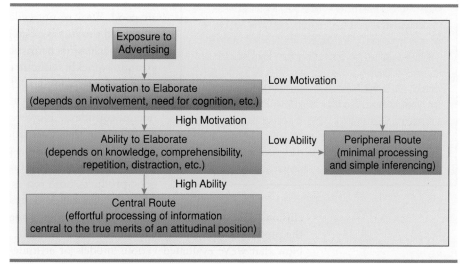

FIGURE 7.6 THE ELABORATION LIKELIHOOD MODEL OF PERSUASION

The elaboration likelihood model indicates that facts and reason are important when consumers follow the central route to persuasion, but not when consumers follow the peripheral route to persuasion. The model also indicates that celebrities, authority figures, humor, and pleasant background music and scenery are important when consumers follow the peripheral route to persuasion, but not when consumers follow the central route to persuasion. In other words, consumers use different types of information depending on which route to persuasion they are following. Furthermore, the central route to persuasion leads consumers to form strong attitudes that are accessible from memory, persistent, resistant to change, and that have a strong influence on other judgments and behavior. Conversely, the peripheral route to persuasion leads consumers to form weak attitudes that are not accessible from memory, not long-lasting, not resistant to change, and that have a weak influence on other judgments and behavior.

The Heuristic/Systematic Model

Another dual-process model of persuasion, the heuristic/systematic model, also suggests two routes to persuasion. When involvement is high and when consumers are able to think carefully about a persuasive message, consumers follow the systematic route to persuasion. In so doing, they analyze all information for its relevance to an attitude and integrate all relevant information into an attitude.

When involvement is low or when consumers are unable to think carefully about a message, consumers follow the heuristic route to persuasion and use persuasion heuristics or shortcuts to form an attitude. A heuristic or mental shortcut is quick and simple; it allows consumers to form an attitude rapidly, but it also encourages them to overlook

As recently as 10 years ago, marketing was a dirty word in the charity business, but today, American charities are embracing many marketing principles.[25] The American Heart Association's hip new slogan, "learn and live," has replaced its old and boring slogan, "fighting heart disease and stroke." The American Heart Association has also declared February 3 as "Wear Red Day" to increase awareness of heart disease. This marketing campaign is bolstered with red pins and red-lit national icons, including the Empire State Building and Niagara Falls, which were lit with red lights on February 3. These efforts have been highly successful. The American Heart Association raised $540 million in 2005, compared to $326 million in 1998. Is it ethical for charities and other non-profit organizations to use marketing methods? Do you think that charities use their brand logos and promotions as peripheral cues in an effort to persuade consumers?

a good deal of information that they might have needed to form an accurate attitude. Good examples of persuasion heuristics are "experts are usually correct," the "majority is usually correct," and "length implies strength," i.e., long messages imply there are a lot of valid reasons for liking an advertised product. Strong brand names on a product, such as Sony, Disney, and so on, imply that these products are good. Weak or unfamiliar brand names imply that an advertised product is a bad product.

All persuasion heuristics enable consumers to form attitudes quickly without much thinking. If consumers are sufficiently confident that their attitudes are correct, they stop thinking about a persuasive message. If they're not as confident. However, they think more carefully by following the systematic route to persuasion. When both routes to persuasion point to the same conclusion (i.e., both routes imply that the advertised product is a good product), both routes influence attitudes. However, when the two routes to persuasion point to opposite conclusions (i.e., one route implies that the product is good, and the other implies that the product is bad), the systematic route overrules the heuristic route to persuasion. Now that we've evaluated various models of attitude formation, let's consider the range of information used in judgment and some general approaches for changing consumer attitudes.

OBJECTIVE 5

Parameters of Judgment

Nearly all types of information can be used in consumer judgment. Information from marketing communications, consumer magazines, other consumers, and prior knowledge and experiences retrieved from memory influence judgment. The information used and how it is used, however, depend on five important parameters:

- perceived relevance of the information
- task demands
- cognitive resources
- nondirectional motivation
- directional motivation[22]

The greater the perceived relevance of a piece of information, the more heavily that information is weighted or used in judgment. For example, word-of-mouth communications are often weighted more heavily than marketing communications because consumers trust their friends and other consumers more than they trust marketers.[23] As the difficulty or complexity of a judgment task increases, consumers are more likely to rely on information that is easy to use (e.g., simple information with straightforward implications). As cognitive resources, or the ability to think carefully about a judgment task or choice task decrease, consumers are more likely to rely on information that is easy to use.

Motivation also influences how extensively consumers use information. Nondirectional motivation refers to a preference to acquire and to think carefully about all judgment-relevant information, regardless of its direction or its implications. As nondirectional motivation increases, consumers typically use more information and think more carefully about the implications of this information. Nondirectional motivation also encourages balanced information processing, or an attempt to use all relevant information, regardless of its ease of use. Directional motivation, on the other hand, refers to a preference for information that supports a consumer's preferred conclusion. This is also knows as wishful thinking. For example, after buying an expensive automobile, a consumer usually focuses only on information that suggests that he or she made a wise purchase. The consumer typically prefers to avoid information that discusses potential problems with the car or that better alternatives are available. Wishful thinking often leads a consumer to use less information and to use one-sided information that supports a preferred conclusion, rather than taking a more balanced approach. Together, the five parameters of judgment determine how much information is used, what information is used, and how heavily or lightly this information is weighted in consumer judgment.

General Strategies for Changing Attitudes

All complete theories of persuasion or attitude change suggest that it is important to choose an appropriate source or spokesperson, to use a suitable message or type of message, and to tailor the message to appeal to the intended audience or market segment. Source factors, message factors, and recipient factors are all important, and the study of persuasion concerns the study of who says what to whom. *Who* refers to the source, *what* refers to the message, and *whom* refers to the recipient.[21]

Effective sources tend to be attractive, likable, knowledgeable, trustworthy, and credible. The effectiveness of a particular type of source depends on the situation. For example, expert sources are most effective when the message is complex, and attractive sources are most effective when the message is simple. Factual messages are most effective when consumers are likely to think carefully about the message, but emotional messages are most effective when consumers are unlikely to think carefully. Two-sided messages that discuss the pros and cons of an advertised product are most effective for knowledgeable consumers. On the other hand, one-sided

Factual messages are most effective when consumers think carefully about an advertisement.

messages that discuss the pros only are most effective for consumers who know little about the product.

To a large extent, persuasion depends on the likelihood that consumers will receive and comprehend a message and on the probability and strength of counterarguments.[21] More formally, $A = R(1 - CA)$, where A refers to attitude, R refers to the likelihood of receiving and comprehending a message, and CA refers to the likelihood of counterarguing. This equation implies that persuasion is greater when R and CA are moderate than when both are high or both are low. Consequently, distraction can increase persuasion when it decreases the ability to counterargue more than it decreases the ability to receive and comprehend a message. Counterarguing is most likely when a message is inconsistent with consumers' prior beliefs. However, when a message is consistent with what consumers already believe, consumers are likely to think of support arguments rather than counterarguments. When this is the case, distraction decreases persuasion.

Chapter Summary

Beliefs are nonevaluative judgments, and attitudes are evaluative judgments. Marketers frequently try to change consumers' beliefs and attitudes through using advertising and other persuasion techniques. Attitudes influence and are influenced by cognition, affect, and behavior. The theory of reasoned action suggests that attitudes and subjective norms influence intentions, and intentions influence behavior. This theory also suggests that beliefs are added together to form attitudes. Information integration theory suggests that beliefs are averaged together to form attitudes, and consequently, it is better to tell consumers about a few very positive features of a product than to tell consumers about many fairly positive features of a product.

Dual-process models of persuasion suggest that consumers think carefully about a persuasive message when involvement is high and when they are able to think carefully. The most famous dual-process models are the elaboration likelihood model and the heuristic/systematic model. The elaboration likelihood model predicts that consumers will follow the central route to persuasion when they think carefully about a message and the peripheral route to persuasion when they don't think carefully about a message. The heuristic/systematic model predicts that consumers follow the systematic route to persuasion when they think carefully, but the heuristic route when they don't think carefully. Both theories suggest that it is important to predict how carefully consumers will think about a message before designing a persuasive message. An effective persuasive message uses an appropriate source and an appropriate argument and targets appropriate recipients.

Key Terms

belief	attitudes	information integration theory
judgments	evaluative-cognitive consistency	dual-process models
search attribute	zanna and rempel's model	elaboration likelihood model
experience attribute	semantic differential scale	heuristic/systematic model
credence attribute	likert scales	central route
descriptive beliefs	involvement	peripheral route
informational beliefs	expectancy-value models	
inferential beliefs	theory of reasoned action	

Review and Discussion

1. How do beliefs influence attitudes?

2. How do attitudes influence beliefs?

3. When are search attributes likely to be more important than experience attributes?

4. When are experience attributes likely to be more important than search attributes?

5. What is involvement? What variables influence involvement? How can you create an ad that increases involvement?

6. Think of questions you would ask to measure brand awareness using several semantic differential scales.

7. Think of questions you would ask to measure beliefs about advertising using several Likert scales.

8. When are factual arguments likely to be important? When are emotional appeals likely to be important?

9. In what ways are the elaboration likelihood model and the heuristic/systematic model similar?

10. In what ways are the elaboration likelihood model and the heuristic/systematic model different?

Short Application Exercises

1. Design an ad for a car using the theory of reasoned action. What attributes should you use and how many should you describe? Remember, an adding model implies that more is better.

2. Design an ad for a digital camera using information integration theory. What attributes should you use and how many should you describe? Remember, an averaging model implies that less is more.

3. Design an ad for a new product using the elaboration likelihood model and the heuristic/systematic model.

4. Form groups of two and ask each other which food is disliked the most. Then, take turns trying to convince the other person that the food he or she dislikes is excellent. What persuasion principles did each of you use?

MANAGERIAL APPLICATION

Imagine you work for a well-known market research firm. Your supervisor has asked you to calculate numerical values for consumer attitudes using the Fishbein expectancy-value model, $A = \Sigma be$. In your preliminary research for a client that manufacturers LCD HDTVs, you learned that the key attributes are picture resolution, screen size, viewing angles, reliability, and easy-to-use inputs. Using the data below, compute attitude scores for consumer A, a highly knowledgeable consumer, and for consumer B, a consumer who knows relatively little about HDTVs.

Attribute	Consumer A		Consumer B	
	b	e	b	e
1080i	7	7	3	4
47-inch screen	6	6	7	7
Viewing angles	6	5	4	3
Reliability	5	6	3	3
Inputs	7	7	2	3

YOUR CHALLENGE:

1. Compute attitudes for both consumers. Which consumer likes the product more and why?

2. For the knowledgeable consumer, which attribute(s) need improvement?

3. For the consumer who knows little about the product, which attribute(s) need improvement?

4. Explain how to influence b and how to influence e for consumer A and for consumer B.

AFFECT AND MOTIVATION

NOSTALGIA SELLS

Many firms use nostalgia to stir up positive emotions and feelings, such as those consumers experience when they reminisce about pleasant childhood memories.[1] Feelings of nostalgia are very powerful, transporting you back to a time when life was simple, you were healthier and happier, and life was grand—at least that is the way you remember it.

A new trend is the nostalgic brand. Marketers are taking successful old brands, updating them, and relaunching them with the hope of leveraging consumer nostalgia. For example, BMW's Mini Cooper is an old brand revived, as is the classic Ovaltine chocolate drink mix. American Greetings has reintroduced Care Bears, popular cartoon characters from the 1980s. It seems that teenage girls are drawn to the colorful and tacky creatures, which shows that even the young are nostalgic at times.

Nostalgia is most often used in advertising campaigns. For example, many automobile manufacturers run ads featuring music from the 1960s to capture the attention and interest of baby boomers. Television ads for Werther's old-fashioned candy show a smiling kindly old grandfather giving Werther's candy to his smiling, eager grandson. The ad also shows that grandson many years later as grandfather himself, now offering Werther's candy to his lucky grandson. In a similar commercial, a grandmother is feeding Cheerios to a baby in a high chair. The baby has his mouth open, and he's waiting for the cereal, but the grandmother keeps playing with the Cheerios by using them as points on an imaginary map to show the baby where his relatives live. Children aren't the only ones who like to play with Cheerios: grandmothers do, too! Emotional experiences and responses are surprisingly powerful and motivating, as is discussed in this chapter.

Image courtesy of The Advertising Archives

An Overview of Motivation and Emotion

Motivation (needs or drives) and emotions (or feelings, affective responses) encourage consumers to act. **Motivation** is a driving force that moves or incites us to act and is the underlying basis of all behavior. Individuals are driven to satisfy their needs, wants, and desires. **Emotion** (or *emotional* and *affective responses*) is a person's affect—feelings and moods—plus arousal.

Motivation and emotion are linked in a number of ways, which is why they are covered together in this chapter. Motivations and emotions are linked because consumers feel positive emotions when motivations are satisfied and negative emotions when motivations are not satisfied. Consumers also often describe motivations and emotions similarly, saying, "I feel like eating some Pizza Hut pizza," or "I feel like drinking Coca-Cola," or "I feel like reading my Consumer Behavior textbook," and so on. Furthermore, motivations and emotions focus attention and energize behavior. Motivations focus attention on goal-relevant objects, and emotions focus attention on emotional objects.

This chapter examines how motivation and emotion influence consumer behavior by examining the process of motivation and several motivation and emotion theories.

The Process of Motivation

What creates the driving force of motivation in a person? Motivation begins when a person feels a need that requires satisfaction. In general, **needs** are desires that arise when a consumer's current state does not match the consumer's preferred state. Physiological needs, such as the need for air, water, food, sex, and protection from the environment (clothing and shelter), are *innate needs* or *primary needs*. Psychological needs are learned as we grow and are socialized, such as needs for affection, companionship, power, self-esteem, and intellectual stimulation. These are *secondary needs*. Needs should also be distinguished from wants. Although some people tend to use these two terms synonymously, there are differences. Needs are automatic and required; if you wake up at 2 A.M., "dying" of thirst, for instance, you need something to quench it. Wants are learned manifestations of our needs, e.g., only a glass of chocolate milk will take care of your 2 A.M. problem. Some marketers also distinguish between needs and wants by classifying wants as product-specific needs.

Chocolate milk is a product-specific need.

PRNewsFoto/San Francisco Chocolate Factory/AP Photo

Needs are aroused via three routes: physiological, emotional, and cognitive. We have already touched on physiologically based needs. Physical changes in the body trigger need **arousal**. For example, your stomach growls when you haven't eaten in several hours; you shiver when your body temperature drops; and your eyes blur and feel scratchy when you are deprived of sleep. Emotions also lead to need arousal. For example, feeling bored or frustrated at work may lead to the need for a vacation; feeling lonely may lead to a need to go to a social event. Finally, arousal can come from our thoughts. Recalling the date of your mother's birthday may prompt a need to purchase and send her a gift. Cognitive arousal is tied closely to the environment because environmental situations and stimuli often trigger cognitive arousal. For example, seeing your roommate's new pair of tennis shoes may remind you of how old your own shoes are and trigger the need to shop.

Once a need is aroused, a state of tension is created that energizes a person to reduce or eliminate the need, returning to a preferred state, called the **goal** (or *goal-object,* *goal-state*). This tension is called a **drive,** and the degree or amount of tension influences the urgency with which actions are taken to return to the desired goal-state. Thus, motivation focuses attention on **goals** and drives us to act.

Motivations focus attention by producing a **valuation effect** and a **devaluation effect**.[2] When consumers are extremely hungry, they rate food products as more desirable (the valuation effect), and they rate non-food products as less desirable (the devaluation effect). Similarly, when consumers are extremely thirsty, they rate beverages as more desirable (the valuation effect), and they rate non-beverages as less desirable (the devaluation effect). Surprisingly, hungry or thirsty consumers devalue money, even though money can be used to buy food or beverages. Furthermore, the devaluation effect is usually larger than the valuation effect, and these effects occur only when powerful motivations are present. For example, a famished consumer is motivated to attain one goal—to satisfy his hunger immediately. Thus, he will devalue any objects (including money) in an attempt to reduce hunger. This is one reason some consumers stand in line and pay exorbitant prices for food and beverages at amusement parks and sporting events. In this situation, they value food and beverages and devalue both time and money.

Motivations also influence the direction of behavior. Two directions are possible: **approach,** or movement towards a desired object or outcome, and **avoidance,** or movement away from an undesired object or outcome. For example, most consumers seek good entertainment; lack of such entertainment causes dissatisfaction. On the other hand, many consumers don't enjoy shopping in crowded retail environments and are likely to avoid shopping at peak times unless forced to do so. Motivations also influence what goals consumers pursue and how intensely and persistently consumers pursue these goals. For example, our hobbies, interests, and needs influence what goals we pursue and how intensely and persistently we pursue these goals. Consumers who love collectible objects (e.g., wine, comic books, stamps, coins, works of art) pursue these objects frequently (e.g., they search for these objects often), intensely (they search everywhere, including stores, flea markets, and the Internet), and persistently (they search for years).

Motivation and Human Needs

Whatever the direction of motivation, needs are the root of the motivational process. Several psychologists and researchers have developed theories and models related to human needs. Some of the most popular are reviewed next.

Drive Theory and Maslow's Hierarchy of Needs

Drive theory is one of the earliest theories of motivation.[3] Drive theory maintains that people have several basic physiological needs, such as needs for food, water, air, etc. When people do not get enough food, water, air, or other basic requirements for survival, a source of energy known as drive compels people to behave in ways that reduce these drives. For example, eating reduces the drive for food. Drinking reduces the drive for water, and breathing reduces the drive for air.

Physiological needs are the most basic needs experienced by people. Building on drive theory, Abraham Maslow suggested that people also have higher-order needs and desires.[4] After all physiological needs are met, people become preoccupied with safety and security needs, including needs for shelter and protection. Once safety and security needs are met, people move on to the next level of social needs, i.e., the need for belongingness and love. Social relationships, affection, belonging, and choosing the right spouse become important at this level. After these needs are met, people advance to the ego or esteem level. At this level, people need to feel competent and important. Finally,

OBJECTIVE 2

the highest level is self-actualization, which is the state of mind of people who feel that they have reached their full potential. Theoretically, relatively few people have reached this ultimate level. Finally, while each need is defined separately, overlap occurs among the categories. No need is ever completely satisfied, but a person cannot progress upward along Maslow's hierarchy until lower level needs are primarily satisfied.

FIGURE 8.1 MASLOW'S HIERARCHY OF NEEDS

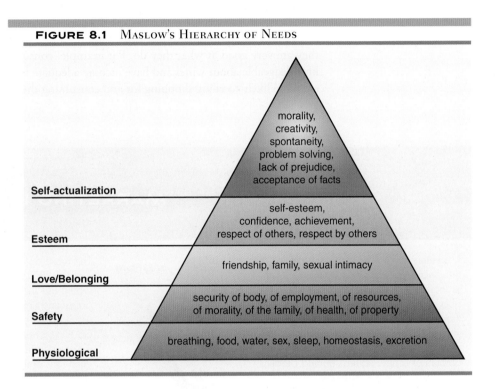

Marketers design clever promotions to appeal to all levels of needs in Maslow's hierarchy. For instance, watch any late night television show, and you will see big, juicy hamburgers and hot, crispy fries floating across the screen to tempt late night cravings. Companies that market home security systems, insurance policies, and even clothing, promote safety and security needs. The Land's End clothing catalog has featured a story about how one of the brand's winter coats kept a person stranded in the wilderness alive. Products consumed in social groups, such food, beverages, and social gathering places stress good friends, good times, and a feeling of belonging. E-Harmony, on online dating service, emphasizes the importance of finding "that true soul mate," while Kodak tells you to "share moments, share life". Examples of esteem needs are everywhere from health and beauty ads to automobile ads. L'Oreal says that you're "worth it"; Lexus is for when "you've arrived"; Maybelline asks, "Maybe she's born with it?" Finally, self-actualization needs, while realized by relatively few, are certainly pursued, and marketers use these needs to help people reach for more. The U.S. Army and Air Force tap into this need with their slogans, "Be all that you can be," and "The sky's the limit." Gatorade asks, "Is it in you?" and Nike says, "Just Do It!"

Self-Determination Theory

Self-determination theory builds on **Maslow's hierarchy of needs** by distinguishing between **intrinsic motivation** and **extrinsic motivation**.[5] Intrinsic motivation refers to the desire to pursue an activity or goal for its own sake, rather than for an extrinsic reward, such as money. Extrinsic motivation refers to the desire to pursue an activity or goal in order to receive a reward, such as money or praise. This distinction is important because people are usually more creative, hard-working, and more fulfilled and happy when they pursue intrinsic goals rather than extrinsic goals. According to self-determination theory, intrinsic motivation is highest when autonomy, belongingness, and competence (the ABCs of self-determination) are high. This means that intrinsic motivation is greater when people feel that they have free choice (i.e., they are not forced to do something), are part of an important group or organization, and feel that they are very good at what they do. For example, consumers who view themselves as knowledgeable about wines and have income adequate to purchase high quality wines are more likely to enjoy shopping for and consuming these products.

MARKETING IN ACTION
Implementation Intentions

Marketers are constantly trying to think of new ways to get consumers to use more of their products. The greater the amount of a product that consumers use, the more they will need to buy. A leading consumer marketing firm recently succeeded in getting consumers to use three times the amount of a new liquid cleaning product than they would normally use. The firm achieved this through implementation intentions.[23]

Implementation intentions are detailed plans concerning when and how a consumer intends to use a product or service.

©tacojim/iStockphoto.com

The more detail the better: consumers were asked to think about when they would use the product (i.e., using specific dates and times) and how they would use it (i.e. they were asked regarding a cleaning product, what specific objects will you clean?). Forming implementation intentions creates associations in memory between intentions to use a product and the specific situations in which the product will be used. The stronger the associations are, the more likely people will use the product when the specific usage situations arise.

The Trio of Needs

Some consumer researchers believe that Maslow's list of needs can be simplified to three key elements particularly important for consumer behavior. The need for *power* refers to the consumer's desire to control other people, objects (e.g., money), and the environment (e.g., one's home or work) because power increases the likelihood that the consumer can acquire the things he or she wants. The need for *affiliation* refers to the need for belongingness and friendship or the desire to be a member of a personally important social group. People with high affiliation needs are socially dependent and choose products they feel others will approve of. The need for *achievement* refers to the need to accomplish difficult tasks (e.g., completing a college degree, getting a high-paying job) and to be successful. After all, no one wants to be a loser. High achievement is a valuable promotional tool when targeting well-educated and affluent consumers.

Need for achievement.

Image courtesy of The Advertising Archives

So far, we have seen that consumers have many different motivations and needs. Some are physical (e.g., food, water, air) and some are emotional (e.g., belongingness). Next, let's switch gears and discuss cognitive needs. Cognition refers to purposeful thinking or information processing. Some types of thoughts and ideas "feel right" and make consumers feel at ease and comfortable. Others feel bad and make consumers feel awkward or uncomfortable. People have a need for cognitive consistency.[6] Typically, consistent thoughts feel right, and inconsistent thoughts feel wrong. Three consistency theories provide explanations for consumers' need for consistency in their thinking: attitude function theory, balance theory, and cognitive dissonance theory.

Attitude Function Theory

Attitude function theory describes four major types of attitudes.[7] Attitudes that serve the *knowledge function* summarize large amounts of information to simplify the world and help consumers make decisions. Attitudes that serve the *value-expressive function* communicate important beliefs to others and help consumers interact with each other more efficiently. Attitudes that serve the *ego-defensive function* help consumers feel safe and secure and good about themselves. Finally, attitudes that serve the *adjustment function* help consumers approach pleasure and avoid pain more quickly and efficiently. Persuasive messages that are positive and consistent with the underlying function of a consumer's attitude are more likely to feel right and are be effective. On the other hand, persuasive messages that are inconsistent with an attitude function are more likely to be ignored. Thus, it is critical for marketers to understand which functions consumers draw on when evaluating their products.

Different persuasion techniques are needed for different attitude functions. Information and facts are useful for changing attitudes that serve the **knowledge function,** but not for changing attitudes that serve other functions. Image appeals are useful for changing attitudes that serve the **value-expressive function**. Authority and fear appeals are useful for changing attitudes that serve the **ego-defensive function**. Finally, hedonic (or pleasure/pain) appeals are useful for changing attitudes that serve the **adjustment function**. Should anyone doubt the power of attitude functions, observe someone trying to change another person's religious attitudes (which serve the ego-defensive function) with facts (which serve the knowledge function). Similarly, try changing someone's attitudes about a favorite guilty pleasure such as smoking (which serves the adjustment function) with imagery such as yellow teeth (which serves the value-expressive function).

Understanding a consumer's regulatory focus is also important. **Regulatory focus theory** suggests that consumers regulate or control their behavior by using either a **promotion focus** or a **prevention focus**.[8] A promotion focus is concerned with the presence or absence of positive outcomes and with aspirations and accomplishment. A prevention focus is concerned with the presence or absence of negative outcomes and with protection and responsibilities. Some consumers are usually more promotion-focused, while others tend to be more prevention-focused. Messages that encourage consumers to think about their aspirations and accomplishments encourage a

OBJECTIVE 3

FIGURE 8.8 TYPES OF ADVERTISEMENTS AND THE CONDITIONS UNDER WHICH EACH WILL BE MOST EFFECTIVE

Attitude Function	Promotion-Focused Ads	Prevention-Focused Ads
Knowledge	Factual appeals Logical arguments Comparative advertising	Mystery ads Surprise Confusion
Value expression	Image appeals Celebrity advertising	Nerd alert ads
Ego defense	Authority figures Experts	Fear appeals
Adjustment	Pleasure	Pain

SOURCE: Adapted from Kardes & Cronley (2000).

promotion focus. Messages that encourage consumers to think about protection and responsibilities encourage a prevention focus.

Combining attitude function theory and regulatory focus theory results in a 4×2 matrix of persuasion techniques.[9] For maximum effectiveness, persuasive messages must match consumers' attitude functions and regulatory focus. Figure 8.2 lists major persuasive message types and the conditions under which each is most effective.

For example, many ads for personal computers and other high-tech products provide information about brand attributes and benefits to inform consumers about these complex products. Usually, consumers need to be at least somewhat knowledgeable about these products to makes sense of the information. Rather than try to inform consumers, prevention-focused knowledge appeals attempt to confuse consumers by using unfamiliar technical information or surprising and unexpected information that leads consumers to rethink their attitudes. Mystery ads, or ads that do not reveal what is being advertised until the end of the message, can also encourage consumers to think more diligently about their attitudes.[10] Many dot.com companies use this approach, as did early ads for the Infinity automobile.

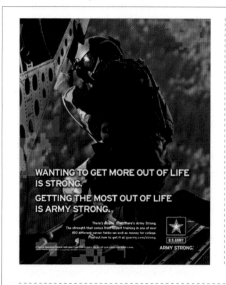

Promotion-focused value-expressive appeals.

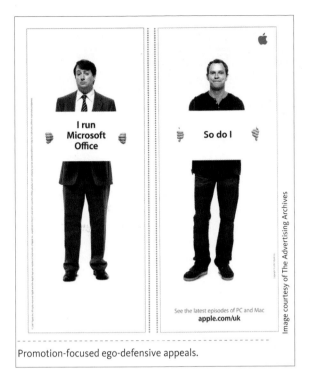

Promotion-focused ego-defensive appeals use authority figures (e.g., political leaders, religious leaders, police officers) or experts (e.g., doctors, lawyers, executives) to convince consumers to change their attitudes about products and services that offer protection against accidents (e.g., insurance), theft (e.g., home and car security systems), and other uncertain, negative events. Such appeals are particularly useful for influencing political attitudes. Stereotypes, or negative attitudes toward specific groups, also serve an ego-defensive function by helping people feel better when they compare themselves to a group they perceive as inferior.

Adjustment appeals focus on simple hedonism, or the pleasure/pain principle. Consumers buy some types of products simply because they taste good (e.g., ice cream, candy, and other unhealthy but good-tasting foods and beverages) or feel good (e.g., alcohol, caffeine, cigarettes). In the same vein, consumers avoid some types of products because they taste bad (e.g., mouthwash, fiber cereals), or feel bad (e.g., pharmaceuticals that improve one's health despite aversive side effects, such as blood pressure medicines). Promotion-focused adjustment appeals focus on the benefits of guilty pleasures, such as high-calorie foods and beverages, and en-

Promotion-focused ego-defensive appeals.

tertainment products that no one wants to admit they like (e.g., movies such as *Dumb and Dumber* and gossip magazines). Facts and figures do not promote such products effectively (e.g., statistics do not convince consumers to quit smoking). Neither does image, because many guilty pleasures are consumed privately rather than publicly. Ego-defensive appeals are similarly ineffective because people like what they like, no matter what authorities or experts think.

Prevention-focused adjustment appeals are particularly useful for products that help consumers avoid pain, such as pain relievers (e.g., aspirin, Tylenol, antacids, seltzers, laxatives, ointments). A recent ad for Excedrin, for example, shows an actor saying he does not know why or care how the product works, it just works. In other words, no complex arguments; no celebrities; and no experts are needed. Consumers want a product that eliminates headaches, and they do not care why the product works.

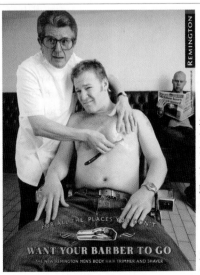

Prevention-focused ego-defensive appeals.

EYE ON INTERNATIONAL

CULTURE AND REGULATORY FOCUS

Most of the research published in leading scientific consumer behavior journals report the results of experiments conducted in the United States. Of course, the United States is a western culture dominated by people with an independent self-view (Canada and Western Europe are similar in this dimension). This means that western consumers are primarily interested in maximizing their own outcomes and are not always concerned about what happens to other people. By contrast, in eastern cultures, such as those of Japan, China, and Eastern Europe, people have a more interdependent self-view. This means that these consumers are primarily interested in maximizing the outcomes of important groups in their lives, such as their families, friends, and co-workers.

PRNewsFoto/DZP Marketing Communications/
AP Photo

Recent research on culture and regulatory focus shows that consumers with independent self-views often adopt a promotion focus.[24] These consumers are therefore more sensitive and responsive to promotion-focused ads because these ads match their promotion-focused regulatory orientation. By contrast, consumers with interdependent self-views often adopt a prevention focus. These consumers are more sensitive and responsive to prevention-focused ads because these ads match their prevention-focused regulatory orientation. Hence, cultural backgrounds have a powerful influence on regulatory focus, and regulatory focus has a powerful influence on the relative effectiveness of promotion- versus prevention-focused advertisements.

OBJECTIVE 4

Balance Theory

Balance theory focuses on the degree of consistency among three elements:

- p, the person or consumer who receives a persuasive message
- o, the other person (e.g., a friend, salesperson, or spokesperson) who recommends a particular product or service
- x, a stimulus such as a particular product or service[11]

Balance exists when the relationships among all three elements are positive (e.g., p likes o; o likes x; therefore, p should like x) or if two relations are negative and one is positive (e.g., my enemy's enemy is my friend). Balanced relationships are learned more quickly, are more memorable, and are rated as more pleasant. Consumers like balanced triads. However, the converse is also true. Consumers do not like imbalanced triads, where all three relations among the elements are negative (e.g., p dislikes o, o dislikes x, and p dislikes x) or two relations are positive and one is negative (e.g., p likes o, o likes x, and p dislikes x). Imbalanced triads produce unpleasant tension, and consumers are motivated to reduce this tension by changing one (or more) of the perceived relations within the p-o-x triad.

Let's take an example. If p is you, o is Tiger Woods, and x is Nike, imbalance exists if you like Tiger (p likes o), Tiger uses Nike golf equipment (o likes x), and you dislike Nike (p dislikes x). There are three ways that you can bring about balance to this triad:

1. change your attitude
2. deny the relationship
3. differentiate the relationships

First, you could change your attitude toward Nike (*p* likes *x*) or change your attitude toward Tiger (*p* dislikes *o*). Second, you could deny Tiger's relationship with Nike by suggesting that he doesn't really prefer Nike products; he just uses the equipment to gain huge endorsements. Third, you could resolve the imbalance through differentiation by indicating that you like Tiger Woods the athlete, but not Tiger Woods the celebrity. See Figure 8.3.

FIGURE 8.3 BALANCE THEORY

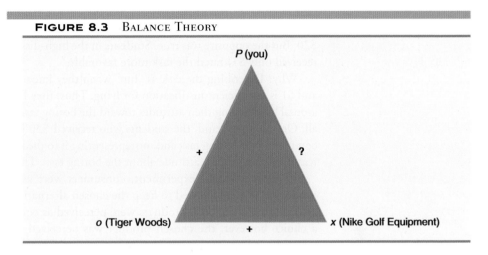

This type of analysis can be applied to almost any set of three elements. For example, consumer, *p*, likes cigarettes, *o*, which are linked to heart disease, *x*. It seems reasonable to assume that the consumer dislikes heart disease (*p* dislikes *x*). Therefore, the consumer must resolve the imbalance through attitude change (e.g., disliking cigarettes and quitting), denial (e.g., cigarettes do not cause heart disease), or differentiation (e.g., the consumer likes the way cigarettes make him feel but dislikes the long-term side effects). Many ads feature a likable celebrity, *o*, endorsing a new product, *x*. If the consumer, *p*, likes *o*, and if *o* likes *x*, subtle pressure toward consistency induces the consumer to form a favorable attitude toward *x* so that the triad is in balance. It's easy to see how balance theory explains why celebrity advertising can be highly effective.

Cognitive Dissonance Theory

Most people assume that attitudes influence behavior, but **cognitive dissonance theory** suggests the reverse: behavior can also influence attitudes. According to cognitive dissonance theory, consumers strive for consonance, or consistency between a specific behavior and an attitude related to that behavior. Dissonance, or behavior-attitude inconsistency, produces an unpleasant tension, referred to as dissonance arousal. When it occurs, people are motivated to reduce the dissonance by changing their attitude to match the behavior that was performed. The shift in attitude that increases behavior-attitude consistency is known as s, the dissonance effect. It often involves effort justification, or attempts to rationalize the initially undesirable behavior. Sometimes people are persuaded to do things that they really don't want to do. For example, parents talk children into cleaning their rooms, professors talk students into doing their homework, and bosses talk employees into doing their jobs. As the amount of effort involved in performing a disliked activity increases, the more people change their attitudes to convince themselves that the effort was worthwhile. This attitude change then leads to future behavior change.

In a classic experiment, college students were asked to perform a senseless and boring task: to turn a series of pegs on a pegboard one quarter of a turn.[12] After turning each peg, they were asked to return the peg to its beginning point and repeat the task. This continued for about a half hour. In the high-dissonance condition, each subject was asked to tell the next person that the task was "exciting and fun." These students received $1 for performing the task and describing it as "fun" to the next participant. In the low-dissonance condition, a separate group of students received $20 for performing the task and telling the next participant that it was "fun." Which group do you think rated the task more favorably, the group who received $1 or the group that received $20? At first glance, one might think the low-dissonance group (those who received $20) rated the task more favorably because they were happy to receive $20. But the opposite was true. Students in the high-dissonance condition (those who received only $1) rated the task more favorably.

Why? Describing the task as "fun" when they knew it was boring is inconsistent, and $1 is insufficient justification for lying. Thus, they had to reduce their dissonance arousal by changing their attitudes toward the boring task. Maybe it wasn't so bad after all. On the other hand, the students who received $20 had sufficient justification for completing the boring task and misrepresenting it to the next participant. There was no reason to change their attitude about the boring task. They were paid to do it!

In another classic experiment, consumers were asked to choose between two products and were allowed to keep the chosen alternative as a gift.[13] Before consumers made a choice, both products were perceived as equally attractive. After making a choice however, the chosen product was perceived as highly attractive, and the rejected product was perceived as less attractive. This "spreading of the alternatives" occurs because making a decision is difficult, and people need to readjust their attitudes to justify their decisions. The more difficult a decision, the more people convince themselves that the chosen product is desirable and the rejected product is undesirable.

Almost any type of decision can set the stage for dissonance effects. For example, suppose a consumer makes a bad decision and buys a product that performs poorly. This behavior is likely to produce dissonance arousal because the behavior is inconsistent with the belief or desire to make good purchase decisions. Post-purchase dissonance is especially likely when the decision

1. Is important
2. Involves giving up positive features of a rejected alternative or accepting negative features of a chosen alternative
3. Involves alternatives that are similar in terms of overall desirability

Making purchase decisions is not the only difficult activity that people perform. Joining a fraternity or sorority, getting into college, getting a job, landing a sale, and losing weight are also difficult activities. Research has shown that the more difficult the activity (e.g., hazing, interviewing, negotiating) is, the more people value their fraternities, sororities, universities, jobs, clients, and health clubs. Consequently, people remain loyal members of their fraternities, sororities, universities, places of employment, and health clubs for longer periods of time.

ETHICS

Approximately 25 percent of the population of the United States is obese. Obesity is a huge (pardon the pun) social problem because of the health risks associated with it, including increased risk for heart attacks, diabetes, and other health problems. Of course, fast food restaurants, such as McDonald's, Burger King, and Wendy's, are very popular in the United States, and this popularity may contribute to the obesity problem. Recently, some morbidly obese U.S. consumers have brought lawsuits against McDonald's based on the fact that McDonald's food is very fattening and unhealthy and therefore, McDonald's food is a major cause of the plaintiffs' obesity problems. The plaintiffs claim that McDonald's is slowly killing them. Does McDonald's have a moral responsibility to produce and market healthier food to help reduce the serious obesity problem in the United States? Or, is it up to the individual consumer to decide what foods and how much food are reasonable to consume? What do you think? What is the role of motivational psychological processes in wanting to eat unhealthy food in large quantities? Can individual consumers be expected to control the physiological and motivational processes that regulate their urge to eat?

Blend Images/Jupiter Images

Emotion

The previous sections have shown that motivations focus attention and influence a wide variety of consumer behaviors. We now turn to feelings and emotions and show how these also focus attention and influence consumer behavior. Even very simple feelings, such as positive affect or positive mood, can have surprisingly powerful and complex effects on behavior. Little things, like nice weather, finding a dollar on the sidewalk, receiving a small gift or a compliment, remembering a positive event, and so on, can induce positive affect. When people are in a good mood, they are more helpful, more creative, and more willing to try new products.[14] Positive affect also helps consumers make better and more satisfying purchase decisions.

The **mood-as-information model** suggests that mood is often treated like any other piece of information and is integrated along with other information when consumers form an overall evaluation of a product.[15] Consequently, a good mood often results in a more favorable evaluation, while a bad mood is likely to result in a less favorable evaluation, even when mood has nothing to do with the product. For example, nice weather, finding a dollar, receiving a compliment, remembering a positive event, and other extraneous sources of mood can enhance product evaluations. This effect can backfire, however, when consumers recognize that their mood may have influenced their evaluation. In this case, consumers attempt to subtract the mood effects. The mood-as-information effect is also qualified by the type of product consumers evaluate. The effect is more pronounced for **hedonic products**, or products consumers use to enjoy positive experiences, than for **instrumental products**, or products consumers use to solve a problem.[16]

The **affect confirmation model** suggests that affect or mood can also influence how consumers use product attribute information.[17] Instead of a direct input for judgment, as the mood-as-information model suggests, mood can alter the weighting of product attribute information. When consumers are in a good mood, positive attributes tend

FIGURE 8.4 Types of Affect and Emotion[18]

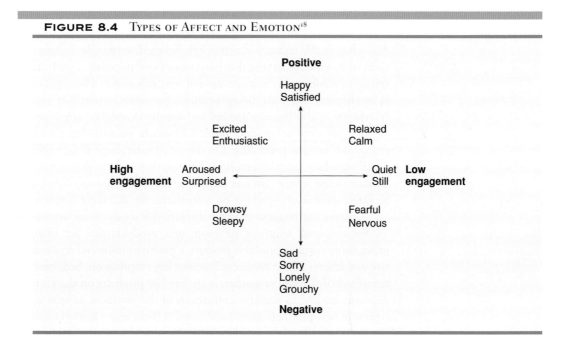

to be weighted more heavily. When consumers are in a bad mood, negative attributes tend to be weighted more heavily. For example, a consumer who is in a good mood may consider a positive feature of *Polo* clothing (e.g., prestige) more important than when he is in a bad mood. Alternatively, a consumer who is in a bad mood may think more about a negative feature of *Polo* (e.g., expensive). Hence, mood can have many different effects on consumer judgment.

Affective experiences or feelings are intensified when they are accompanied by physiological arousal or excitation of the sympathetic nervous system. As stated previously, emotion is defined as intense affect or affect plus physiological arousal. Emotion is more specific than affect because it reflects an appraisal process (e.g., happiness, sadness, anger, fear).[19] Exciting events like action movies, major sporting events, and intense interpersonal interactions produce emotion. Exercise also increases physiological arousal levels and can produce emotion. Chemicals, such as caffeine, adrenalin, norepinephrine (synthetic adrenalin), and other stimulants also produce emotion.

Although people are good at detecting changes in their arousal levels, they are often surprisingly bad at interpreting their own emotions. For example, in a classic study, people were injected with norepinephrine (which produces arousal) and were asked to stay in a waiting room for the next phase of the experiment.[20] Another person was also waiting there. Although this person seemed like another participant in the experiment, he was actually an accomplice of the experimenter. In "happy" conditions, the accomplice seemed to be overjoyed: he smiled a lot and threw paper airplanes. In "angry" conditions, the accomplice seemed to be annoyed and mad: he frowned a lot and complained about having to wait for so long. During the next phase of the experiment, participants were asked to fill out a questionnaire asking them about their current emotional states. Participants who received norepinephrine and saw the happy accomplice perceived themselves to be happy. Participants who received norepinephrine and saw the angry accomplice perceived themselves to be angry, just like him. In other words, people used the accomplice's behavior as a contextual cue to help them interpret their own emotions. In general, studies like this have found that people are bad at interpreting their own emotions without the help of such contextual cues.

Discrepancy-Interruption Theory

According to discrepancy-interruption theory, discrepancies or surprises and interruptions or unexpected events that prevent us from pursuing a goal that we are currently trying to achieve also increase arousal and emotion.[21] Discrepancies increase arousal or alertness and wake us up because they often require our immediate attention. Interruptions also increase arousal and require immediate attention. Small discrepancies or small surprises produce positive emotions because they are usually mildly interesting and thought-provoking. On the other hand, large discrepancies or big surprises usually produce negative emotions because they suggest that our current expectations are completely wrong. No one likes to be completely wrong. Similarly, no one likes to be interrupted while working on something. So, the more important the task is, the more intense our negative emotional reaction is when we are interrupted.

Because small surprises are good, new products that are slightly different from other, more familiar products produce a positive emotional response, leading to positive evaluations of the products. Because big surprises are bad, new products that are completely different from other, more familiar products produce a negative emotional response, leading to negative evaluations of the products, at least initially. Hence, designers of new products should add features (bells and whistles) that are mildly surprising and interesting because these make new products more interesting. Developing a

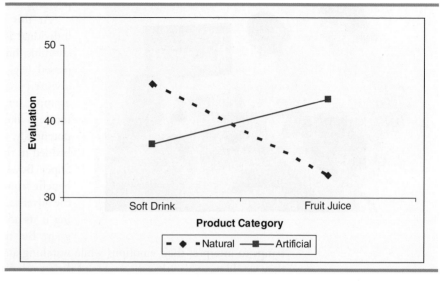

FIGURE 8.5 DISCREPANCY-INTERRUPTION THEORY

completely new product is risky because consumers will not know how to react to it or use it, leading to negative emotions, at least initially. Time and money are often required to educate consumers about completely new products to help them fully appreciate the benefits of an innovation. Televisions, computers, personal digital assistants, and other high-tech products were not overnight sensations.

Consistent with discrepancy-interruption theory, research shows that brands that are moderately different from other brands in a particular product category engender positive arousal and are evaluated more favorably than brands that are typical of a product category.[21] For example, most soft drinks are high in preservatives and artificial ingredients. However, new all-natural soft drinks (e.g., vitamin water) taste different and interesting and are evaluated positively in blind taste tests. Conversely, most fruit juices are all natural, and consequently, a fruit juice that is high in artificial ingredients tastes different and interesting. This results in more favorable evaluations in blind taste tests as well. See Figure 8.5.

OBJECTIVE 5

Excitation Transfer Theory

Because consumers are bad at interpreting their emotional states, the excitation or arousal produced by one stimulus (e.g., exciting media events, exercise, stimulants, discrepancies, interruptions) can transfer or spillover to other stimuli.[22] Excitation transfer theory rests on four key principles of emotion:

1. Arousal is non-specific with respect to emotion (i.e., arousal intensifies both positive and negative emotions)
2. People are insensitive to small changes in arousal
3. People often look for a single cause for their arousal, even when there are multiple causes
4. Physiological arousal dissipates at a slower rate than perceived arousal

These principles suggest that a narrow window exists in which arousal can transfer from one stimulus to the next, thereby intensifying the emotional experience attributed to the second stimulus. Initially, little transfer occurs because a single, salient stimulus is perceived to be the cause of the arousal (e.g., an exciting movie). After a long period of time, arousal goes away, and nothing is left to be transferred. After a moderate

Tetra Images/Jupiter Images

period of time, however, excitation transfer is possible.

At this intermediate point in time, an individual is still aroused from the original stimulus, but because the stimulus event has passed (e.g., the movie is over), the person doesn't perceive that he is still aroused. For example, an exciting sporting event or action movie is likely to produce arousal that could, potentially, transfer to an advertisement embedded in the program. Ads aired during the Super Bowl and other exciting events may benefit from this excitation transfer process: the advertised product may seem more exciting if its ad is aired during an exciting program. But timing is crucial. If consumers attempt to interpret their emotions while watching an exciting movie or TV program, they would recognize that the source of their arousal is the program, not the products advertised during commercial breaks. However, if people attempt to interpret their emotions shortly after an exciting event, they are more likely to confuse their arousal from the event with interest in the advertised brand.

It's no surprise that watching a scary movie at a theater can produce arousal, and this arousal can later be transferred to your date! In fact, transference produces a more intense emotional response than the original arousal. Furthermore, because people are bad at interpreting their emotional states, the fear produced by a horror movie can be misinterpreted as romantic attraction to the date. Again, timing is crucial. If people attempt to interpret their emotions while watching the horror movie, they should recognize that they are feeling fear. If people attempt to interpret their emotions shortly after the horror movie, however, they are more likely to confuse romantic attraction for fear. Of course, the mass media can produce all kinds of emotions (e.g., love, hate, fear, anger, sadness), and if the timing is right, arousal will transfer to other stimuli (e.g., other people, advertised products, products consumed while watching an exciting event). See Figure 8.6.

FIGURE 8.6   MISATTRIBUTION OF AROUSAL

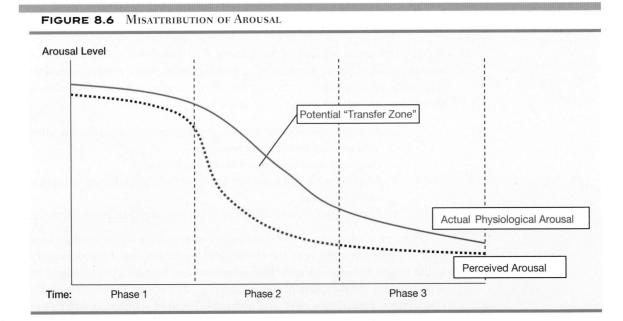

Chapter Summary

Motivation and emotion focus attention and energize behavior. When consumers desperately need something, goal-relevant products are overvalued (the valuation effect) and goal-irrelevant products are undervalued (the devaluation effect). Basic physiological needs must be satisfied before consumers pursue higher-order goals, such as safety, belongingness, and, finally, self-actualization. In addition to these needs and goals, consumers need cognitive consistency. Several types of cognitive consistency are important, including attitude function consistency, balance (consistent relationships among *p-o-x* elements), and behavior-attitude consistency. According to cognitive

dissonance theory, when behaviors and attitudes are inconsistent, consumers are motivated to change their attitudes to make them consistent with their behaviors.

Positive affect increases helpfulness, creativity, and the quality of decision making. Emotion is intense affect or affect plus arousal. Exciting events, unexpected events, interruptions, exercise, and stimulants increase arousal and intensify emotional experiences. Because consumers are bad at interpreting their emotions without the help of contextual cues, one emotion can be confused for another, and arousal produced by one stimulus can be transferred to another.

Key Terms

motivation	Maslow's hierarchy of needs	balance theory
emotion	self-determination theory	cognitive dissonance theory
needs	attitude function theory	arousal
goals	regulatory focus theory	positive affect
drives	affect confirmation model	discrepancy-interruption theory
valuation	instrumental product	excitation transfer theory
devaluation	knowledge function	mood-as-information model
approach	value-expressive function	hedonic product
avoidance	ego-defensive function	
drive theory	adjustment function	

Review and Discussion

1. How does motivation focus attention?
2. How does motivation energize behavior?
3. List the hierarchy of needs from the most basic level to the most advanced level.
4. What factors increase self-determination and intrinsic motivation?
5. Use balance theory to analyze how a specific consumer segment should be linked with a specific celebrity and a specific brand.
6. Discuss some ways people can be tricked into behaving in ways that are not consistent with their attitudes.

7. Think of an ad that, in your opinion, is particularly good at making you feel a strong emotion. How did the advertiser accomplish this?

8. Think of a product so new and different that it made you feel negative emotions at first. How do you feel about this product now?

9. In what ways are motivations and emotions similar?

10. In what ways are motivations and emotions different?

Short Application Exercises

1. Managers are constantly trying to develop ways to motivate their employees to work harder without paying them more. Think of some ways you might be able to accomplish this.

2. Think of some ways you could use advertising to motivate consumers to find out more about your product.

3. Think of some ways excitation transfer theory can be used to make your product more exciting.

4. Form a small group and take turns pretending one person is an actor and the others are the audience. The actor should think of a past emotional event and make a face consistent with the emotion. The actor should use only facial expressions and no verbal communications. The actor should pretend to have several different emotions (e.g., happiness, sadness, anger, fear, anxiety). How good is the actor at expressing emotions nonverbally, and how good is the audience at interpreting the actor's emotional expressions?

MANAGERIAL APPLICATION

Imagine that you work for a large advertising agency. Your supervisor has asked you to analyze the attitude functions of large consumer segments for several different clients. For each client, you need to analyze the need or the desire served by the client's product or service. This provides clues about the attitude function that is most likely to be associated with each product or service. Based on this functional analysis, design an ad that tailors different persuasion techniques to different attitude functions.

YOUR CHALLENGE:

Perform a functional analysis and design appropriate ads for each of the following clients:

1. General Motors

2. Carnival Cruises

3. A local hospital

4. A candidate for U.S. Senator from your state

5. Your university

CHAPTER

9

THE ROLE OF LEARNING AND MEMORY

OBJECTIVES *After studying this chapter, you will be able to...*

1 | Explain how classical conditioning works in advertising.

2 | Explain how operant conditioning works in sales promotion.

3 | Identify misleading ads that encourage consumers to form incorrect inferences.

4 | Define the seven sins of memory.

MARTINI & ROSSI

Martini & Rossi uses advertising to educate consumers about its product.

Most people don't like martinis the first time they try them. The first sip often seems surprisingly dry, medicinal, and high in alcohol. However, preferences change over time as people learn and change. Even if people don't like martinis at first, many learn to like martinis the more they drink them. Companies like Martini & Rossi count on this type of change. Martini drinkers also often learn to appreciate subtle differences among different brands of gin (e.g., Boodles, Bombay Sapphire, Tanqueray) and different brands of vermouth (e.g., Martini & Rossi, Nouilly Prat, Vya). They also often experiment with different brands of olives and appreciate martini glasses. Martini & Rossi uses advertising and other promotional efforts to educate consumers about its product and its uses, in addition to simply get consumers to purchase the product to aid in this learning process. How do consumers acquire a taste for products that weren't appealing initially? What role does learning play in preference formation? How does learning influence memory and the stability of preferences over time? We will explore these questions in this chapter.

OBJECTIVE 1

The Importance of Learning and Memory

In our continuing discussion of consumer information processing, this chapter discusses the role of learning and memory in consumer behavior. *Learning*, as it pertains to consumer behavior, is the process of acquiring new information and knowledge about products and services for application to future behavior. As learning increases, the amount of knowledge about products and services stored in a consumer's memory also increases. *Memory* enables past experiences and learning to influence current behavior. Without memory, we cannot physically function in society. People often underestimate how important memory is for everyday behavior; most people don't fully appreciate how essential memory is until this function is seriously impaired as a result of health conditions such as Alzheimer's, Korsakov's syndrome, or serious head trauma.

Consumer behavior research shows that learning plays an important role in preference formation.[1] Learning changes the way consumers think about and use products. The more consumers learn about a product category, the more likely they are to use new words and phrases to describe their consumption experiences, and the more likely they are to focus on product attributes that didn't seem as important when they first tried the product. In other words, learning enriches consumers' experiences with products and services, and of course, influences their potential future behavior related to the product.

Types of Learning

People learn in many ways. How people learn has been studied extensively in medicine, psychology, sociology, and education, and a number of learning theories have been developed. Two of these theories, classical conditioning and operant conditioning, are discussed next.

Classical Conditioning

Learning leads to knowledge. *Knowledge* is created when a person makes associations between concepts. For example, associating touching a hot stove burner with pain creates knowledge about how to behave around stoves. One way associations between concepts are formed is by simply thinking about the concepts. Thinking about two objects or ideas (like the hot stove burner and pain) at the same time is enough to form an association in memory; repeatedly thinking about two things at the same time increases the strength of the association. The nature of the objects or ideas and the timing are also crucial for learning, as we shall see shortly.

Classical conditioning (or Pavlovian conditioning) is a learning theory centered on creating associations between meaningful objects or ideas (or what researchers call *stimuli*) to elicit desired responses. In a classic example, a researcher named Ivan Pavlov in the 1920s illustrated classical conditioning with a dog, some food, and a bell. Pavlov would place food in front of a dog, which made the dog salivate, naturally. Every time Pavlov fed the dog, he would also ring a bell. Eventually, the dog would begin to salivate simply at the sound of the bell, without the food present.

According to the theory, learning results when a meaningful object, called an **unconditioned stimulus** (the dog's food), is paired with another object, called a **conditioned stimulus** (the bell). The unconditioned stimulus has a known response called an **unconditioned response** (salivation). Over time, the pairing leads to the response, without the original unconditioned stimulus, which is called the **conditioned response** (salivation at the sound of the bell without the food present).[2]

In a consumer behavior setting, advertisers use a wide variety of meaningful unconditioned stimuli, including catchy music, sexy models, likable celebrities, cute animals, pretty scenery, and so on.[3] These positive unconditioned stimuli produce positive unconditioned responses, such as amusement, joy, happiness, attraction, etc. Negative unconditioned stimuli produce negative unconditioned responses or feelings. The brand serves as the conditioned stimuli (just like the bell in Pavlov's experiment). By pairing meaningful unconditioned stimuli with the brand, the advertiser hopes to *condition* consumers to feel positively about the brand. Hence, it is crucial for advertisers to select unconditioned stimuli that appeal to the target market.

Pairing an unconditioned stimulus with an unconditioned stimulus repeatedly leads to *stimulus generalization*, or to similar responses to both stimuli. This means that people learn to associate the unconditioned stimuli or the background elements of the ad with the conditioned stimulus, the brand itself. Once an association is learned, people respond similarly to the conditioned stimulus and to the unconditioned stimulus. Importantly, this occurs even when the conditioned stimulus is presented alone. After learning an association between an advertised brand and the positive background elements of an ad, consumers often encounter the advertised brand alone in a store. To the extent that learning or conditioning was effective, the same feelings generated by the advertisement should occur when the brand is encountered in the store without any advertising.

Timing is crucial. Greater learning or conditioning occurs when the conditioned stimulus is presented before the unconditioned stimulus. This is known as **forward conditioning** because the presence of the conditioned stimulus can be used to predict the subsequent occurrence of the unconditioned stimulus. Many advertisements, however, use **backward conditioning**. That is, the conditioned stimulus (the advertised brand) is presented after the unconditioned stimulus (e.g., likable music, people, places, or things). Learning still takes place, but the associations are weaker; higher levels of repetitive advertising are needed for learning to occur. Furthermore, many ads use unconditioned stimuli that are ineffective because they were previously encountered alone without pairing (the unconditioned stimulus **pre-exposure effect**). For example, a popular song that has been repeatedly encountered alone is not a good candidate for classical conditioning because consumers have been pre-exposed to the music. The familiar song is not likely to become associated with a brand. Classical conditioning is also less effective for old, familiar brands than for new, less familiar brands.[4]

Classical conditioning is also less effective when multiple conditioned stimuli predict the subsequent occurrence of an unconditioned stimulus.[5] Conditioned stimuli compete with one another for predictive strength. Consequently, as the predictive strength of one stimulus increases, the predictive strength of other stimuli decreases. Again, timing is paramount. The order in which stimuli are presented has an important influence on subsequent learning. For example, after consumers learn that a target attribute (e.g., brand name) is useful for predicting quality, other cues (i.e., other attributes) seem unpredictive. This is known as **blocking** because the first predictive stimulus blocks or prevents learning for other predictive stimuli encountered later. During the learning phase of a recent study on blocking, participants received

EYE ON INTERNATIONAL

MEXICAN "CHAMPAGNE"

To facilitate learning about international marketing, Professor James Kellaris of the University of Cincinnati led a group of students on a field trip to Mexico. The students received a 45-minute tour of the Freixenet manufacturing facility conducted by a representative of Freixenet. Freixenet is a Mexican "champagne," or more accurately, a Mexican sparkling wine. At the end of the 45-minute tour, the Freixenet representative asked if there were any questions. One of the students pointed to a large container and asked, "Is there wine in there?" What does this question reveal about the learning process? It demonstrates that exposing people to a large amount of information is not sufficient to produce learning. Learning requires motivation, attention, and most importantly, relating new information to old information stored in memory and thinking about the implications of new information.

Screen shot provided by Freixenet USA/Intwine Marketing

Even though the same grapes (usually a blend of chardonnay, pinot meunier, and pinot noir) and the same process (méthode Champenoise) are used to make sparkling wine worldwide, sparkling wine can be called champagne only if it is made in the Champagne region of France. Dom Pèrignon is a classic example of French champagne, and it is very famous because it is the pioneering brand or the first "sparkling" wine ever produced. Excellent sparking wines are made in many other countries also, including Freixenet of Mexico, Domaine Carneros of California, in the United States, Asti Spumanti of Italy, Cava of Spain, and the sparkling wines of Australia. Why do you think it is important to the French that the term "champagne" be reserved for sparkling wines made in the Champagne region? Why do you think sparkling wine is such a popular product in many different countries?

attribute (airecell or closed-cell compartments) and brand name (Hypalon or Riken) information for several products in an unfamiliar category (rafts).[6] Either the type of compartment or the brand name predicted quality ratings. During a second learning phase, a redundant cue (tubular or I-beam floor) also predicted quality ratings. During the test phase, participants judged the quality of several new raft products. Learning about the importance of a redundant cue was blocked by prior learning about the first predictive cue, regardless of whether the first predictive cue was a brand name or an attribute.

In a follow-up study, researchers investigated the competition between attribute versus brand name information as signals for quality by manipulating the predictive strength of attribute and brand cues (experimental conditions) or brand cues only (control conditions).[7] During the learning phase, participants received attribute (Alpine class down fill or regular down fill) and brand name (Hypalon or Riken) information for several products in an unfamiliar category (down jackets). During the test phase, participants judged the quality of several new products. The results showed that the brand name had a weaker effect on quality judgments when the target attribute was predictive (vs. unpredictive) of product quality. This pattern was observed for new products in the original product category (down jackets), as well as in a different product category (wool sweaters). This effect is reduced when brand–quality associations are learned prior to attribute–quality associations or when no information about quality is provided during the learning phase. Although conventional wisdom suggests that building strong brands requires marketers to design products with high-quality attributes, the results of these studies show that attribute equity undermines brand equity when unambiguous information about quality is available.

Learning via classical conditioning is important in advertising and in many other situations as well. Think about the importance of timing for learning about the benefits and costs of using credit cards to buy products. The benefits of credit card use are immediate: the product or service is yours to enjoy as soon as you use your card. Consequently, strong credit card–benefit associations are learned by consumers. However, the costs of credit card use are delayed: the credit card bill arrives days or weeks after the credit card purchase is made. Consequently, weak credit card–cost associations are learned by consumers. In other words, the benefits of using credit cards are more strongly associated with credit cards than are the costs of using credit cards. This conditions or brainwashes consumers into spending more when they use their credit cards.

To test this idea, a study of credit cards and classical conditioning examined the average size of tips left by restaurant patrons who paid using credit card versus those using cash.[8] Customers who paid by credit card left larger tips. In a follow-up study, consumers were asked to play a "Price Is Right" game by guessing the prices of several products shown on a computer monitor. In the experimental condition, a small plastic MasterCard sign was placed next to the computer

Consumers spend more and reach the decision to spend more quickly when credit card symbols are present.

monitor. In the control condition, the sign was removed. Higher price estimates were formed when the MasterCard sign was present than when the MasterCard sign was absent. In another follow-up study, several products and their prices were displayed on a computer monitor, and consumers were asked to press one key if they were willing to buy each product and a different key if they were unwilling to buy the product. Decision times to buy the product were faster when the MasterCard sign was present than when the MasterCard sign was absent. A final study found that college students donated more to charity (The United Way) when the request to donate was made in a room containing credit-card logos, despite the fact that the donations had to be cash! Together, these results show that consumers spend more and reach the decision to spend faster when credit card symbols are present rather than absent. As a result, retailers, catalog marketers, and Internet marketers should prominently display credit card symbols in menus, point-of-purchase displays, catalogs, Web pages, and other marketing communications, because it is very likely that their customers will make larger purchases if they know they can use their credit cards.

OBJECTIVE 2

Operant Conditioning

In classical conditioning, the stimulus precedes the response, but in **operant conditioning** (or instrumental conditioning), the stimulus follows the response.[9] **Positive reinforcement**, or the presence of a reward, increases the probability of a response, while **negative reinforcement**, or the absence of **punishment,** also increases the probability of a response. **Extinction**, or the absence of a reward, decreases the probability of a response. The presence of punishment also decreases the probability of a response. Learning via operant conditioning is faster under conditions of **continuous reinforcement**, or when reinforcement occurs every time the desired response occurs. However, learning via operant conditioning is more persistent under conditions of **partial reinforcement**, or when reinforcement occurs only some of the times the desired response occurs.

Rewards used in marketing include coupons, bonus points, rebates, and prizes given to consumers who buy your product. Rewards increase the probability of repeat purchase. Operant conditioning can also be used to influence consumers who do not currently use your product. Negative reinforcements in marketing include eliminating expensive shipping terms, reducing paperwork associated with rebates and warranties, or eliminating long waiting lines or delivery times. **Shaping**, or reinforcing successive approximations of the desired response, also can be used to encourage current non-users to buy your product. For example, a retailer may first reward non-users to visit the mall where the store is located by offering a free fashion show. Then, the retailer may encourage non-users to visit the store by offering a door prize. Next, the retailer may encourage non-users to buy products by offering a discount on products purchased in the store using a store credit card. Finally, when consumers buy products, the retailer can reward them by offering frequent-user bonus points for each purchase.

Comprehension and Miscomprehension

Comprehending or understanding information requires relating new information presented in the environment to old information stored in memory.[10] Because new information is typically incomplete, consumers must form inferences to fill in missing details to make sense out of the new information. For example, when reading a story

ETHICS

Some ads take advantage of consumers' assumptions about advertising claims that are literally true but figuratively false.[37] Because the claims are literally true, advertisers can argue that they are not lying. However, consumers' assumptions about the meaning of the advertised claims can make the claims misleading. For example, the word "may" implies maybe yes and maybe no. However, consumers often assume that "may" probably means yes. So, when an ad states that Brand X may relieve pain, consumers often assume that yes, Brand X does relieve pain.

Comparison omission can also mislead consumers. When an ad states that Brand Y gasoline gives you greater mileage, consumers typically assume that this means that Brand Y gives you greater mileage than other brands of gasoline. The ad never stated this directly, and after all, Brand Y does give you greater mileage than water. Piecemeal information can also make a product seem better than it actually is. For example, an ad stating that a Brand Z car had more head room than a Mercedes Benz, more leg room than a BMW, and more trunk space than a Lexus implies that Brand Z is better than each of these luxury automobiles. In reality, the differences were trivial: Brand Z has 1/10th of an inch more head room than a Mercedes Benz, 1/5th of an inch more leg room than a BMW, and 1/15th of an inch more trunk space than a Lexus. Thus, each of the piecemeal claims are literally true, but the actual differences are trivial. What are the ethical implications of misleading ads that are literally true but figuratively false? Should firms be allowed to exploit consumers in this manner? What is the best way to protect consumers from misleading advertising?

stating that Bob pounded a nail into the wall, people automatically infer that Bob used a hammer even though the story never stated this.[11] Similarly, when reading an ad for a new automobile, consumers automatically infer that the automobile has standard features, such as automatic transmission, anti-lock brakes, etc., even if the ad never mentions these features. Background knowledge helps people fill in missing details to make sense of new information. However, sometimes new information is so extreme, it invites consumers to form specific inferences. For example, the features of a Lexus are so luxurious that it is difficult not to infer that the Lexus is a luxury automobile while examining it. Consumers' goals also influence what inferences consumers are likely to form. For example, consumers with the goal of purchasing a luxury automobile are likely to evaluate all automobiles in terms of the attributes that mean luxury to them.

As comprehension increases, memory performance also increases. It is difficult to remember meaningless information. This is why professors use memory tests (e.g., multiple choice exams, fill-in-the-blank questions, short essay questions) to assess comprehension. If a student does not understand the course material, the student is not likely to remember much, and will probably perform poorly on the exam. Controlled laboratory studies show that students have great difficulty memorizing meaningless statements, such as "the notes went sour because the bag was ripped."[12] However, these statements were easy to remember when the students were given a theme word (e.g., "bag pipe") that made the statements more meaningful. Ideally, students should always try to make new course material more meaningful by relating it to prior knowledge.

OBJECTIVE 3   Because consumers use background knowledge to fill in missing details, ads can mislead consumers by presenting claims that are literally true but figuratively false. Claims stating that a product *may* be effective, or is *more* effective, or is *recommended* by experts often lead consumers to assume that the product is better than it actually is.[13] When consumers see an ad stating, "Be popular! Brush with UltraBrite!" they often assume that brushing with UltraBrite will make them more popular, even though the ad never directly stated this. When consumers see an ad stating, "Women who look younger use Oil of Olay," they often assume that using Oil of Olay will make them look younger, even though the ad never stated this. Advertisements often imply much more than what is actually stated, and such implications can be misleading.

Visual images can also contain false implications.[14] For example, a Milky Way ad transforms a glass of milk into a candy bar, implying that the candy bar is as nutritious as a glass of milk. A Mattel advertisement uses extreme close-ups and camera angles that make Hot Wheels toy cars appear much faster than they actually are. A Campbell's soup ad shows a bowl of soup with meat, potatoes, and vegetables bursting above the broth level. What consumers do not know is that marbles are in the bottom of the bowl, pushing the solid ingredients above the broth level.

A Black Flag ad shows two glass tanks filled with cockroaches. One tank is sprayed with Black Flag, and most of the cockroaches die. The other tank is sprayed with another leading brand, but few cockroaches die. What consumers are not told is that the cockroaches in the second tank are bred to be resistant to the other leading brand of insecticide.

Misleading advertising practices are unfair because consumers must form inferences and make assumptions to comprehend advertising claims. Sometimes the Federal Trade Commission (FTC) orders advertisers to air **corrective advertising** that states that a previous ad was misleading, as in the famous Listerine case. A Listerine ad stated that Listerine kills germs that cause colds, which simply was not true. Listerine's corrective ad stated that Listerine does not help prevent colds. Nevertheless, extensive research has shown that corrective advertising is typically ineffective[15] because consumers have difficulty changing their beliefs dramatically, even when they realize that those beliefs are wrong.[16]

Memory

Memory researchers often use a computer metaphor to explain how memory works.[17] A computer has a hard drive that can store a large number of inactive files. A computer also allows users to retrieve a file from the hard drive and bring it into active memory so the file can be processed (e.g., edited or used). Similarly, people have a long-term memory system that stores a large amount of inactive data or knowledge. To use such knowledge, however, people must retrieve a "file" from long-term memory and bring

© Dave Teel/CORBIS

in into short-term memory to process it further. All thinking and reasoning occurs in short-term memory, but only a small amount of information can be held in short-term memory at any given time (7 plus-or-minus 2 chunks or units). If this information is not used, it is lost less than 18 seconds later (hence, the name "short-term memory"). By contrast, long-term memory appears to store an unlimited amount of information for a long period of time. Nevertheless, three different types of forgetting can occur in long-term memory:

1. Original information is not maintained
2. New information is not successfully stored in memory
3. New knowledge overrides existing information, or vice-versa

Information held in long-term memory can also be distorted or changed over time. Furthermore, sometimes consumers can't forget things that they'd prefer to forget. We discuss how consumers forget information in the next section.

(O B J E C T I V E 4)

The Seven Sins of Memory

Although memory influences nearly every thought and action we take, memory can also be fallible. There are seven basic mistakes or "sins" of memory: transience, absent-mindedness, blocking, misattribution, suggestibility, bias, and persistence.[18] The first three sins refer to three different types of forgetting. The second three refer to three different types of distortion. Persistence refers to the inability to forget things one wants to forget.

TRANSIENCE   **Transience** refers to forgetting over time. If you don't use it, you lose it: If knowledge is not used for a long period of time, information loss can occur. Recently processed information is more **accessible** or easy to retrieve, relative to information that was processed long ago. Information accessibility decreases with the passage of time. Hence, it is easier to remember commercials we viewed recently than to remember commercials we viewed long ago. However, the passage of time is not the only variable that influences forgetting. Forgetting can also occur as a result of shallow processing (absent-mindedness) or interference from other information stored in memory (blocking).

ABSENT-MINDEDNESS   **Absent-mindedness** refers to forgetting as a result of shallow or superficial processing of information during encoding or retrieval. **Encoding** refers to attention, comprehension, and the transference of information from short-term memory to long-term memory. **Retrieval** refers to the transference of information from long-term memory to short-term memory. Lapses of attention or effort during encoding or retrieval can lead to forgetting. If consumers are unmotivated to process information carefully because of a lack of interest in a product, or if they are unable to process information carefully because of distractions or attempts to perform several cognitive tasks simultaneously (divided attention), absent-mindedness and the forgetting associated with it are likely to occur.

Depth-of-processing research shows that memory performance improves with effort.[19] A given word is easier to remember if it is processed at a deep level rather than at a shallow level. Level of processing can be manipulated experimentally by varying the difficulty of the questions we are asked about a word. For example, shallow encoding occurs when people are asked a simple question: Is TIDE printed in uppercase letters? Deeper encoding occurs when people are asked a more difficult question: Is TIDE a type of detergent? The word TIDE is more likely to be remembered when it is processed intensely rather than superficially. Consequently, ads that encourage consumers to think deeply about a product are more memorable than ads that encourage cursory processing. In a similar vein, simply reading a bunch of words is a bad way to prepare for an exam. Thinking deeply about the concepts, generating examples of the concepts, and relating the concepts to prior knowledge and experience is a much better way to study. Research on the **generation effect** shows that memory performance is enhanced when people generate their own answers to questions rather than simply reading them.[20] This occurs because generating answers requires more effort than simply reading answers, and memory improves as effort increases.

Absent-mindedness can also occur at the time of retrieval. When distracted, consumers often forget to perform actions they intended to perform. Consumers forget to take their medicine, pick up certain items at the grocery store, or keep appointments. In each example, consumers forget to perform a future action even though

Memory aids such as electronic devices help eliminate absent-mindedness.

Image courtesy of The Advertising Archives

they intended to do so. Memory aids such as post-it notes, pocket calendars, PDAs, and even tying string around a finger are often used to prevent this type of forgetting.

BLOCKING   Forgetting frequently occurs because the information one is trying to retrieve is temporarily inaccessible as a result of **blocking** or interference from related information. The information one is trying to retrieve is stored in memory; it has not been lost over time; it had been encoded deeply; but the search for it in one's memory is not always successful. Sometimes people know they know the answer to a question, but they cannot quite put their finger on it. This is known as the **tip-of-the-tongue effect**: The answer seems to be on the tip of your tongue, but you can't quite retrieve it.[21] Students often complain that they knew the answer to an exam question, but couldn't retrieve it until after the exam was over. The answer was temporarily inaccessible because "ugly sisters" blocked or prevented retrieval of the correct answer. The name "ugly sisters" comes from the story of Cinderella, in which the nice Cinderella was dominated by her mean older sisters. In memory research, ugly sisters are incorrect answers related to the correct answer, and they are retrieved repeatedly instead of the correct answer.

The tip-of-the-tongue effect shows that forgetting can occur even when the answer to a question is stored somewhere in long-term memory. The answer did not fade or decay over time. Instead, the answer is temporarily inaccessible because of interference from related information. Studies of very long-term memory show that people can remember information learned in high school (e.g., foreign languages, mathematics) even more than 50 years![22] Again, this shows that long-term memories do not necessarily fade or decay over time.

Studies of relearning provide the best evidence for forgetting without information loss. Relearning something you thought you forgot (e.g., foreign languages, mathematics) is easier than learning something for the first time.[23] In classic relearning studies, participants learned 20 pairs of numbers and words (e.g., 43-dog). Two weeks later, participants forgot about 25 percent of this material. In the relearning condition, participants relearned the same 20 pairs of numbers and words. In the control condition, participants learned new words paired with old numbers for all forgotten pairs (e.g., the original 43-dog was changed to 43-house). Memory performance was far better in the relearning condition than in the control condition. This result could not occur if forgotten information were lost forever.

According to the association principle of long-term memory, each **node**. idea, or piece of information stored in memory is connected to other nodes that are conceptually related by links known as **associations**.[24] Associations are learned via classical conditioning and operant conditioning. Related nodes are connected in a complex **associative network,** in which closely related nodes are connected directly by a single association, and distantly related nodes are connected by a chain or series of associations. **Activation** or retrieval refers to the transfer of information from inactive long-term memory to active short-term memory. **Spreading activation** refers to the idea that when people retrieve a particular node, they automatically think about other closely related nodes. An associative network is like a complex system of irrigation ditches; each node is like a pool of water connected to other pools via a system of ditches. When one pool is filled with water, the water spills out to other nearby pools. The more water poured into a pool, the farther the spillage spreads. Eventually, the water runs out and the spreading stops.

For example, whenever consumers think about a brand name, like McDonald's, they start thinking about associations to the brand (e.g., Big Macs, fries, shakes, Ronald

FIGURE 9.1 ASSOCIATIVE NETWORK

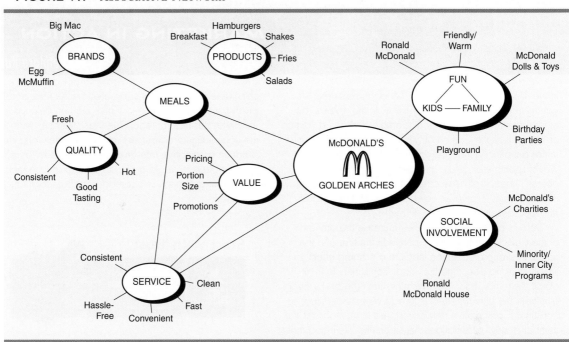

McDonald). A strong association leads to a **priming effect**: Simply thinking about the brand leads consumers to think about closely related concepts. The priming effect can be reduced or eliminated by adding new associations to consumers' associative networks. As the number of new associations increases, the likelihood that consumers will think about a particular old association decreases. New associations increase the complexity of consumers' associative networks and produce **associative interference**, in which the new associations compete with and block old associations.

Associative interference is commonly observed in advertising.[25] Old ads compete with new ads, and vice versa. **Proactive interference** occurs when information learned earlier blocks memory for information learned later. **Retroactive interference** occurs when information learned later blocks memory for information learned earlier. Both types of interference are common in advertising. Furthermore, greater proactive and retroactive interference occurs with advertisements for brands in the same product category (e.g., ads for different brands of cereal) than for brands in different product categories (e.g., ads for cereal and for cars).

Blocking is often frustrating because people realize that they know the answer they're looking for, but they can't find it. How can blocking be reduced? According to the **encoding-specificity principle**, memory is context dependent.[26] Contextual or background cues have a surprisingly powerful influence on memory performance. During encoding, contextual cues are encoded along with the target information one is trying to remember. Later, during retrieval, the contextual cues may be the same or different. Memory performance is enhanced when the contextual cues at the time of encoding and at the time of retrieval match or are highly similar. As the degree of similarity decreases, memory performance decreases.

For example, students typically attend lectures and take exams in the same classroom. In this case, the contextual cues (e.g., lighting, seating, background noise level, etc.) are the same during encoding (learning) and retrieval (taking an exam), and this

MARKETING IN ACTION

Marketplace Rumors

In the 1970s a rumor started that McDonald's used worms in its hamburger meat mixture. In the 1980s, another rumor said that Procter & Gamble donated a portion of its profits to the Church of Satan. In the 1990s, a third rumor announced that parked Audi 4000s automobiles would spontaneously slip into gear and crash into large objects. In each of these cases, the firms reacted by denying the rumors. However, sales of each of these brands dropped despite the denials. Why?

Denials backfire because they increase the strength of the association in memory between the firm and the rumor. A strong association leads to a **priming effect**: simply thinking about the firm leads consumers to think about the rumor associated with the firm. The best way to eliminate the priming effect is to add new associations to consumers' associative networks stored in memory. As the number of new associations increases, the likelihood that consumers will think about the rumor decreases.

New associations can include information on the various products and services offered by a firm, the charitable organizations sponsored by the firm, and the prestigious organizations to which the firm belongs (e.g., the Better Business Bureau). New associations increase the complexity of consumers' associative networks and produce **associative interference**. That is, new associations compete with old associations and reduce the probability that activation will spread to old associations.

Council of Better Business Bureaus

improves memory. If a professor wants to be mean, he or she could lecture in one room and give exams in a different room. In this case, the contextual cues present during encoding and during retrieval are different, and this reduces memory performance. Even small seemingly irrelevant background differences can have dramatic effects on memory performance. Larger background differences have even more dramatic effects. For example, students often hurt themselves by studying for an exam late at night while drinking lots of coffee. Then they take the exam in the morning without coffee. Nighttime contexts differ from daytime contexts in many respects (e.g., lighting, seating, fatigue levels, hunger levels, etc.) and high caffeine contexts differ from low caffeine contexts in many respects (e.g., alertness levels, thirst levels, etc.). The greater the differences between encoding contexts and retrieval contexts, the more memory performance decreases.

Marketers can use the encoding-specificity principle to their advantage by trying to increase the similarity of contextual cues present during encoding and during retrieval. Consumers often encode information about products while watching TV at home. Later, while shopping at a grocery store, they are likely to retrieve information about products to make informed purchase decisions. Obviously, large contextual differences exist between the home environment and the grocery store environment. These differences can be reduced by placing characters from advertisements viewed at home in the grocery store environment. For example, Life cereal's TV commercials feature Little Mikey, and Little Mikey's picture appears on boxes of Life cereal in grocery stores. Other advertising characters (e.g., the Pillsbury doughboy, Tony the tiger, the Keebler elves, Juan Valdez) are also featured on product packages or point-of-purchase displays to help consumers remember information from advertisements they viewed in different contexts.

MISATTRIBUTION   Forgetting isn't the only memory problem consumers encounter. Memory can also be distorted from **misattribution**. Three different types of memory misattributions or confusions are possible:

1. source confusion
2. feelings of familiarity
3. false memories

Source confusion occurs when consumers remember reading a fact about a product but misremember where they read it.[27] Sometimes consumers believe that they read the information from a credible source (e.g., *Consumer Reports*), but they actually read it from a noncredible source (e.g., *National Enquirer*). Sometimes consumers believe that the conclusions they drew after reading a message about a product were actually stated in the message. In short, source confusion can lead consumers to trust product information more than they should.

The second type of memory misattribution is the tendency to confuse feelings of familiarity with a wide variety of possible judgments, including fame, confidence, liking, and truth.[28] The more familiar a brand name seems, the more famous and popular the brand seems to be. Answers to questions that come to mind readily are held with greater confidence. The more familiar an initially neutral product becomes, the more consumers like the product. This is known as the **mere exposure effect** because repeated exposure to a product increases familiarity and liking. This is one reason why consumers learn to like novel foods (e.g., sushi), beverages (e.g., martinis), words (e.g., afworbu), and songs (e.g., new tunes heard on the radio) more over time. As the familiarity of a product claim increases, the more consumers believe the claim. This is known as the **truth effect**.[29] Simple repetition (e.g., repetitive advertising) is one way to increase the familiarity of a product, a claim, or an idea, and simple repetition can increase judgments of fame, confidence, liking, or truth. Increasing the ease with which consumers can perceive, read, or comprehend product information also increases familiarity. Consumers are most likely to confuse familiarity with fame, confidence, liking, or truth when their attention is divided during encoding, retrieval, or both.

Stefan_Redel/iStockphoto.com

The third type of memory misattribution is a false memory, or the tendency to remember items or events that never happened.[30] In a typical false memory experiment, people study a list of words that are closely related to a non-presented word. For example, the words "sugar," "sweet," "chocolate," and "tasty" are closely related to the non-presented word "candy." When people are later asked to recall as many words from the list as possible, they frequently recall the word "candy," even though it was not presented. This occurs because it is easier to remember the gist or the general meaning of the presented words than to remember the specific presented words themselves.

SUGGESTIBILITY   Misleading questions and suggestions can also lead to memory distortion.[31] For example, people who witness an automobile accident remember different events when they are asked, "How fast was the car going when it ran past the stop sign?"

versus "How fast was the car going when it ran past the yield sign?" They also remember different events when they are asked, "How fast was the car going when it smashed into the other car?" versus "How fast was the car going when it bumped into the other car?" Similarly, adults asked to remember their childhood experiences are more likely to remember instances of child abuse if they receive suggestions of child abuse from a psychotherapist. Advertising can also produce memory distortion. For example, after tasting a bland orange juice, consumers are more likely to misremember the orange juice as flavorful after seeing an ad suggesting that the product is flavorful than after seeing no ad. Advertising can distort memory for past experiences with a product.

BIAS   Previously viewed advertising can also influence what is learned from current product experiences.[32] Advertising influences consumers' expectations, and expectations subsequently color what consumers see. To the extent that product experiences are ambiguous or open to multiple interpretations, expectations guide the interpretation of product experiences. Products seem larger, smaller, heavier, lighter, tastier, or more comfortable if consumers expect them to be larger, smaller, heavier, lighter, tastier, or more comfortable, respectively. Prior beliefs can bias current beliefs and experiences.[33] Consequently, learning from experience becomes difficult because prior beliefs and current experiences are perceived as more consistent than they actually are.

The opposite is also possible. Current beliefs can bias memory for prior beliefs and experiences. In a recent study, marketers were led to prefer supplier A over supplier B. Three weeks later, the same marketers were led to prefer supplier B over supplier A. When they were asked about their earlier preference, the marketers indicated that they always preferred supplier A.[34] Even when preferences change dramatically over time, people often assume that their earlier preferences were the same as their current preferences. Consequently, people often believe that their preferences are more consistent than they actually are.

PERSISTENCE   Sometimes people can't forget things they want to forget. Traumatic events are often difficult to forget. Some songs and advertising jingles get stuck in our heads. This is known as earworm.[35] Try not to think about a catchy song (such as "Who Let the Dogs Out") or advertising jingle (such as the Subway jingle) that you've heard recently. Simple, catchy, repetitive tunes are especially likely to produce earworm. Trying not to think about a specific song, object, or issuep is surprisingly difficult. After trying not to think about a specific topic, people are more likely to think about it later when they are no longer trying not to think about it! Momentary distractions can also lead people to think more about a topic they are trying not to think about. The **persistence** of unwanted thoughts can be frustrating, distracting, and sometimes depressing.

Chapter Summary

Learning produces knowledge about products, and memory determines how knowledge about products is accessed and used. Associations between unconditioned and conditioned stimuli are learned via classical conditioning. Associations between responses and consequences are learned via operant conditioning. Associations are the building blocks of knowledge stored in memory. Although memory influences nearly all aspects of consumer behavior, most consumers underestimate the importance of memory. The seven sins of memory are side effects of an otherwise adaptive memory system. The sins of forgetting are transience (forgetting over time),

absent-mindedness (forgetting because of a lack of effort during encoding or during retrieval), and blocking (forgetting as a result of interference resulting from cue competition). The sins of distortion are misattribution (distortion as a result of confusion), suggestibility (distortion as a result of the questions and suggestions of others), and bias (distortion because of overestimating the consistency of the past and the present, and vice versa). The sin of persistence refers to the inability to forget what one wants to forget. Despite these sins, memory enables consumers to perform remarkably complex thinking, reasoning, and decision-making activities.

Key Terms

classical conditioning	negative reinforcement	absent-mindedness
unconditioned stimulus	punishment	blocking
conditioned stimulus	extinction	misattribution
unconditioned response	shaping	suggestibility
conditioned response	continuous reinforcement	persistence
forward conditioning	partial reinforcement	priming effect
backward conditioning	encoding	associative interference
pre-exposure effect	retrieval	proactive interference
operant conditioning	accessibility	retroactive interference
positive reinforcement	transience	encoding-specificity principle

Review and Discussion

1. What are the differences between classical conditioning and operant conditioning?
2. How does learning influence memory?
3. How does memory influence learning?
4. Discuss three different ways forgetting occurs.
5. Discuss three different ways memory distortion occurs.
6. Discuss some ways that forgetting influences consumer behavior.
7. Discuss some ways that memory distortion influences consumer behavior.
8. What are the three types of memory misattributions?
9. When and how does previously viewed advertising influence current beliefs?
10. When and how does advertising viewed today influence memory for past product experiences?

Short Application Exercises

1. Think of some ways you could use classical conditioning in advertising.

2. Think of some ways you could design an advertisement that would improve memory for the advertised brand and for claims about the advertised brand.

3. Think of some ways you could design an advertisement that would block memory for competing brands and for claims about competing brands.

4. Form a small group and create a memory test for other small groups. Each group should pick a product category, write down a list of ten brands, and purposely omit one leading brand. Read the list quickly to the memory test takers and ask them to count backwards from 100 by threes for about 20 seconds. Then ask the test takers to recall as many brand names as possible. How many test takers mention the omitted leading brand? Is it possible to create false memories in only 20 seconds?

MANAGERIAL APPLICATION

Imagine that you work for the Consumers Union, the consumer protection organization that publishes *Consumer Reports*. Your supervisor asked you to test the effectiveness of several subliminal self-help CDs that are currently on the market. Before designing your experiment, you performed a literature review and found a classic experiment on the effectiveness of subliminal self-help audiotapes. Students were randomly assigned to conditions in a 2 × 2 factorial design in which expectations and audiotape contents were manipulated experimentally.[36] Half the students were told that the audiotape improved memory performance. The other half were told that the audiotape improved self-esteem.

Half of the students received the memory audiotape, and half received the self-esteem audiotape,

regardless of what they were told earlier. Hence, in half of the conditions, expectations and content matched (e.g., students expected the audiotape to improve memory and the audiotape was supposed to actually improve memory). For the remaining half, expectations and content were mismatched (e.g., students expected the audiotape to improve memory, but the audiotape was supposed to actually improve self-esteem). The results showed that expectations influenced memory performance and self-esteem ratings and that the content of the audiotapes had no effect. Imagine that you conducted a replication experiment using currently available subliminal self-help CDs and that you obtained the same pattern of results.

YOUR CHALLENGE:

1. Explain your results. Which of the seven sins of memory is at work here and how is it operating?

2. Placebo effects are common in medical research. Which of the seven sins of memory is responsible for placebo effects? How do medical researchers design experiments to test for placebo effects?

3. How are marketing expectation effects and medical placebo effects similar?

4. How would you protect consumers from subliminal self-help CDs that don't work?

AUTOMATIC INFORMATION PROCESSING

OBJECTIVES *After studying this chapter, you will be able to...*

1 | Define automatic information processing.

2 | Explain the benefits of unconscious thought.

3 | Explain thin slice theory.

4 | Identify many different types of priming effects.

5 | Describe subliminal priming and persuasion.

EFFECTS OF FRENCH VS. GERMAN MUSIC ON PURCHASE BEHAVIOR

Chiyacat/iStockphoto.com

Can the background music played in a store influence consumer choice? To answer this question, an experiment was conducted in which either French music or German music was played in a store.[1] The results showed that consumers bought more French wine when French music was played. The results also showed that consumers bought more German wine when German music was played. These results were surprising because the consumers did not think that the music had any influence on them. Furthermore, France is famous for dry red wines, like the cabernet sauvignon-merlot blends of Bordeaux and the pinot noir of Burgundy. However, Germany is famous for sweet white wines, like Riesling, Gewurtztraminer, and Kabinett. Even though the styles of wine are very different, background music influenced choices and did so without consumers' awareness or intention.

What Is Automatic Information Processing?

Automatic information processing refers to mental processes that occur without awareness or intention, but nevertheless influence judgments, feelings, goals, and behaviors.[2] Consumers do many things without their conscious awareness. For example, in a classic study, consumers were shown four pairs of nylon stockings and were asked to choose the best pair.[3] The stockings were arranged from left to right on a table, and the results showed that most consumers preferred the right-most pair. However, when they were asked why they liked this pair best, they were unable to explain it. Some said that they thought that this pair of stockings was higher in quality than the other pairs. This was not correct, however; the study participants were tricked: all four pairs of stockings were identical. So, when consumers are not sure why they like one product better than another, they often make up an answer that seems reasonable, but maybe—and often is—wrong.

When shopping for groceries, consumers often buy impulsively. These impulse purchases are usually made with little or no conscious thought; later, when it's time to pay for the groceries, consumers are often surprised by how high their bills are. Impulse buys are sometimes made without awareness. That is, consumers sometimes do not realize that they are putting certain items into their shopping carts. Impulse buys are usually made without intention. That is, consumers usually do not intend to make impulse purchases. Research shows that grocery shoppers are more likely to make impulse purchases when they are hungry and even more when they don't have a shopping list.[4]

How do consumers make decisions with minimal thought? Some decisions are based on attitudes that come to mind automatically whenever consumers see

Impulse purchases are more likely when consumers don't use a shopping list.

or think about a particular product.[5] Rather than thinking about all the pros and cons associated with a product, consumers simply think about whether they like the product. This does not occur for all products, but it does occur for highly familiar products. For example, consumers do not need to think about the pros and cons of Snickers candy bars if they already know that Snickers candy bars are among their favorites. Consumers do not need to think about the pros and cons of canned spinach if they already know that they detest canned spinach. For products associated with strong attitudes that are highly accessible from memory, responses come to mind quickly and unintentionally whenever these products are encountered.

OBJECTIVE 2

The Adaptive Unconscious

How does a mental process become automatic? The answer is practice. Learning how to drive a car for the first time is painstakingly difficult. It is important to pay close attention to the road, to other cars, to the pedals, and to the controls on the dashboard. However, with lots of practice, driving becomes easy because it becomes automatic. Instead of paying close attention to everything, practice makes it possible to receive all the information you need with just a glance. Practice can also make it easy to play a new sport, solve math problems, or make purchase decisions.

What are the benefits of automatic information processing? When a mental process becomes automatic and subject to unconscious control, it becomes easier to pay attention to novel objects and ideas that require careful attention and thought. Here, the subconscious mind frees up mental resources for the conscious mind. It would be difficult, if not impossible, for the conscious mind to navigate our complex environment without assistance from the unconscious mind.

Note that this view of the unconscious is quite different from the Freudian view. Freud thought that the unconscious hid important thoughts and ideas from us, and that this causes mental illness. The purpose of psychotherapy, according to Freud, was to uncover these hidden thoughts and ideas. In sharp contrast, the modern view of the **adaptive unconscious** suggests that the unconscious mind can be trained to perform routine mental activities. This is beneficial, rather than harmful, because it enables people to devote more attention and thought to non-routine mental activities. For example, shopping for routine products, such as milk, butter, and eggs, requires little time or energy. So, time and energy are thus freed up for thinking more carefully about non-routine purchases, such as the special ingredients for a new dish you want to try.

It becomes easier to appreciate the importance of the unconscious mind when one compares normal people to people whose brain injuries prevent them from experiencing emotions and learning unconsciously.[6] In an important experiment, groups of participants were asked to play a gambling game in which they drew cards from four decks. Two of the decks were high-risk decks with high payoffs or high losses, with losses more likely to occur than payoffs. Two decks were low-risk decks with low payoffs or low losses, but in this case, payoffs were more likely. Normal people quickly

> **ETHICS**
>
> There are many different types of marketing placebo effects. If a consumer believes that a product will be highly effective, the product is often more effective. Marketing placebo effects have been observed for self-help tapes, energy drinks, coffee, and other products. Even when two products are identical, the higher-priced product or the product with the more prestigious brand name often seems better. Is it ethical to market subliminal self-help tapes that don't work? Is it ethical to market products that produce placebo effects, like homeopathic medicines, herbal remedies, and New Age cures? Where should the FDA draw the line?

and unconsciously learned to draw mainly from the low-risk decks. Interestingly, they learned to do this long before they could explain why they did this. People with brain injuries that blocked emotions, but who were otherwise highly intelligent, drew mainly from the high-risk decks and lost more money. The absence of emotional responses and gut feelings prevented them from learning to avoid high-risk situations.

(OBJECTIVE 3)

Thin Slice Theory of Informational Processing

People can learn a surprisingly large amount of information from very quick first impressions. "Thin slices," or brief observations of another person's behavior, provide surprisingly accurate information about this person's personality traits and current feelings and goals.[7] Research shows that what people learn from thin slices of behavior typically occurs in less than five minute intervals. Ironically, first impressions are often more accurate when they are based on very brief observations than when they are based on longer observations. Also, first impressions are often more accurate when people focus on nonverbal information, such as facial expressions, gestures, voice tone, and body movements, than when they focus on verbal information. This occurs because people have less control over nonverbal cues than they do over their verbal communication.

In a recent study of thin slicing, consumers were asked to make inferences about sales management job applicants based on 20-second audiotapes of random portions

MARKETING IN ACTION
The Marketing Placebo Effect

The more consumers pay for a product, the better they expect the product to perform. Some retailers charge a high price, and some charge a low price for exactly the same product, however. Does the price of a product influence how well the product performs even if different prices are charged for the same product? In an experiment designed to answer this question, consumers were told that SoBe Adrenaline Rush either sold for a high price or a low price.[31] After tasting this beverage, consumers were asked to solve intellectual puzzles. The results showed that consumers solved more puzzles after drinking the high-priced beverage than after drinking the low-priced beverage, even though all

Priming activates concepts from memory.

consumers drank exactly the same beverage.

These results suggest that pricing information influences consumers' expectations, which then influence behavior without awareness and without intention. This phenomenon is known as a **placebo effect**. This effect is especially common in medicine: If people think that a pill will make them feel better, it often makes them feel better, even if the pill has no real effect. The placebo effect also occurs in marketing: If consumers believe that a product will be effective, it seems more effective.

of job interviews. These inferences were compared to those of the expert sales managers who conducted the interviews. The results showed that consumers formed remarkably accurate inferences about the social skills and the anxiety levels of the job applicants based on thin slices of behavior. Accuracy was even higher when the audiotapes were content-filtered, so that consumers could listen to voice tone but the verbal message was garbled. Sometimes less is more.

Sometimes snap judgments are more accurate than judgments resulting from a great deal of thought. In a strawberry jam taste test, some consumers were asked simply to indicate which jams they liked best.[8] Other consumers were asked to explain why they liked one particular jam better than the others. The researchers then compared the ratings of these consumers to the ratings of experts. The results showed that the consumers who simply indicated their preferences without explaining them were more accurate than the consumers who were asked to explain their preferences. In a follow-up study, consumers were asked to choose one of several decorative posters to keep for free.[9] Again, half simply indicated their preferences, and half explained their preferences. Three weeks later, the consumers who simply indicated their preferences were more satisfied with their decisions than the consumers who explained their preferences. Sometimes too much thinking can lead to bad decisions.

When should consumers trust their **intuition** and when should they think carefully about a decision problem? Some types of decisions, like picking strawberry jams or decorative posters, should be made intuitively. Other types of decisions, like buying a car or a kitchen appliance, should be made deliberatively. In a study of intuitive versus deliberative judgment, participants were asked either to provide simple answers to various questions or to explain their answers.[10] Some of the questions were subjective, such as "Which advertisement would consumers like best?" Other questions were more objective, such as "What is the length of the Amazon River?" The results showed that intuition worked best for questions with subjective answers, and deliberation worked best for questions with objective answers.

Thin-slice inferences are more accurate for questions having subjective answers. Thin-slice inferences are also more accurate when consumers have a lot of practice forming these inferences and when they receive a good deal of accurate feedback about the quality of their inferences.[11] The best type of feedback occurs frequently and quickly. A great deal of learning takes place under these conditions. On the other hand, learning is difficult when feedback is infrequent or delayed. Learning also depends on the consequences of one's mistakes. It is easier to learn from one's mistakes when mistakes are obvious. However, it is difficult to learn from one's mistakes if it is unclear whether a mistake actually was made. For some types of decisions, nearly any reasonable judgment turns out well. For example, most brands of CD players are very good. Consequently, consumers are likely to be satisfied with nearly any brand of CD player they choose, even if they make a mistake and fail to choose the best brand.

OBJECTIVE 4

Implicit Memory

Sometimes consumers purposefully try to retrieve information from memory. When consumers are aware that they are searching for information stored in memory and/or when they intend to do so, they are performing an **explicit memory** task. However, sometimes consumers are not aware that they are using memory as a tool to perform some task. When memory is used as a tool without awareness or intention, consumers are performing an **implicit memory** task. The priming effect is the most common type of implicit memory phenomenon.

THE PRIMING EFFECT   Priming occurs in situations in which consumers are subtly lead to think about a concept, such as a brand name, a product category, an attribute, a benefit, or any idea.[12] For example, watching TV primes concepts related to products (e.g., information conveyed in ads), politics (e.g., information conveyed in news shows), and entertainment (e.g., television shows featuring sex, violence, comedy, action, etc.). Crossword puzzles and other types of intellectual puzzles (e.g., find-a-word puzzles, scrambles) also prime ideas. Fiction and non-fiction books and magazines also prime ideas. Once an idea has been primed, it influences how people think about related ideas. People are usually unaware of this influence.

Simply thinking about a concept activates that concept from memory. Once a concept has been activated, it influences how consumers think about subsequent topics. For example, in a study on pricing, consumers were asked to fill out a find-a-word puzzle.[13] In expensive prime conditions, the puzzle contained brand names of expensive automobiles (e.g., Mercedes-Benz, Rolls Royce, Ferrari, Porsche). In inexpensive prime conditions, the puzzle contained brand names of inexpensive automobiles (e.g., Chevette, V W Beetle, Ford Pinto, Ford Fiesta). Participants were asked to find the hidden names and circle them. This simple task resulted in the activation of either expensive or inexpensive automobiles in the minds of the participants. Later, consumers were asked to judge the expensiveness of a moderately priced automobile, called the target. In the ambiguous condition, participants were asked to rate a moderately priced car with a concealed brand name. In the unambiguous condition, different participants rated the

MARKETING IN ACTION
Subliminal Advertising

In 1957, market researcher James Vicary claimed that he flashed the messages "Eat Popcorn" and "Drink Coke" on a movie screen at 1/3,000th of a second during the airing of a popular film called *Picnic*.[14] Although no one could see these messages, Vicary claimed that popcorn sales increased by 58 percent and Coke sales increased by 18 percent. Later, he admitted that he made up these data and

that he never flashed any subliminal messages on the screen. Subliminal messages cannot be seen by the eye or interpreted by the conscious mind, but presumably can be "seen" by the subconscious mind. Despite Vicary's admission, many consumers were and still are frightened by the possibility of unconscious mind control. This is because most consumers do not understand how the unconscious mind works. The unconscious mind is the focus of this chapter.

were presented, participants made lots of errors. However, some errors were more common than others. In fact, participants were more likely to believe false statements to be true than true statements to be false. This is because believing is easier than unbelieving.

Naturally, consumers do not ultimately believe everything they see and hear, but the important point is that unbelieving or rejecting false claims requires an additional step beyond simply understanding the claim. When consumers are overloaded with too much information, when they need to make a judgment or decision quickly, or when they try to do too many things at once, they are less able to engage in the extra effort required for unbelieving. So, under these circumstances, they are more likely to believe false claims to be true. Information overload, time pressure, and multi-tasking are facts of contemporary everyday life, so consumers may have difficulties rejecting false claims even more today than in previous decades.

Can distraction affect important decisions? Evidence indicates that it can. In a fascinating study, participants read statements about two crime reports that crawled across the bottom of a television screen, just like a weather, business, or sports bulletin. True statements were printed in black and false statements were printed in red. The false statements suggested that the first defendant was innocent and the second was guilty, or vice versa. Participants were sometimes distracted by multi-tasking while they read the crime report. The distraction greatly influenced their judgments. On average, distracted participants recommended 11 years in prison for the accused party when the false statements were exacerbating (made to appear worse) and only six years in prison when the false statements were extenuating (accompanied by an explanation). In contrast, participants who were not distracted recommended approximately the same prison sentence (about six years) in both cases. Thus, distracted participants had difficulty unbelieving false statements, despite the fact that true statements were printed in black, and false statements were printed in red. Of course, unbelieving false statements is even more difficult when the real-world mass-media fails to provide such color differentiation!

OBJECTIVE 5 Subliminal Advertising Revisited

When combined with accessible needs, subliminal priming can increase persuasion.

At the beginning of this chapter, we discussed the case of James Vicary, who claimed he was able to increases sales of popcorn and Coca-Cola by subliminal suggestion during a movie. Consumer behavior is too complex to be controlled by simple subliminal messages. However, as this chapter illustrates, memories of past experiences can influence a wide variety of judgments without intention or awareness. Furthermore, recent research shows that subliminal priming can influence behavior without intention or awareness.[32] In one research project, all participants were asked not to eat or drink for three hours prior to the experiment. At the beginning of the experiment, participants were randomly assigned to a thirsty condition (i.e., they were not allowed to drink any water) or a non-thirsty condition (i.e., they were allowed to drink as much water as they wanted). Next, words were flashed for 16 milliseconds on a computer screen followed by a mask, or a string of letters that made it even more difficult to see a briefly flashed word. Participants were randomly assigned to a thirst-related words condition (i.e., thirst, dry) or a control condition in which neutral words were flashed (i.e., pirate, won). Finally, participants were asked to perform a taste test for two different kinds of Kool-Aid, and they were allowed to drink as much of this beverage as they wanted. The results showed that thirsty participants who were exposed to thirst-related subliminal primes drank more Kool-Aid than did participants in the other conditions.

In a follow-up experiment, thirst-related primes increased preferences for a drink that was advertised as thirst-quenching ("SuperQuencher") over a drink that was advertised as energizing ("PowerPro"). Again, however, this effect was observed only in participants who were already thirsty. Hence, subliminal priming by itself does not increase persuasion. But subliminal priming combined with an already accessible need or goal can increase persuasion.

Chapter Summary

Automatic information processing refers to mental processes that occur without awareness or intention, but that influence judgments, feelings, and behaviors. Automatic information processing is useful and adaptive because it enables people to perform some simple tasks without thinking. This allows people to think more carefully about other tasks they need to perform. A response becomes automatic via practice and repetition. One particularly useful skill that people have learned automatically is thin-slice inferencing. Thin slices or brief observations of another person's behavior often tell us a surprisingly large amount of information about the person.

The priming effect is another important example of automatic information processing. Recent or frequent exposure to an idea presented on television, on the radio, in a magazine, in a book, or in a conversation can change the way people think about subsequently encountered ambiguous information. An unfamiliar product can seem expensive or inexpensive, versatile or easy to use, or good or bad depending on what information was primed before examining the product. Priming can also influence behavior as well as judgment. People often behave in a manner consistent with the implications of a prime and do so without awareness or intention.

Key Terms

automatic information processing

adaptive unconscious

placebo effect

intuition

thin-slice inferences

explicit memory

implicit memory

assimilation effect

contrast effect

procedural priming effect

mindset priming effect

Implicit Association Test (IAT)

implicit attitudes

explicit attitudes

truth effect

distraction effect

subliminal advertising

Review and Discussion

1. What is automatic information processing?
2. Give some examples of automatic information processing.
3. When are attitudes likely to come to mind automatically?
4. How does a mental process become automatic?
5. What are the benefits of automatic information processing?
6. Why do people trust their intuition more than they should?
7. Give some examples of thin-slice inferences.
8. Give some examples of the priming effect.
9. What is the IAT?
10. When is the IAT most useful?

Short Application Exercises

1. Subliminal sexual images are sometimes used in ads for alcohol. Do people have a strong association in memory between sex and alcohol? Why are people afraid of subliminal advertising? Should they be afraid?
2. Discuss ads for Cialis, Viagra, and other drugs for erectile dysfunction. What automatic information processing principles would be most useful for selling these types of products?
3. Describe the ways the priming effect could influence you after watching TV, reading the newspaper, and reading a novel.
4. Visit the Web site for the IAT (www.implicit.harvard .edu) and take the test. What have you learned from this test?

MANAGERIAL APPLICATION

"What's in a name? A rose by any other name would smell as sweet." Although this may be true in Shakespeare, it's not true in marketing. Because of thin-slice inferences, a brand name often tells consumers quite a bit about the brand, including information about its identity and personality. A good brand name is easy to pronounce, because brand names that are easy to pronounce are easier to think about and are more memorable. A good brand name also primes product applications, the appearance of the product, the key features of the product, and an appropriate mindset. A good brand name could also prime a specific consumer lifestyle, so as to appeal to members of a target consumer segment.

YOUR CHALLENGE:

Keeping all of these thin-slice inferences and priming effects in mind, generate three good brand names for each of the following products, and explain why each brand name could be effective:

1.   Personal computer

2.   PDA (personal digital assistant)

3.   3-D TV

4.   Hawaiian vacation package

THE ROLE OF PERSONALITY AND SELF-CONCEPT

OBJECTIVES · *After reading this chapter, you should be able to...*

1 | Define self-concept, extended self, and love objects.

2 | Describe the three components of impression management.

3 | Explain how self-monitoring is related to consumer behavior.

4 | Describe multiple-trait theory and how it is linked to brand personality.

5 | Discuss cognitive factors relating to single-trait theory of personality.

GAP'S KHAKIS HAVE PERSONALITY

A favorable brand personality can be critical to the success of any product. Many of the world's top brands seem to possess human-like traits, which helps consumers decide if they are compatible with a particular brand.[1] For example, Coca-Cola is reliable; IBM is intelligent; G.E. is a planet protector; Disney is cheerful; McDonald's is friendly; Nokia is fashionable yet affordable; Volkswagen is down-to-earth; Harley-Davidson is rugged; and Mercedes Benz is sophisticated. Firms have even branded commodities, such as chicken (Purdue), potatoes (Idaho), and fruits (Sunkist). With a little help from the late Marvin Gaye, the California Raisin Advisory Board transformed raisins from nerdy to hip. But khakis? How can you give basic trousers a personality?

Khakis are easy to get along with. You can throw them in the washer, hang them up to dry, and they look fine without ironing. Pleated or plain, cuffed or straight, baggy or trim, they go well with everything from T-shirts to blue blazers. And they're not too expensive. But there is a downside to their appeal. No matter where you buy them, they all look alike. Consequently, khakis have been treated like a commodity—until Gap decided to give khakis some soul.

In 2007, Gap launched an advertising campaign emphasizing the personality of their khakis. In one particular ad, a young man is wearing "Khakis with Attitude." As he puts his right leg into his new Gap pleated-front, cuffed, baggy khakis, the pants twist and shout, "Get your leg outta there, man!" The young man screams, crashes against the wall and looks in terror at the crumpled trousers. The pants continue, "Yo. Listen to me. You bought khakis with attitude. You saw the sign. That's what I got. Now put me back in the closet. I'll go out with you when it warms up."

In another ad, a young woman is sporting "The Boyfriend Trouser." As she slips on her new Gap khakis, she feels an odd sensation, as if the pants are gently moving. With a cry of fright, she tears off the pants. "Please! I love you!" the pants proclaim. The young woman assumes the kung-fu attack position she learned in a personal defense class and confronts her trousers. "What the hell are you?" she demands. "I'm the boyfriend trouser. I thought that's why you bought me . . . that you needed a boyfriend." She withdraws in disgust. The Gap campaign was a winner. Gap differentiated its commodity khakis from all the others by injecting their pants with personality, offering "pants with an attitude."[2]

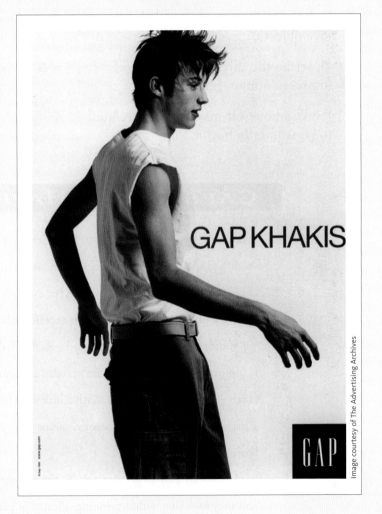

OBJECTIVE 1 # Self-Concept Defined

Most people are preoccupied with discovering who they are. Indeed, "Who am I?" is a question that most of us consider throughout our lives. Our unique answers to this question provide insight into our **self-concept,** the beliefs and attitudes we hold about ourselves. Although no precise definition of self-concept exists in the consumer behavior literature, self-concept is often described as the totality of an individual's thoughts and feelings regarding him/herself as an object.[3] Self-concept is complicated and multidimensional. Consumers have been characterized as describing themselves on three dimensions: role identities, personal qualities, and self-evaluations.[4]

Role identities represent the numerous *positions* that people occupy in society such as student, friend, son or daughter, and consumer. People construct these identities by observing how they behave and the reactions that others form about them in each of their roles.[5] Although society imparts role expectations on its members (e.g., friends should be loyal), individuals usually have plenty of room to improvise. It may be helpful to think of consumers as *shaping* their role identities within the broad boundaries set by society. For example, all people playing the role of customer do not respond the same way to sales promotions. Some people are passionate "bargain-hunters," while others play a more indifferent role toward sales. Because people create roles in unique ways, each person derives a different role identity even when they occupy the same position. Moreover, these differences vary widely across product category. For example, a person who is a 'bargain hunter" for shoes may demand an expensive brand when it comes to coffee, or vice versa.

When people identify their roles, they often start with occupational or educational groups (e.g., college student). Consumers have convenient acronyms that provide ready shortcuts, especially in the professions. "She's an MBA" labels someone as having obtained a master's degree in business and someone who is probably quite practical. "I'm an M.D." self-identifies a medical doctor, which is different than a D.O. (doctor of osteopathic medicine) or a D.D.S. (doctor of dental surgery). Consumers also identify social categories such as religion (e.g., Protestant), race (e.g., African American), and ethnicity (e.g., Lebanese). Consumers' role identities are played out in public, and hence, they are more transparent than their personal qualities and self-evaluations, which describe idiosyncratic parts of the self-concept that are not so clear-cut. People's notions about how friendly, athletic, and easy-going they are may not match the way others perceive them.

Personal qualities involve modes of interpersonal behavior that distinguish people from one another, such as sense of humor or friendliness. They also include internal psychological styles, such as optimism or cheerfulness, that influence role identities.[4] Personal qualities can be thought of as **traits,** or tendencies to behave a certain way across similar situations. Psychologists believe that traits are developed at an early age, remain relatively consistent across similar situations, and endure. Personal qualities provide consumers with opportunities to play out their role identities. For example, people respond differently to product failures and malfunctions. Some people exhibit anger and aggression, while others are more "laid back" in response to these disappointments. Similarly, consumers who are technologically savvy may play the role as an expert whom friends and family members contact when it is time to shop for a personal computer or digital video recorder. Consumer psychologists also know that traits play out differently in different contexts. For example, a person who is classified as anxious is unlikely to express anxiety in the same way in all contexts, e.g., with a friend, policeman, or professor. Thus, using personality traits to predict consumer behavior can be a tricky business.

Launched in the UK during 2003, *Dove's* "Real Beauty" campaign celebrates women of all shapes, sizes, and colors.

"Real Beauty" was conceived based on the results of a multinational study of 3,500 women. The study revealed that two-thirds of women believe that the media endorse an image of beauty unattainable by most women. Moreover, just two percent of respondents reported that they considered themselves beautiful. Consequently, Unilever overhauled *Dove's* global advertising message to challenge the imagery traditionally associated with beauty and personal care products. "Real Beauty" made it to the U.S. in 2005 with ads for hair, skin, and body products featuring images of wrinkled skin for skin care; rotund bodies for moisturizers; and short, curly coifs for hair care products. Two TV ads in the series featured women—wrinkled, freckled, and stretched by pregnancy—to promote *Dove's Body Nourishers* lotion line. Other ads revealed six curvy, unapologetic women dressed in underwear to promote a new *Dove Intensive Firming Lotion*. To promote hair care for all types of hair, *Dove* had women rip off blonde wigs in unison to reveal their own variety of hair styles and colors.[85]

In 2006, *Dove* ran its first Super Bowl ad with an inspirational message designed to raise girls' self esteem. Helping girls accept themselves is a mission of *Dove's* five-year marketing strategy. In the ad, one dark-haired girl "wishes she were blonde." Another "thinks she's ugly." A red-haired girl "hates her freckles." The background music is Cyndi Lauper's *True Colors*, sung by the Girl Scout Chorus of Nassau County, N.Y. The ad also promoted *Dove's* Self-Esteem Fund that supports the Girl Scouts' Uniquely Me program. It encourages viewers to "get involved" at www.campaignforrealbeauty.com.[86]

But is the "Real Beauty" campaign for real? Some consumers see it as just another marketing stunt aimed at selling soap.

Perhaps the heart of the issue is whether the campaign makes women feel good about themselves.[87] On one hand, there are certain classic looks that women would all secretly love to possess. When they see a beautiful model promoting a brand, women respond imaginatively and, for a moment or two, feel beautiful, too. Although they know the product will not change them, the power of association is so great that, deep down, women feel as though a little of the model's magic has rubbed off—this is the ideal self-concept speaking. On the other hand, contemporary, self-confident women want to see figures and faces like their own featured and celebrated in advertising—this is the actual self-concept speaking. Which self-concept wins? Research suggests that when evaluating brands, it's usually the ideal—not the real—that matters, which is an ominous sign for *Dove's* "real beauty" campaign.

People also perform **self-evaluations** by considering the adequacy of their performances in various role identities. Am I a good student or a thoughtful boyfriend/girlfriend? Am I a smart shopper? Usually, these evaluations focus on competence, perseverance, morality, and social unity. Self-evaluations also influence role identities. For example, people who perceive themselves as "athletic" are more likely to engage in organized sports than those with poorer self-evaluations. In a similar vein, consumers who see themselves as competent Internet shoppers often share their knowledge with less experienced friends. One consumer might say to another, "Just type in www.fedex.com, click 'track by number,' and type in your tracking number. You can follow your package all the way to its destination." If this advice is well received, then the e-shopper's self evaluation is enhanced and s/he is more likely to perform this role identity in the future.

The sum of all self-evaluations determines **self-esteem,** the overall evaluative component of a person's self-concept. Self-esteem can be considered a person's general attitude toward him or herself. Research shows that high self-esteem is associated with active and comfortable social interactions, but low self-esteem can be depressing and debilitating.[1] People with low self-esteem tend to view social situations as threatening, feel more negative toward others, and hence, are easily wounded by criticism. In addition, they yield more to other's requests.[3] It is probably best to think of self-esteem and behavior as a two-way street. People with high self-esteem tend to be more confident and hence, more influential. And yet, the behavior of influencing others may lead to increased self-esteem, a virtuous cycle.

The opposite may be true for those with low self-esteem. With little faith in their ability to succeed, people with low self-esteem may fulfill their low expectations, which leads to even lower self-esteem—a vicious cycle. Research provides evidence that marketing activities can affect a consumer's self-esteem. Exposure to idealistic standards can produce unpleasant consequences regarding how we view ourselves.[6] On the other hand, marketing stimuli can also cause our self-evaluations to converge toward these higher standards, subsequently increasing self-esteem.[7] Some marketers have attempted to enhance image-related self-esteem through the inclusion of more realistic and attainable role models. See the Ethics Box regarding Unilever's "Real Beauty" campaign for Dove.

A consumer's self-concept is comprised of two key dimensions: (1) *self-focus* (actual versus the ideal) and (2) *self-location* (private versus public). Each dimension has two parts. Regarding focus, the **actual self-concept** represents how consumers in fact perceive themselves, while the

ideal self-concept describes how consumers would like to be. The gap is referred to as self-discrepancy. With respect to *self-location,* the **actual public-concept** embodies others' true perceptions of a consumer, while the **ideal public-concept** represents how consumers would like others to see them. The gap between actual public and ideal public concepts is known as a public-discrepancy. This four-part self-concept is shown in Figure 11.1.

Depending on the purchase situation, consumers are likely to emphasize a different self-concept. For privately consumed products, consumers may simply rely on their actual self-concept. In contrast, when purchasing products that will be consumed in public, consumers may draw on their actual public-self image to appear consistent with others' expectations, or they may employ their ideal public-concept to change how others view them. Let's take a closer look at the joint interplay of marketing activities and self-concept, with particular emphasis on the actual versus ideal self-concepts.

FIGURE 11.1   THE TWO-DIMENSIONAL SELF-CONCEPT

		Self-Focus	
		Actual	**Ideal**
Self-Location	Private	Actual self-concept	Ideal self-concept
	Public	Actual public-concept	Ideal public-concept

Source: Cline, T. W. (2009). Working paper, Saint Vincent College, Latrobe, PA. Reprinted by permission of the author.

The Role of Self-Concept

Self-concept is important to marketers because consumers' self-perceptions influence their attitudes towards product categories and specific brands and subsequent purchase behavior.[8] Consequently, brands deliberately convey images that extend beyond their purely functional characteristics. For example, *Harley-Davidson* evokes mental imagery quite distinct from that of *Honda* or *Suzuki,* and *Nordstrom* conveys a different image than *Kmart* or *Sears.* Research suggests that some consumers like to express themselves in their brand choices. Thus, promotional efforts to image-conscious consumers are more effective if they portray product images that are consistent with consumers' self-concepts.[9] But which self-concept should marketers embrace—the actual or ideal? The answer is "it depends."

Because self-concept is relatively important to everyone, consumers tend to maintain or protect their self-concepts on the one hand, and enhance them on the other. The former is referred to as the self-consistency motive; the latter is called the self-esteem motive. Consumers motivated by self-consistency act in accordance with their self-concepts—even in the face of challenging evidence.[1] In contrast, consumers motivated by self-esteem engage in activities that lead to more positive self-evaluations.[10] Both motives coexist within an individual, but they can tug us in different directions, depending on the task at hand.

Advertisers want us to remember their brands and evaluate them favorably, but recall and evaluation are two different tasks. If a consumer's task is to recall the brand name or its attributes, then s/he is more likely to remember information consistent with her/his *actual* self-concept, rather than information consistent with her/his *ideal* self-concept. Why? Consumers generally possess well-developed, actual self-schema with rich associative networks in their memories. **Self-schemas** are cognitive structures that help us make sense of who we are. Schemas can be thought of as basic sketches of what people know about something. People are generally knowledgeable (if not altogether happy) about who they are. Consequently, people are likely to attend to and retrieve information congruent with their actual self-schema.[11] Recalling congruent information also enables consumers to maintain a state of cognitive consonance. In general, consumers are motivated to maintain harmony in their belief systems and between their attitudes and behavior. Thus, if marketing communication fits with consumers' understanding of who they are, the communication facilitates this desired balance.

The situation is quite different if a consumer is focused on evaluating or judging a product. Because consumers are aware of not only who they are, but also who they would like to be, a gap between the actual and ideal self-concepts represents a state of inconsistency. As such, the ideal self-concept can serve as an important moving target, a goal that consumers seek to attain. Thus, when consumers evaluate a brand, they are more likely to be influenced by whether the brand fills the gap, i.e., advances them toward their ideal self-concepts. It follows that brands congruent with a consumer's ideal self-concept are evaluated more favorably than those congruent with a consumer's actual self-concept. For example, a consumer who wants to achieve "preppiness" may meet that goal by endorsing *Lacoste, Izod, J. Crew,* or *Polo Ralph Lauren*. On the other hand, if a consumer's ideal self-concept is more "edgy," s/he may wear clothing from *Karl Kani* or *Timberline*. In sum, if marketers want consumers to remember their brand names, attributes, and benefits, they should create communications that are consistent with consumers' actual self-concepts. In contrast, if changing attitudes is important, marketers should communicate information that is congruent with consumers' ideal self-concepts.

The notion of positioning brand images to be congruent with consumers' self-concepts reflects the general practice of market segmentation (see Chapter 2). Marketers identify patterns of self-concepts residing in specific demographic groups and find media that communicate directly to these groups. This practice is not new. For decades, *Virginia Slims* cigarettes attempted to match their slogan, "You've come a long way, baby" with women's ideal self-concepts regarding social independence. Similarly, *Harley-Davidson* motorcycles convey raw excitement to consumers seeking to improve their ideal self-concepts regarding freedom and adventure. Non-profits and government organizations have also used this approach. The U.S. Army's recent ad campaign, "Army Strong," targets prospects with messages of self-empowerment and self-determination. The other military services also rely on slogans to appeal to consumers' ideal self-concepts. The U.S. Air Force recently abandoned its "Cross Into the Blue" to "Do Something Amazing." Since 2001, the U.S. Navy has promoted with "Accelerate Your Life," and the Marines have relied on "The Few...The Proud," targeting prospects who are motivated by self-esteem.

MARKETING IN ACTION

The U.S. Army "Targets" Recruits' Self-Concepts

Early in 2001, the U.S. Army abandoned its 20-year ad campaign, "Be All You Can Be." Instead, the Army committed its $150 million advertising budget and its recruiting goals to "An Army of One." The campaign emphasizes that young people can maintain their sense of identity and attain self-fulfillment while serving in today's Army. One promotion in the new campaign featured a solitary soldier running outdoors while a voiceover says, "I am an army of one, even though there are 1,045,690 soldiers like me." Another ad emphasizes technology and training, encouraging potential recruits to log onto the Army's Web site at goarmy.com.

The change in campaign was not without controversy. Advertising expert Jerry Della Famina thought it was a mistake. He argued that the Army benefited from one of the greatest campaigns in history. In fact, *Advertising Age*, an industry publication and information leader, ranked the "Be All You Can Be" campaign as the second best of the 20th century.

However, although "Be All You Can Be" was embedded in the culture of the nation, apparently it had lost its connection with the Army's target audience of over 20 million young adults between the ages of 18 and 24. An important part of that target market is African American youth. "We are aware of how popular 'Be All You Can Be,' is with the Army," said Bob McNeil, president of Atlanta-based IMAGES USA, the Army's African American marketing agency. McNeil noted that "Army of One," speaks directly to African American youth who need culturally relevant information to have it stay with them.[79]

During the fall of 2006, however, "Army of One" was itself retired. Army officials said the "Army of One" campaign was not a failure, but it had not been highly effective. The Army missed its recruiting target in 2005 by the widest margin in more than 20 years.

In hopes of connecting better with potential recruits, the Army introduced its new pitch, "Army Strong," accompanied by a $200 million annual advertising contract with McCann Worldgroup, on November 9, 2006, to coincide with the Veterans Day weekend. The five-year contract between the Army and McCann Worldgroup is valued at $1 billion.

So far, this campaign appears to be meeting its goals. The Army met its 2006 recruiting goal of signing up 80,000 new soldiers. The new slogan, developed after numerous focus groups and interviews with soldiers, is designed to communicate the idea that if you join the Army, you will gain physical and emotional strength as well as strength of character and purpose.[80] These ideas are aimed directly at recruits' ideal self-concepts.

Dates	Campaign Slogan[81]
1971–1973	Today's Army Wants to Join You
1973–1979	Join the People Who've Joined the Army
1979–1981	This is the Army
1981–2001	Be All You Can Be
2001–2006	Army of One
2006–present	Army Strong
Slogans of historical U.S. Army advertising campaigns	

Courtesy of U.S. Army

The Extended Self

Some products are so important to consumers that they are used to confirm their self-concepts. The relationship between a consumer's self-concepts and his/her possessions is called the **extended self**.[12] The idea that our belongings represent an extension of ourselves dates back to 1890, when William James claimed that we are the sum of our possessions.[13] In a more recent and highly regarded essay, Russell Belk maintains that the extended self is not limited to personal possessions, but also includes people, places, and group possessions. This view is consistent with the notion that external objects become a part of us when we are able to exercise significant control over them. In this sense, even body parts are viewed as part of the extended self.[14] Research confirms that people consider the following categories as possessions:

- Their bodies
- Personal space

- Consumable goods

- Durable goods

- Home and property

- Significant others

- Children

- Friends

- Mementos

- Pets[15]

Thus, marketers need to understand the variety of ways consumers express themselves through their possessions. And they do. Unilever appeals to consumers' view of their bodies with *Lever 2000,* "for your 2000 body parts," an enormously successful campaign, Unilever extended the *Lever 2000* brand to include body washes with Ginseng and vitamins (Energize), cucumber extracts (Fresh Aloe), and a rain scent (Refresh). 3M understands consumers' desire to "possess" their own personal space or sense of privacy. They developed a new product to restore privacy to computer screens called the *Notebook Privacy Computer Filter.* By slipping a thin sheet of plastic in front of a computer screen, the images on the screen can no longer be viewed from the side.

For consumers who view their pets as an extension of themselves, PetSmart, Inc., the world's largest specialty pet retailer of products and services, offers in-store PetsHotels, Doggie Day Camps, pet training, pet grooming, and adoption programs.

While acquiring and investing in possessions can extend who consumers think they are, the loss of important belongings can reduce their extended selves. Burglary victims report a diminished sense of self when their possessions are lost to theft. Research suggests that grief and mourning follow theft, just as it does when someone loses a loved one.[16] Similarly, natural disaster victims report going through a grieving process, including denial, anger, depression, and finally acceptance.[17] ADT knows that homeowners fear the loss of possessions resulting from burglary. In fact, ADT advertises that its customer monitoring centers "help protect the people and things you value most," i.e., the extended self. Insurance companies like Allstate understand that natural disasters can damage more than homeowners' property. They can also destroy a consumer's extended self. Accordingly, these firms offer catastrophe and disaster insurance for those willing to pay the premiums.

Research also suggests that for many Americans, the automobile is an important part of their extended selves and ideal self-concepts.[18] The process of creating one's extended self through an automobile occurs when people customize their cars or painstakingly wash and maintain them. Some consumers build special sound systems for their cars; others spend hours washing and

PRNewsFoto/ADT/AP Photo

Burglary victims often feel a diminished sense of self.

waxing their vehicles. To these consumers, their automobiles represent a significant part of their extended selves. Marketers of *Turtle Wax* and *3M Car Care* run advertisements that encourage people-car relationships. They feature beautifully conditioned automobiles, lavishly maintained by their owners, who caress and talk to their cars as though they are lovers. When car aficionados damage their vehicles, they often behave as though their own bodies have been wrecked, and they work anxiously to restore the automobiles to their original condition. Not surprisingly, for car aficionados, collision centers act as surrogate "emergency rooms."

How do possessions become extensions of consumers? First, they facilitate *action* by allowing consumers to do things they otherwise couldn't do. For example, without an *ipod*, consumers would not be able to share their favorite songs with their friends, songs that also represent part of the extended self. Second, consumers' belongings *symbolically* extend who they are. For instance, trophies and awards highlight individual accomplishments; diplomas exhibit academic credentials; and photographs and artwork present vivid illustrations of what people deem important. Third, possessions bring consumers *power and prestige*. Accumulating antiques and other scarce items, for example, conveys a certain status, because rare items are expensive. Fourth, possessions allow consumers to associate themselves with desirable *people, places, or times*. Autographs of a favorite celebrity; memorabilia acquired on a trip to Paris; and family heirlooms extend who consumers are by linking them to these desirable entities.[10] Some possessions so are important that consumers develop a deep affection for them. These items are known as "loved objects."

Loved Objects

The people and things that consumers love impart a strong influence on their self-concepts. The word "love" is commonly used to describe activities, places, and possessions: "I love to golf," "I love Paris," "I love your hair style," "I love that movie." Research shows that consumers not only "love to shop," but they also "fall in love" with the products they buy.[19] In fact, love is the second most common word consumers use to describe their feelings about possessions (happiness ranks first). Of all the possessions that consumers acquire and divest throughout their lives, only a few attain loved status. Loved objects, a special subset of all possessions that comprise the extended self, play a central role in our knowledge of who we are as people. Recent research provides evidence that loved objects can be part of a synthesizing solution to a specific identity conflict. In fact, **loved objects** are shown to derive much of their emotional status by helping resolve these internal conflicts.[20] For children, a favorite stuffed animal provides comfort during times of psychological conflict. For adults, beloved sports cars can compensate for lack of social power, and chocolates can be used as rewards. Loved objects can also resolve role conflicts. For example, if a man experiences a psychological conflict between his role as a businessperson and his role as an art connoisseur, he might come to love his paintings and sculptures as a way of preserving his artistic persona and compartmentalize his business as simply a pragmatic choice. "It's just a job," he says. He might also identify his unloved objects, such as furniture, as practical and mundane—like his job. Similarly, if a woman has a conflict between her feminist and traditional ideals, she may identify loved objects to help resolve this conflict. Perhaps her collection of antique and delicate porcelain figurines raises good feelings about a time (the 1950s) in which women were relatively repressed.

Even a favorite pair of blue jeans can resolve internal role conflict. Perhaps a young manager has misgivings about working on Saturday. By dressing in her favorite, well-worn blue jeans, she can exercise some autonomy. "If I have to work on the weekends, at least I'll be comfortable," she says. In a positive sense then, loved objects can provide a mechanism for psychological conflict resolution. Now that we've discussed the importance of the extended self and loved objects, let's examine how individuals manage their social behavior.

OBJECTIVE 2

Self-Monitoring

The extent to which consumers use situational cues to guide their social behavior is known as **self-monitoring.** People who routinely modify their behavior to meet the expectations of others are known as *high self-monitors.* Conversely, people who act primarily on the basis of their internal beliefs and attitudes are known as *low self-monitors.*[21] Put simply, high self-monitors tend to behave like social chameleons, constantly changing and adapting their behaviors to different situations and different people. Low self-monitors march to the beat of their own drums. Research shows that *low* self-monitors exhibit greater attitude-behavior consistency than high self-monitors.[22] Research also demonstrates that *high* self-monitors show more concern for the self-image they project in social situations.[23] As a result, high self-monitors are more likely to respond to image-based appeals that promise to make them look good, while low self-monitors are more likely to evaluate the functional benefits of a product.[24] Self-monitoring typically involves three somewhat distinct individual differences:

- Willingness to be the center of attention

- Concern about the opinions of others

- Ability and desire to adjust one's behavior to induce positive reactions in others

Like many individual difference variables, self-monitoring can be measured by a survey instrument. Low self-monitors tend to endorse statements like "My behavior is usually an expression of my true inner feelings, attitudes, and beliefs." High self-monitors agree with statements such as "When I am uncertain how to act in a social situation, I look to the behavior of others for cues."

Self-monitoring can be helpful in resolving the personality-versus-situation debate in consumer behavior, which focuses on the relative influence of personality traits versus situational factors on consumers' attitudes and behaviors. Advocates of the personality approach argue that an individual's personality determines his/her behavior. Conversely, advocates of the situation approach believe that the nature of circumstances drives behavior.[25] Research suggests that both approaches can be correct, depending on an individual's self-monitoring. The importance of personality traits is discussed later in this chapter.

The term **malleable self** refers to a multifaceted self-concept that includes a *good self, bad self, not-me self, desired self, ideal self, ought-to-be self.* Any of these **self-conceptions** are accessible at any given moment.[26] In this sense, self-concept is regarded as both stable and malleable. On one hand, the self-concept contains an enduring set of self-conceptions. On the other hand, consumers access and use different self-conceptions, depending on the task at hand—like tools in a toolbox. Classic research indicates that people prefer brands that match their self-conceptions. But which self-conceptions do consumers use to compare themselves to brands? Recent research shows that high self-monitors use social cues to select self-conceptions, and low self-monitors draw on their internal traits.[27]

Photodisc/Getty Images

The extent to which consumers use situational cues to guide their social behavior is known as **self-monitoring**.

Let's take a real-world example. Suppose a first-year college student goes dancing three nights during the first week of school. Does this mean that she is extroverted (a stable personality trait) or did she go dancing to reduce the stress associated with her new school environment (a temporary situation)? Self-monitoring provides a third and more complete explanation. Perhaps this individual is neither unusually extroverted nor extraordinarily stressed. She is, however, interested in joining a social sorority (a brand), whose members have been frequenting the night clubs this week. As a high self-monitor, she evaluated the situation and drew on her "desired self," i.e., her desire to be a member of this sorority. Next, she adapted her behavior to appear extroverted and outgoing because she believes this would increase her chances of being invited to join the sorority. Alternatively, if she were a low self-monitor, she would probably stay at home. Her choice of a sorority would be guided predominately by her internal beliefs and attitudes, and she would not attempt to construct a desired image. Perhaps charity is an important part of her self-schema, or actual self. Accordingly, she might evaluate sororities on the basis on their community service record and search for a sorority accordingly.

Consider also a high self-monitoring consumer who wants to project an image of intellect and culture to his dinner party guests. In addition to choosing appropriate words and mannerisms, he selects and displays the brands of food, wine, and music that support an intellectual and cultured image. Conversely, the low self-monitor would not be influenced by these social cues. Instead, he would select a decorum that fits his actual self-concept, i.e., who he really is.[28] Some level of self-monitoring is inherent in all social situations. People must adapt to their environments in order to interact. Nevertheless, some individuals present themselves in such a way as to create exaggerated or misleading images. Motivation for this behavior is explored next in a discussion of impression management theory.

OBJECTIVE 3

Impression Management Theory

The process of creating desirable images of ourselves for others is known as **impression management.** In general, people practice impression management to increase control over valued outcomes, such as praise, approval, sympathy, and special treatment. Individuals engage in impression management to make people like them (ingratiation); to generate fear (intimidation); respect (self-promotion); to lift up their morals (exemplification); and to engender pity (supplication).[29] Consumers employ at least three tactics to manage the images that others form about them:

1. Appearance management
2. Ingratiation
3. Aligning activities

APPEARANCE MANAGEMENT   By controlling the selection of clothes, grooming, habits (e.g., smoking), verbal communication (e.g., jargon, accents), and the display of possessions, consumers convey desired images to others.[30] The decisions regarding how consumers control their physical appearances and surroundings comprise their **appearance management.** Research supports the notion that consumers pay close attention to their physical appearance in order to claim certain identities. Job applicants have been shown to manage their physical appearance to match the interviewer's stereotyped expectations. If the interviewer is thought to be conservative, the applicants dress more traditionally than if the interviewer is thought to be progressive.[31] Likewise, salespeople spend considerable time and money on clothing and grooming. People also pay close attention to their props (items in their physical environments). Do you arrange your dormitory or apartment differently depending on whether your

Fathead appeals to consumers who like to prop their surroundings with sports and entertainment figures.

parents or friends will be visiting? You are not alone; most consumers use props. Executives arrange their offices to convey prestige; children prop their bedrooms with colorful posters; and professors always seem to have piles of books on their desks and tables (they must be busy). Have you noticed that U.S. politicians always have the American flag propped in the background and an American flag pin in their lapels for photo ops and speeches? *Fathead* targets consumers who want to prop their surroundings with sports and entertainment figures.

INGRATIATION   It is inherently pleasing to be liked by others. One of the tactics people use to get others to like them is **ingratiation,** a set of strategic behaviors designed to increase the probability of gaining benefits or favors from another person. One can ingratiate with self-presentation, opinion conformity, and flattery.

Self-presentation involves either *self-enhancement* or *self-deprecation.* The former occurs when people promote their good qualities, such as during interviews or on first dates. Self-enhancement can backfire, however, if the claims are viewed as conceited[32] or exaggerated and later discredited.[33] When employing self-deprecation, people make humble or modest claims about themselves, often downplaying their positive attributes or their role in a successful outcome. This tactic can also backfire if the self-deprecation is excessively negative and perceived as an attempt to elicit reassurance from others.[34] Taken together, self-presentation is a trade-off between favorability and plausibility—modest claims may signal incompetence, and yet, highly favorable claims may not be credible.

Think about your strategy on a first date. On one hand, if you describe all of your accomplishments and talents, you may be perceived as boastful and turn off your date. On the other hand, if you fail to mention your positive capabilities, your date may regard you as mediocre. Either way, you probably don't get a second date. Thus, self-presentation involves striking a balance between the opposing forces of self-enhancement and self-deprecation.[35] Research demonstrates that the optimal balance shifts, depending on whether people are interacting with friends or strangers.[36] Self-presentations are more likely to be self-enhancing to strangers and modest to friends. Why? Strangers usually have little information, so an individual's performance record may be difficult to verify. Consequently, by presenting highly favorable information to strangers, people willingly sacrifice likeability in exchange for perceptions of competence. The strategy is different with friends. Because they have more background information about you, friends can easily disconfirm an exaggerated claim. Moreover, people share common interests with friends and expect many future interactions. Thus, people maintain friendships by increasing likeability through a more modest self-presentation. Let's return to the strategy for a first date. Research suggests that if a new acquaintance is aware of something you've done well, s/he will like you more if you are modest about it. On the contrary, if s/he is completely unaware of a particular talent, modesty is simply interpreted as mediocrity.[37] In sum, if you've got it, flaunt it—but only if your date doesn't already know about it.

Opinion conformity entails expressing insincere agreement on important issues. Subordinates often use this tactic with supervisors, because people generally like those who share their opinions.[38] But it can backfire if the target of opinion conformity perceives the ingratiator as pandering. Thus, a clever mix of disagreement on unimportant issues and agreement on critical issues reduces suspicion.

Flattery involves excessive compliments or praise designed to make someone feel good about her/himself. Flattery does not have to be insincere. In fact, effective flattery should be targeted at important attributes where people feel uncertain about their abilities or performance. For example, if a friend expresses anxiety about his performance on an important and recently delivered speech, an earnest comment such as "I appreciate that you spoke slowly and clearly" is likely to gain favor for the ingratiator. Similarly, when a salesperson flatters a potential customer regarding an important but uncertain attribute, the customer is likely to respond favorably. For example, a consumer may have reservations about his weight and expresses those concerns while trying on business suits. A clever salesperson may flatter the customer by remarking that he is "in better shape than most men his age." Recent research demonstrates that if customers perceive flattery to be sincere, it matters not whether the remark is perceived to be accurate, as both genuine compliments (sincere and accurate) and opaque flattery (sincere and inaccurate) appear to generate positive intentions to continue working with a salesperson.[39] Figure 11.2 provides a multidimensional model of Consumer Ingratiation.

ALIGNING ACTIVITIES   Sometimes consumers behave in ways that violate existing cultural norms. **Aligning activities** consist of comments that attempt to realign our behavior with norms.[40] **Disclaimers** are verbal assertions, made in advance, to offset the potential negative effects of a behavior.[41] A celebrity endorser may use a disclaimer such as "I'm no expert, but …" to avoid responsibility for a product's performance. A salesperson may remark, "Please hear me out before you refuse this offer" to keep potential customers from prematurely rejecting an offer. **Accounts** entail *excuses* and *justifications.* The former reduce or deny one's responsibility for inappropriate actions; the latter acknowledge responsibility but rationalize the behavior as appropriate, given the circumstances.[42] Both excuses and justifications are designed to reduce perceptions of wrongdoing. For example, a customer service representative from Dell Computer Co., who claims that your computer crashed because you installed incompatible software, is excusing Dell from any responsibility for the problem. In contrast, the service rep may justify the computer crash on grounds that the computer is seven years old and well beyond its useful life. In a similar vein, one salesperson may explain a late delivery as a shipping or supplier problem—an excuse; another may explain the late delivery as a function of building a custom order—a justification. Accounts work best when the individual delivering them is of superior status and when the violating behavior is not serious.[43] What about students, who are not in a superior position to account for serious violations such as late assignments and missed exams? Research suggests that students' excuses and justification are better received if they are truthful and apologetic. It also helps if the account is reasonable.

It should be clear that people employ various tactics to manipulate the impressions others form of them. Consumers and salespeople manage their appearances; they ingratiate themselves through selective presentation, opinion conformity, and flattery; and they try to repair their identities when their conduct is questionable. Next, let's take a look at what makes an individual unique and how that influences his/her behavior as a consumer.

FIGURE 11.2 A MULTI-DIMENSIONAL MODEL OF CONSUMER INGRATIATION

POSITIVE INGRATIATION		Sincerity [Perception of the Ingratiator's Motive]	
		Insincere [self-enhancement] *manipulative*	**Sincere** [other-enhancement] *genuine*
Accuracy [Perception of the accuracy of the remark]	**Accurate** [true positive]	***Phony Compliment*** *[smooth talk]*	***Genuine Compliment*** *[positive feedback]*
	Inaccurate [false positive]	***Transparent Flattery*** *[brown-nosing]*	***Opaque Flattery*** *[friendly behavior]*

NEGATIVE (anti) INGRATIATION		Sincerity [Perception of the Ingratiator's Motive]	
		Insincere [self-enhancement] *manipulative*	**Sincere** [other-enhancement] *genuine*
Accuracy [Perception of the accuracy of the remark]	**Accurate** [true negative]	***Disparagement*** *[malicious Criticism]*	***Negative Feedback*** *[useful Criticism]*
	Inaccurate [false negative]	***Sarcasm*** *[harmful Criticism]*	***Hyper Critique*** *[ineffectual Criticism]*

Source: Thomas W. Cline, D.P. Mertens, N.S. Vowels, and A. Davies, "All ingratiation is no equal: A two dimensional model of consumer ingratiation," Society for Consumer Psychology 2009 Winter Conference. Reprinted by permission of Thomas W. Cline.

Personality

Personality is a set of unique psychological characteristics that influence how a person responds to his or her environment, including cognitive, affective, and behavioral tendencies. Understanding a consumer's personality can help predict his/her responses to marketing activities—but it is a tricky business. People don't necessarily behave the same way in all situations, and an individual's personality can change over time. Consumers' personalities mature along with their physical growth. For example, advanced education may affect consumers' personalities by teaching them to be more open-minded and inquisitive. Similarly, the process of aging often ushers in self-reflection, increasing consumers' desire for reading and experiential travel. Some people become more cynical over time, while others become more trustful. Few consumers respond to products and services today as they did as children or teenagers.

Major life events can also produce "shocks" in a consumer's personality. Often, a full-time job can increase a person's need to be conscientious, and marriage frequently brings a spirit of cooperation (at least initially!). Having children, changing occupations, chronic illness, and the death of loved ones can also engender significant shifts in one's personality. Nevertheless, it's difficult to ignore the enduring qualities of personality; in fact, personality has uniformly been considered to be constitutional, i.e., an essential and stable characteristic of individuals Some people just seem consistently grouchy, while others routinely act pleasingly. In the same vein, some of your friends probably assert themselves without fail, while others predictably withdraw from confrontations. Earlier in this chapter, we described these individual nuances as traits. Indeed, scholars have approached the study of personality from a variety of angles, producing many interesting theories, including Freudian Systems,[44] Neo-Freudian Theories,[45] and trait theories.[46] The most useful approach for consumer behavior is multiple trait theory.

OBJECTIVE 4

Multiple Trait Theory

Multiple trait theory maintains that **personality traits** represent consumers' tendencies to respond in a certain way across similar situations. Traits vary from one person to another, and although an individual's traits can shift, they are generally stable over a reasonable time frame. Think of traits as those specific qualities and mannerisms that distinguish one person from another. Consider, for a moment, your best friend. How would you describe his/her personality? Is this person generally outgoing, smart, shy, or moody? How does s/he respond to new situations? Is s/he optimistic, dramatic, or indifferent? How does this individual react to marketing stimuli? Is s/he a bargain hunter or an impulsive shopper? Longstanding research interest in personality and consumer psychology has produced a host of measurable personality traits. Among the most popular multiple trait theory taxonomies is the **Five-Factor Model**.[47] This multi-factor structure identifies five basic traits that derive primarily from an individual's genetics and early childhood learning.[48] The five basic traits have traditionally been numbered and labeled as:

1. Surgency (outgoingness)
2. Agreeableness
3. Conscientiousness
4. Emotional stability
5. Intellect

Figure 11.3 provides specific characteristics of the five core traits.[47]

The Five-Factor Model enables marketers to categorize consumers into different groups based on several traits. Thus, trait theory is a special case of market segmentation. Research shows that important personality traits can be linked to specific consumption behavior, such as **compulsive buying,** i.e., the drive to consume uncontrollably and to buy in order to avoid problems. Specifically, consumers who score low on conscientiousness

FIGURE 11.3 THE FIVE-FACTOR MODEL OF PERSONALITY

	DIMENSION	
Those scoring low are...	**Surgency**	*Those scoring high are...*
Introverted		Extraverted
Shy		Talkative
Quiet		Assertive
Reserved		Verbal
Untalkative		Energetic
Inhibited		Bold
Withdrawn		Active
Timid		Daring
Bashful		Vigorous
Those scoring low are...	**Agreeableness**	*Those scoring high are...*
Cold		Kind
Unkind		Cooperative
Unsympathetic		Sympathetic
Distrustful		Warm
Harsh		Trustful
Demanding		Considerate
Rude		Pleasant
Selfish		Agreeable
Uncooperative		Helpful
Those scoring low are...	**Conscientiousness**	*Those scoring high are...*
Disorganized		Organized
Careless		Systematic
Unsystematic		Thorough
Inefficient		Practical
Undependable		Neat
Impractical		Efficient
Negligent		Careful
Inconsistent		Steady
Those scoring low are ...	**Emotional Stability**	*Those scoring high are ...*
Anxious		Unenvious
Moody		Unemotional
Temperamental		Relaxed
Envious		Imperturbable
Emotional		Unexcitable
Irritable		Undemanding
Those scoring low are...	**Intellect**	*Those scoring high are...*
Unintellectual		Intellectual
Unintelligent		Creative
Unimaginative		Complex
Uncreative		Imaginative
Simple		Bright
Unsophisticated		Philosophical
Unreflective		Artistic

Source: Adapted from Goldberg, L. R. (1992). The Development of Markers for the Big Five-Factor Structure. *Psychological Assessment*, 4:26–42.

or high on agreeability demonstrate a propensity to shop compulsively.[49] This negative link between conscientiousness and compulsive buying suggests that individuals who have difficulty controlling their buying may also lack organization, precision, and efficiency. The positive relationship between agreeability and compulsive buying implies that uncontrolled shopping is associated with tendencies to be kindhearted, sympathetic, and not rude to others.[50] The Five-Factor Model has also been used to explain consumers' bargaining and complaining behavior,[51] voting behavior,[52] and alcohol abuse.[53] Research also shows that the Five-Factor Model can provide a framework to tap the dimensions of a brand's personality.

Brand-Personality

Earlier in this chapter, we learned that consumers prefer brands that enhance their self-concepts. In some cases, consumers prefer products that reflect who they are, i.e., their actual self-concepts. For example, "These blue jeans aren't for me. They're too risqué." In other cases, consumers buy products that help them express who they'd like to be, i.e., their ideal self-concepts. For example, "I'll take these preppy jeans; I need to upscale my image." Brands such as *Nike* and *Nokia* often conjure up specific **brand images,** which comprise all the thoughts and feelings consumers have about a particular brand. Consumers' thoughts and feelings are evoked through the stimuli they associate with a brand, such as logos, slogans, endorsers, price, distribution channel, typical users, and use situations. Though somewhat elusive, brand image can be estimated by asking consumers the first words that come to mind when the think about a brand. What comes to mind when consumers think of *Mountain Dew, Yahoo!, Apple, Kellogg's, McDonald's,* and *Louis Vuitton?*

A considerable amount of research demonstrates that, like people, brands exhibit personality traits. **Brand personality** refers to the set of human characteristics associated with a brand. Brand personality comprises the human side of a brand's image. For example, *Absolut vodka* is typically described as a cool, contemporary, 25-year old, while *Stoli's vodka* is an intellectual, conservative, older man. Would consumers describe the personality of *Sky vodka* any differently? Drawing on the Five-Factor Model of personality, Jennifer Aaker developed a framework to measure a brand's personality. She identified five distinct personality traits:

1. Sincerity
2. Excitement
3. Competence
4. Sophistication
5. Ruggedness[54]

Each of these factors includes various descriptors, as shown in Figure 11.4.

Three of the five dimensions of brand personality relate to the "Big Five" human personality dimensions. *Agreeableness* matches up with *sincerity* to capture warmth and acceptance; *Conscientiousness* parallels *competence,* as both embody responsibility, security, and dependability; and *extroversion* and *excitement* mutually describe energy, activity, and sociability. Two dimensions of brand personality (*sophistication* and *ruggedness*), however, stand apart from the Five-Factor Model. This suggests that consumers may not recognize these particular traits in themselves, but rather aspire to attain them. This notion is consistent with existing marketing activities surrounding archetypal sophisticated brands such as *Gucci, Lexus, Hennessy,* and *Rolex* that feature glamorous and high-class images. Similarly, rugged brands such as *Marlboro, Timberline, Jeep,* and *L.L. Bean* symbolize tough, outdoorsy ideals that appeal to consumers' ideal self-concepts.[54]

Image courtesy of The Advertising Archives

What is Gucci's brand personality?

PART THREE How Consumers Process Information

FIGURE 11.4 THE DIMENSIONS OF BRAND PERSONALITY

```
                        Brand Personality

   Sincerity      Excitement     Competence    Sophistication   Ruggedness

 Down-to-earth    Daring          Reliable      Upper class      Outdoorsy
 Honest           Spirited        Intelligent   Charming         Tough
 Wholesome        Imaginative     Successful
 Cheerful         Up-to-date
```

Source: Schoen, H., and Schumann, S. (2007). Personality traits, partisan attitudes, and voting behavior: Evidence from Germany. Political Psychology, 28, 471-498. Reprinted by permission of John Wiley and Sons, Inc.

Brand personality traits maintain an important relationship with human personality traits. First, human traits are characterized based on a consumer's observable behavior, manifest beliefs and attitudes, and physical and demographic characteristics.[55] For example, "He's a sophisticated manager, always in a hurry and up-to-date with technology." In contrast, brand traits are characterized based on a brand's *typical user*, i.e., the set of human characteristics associated with those who routinely endorse the brand. Thus, if technologically inclined, sophisticated managers are typical users of *Bluetooth technology*, then these particular personality traits are likely to be transferred to the *Bluetooth* brand.[56]

EYE ON INTERNATIONAL

THE DIMENSIONS OF BRAND PERSONALITY DEPEND ON CULTURE

Brand personality may be critical to developing brand loyalty, but the specific dimensions that describe a brand's personality are far from universal. For example, researchers from China and the UK found that one particular dimension important to Americans, but not to Chinese, is ruggedness, i.e., "rugged or tough."[82]

One explanation for the absence of this dimension among Chinese consumers may reside in their social norm of non-aggression. Many Chinese are influenced by the doctrine of Way (Tao), which emphasizes politeness and harmony, and the doctrine of Mean (Yau), which urges people to avoid competition and conflict in order to maintain inner harmony.

©Phil Date, 2009/Used under license from Shutterstock.com

Understandably, "tough" and "rugged" signal undesirable meanings in China because these adjectives appear to oppose desirable personal attributes, such as "gentle," "polite," and "elegant."

The marketing implications for brands that rely on ruggedness, such as Marlboro cigarettes, are complicated. Should Marlboro remain consistent over time and space when advertised in foreign countries or shift the meaning of the brand, e.g., associate Marlboro with less rugged but more exciting images? Research suggests the latter. The American cowboy need not be rugged and tough to connect with the Chinese. He could be well-mannered, intelligent, and reliable.

Consumers also extract cultural meaning from the brands that they purchase. Thus, the process is a paradoxical two-way street. A brand's image is shaped by those who use it, and yet, the users construct their identities through a brand's personality. Research also suggests that brand personality includes the demographic characteristics of the typical users, such as gender, class, and age. For example, *Revlon* is predominately female; *Budweiser* is male; and *Starbucks* is gender-neutral. *Chevy* is middle-class, but *Cadillac* is upper class. Apple's *Mac* is young; and *HP* is old.

Brand traits can also be inferred through *typical use situations,* which represent the various ways a brand is consumed or used. For example, *McDonald's* is a popular destination for single parents to treat their children to a pre-made meal in a colorful, quick-serve environment. *Big Boy* also appeals to this demographic, offering a similar menu and remarkably comparable brand symbols (Ronald McDonald versus Big Boy). However, the use situation at *Big Boy* is sit-down and typically includes the entire family. For another example, consider the desktop computer. *Apple Computers* are typically used for creative applications and hobbies. Quite the opposite, PCs tend to be all about business applications. The popular "I'm a Mac. I'm a PC." ads by Apple attest to this dichotomy.

Like human traits, brand traits can also be inferred indirectly through *product associations,* such as attributes (e.g., the *iPhone's* features are imaginative), product-category (e.g., motorcycles are daring), names (e.g., Smucker's is down-to-earth), and logos (e.g., Nike's swoosh is spirited).[57] Finally, a brand's personality can be formed by using characters and celebrities to endorse the brand. See Figure 11.5 for a model of brand personality.

In contrast to a brand's tangible attributes (e.g., dress or pants size), brand personality tends to serve a symbolic or self-expressive function for consumers.[58] The symbolic use of brands occurs because consumers instill brands with human personality traits. Marketers understand the importance of symbolic meaning and often use characterization to communicate brand personality.

FIGURE 11.5 A MODEL OF BRAND PERSONALITY

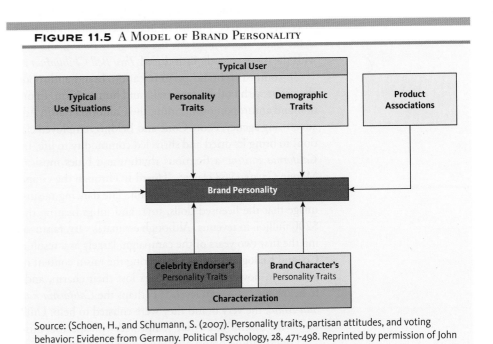

Source: (Schoen, H., and Schumann, S. (2007). Personality traits, partisan attitudes, and voting behavior: Evidence from Germany. Political Psychology, 28, 471-498. Reprinted by permission of John Wiley and Sons, Inc.

Characterization

Two strategies provide brands with characterization. **Brand personification** involves giving non-humans human-like traits, while **brand anthropomorphism** assigns both human form and human traits to non-humans. Marketers use both strategies to build brand personality. For example, *Geico's* talking gecko represents brand personification. The gecko's English accent and delightful mannerism are unmistakably human, but he retains the form of a lizard. In fact, this laid-back ambassador of great customer service and quick insurance rate quotes was voted America's favorite advertising icon in 2005.[59] The idea for the gecko emerged from a creative session at the Martin Agency in Richmond, Virginia. For years, the company's name, "Geico," an acronym for Government Employees Insurance Company,

The M&M characters represent brand personification.

PRNewsFoto/Carvel Corporation/AP Photo

had been incorrectly pronounced as "Gecko." Thus, the gecko was created to turn consumers' mispronunciations into an amusing memory aid. The famous gecko first aired on national television in 1999. But the gecko had, and still has, competition—in the form of the Aflac Insurance duck. Also debuting in 1999, Aflac's duck—voiced by Gilbert Gottfried—"quacks" out the company's name in frustration to prospective policyholders who can't seem to remember it. This is a deliberate attempt to facilitate brand name recall and link the crazy character traits of the duck to an otherwise boring product, supplemental insurance.

Brand personification need not involve animals. The M & M characters appear in lighthearted commercials for Mars, Inc., one of the largest privately owned businesses in the world. The M & M characters have been assigned human traits but their forms are primarily non-human, i.e., they have faces on a body reminiscent of actual M & Ms. To emphasize the M & M's brand personality, Mars has even named their "spokescandies." The cynical and sardonic *red* duo serve as mascots for milk chocolate M & Ms, and happy and gullible *yellow* duo represent peanut M & Ms. In a 2004 online poll sponsored by *USA Today* and *Yahoo!,* the M & M candy characters were voted America's favorite advertising icons.[60] It's no wonder, as consumers can visit the www.mms.com (planet M & Ms) and create their own look-alike M & M characters. The list of brand personifications is lengthy, including classics such as the *Budweiser Clydesdales,* the *Energizer Bunny,* and *Star-Kist's Charlie the Tuna* along with the more recently introduced *Taco Bell Chihuahua* and the *Chic-fil-A cows.*

In contrast to brand personification, brand anthropomorphization enlists fictitious characters with both human traits and human form. In one of the most fascinating cases of brand anthropomorphization, the California Raisin Advisory Board, working with its advertising agency, Foote Cone and Belding, employed claymation (stop-motion animation) to bring its dried and shriveled commodity to life. In 1987, the agency created *The California Raisins,* a fictitious rhythm and blues musical group, that debuted singing Marvin Gaye's 1968 classic, "Heard It Through the Grapevine." The annual advertising budget was estimated at $40 million. The dancing raisins created such a popular brand image that the licensed dolls, toys, and mugs bearing their likenesses generated nearly $200 million in revenue. Although estimates vary, raisin sales increased dramatically during the first two years of the campaign, largely as a result of cereal marketers Post Cereal Co. and Kellogg Company bolstering the raisin content of their brands. Fewer than five years later, however, the characters lost their charm, and sales of raisins had decreased to below pre-campaign levels.[61] Perhaps the *California Raisins* overpowered the image of *Sun-Maid,* the very brand they were enlisted to help. Unlike the M & M characters, the *California Raisins'* faces were sculptured with specific, human features.

Longstanding brand anthropomorphizations dot the marketing landscape, including the *Jolly Green Giant, The Pillsbury Dough Boy, Mr. Clean, McGruff the Crime*

Dog (National Crime Prevention Council), *Planter's Mr. Peanut, Kellogg's Rice Krispies Snap, Crackle, and Pop, Mrs. Butterworth, the Quaker Oats man, and the Kool-Aid man.* Each is designed to "humanize" and distinguish the brand from its competitors. In a more recent example of brand anthropomorphization, the ABC network developed a comedy called "Cavemen," adapted from Geico Insurance commercials as an offbeat commentary on ethnic prejudice from the perspective of three prehistoric guys trying to make their way in the modern world. The television show debuted in fall 2007, but didn't survive the entire season.

In sum, brand personality has long held the attention of marketing professionals, who are interested in "striking the right cord" with their target markets.[62] Research has demonstrated that consumers purchase brands not only for their functional benefits, but also for their symbolic roles. Brand personality dimensions can affect consumer behavior as a result of self-expressive needs expressed when consumers choose brands representing an extension of their actual or ideal-self concepts. Furthermore, brands are also capable of affecting consumers' self-concepts. Recent research provides evidence that a brand's personality can be transferred to consumers.[63] Specifically, when consumers think about "sincere" brands, they view themselves as more agreeable. When consumers consider "competent" brands, they see themselves as more sophisticated. These findings highlight the extraordinary power of brand personalities. Not only do consumers choose brands because they want to underscore some aspect of who they are or who they want to be, but—to some extent—brands also make consumers who they are.

OBJECTIVE 5

Cognitive Factors

One critical difference between the social sciences (e.g., consumer behavior) and the natural sciences (e.g., biotechnology) is that the former recognizes the importance of **cognitive personality variables,** those personality traits that describe an individual's mental responses to objects. Individual differences in cognition can explain how consumers respond differentially to various marketing activities. Earlier in this chapter, we learned that high self-monitors, individuals who are sensitive and responsive to social cues, constantly change and adapt their behavior to match the particular social situation. Conversely, low self-monitors behave more consistently across various situations. Similarly, **locus of control** describes the extent to which an individual possesses internal or external reinforcement beliefs. Individuals with an external locus of control believe that their outcomes are controlled primarily by fate, luck, or more powerful others.[64] Consequently, their behaviors seem to vary almost randomly across situations. Individuals with an internal locus of control, however, believe that they are masters of their own destinies and so, are more likely to behave in accordance with their internal states, i.e., opinions, beliefs, and attitudes.[65]

In contrast to multiple trait theory, cognitive approaches often identify one particular cognitive trait relevant to consumers' beliefs, attitudes, and intentions regarding products and services. Traits labeled as "needs" generally reflect consumers' desires or tendencies to engage in specific mental activities. Three of these motivational traits—need for cognition, need for humor, and need for cognitive closure—are discussed next.

Need for Cognition

Just as there are situational differences that enhance consumers' motivations to carefully evaluate persuasive messages, personality differences can also affect consumers' processing motivation in persuasive situations. **Need for cognition** (NFC) measures an individual's natural tendency to engage in and enjoy effortful cognitive activities.

Specifically, individuals high in NFC are more intrinsically motivated to engage in effortful cognitive analyses than are those individuals low in NFC.[66] Research shows that consumers who score high in NFC focus primarily on the product-relevant information in an advertisement. Motivated to evaluate the cogency of the message, these consumers are relatively unaffected by irrelevant background appeals, such as celebrity endorsements. On the other hand, consumers who score low in NFC pay attention to ancillary message cues, such as celebrities and attractive people in the ad. Related research reveals that when presented with unfamiliar brands, the attitudes of high NFC individuals are based on evaluation of product attributes, while those low in NFC develop attitudes based on simple peripheral cues.[67]

Need for cognition can also explain consumers' Internet preferences. Research evaluating individual differences in Web usage shows that those high in NFC use the Web to search for product information, current events and news, and for general education purposes. In contrast, Web users low in NFC are more likely to use the Web for entertainment purposes.[68] In general, those high in NFC, who enjoy thinking and effortful intellectual pursuits (e.g., chess, bridge, crossword puzzles, Sudoku), tend to be more heavily influenced by rational appeals, whiles those low in NFC—who do not enjoy effortful cognitive exercises and who think carefully only when necessary—are influenced more by emotional appeals.[69]

Need for cognition can provide helpful guidelines for public policy makers, who have embraced the use of marketing activities to improve public health by preventing the spread of HIV infection. A recent study shows that high NFC individuals develop a better understanding of the risks of unsafe sexual conduct when the information is presented in a written (versus comic strip) format. The opposite is true for those low in NFC.[70] Results of another study demonstrated the usefulness of need for cognition in reducing addictive behaviors, such as smoking. As their perceived vulnerability to the negative health effects of smoking increased, smokers more correctly inferred that smoking-cessation gimmicks (e.g., Quest Cigarettes) were no healthier than regular cigarettes, especially when their NFC was high. This finding was consistent with previous studies demonstrating that increased levels of motivation to process a persuasive communication are associated with more critical appraisals of that communication.[71]

Fly American, and you could kick yourself. Literally.

While American Airlines has been busy putting seats back in their planes to reduce legroom, we've been busy taking seats out. So it's not surprising that Economy Plus has now been voted the best premium economy class in the world. And that includes Chicago.

united.com   A STAR ALLIANCE MEMBER

✈UNITED
It's time to fly.

PRNewsFoto/United Airlines/AP Photo

Need for Humor

Humor is such a key ingredient in social communication that it is unusual to witness a casual conversation in which jokes and other humorous stimuli are *not* attempted. Similar to the need for cognition, individual differences in an individual's need for humor play an important role in the processing of persuasive communications. **Need for humor** (NFH) represents an individual's tendency to crave, seek out, and enjoy humor, a construct more motivationally driven than sense of humor.[72] The domain of NFH includes amusement, wit, and nonsense. Research suggests that the influence of humorous ad appeals are shaped by the joint interplay of the level of humor present in an ad and an individual's NFH.[73] Specifically, those consumers low in NFH appear indifferent to the level of humor in the ad, while those high in NFH not only form more favorable attitudes towards humorous ads, but are also turned off by understated or weak humor.

More interesting, NFC (need for cognition) may act as an "on-off switch" regarding consumers' NFH. People high in NFC are motivated to process issue-relevant ad claims rather than peripheral cues, so their NFH may be switched "off" during message evaluation. As a result, the level of humor in an ad has little effect on their attitudes. In contrast, those low in NFC are not motivated to critically evaluate the message; they are interested in peripheral cues, such as humor. Consequently, their NFH is switched "on." Taken together, consumers who are *low* in NFC and *high* in NFH tend to respond most favorably to humorous ad appeals. Finally, related research indicates that NFH can influence message recall. Individuals with low NFH recall more ad claims if they do not anticipate humor to be present in the communication, i.e., the humor is completely unexpected.[74]

On the basis of humor's prevalence in advertising and the belief in its universal effectiveness, NFH may be useful as a segmentation tool. For example, it may be helpful in identifying audiences who are more likely, under certain conditions, to respond favorably to humorous ads. NFH can differentiate subjects' attitudes under varying conditions of humor content. Thus, if marketers' objectives include attitude change, humor targeted at audiences high in NFH may produce favorable results. As with other "need" traits, it is rarely practical to survey members of target audiences; however, market research may identify media vehicles that draw audiences characterized by high NFH. For example, *National Lampoon* readers, *Comedy Central* watchers, and *Twitter* users may tend to score high in NFH. Advertisers could use this information to determine which product categories or brands tend to be popular with users of these media. For instance, *Comedy Central* viewers may also be heavy users of B-films and video games. In a similar vein, research firms such as SRI-CBI use values and lifestyle data (VALS) to identify marketing opportunities by segmenting on the basis of key personality traits that motivate consumer behavior. The premise of VALS is that consumers express their personalities through their actions. Accordingly, VALS defines consumer segments on the basis of those personality traits that affect consumer behavior. By including NFH as a key personality variable, VALS might discover that consumers who score high in NFH are more likely to perform karaoke, attend amusement parks, and watch comedy. Thus, NFH may be helpful both in media selection and in targeting audiences for specific products and services.

Need for Cognitive Closure

When making decisions, consumers must frequently make the difficult trade-off between speed and accuracy. Some decisions require immediate action, and consumers must make quick judgments. Other tasks afford consumers the opportunity to think about the decision more carefully and for longer periods of time. A quick decisions may serve as only a temporary and partial solution to a consumer's problem. For example, consumers may select a brand based on familiarity or other heuristic choice strategies. Unfortunately, the brand may not satisfy a consumer's future needs. Let's say a consumer wanted a docking station to charge and play her *Ipod*, and she also wanted an alarm clock feature built-in. If this consumer purchased an *Ihome,* she may later discover that the sound reproduction is inferior to such brands as *Bose.* Accordingly, longer deliberations generally result in better decisions. Research dealing with the **theory of lay epistemology,** the formation and use of everyday knowledge, suggests that individuals differ in the degree to which they make the important trade-off between speed and accuracy.[75] The **need for cognitive closure** (NFCC) describes a consumer's desire for definite knowledge of any kind to reduce confusion or ambiguity. As the need for cognitive closure increases, people consider fewer alternatives, consider smaller amounts of information about each alternative, make snap judgments that have obvious and immediate implications for action, and are insensitive to evidence inconsistent with their judgments. Ironically, they exhibit high levels of confidence in the appropriateness of their judgments, decisions, and actions.

In short, the need for cognitive closure promotes *epistemic seizing* and *freezing*. *Seizing* refers to the tendency to attain closure quickly, even if this means oversimplifying an issue or failing to carefully consider all sides of an issue. Alternatively, *freezing* refers to the tendency to maintain closure as long as possible, even if this means being closed-minded or unwilling to consider other options. People differ in their NFCC—some are strongly motivated to reach conclusions quickly at the risk of overlooking important qualifiers and limiting conditions; others are willing to deliberate carefully for long periods of time at the risk of appearing indecisive or to lack confidence. Situations also differ in the extent to which they increase or decrease NFCC. Time pressure increases the motivation to attain closure quickly. Concerns about accuracy and the long-term consequences of one's actions decrease motivation to attain closure quickly.

Recent research shows that the degree to which price is perceived to predict quality (the price-quality heuristic) is overestimated when consumers' NFCC is high. For people with a heightened NFCC, attaining closure quickly and perpetuating that closure is paramount. For these consumers, selectively focusing on belief-consistent information and ignoring potentially disconfirming evidence promotes closure because it allows one to reconfirm and maintain preexisting beliefs.[76] Research also reveals that when the attributes of a brand under consideration (target brand) cannot be readily compared to a previous brand (referent brand), evaluations for the target brand suffer, particularly if a consumer has a high NFCC.[77] Need for cognitive closure also provides insights into criminal investigations. Recent evidence suggests that investigators with high NFCC are less likely than those low in NFCC to acknowledge observations that are inconsistent with their hypothesis about the crime.[78]

Chapter Summary

Self-concept is the totality of an individual's thoughts and feelings about him or herself, including role identities, personal qualities, and self-evaluations. Role identities represent the various positions that consumers occupy in society. Personal qualities involve personality traits, or tendencies to behave in a certain way across similar situations. Self-evaluations are constructed when consumers consider the strength of their performances in various roles. The sum of all self-evaluations comprises self-esteem, which is the overall evaluative component of self-concept. The self-concept can be broken down into two dimensions—the actual versus ideal, each with two parts. The actual self-concept represents how consumers perceive themselves, while the actual public-concept embodies others' true perceptions of a consumer. The ideal self-concept describes how consumers would like to see themselves, and the ideal public-concept represents how consumers would like others to see them.

Self-concept is important to marketers because consumers' self-perceptions influence their attitudes towards products and subsequent purchase behavior. If marketers

want consumers to recall something about their brands, they should create communications that are consistent with consumers' actual self-concepts. Alternatively, if marketers' goals involve creating positive attitudes or images about their brands, they should communicate information that is congruent with consumers' ideal self-concepts. The relationship between a consumer's self-concept and his/her possessions is called the extended self. Possessions for which we develop a deep affection are known as "loved objects." Loved objects can help consumers resolve internal psychological conflicts.

The term "malleable self" refers to the notion that consumers can hold various self-concepts about themselves. Consumers will employ a particular self-concept, depending on the situation and their level of self-monitoring, which describes the extent to which consumers use situational cues to guide their social behavior. People who change their behavior to meet the expectations of others are known as high self-monitors, while people who act primarily on the basis of their internal beliefs and attitudes are known as low self-monitors.

The process of creating contrived images for others is known as impression management. Impression management involves our appearance, ingratiation, and aligning actions. Consumers control their selection of clothes, grooming, habits, language, and possessions. Ingratiation is the purposeful attempt to gain benefits or favors from others. Aligning activities are attempts to realign our behavior so it comes close to matching norms.

A consumer's personality consists of a set of unique psychological characteristics that influence thoughts, feelings, and behavior regarding products and services. Multiple trait theory holds that individuals' personality traits describe their tendencies to respond in given ways across similar situations. Brands also have personalities, comprised of the human characteristics we associate with them. Brand personalities are derived from the typical user, typical use situation, product associations, and brand characterization.

Personality differences can affect consumers' motivation to respond favorably to marketing activities and brands. Need for cognition (NFC) describes a consumer's tendency to engage in and enjoy effortful cognitive activities. Need for humor (NFH) represents an individual's inclination to crave and engage in humor. Finally, need for cognitive closure (NFCC) explains a consumer's desire for any kind of knowledge that reduces confusion or ambiguity.

Key Terms

self-concept	self-monitoring	personality traits
role identities	malleable self	five-factor model
personal qualities	self-conceptions	compulsive buying
traits	impression management	brand image
self-evaluation	appearance management	brand personality
self-esteem	ingratiation	brand personification
actual self-concept	self-presentation	brand anthropomorphism
ideal self-concept	opinion conformity	cognitive personality variables
actual public-concept	flattery	locus of control
ideal public-concept	aligning activities	need for cognition
self-schemas	disclaimers	need for humor
extended-self	accounts	theory of lay epistemology
loved objects	personality	need for cognitive closure

Review and Discussion

1. What is the difference between the actual self-concept and the actual public-concept? How do the ideal self-concept and ideal public-concept differ?

2. When consumers try to recall brand information, are they more likely to reference their actual or ideal selves? When they evaluate brands, which self-concept is activated? Explain.

3. How do loved objects help consumers resolve internal (personality) conflicts?

4. How does self-monitoring help explain how consumers use their malleable self?

5. Review the three tactics of impression management. When students conjure up excuses for late assignments, what are the best tactics?

6. Review the Five-Factor Model of personality. Explain how it might be used to account for consumer complaining, compulsive shopping, and binge drinking.

7. As the marketplace becomes more crowded with brands, do you think brand personality will be more or less important to consumers? Explain.

8. Select one of your favorite brands and describe it's brand personality based on the model provided in Figure 11.5. Be sure to include descriptions of the brand's *typical users, typical use situations, product associations, celebrity endorser's personality traits,* and *brand characterizations.*

9. Explain how brand characters such as *Tony the Tiger, Captain Morgan,* and the *Budweiser Clydesdales* can be useful in global marketing.

10. Review the cognitive variables, NFC, NFH, and NFCC. How can they be used to help marketers identify suitable target markets?

Short Application Exercises

1. On 15 numbered lines, write down 15 different things about yourself. Write the answers in the order that they occur to you. Do this prior to reading the next sentence. Now label each of the 15 descriptions about yourself as either:

   A. Role Identities—personal relationships, ethnic/religious groups, professional/hobby groups

   B. Personal Qualities—abilities, attitudes, emotions, interests, motives, opinions and traits

   C. Extended self—tangible objects that refer to your body or your possessions. Which of the three categories of your self-concept is most prevalent?

2. Consider the Ethics Box describing Unilever's "Real Beauty" campaign for Dove. From the viewpoint of a marketer, develop a list describing positive and negative aspects of such a campaign. Make the same list from the viewpoint of the consumer. Compare and contrast your responses.

3. Identify brands that have become a part of your "extended self" in five of the following ten categories:

   1. body
   2. personal space
   3. consumable goods
   4. durable goods
   5. home and property
   6. significant others
   7. children
   8. friends
   9. mementos
   10. pets

   For example, *Boflex* or *Lean Cuisine* may help consumers view their bodies as their extended self. Golf lessons for a golf professional's daughter may allow the pro to see his daughter as an extension of himself.

4. Conduct a mini-experiment with 15 friends. First, ask each of them to indicate, on a seven-point scale, the importance of the brand name versus the warranty for a laptop. Then, administer the self-monitoring scale to each. Evaluate whether low or high self-monitors found brand name to be more important.

MANAGERIAL APPLICATION

Imagine you work in the marketing department of a major athletic shoe firm. Your supervisor wants to understand how consumers view the top competitors in terms of brand personality. Use the five dimensions of brand personality discussed in the text as a framework (see Figure 11.4).

YOUR CHALLENGE:

1. Conduct a mini-experiment regarding brand personality. Ask 20 friends to write down the first several words that come to mind when they hear the brand names *Nike, Adidas, and Reebok.*
2. From these descriptions, summarize each of the three brands' personalities.
3. Describe the possible differences in target markets based on your research.
4. Select one particular brand and design a magazine ad that reflects what you learned from your research.
5. Explain which magazine would be an appropriate media vehicle for your ad.

The part video is designed to expand and highlight the consumer behavior concepts in this part of the book. To view the videos, go to **http://www.cengage.com/international,** and click on the student companion site link. After viewing the video, answer the following questions to test your knowledge on the part content and its application to the video case.

Harley-Davidson

Harley-Davidson has been in the motorcycle business since 1903. According to the company's Web site, its mission is "... in fulfilling dreams and providing extraordinary customer experiences through mutually beneficial relationships with our stakeholders." This video case examines how Harley-Davison uses company-sponsored activities to deepen relationships with customers.

1. What is the Harley-Davidson "experience" in terms of customers' motivations, attitudes, and emotions? How does Harley-Davison foster this "experience" through its marketing strategies?
2. What might a Harley-Davidson customer's associative network look like for the brand? What unique characteristics and values are present in an associative network for Harley-Davidson that would lead a consumer to pick a Harley-Davidson over a competing brand?
3. How important are the firm's use of H.O.G activities and functions to attract new customers (not just engage current customers)? Develop a new face-to-face activity to specifically appeal to potential new female customers.

The Influence of the Social Environment and Contemporary Strategies for Marketers

CHAPTERS

Professor of Marketing
UNIVERSITY OF WISCONSIN
Executive Director
Brand and Product Management Center
UNIVERSITY OF WISCONSIN

Thomas O'Guinn is Professor of Marketing at the University of Wisconsin. He is also executive director of the Brand and Product Management Center at UW. He studies brands and their communication as well as aspects of the sociology of consumption, i.e., how membership in various groups and social strata affect consumer behavior. He is the author of several award-winning articles and a leading book on advertising and integrated brand communication.

Q Could you comment on the role of the many different paradigms or "camps" in the field of consumer behavior and on your position with respect to these camps?

I don't fit particularly well in any of these camps. I had the opportunity to study several different paradigms when I was in graduate school and did some qualitative work on how people watch television and use advertising. A lot of that work was federally funded to understand how children watch television. Those methods, in that context, became very accepted, even with NSF money, to really understand how kids watch TV and how advertising works in real homes with real kids. At the same time, I was working in social and developmental psychology labs doing experiments . . . again, federally funded. So, I got a wonderful opportunity to cross paradigms in the same substantive domain. That was an education. I loved the clean nature of experiments AND the messy nature of *in situ* observation. Television viewing is one of those social behaviors that are so hard to replicate in the lab. It's very hard to bring people into a lab and say watch this . . . pretend you are at home. And there are long-term processes; the significant effects of television do not occur in an hour or a day, or even a year. I was always one of those people who was inclined, just by virtue of chance and by training, to be very multidisciplinary and to use multiple methods. I'm very driven by the phenomena, so sometimes it's entirely appropriate to be in the lab; it's the only way you can get it done. Other times, there are phenomena that I don't know how you could possibly do in a lab. So, to me, it's always the question that tells you which are the tools out of the toolbox you need to apply. And I think,

in my work I've always been less concerned about, "I am an experimentalist; I should do it this way," than I was about, "this is the phenomena; how am I going to understand it?" I also like to work with other people because they bring something to the project, and they make me stay on deadline. I get bored pretty easily.

Q How did you get interested in the topic of consumer compulsiveness, and what insights does your research provide on this important topic?

That came about literally when Ron Faber and I were at ACR in Las Vegas. And we're watching people gamble. I said to Ron, "I know people who shop like these people gamble." And we started this conversation. And on the way home I'm reading an in-flight magazine, and there is this woman talking about people who shop too much and this and that. So I get back home and I think, you know this is a pretty interesting thing. And that was one of those things we knew nothing about. And we spent a good two and a half years learning it before we ever put anything on paper because we didn't want to look like idiots. We found this group out in the Bay Area that was the largest self-help group for shopaholics. But at first it had this kind of carnivalesque feel about it . . . . I didn't like this. When you really saw the suffering, it was no longer funny. And we went out there, and we spent a lot of our own money, a lot of time. I remember sleeping on the floor at San Francisco International Airport one night because we were both young and didn't have money. We went out there and got with these self-help groups and spent I don't know . . . a good two and a half years doing qualitative work, trying to understand what it was and what it wasn't. And then we went into a more quantitative phase where we used our qualitative data to develop instruments. And then we were able to piece together enough money through different funding to do a big sample—the State of Illinois matched to a national list of self-reported compulsive buyers. We went to a Survey Research Lab in Illinois and did the adjustment to make these comparable. Seymour Sudman helped us. When we finally came out with a series of papers, we felt really good about them because we had done the work. We had used the qualitative data largely in a developmental phase. Although I don't want to say that was all it was used for, because that would diminish the nature of those data. We did use verbatims from it occasionally as exemplars of what we were talking about. But, we also used those data as you would any data . . . to drive understanding. I came out of a survey research background, and Ron came out of an experimental background. I think that we both, at least on that project, saw that the qualitative results could have stood alone. But I don't think so now. I think it needed the numbers side as well; their convergence helped. So when we wrote two or three, four or five papers from it, we really felt good about it. We thought they were solid. We felt like we could actually go talk at a conference and not look foolish because you know the topic was so easy to lampoon or dismiss. And we didn't want that because we had actually seen these people. You know these people literally had impulse control disorders; they couldn't not do this. And the co-morbidity between them and compulsive gamblers, most of these people, they just floated from one impulsive control to another. These were a lot of people who were in a lot of serious trouble. And the other thing that we didn't want made light of was that they were 90 percent women. There are two reasons for that. One is the self-report bias for women: they are much more likely to seek therapy (and report it) than men. If you go back to the 1940s, a woman is upset with a man, "Here, honey, here's some money, go buy a hat." We didn't want to contribute to that. Stratification differences in income and work status, as well as gender stereotyping, kind of made it "a woman's problem." So when the *New York Times* and National Public Radio and the *Wall Street Journal* start calling you for interviews, you are very aware of the potential for harm. The first thing out of our mouths was, "We're not clinicians, we are not . . ." But I think we were able to talk about it in a sensitive enough way that we didn't just run out, do some kind of goofy study, make fun of these people and leave, which does happen in the field. I think there are people in our field that I think regrettably do that. They see something in the news; they run out; they do a study. And it's

topical, but I think sometimes if you don't do the work, if you don't do the two or three years of homework on it, you can either make a fool of yourself or you can make light of something that's actually serious.

Q **Does your work have implications for helping consumers to adopt healthier lifestyles?**

Yes, but my co-author Ron Faber is much better at talking about that. Ron and I are still working on some things together, but he's more interested in psychological issues. He's hooked up with some people at the medical school at [the University of] Minnesota and has done some brilliant work on this. I was more interested in the why consumption question, the social question. Why does this manifest as buying? And that turned out to be a substantive but easy answer: because we live in a consumer culture. And I think Ron's work, the work that came out of our work that I have some part of, I think it does help. He's gotten involved in—well, our screener that we developed for the second paper, third paper. One of the cool things about that is that's becoming the preferred clinical and diagnostic screener. The psychometrics of it are just very strong, and it's a lot of luck. Then a guy at the Stanford Medical School got very fascinated in this topic. They adopted it as their screener. And then once they adopted it, so did a lot of folks. And so, that helps people screen for compulsive buying. And then I think just what Ron has been able to do with understanding the co-morbidity of this with other impulse control disorders and their response to certain anti-depressants. I mean Ron and his MD colleagues actually do help people; a lot of these people do respond really well to certain antidepressants. And I think our work also informs how therapists talk to people about compulsive buying. I think the most interesting thing we found out is that these people, at least on materialism scales, are no more materialistic than anybody else. What's interesting is they don't use the products. It's all about the acquisition. They store them under their beds, they hide them. They will go out and buy ten of the same thing. And it is about their relationship with the store. It's about the thrill of shopping; it's not the thrill of owning or using. It's the buying. To me, that really challenged what were then the dominant models of consumer behavior. I'm proud of that. The things purchased often remain unopened. And their social networks often are, not surprisingly, comprised of shopping clerks and delivery people. Compulsive buyers often consider the shopping clerks their friends. So there's more to the phenomenon than simple acquisition. It's the buying. That, I think, has helped clinicians. I think we have helped some consumers and I'm proud of that.

Q **Let's switch gears and talk about your work on advertising.**

You know it's funny I hardly ever wrote about advertising until this book and then lately, for whatever reason, I've started doing more advertising-related research. I've always been interested in mass media, but mostly program content, consumption in program content. But now that those lines between ads and content have started to disappear, I've become interested in branded entertainment. Also, I've always been fascinated how different social strata—stratification issues, social class issues—play out in ads and through ads. Target is one of the brands I use as an example because of how they have leveraged those sociological phenomena and how they do it with their ads and other ways. Here's a retailer that has done what was thought to be impossible. Sears tried to be everything to everybody for a hundred and something years. And I knew a lot of people who worked on Sears' business, and the problem was always that not many people wanted to buy a little black dress where they bought their socket sets. It just didn't work.

Target, however, has been able to do that, at least much more effectively. Part of the reason they have is what has happened demographically and how those demographics relate to what we call taste. So, it used to be we identified the wealthy through their display of certain types of consumption. For a long time, handmade had a certain social marker status. Well, now robots make much better things than handmade. Handmade is actually inferior. Several people write about this in sociology—the democratization or collapse of traditional status hierarchies in consumption. John Seabrook (NOBROW) writes about the case where high-end brands are now replicating low-end stuff like the sort of torn, beaded jeans for $3,500 from Gucci to look like something you would see, you know, in a very different social milieu from 5th Avenue. And this collapse of traditional status hierarchy is flattening taste cultures. Target management picked up on this beautifully, this whole design for the masses that Target has done so well.

Some of this matches up with my interest in design thought. I got lucky because when I came to the University of Wisconsin-Madison to run this brand center, one of my donors earmarked some money to look into design issues. I took a group out to the design school at Stanford, and now UW-Madison is partnering with a wonderful design company in Madison, Design Concepts, Inc. And one of the things we're all interested in, companies as well, is how do these things convey social meaning, map onto strata; how do they convey taste and culture? So, here again, a lot of interests: visual thought, design thought, social strata, and markers of taste all converge. I'm lucky: lots of nice toys.

Q **This leads into the next question. What are some of the key implications of the sociological and anthropological perspectives for managers?**

You don't have to convince managers of the value of qualitative research. It's one of the funniest things. In the academic field, it's been harder to convince people; they want so desperately to be real scientists. Well, maybe it's not that hard now, but there was a time when it was difficult to convince academic marketing colleagues that there was any value at all in doing fieldwork. I understand that because I came out of that tradition, too, and people want to see hard numbers and heavily controlled experiments, and I'm a believer in that too. But you know, I was listening to Scott Cook from Intuit talk. He is such a believer in going out and watching people use the product. You have to go see people actually use products and figure out what it is that they need. Eric von Hippel's (MIT) early work on using lead users and not being trapped by the present was so right. I've yet to run into a company that thinks that doing fieldwork is weird, in fact quite the opposite. It's more an academic concern. Now, the implications I think come in a lot of forms. Usually it's called, you know, consumer insights. They almost always think of fieldwork and in-home visits and all that as consumer insight. And that's just a big basket term for what they are learning in the field. But I think it's more the exception to hear them say that they didn't do that. They all sort of believe that. Now, some of them still do a lot of attitude work, you know particularly tracking studies. But I think they drive the front end with qualitative work. They all want metrics, some remain attitudinal, but I don't think they get used much beyond that sort of behavioral bean-counting. I do think, in my experience over the last 20 years, that there has been increasing skepticism about some of the metrics. Not about doing metrics, but about some of the metrics. And how sometimes their internal metrics on a brand mix will get in the way. We need to think about brands in terms of meaning rather than mere attitudes. Now, do I think attitudes and any of those other things are valuable? Sometimes.

Academic research often has different goals than managerial research. I try not to confuse them, but I also try to let one at least partially inform the other when that makes sense.

AN INTERVIEW WITH ROBERT CIALDINI

Courtesy of Robert B. Cialdini

Regents' Professor of Psychology and Marketing
Distinguished Graduate Research Professor
ARIZONA STATE UNIVERSITY

Robert Cialdini is the Regents' Professor of Psychology and Marketing at Arizona State University. He is also a Distinguished Graduate Research Professor at ASU. He is a recipient of the Distinguished Scientific Achievement Award of the Society for Consumer Psychology; the Donald T. Campbell Award for Distinguished Contributions to Social Psychology; and the Peitho Award for Distinguished Contributions to the Science of Social Influence. He studies persuasion and influence, altruism, and the tactics of favorable self-presentation.

Q How did you get interested in social influence?

As I say at the outset of a book I wrote on the topic, I think my initial interest in social influence was grounded in a personal weakness: I was always finding myself contributing to charities I knew nothing about or buying things I didn't really want from salespeople at my door. So, out of self-defense, I figured I'd better learn how this worked.

Q What role does social influence have in consumer behavior and marketing?

I believe there is a central role for social influence in these areas. After all, social influence involves the ability of one person to change the attitudes, beliefs, or behaviors of another; and this is frequently the primary goal of consumer-related messaging and marketing.

Q You once told me that the timing of the various elements of a request is crucial. Can you elaborate on this point?

I believe that there are particular moments in the course of an interaction when a request, recommendation, or

proposal is likely to be most successful. In fact, I am planning to write a book on the subject titled *Moments of Power*. It will not be so much about what to say for optimal influence as when to say it.

Q There are some publications in the marketing literature suggesting that high self-monitors are more effective salespersons relative to low self-monitors. Does this finding apply to the application of the weapons of influence, or can anyone learn to apply these tools? Do some types of individuals have an advantage in terms of their ability to influence consumers?

For a long time, persuasion was thought to be an art, something people were just naturally good (or not so good) at. I do believe that's true. At the same time, we now know that persuasion is also a science; consequently, it can be taught and learned. Therefore, even those of us who were not born with the artist's touch of a persuasion master can be trained to use scientifically proven principles of persuasion to become significantly more influential at work, at home, and beyond.

THE ROLE OF VALUES AND CULTURE

OBJECTIVES *After reading this chapter, you should be able to...*

1 | Define culture, cultural values, and subculture.

2 | Describe how cultural meaning moves from society to consumer products and eventually to individual consumers.

3 | Explain the differences among the four consumer rituals: exchange, possession, grooming and divestment.

4 | Explain how the Returns Potential Model shows the importance of various norms.

5 | Explain how product attributes and benefits may lead to instrumental and terminal values for consumers.

CHEATERS PROSPER

Commencement speeches at American universities and high schools typically feature inspirational themes designed to encourage freshly minted graduates to pursue honorable life goals. How would you feel about a speech that extols the virtues of cheating? Luca Cordero de Montezemolo, president of Ferrari and head of the Italian employers' federation Confindustira, did just this in a speech to graduates at Rome's Luiss University. Mr. Montezemolo recounted his skill at cheating in school. "I was the world champion copier when I was in school. I think I had no rivals for technique and sophistication. I always found a way to sit near someone clever and generous who would let me copy. This goes to show that there is hope even for one who copies, because even that way you can learn something." Mr. Montezemolo is also the president of Luiss University.

Can you imagine Steve Jobs (Apple), Bill Gates (Microsoft), or Jimmy Carter inspiring, the graduating class at Yale with such advice? There lies one major difference between cultures. Americans are told at an early age, "cheaters never prosper" and "honesty is the best policy." Stories about the integrity of George Washington and Abe Lincoln—if mythical—are nevertheless American staples. In contrast, other cultures are replete with such Calabrian proverbs as "He who behaves honestly, comes to a bad end."

In fairness, a plethora of websites based in the United States selling term papers demonstrate that Americans are both enthusiastic and entrepreneurial in their ability to cheat. But at least they have a bad conscience about it. In Italy, the concept of copying schoolwork reflects a specific cultural view about competition. Italian culture tends to favor community over rivalry. In the United States, the opposite is true. Mr. Montezemolo's remarks may simply describe a cultural attitude that students who allow others to copy their schoolwork are expressing loyalty and solidarity with their classmates. Cultural differences in the use of words to describe student-to-student plagiarism may explain this apparent inconsistency between the Anglo-American and Italian worlds. The U.S. student "cheats" his classmates by stealing their work, but the Italian students share their knowledge by letting their peers "copy." So, although it may be true that cheaters never prosper, it may also be true that copiers thrive.[1]

syagci/iStockphoto.com

(OBJECTIVE 1) # Culture Defined

Culture is a lot like humor—it's easy to recognize but difficult to define. In fact, countless definitions of culture exist in various disciplines such as anthropology, sociology, and social psychology. Some behavioral scientists define **culture** as the patterns of meaning acquired by members of society expressed in their knowledge, beliefs, art, laws, morals, customs, and habits. Edward B. Tylor, a British anthropologist, introduced this notion of culture in 1871.[2] Although we can see the manifestations of a culture, its meaning only exists in the collective minds of a society. As a result, culture is abstract, fragile, and dynamic. Geert Hofstede conducted a comprehensive study on how culture influences values. He defines culture as "the collective programming of the human mind that distinguishes the members of one human group from those of another." In this sense, culture can be thought of as a system of collectively held values.[3] **Cultural values** comprise a collective set of beliefs about what is important, useful, and desirable. Simply put, culture reflects the *personality* of a society. **Subcultures** are smaller groups of a larger culture that share some cultural values with society overall and yet demonstrate unique cultural values and patterns of behavior within the individual subgroup. Subcultures provide opportunities for marketers to segment society into more manageable groups that are likely to respond similarly to products and services based on their similar needs and wants. Geography, gender, age, race, nationality, religion, and social class form important subcultures. This chapter, however, provides a broader focus than a discussion of individual subcultures. Instead, we examine, in general, how cultural values move from the collective minds of society to individual consumers, with the help of marketing efforts and the fashion system.

Although we do not investigate individual groups such as Hispanic and African-American subcultures, Jewish consumers, Generation Y, or working women, we provide key references to help understand these important subgroups on our Cengage Learning website. For example, the U.S. Census Bureau (www.census.gov) provides information regarding the size and trends of all races in the United States, and detailed information on the demographic, economic, and social characteristics of individual cities and counties throughout the country. We encourage our readers to visit our book companion website **http://www.cengage.com/international** to find more interesting resources for understanding subcultures.

The opening vignette in this chapter provides a glimpse of cultural differences regarding cheating in school. At the very heart of this dissimilarity, differing systems of values exist—one culture emphasizes group solidarity, while another culture stresses individual integrity. Consumers who travel to foreign countries often encounter cultural differences. If these differences are extreme, they experience "culture shock," a state of anxiety associated with trying to deal with this new and unfamiliar environment. Cultural differences can also create vast differences in consumer behavior.

Consumer behavior is concerned with all consumer activities associated with the purchase, use, and disposal of goods and services, including the consumer's cognitive, affective, and behavioral responses that precede, determine, or follow these activities. Accordingly, this chapter discusses the characteristics of culture that are most likely to influence consumer behavior: language and symbols, customs and rituals, norms, and consumer values. Before discussing these specific aspects of culture, let's look as some theories that offer understanding on how culture evolves in a consumer society.

A Cultural Framework for Consumer Behavior

Anthropologist Grant McCracken provides a framework that describes the mobility of cultural meaning and the instruments that transfer this meaning from society to consumer products, and then from consumer products to individual consumers.[4] Figure 12.1 illustrates this movement of cultural meaning.

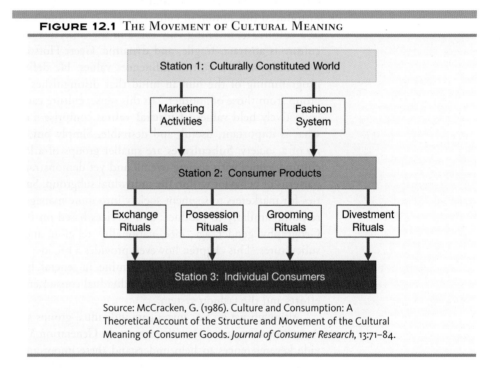

FIGURE 12.1 THE MOVEMENT OF CULTURAL MEANING

Source: McCracken, G. (1986). Culture and Consumption: A Theoretical Account of the Structure and Movement of the Cultural Meaning of Consumer Goods. *Journal of Consumer Research*, 13:71–84.

OBJECTIVE 2

The Culturally Constituted World

Consumers' broadest understanding of culture resides in the **culturally constituted world,** where all consumer experiences are shaped by the intangible beliefs and values of society. This is Station 1 in Figure 12.1. It is helpful to think of the culturally constituted world as a place where society's widely shared values are collected and stored. But note that these values are ever changing. As a warehouse for society's values, the culturally constituted world supplies meaning for consumers via two interrelated concepts: cultural categories and cultural principles. **Cultural categories** help organize a society by dividing the world into specific and distinct segments of time, space, nature, and people. Categories comprising people, such as age, gender, social class, and occupation, are most important to the study of consumer behavior. Cultural categories are the ancestors of market segments, but their purpose is not to identify groups of potential customers. Instead, cultural categories exist to help people understand the world in which they live, and although abstract, their meaning can be substantiated through the visible consumption of goods and services. In short, consumer products provide a tangible explanation for the existence of intangible cultural categories. For example, in most cultures, women typically use more cosmetic products than do men; seniors purchase a majority of health care services; and the upper class is most likely to own yachts. Here, gender, age, and social class categories help us understand the culturally constituted world by allowing us

Consumers' clothing can communicate cultural categories such as age, gender, religion, and social class.

to examining specific products chosen by distinct subgroups within each category. More subtle differences also exist within each category, such as gender. Recent research demonstrates that young men typically stress functional buying motives, whether shopping online or in conventional stores. In contrast, young women emphasize the social and experiential value of conventional shopping but show similar functional motives as men when shopping online.[5] Thus, a cultural shift from conventional to online shopping requires more attitude change for women, which provides one explanation as to why women are often less satisfied than men with online shopping.[6]

Cultural principles are the *ideas* that help guide the construction of cultural categories. Consumer products also illustrate cultural principles. For example, clothing can communicate "refinement" for the upper class and "rebellion" for the hip-hop culture. Similarly, women's clothing communicates something about the "feminine" nature of women, while men's clothing shows the "masculine" characteristics of men. Here, cultural principles work hand-in-hand with cultural categories. In sum, cultural principles give us the reasons for performing segmentation, and cultural categories provide useful descriptors for these segments. Both can be seen in consumer products.

Station 2 in Figure 12.1: Consumer Products

Cultural meaning is transferred from the culturally constituted world to consumer products. Consumer products represent the second stop in the journey to understanding the movement of cultural meaning. Consumer products serve as Station 2 in Figure 12.1. *Marketing activities* provide one important conduit for this movement. Through deliberate marketing efforts, such as advertising, promotion, distribution, and pricing, products take on cultural meaning. For example, cellular phone products reflect society's desire for convenient, global, person-to-person communication. Advanced cellular products offer connection to the Internet, email options, and access to a consumer's home computer. These innovations depict a specific cultural category or segment (e.g., high tech-oriented consumers), as well as the cultural principle that helped create it (e.g., multi-tasking increases productivity). Because culture is dynamic, however, products continually give up old meanings and take on new ones. SUVs, a specific category of automobile, once communicated outdoor- and sports-related cultural principles. Now, they may also reflect consumer extravagance and excessive fuel consumption. Accordingly, the marketplace offers new, smaller, more fuel-efficient SUVs. As active participants in the marketing process, consumers are informed about the most current cultural meanings in consumer products through marketing communication. Marketing activities, particularly advertising, provide a pipeline through which cultural meaning moves from the culturally constituted world to consumer products.[4]

Although highly complex and more difficult to observe than marketing activities, the *fashion system* is equally important in transferring cultural meaning from the culturally constituted world to consumer products. The fashion system is not just limited to clothing and body adornment; it includes various forms of social expression such as music, art, architecture, journalism, politics, speech, entertainment, and technology. The fashion system transfers meaning to consumer products in three ways. First, it takes new styles of clothing, music, etc., and associates them with established cultural categories and principles.[7] For example, new styles of dress (e.g., business casual) may reflect the existing cultural principle productivity, which is linked to the existing cultural category time (work versus leisure). Here, the joint interplay of comfort and productivity are reinterpreted within the context of work time, i.e., comfort increases productivity in the white-collar world. Similarly, new forms of automobiles (e.g., hybrids) highlight a culture's existing desire for environmental stewardship. Hybrid automobiles, a new fashion, joins the category fuel-efficient automobiles through the principle "the natural environment is worthy of being preserved." Both category and principle existed earlier, but the changing fashion system revised the cultural meaning surrounding cars and the environment.

Second, the fashion system invents completely new cultural meaning by enlisting opinion leaders who modestly shape and refine existing cultural principles and categories. **Opinion leaders** are individuals who, by virtue of birth, beauty, talent, or accomplishment, are held in high esteem and provide cultural meaning to those of lesser standing.[8] Rain, a South Korean pop singer, whose albums have topped the charts in China, Japan, Thailand, Indonesia, and South Korea, has prompted new cultural meaning in music. Nelson Mandela, former president of South Africa, led his nation out of apartheid. By virtue of his character and decency, Mandela remains one of the most compelling moral and political opinion leaders of our time. Actress Angelina Jolie has become an opinion leader regarding humanitarian causes, including eradicating poverty and reversing the spread of HIV/AIDS throughout the world. She reportedly raised $10 million for charities by selling pictures of her and Brad Pitt's baby, Shiloh, to popular magazines. Warren Buffet is the second richest man in the world, worth over $50 billion. He is also the foremost opinion leader in personal investing. Eldrick (Tiger) Woods is perennially ranked number one in golf in the world and is among the most successful golfers of all time—at age 34. He has accomplished more wins on the PGA tour than any other active golfer. As a multi-racial athlete, he has opened the door for minorities to enjoy golf, and his rigorous physical training has changed the way golfers view strength and conditioning. All these opinion leaders invent and deliver new cultural meaning by passing along modest changes in their styles, values, and attitudes to other members of society, who then imitate them.

EDWARD PARSONS/AFP/Getty Images

Actress Angelina Jolie has become an opinion leader for humanitarian causes.

The third way the fashion system passes on meaning from the culturally constituted world to consumer products is via radical reform. According to Claude Levi-Strauss, Western societies willingly accept—even encourage—radical reform.[9] As a result, Western cultures constantly undergo systematic change. The fashion system serves as an important conduit to capture and move radical and innovative cultural meaning. Who are the people responsible for this radical reform? The people responsible are those at the very fringes of society, such as hippies, punks, and rappers.[10] These radical and innovative groups redefined cultural categories by overturning the established order. For example, hippies protested the Vietnam War and established the recreational drug culture; people in the gay community have reshaped the cultural category gender; and rap artists have influenced such cultural categories as clothing, jewelry, and patterns of speech.

MARKETING IN ACTION
Cultural Change via Hip-Hop Fashion

Often, the groups responsible for a radical departure from the culturally constituted conventions of Western societies are those existing at the margins of society.[4] The hip-hop culture, broadly recognized by its rap music, beatboxing, breakdancing, and urban graffiti, has created an entirely new clothing fashion. The diffusion of hip-hop fashion into the mainstream illustrates the power that less privileged groups can exercise over the whole of society. Today, hip-hop fashion is a prominent part of popular global fashion for all races and ethnicities. But it didn't start that way. It began with inner city, African-American youth in New York and Los Angeles.

In the early 1980s, hip-hop fashion was novel. *LL Cool J* wore brightly colored sweat suits, bomber jackets, and Adidas sneakers with "phats," i.e., oversized shoelaces. *Big Daddy Kane* wore heavy gold chains, and *Salt-N-Pepa* donned oversized earrings. Then came the 1990s. Dance rappers like *MC Hammer* popularized blousy pants, and *Left Eye* helped popularize baseball caps and neon-colored clothing. *Public Enemy* wore dreadlocks, matted ropes of hair that originated in ancient dynastic Egypt. Polka-dot clothing made a brief but impressionable appearance, thanks to rapper *Kwamé,* and Starter jackets and Air Jordan sneakers emerged as status symbols. Hip-hop fashion crossed over to high fashion when models began wearing heavy gold jewelry and bomber jackets with thick fur collars. Among the most interesting hip-hop trends of the early 1990s, *Treach* of *Naughty by Nature* dressed in metallic chain-linked padlocks, in apparent solidarity with "all the brothers who are locked down."[40] This particular trend did not last. Gangsta rap emerged in the mid-1990s with black-ink tattoos, bandanas, and baggy pants without belts. In addition, new street-slang, such as "homeboy," emerged. Interestingly, gangsta rap was influenced to

attator/iStockphoto.com

some extent by the gangster styles of the 1930s, shown by a resurgence in the wearing of bowler hats, silk shirts, alligator-skin shoes, and double-breasted suits.

Fashion design houses Polo, Calvin Klein, and Tommy Hilfiger embraced hip-hop fashion in the 1990s. In fact, when *Snoop Doggy Dogg* donned a Hilfiger sweatshirt during *Saturday Night Live*, this article of clothing was sold out in New York City stores the next day. The late-1990s witnessed the rise of platinum jewelry and aviator warm-up suits, largely inspired by rap star Sean Combs, who is also known as *Puff Daddy* and *P. Diddy.* Do-rags became a hit, supporting the popular African-American hairstyles with cornrows and Caesar low-cuts. Afros also reemerged after 30 years of dormancy. Rappers like *Jay-Z* and *The Hot Boys* started the *Bling* movement, which featured ostentatious jewelry, including *grills,* or removable platinum-jeweled teeth covers.

The 2000s ushered in new hip-hop styles, including *prep-hop,* featuring polo shirts with popped collars, large, elaborate belt buckles, and fitted caps with straight bills worn sideways. Shorter, tighter T-shirts replaced long Ts in an effort to show off decorative belt buckles. More recently, the baggy pants style appears to be waning. Today, hip-hop fashion has become mainstream. It has moved from the inner cities to the suburbs, even into the boardrooms of McDonald's, Coca-Cola, and Nautica. Young people of all races and nationalities have embraced the hip-hop culture—its music, clothing, street-slang, tattoos, jewelry, movies, and magazines. Hip-hop artists are "meaning suppliers" for culture. Like the hippies and punks who preceded them, hip-hop artists utilize the fashion system to overturn the established cultural order and inspire new cultural principles and categories. They will not be the last innovative group to effect cultural change.[41]

OBJECTIVE 3

Station 3 in Figure 12.1: Consumers

All high-involvement consumer products (e.g., clothing, body adornment, transportation, architecture, music, food) express the beliefs and values present in the culturally constituted world. This meaning continues its journey from consumer products into the day-to-day life of consumers. Consumers represent Station 3 in Figure 12.1. The instruments that transfer meaning to consumers are known as **rituals.** Rituals are symbolic actions that occur in a fixed sequence and are repeated over time.[11] Consumers use four rituals to affirm or revise cultural meaning: exchange, possession, grooming, and divestment. Each represents a different stage by which cultural meaning moves from product to consumer.[4]

Exchange rituals involve one person or a group of people purchasing and presenting consumer products to another. This movement of products from giver to receiver allows the giver to transfer deliberated cultural properties to the receiver. A son who receives books in exchange for good performance in school is also made the recipient of a specific concept about himself as intellectually curious. An engaged daughter who receives a down payment on a new home in lieu of an expensive wedding celebration may come to see herself as practically minded. Western gift exchange rituals—particularly at birthdays and Christmas—provide powerful opportunities for the giver to pass on cultural meanings to the receiver.

Unfulfilled requests can be equally important in passing on cultural meaning. A child's request for and his parents' subsequent refusal to give him toy guns and soldiers signals something about cultural attitudes toward warfare. Similarly, presenting substitute gifts conveys important cultural meaning. Children who receive *Nancy Drew* computer games as substitutes for *World of Warcraft* games or *Civilization* instead of *Sims* may decode messages about acceptable forms of fantasy. Giving a young person a mobile phone that does not include text messaging and digital photography options may emphasize the serious nature of the mobile communications, i.e., the phone is for safety. Substituting a trip to Cedar Point in Ohio for Disney World could highlight a family's scarcity of time or money. Recent research suggests that sharing music files from sources such as Napster, Limewire, or Itunes represents a special case of gift giving.[12] Sharing music and movies provides rich insight into the cultural values being passed to the receiver. What kind of message is being sent along with the "gift" of *Beethoven*? How about *Fifty Cent*? The *Rolling Stones*?

Gift-wrapping can also express important cultural meaning. In Japan, for example, the economic value of the gift is subordinate to its symbolic meaning. Consequently, the wrapping paper and adornments are paramount. Many Japanese view giving gifts to friends and family as a reciprocal obligation, known as *kosai*. They perform ritualized activities when giving gifts to both personal and professional acquaintances, all of which can be very stressful. Consistent with the Japanese cultural principle of "saving face," gifts are rarely opened in the presence of the giver, just in case the receiver responds unfavorably to the contents inside the elaborate packaging.[13]

Possession rituals occur when consumers discuss, compare, reflect upon, and display their belongings. "Claiming" takes place when consumers adopt into their existing personalities the specific qualities of a product assigned to it by marketing activities.[4] For example, marketing teaches us that motorcycles represent freedom, power, and rugged individuality. Thus, discussing one's motorcycle may transfer the cultural principle, freedom, from the product to a consumer's personality. Friends who compare the features of their minivans may be emphasizing the nurturing dimension of their personalities—or simply underscoring their pragmatism. Sorting and organizing one's photographs (in traditional scrapbooks or digitally on the computer) reinforces existing cultural principles and categories. Photos of vacations depict the category, time, and offer some insight into the cultural principle surrounding leisure. Photographs of the consumer at various stages of her life illustrate the category, age, and the principles associated with age-relevant behaviors. Through possession rituals, consumers draw on the ability of consumer products to discriminate between cultural categories and principles. "He's a BMW guy," really means that he's a yuppie (young urban professional).

"She's a Target woman," suggests a practical but chic personality. Rolex and Kmart signal class categories and the principles associated with upper versus lower class. Work boots and hard hats represent more than protection; they are symbolic of blue-collar occupations. Trips to Cancun, Mexico, paint a different picture than do excursions to Barcelona, Spain. Interestingly, possession rituals can be equally instructive when consumers fail to embrace the cultural properties of their possessions. "I sold the motorcycle. It wasn't me," provides insight into a consumer's value system. "I no longer shop at Target because they don't carry the brands that I like" similarly reflects a consumer's attitude regarding brands and shopping. Possession rituals help complete the second stage of cultural movement from products to consumers. Consumers extract the meaningful properties of consumer products and adopt or reject them as part of their lives.

Many consumer products do not last indefinitely. Accordingly, **grooming rituals** allow consumers to extract cultural meaning from perishable possessions through repeated use. Products such as shampoo, cosmetics, and clothes facilitate daily grooming rituals. The ritual of "going out" is an example of a more elaborate grooming ritual. Women sometimes describe applying cosmetics as "putting on their faces," while men sometimes behave as though they are preparing for an athletic event when they get dressed in the morning. Pep talks, changing and re-changing clothes, painstakingly styling one's hair, and meticulous shaving all demonstrate consumers' desire to cultivate consumer products and absorb the products' meanings into their personality. "Because you're worth it" (L'Oréal), "Create a storm," (Monsoon), "Gentlemen prefer Hanes," "Because life is not a spectator sport" (Reebok), and "Every kiss begins with Kay" (Kay Jewelers) embody marketing-created meanings that can be transferred from the product to the consumer via grooming rituals. In sum, grooming rituals help draw cultural meaning out of products and invest them in the consumer.[14]

Consumers use **divestment rituals** for two purposes. First, if consumers purchase previously owned items such as cars or homes, elaborate cleaning and redecorating rituals help erase meanings associated with the previous owner. This allows the new owner to free up the cultural meaning of the product and re-associate it with him/herself. Second, when consumers sell or otherwise dispense with a product, they attempt to erase the meaning that they invested in the item. Prior to selling a beloved automobile, consumers remove all personal artifacts, sometimes even the floor mats, and prepare the car for its new owner. Nevertheless, consumers may feel awkward seeing the new owner with his/her old possession. If the products provided cultural meaning for consumers, they may feel strange about someone else driving their cars, wearing their jackets, playing with their golf clubs, sitting on their lawn furniture, or riding their bicycles. Divestment rituals clearly suggest that consumers *believe* cultural meaning can be transferred from products to people.

All four personal rituals help the transfer of cultural meaning from consumer products to consumers. Exchange rituals allow one consumer to impart desirable meaning to another, while possession rituals help reinforce the relationship between a product and its owner. Grooming rituals provide an opportunity to continually extract meaning from perishable goods, and divestment rituals empty products of their meaning before they assume new ownership.

Cultural meaning, which began in the collective minds of society (the culturally constituted world), is transferred to consumer products by deliberate marketing activities and the fashion system. Cultural meanings "get into" consumer products through marketing activities because ads and promotions make clear reference to existing cultural symbols. Similarly, opinion leaders and reference groups provide meaning to products by the associations that consumers hold regarding those groups. Then, consumers extract cultural values from the products they purchase by employing rituals. Through their brand choices, consumers express and build their identities. In the end, cultural meaning—beliefs about what is important, useful, and desirable—resides at all three stations simultaneously: the culturally constituted world, consumer products, and consumers. Next, we explore how consumers learn about their cultures.

Enculturation and Acculturation

Anthropologists refer to learning about one's own culture as **enculturation.** McCracken's cultural framework includes *cultural agents,* who help with this process. Cultural agents gather meaning in one station and help transfer it to the next. Marketing and fashion agents help give meaning to their products. Specifically, marketing agents such as product designers and advertisers decide which product benefits—such as convenience, style, durability, and economy—reside in the culturally constituted world and then promote these benefits to the most responsive consumer markets. Some cultures, such as the United States, appear time-impoverished and respond favorably to any innovation that saves time. In contrast, Latin American cultures rarely feel pressured by time.

Fashion agents such as architects and artists, clothing creators, and automobile designers use the fashion system to inject their creations with cultural meaning. Media agents such as journalists, reporters, and experts observe cultural innovation and decide what is "hot" and what is "not." Other cultural agents such as parents, peers, and teachers impart their cultural values to consumers. Often, these values are reflected in consumers' rituals and help transfer meaning from consumer products to consumers. Thus, cultural agents exist at and between every station in the model (Figure 12.1).

The process of **acculturation** occurs when people in one culture adapt to meanings in another culture.[15] Acculturation has become increasingly important as a result of global immigration, which can profoundly influence a nation through language and other cultural differences. In France, for example, immigration is expected to be a major political issue, in no small part because of the 2005 riots in the eastern suburbs of Paris involving French Muslims who had immigrated from Northern Africa. In the United States, the foreign-born population is growing more than six times faster than the native-born population. The most recent census data report 31.1 million immigrants, more than twice the 14.1 million recorded in 1980. Nations with large immigrant populations, like the United States, must deal with important acculturation issues surrounding language.

Language

Perhaps the most obvious differences among cultures lie in their verbal communication systems. Consumers who travel to foreign countries understand the challenges of both oral and written communication. In order for people to function as consumers—nonetheless in a society—they must be able to interact with the prevailing language. Language is not merely a collection of words. Language expresses the beliefs and values of a culture. Anthropologist Benjamin Lee Whorf maintained that language actually shapes the worldview of consumers, their behavior toward others, and their manners of acting.[16]

Linguists divide the study of verbal language into four categories. *Syntax* comprises the rules of sentence formation; *semantics* deals with systems of meaning; *phonology* deals with sound patterns; and *morphology* involves word formation. A fifth category, *nonverbal communications*, includes body language, gestures, and other forms of unspoken communication. Taken together, all five categories comprise the broader field known as *semiotics*. Figure 12.2 provides several examples of linguistic differences between English, Russian, Spanish, and Japanese.

FIGURE 12.2 LINGUISTIC DIFFERENCES[43]

Linguistic Category	Examples
Syntax	English has relatively fixed word order, while Russian has relatively free word order. In Spanish, the adjectives follow nouns; in English, adjectives precede nouns.
Semantics	Japanese words communicate nuances of feeling for which other languages lack exact translations. For example, "yes" and "no" can be interpreted with finer distinction in Japanese than in other languages
Phonology	Japanese does not distinguish between "L" and "R" sounds. Rs are "rolled" in Russian. In Spanish, two Ls, one after another, are spoken like a "y."
Morphology	Russian is a highly inflected language, with six different endings for nouns and adjectives.

The semantics of the "got milk?" campaign was misunderstood in Mexico.

PRNewsFoto/Milk Processor Education Program/AP Photo

Solid communication linkages must be established between marketers and customers or *translation problems* are likely to occur. Attempts to translate marketing communications from one language to another often fail because of problems with *semantics*, as illustrated by the following examples. During the late 1990s, Nike aired a television commercial for hiking shoes in Kenya using Samburu tribesmen. The camera closed in on the one tribesman who speaks in the native Maa language. As he speaks, the Nike slogan "Just do it" appears on the screen. The Kenyan is really saying, "I don't want these. Give me big shoes." Similarly, the Dairy Association's huge success with the "got milk?" campaign prompted them to expand their advertising to Mexico. Unfortunately, the Spanish translation read "Are you lactating?" Each of these translation blunders occurred because of semantics, i.e., finding words with equivalent meanings.

Phonology frequently complicates cross-cultural communication. Mars, Inc., the $18 billion privately owned candy conglomerate, had difficulty making the M&M's name pronounceable in France, where neither ampersands nor the apostrophe "s" plural form exists. Similarly, Whirlpool struggled with a brand name that is nearly impossible to pronounce in Spain, Italy, France, and Germany.[17] The name Coca-Cola in China was first rendered as Ke-ke-ken-la.

Unfortunately, Coke did not discover until after thousands of signs had been printed that the phrase means, "bite the wax tadpole" or "female horse stuffed with wax," depending on the dialect. Coke then researched 40,000 Chinese characters and found a close phonetic equivalent, "ko-kou-ko-le," which translates as "happiness in the mouth," a much better choice.

Cultural Translation

Jean-Claude Usunier maintains that many problems in translation are **cultural translation** difficulties, i.e., problems related to the spirit of the language. Some words simply have no foreign equivalent because the meaning may not be relevant to a foreign culture. The English word "upset" for example, does not have a French equivalent, because the English meaning of the word suggests something of an inner personal disruption and loss of self-control. The French cannot be "upset" because generally they are not afraid to show their feelings and emotions to others.[18] In contrast, it is well known that in the language of peoples who live near the Arctic Circle, nearly a dozen different terms are used to describe the English word "snow." The following translation blunders illustrate problems with *cultural translations*.

Samarin is a Swedish over-the-counter remedy for upset stomachs. It is similar to Alka-Seltzer. Several years ago, their ads featured comic strips without text; they used three pictures. The first picture showed a man grasping his stomach, obviously ill. In the second picture, the man drank a glass of Samarin. In the final picture, he appeared smiling. Although the ad campaign was a success in Europe, it failed when printed in Arabic-speaking newspapers. Why? Arabic languages are read from right to left!

In 2003, the Hong Kong Tourist Board was unable to change an advertising campaign that was on billboards throughout Hong Kong and in British versions of *Cosmopolitan* and *Condé Nast Traveller*. The slogan was, "Hong Kong: It will take your breath away." Unfortunately, the campaign coincided with the SARS epidemic that resulted in numerous deaths. Shortness of breath is one of the main symptoms of SARS. Figure 12.3 illustrates 10 classic marketing translation *faux pas*; most are rooted in semantic or cultural translation problems.

Body Language

Although familiarity with verbal language is critical to understanding a culture, it is not the only way cultures express their personalities. Derived from the Greek word *kinein*, meaning "to move," *body language* involves the silent movement of body parts, including *facial expressions* such as scowls, smiles, and stares, *gestures* such as hand and arm signals, *postural shifts* such as leaning forward or crossing one's arms, and forms of *touching*, including slapping and caressing. *Interpersonal spacing* is also an important form of nonverbal communication. Different cultures prefer standing relatively close or far away, facing head-on versus to one side. Latin Americans, Arabs, and Africans typically stand within 18 inches when speaking to a business acquaintance. To them, it is a sign of confidence. In contrast, Germans, Nordics, and Asians generally consider at least 36 inches as their personal space.

Like written and spoken language, nonverbal languages are mostly learned rather than innate. Consequently, the meanings of nonverbal expressions such as gestures can vary from culture to culture. One catalogue retailer learned this the hard way by printing the "OK" finger sign on each page of its catalogue. Unfortunately, in many parts of Latin America such as Brazil, this sign is considered an obscene gesture. The catalogues were scrapped and re-designed to better reflect resident body language. Similarly, Mountain Bell Company marketed its telephone services in Saudi Arabia. One of the ads portrayed an executive talking on the phone with his feet propped up on the desk, showing the soles of his shoes. Arab culture considers the display of one's soles to be disrespectful.

FIGURE 12.3 TEN CLASSIC MARKETING TRANSLATION FAUX PAS

1. Colgate's Cue toothpaste sold poorly in France because the term "cue" is slang for derrière.

2. Managers of an American company were startled when they discovered that the brand name of the cooking oil they were marketing in a Latin American country translated into Spanish as "Jackass Oil."

3. A firm marketed shampoo in Brazil under the name "Evitol." The name translates into "dandruff contraceptive."

4. Esso Oil discovered that its name translates into "stalled car" in Japanese.

5. American Motors marketed its car the Matador based on the image of courage and strength. However, in Puerto Rico, the name means "killer" and was not well received, given the hazardous roads throughout the country.

6. In 2002, UK sports manufacturer Umbro had to withdraw its new sneakers named Zyklon from German markets. They discovered that Zyklon was the name of the gas used in Nazi concentration camps. Hoover made the same mistake when they named one of their brands Zykon, which was supposed to translate as "cyclone."

7. Several companies become tangled up with bad translations for products resulting from misusing the word "mist." "Irish Mist" (an alcoholic beverage), "Mist Stick" (a curling iron from Clairol), and "Silver Mist" (a Rolls Royce car) all bombed in Germany because "mist" translates into "dung" or "manure."

8. Kellogg had to rename its Bran Buds cereal in Sweden; the name roughly translated to "burned farmer."

9. PepsiCo advertised in Taiwan using the slogan "Come Alive With Pepsi," which translated into Chinese as "Pepsi brings your ancestors back from the dead."

10. In Italy, a campaign for Schweppes Tonic Water translated the name into "Schweppes Toilet Water."

In contrast, emotion expressed by the face tends to contain universal meaning. Research demonstrates that most cultures communicate five different emotions by distinct facial expressions: happiness, sadness, fear, surprise, and anger. Happiness is easily detected in the lower face, while sadness and fear are best understood from the eyes.[19] Still, the rules for using these facial expressions may vary from culture to culture. For example, Americans consider direct eye contact while speaking a sign of trust. South Koreans, however, view this as rude and disrespectful. The French maintain that Americans smile too much. In addition to language, both verbal and nonverbal, marketers must understand the social setting of a culture.

High- and Low-Context Cultures

The social setting, or *context*, can affect intercultural communications. Some cultures are *low-context* and emphasize explicit messages. The meanings of such messages are largely independent of the situation and people involved, and the words are relatively precise in meaning. Other cultures are *high-context* and communicate more implicit meanings. The meanings of the words change depending on who is speaking to whom and under what circumstances. Nonverbal messages such as gestures and body language are important in high-context cultures. Figure 12.4 depicts various cultures on this message-context continuum.[20]

FIGURE 12.4 CULTURAL MESSAGE-CONTEXT CONTINUUM

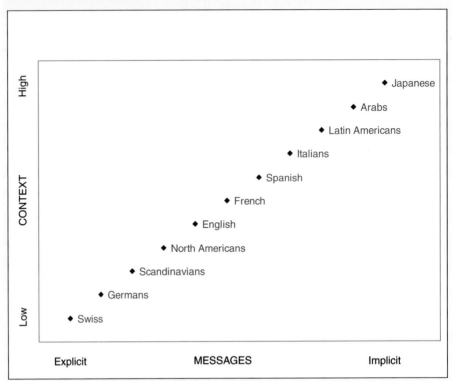

Source: Usunier, J. (1993). *International Marketing: A Cultural Approach.* Englewood Cliffs, NJ: Prentice Hall International (UK) Limited.

Highly explicit messages can be thought of as unambiguous computer commands; they tend to go with low-context cultures. Conversely, highly implicit messages, usually associated with high-context cultures, are more ambiguous. The Swiss are represented at the extreme lower-left portion of the graph. There is a great deal of precision in their verbal communication. This suggests that Swiss speed limits, contracts, and appointment times should be taken literally. In fact, patients pay a fine if they are late for a doctor's visit. The Germans, Scandinavians, and North Americans also fall in the low-context/ explicit message range. In contrast, the Japanese are represented at the upper-right portion of the graph, where context plays a critical role in communication. For example, when a consumer from a Western culture says "no" in negotiating, s/he is usually saying "I *reject* the deal." The Japanese, however, have at least 14 ways of saying "no."

The Arab and Latin American cultures also tend to be high-context and implicit with their messages. Day-to-day consumer behavior in Arab countries differs greatly from that in the West. Consumers are expected to negotiate deals and bargain—even for perishable food products. But cultures do not always fall at the extremes. The Latin-European countries such as Italy, Spain, France, and England tend to be more intermediate in terms of context and message. Language plays a prominent part in cross-cultural communication, but it is not the only cause of cultural misunderstandings. To communicate effectively, consumers and marketers must possess a common understanding of symbols.

FIGURE 12.5 Fourteen Ways to Say "No" in Japanese[18]

1. Vague "no."
2. Vague and ambiguous "yes."
3. Silence.
4. Counter-offer.
5. Unrelated response.
6. Physically withdrawing from the conversation.
7. Feigning equivocation or making an excuse.
8. Taking issue with the question.
9. Refusing to acknowledge the question.
10. Conditional "no."
11. Conditional "yes."
12. Delayed response, i.e., "we'll get back to you."
13. Apology.
14. The (rare) equivalent of an English "no."

New Campbell's Souper Stars.
Twice the Stars. Twice the Fun.

Courtesy of the Campbell Soup Company

Symbols

Objects created by a culture cannot be communicated solely by their physical characteristics, and consumer products are no exception. Goods and services always contain symbolic elements such as exclusivity, utility, and style. *Symbols* are communication devices that convey meaning through representation. Important marketing symbols include *words* such as brand names, *images* like brand logos, and *actions* such as body language and gestures. Symbols can be verbal or nonverbal. **Brand jingles** are short, catchy tunes—with or without words—that represent a brand or organization. Marketers understand that music facilitates recall. Children learn much about their world by putting words to songs. Many adults still recall the tune that accompanied the alphabet song. Jingles such as "Mm-Mm-Good" (Campbell's Soup) and "Like a Rock" (Chevy) take advantage of the "stuck song syndrome," or "earworm." Marketing professor and professional musician James Kellaris discovered that although people generally have their own unique earworms, "YMCA," "We Will Rock You," and "The Lion Sleeps Tonight" rank in the top-ten list. According to Kellaris' **theory of cognitive itch**, certain properties of music may be analogous to biochemical agents, such as histamines, which cause an itch on the skin. Exposure to such music may cause a sort of "cognitive itch" in one's mind. The only way to scratch a cognitive itch is to repeat the offending music mentally. But this only exacerbates the itch, trapping the hapless victim in an involuntary cycle of repeated itching and scratching.[21] Thus, advertisers do well to plant their jingles in our heads. But jingles need not contain words to be effective. The Nabisco "ding," the Avon "ding-dong," and the four musical notes representing *Intel Inside* employ only tones to catch our attention and keep their jingles recycling.

Brand logos take a variety of forms, including colors, shapes, words, and other images. For example, the McDonald's brand includes a *word mark* consisting of the word "McDonald's" written in white lettering across the "golden arches," and superimposed against a red background. The "golden arches" represent a *non-word mark logo*, or *brand symbol*. Many firms use non-word logos to create a distinctive image designed to catch a consumer's eye and trigger positive thoughts about the brand. The AT&T globe, the Mercedes-Benz three-pronged star, Captain Morgan's sea captain, Target's bull's eye, and the Nike swoosh all transcend language with symbolic meaning. What messages do the Hot Wheels flame and pink-scripted *Barbie* symbolize to consumers? What do the Olympic "rings" communicate? What does the NBA logo symbolize? Given the substantial investment of creative energy and resources, firms register their brand names, logos, and other brand elements as either *trademarks* or service marks; both provide a form of legal protection for the brand, which is considered intellectual property.

Safeguarding brand logos is an important issue in consumer behavior. On March 16, 2007, AT&T filed suit in U.S. District Court in Atlanta, demanding that NASCAR allow an AT&T-sponsored car to change its rear quarter to reflect the retirement of the Cingular brand name and the introduction of the AT&T global logo. The car, No. 31, owned by Richard Childress Racing, was driven by Jeff Burton, the third-ranked NASCAR driver.[22] The lawsuit claims that by not adding the new AT&T logo to the existing Cingular car, NASCAR was doing substantial and irreparable harm to AT&T.

Failure to recognize the cross-cultural implications of symbols can cause problems for marketers and consumers. In Japan, for example, a Western golf ball manufacturing company packaged golf balls in packs of four for convenience. Unfortunately, items packaged in fours are unpopular because the pronunciation of the word "four" in Japanese connotes "death." Nike may have offended Muslims in 1997 when the "flaming air" logo for its Nike Air sneakers appeared too similar to the Arabic form of God's name, "Allah." Subsequently, Nike pulled more than 38,000 pairs of sneakers from the market. Similarly, a soft drink was introduced into Arab countries with an attractive label featuring six-pointed stars. Some Arab people interpreted this symbol as pro-Israel and refused to buy it. Consequently, another label was printed in ten languages, one of which was Hebrew. Again, it sold poorly. When Pepsodent marketed toothpaste in

EYE ON INTERNATIONAL

THE MERCEDES-BENZ BRAND LOGO

Although registered more then a century ago, the Mercedes-Benz brand name initially did not have a logo associated with it. The idea for the "Star" logo originated with Paul and Adolf Daimler, the sons of the company's founder. They recalled that their father had once used a star symbol in his family correspondence. Their father, Gottlieb Daimler, was technical director of the Deutz gas engine factory from 1872 until 1881. During this time, Daimler had marked a star on a postcard of Cologne, and Deutz predicted that a star would one day shine over Daimler's own factory, symbolizing its prosperity.

AP Photo/David Zalubowski

In June, 1909, Mercedes-Benz registered both a three-pointed and a four-pointed star as trademarks. Although both designs were legally protected, only the three-pointed star was ever used. Beginning in 1910, the three-pronged star appeared as a design feature on the radiators of the automobiles. Apparently, the three points of the star represented Daimler's ambition of universal motorization on land, water, and sea. Over the years the logo evolved to include the "Benz" laurel wreath. Then in 1923, the three-pointed star was enclosed in a circle and registered as a trademark. The brand logo has changed very little since 1923.[42]

On May 2, 1989, 15-year-old Michael Thomas, a ninth grader at Meade Senior High School in Anne Arundel County, Maryland, was strangled by a fellow student who took Thomas' two-week-old Air Jordan basketball shoes and left Thomas' barefoot body in the woods near the school. Young Thomas love Michael Jordan and the shoes Jordan endorsed. He loved them both so much, he paid $115.50 (approximately $250 in today's dollars) to "be like Mike."

This was not the first crime relating to sneakers, but perhaps the most infamous. This particular story was told in Sports Illustrated's May 14, 1990, issue. There have been other such crimes for not only Air Jordans, but for other brands of athletic shoes, jackets, and caps bearing sports insignia. If you think killing for sneakers was a 1980s thing think again. On February 14, 2004, three 16-year-old teens viciously beat and stabbed Huang Chen to death, beyond recognition. The teens called a food order into Chen's family's takeout shop. When Chen delivered the order, the three teens murdered him to obtain money for sneakers.

Sociologist Elijah Anderson has argued that crimes among young black males involving apparel can be linked to inequalities in class and race. "The uneducated, inner city kids don't have a sense of opportunity. They feel the system is closed off to them. And yet they're bombarded with the same cultural apparatus [advertising] that the white middle class is. They don't have means to attain the things offered and yet they have the same desire. So they value these 'emblems,' these symbols of supposed success. The golf, the shoes, and the drug dealer's outfit—those things all belie the real situation, but it's a symbolic display that seems to say that things are all right." Professor Anderson argues that advertising fans the flames of this process by presenting images that appeal to inner city, black youth, and the shoe companies capitalize on the situation. Anderson stops short of laying all of the blame with marketers. "This is, after all, a free market," he notes.

NBA star Stephon Marbury of the New York Knicks is working on a solution. In September 2006, Marbury announced that he was producing a line of less expensive athletic apparel. In fact, Starbury brand shoes retail for about $15, a far cry from the $150 to $300 for Nike or Adidas shoes. Marbury's hope is to "keep kids a little safer." He reasoned that children wearing low-priced jackets and sports shoes would be less likely to become crime victims. Do you think this will help?

Source: Telander, R. (May 14, 1990). Your sneakers or your life. Sports Illustrated, 36-49.

Southeast Asia, its ad campaign emphasized "teeth whitening." However, some local natives chew betel nuts to blacken their teeth because they find dark teeth attractive. A U.S. telephone company promoted its products and services in Latin America by showing a commercial in which a Latino wife tells her husband to call a friend and explain that they would be late for dinner. The commercial was not received well for two reasons. First, Latino women rarely communicate commands to their husbands. Second, the concept of "lateness" in Latin America is viewed differently than in the United States. Not arriving on time for dinner is *not* considered being "late."

Even within a culture, the meaning of symbols can change over time. Crayola has changed its color names because of the civil rights movement and other social pressures. In 1962, Binney & Smith replaced "flesh" crayons with "peach," in recognition of the global variety of skin tones. In 1999, they changed "Indian Red" to chestnut. Interestingly, the color was not named after Native Americans, but for a special pigment originating in the country India. Mercedes-Benz understands the importance of their symbol. It has remained relatively unchanged for more than a century.

Norms

Earlier, we described **cultural values** as a collective set of beliefs about what is important, useful, and desirable. From these cultural values flow **norms**, which specify appropriate responses in specific situations. In short, norms are culture's rules of behavior. **Enacted norms** explicitly and formally prescribe acceptable behaviors. For example, restrooms in the United States provide gender placards, indicating facilities for men to use and for women to use. In contrast, in France, the same restrooms can be shared by both sexes. **Crescive norms** are implicit and learned only through interacting with other members of a culture. Crescive norms include customs, morés, and conventions. **Customs** are overt behaviors that have been passed down from one generation to the next. Consumer customs may include routine, everyday activities that have been handed down from the past, such as drinking coffee with breakfast and brushing one's teeth at night. They can also be formal and elaborate, such as anniversary celebrations and funerals. Earlier in this book, rituals were described as a series of behaviors in a fixed sequence. Customs are more broadly defined than rituals. It is best to think of a custom as an entire category of behavior (e.g., a wedding) and a ritual as the individual parts (e.g., each of the steps in exchanging vows).

Another form of custom is a **moré** (more-ay), which is a custom with strong moral implications. Morés typically prescribe right and wrong ways of behaving and involve taboos, or forbidden cultural activities involving eating, sex, gender roles, vulgarity, and the like. When consumers violate customs and mores, they are likely to receive strong sanctions from other members of society. For example, in the United States, consumers who "cut in line" at retail stores, restaurants, or amusement parks typically receive strong scoldings from other shoppers and patrons. In extreme cases, aberrant consumers may be removed from the premises. Similarly, in Arab cultures it is forbidden to feature women in advertising. Firms that do so risk serious consumer backlash. By contrast, **conventions** are norms that deal less with right or wrong or tradition, but rather with what is more or less "correct." A list of conventions in Western countries might include how to host a birthday party, how to complement clothes with scarves, how to maintain one's lawn, and how to coordinate a golf outing.

Customs, mores, and norms interact to guide culturally appropriate behavior. For example, a *moré* might tell consumers what gifts are appropriate for a boss or superior. A custom would guide consumers on *when* the gift should be presented, and a convention might suggest *how* to present the gift. In Japan, for example, mores indicate that periodically giving gifts to bosses is appropriate—even expected. The giving of year-end gifts, called *oseibo*, is a Japanese custom. Spending approximately 5,000 yen (about $40) for a store-delivered gift is the convention.

Conducting business in Saudi Arabia can be challenging for Western women. Although the environment is changing, gender separation still exists. It is taboo for women to dine without their husbands. Therefore, public places, such as hotels and restaurants, provide family rooms where women are served with their husbands. Also, women are forbidden to drive. The norm for women is to dress conservatively—long skirts, sleeves of elbow length or longer, and unrevealing necklines. Finally it is not customary for Muslim men to shake hands or to engage in conversational body contact with women, but such gestures are common when speaking with other men.

O B J E C T I V E 4

Return Potential Model

Because norms are based on a group's cultural values, they not only coordinate the behavior of the culture, they also prescribe behaviors that prolong such values. Norms can also help define and enhance the identity of a culture through the use of distinct clothing, speech dialects, or hairstyles. Perhaps most importantly, norms can provide feedback on how much or how little a behavior is desired. The **return potential model** describes norms on two dimensions. The *behavioral dimension* specifies the amount of behavior regulated by the norm, and the *evaluation dimension* shows the cultural response to that behavior.[23] To illustrate, Figure 12.6 depicts three norms, A, B, and C. Each norm takes a different functional shape based on how much behavior relating to that norm is desired. For example, let's call Norm A "integrity." Approval for Norm A is a positive linear function of the behavior relating to Norm A (e.g., honesty), i.e., more is always better. Let's define Norm B as "infidelity." Cultural approval for Norm B is a negative linear function. Here, indifference is returned for the lowest level of behavior characterizing infidelity (fidelity is the norm), and increasing levels only bring greater disapproval. Let's call Norm C "sense of humor." Norm C appears as an inverted U-shaped function. Here, cultural disapproval exists for very low levels of behavior relating to humor. In other words, lacking a sense of humor is met with disapproval. Similarly, very high levels of behavior relating to humor are not approved, either. Too many jokes and funny stories may be considered in bad taste. The middle ground is best for Norm C. A moderate level of humor *returns* the greatest approval.

Figure 12.6 also specifies acceptable levels for the three norms at points where the functions lie above the horizontal behavioral line. No level of infidelity (Norm B) is acceptable. Low levels of infidelity are expected, and clearly more is always worse. In contrast, behaviors representing integrity (Norm A) attain acceptance only at moderate or high levels. Sense of humor (Norm C) is like a roller coaster. Too little (slow) is no fun, and too much (fast) is overkill. Moderately low to moderately high levels of behaviors demonstrating sense of humor return cultural acceptance. Finally, the return potential model identifies the various levels of *intensity* for each norm by observing the range from the highest point to the lowest point on the *evaluation dimension*. For example, Norms A and B exhibit large distances between high and low points of approval. In contrast, Norm C's range of high and low approval is very small. Thus, one could infer that members of this culture feel more strongly about Norms A and B than they do about Norm C.

FIGURE 12.6 RETURNS POTENTIAL CURVES

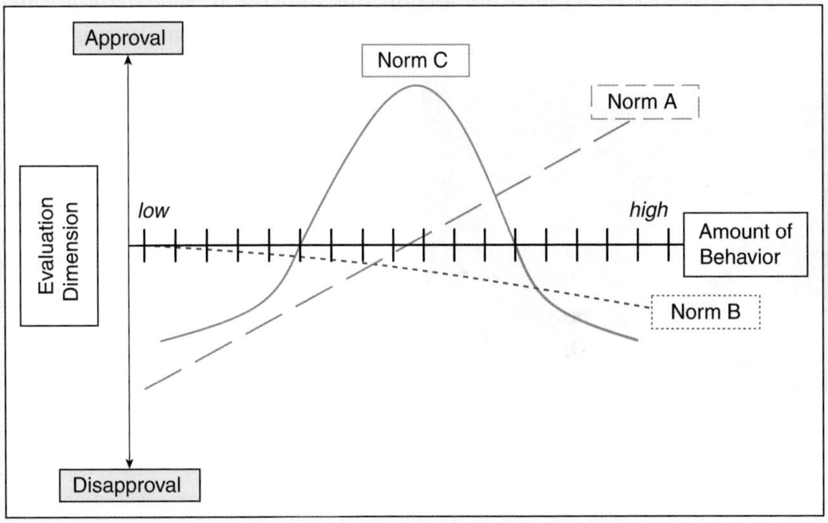

Source: Jackson, J. (1965). Structural Characteristics of Norms. In I. D. Steiner and M. Fishbein (eds.). *Current Studies in Social Psychology*. New York: Holt, Rinehart and Winston, Inc.

In summary, norms exert tremendous influence on consumer behavior by prescribing which actions are appropriate in specific situations. The Returns Potential Model helps explain how much of these actions are desirable and what *return* consumers can expect. The next section further describes how cultural values are adopted by individual consumers.

Consumer Values

Core Values

Pervasive and enduring cultural values are called *core values*. These important values reflect and shape the collective personality of a culture. Organizational anthropologist Geert Hofstede identified five dimensions of cultural values. Three of the dimensions center on expected social behavior; the fourth describes the search for "truth"; and the final dimension deals with the importance of time.[24] *Power distance* describes the extent to which the less powerful members of a culture tolerate large gaps in power structure. For example, the Hong Kong and French cultures exhibit high power distance; they expect power to be unequally distributed. In contrast, Germans, Austrians, and Scandinavians tend to exhibit low power distance. *Individualism* reflects the degree to which society is partitioned into groups. Individualistic cultures, such as the United States, tend *not* to emphasize group cohesion, while collectivist cultures, such as Japan, emphasize group solidity. *Masculinity* describes the extent to which men are expected to be competitive and ambitious and women are expected to be nurturing and concerned primarily with children and family. Japan exhibits high masculinity, while Spain and Taiwan rank low on this dimension. *Uncertainty avoidance* captures the extent to which a culture is uncomfortable with ambiguous and unstructured situations. Cultures such as Greece and Portugal tend to believe in absolute truth and so, score high on this dimension. Conversely, Southeast Asia and India tend to behave contemplatively, and so, score low on this dimension. *Long-term orientation (LTO)* represents a culture's search for virtue (versus truth). This dimension measures cultural characteristics such as persistence, social hierarchies, thrift, and a sense of shame. Hong Kong and Taiwan score very high on LTO; Spain and Portugal score low. Differences in cultural core values can explain why some marketing efforts succeed in one culture and fail in another. For example, research shows that North American consumers exhibit more favorable attitudes toward advertising messages that focus on individualistic core values such as self-reliance, self-improvement, and achievement of personal goals. In contrast, South Korean consumers prefer ads that emphasize collectivistic core values including goals, family integrity, and group harmony.[25]

©Gina Smith, 2009/ Used under license from Shutterstock.com

At the individual level, core values are central to a consumer's **self-concept,** i.e., his/her awareness and perceptions about him/herself. As such, core values significantly influence consumers' beliefs, attitudes, and behaviors in the marketplace. Understanding consumers' core values helps marketers uncover the basis for the customer-product relationship. Means-end chains help explain how consumers derive core values in the marketplace.

OBJECTIVE 5

Means-End Chains

Cultural meaning moves from the broader society to consumer goods, and consumers extract meaning from their products and merge these meanings into their own personalities. For example, Red Bull users often differ from Starbuck's drinkers, and Corvette owners exhibit personality characteristics that may differ from Cadillac owners. Clearly, consumers do not invite all products to become a part of their self-concept.

A useful approach to understanding how consumers view products is through a means-end chain. A *means-end chain* combines three levels of a consumer's product knowledge—attributes, consequences, and values—to form a sequential network of meaning.[26]

ATTRIBUTES   A means-end chain begins with **attributes,** the basic characteristics of goods and services. Attributes can be *tangible*, such as the processing speed and memory capacity of a computer, the miles per gallon of an automobile, or the fabric of a dress. Attributes can also be *intangible*, such as the style of a house, the design of a jacket, or the comfort of a shoe. Furthermore, attributes are not limited to physical goods. Services, such as banks, offer tangible products such as interest-bearing checking accounts and ATMs and provide intangible attributes such as speed of service, friendliness of staff, and convenience of location. Tangible attributes are easily measured. For example, miles per gallon is a numeric value calculated from gas consumption and distance traveled. Similarly, megahertz is the unit of measure for computer processing speed. Intangible attributes, although largely abstract, can also be measured. Consumers' attitudes toward quality, comfort, and convenience can be measured by survey instruments such as *Likert* (agreement) and rating scales (1–10).

BENEFITS   Consumers rarely evaluate brands solely on the basis of their physical or abstract attributes. Instead, they are interested in what these attributes can do for them. **Benefits** represent the second stage in a means-end chain and embody consumers' perceptions about the outcomes or *consequences* provided by the attributes. Miles per gallon, for example, doesn't mean much as an attribute. It takes on meaning only because it indicates a certain level of economy. Similarly, computer-processing speed is meaningful because it allows for efficient multi-tasking. Benefits can be classified as *functional* or *psychosocial. Functional benefits* are tangible outcomes that result from consuming or using a product. For example, the functional benefit of a large engine is greater power and speed, and the functional benefit of consuming 12 ounces of Gatorade is replenishing electrolytes lost during exercise.

Functional benefits are tangible outcomes such as the electrolytes offered in *G*.

In contrast, *psychosocial benefits* include the internal *psychological* and external *social* consequences of using or consuming a product. Often, consumers enhance their self-concepts by purchasing items that make them feel stylish or beautiful. Consumers also derive social benefits from wearing stylish clothes if their peers make positive comments about them publically. A consumer may benefit psychologically by eating a vegetarian diet and feeling positive about *not* consuming animals.[27] Similarly, a consumer may benefit socially if a colleague champions her vegetarian diet to another colleague.

VALUES   Just as cultural values collectively represent what is important, useful, and desirable, *consumer values* embody consumers' priorities and preferences about their life goals and how products can help them attain these goals. For example, consumers who place a high priority on education may attend graduate school, despite the difficult regimen and foregone income. Consumers who strongly prefer American-made products may purchase only American cars and trucks. In fact, research shows that values relate to a wide variety of consumer behaviors, including automobile purchasing,[28] choice of occupation,[29] and media use.[30] Broadly speaking, values can be classified as instrumental or terminal.[31]

Instrumental values represent preferred modes of behavior. They are actions or "instruments" that provide positive value for consumers. In this sense, instrumental values are mostly transitional, i.e., a means to an end. For example, jokes are instruments for amusement; exercising is an action that provides feelings of vigor; and studying makes students feel responsible and informed. All these behaviors (jokes, exercise, and studying) may be employed to serve higher-level goals (pleasure, fitness, and accomplishment) or *terminal values,* which represent psychological states of being. In this sense, terminal values serve as the end points for a set of actions. Figure 12.7 provides a list of instrumental and terminal values.[32] Whether instrumental or terminal, consumer values represent the final destination of the means-end chain.

FIGURE 12.7 INSTRUMENTAL AND TERMINAL VALUES

Instrumental Values	Terminal Values
Ambitious	The good life
Open-minded	An exciting life
Capable	World peace
Cheerful	Equality
Clean	Freedom
Courageous	Happiness
Forgiving	National security
Helpful	Pleasure
Honest	Salvation
Imaginative	Social recognition
Independent	True friendship
Intellectual	Wisdom
Logical	World beauty
Loving	Family security
Obedient	Mature love
Polite	Self-respect
Responsible	Sense of accomplishment
Self-controlled	Peace of mind

Source: Pollay, R. W. (1983). Measuring the Cultural Values Manifest in Advertising. *Current Issues and Research in Advertising,* 6:71–92.

Because means-end chains are constructed at the individual level, they are likely to differ greatly among consumers. Also, not every means-end chain leads to a instrumental or terminal value. In fact, a functional benefit may represent the conclusion of a means-end chain. Consider a consumer who is so thirsty that the functional outcome (quenching her thirst) is the only *end* she is seeking. Any *means* (e.g., water, juice, soda) would suffice. In the same vein, a psychosocial benefit can serve as the final end point (e.g., buying a particular hat makes a consumer fit in with his friends). Finally, some products may have missing levels in the means-end chain (e.g., I don't know why, but this golf ball really flies a great distance) and some products have multiple means-end chains because more than one attribute or benefit is important (e.g., distance and feel are important in a golf ball). Figure 12.8 illustrates a detailed means-end-chain and provides examples and explanations for each stage.[33] Tangible attributes (e.g., silk fabric) typically provide functional benefits (e.g., comfort), and intangible attributes (e.g., stylish design) generally lead to psychosocial benefits (e.g., I feel attractive; others have complimented my choice of style). Both functional and psychosocial benefits can fulfill instrumental values (cheerful), and instrumental values (e.g., cheerful) can lead to terminal values (e.g., happiness).

FIGURE 12.8 THE MEANS-END CHAIN PROCESS[33]

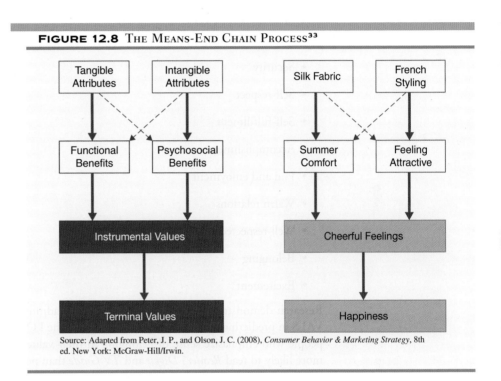

Source: Adapted from Peter, J. P., and Olson, J. C. (2008), *Consumer Behavior & Marketing Strategy*, 8th ed. New York: McGraw-Hill/Irwin.

Rokeach Value Survey

Because instrumental and terminal values can help predict consumer attitudes and behaviors towards brands, researchers have begun to use value models in consumer behavior studies, such as the **Rokeach Value Survey (VALS)**.[24] This widely used survey instrument is designed to provide insight into global value systems by linking them with consumer beliefs, attitudes, preferences, and behaviors. Some evidence suggests that differences in values across cultures can translate into product- and brand-specific consumer preferences. One interesting study compared adult Brazilians across six terminal value segments using the Rokeach Value Survey.[34] Segment A (13 percent of the sample) was primarily concerned with world peace, followed by inner harmony and true friendship. Relatively less materialistic in their value system, this group was more likely to be involved in activities such as reading, gardening, and visiting with family members. As consumers, this group was less likely to invest time and money on new products. By comparison, the more self-centered, achievement-oriented pleasure seekers found in Segment B (9 percent of the sample) were extravagant dressers who value the latest fashions. This segment was more likely to try new products. A third segment (21 percent of the sample) included relatively younger and more educated individuals who mostly value inner harmony and freedom. This group was motivated to attend artistic and cultural activities and preferred living in large cities. They viewed clothing as more than just bodily protection, but they stopped short of using it as a fashion statement.

The List of Values (LOV)

Similar in purpose to the Rokeach Value Survey, the **List of Values (LOV)** was developed at the University of Michigan Survey Research Center to identify nine consumer value segments and link them to value-related consumer behavior.[35] The nine segments are:

- Security
- Self-respect
- Self-fulfillment
- Accomplishment
- Fun and enjoyment
- Warm relations
- Well-respected
- Belonging
- Excitement[36]

Research demonstrates that the LOV is easier to administer and performs as well as VALS in predicting consumer behavior trends.[37] The LOV has been used to show that people who emphasize sense of belonging in their value system tend to be older and more likely to read *Reader's Digest* and *TV Guide* than people who do not endorse this value. People who endorse excitement in their value system are younger and prefer *Rolling Stone* magazine.[38] Finally, LOV has been used to help predict the purchase of several categories of durable goods. For example, consumers who valued security, respect, and sense of belonging showed greater preference for sports, exercise, and luxury products. Those who valued fun and excitement revealed a greater preference for home entertainment products and pets.[39]

Chapter Summary

Culture is often defined as the patterns of meaning acquired by members of society expressed in their knowledge, beliefs, art, laws, morals, customs, and habits. Put simply, culture can be thought of as a system of collectively held values or the *personality* of a society. Cultural values comprise a collective set of beliefs about what important, useful, and desirable. The meaning of cultural values is mobile within a given society. Cultural meaning begins in the collective minds of society and is transferred to consumer products by marketing efforts and the fashion system. Consumers then adopt cultural values from the products they purchase by employing exchange, possession, grooming, and divestment rituals. Enculturation refers to learning about one's own culture; acculturation occurs when people in one culture adapt to meanings resident in another culture.

Written and spoken language is perhaps the most obvious characteristic of a culture. Many of the problems in translating languages verbally stem from fundamental differences in cultures. Some words and phrases have no translation because the meaning may not exist in a different culture. Nonverbal communication, such as body language and symbols, is also important to cultures. Facial expressions, gestures, postural shift, and touching differ among cultures. A familiar hand signal may have an obscene interpretation in another culture. Different cultures also prefer standing relatively close or far away, depending on their attitudes toward interpersonal spacing. Symbols help convey meaning through representation. Important marketing symbols include brand names and brand logos. Because organizations spend considerable money and effort creating brand symbols, legal protection for these symbols has become paramount.

Norms serve as a culture's rules for behavior. Enacted norms explicitly and formally prescribe acceptable behaviors, while crescive norms are implicit and learned only through experience; these include customs, morés, and conventions. Customs are behaviors that have been passed down from previous generations. A moré is a custom that implies a moral right or wrong way of behaving. Conventions are norms that describe the best or "correct" way of doing something. Because norms differ greatly across cultures, it is important to understand different behavioral expectations prior to traveling or doing business with a foreign culture. The return potential model describes norms on behavioral and evaluation dimensions. Too much or too little behavior, such as humor, can be evaluated either positively or negatively, depending on the cultural norms.

A means-end chain combines three levels of a consumer's knowledge about attributes, consequences, and values to form a chronology of product meaning. Attributes are the fundamental characteristics of features of a product. They can be tangible, such as weight or size, and they can be intangible, such as style or quality. Knowledge about product attributes leads consumers to evaluate the benefits that derive from attributes. Benefits can be functional or psychosocial. Functional benefits provide easily measured outcomes, such as speed and durability, while psychosocial benefits involve the psychological or social consequences of using or consuming a product. Product benefits can provide value satisfaction for consumers. Values are classified as instrumental or terminal. Instrumental values represent actions or modes of behavior, such as imaginative or honest. Terminal values represent psychological end states, such as happiness or freedom. The Rokeach Value Survey and List of Values (LOV) are survey instruments that help consumer psychologists and marketers predict consumer attitudes and behaviors towards brands.

Key Terms

culture	divestment rituals	morés
subcultures	enculturation	conventions
cultural values	acculturation	return potential model
culturally constituted world	cultural translation	self-concept
cultural categories	brand jingles	attributes
cultural principles	theory of cognitive itch	benefits
opinion leaders	brand logos	instrumental values
exchange rituals	enacted norms	Rokeach Value Survey (VALS)
possession rituals	crescive norms	List of Values (LOV)
grooming rituals	customs	

Review and Discussion

1. Locate Aesop's fables (you can find them on the Internet). Select your favorite one and explain the cultural value being communicated.

2. Cultural values comprise a collective set of beliefs about what is important, useful, and desirable, i.e., the *personality* of a society. Select a culture or sub-culture to which you belong and explain this group's cultural values.

3. Identify the three stations in McCracken's theory regarding the mobility of cultural meaning. Explain how marketing activities and the fashion system transfer cultural meaning to consumer goods and how consumers adopt for themselves that meaning via rituals.

4. Think about the last time you sold or gave away an important possession (e.g., car, clothing, collection, etc.). Identify the divestment rituals that you conducted before giving it up.

5. Acculturation is a challenge for nations with diverse populations. Explain why the United States has so much at stake regarding acculturation of its immigrants.

6. Why is body language so important for a high-context culture?

7. Identify a brand jingle that got "stuck in your head." Why was this jingle successful at creating a "cognitive itch"?

8. Select your favorite brand logo. Describe its elements in detail and explain whether the symbols are likely to translate successfully into foreign cultures.

9. Identify one of your family customs and describe it in one phrase. Next, explain the various rituals involved with this custom in one paragraph.

10. Construct a means-end chain for the brand *Ipod*. Identify tangible and intangible attributes, functional and psychosocial benefits, and instrumental and terminal values that derive from this product.

Short Application Exercises

1. If you have traveled to a foreign nation, describe specific characteristics of the culture that created for you the greatest "culture shock." Identify specific differences in cultural values, verbal language, body language and symbols, and norms. If you have not traveled abroad, interview someone who has and ask him or her to identify the cultural differences above.

2. Select one specific value from your culturally consti-tuted world (e.g., individuality, freedom, ambition, responsibility) and trace its movement from society to consumer goods, all the way to consumers. Draw on McCracken's framework for the mobility of cul-tural meaning. Identify marketing activities and ele-ments of the fashion system that transfer your select-ed value to consumer products. Select various rituals that subsequently transfer this meaning to individual consumers.

3. Conduct an in-depth interview with a consumer from your parent's generation. Ask questions about the kinds of gifts they gave their children for their birthdays. Try to identify indirectly the cultural meaning that resides in their exchange rituals.

4. Research the business practice of using "bribes" in Middle Eastern cultures. Explain how this Western concept (bribe) does not take on a pejorative mean-ing among Arabs.

5. Select a popular slogan from an American product and translate it into a foreign language of your choice. Identify at least three points of confusion regarding the translation. Focus not only on seman-tics and phonology, but also on cultural translation issues.

MANAGERIAL APPLICATION

Imagine you work in the marketing research department for a major television network. The network is considering developing a new show targeted at various college subcultures. The network is interested in uncovering core values for this subgroup.

YOUR CHALLENGE:

1. Use the Norm Potential Model as a framework to illustrate the values of (a) politeness, (b) cheerfulness, and (c) conscientiousness in your most important college subculture (e.g., marketing club, drama club, fraternity, sports team, religious group).

2. Interview several members of this subculture regarding the desirability of these three values.

3. Using Figure 12.6 as a framework, draw curves for all three values.

4. Are the functions for politeness, cheerfulness, and conscientiousness simply linear (i.e., is more always better) or do diminishing returns exist?

5. With respect to these three values, how would you advise the network to proceed in designing the show?

PERSUASION THROUGH SOCIAL INFLUENCE

OBJECTIVES *After reading this chapter, you will be able to . . .*

1 | Define behavioral compliance

2 | Explain the automaticity arinciple

3 | Explain the commitment and consistency principle

4 | Explain the reciprocity principle

5 | Explain the scarcity principle

6 | Explain the social validation principle

7 | Explain the liking principle

8 | Explain the authority principle

AN INFLUENCE AGENT AT WORK

This spring John visited Sears to shop for a new lawn tractor. After several hours comparing a number of different models, John was mentally exhausted and ready to return home and cut the lawn by hand. Luckily, he encountered an eager salesperson.

The salesperson's approach was unassuming. "I'm here to help you find the right tractor for your needs." At first, the salesperson seemed more interested in John and his family than in selling a tractor. "Where do you live? Tell me about your children. What are your hobbies?" As it turns out, the salesperson seemed remarkably *similar* to John. He enjoyed the same hobbies, listened to the same music, and rooted for the same sports teams.

John was initially overwhelmed with all the possible attribute combinations available in different models of lawn tractors, such as engine size, deck size, manual versus hydrostatic transmission, twin versus triple hi-lift blades, fuel capacity, turning radius, and so on. The salesperson indicated that he could simplify the decision. He asked John a series of questions about his lawn. After a few calculations, the salesperson recommended the *Craftsman 80th Year Anniversary Edition*, which happened to be on sale this weekend only for $1,499, or $200 off the original price. In fact, according to a Sears riding equipment brochure, *The 80th Anniversary Edition* was listed as a "best buy" in a leading consumer magazine. "Thousands of satisfied customers had already chosen it; they can't all be wrong," claimed the salesperson. This particular model was so popular the salesperson said he needed to check the remaining inventory. "It may be sold out," he said cautiously. After checking the local warehouse, however, the salesperson was able to find just one remaining unit. He said, "If I were you, I'd purchase this tractor before another associate with access to our warehouse claims it."

Now that John had become committed to the *80th Anniversary Model*, he seized the opportunity to buy the last remaining unit. The salesperson told John, "Standard in *The 80th Anniversary Edition* model is a 46-inch deck. Unfortunately, the only remaining unit has a custom 54-inch deck. The price difference is only an additional $190." The salesperson went on, "Delivery and assembly is an additional $90, and the earliest delivery date that I have available is in two weeks." With somewhat diminished enthusiasm, John handed over his (old) Sears credit card to commence the transaction. "I assume that you would like the five-year extended warranty?" the salesperson asked. "It covers defects, on-site service with no trip charge, non-technical service calls, and common repairs due to normal use. That's an additional cost of $399, but it practically pays for itself in two years," the salesperson noted. John wasn't expecting an expensive warranty fee, so he declined this particular add-on. "I understand," the salesperson

©Mike Heittola, 2009/Used under license from Shutterstock.com

remarked sympathetically. "How about the one-year warranty for only $199?" John quickly accepted this more reasonable deal.

On the way home, John reflected on his experience. Shopping at Sears had consumed two hours, and he had spent more than $2,000 on a tractor that would not be delivered for two weeks. How did all of this happen? It was the work of a well-trained salesperson who understood the principles of social influence.

OBJECTIVE 1

Defining Compliance

The Sears salesperson is not the only influence agent in the marketplace. Fundraisers, politicians, con artists, bosses, parents, friends, family members, and even professors use a variety of techniques to get consumers to say "yes." The wording of their requests is crucial—a request worded one way may be effective, but if the same request were worded just a little differently, it may be completely ineffective. Timing is also important, as the window of opportunity when people may be susceptible to a request is narrow. Consumer psychologists use the word **verbal compliance** to describe a situation where someone says "yes" to a specific request. The term **behavioral compliance** describes a situation where someone actually carries out that request. Robert Cialdini has conducted many pioneering scientific investigations of behavioral compliance techniques and has uncovered numerous principles about their effectiveness. You can be sure that con artists and others who like to persuade us wish that Professor Cialdini had kept his findings to himself.[1] This chapter discusses some findings uncovered by Cialdini and other researchers and offers a glimpse of the interesting experiments that generated the principles. Specifically, seven key principles of behavioral influence are explained: automaticity, commitment and consistency, reciprocity, scarcity, social validation, liking, and authority. Knowing these principles helps consumers become more influential with people. Perhaps even more importantly, understanding how these principles work helps consumers stay on guard against unwanted influence.

OBJECTIVE 2

The Automaticity Principle

People often use simple heuristics when evaluating the requests of others, sometimes automatically. The **automaticity principle** is the cornerstone of all influence techniques. As the name suggests, this principle asserts that people often think mindlessly and as a result, behave automatically, without fully evaluating the consequences of a request. Harvard University psychologist Ellen Langer[2] finds that people typically spend a large portion of their day in a mindless state. Routine, habitual behaviors (like answering a cell phone or responding to "good morning") are performed over and over with relatively little conscious thought because people don't have the time or resources to think carefully about everything they do. Only a few important behaviors receive careful consideration; others are carried out mindlessly.

Suppose a student is about to use the photocopier in the school library and another student approaches her and says, "Excuse me, I have five pages. May I use the copy machine?" Such a small request typically involves little thought, and many people simply agree without considering the consequences. After all, five pages isn't much. Moreover, people are more likely to comply with a small request if you give them a real reason to comply. In fact, this is precisely what happened in a classic field experiment conducted by Langer and her colleagues.[3] (A field experiment is an experimental study conducted in the real world, as opposed to a laboratory setting.) When the request was basic (i.e., no additional information was provided), compliance was 60 percent. This is called the control group. In contrast, when the request included real information (e.g., "Excuse me, I have five pages. May I use the photocopier *because I'm in a rush*?"), compliance rates increased to 94 percent. The most interesting results, however, occurred when the word *because* was used without any real information (known as placebic information). The request "Excuse me, I have five pages. May I use the photocopier *because* I have to make copies?" generated compliance of 93 percent, statistically equivalent to compliance for the real request. How could this happen? Clearly, placebic information is less compelling than real information. According to the **because heuristic,** however, people tend to process small requests mindlessly. So, merely hearing the word *because* may be enough to trigger compliance. With mindless processing, people don't evaluate the specific reasons for a request. If they hear the word "because," they simply move forward with compliance. "Because" is a signal—a green light for carrying out the request. But that's not the entire story. When the request was changed from small (5 copies) to large (25 copies) the results also changed. People don't automatically agree to everything. Relatively larger requests tend to encourage more purposeful thinking, which reduces the likelihood of using the because heuristic. This is exactly what happened in Langer's study. When the request was "Excuse me, I have 25 pages. May I use the photocopier?" compliance rates dropped to 24 percent. Furthermore, the because heuristic did not increase compliance in this large request condition; it remained at 24 percent. In contrast, when real information was given with the large request, compliance increased from 24 percent to 42 percent. These findings suggest that when people have a substantial request, providing real information is the best strategy. In contrast, if a request is relatively small, people may respond favorably simply by hearing the magic word "because." There's no need to come up with elaborate excuses. Figure 13.1 provides a summary of this interesting study.

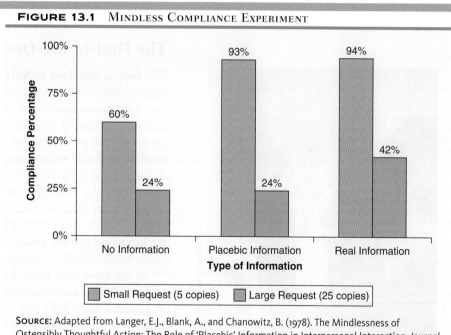

FIGURE 13.1 MINDLESS COMPLIANCE EXPERIMENT

SOURCE: Adapted from Langer, E.J., Blank, A., and Chanowitz, B. (1978). The Mindlessness of Ostensibly Thoughtful Action: The Role of 'Placebic' Information in Interpersonal Interaction. *Journal of Personality and Social Psychology*, 36:635–642.

The because heuristic involves the use of only one cue or piece of information—the word "because." Other, potentially more relevant pieces of information tend to be neglected. Although the rationale provided *after* the word "because" should be important, people often ignore it as a result of mindless thinking. They respond automatically.

OBJECTIVE 3

The Commitment and Consistency Principle

Pressure to maintain consistency is surprisingly powerful. People are expected to exhibit beliefs, attitudes, and behaviors that are stable and coherent. Inconsistencies often invite interpretations of personality flaws or, in extreme cases, mental illness.[4] This principle is known as the **commitment and consistency principle.** When people identify an inconsistency in their pattern of beliefs, they often change one or more beliefs to balance the system. People also attempt to keep their relationships and attitudes consistent. Similarly, when people initially say "yes" to a request or offer, they are likely to continue to say "yes" to subsequent requests regarding the same topic or task. After complying with an initial small request, people tend to comply with larger requests. And after initially saying "yes" to a deal, people tend to stick with their initial commitment—even if the deal changes.

The influence of commitment and consistency extends to fund-raising drives. An interesting study shows that consumers' own self-prophecy can increase their donations.[5] Self-prophecy is founded on two psychological effects. First, asking people to make predictions about socially influenced behaviors can cause people to respond as they think they should. Second, when later asked to perform those same behaviors, people tend to remain consistent with their predictions. In this particular study, when asked to predict whether they would donate to their university fund drive, 49 percent of the people predicted they would do so. In contrast, only 30 percent of the group that was simply asked to donate up front actually did so.

The Foot-in-the-Door Technique

The **foot-in-the-door technique** involves a making a small request followed by a larger one. Telemarketers, sales reps, and fund-raisers apply this technique frequently and with considerable success. First, they make a small request. Then comes the real pitch. For example, some unscrupulous telemarketers pretend to be survey researchers. They ask people if they are willing to share their opinions about a subject of general interest. If people comply with this initial request, they are more likely to continue to appear helpful by purchasing a product or service. However, had they known from the beginning that the phone call was primarily for sales purposes, they would have been more resistant.

In the same vein, many fund-raisers know that past donors are likely to continue to donate and at greater levels than in previous years. Sales reps also understand that customers who have recently placed small orders are likely to continue to buy and in larger quantities. Are these customers genuinely loyal to the cause or product, or are they simply falling prey to the foot-in-the-door technique? "Start small and build" foot-in-the-door tactics are surprisingly simple to recognize and dangerously effective.[6]

In another classic field experiment, people went door-to-door asking California residents to post a large, ugly sign in their front lawns.[7] The sign read "Drive Carefully." Not surprisingly, only 17 percent agreed to this target request. The

Foot-in-the-door tactics often involve asking consumers for their opinions, followed by a sales pitch.

©EdBockStock, 2009/ Used under license from Shutterstock.com results changed dramatically, however, when the foot-in-the-door technique was applied. When people were first asked to carry out a small favor (posting a small "Be a Safe Driver" sign in their yards), 76 percent complied with the larger, target request and posted the bigger, uglier sign. These results are even more interesting when you realize that the large request was made nearly two weeks after the small request and that two different people made the requests. In contrast, if the small favor dealt with a *topic* that was unrelated to the large request (e.g., posting a small "Keep California Beautiful" sign instead of a "Drive Carefully" sign) or if the initial, small *task* was different from the larger request (e.g., sign a petition instead of posting a small sign), compliance for the larger, target request decreased significantly from 76 percent to 48 percent. These results demonstrate a critical lesson. The foot-in-the-door technique is not as effective if the task or topic of the initial, small request is unrelated to the larger, target request. In both cases, people feel less connected to the original request and so, their need to behave consistently attenuates.

The most widely accepted psychological explanation for the foot-in-the-door technique is based on self-perception theory.[8] **Self-perception theory** suggests that complying with a small request leads people to label themselves as helpful, good citizens or as reasonable people. Once people have labeled themselves as such, they have a strong desire to maintain this self-perception, and they are likely to continue complying. Figure 13.2 is a bar graph depicting the findings of research on foot-in-the-door technique.

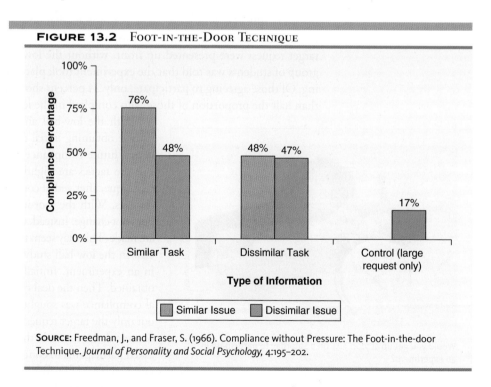

FIGURE 13.2 FOOT-IN-THE-DOOR TECHNIQUE

SOURCE: Freedman, J., and Fraser, S. (1966). Compliance without Pressure: The Foot-in-the-door Technique. *Journal of Personality and Social Psychology*, 4:195–202.

The foot-in-the-door technique is surprisingly easy to apply. Complying with small requests like "Will you do me a small favor?," "Would you like to test drive this vehicle?," "Would you like to try on this suit?," and "Try a sample of this perfume," is all that is necessary to establish an initial commitment. Once the foot is in the door, consumers too often comply with the larger, more substantial request that follows.

The Low-Ball Technique

Car salespersons are notorious for their use of the **low-ball technique**. They try to get an initial commitment, and then they change the deal. First, the salesperson offers a consumer an attractive deal. Next, the consumer completes half a dozen forms and falls in love with the car. But after the consumer is committed, the deal changes. The consumer learns that the car is actually more expensive than originally thought. Perhaps the salesperson made a mistake, or the cost of an expensive option was not included. Maybe the salesperson's boss did not approve the sale. Sometimes the deal changes at the last possible moment, even when the consumer is signing the financial agreement. Whatever the case, once consumers commit to a deal, they tend to stick with it, even when it is no longer as attractive.

Professor Cialdini first learned about the low-ball technique while pretending to be a sales trainee at a Chevrolet dealership. After experiencing the technique first hand, he returned to his psychology lab and began conducting a series of experiments.[9] Both experiments involved college students. In the first study, students were approached on their way to classes and asked if they would be willing to participate in an experiment. This is a reasonable request. Experiments can be fun, and so most students said, "Yes." But then the deal changed. After agreeing to participate, students were told that the experiment would begin at 7:00 A.M. Saturday morning. That's a different arrangement altogether! Nevertheless, more than half (56 percent) of the students who said "yes" to the initial request actually agreed to the target request and showed up for the experiment at 7:00 A.M. This alone, however, doesn't demonstrate support for the low-ball technique. We need to know what proportion of students would have shown up if the target request were presented up front, without the low-ball technique. So, a second group of students was told that the experiment took place at 7:00 A.M. Saturday morning. Of those agreeing to participate, only 24 percent showed up at the lab. That's fewer than half the proportion of those who complied in the low-ball condition.

Both the low-ball and foot-in-the door techniques involve obtaining initial compliance in hopes of engendering future compliance through mindless consistency. But the tactics are slightly different. With the low-ball technique, after verbal commitment is obtained, the deal changes. With the foot-in-the-door technique, the deal does not change. Instead, two separate behavioral requests are made. This may seem trivial, but the distinction is crucial. In the low-ball study, students agreed to participate in an experiment. Initially, only verbal compliance was obtained. Then the deal changed and students' behavioral compliance was sought. Students were asked to carry out only the target request (e.g., show up at 7:00 A.M. on Saturday). In contrast, the foot-in-the-door experiment asked participants to comply behaviorally with two separate requests. After first agreeing and complying with a small request (posting a small sign), they were asked to comply with the second, target request (posting a larger sign). The low-ball technique is convincing. But so is the foot-in-the-door technique. Which is more influential? Professor Cialdini matched the two techniques, head-to-head, in his second study.

In this field experiment, students were approached in their dorms. In the low-ball condition, students were first asked if they would be willing to help with the United

Would you get up at 7:00 A.M. on a Saturday to participate in an experiment?

LeggNet/iStockphoto.com

Way—a request requiring verbal compliance only. After obtaining the crucial "yes," the deal changed and students were then told that they needed to go to the dormitory's front desk to get the door posters. This was the target request. In the foot-in-the-door condition, students were first asked to display a small window poster that was given to them—a small behavioral request. If they complied with this small request, they were asked to go to the dormitory's front desk to get the door posters, the same target request as in the low-ball condition. In the control group, students were simply asked, up front, to go to the dormitory's front desk to get the door posters. The low-ball technique was the winner. Only 10 percent of the students complied with the target request in the foot-in-the-door condition, but 60 percent complied when the low-ball technique was employed. Interestingly, 20 percent complied in the control condition.

Why is the low-ball technique so effective? Research shows that it works through the principle of commitment and consistency. **Commitment theory** suggests that the purpose of obtaining an initial commitment is to impart resistance to change. People don't like to change their minds. It suggests internal contradiction that creates psychological disharmony. The low-ball technique works by first gaining closure and commitment to an idea or deal. When people become committed to a deal, they feel compelled to behave in such a way that maintains their consistency. Thus, they sustain their commitment, even after the deal changes. Let's return briefly to the opening vignette in this chapter. The Sears salesperson applied the low-ball technique when he told John that the only model available was the 54-inch deck, and it was $190 more expensive. He knew that after more than an hour evaluating various products and settling on a particular brand, John was committed.

It is important to recognize that car salespeople and experimenters are not the only ones who use the low-ball technique. People get low-balled every day. The low-ball technique is particularly effective when the initial agreement is a no-brainer—quick and easy. Obtaining public commitment is also crucial. People are especially resistant to change when others hear them agree to a deal. People don't want to appear wishy-washy in front of others. Finally, research shows that the low-ball technique is most powerful when people believe that they agreed to the initial request by their own free will. So, the next time someone asks, "Would you do me a favor?" the correct answer is, "It depends. Tell me what the favor is *first*."

The **bait-and-switch** tactic is a special case of the low-ball technique. Sometimes known as the *lure procedure,*[10] this approach "lures" customers by advertising a low-priced product or service. When customers discover that the product is not available, a salesperson encourages them to purchase a substitute that, of course, costs more. Bait-and-switch is considered fraud if the supplier is not capable of actually selling the advertised product. However, if the seller is able to sell the advertised product, but simply chooses to aggressively promote a competing product, no fraud exists. The bait-and-switch tactic operates under the same principle as the low-ball technique. Customers become committed to the low-priced "bait." When the good deal is taken away, customers feel uncomfortable and seek to reduce this discomfort by accepting the "switch," so long as the new offer is a reasonable substitute.

(OBJECTIVE 4)　　# The Reciprocity Principle

When someone does you a favor, you feel obligated to return it in kind. This is the premise of the **reciprocity principle.** It is not just a principle of social etiquette; it's also a surprisingly powerful influence technique. The problem is that people are often tricked into returning much larger favors than they receive. For example, nonprofit organizations often give people small gifts—such as flowers, buttons, and books—and then ask for charitable donations in return. After accepting a small gift, people have a surprisingly difficult time refusing to donate. University groups, such as alumni associations, apply this technique extensively. They send free bumper stickers, refrigerator magnets, and calendars to their alumni and then follow up with appeals for donations. Sales reps give their clients specialty gifts, such as coffee mugs, pens, and t-shirts, in hopes of creating a feeling of reciprocity.

Have you noticed all of the free samples given in shopping malls? Japanese cuisine on a toothpick, free makeovers at cosmetic boutiques, demonstrations of stain removal products, free bite-sized cookies. It's hard to walk away after accepting free samples. Door-to-door distributors such as Amway also understand the principle of reciprocity. Their salespeople offer free "test drives" of their products. For example, the BUG consists of a bag of Amway products (e.g., furniture polish, window cleaner, detergent, shampoo, deodorizer, pesticide). Amway salespersons leave the BUG with clients for a few days and ask them to try the products for free. After accepting the BUG bait, people are more likely to purchase items from Amway.

Infomercial sponsors are particularly skilled at applying reciprocity. Proactive Solutions, Boflex Extreme, Total Gym 1500, One-Touch Can Opener, Magic Bullet Blender, Hip-Hop Abs, and Core Secrets all offer "no-obligation" deals, which operate similar to free samples. Even children's magazines, such as Highlights®, offer evaluation samples to induce trial for their brands. Of course, after consumers use the products in their homes for several weeks, the likelihood of returning them is low.

The Door-in-the-Face Technique

Invoking the reciprocity principle need not involve free gifts, samples, or test-drives. More subtle approaches are also used. For example, following up a large, unreasonable request with a smaller, more sensible request usually improves behavioral compliance. This is known as the **door-in-the-face technique.** The design is opposite of the foot-in-the-door technique, which involves a small request followed by a large request. Instead, when influence agents make a large request that is rejected, they often follow up with a smaller, more sensible request. The smaller request is a concession, and it often engenders reciprocity. When someone tries to act reasonably with us, we feel compelled to reciprocate and act reasonably in return. The technique is sometimes referred to as "rejection followed by moderation." Salespersons and other influence agents know full well that the initial, unreasonable request will be rejected, and the likelihood of obtaining compliance will increase with the second, more moderate request. For example, salespersons often try to sell expensive three-year service plans and extended warranties. Initially, they use fear tactics to sell the general idea of a warranty. After the expensive plan is rejected, they offer a less expensive, one-year service plan. On the basis of reciprocity, consumers often accept the more reasonable offer. Returning again to the opening story in this chapter, the salesperson offered John an expensive three-year warranty for $399. When he rejected it, the salesperson quickly offered a more reasonable, one-year warranty for $199—which John accepted without resistance.

A series of interesting field experiments was designed to test the effectiveness of the door-in-the-face technique.[11] In the first experiment, college students were approached on their way to class and asked to work for two years as unpaid volunteers for the Juvenile Detention Center. Not surprisingly, no one complied. Immediately after rejecting this request, students were asked to volunteer to take a group of juveniles to the zoo for two hours. Fifty percent agreed to this more reasonable target request. But is the door-in-the-face technique more effective than simply making the target request up front? A control condition was included to test this possibility. A separate group of students was simply asked to volunteer to take a group of juveniles to the zoo for two hours. Only 17 percent agreed. In other words, the door-in-the-face technique was more effective than simply making the target request up front.

Still, it is possible that the 50 percent who verbally complied did so not because of their feelings of reciprocity but because of a simple contrast effect. After all, two hours of volunteer work looks relatively small when contrasted with two years. A third experimental condition tested this hypothesis. A separate group of students was asked, up front, to choose directly between the two alternatives (volunteer for two years *or* two hours). In this condition, only 25 percent agreed to take the juveniles to the zoo for two hours (half the rate of the door-in-the face technique). This provides strong evidence that the door-in-the-face technique does not operate through a simple compare and contrast effect.

Although the door-in-the-face technique appears not to operate via contrast, a second study evaluated reciprocity as the underlying mechanism. In this experiment, students were asked to serve as unpaid volunteers for a group of low-income children (not juvenile delinquents). After this request was rejected, students in the door-in-the-face group were asked to take the children to the zoo for two hours (the same target request as in the first study). Again, the door-in-the-face technique was effective, as 54 percent agreed to the target request. A second group of students was also exposed to the door-in-the-face technique, with one critical twist: Two different people made the requests. One individual made the initial large request, and a different individual made the second, more reasonable request. Consistent with the reciprocity principle, the two-requestor condition approach was less effective, as only 33 percent complied. Thus, a concession occurs only when the *same* individual makes both requests. This is intuitively appealing. Reciprocity is about relationships. People feel reciprocity to other people—not objects or ideas.

Which is more effective, the door-in-the-face technique or the foot-in-the-door technique? You probably know the answer already: "It depends." In a study that directly compared the two techniques, the timing of the requests was varied.[12] In a no-delay condition, the initial and target requests were administered back-to-back, as in the previous studies. In the delay condition, however, seven to ten days separated the requests. The target request was the same for both techniques. Participants were asked to distribute 15 traffic safety pamphlets to their neighbors. In the door-in-the-face condition, this request was preceded by a very large unreasonable request: "Would you keep a record of traffic flow at a busy intersection for two hours?" In the foot-in-the-door condition, the target request was preceded by a very small request: "Would you answer a few short questions about driving safety?" The results of the study clearly indicate that the door-in-the-face technique was more effective than the foot-in-the-door technique when there was no delay in the requests. Conversely, the foot-in-the-door technique outperformed the door-in-the-face technique when the second request was delayed. The illusion of concession is shattered after a period of several days. Consumers' feelings of reciprocity dissipate over time, and thus, the rejection-then-moderation approach is only effective when the requests are close in time. Consistent with the self-perception explanation of the foot-in-the-door technique, the start-small-and-build approach is effective regardless of the timing of the requests. Labeling oneself as helpful and compliant apparently has more long-lasting consequences than does reciprocity. Thus, these two multiple-request techniques operate by different psychological processes. Figure 13.3 provides a visual summary of the findings.

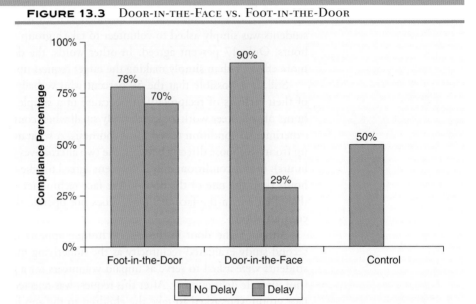

FIGURE 13.3   DOOR-IN-THE-FACE VS. FOOT-IN-THE-DOOR

SOURCE: Cann, A., Sherman, S. J., and Elkes, R. (1975). Effects of Initial Request Size and Timing of a Second Request on Compliance: The Foot-in-the-door and Door-in-the-face. *Journal of Personality and Social Psychology*, 32:774–782.

Firms that sell knives and other household items via infomercials often use the that's-not-all technique.

Photodisc/Getty Images

The That's-Not-All Technique

The Ginsu knife, blue-light specials at Kmart, and vacation packages to Cancun, Mexico, are classic examples of the **that's-not-all technique.** Infomercials and shopping networks are notorious for applying this technique to drowsy viewers at 3:00 A.M. How does it work? Opposite of the low-ball-technique, the that's-not-all technique starts high and builds in a downward fashion. The initial deal is changed into an even better deal *before* the consumer has an opportunity to reject the first offer. Long before the consumer can generate counterarguments, extra gifts, deeper discounts, and more attractive financing are incrementally added to the original offer (e.g., "Today only, the Ginsu Stainless Block Set has been reduced in price from $129.95 to $89.95. But that's not all. Order today and you get a free pair of kitchen shears. And if you order with a credit card right now, we'll make the first payment for you!"). The that's-not-all technique invokes the norm of reciprocity: With each increment, the sponsor appears to be offering a better and better deal, so the customer feels an increasing obligation to comply in response to these concessions. It is all part of a social norm—a general rule of behavior.

Professor Jerry M. Burger conducted a series of field experiments to test the effectiveness and underlying causes of the that's-not-all technique.[13] In the first experiment, customers in the that's-not-all condition were offered a cupcake for 75 cents at a college bake sale, but the deal was sweetened (literally) by adding two free cookies before the customers had a chance to respond. In the control condition, customers were told up front that for 75 cents, they got a cupcake and two cookies. Although the deal was identical for both conditions, a larger proportion of customer agreed to the deal in the that's-not-all condition (73 percent compliance) than did those in the control condition (40 percent compliance).

In the second experiment, similar results were obtained—this time by reducing the price rather than by adding a free product to the deal. In the that's-not-all condition, customers were first offered a cupcake for $1.00, but the price was reduced to 75 cents before they had a chance to say "no." In the control condition, customers were offered a 75-cent cupcake up front. The that's-not-all technique again generated 73 percent compliance, while the control condition produced only 44 percent compliance.

Similar to the door-in-the-face technique, the that's-not-all tactic works by seducing customers into a negotiating situation. The seller has come down from the original price or improved the deal with an additional product. Abiding by the reciprocity norm, customers often feel an obligation to reciprocate the seller's negotiating actions and purchase the product. On the other hand, if the seller's actions are seen as something they are forced to do, then there should be no need to reciprocate. A third experiment addressed this very hypothesis by including a condition where the seller made a mistake in price rather than reducing it of her own free will. The results support the reciprocity explanation, as only 37 percent agreed to the deal when the price was reduced as a result of a mistake. On the other hand, 57 percent complied when the seller negotiated the price downward.

The next experiment tested a simple contrast-effect explanation. Is reciprocity really the motivation for complying, or does 75 cents simply compare favorably to $1.00? One group of customers was told that the cupcakes sold for 75 cents; a second group was told that they cost $1.00. Next, both groups were asked how much they would be willing to pay for the cupcakes. The groups estimated similar price points. This indicates that a contrast effect is not driving customers' decisions.

A follow-up experiment compared the that's-not-all-technique against a common bargain technique. Prices were raised beyond the prices in the earlier studies to reduce mindless compliance. In the that's-not-all condition, $1.25 cupcakes were reduced to $1.00 because the students wanted to close down the bake sale. In the bargain condition, customers were told, "These are only a dollar now. We were selling them for $1.25 earlier." Compliance was significantly higher in the that's-not-all condition (55 percent) than in the bargain condition (25 percent). This provides evidence that a perceived bargain cannot account for the effectiveness of the that's-not-all technique.

If reciprocity is the underlying motive for both the that's-not-all and the door-in-the-face techniques, which tactic is superior? In the final experiment, these two techniques were matched head-to-head. Recall that the door-in-the-face technique allows customers the opportunity to refuse the initial deal or request and a second, more reasonable offer follows. In contrast, the that's-not-all technique offers a better deal immediately, eliminating the opportunity to refuse the initial offer. In the that's-not-all condition, the price of the cupcakes was reduced from $1.25 to $1.00 as in the previous study. In the door-in-the-face condition, cupcakes were initially offered for $1.25. If customers refused this deal, *then* the price was reduced to $1.00. In the control condition, cupcakes were sold for $1.00 up front. Compliance was highest in the that's-not-all condition, second for door-in-the-face, and lowest in the control condition.

There are two important lessons to learn from Professor Burger's field studies. First, the that's-not-all technique operates through the principle of reciprocity. When salespeople offer better and better deals, customers often feel obligated to reciprocate these acts of concession. So, consumers can avoid unnecessary feelings of reciprocity by focusing only on the final deal—without considering the incremental offers. Second, similar to the because heuristic, the that's-not-all technique is only effective when consumers behave mindlessly. Of course, consumers can avoid the negative consequences of mindless behavior by concentrating on real information—evaluating the substance, not the fluff.

The Multiple-Deescalating-Requests Technique

The door-in-the-face technique involves two separate requests—a large request followed by a smaller, more reasonable appeal. The **multiple-deescalating-requests technique** involves more than two requests. However, it differs from the that's-not-all technique in that once a request is refused, additional requests follow—one after the other—until one is finally accepted. In contrast, the that's-not-all technique provides multiple offers without allowing customers to respond until the final deal is presented. Research shows that the multiple-deescalating-requests technique can be effective in the context of university fund-raising.[14] Telemarketers initially request $1,000 donations for their university. If this request is rejected, a request of $750 follows. If this fails, there is an appeal for $500, and so on. This approach yields greater compliance rates and donation amounts compared with a standard request. Moreover, the multiple-deescalating-requests technique is more effective than presenting statistical information about typical donation levels and ranges (a common fund-raising technique). In fact, presenting statistical information is no more effective than the standard request. These results are consistent with the automaticity principle and with research on consumers' tendency to neglect statistical information.

The Even-a-Penny Technique

Influence agents can appear to be reasonable and induce clients to comply through a wide variety of reciprocity-based tactics: free gifts, concessions, or multiple concessions. Another way to appear reasonable is to make extremely small requests. This approach is known as the **even-a-penny technique**, and it involves the legitimization of trivial contributions (a penny, a dollar, one minute of your time). Research

© Craig Wactor, 2009/Used under license from Shutterstock.com

shows that this approach can be effective in increasing compliance rates without decreasing the average amount donated by contributing individuals in fund-raising efforts. One field study tested the effectiveness of the even-a-penny technique by soliciting donations door-to-door for the American Cancer Society.[15] In the control group, potential donors were given the standard plea, "Would you be willing to help by giving a donation?" In the even-a-penny condition, the solicitor added, "Even a penny will help." The even-a-penny technique generated almost twice the compliance rate (50 percent) as the control condition (28 percent). More interesting, the median dollar contributions by individuals were identical. This is a powerful lesson for nonprofit organizations: The even-a-penny technique does not sacrifice dollar contributions for higher compliance rates. Further research shows this technique can increase donations to the American Heart Association[16] and the Reye's Syndrome Foundation. Finally, this reciprocity-based technique appears to be equally effective in both face-to-face and telemarketing contexts.[17]

OBJECTIVE 5

The Scarcity Principle

"While Supplies Last," "Limited Edition," "Sale Ends Soon," and "One-Time-Offer" all proclaim a sense of urgency to imply scarcity for products and services. Do consumers prefer items that are abundant or rare? According to the **scarcity principle,** people often want what they cannot have. Consumers also want things that may not be available in the future. Stamp collectors covet the rare *Curtis Jenny* inverted airmail stamp. Only 100 were created in 1918, all on a single sheet created by a printer error. Baseball card collectors dream about the scarce 1909 T206 Honus Wagner tobacco card, also known as the "Holy Grail of baseball cards." Incredibly, this 1-7/16" × 2-5/8" card was once owned by hockey great Wayne Gretzky and recently sold for $2.35 million at a sports memorabilia show in Atlantic City.[18] The scarcity principle rests on the premise that because valuable objects are rare, it follows that rare objects must be valuable. This backwards logic is known as **affirmation of the consequent,** or confusion of the inverse. In fact, there are lots of scarce items that have little value—obsolete mainframe computers, turntable record players, and manual typewriters, to name a few. Still, consumers associate scarcity with value. Clever marketers create scarcity by limiting production or supply. Some manufacturers, including Harley-Davidson and Porsche, deliberately limit production on expensive models. In the case of Harley-Davidson, some customers are willing to wait more than a year to take title to their new motorcycles. Other marketers influence perceptions of scarcity by limiting distribution. Until July 2000, L.L Bean resisted expanding its bricks-and-mortar retail stores beyond its single outlet in Freeport, Maine. White House Black Market (WHBM), a high-end women's clothing boutique, does not distribute its products through discount retailers such as Walmart. Firms like WHBM understand that consumers' perceptions of exclusivity are inversely related to distribution intensity and that exclusive (or scarce) products command higher margins. For decades, the DeBeers Company has successfully convinced consumers that diamonds are rare. Diamonds, which are basically compressed carbon, have not been "rare" since their discovery in South Africa in 1867. Today, diamonds are mined in about 25 countries, on every continent except Europe and Antarctica.

Inverted Jenny postage stamp, courtesy of the Smithsonian National Postal Museum

Stamp collectors covet the extraordinarily rare Curtis Jenny inverted airmail stamp.

Government attempts to limit the availability of a product via prohibition or censorship often backfire because telling us we cannot have a product makes us want it even more. During the Prohibition Era in the United States, alcoholic beverages became scarcer and so, more desirable. Consequently, consumers went to great lengths (even committing crimes) to obtain alcohol. Similarly, telling us *not* to do something makes the behavior more desirable. For example, some research raises questions about the effectiveness of the D.A.R.E. Program (Drug Abuse Resistance Education).[19] Similar criticisms have been raised against programs aimed at reducing teenage smoking and alcohol consumption. In the mind of a teenager, "If everyone is telling us not to do it, it must really be good." Censorship can also increase demand. The publication of Salman Rushdie's *The Satanic Verses* in 1988 provoked violent reactions from radical Muslims because it was perceived as irreverently portraying the prophet Muhammad. Rushdie received threats and a fatwa issued by Ayatollah Khomeini, calling for his execution. How did the book sell? It headlined on the *New York Times* bestseller list for more than a year and has produced 14 hardcopy editions since, quite a feat for a modern-day novel.

Research on the effects of scarcity show that reducing availability increases desirability. Field experiments demonstrate that something as simple as the number of chocolate chip cookies in a jar can exert a surprisingly powerful effect on the desirability of a product.[20] Participants in a field study selected more cookies when there were only two (versus ten) cookies in the jar. This effect was more pronounced when limited product availability was the result of an accident (i.e., the experimenter grabbed the wrong jar). Moreover, desire for the scarce cookies was highest when product availability was reduced because of demand (i.e., the product was chosen frequently by previous participants). Interestingly, these scarcity effects did not occur because of preferences in taste.

It is important to guard against the power of the scarcity effect when marketers inundate us with claims of product shortages or limited time offers. Remember the X-box 360 shortage during Christmas, 2005? Rumors of retail shortages sent consumers scurrying to *eBay* to buy the product for as much as $3,000. The bidding wars that ensued only pushed prices higher (the manufacturer's suggested retail price was about $399). Judging by the thousands of X-box 360 listings on *eBay* during that holiday season, one might wonder if the shortage was real or simply crafted to benefit the scalpers.

(O B J E C T I V E 6)   # The Social Validation Principle

Thousands of satisfied customers can't be wrong, and firms like Procter & Gamble, Toyota, and Verizon Communications spend more than $1 billion in advertising each year reminding us of the popularity of their brands. For decades, McDonald's proclaimed "over one billion [hamburgers] sold." Public broadcasting stations, charity telethons, and university fund-raisers delight in presenting long lists of names of individuals who have been involved in their causes in the past. Salespeople often provide prospects with their list of clients, emphasizing that some of the names are friends or acquaintances of the prospect. In televised fund-raising drives, dozens of telephones are ringing and volunteers are answering them, supposedly taking the names of eager contributors. Shopping networks show a digital count of the number of units sold along with the time remaining, and eBay displays the cumulative number of bids and times the page has been visited for each auction item. Bartenders, street musicians, and deli-clerks, among others, salt their tip jars to give the impression that many people leave tips—and large ones. Nightclub ushers limit the number of people allowed into the club so that long lines form outside the door, suggesting that the club is extremely popular. Canned laugh tracks are still used on television sitcoms to make the shows seem funnier (even though people claim not to like canned laughter).[21]

What do all these examples have in common? They are applications of the **social validation principle,** also know as "proof in numbers." The social validation principle maintains that the perceived validity (or correctness) of an idea increases as the number of people supporting the idea increases. In fact, the opinions of other people can be extremely informative, especially under conditions of ambiguity or uncertainty.[22]

Presenting a list of supporters or donors to a prospect is known as the **list technique.** Research on the list technique shows that it can significantly increase compliance. In a door-to-door fund-raising campaign for the American Heart Association, one group of prospective donors was shown a long list of names of previous donors prior to the request. The control group received only the standard request for a donation. Forty-three percent donated in the list technique condition, but only 25 percent donated in the control condition.[23]

People also look to the behavior of others when they decide *not* to do something. On March 13, 1964, Catherine "Kitty" Genovese parked her car by the Long Island Railroad parking lot and began walking home. Winston Mosley chased her down and began attacking her. Injured and terrified, Kitty screamed, "Oh my God! He stabbed me! Please help me!" Mosley fled when nearby apartment lights went on and a man shouted, "Let that girl alone," but Mosley returned and stabbed Kitty again when no one actually came forward to help. At 3:25 A.M., Mosley returned a third time and stabbed Kitty as she lay inside the front door of her apartment. It wasn't until 3:50 A.M. that the police finally received a call from one of the 38 witnesses to the murder. Tragically, by the time police reached Kitty, she was already dead.[24] Why did none of the witnesses help? What kind of people would simply watch and not intervene? These questions have been asked over and over again. The truth is, the witnesses' behavior—though disturbing—is fairly normal. Classic research on bystander nonintervention shows that people are less likely to help a person when many other people are present.[25] One explanation for this bystander nonintervention is that people don't think others need help if no one else appears alarmed or concerned. People look for cues from other group members. If no one quickly steps forward to act, then the likelihood of anyone acting decreases and a snowball of pluralistic ignorance ensues. This peculiar inaction among group members is known as the **diffusion of responsibility.** In fact, people are much more likely to help when they perceive themselves to be the only person available to help, i.e., responsibility for helping the person in need cannot be diffused.

Do consumers diffuse their responsibilities in the marketplace? Do they ignore good causes when few people seem to support them (e.g., world literacy)? Do consumers shy away from superior products that lack advertising clout (e.g., blood pressure monitors)? Conversely, do they jump on the bandwagon of brands because we see others buying them (e.g., *Ipods, BlackBerry* devices, and *Crocs*)? Classic research indicates that people observe and model (imitate) the behavior of others.[26] Moreover, the effects of peer pressure and conformity on consumers' perceptions of what is correct can be powerful.[27]

Cultural and Individual Differences

All consumers are not equally susceptible to peer pressure. High self-monitoring individuals (those who are highly sensitive and responsive to social cues) are more susceptible to social influence than are low self-monitors.[28] Individuals from collectivistic (versus individualistic) cultures are also more given to social influence.[29] Members of individualistic cultures tend to define themselves as independent from groups and focus on personal goals, while members of collectivistic cultures define themselves in terms of group membership and emphasize group goals. In general, Western cultures such as North America and Western Europe are individualistic and Eastern cultures such as Japan, South Korea, and China are more collectivistic. Even within a culture, however, people differ. Those with a strong collectivistic (versus individualistic) orientation tend to be more responsive to social influence, regardless of the prevailing culture. In fact, research indicates that individual differences may be more important than cultural differences.[30]

An interesting study tested the effectiveness of social-validation procedures versus commitment and consistency techniques for influencing consumers in the United States and Poland. The United States is considered an individualistic culture, while Poland is considered relatively more collectivistic. Individual differences were also

EYE ON INTERNATIONAL

MAC ADJUSTS ATTITUDE IN JAPAN

Collectivistic and individualistic cultures often respond differently to humorous advertising. When Apple Inc. introduced its "Mac versus PC" ads to global markets, it faced a common but difficult issue: What seems funny in one culture may seem ill-mannered in another. In the American ads, a nerdy PC guy (John Hodgman, who bears a striking resemblance to Bill Gates) keeps getting trumped by his hip Mac counterpart (Justin Long), who unassumingly shows the audience that Macs are superior. In one spot, PC is proudly getting a camera taped to his head so he can do video chatting, only to discover that Mac already has a built-in camera. In another spot, PC is flanked by an officious security guard who insists on granting (or denying) permission each time Mac tries to say something to PC. This is meant to represent the cumbersome security functionality in Microsoft's Vista operating system for PCs.

The ads may elicit humor in America, but in Japanese culture, where direct-comparison ads have long been frowned

ayzek/iStockphoto.com

upon, it is considered rude to brag about one's strengths. Accordingly, the Japanese versions of the ads include two local comedians from a group called the Rahmens. In the Japanese ads, the dialogue emphasizes that Macs and PCs are not that different. Instead of clothes that cast PC as a nerd and Mac as a hipster, PC wears plain office attire and Mac wears more casual attire, highlighting the work/home divide between the devices more than brand personality differences. In the first ad of the series, Mac even gives PC a nickname: *waaku*, which is a playful Japanese version of the word "work." In the Japanese spots, PC's body language is the primary source of humor. Mac looks embarrassed when PC touches his shoulder or hides behind Mac's legs to avoid viruses. "PC constantly makes friendship-level approaches that Mac rejects in a friendly-irritated way," says Oliver Reichenstein, the founder of Tokyo-based interactive brand consultancy, Information Architects Ltd. "The western Mac ads would backfire in Japan, because the Mac would appear to lack class."[59]

measured using an individualistic/collectivistic personality scale. Students were asked to imagine that they had been approached by a representative from the Coca-Cola Company who wished to ask them some questions about Coca-Cola. In the social-validation condition, students were told that all (or half) their classmates had agreed to participate. In the commitment and consistency conditions, students were told that, in the past, their classmates had always (or never) complied with survey requests. Two important findings emerged. First, the social-validation procedure was more effective with the Polish students, but the commitment and consistency technique worked better with the American students. Second, students' personal orientation (individualistic versus collectivistic) had a stronger impact on their compliance than did the overall cultural orientation.[30]

Injunctive Versus Descriptive Norms

Sometimes well-intended communications may actually send the *wrong* message. In 1971, Keep America Beautiful, Inc., created a dramatic public service announcement hoping to convince Americans to stop littering. The first spot aired on Earth Day and featured *Iron Eyes Cody*, a famous Native American actor, quietly canoeing through a polluted river. As Iron Eyes Cody emerged from the river near a busy highway, a motorist threw a bag of garbage, which splattered at the Indian's feet. The ad ended with a close-up of Iron Eye's solemn face, and a tear trickles down his cheek (this classic PSA can be viewed online at www.kab.org, Media Center). Titled "People Start Pollution, People Can Stop It," the ad became a classic and was partially credited with helping to establish the nascent environmental movement in the United States. But did it send the wrong message?

Despite the drama created by the "Iron Eyes Cody spot," research shows that the ad contains features that may encourage behavior opposite of that supported by the sponsors.[31] Recall that **norms** serve as important behavioral guidelines for a culture. Professor Cialdini's research suggests that Keep America Beautiful, Inc., may have unwittingly pitted two specific types of social norms against one another—descriptive and injunctive norms. **Descriptive norms** involve perceptions of which behaviors are common or popular, i.e., what is everyone doing? Previous research has demonstrated the powerful influence of descriptive norms. For example, by increasing the number of people looking up from a street corner to a bogus image in the sky, experimenters increased the number of pedestrians who also stopped and looked up.[32] By observing what most other people are doing, people can imitate these common actions and usually make good choices.[33] Have you ever attended a church, synagogue, or mosque that was foreign to you? If so, you understand the importance of descriptive norms. Marketers understand descriptive norms, too. By showing crowded stores, excited customers, and declaring their brands as "best sellers," marketers are implying that their products are desirable. The proof is in the numbers.

In contrast, **injunctive norms** involve perceptions of which behaviors are accepted or rejected by society. While descriptive norms tell us what *is* done, injunctive norms tell us what *should* be done. Injunctive norms motivate us with social rewards for appropriate behavior and social punishment for inappropriate actions. Both kinds of norms motivate human action because people tend to do what is popular *and* what society approves.[34] As such, the two norms could be potential competitors, descriptive norms pulling consumers in one direction and injunctive norms tugging the other way. Could it be that the "Iron Eyes Cody spot" sends a mixed message to its audience by showing a regrettable but common behavior? By featuring a littered environment, the audience may simply interpret the message as validating their belief that everyone litters. Worse, if the ad focuses attention on the undesirable behavior (e.g., showing someone in the act of littering), then the effect may be to increase that very undesirable behavior. If everybody's doing this, it must be normal. Here, the descriptive norm (what people actually do) may win the battle against the injunctive norm (what people ought to do). Even the voice-over for the ad, "People Start Pollution . . ." invokes a descriptive norm—everyone pollutes.

Professor Cialdini tested this hypothesis in a field study.[31] Flyers regarding automotive safety week were tucked under the windshield wipers of parking garage patrons. One area was filled with litter; the other was clean. In addition, patrons either witnessed a person drop a large flyer on the floor (littering condition) or witnessed a person walk by (walk-by condition). The results showed that parking patrons were more likely to litter in the littered environment than in the clean environment. More important, patrons who witnessed a person litter in the littered environment also littered more (54 percent) than did those who patrons who saw no littering in the littered environment (32 percent). Finally, patrons who witnessed a person litter in the clean environment littered less (6 percent) than did those patrons who saw no littering in the clean environment (14 percent). This important interaction is depicted in Figure 13.4.

FIGURE 13.4   DESCRIPTIVE VS. INJUNCTIVE NORMS

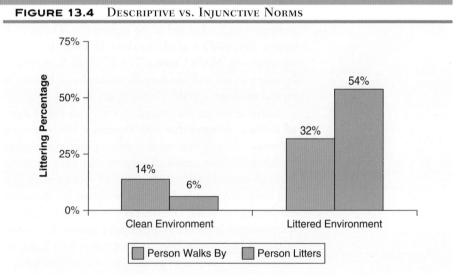

SOURCE: Adapted from Cialdini, R. (1996). Activating and Aligning Two Kinds of Norms in Persuasive Communications. *Journal of Interpretation Research*, 1:3–10.

The results of this study are intuitively appealing. The rationale to litter in a dirty garage may involve something like, "Littering won't do much additional damage here; it's already a mess." Moreover, observing someone else litter in a dirty environment increases littering behavior (54 percent). Here the descriptive norm (everyone litters) overpowers the injunctive norm (littering is wrong). Conversely, witnessing someone litter in a very clean environment may invoke a more powerful injunctive norm, "Why would he litter? This place is clean!" The lesson from this research is important. When communicating that a particular behavior is socially objectionable, advertisers should not portray the undesirable behavior as common. Instead, they should focus their message on the desired outcome. Otherwise, they run the risk of emphasizing the descriptive norm (e.g., lots of people perform the unwanted behavior) over the injunctive norm (e.g., the unwanted behavior is wrong).

MARKETING IN ACTION

Back by Popular Neglect

Research in consumer behavior can be helpful to non-profit organizations looking for solutions to national problems, such as littering. Professor Cialdini's 1996 study demonstrates that previous techniques aimed at stopping littering may actually endorse and increase littering behavior.[32] Keep America Beautiful, Inc.'s (KAB) 1971 Iron Eyes Cody public service announcement is a perfect example. By showing a littered environment to the audience, with an implicit warning that littering is harmful, the audience actually views a scene validating their belief that everyone litters. Keep America Beautiful, Inc., didn't know about Cialdini's research in 1971. But they did in 1998.

First aired on April 21 (Earth Day) in 1998, Keep America Beautiful's sequel to the 1971 ad recalls the famous face and tear of Iron Eyes Cody. The ad begins with a scene at an urban bus stop. Prior to climbing on the bus, a young, African American woman prepares to litter her gum, a middle-aged Caucasian businessman litters his newspaper, an African American man innocently places his Styrofoam cup on the ground, while a casually dressed white man tosses his cigarette and extinguishes it with his foot. After the litterbugs get on the bus, the ad focuses on the littered environment, where a breeze tosses the trash about. Finally, the camera pans to a large poster of Iron Eyes Cody, which is strategically positioned inside the bus stop shelter. In high drama, a tear rolls down his face—the same tear he cried some 35 years ago. Unfortunately, the same effects are also likely to occur. Once again, the ad features both a littered environment and copious littering behavior, and this time the message is even stronger—people of all races, genders, and socioeconomic backgrounds litter. It's a recipe for misinterpretation and an invitation to litter. The tagline, "Back by Popular Neglect," refers to environmental neglect. However, it could just as easily refer KAB's disregard for consumer research.

So what is the correct approach? According to research, the lowest frequency of littering occurs when people view *one* thoughtless person littering in a *clean* environment. This approach would send the message that *few* people litter, and any individual who does so significantly harms the environment. How about a scene

of Iron Eyes Cody wiping away his 35-year-old tear and replacing it with a smile as a sole litterbug changes his course by picking up not only his litter but also a misplaced item near a tidy and conspicuously positioned recycling bin?

KAB isn't the only organization that appears to eschew the recommendations of consumer research. In 2007, the National Highway Traffic Safety Administration (NHTSA) began a national highway seat-belt enforcement campaign, "Click It or Ticket." The ads show various scenes of police officers ticketing motorists (of all races and ages) who have failed to buckle-up. The NHTSA cites the campaign as helping create 82 percent seat-belt usage nationwide. One can't help but wonder how high usage would be if the NHTSA's ads featured a majority of drivers buckling-up and avoiding traffic tickets.

AP Photo

Changing behavior is important for many nonprofit organizations and cause-related marketers. Stopping smoking, driving under the influence, and unsafe sex all require cessation of a negative behavior. In contrast, getting mammograms, exercising regularly, and eating healthy foods all involve the adoption of a positive behavior. In both cases, marketers who understand descriptive and injunctive norms are better equipped to obtain the desired outcome. In *The Tipping Point*, Malcolm Gladwell discusses how social phenomena like fashion trends and crime begin, gather momentum, and finally "tip" to become epidemics.[35] He also argues that America's anti-smoking messages during the previous two decades may have backfired. Recent data from the American Lung Association indicate that approximately 20 percent of college students currently smoke. But the American Lung Association notes that smoking rates among students fluctuate greatly, and they attribute the most recent decline to higher prices for cigarettes and more regulations barring smoking in public areas and colleges.[36] Gladwell argues, however, that health organizations should stop trying to change attitudes about tobacco. Smoking, *per se,* has never been cool. But it is the *smokers* who are cool. From James Dean to Steve McQueen to Sarah Jessica Parker, each embodies rebellion, sexuality, and most of all, sophistication. Though Gladwell makes a case for limiting the nicotine in cigarettes and reducing smoking by understanding its links to depression, he would probably agree that emphasizing injunctive norms (smoking is bad) just fuels teenage interest in smoking. Ad campaigns that portray teenage smokers as delinquent or antisocial simply acknowledge the frequency of the behavior. Besides, teenagers are often drawn to rebellious behavior; it's part of being a teenager. The current anti-smoking campaigns run parallel to the Keep America Beautiful's campaign. Both emphasize the common, descriptive norms over the prescriptive, injunctive norms. And the descriptive norms are likely to win; in other words, if everyone is doing it, it must be normal.

OBJECTIVE 7

The Liking Principle

The **liking principle** is remarkably simple—we tend to comply with the requests of those whom we like. So, the more an individual likes you, the more power you have over him or her. Your overall social power is proportionate to the number of people who like you. Take Joe Girard, for example. Joe is the famous Chevrolet salesman who won the title "Number One Car Salesman" 12 years in a row and earned more than $200,000 annually.[1] Girard is also listed as the world's greatest car salesman in the *Guinness Book of World Records.* How does he do it? Joe claims people like him because he offers his customers a fair deal. But he does something else. Each month, Joe sends more than 13,000 greeting cards to his customers. The message inside is always the same three words, "I like you." Let's explore the formula for the liking principle. It rests on four primary factors: familiarity, attractiveness, similarity, and ingratiation.

Familiarity

The *mere exposure effect* suggests that the more familiar we become with an object, the more we like it. This explains why an initially unfamiliar stimulus such as a new song becomes more likable over time. We aren't too sure about the song the first time we hear it. After repeated exposure, however, the tune becomes more familiar; by the third or fourth play, we are singing along. Recent research shows that the mere exposure effect is also applicable to our familiarity with specific people. In a recent study, participants repeatedly viewed photographs of people's faces and then viewed the same photographs again, along with photographs of new (similarly attractive) faces. The familiar faces were rated as more likable and evoked more smiles than did the unfamiliar faces.[37] The lesson is simple. We tend to like familiar people.

Physical Attractiveness

Of all the factors influencing likeability, physical attractiveness may be the most intriguing. Research shows that we automatically assume attractive people to be intelligent, kind, and honest.[38] This *halo effect* suggests that we over-generalize, assuming that one positive trait (e.g., physical attractiveness) implies the presence of many other positive traits. Accordingly, successful salespeople closely attend to the latest fashions and try to appear attractive. And they should. Research demonstrates that well-groomed job candidates can receive more favorable hiring decisions.[39] Another study shows that attractive employees earn approximately 12 to 14 percent more income than their less attractive colleagues.[40]

Attractiveness bias doesn't end in the workplace. A mesmerizing criminal trial, known as "The Preppy Murder Trial," began during 1986. Robert Chambers was charged with and tried for the second-degree murder of Jennifer Levin, whose semi-clad body was found by a bicyclist near Fifth Avenue and 83d Street, behind the Metropolitan Museum of Art in New York. Robert Chambers was an attractive young man. Standing 6'4" and weighing 200 pounds, his blue eyes and movie-star proportions won favor

AP Photo/Mario Suriani

with the media. Chambers was described as a handsome "altar boy" with a promising future. In contrast, the media attacked Levin's reputation. Although the jury was deadlocked for nine days, Chambers' legal team ultimately struck a plea bargain—manslaughter. In the end, Chambers was sentenced to serve only 5 to 15 years in prison. He served all 15 years, mostly because of his bad behavior while incarcerated.

Does physical attractiveness affect the legal process? An experiment demonstrates that attractive defendants who serve time are less likely to return to jail than their less attractive counterparts.[41] A group of New York City inmates underwent plastic surgery to remove facial disfigurements. A second group received only the typical rehabilitation services, such as counseling and training. The group who received cosmetic surgery was significantly less likely to be re-incarcerated. There's more. Attractive people are more likely to receive help in times of need (from both sexes) than are less attractive people.[42] Finally, physically attractive politicians have been shown to receive more than twice as many votes as their less attractive opponents.[43] Overall, attractive people enjoy significant social advantages in our culture. They are viewed as more intelligent, earn higher incomes, and receive preferential treatment. Given this background, it's not surprising that *Hooters of America, Inc.* quickly settled a class action lawsuit for more than $3 million in exchange for the right to hire only (attractive) women as waitresses. Men are permitted to work at the Hooters restaurants,

Plastic surgery has become a family tradition. Doctors report that children are more likely to consider a cosmetic surgery if another family member has had the same. Surprisingly, some parents are even giving it to their children as graduation gifts. Forget the trip to Cancun or even a new car. Some high school graduates are opting for cosmetic surgery instead. Charlie Baase, a spokesperson for the American Academy for Cosmetic Surgery, said the organization's member surgeons have reported a slight increase in the number of teens wanting to change something about their appearance around graduation time. The most common procedures range from ear pinning and nose jobs to less invasive procedure such as microdermabrasion or Botox injections.

There appears to be a slow but steady rise in teens getting cosmetic surgery, with an average annual increase of about 2.5 percent over the last four years, according to Dr. Richard A. D'Amico, president-elect of the American Society of Plastic Surgeons. Breast augmentations among young women ages 18 to 19 increased about 12 percent between 2005 and 2006. "I've seen an increase in teens having plastic surgery, and certainly for graduation," said Dr. Stephen T. Greenberg, a New York plastic surgeon and the author of *A Little Nip, a Little Tuck.*[60]

"Parents buy this as a gift because the child has everything else," said Dr. Diana Zuckerman, president of the National Research Center for Women and Families. "It should be considered with the same seriousness as any other surgery, not with the same seriousness as buying a graduation dress."

Zuckerman added that there's a difference between getting a nose job, for instance, and wanting breast implants as a teen. Liposuction and breast augmentation, she warned, can have more immediate and dangerous complications, including allergic reactions. She also warned that it is important to recognize that the U.S. Food and Drug Administration has not approved the marketing and use of silicone gel-filled breast implants for women under the age of 22.

Research shows that young people looking to have cosmetic surgery may suffer from body dysmorphic disorder, a preoccupation with a perceived flaw in one's appearance. "Individuals who suffer from body dysmorphic disorder and turn to cosmetic surgery almost uniformly report no improvement of their bodies after surgery," said Dr. David Sarwer, associate professor of psychology at the Center for Human Appearance at the University of Pennsylvania School of Medicine. "They then become preoccupied with another aspect of their appearance." But for some patients, like 15-year-old Robin Kushner, rhinoplasty surgery (nose job) has improved her self-esteem. Her friends say that she looked good before, but looks even better now. "It's easy for people to say to look on what's on the inside, not the outside," said Antell. "That's being naive. We all judge books by the cover. I'm not saying its right, and I'm not saying it's wrong. I'm saying it's reality."[60]

but only as cooks, dishwashers, and managers. The company Web site argues that "Hooters Girls" have the same right to use their natural female sex appeal to earn a living as supermodels. Hooters understands that attractiveness generates liking, and liking generates power.

It also should come as no surprise that in 2006, almost a quarter of a million cosmetic procedures were performed on young people ages 13 to 19, including about 47,000 nose jobs and 9,000 breast augmentations. This represents nearly a 10 percent increase in teen cosmetic surgeries since 2002.[44] At a more mundane level, how many men have grown mustaches or beards, and how many women have changed their hair color? How many people wear contact lenses to improve their youthfulness or lose weight in order to improve their body appearance? Perhaps these measures are less extreme than surgery, but they are still just a variation on an important theme—attractiveness.

Similarity

For those people who are happy with (or resigned to) their perfectly normal appearance, the *similarity tactic* can be tapped to influence liking. People tend like others who are similar in terms of appearance, attitudes, opinions, lifestyle, personality, or social and educational backgrounds.[45] Of course, the opposite is also true. We tend to dislike those who are dissimilar to us, and this finding has important implications for understanding stereotyping and prejudice.[46] One classic study from the 1970s shows that people are more likely to help those who dress as they do. An experimenter dressed either conservatively or in "hippie" getup and asked college students for a dime to make a phone call (obviously, the study took place in the pre-cell phone era). When the experimenter dressed the same as the students, more than two-thirds of the students complied. In contrast, when the experimenter dressed unlike the students, fewer than half met his request.[47] Even trivial similarities can be influential. Salespeople are trained to find out what hobbies and leisure activities potential clients enjoy and to feign similar interests. Car salespeople are trained to look in the trunks of potential clients' cars for clues! Remember how the Sears salesperson in the opening vignette preferred the same music and sports as the customer? What a coincidence that he liked the same sports teams as the shopper. Because similarities can easily be manufactured and masqueraded, consumers should pay special attention to influence agents who claim to be just like them.[1] In fact, many sales training programs instruct trainees to "mirror" their client's body posture, mood, and verbal style.[48]

Ingratiation

If you suspect that someone is paying you compliments because they want a favor, you're probably right. **Ingratiation** is a tactic commonly used to engender liking. It involves purposefully bringing oneself into the good graces of another person. In fact, we tend to like those who like us, and we are hopelessly addicted to compliments. Research shows that even when consumers realize that they are being flattered, they still like the flatterer. What's more, the ingratiation doesn't have to be accurate to work. Research shows that compliments by an evaluator produced the same liking whether the comments were true or not.[49] Remembering a client's name[50] and asking a person how he or she is doing can also facilitate liking and thus, produce compliance.[51] Ingratiation, however, is not a panacea. It can backfire if the ingratiator goes too far with the flattery, making it exaggerated or inappropriate. This is known as the "ingratiator's dilemma."[52] Thus, ingratiation should be subtle. Some tactics include paying compliments about someone to a third party, agreeing with someone only *after* expressing some initial resistance, and performing useful (versus superfluous) favors, i.e., favors that actually help the target of the ingratiation.[53]

Creating **indirect associations** to a positively evaluated stimulus (such as a popular university, sports team, or brand) can also increase liking for the stimulus. For example, when our team wins, we are more likely to wear hats, hoodies, and T-shirts adorned with the team's logo. This is known as basking in reflected glory, or BIRGing. Although fans don't have much to do with the performance of the team, a victory feels like a personal triumph. On the other hand, when our team loses, it feels like a personal defeat.[54] Simply by wearing NFL gear or drinking from a mug that displays our favorite brand, we increase our likeability for that particular organization. If the team or brand performs poorly, however, we tend to disassociate the brand or cut off reflected failure, also known as CORFing.

People also like to be the first to communicate *good news*—with good reason. The positive feelings created by the good news often transfer to the communicator. **Affect transfer** is a special case of classical conditioning. It occurs when the positive affect (or feelings) created by an unconditioned stimulus becomes associated with a conditioned stimulus. Advertisers are famous for attempting to transfer the positive feelings created by the drama in an ad to the sponsored brand. Conversely, people are reluctant to communicate bad news, because the bad feelings created by unfavorable news can also be indirectly associated with the communicator. The tendency to keep mum about unpleasant messages is called the **MUM effect**.[55] Research demonstrates that the MUM effect is more pronounced when future contact with the message recipient is anticipated, because communicators are concerned about the consequences of their message.[56] In fact, the MUM effect has been around for centuries. Ancient Persian kings used to "kill the messenger" when the news was bad. In summary, the liking principle suggests that how we look and what we say makes a strong impression on others.

OBJECTIVE 8   The Authority Principle

Why do people comply with the requests of police officers, physicians, priests, and flight attendants? They all share one important characteristic—uniforms. According to the **authority principle,** authority figures use titles, clothes (such as uniforms), or expensive possessions that convey status to impress and influence others. Disobeying authority figures can produce obvious negative consequences, but how far will people go when following the orders of someone in authority? Yale University professor Stanley Milgram attempted to answer this question in one of the most influential and controversial studies in the annals of experimental psychology.[57] Participants were told that they would take part in an experiment intended to measure the effects of punishment on learning. Participants playing the role of "teacher" read questions to other persons who played the role of "learner." The teacher was directed to inflict a series of electric shocks on the learner, increasing the intensity of the shocks with each incorrect response. An impressive array of shock switches with very clear labels (i.e., slight shock, strong shock, intense shock, danger—severe shock, and maximum 450 volts) was positioned directly in front of the teachers. As shock intensity increased, the learner screamed louder and louder, begging to be released from the experiment. However, anytime the teacher hesitated, an authority figure (dressed in a while lab coat) told the teacher that s/he must continue. How many people would administer the shocks, all the way to the maximum 450 volts?

These exact experimental procedures were described to a group of 39 psychiatrists who were asked to predict how many participants would "go all the way" and use the maximum shock on the learner. The psychiatrists predicted that only one person in a thousand, or one tenth of a percent, would pull the maximum-volt switch. The actual results are startling. Sixty-five percent of the participants complied. Fortunately, the learner was just an actor, and no real shock was delivered. Milgram was "shocked" by the results, and so he conducted the study with different people, using newspaper ads to recruit subjects from outside the university. Also, he varied the distance between the learner and the teacher and he moved the location of the laboratory away from the university. Nevertheless, the results were similar. When an authority figure in a lab coat was present, a majority of the participants continued to deliver the highest shock. Milgram's experiments showed no significant difference in compliance rates between women and men, and other researchers replicated the results in countries beyond the United States.[58] In an attempt to partially explain the Holocaust, Milgram originally hypothesized that Germans may be more blindly obedient to authority than Americans. In the end, however, Milgram concluded that ordinary people, simply doing their jobs, are astonishingly obedient to authority. He warned that blind obedience to authority could happen anywhere, not just in Nazi Germany.

Do consumers blindly comply with authority figures in the marketplace? A physician prescribes a series of complicated medical tests; a computer technician instructs consumers to purchase new software; an automobile mechanic tells automobile owners that they need new brakes; a beautician recommends supplementary hair products; and a cashier tells shoppers to move to another check-out line. Usually, consumers comply. Waiters escort diners to a table (of the waiter's choice); credit card companies change their lending policies; flight attendants ask customers to switch seats with someone; orthodontists tell parents that their children need braces; even professors change their syllabi. And still consumers comply. In fairness, the cost of disobeying can often be greater than the cost of complying. If patients don't submit the complicated (and expensive) medical tests, they may not survive the consequences. Foregoing anti-virus software may result in the loss of valuable data, and so on. Nevertheless, consumers should avoid *mindless* compliance. Two simple questions usually answer the question of whether consumers should comply: What is the influence agent's motive and what are the consequences of *not* complying?

KarenMower/iStockphoto.com

Uniforms signal authority.

Chapter Summary

People are susceptible to a wide variety of influence techniques. This chapter identified seven key principles of influence on consumer behavior: automaticity, commitment and consistency, reciprocity, scarcity, social validation, liking, and authority. The automaticity principle recognizes that people often think mindlessly, without fully evaluating the consequences their compliance. The commitment and consistency principle indicates that people try to maintain consistency in their belief systems. The foot-in-the-door and low-ball techniques take advantage of consumers' tendencies to choose courses of action consistent with past commitments and decisions. The reciprocity principle shows that consumers often feel obligated to return favors—often beyond the value of what they received. The door-in-the-face, that's-not-all, multiple-deescalating-requests, and even-a-penny techniques capitalize on this tendency. The scarcity principle suggests that because valuable objects are rare, consumers often assume that rare objects are valuable. Marketers create perceptions of scarcity for their goods and services by limiting distribution and emphasizing the uniqueness of their brands. The social validation principle rests on the premise that the validity of an idea increases with the number of people supporting it. In the marketplace, consumer popularity begets more popularity. Conversely, diffusion of responsibility occurs when people look for others to react first. Efforts to influence consumers can backfire if descriptive norms overpower injunctive norms. Likeability is also a powerful weapon of influence, and consequently, similarity, attractiveness, and impression management can be used to increase liking for a person or brand. Finally, most people are compliant with authority figures. Understanding these seven key principles of social influence can help people avoid being unduly compliant.

Key Terms

verbal compliance

behavioral compliance

heuristics

automaticity principle

because heuristic

bait-and-switch tactics

commitment and consistency principle

foot-in-the-door technique

self-perception theory

low-ball technique

commitment theory

door-in-the-face technique

that's-not-all technique

multiple-deescalating-requests technique

even-a-penny technique

reciprocity principle

scarcity principle

affirmation of the consequent

social validation principle

list technique

diffusion of responsibility

descriptive norms

injunctive norms

liking principle

indirect associations

affect transfer

authority principle

MUM effect

Review and Discussion

1. Do you think the "because heuristic" would be more effective when people are busy or in a rush? Explain.

2. Both the door-in-the-face and that's-not-all techniques apply the principle of reciprocity. In fact, they both begin with deals that are eventually improved. Explain the difference between the two techniques.

3. Do you think businesses that give out free samples are mostly applying the reciprocity principle or the foot-in-the door technique? Does it depend on the nature of the sample? Explain.

4. Why do you think Cialdini found the low-ball technique to be more effective than the foot-in-the-door technique? Can you think of circumstances where the foot-in-the-door technique might be superior?

5. The door-in-the-face technique has two important limitations:

   a. The same person must make both requests.

   b. The two requests must be close in time.

How does the principle of reciprocity explain these limitations?

6. Why do you think Cialdini found the that's-not-all technique to be more effective than the door-in-the-face technique? Are there situations where the reverse might be true?

7. What does the scarcity principle suggest about the legalization of marijuana?

8. Aren't *fads* just a special case of the social validation principle? Why do fads lose their appeal?

9. How does the mere exposure effect work?

10. Drawing on your knowledge of descriptive and injunctive norms, how well do you think abstinence programs that emphasize the high rate of teenage pregnancy will work?

Short Application Exercises

1. Conduct your own mini-experiment using the "because heuristic." Test it in the cafeteria or workout room. Compare your findings to those of Langer and colleagues.

2. Make a trip to your nearest Barnes & Noble Bookstore. Observe the behavior at the bargain counter. See if the number of people at the bargain counter increases when two or three stop and browse. How would you explain this behavior?

3. Conduct a mini-experiment comparing the low-ball technique against the door-in-the face technique. Make the target requests identical for both techniques. In the low-ball condition, ask a group of students for a small favor and then change it to the

target request after people initially say "yes." In the door-in-the-face condition, ask a different group of students to complete a very large request. When they say "no," ask for the target request. See which technique produces the higher rate of compliance.

4. Watch 60 minutes of network television, uninterrupted. Keep a log of the commercials, tallying the number using each of the seven principles of influence. Report the findings in a graph or table.

5. Survey 30 adults to find out how often they question their family doctors about a medical prescription. Survey 30 fellow students. Ask them if they have ever contested a traffic ticket. Do your results support the authority principle?

MANAGERIAL APPLICATION

Re-read the opening vignette in this chapter. The Sears salesperson attempted to apply five different behavioral compliance techniques discussed in the chapter. Imagine that you are the manager of that Sears store and you are observing the salesperson's attempts to persuade the customer.

YOUR CHALLENGE:

1. Evaluate each of the five influence techniques attempted by the salesperson. Which technique do you think was most effective? Which technique was most important in generating revenue for Sears?

2. Assume that Sears' total variable cost for the lawn tractor is $1,278. Also assume that the salesperson makes a 5 percent commission on both the selling price and the warranty. How much unit contribution (selling price–variable cost–commission) did the salesperson generate for Sears on this transaction?

3. What could Sears do to reduce the customer's cognitive dissonance relating to the purchase?

4. How could customers like the one at Sears avoid being persuaded by behavioral compliance techniques?

CONTEMPORARY MARKETING STRATEGIES

OBJECTIVES *After studying this chapter, you will be able to . . .*

1 | Define word-of-mouth communication and understand why it is so powerful.

2 | Discuss the ways marketers create and promote word-of-mouth through buzz marketing.

3 | Explain how consumer generated advertising has become a unique way to push the "buzz button."

4 | Discuss how celebrity and athlete endorsers bring unique value to brands and understand how important it is for a marketer to pick the right endorser for a brand.

5 | Explain why product placement is an essential tool for marketers today.

6 | Describe the various types of product placement.

MARKETING ATHLETE ENDORSERS IN CHINA

Liu Wei, the captain of China's national basketball team, averaged 22.3 points per game in 2006 with the Shanghai Sharks, Yao Ming's former team. Mr. Ming, of course, is the center for the National Basketball Association's Houston Rockets. But Liu Wei is not permitted to star in a Chinese Coca-Cola ad. In China, it is not clear as to who owns the rights to a professional basketball player's image: the athlete himself or the government-run China Basketball Association. To be sure, China's socialist system of state control over athletes' careers is not only problematic for the Chinese athletes, but it is a headache for global marketers who would like to use emerging Chinese sports stars to attain coveted market share in a country of 1.3 billion people. Most Chinese athletes join government-run training programs as kids with the promise that they will be taken care of for life. In exchange, they give up most of their earnings and decision-making power to China's sports federations, including those related to appearing in advertising and public relations activities.

Liu Wei is not alone. In 2004, Olympic diver Tian Liang won two gold medals in Athens, Greece. As the marketing deals rolled in, Chinese sports officials accused him of engaging in too many commercial activities and suspended him from the national team. In a similar case, Liu Xiang, a runner who reached fame after his surprising gold medal performance in the 110-meter hurdles in Athens, is required to give half the money he makes to the athletic association, his coach, agents working between the federation and marketers, and his former team. Only a sports federation "knows best how to keep or maintain the athletes' good performance, which is regarded as the key value for the sports stars," says Wang Dawei, the vice president and treasurer of the CAA.

Only one Chinese star truly enjoys the Western-style freedom of a celebrity—Yao Ming, the 7'6" center for the Rockets. How does he do it? Yao's global fame transcends even the Chinese Basketball Association; Yao works for the NBA. Although he is somewhat overexposed in China, marketers claim that Yao's endorsements are worthwhile because his achievements tap into the powerful Chinese national pride. But Yao may have company soon. Basketball player Yi Jianlian, who earlier this year declared his eligibility for June's NBA draft, looks to be the next Chinese superstar with global appeal. He already has endorsement deals with Nike and Amway Corp.

So what is the solution for global brand marketers wanting to have Chinese sports stars other than Yao and Yi endorse their products? Develop close relationships with sports federations to gain access to their stars, of course. Adidas knows this and has been working with Chinese federations for 25 years. "We have a very deep-rooted relationship with coaches, and we have our own scouts within China to help us identify up-and-coming athletes," notes Marcus Kam, Adidas's senior manager of sports marketing in China. However, Chinese coaches and government bureaucrats can be challenging business partners. Scheduling time with some Chinese athletes takes months of planning, and sponsors pay as much as $1.3 million to be associated with someone like Liu Xiang and then may pay nearly $2 million for an ad shoot. Other access to Liu Xiang is denied.[1]

Consumers are all too familiar with the traditional methods that marketers use to reach and persuade them—advertisements on television, radio, on billboards and signs, in newspapers, from telemarketers, in junk mail, and from face-to-face salespeople. But today, companies are turning to alternative means to reach consumers in non-traditional ways. In this chapter, we examine some of the more unique ways marketers reach out to consumers, including word-of-mouth marketing, consumer generated advertising campaigns, celebrity and athlete endorsers, and product placements. Why study these alternative promotional methods and media? Many of the consumer behavior concepts we study are usually researched and taught through the lens of conventional marketing practices like mass advertising only. Understanding non-traditional marketing tactics and strategies enhances our understanding of the nuances of consumer behavior theories and practices.

OBJECTIVE 1

Word-of-Mouth: Pushing the Buzz Button

Some say it is the age of clutter. It seems like there are more and more commercials on television—12 minutes per hour during network primetime.[2] And the costs of those commercial are high. The average cost of a 30-second network television commercial is around $150,000, with prices for the most popular primetime shows reaching over $700,000 per spot. At that kind of investment, companies expect to see results. But the system seems to be at a breaking point. According to media researcher AC Nielsen, network television viewership has been eroding at a rate of about two percent per year, and cable channels now draw larger audiences than network television, resulting in greater fragmentation.[3] In addition, the proportion of time consumers spend with other media, especially the Internet, is growing, as broadband penetration has now reached well over half the households in the United States.[4] Now armed with digital video recorders (DVR's), video-on-demand channels, and shows that can be streamed over the Internet, consumers are skipping over or fast-forwarding through commercials

Websites like Hulu.com now stream television shows over the Internet, further fragmenting traditional television viewership.

©Mike Margol/PhotoEdit.

entirely. Thus, it appears that the effectiveness of traditional television advertising is faltering. So, marketers are turning more attention to non-traditional tactics. One of those tactics is buzz marketing, a technique designed to generate word-of-mouth.

Why Is Word-of-Mouth So Powerful?

Some marketers claim that **word-of-mouth** (or "buzz") is the most powerful form of marketing—period. Word-of-mouth is the act of one consumer talking to another about a brand, and it can happen face-to-face and indirectly via phone, mail, or the Internet. Word-of-mouth has been around as long as human communication (consider one pre-historic hunter telling another where the best hunting spots were). While word-of-mouth can be either positive or negative in nature, marketers attempt to generate positive word-of-mouth about their products and services.

So, why is word-of-mouth so powerful? Word-of-mouth is credible and authentic. Word-of-mouth communication is considered believable because consumers talking to one another rarely involve advertising or sales pitches. The underlying assumption is that the friend, neighbor, co-worker, or chat-room buddy engaged in word-of-mouth is someone whom you know and trust, and their opinions are honest and true, free from ulterior motives. People want to share the benefits of his/her own experiences with fellow consumers. In other words, they want to share their product experiences because they have other people's best interests in mind.

Another reason that word-of-mouth is so powerful is that consumers enjoy discussing their product and service experiences; they like being "in the know." It is appealing to have your peers view you as being on the cutting-edge of a new trend, or your information to be interesting. If a consumer sees a terrific new band play at a local club, he immediately texts or emails his closest friends. If the band stinks, the consumer spreads the word, saving his friends from spending money on poor entertainment.

Finally, thanks to technology, word-of-mouth can spread faster and farther than ever before, through cell phones, email, text messaging, social networking sites, blogs, instant messaging, chat rooms, and message boards. Because of the Internet, the word-of-mouth story can linger for a long time in cyber space. For example, back in the early 2000s, the Firestone brand of automobile tire went through a massive product recall

FIGURE 14.1 TRADITIONAL MARKETING VERSUS WORD-OF-MOUTH

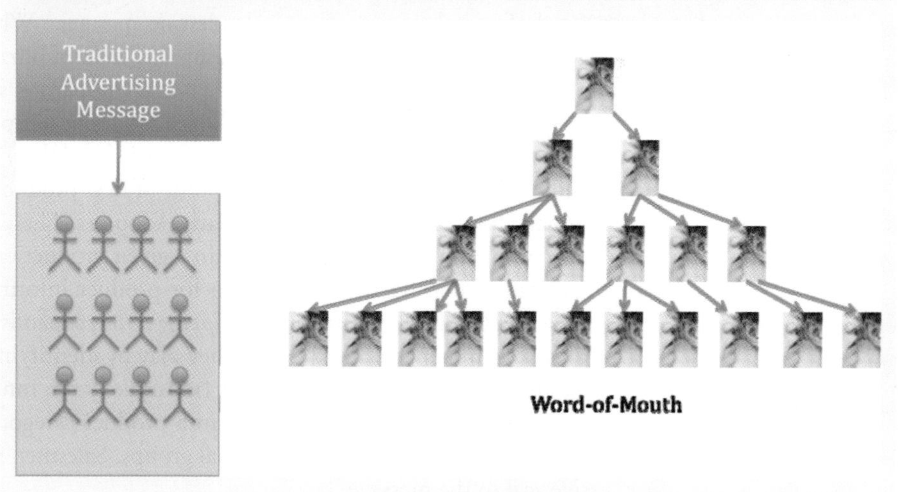

Traditional Advertising Message

Word-of-Mouth

when some of their tires were blamed for causing automobile accidents. Today, a simple Internet search still yields dozens of postings about that incident. Given the ever-increasing power of this marketing medium, it is not surprising that marketers are now trying to take better control of the word-of-mouth process through buzz marketing.

(OBJECTIVE 2)

Buzz Marketing

Word-of-mouth that occurs naturally is called **organic word-of-mouth**. Historically, marketers only *hoped* for positive word-of-mouth, allowing it to generate naturally, as one consumer told another about his/her satisfactory brand experiences. A company might also try to prevent negative word-of-mouth through good service or service recovery following a poor customer experience. In recent years, marketers have become more proactive in trying to deliberately generate and direct word-of-mouth. **Buzz marketing**, also sometimes called **word-of-mouth marketing, viral marketing,** or **stealth marketing**, is the execution of marketing tactics specially designed to generate positive word-of-mouth marketing messages and create a virus-like exponential spread of those messages throughout the population of interest. In buzz marketing, the goal is to get key, influential people from the target market to talk about a product, service, or brand experience. These influencers rapidly spread the word, and then the buzz spreads, getting and bigger and stronger as it goes.

Variations on buzz marketing are viral marketing and stealth marketing. While "buzz," "viral," and "stealth" marketing are sometimes used interchangeably, there are slight variations among them. Buzz marketing is a general term, encompassing any campaign designed at generating word-of-mouth. Viral marketing usually involves the Internet to facilitate the spread of word-of-mouth and spark buzz.

Marketer can try to spark a "virus" on the Internet in many ways. *Viral videos* draw large audiences and spark talk about the brand and the video, thanks to video sharing websites such at YouTube.com. YouTube.com uploads about 30,000 hours of footage every day! For example, T-Mobile, as part of their "Life Is for Sharing" campaign, placed a viral video link on YouTube.com, called "The T-Mobile Dance," that showed a large group of people doing a seemingly impromptu dance routine in a London train station. At the end of the video, the T-Mobile logo is flashed on the screen, and the video has a link to the T-Mobile website. By midsummer, 2009, the video had been viewed more than 12 million times. Other viral marketing techniques engage Internet users through blogs, chat rooms, and social networking websites.

Stealth marketing is a buzz marketing campaign that specifically relies on spreading word-of-mouth in a covert or clandestine manner.[5] While the tactics may not differ appreciably in a stealth marketing campaign than in buzz marketing generally, the consumer is supposed to remain unaware that a company is systematically generating buzz.

Who are the key influencers in buzz marketing campaigns? The popular press gives them names like "opinion leaders, influentials, alphas, trend-translators, hubs, bees, and magic people."[6] From the viewpoint of new product development, they are traditionally known as Innovators and Early Adopters. These individuals are the first to try new products and technologies within a given product category. They tend to be opinion leaders that later buyers rely on for product information and recommendations. Malcolm Gladwell, author of *The Tipping Point*, expands on the notion of tapping into these key influencers and the roles they play by identifying individuals he calls Mavens, Connectors, and Salesmen. Mavens (most likely the Innovators and Early Adopters of new products) are product experts in a product category. Connectors are individuals who hook into and span several social groups. Salesmen feed the fire by adding persuasive zeal to the message.[7]

jfairone/iStockphoto.com

Regardless of what they are called, marketers try to tap into the influence of those who seem to have the ability and willingness to talk about products and brands and generate a buzz. Now, let's examine a few of the strategies and techniques companies and marketers use to generate buzz.

PRODUCT PUSHERS Product pushers are people recruited by a company to get a product prominently seen and talked about in the marketplace. These recruits are usually attractive but approachable and friendly, often from the target market's own key influencer set. A few years ago, Ford Motor Company recruited a few popular opinion leaders in some key college markets and gave them a Ford Focus to drive for six months. In exchange, the brand pushers were supposed to be seen driving the car and hand out Ford promotional materials to anyone who expressed an interest in the car. In a similar campaign, when Italian scooter maker Piaggio wanted to reintroduce a European-style motorbike, it sent beautiful people out to ride and generate buzz for the Vespa.[8] On college campuses, exam time brings out the Red Bull patrol, and someone hired by that company drives around the campus in a specially decorated car, handing out free cans of the stimulating drink. Throughout the term, college students are hired to carry around spare cans of Red Bull and give them to friends and fellow students who look like they could use a Red Bull.

While brand pushers may really be users of the product they are employed to sample, push, and talk about to fellow members of the target market, they can also be more obvious. For example, beer companies have often hired beautiful models to "crash" nightclubs and bars dressed in company logo attire, hand out coupons for free beer, and otherwise generate excitement. Oscar Meyer uses the famous "Weinermobile" to generate excitement and buzz at special events like store openings, where employee hand out free samples and coupons. Employees of Lucky Strike cigarettes, called "Lucky Strike Forces," show up outside office buildings offering free coffee and beach chairs to smokers who are banished from their offices whenever they want to light up.

A special type of brand pusher has emerged on the Web. Companies like BzzAgent provide a forum for people who want to be involved in buzz campaigns, letting consumers do the legwork. Real people who are real consumers sign up to be agents. They volunteer to try to create buzz for a product in their own communities through grassroots efforts. For example, they may tell their friends about the product, ask their local store to carry the brand, or hand out coupons to people they meet in the street. In exchange, the people who sign up as agents occasionally get previews of new products for free and free samples of the brands they promote. These agents are not under any obligation to push a product if they don't like it. But there are plenty of ordinary people willing to participate. BzzAgent currently has more than 300,000 members and has run more than 300 buzz campaigns for companies like Kraft, American Express, Sony, and Kellogg's.[9] Vocalpoint and TremorTeen, word-of-mouth marketing websites run by Procter and Gamble, also have memberships in the hundreds of thousands that aim at attracting moms with kids and teenagers, respectively.[10]

IMITATION EVANGELISTS Imitation evangelists are actors put on the payroll for stealth buzz campaigns. Their task is to slip commercial messages and recommendations into everyday conversations under the consumer's nose, with the hope of igniting a natural buzz. They differ from regular brand pushers because of the stealth nature of the campaigns. The consumer is never supposed to know that the encounter is not authentic. For example, when Sony Ericsson Mobile Communication Company wanted to promote a new camera-cell phone, they created the "fake tourist" campaign. Young, attractive couples posed as tourists in popular vacation spots around the United States. They asked passersby to snap their photo with the phone. The chance encounter became a moment to generate interest and buzz about the product.

Another popular stealth technique is to use "fake shoppers." On the Internet, these people post on blogs, participate in chat rooms, and post product reviews. The music industry has also planted hip shoppers in music stores to chat about new artists so other shoppers overhear. Likewise, cigarette manufacturers sometimes hire women to give packs of cigarettes to smokers because, they claim, "the pack doesn't fit in my purse."[11] Finally, some alcohol manufacturers hire "leaners." These stealth marketers pose as bar patrons, leaning on the bar, ordering the particular brand, and recommending the drink to others around them.

STEALTH CELEBRITY ENDORSERS Celebrities are also sometimes part of stealth marketing campaigns. In a standard celebrity endorsement, a celebrity is paid to appear in a commercial. The viewer knows that the celebrity is being compensated for participating in the commercial. What consumers often don't realize is that celebrities are also sometimes compensated with fees or free merchandise to use or talk about products in their everyday lives as well. For example, when actress Kathleen Turner appeared on ABC's "Good Morning America" and talked about an illness she had, she directed people to a website sponsored by a pharmaceutical company. However, she said nothing about the fact that the drug manufacturer had paid her for her public appearances on its behalf.[12] Celebrities who have discussed their health ailments in media interviews, but have failed to disclose their endorsement deals, have been criticized for taking stealth marketing too far.

The next subject, consumer generated marketing, attempts to combine the advantages of good buzz-generating tactics with traditional advertising.

OBJECTIVE 3

Consumer Generated Marketing

Consumer generated marketing (advertising) is the creation of advertising or other marketing content by the customer. Here, companies leverage their own customers to generate not only interesting advertisements, but also some resulting good press and buzz too. Typically, a company invites participants to create marketing content, often an advertisement, for its brand through some kind of promotion or contest. The content is usually submitted via the company's website. Selected "winners" may have their advertisements appear on the company website or on broad community Internet forums, such as YouTube.com. Occasionally, the content may cross over to television, radio, magazines, etc. For example, when Frito-Lay's Doritos brand chips held its consumer generated advertising campaign, the two winning advertisements were shown during the 2007 Super Bowl game. Frito-Lay also increased customer participation by allowing people to vote to determine the winning spots.[13]

Why would a company solicit consumer generated advertising? The answers are numerous, if not obvious. First, the costs of producing traditional advertising are very high. User-generated content is much cheaper. Second, when customers decide to

Snack Strong.

Courtesy of Frito-Lay

participate, they have to really think about the brand creatively, generating a new depth of interaction with the brand, something that marketers want. Third, the content created is often quite good. A consumer who loves a brand enough to produce creative work can generate truly inspiring and compelling content. Finally, consumer generated advertising is also a great marketing research tool: what better way for marketers to see how people feel about the brand and how the brand is actually positioned in the marketplace? In sum, the goal of consumer generated advertising campaigns is not always to create award-winning advertising, although sometimes this happens. Instead, the goal is to allow consumers to express, in their own words, how they feel about the brand. As a result, these authentic, innovative, and entertaining messages offer greater opportunity for generating positive buzz about the brand than do traditional marketing communications. When consumers are engaged in the process, they feel empowered.

Of course, risk exists in consumer generated advertising. First, such advertising may not be applicable for all products. It is hard to be passionate about toilet paper and fabric softeners. Products that are new, unique, or edgy, or brands with an iconic brand identity are usually better candidates for this type of campaign. For example, even though ketchup is a commodity-type product, the H. J. Heinz Company has managed to inspire a passion and love for its ketchup brand over the years. To cash in on these feelings, the company ran a consumer generated campaign called, "Top This TV Challenge." The commercials submitted were shown on YouTube.com, and the top 15 ads (selected by the company) were also featured on the company's website. The cyber public then voted for the winners. The top five commercials were shown in national television advertising spots, and the winning commercial won $57,000, referencing the number "57," part of the Heinz trademark.

Furthermore, with the good ads also come the bad. When an uncontrollable and unqualified public has free rein to submit anything, a company has to spend time and money sifting through all the bad content to find a few advertising gems—and there's no guarantee there will be any worthy of public display. Heinz had no guarantee that any of the advertisements submitted would be any good, but the company was committed to running the five finalists on national television. Thus, Heinz assumed considerable risk in making the promise to air the winning ads, no matter what.

Finally, brands with passionate devotees also tend to attract consumers who hate the brand as much as the devotees love it. While a firm may reject negative content for its website and marketing activities, harmful information can easily find its way onto the Internet and into the press.

Consumer generated advertising is an interesting new form of customer engagement that leverages the capabilities of digital communications. Will this new form of marketing stick around or will it lose its appeal as the novelty wears off? We don't know the answer to that question, but celebrity and athlete endorsers, our next topic, have secured what appears to be a permanent place in the repertoires of marketing managers.

MARKETING IN ACTION

Chevy Tahoe Lets Everyone Have a Say

When the marketers of Chevrolet automobiles decided to hold an online contest to see who could produce the best television commercial for its newly redesigned Tahoe SUV, they didn't necessarily count on Chevy bashers joining the game. But that's what sometimes happens when marketers ask to hear from the public.

The contest, which coordinated with a sponsorship episode of NBC's "The Apprentice," urged viewers to create and submit videos about the Tahoe on a special Chevy website, Chevyapprentice.com. The response was huge, with more than 30,000 videos submitted in four weeks and 629,000 visitors to the website. The majority of entries were extremely positive, touting the auto's features. But it wasn't long before negative videos started showing up on the site, too, and all over the Web, with sharply satirical advertisements talking about global warming, a war for oil, social injustice, and even connotations related to sexual inadequacies. Chevy was now facing a pivotal decision: yank the negative Chevy-bashing videos off the website or let them stay. The company let them stay, apparently deciding that it was more credible to let *everyone* who wanted to participate have a say. This strategy paid off. The Chevyapprentice.com

website drove people to the Chevy website, and sales rose quickly, outpacing the competition.

In consumer generated advertising, marketers ask customer what they think and how they define the brand. Is this level of customer interaction and brand co-creation risky? While some marketers say it is because it invites brand-bashers to the table, many are realizing that controlling the advertising message and trying to force a brand image onto the consumer doesn't necessarily work any longer. Consumers want a say.[36]

General Motors Corp. Used with permission, GM Media Archives

Celebrity and Athlete Endorsers

Consumers often think of brands in terms of the famous people who endorse them. A **celebrity endorser** is an individual who enjoys public recognition and uses this recognition on behalf of a consumer product by appearing in an advertisement or engaging in some other marketing tactic. Celebrity endorsements are pervasive, particularly in the United States, where some estimates indicate that more than 20 percent of all television advertisements feature a celebrity endorser. While this trend is on the rise now, the fact is that celebrities have been endorsing brands for more than a century. In 1882, British actress Lily Langtrey, a very close friend of King Edward VII, endorsed *Pears Soap*. Mark Twain promoted his own brands of flour and cigars. Former president Ronald Reagan appeared in ads for *Chesterfield* cigarettes, and Sean Connery endorsed *Jim Beam* bourbon. What benefits does Tiger Woods bring to *Nike?* How does martial artist Jackie Chan help *Mountain Dew?* What about Ellen DeGeneres and *American Express?* See Table 14.1 for a sample of celebrity endorsements, both classic and contemporary.

Although research is mixed on the value of celebrity endorsements, under certain conditions, the use of celebrities can increase message recall[14] and aid in brand recognition.[15] Research also shows that celebrities can provide brands with increased levels of trustworthiness, likeability, and persuasion.[16] One interesting study even demonstrates

TABLE 14.1 CELEBRITY ENDORSEMENTS AND BRAND PERSONALITIES

Celebrity		Brand
Name	*Claim to Fame*	*Name*
Paula Abdul	Pop-R&B Singer	*L.A. Gear*
Halle Berry	Actress/Model	*Revlon*
David Beckman	English Football Star	*Gillette*
Cameron Diaz	Actress	*Calvin Klein*
Hillary Duff	Actress/Musician	*Got Milk?*
Jenny McCarthy	Actress	*Candies*
Brad Pitt	Actor	*Tag Heuer*
Justin Timberlake	Musician	*McDonald's*
Tiger Woods	Professional Golfer	*Nike*
Bob Dole	Senator	*Viagra*

that investors react positively to the announcement of celebrity endorsements.[17] Another study shows that celebrity endorsers can reduce consumers' perceptions of risk involved in technology products, provided that the celebrity is a good fit with the product (e.g., Jerry Seinfeld endorsing American Express).[18]

Much of the value of employing celebrities derives from their ability to portray themselves as typical brand users in typical use situations. Research suggests that when a consumer sees a celebrity endorsing a product, the consumer makes correspondent inferences. A **correspondent inference** is the assumption that a person's behavior is a reflection of their beliefs and underlying dispositions, rather than the result of some situational variable. So, a celebrity wearing a certain brand of watch leads the consumer to infer that the celebrity actually likes the brand and is a typical user of the brand. This occurs despite the fact that most consumers are aware that celebrities are paid large sums of money to endorse brands. Along with correspondent inferences, research also suggests that celebrity endorsers come with "cultural meanings." If the endorser and the product are a good "match" so the transfer of cultural meaning is possible, then the endorser is more effective. Consumers usually develop preconceived images about celebrity endorsers, resulting in celebrity images transferring to the brand.[19] Thus, the managerial implication is that the endorser should "fit" the product endorsed.

Beyond the issue of "fit," celebrity endorsement can be risky. Famous stars can over-shadow a brand, and celebrity scandals can tarnish a brand's image. Chrysler dropped Celine Dion, believing her sponsorship sold more music than automobiles. Similarly, Pepsi broke off its relationship with Beyoncè over concern that the brand didn't benefit from the promotion as much as she did. Firms also drop celebrity endorsers quickly when they are linked to negative publicity. In 1989, Pepsi dropped Madonna following the release of her controversial *Like a Prayer* video. In 1991, Ervin "Magic" Johnson lost his endorsement deals after publicly announcing that he was HIV-positive. It was ten years before Johnson landed another endorsement deal, this time with *Lincoln Mercury*. Kobe Bryant's was just beginning to find new endorsement deals in 2009, after accusations in 2003 regarding sexual misconduct, even though the case against him was ultimately dismissed. After years of positioning its brand as youthful and hip, *Dell* dropped Benjamin Curtis ("Dude, you're getting a Dell") after he was allegedly involved with marijuana.

Marketers also vigorously avoid negative political fallout. Sears and Federal Express pulled their sponsorship of *Politically Incorrect* after host Bill Maher referred to Americans as "cowards" for "lobbing Cruise missiles from 2,000 miles away." Sadly, there appears to be no end to celebrity misconduct. In 2007, Michael Vick, the popular quarterback of the Atlanta Falcons, was indicted on federal conspiracy charges for his alleged role in a dog-fighting venture Vick lost about $37.5 million in earnings, including a lucrative deal with *Coca-Cola.* But in the summer of 2009, he was picked up by the Philadelphia Eagles.

Not surprisingly, marketers are adamant about protecting their brand images from the deleterious impact of celebrity misbehavior. Many firms now include morals clauses in celebrity endorsement contracts that allow the company to terminate a deal should a celebrity behave in an unbecoming manner. See Table 14.2 for a *Forbes Magazine* list of the most powerful celebrities

TABLE 14.2   Forbes Most Powerful Celebrities[20]

Rank	Celebrity	$ (millions)
1	Oprah Winfrey	$ 260
2	Tiger Woods	100
3	Madonna	72
4	Rolling Stones	88
5	Brad Pitt	35
6	Johnny Depp	92
7	Elton John	53
8	Jay-Z	83
9	Steven Spielberg	110
10	Tom Hanks	74
11	Howard Stern	70
12	Phil Mickelson	42
13	David Letterman	40
14	Bon Jovi	67
15	Celine Dion	45
16	Simon Cowell	45
17	Michael Schumacher	36
18	Ben Stiller	38
19	Brian Grazer/Ron	70
20	Tim McGraw	37
21	Jerry Bruckheimer	120
22	Kimi Raikkonen	40
23	Jerry Seinfeld	60
24	Oscar De La Hoya	43
25	Gore Verbinski	37

Athlete endorsers have become major factors in today's media culture. Sports celebrities—both famous and infamous—have flourished as a result of the technological advances in broadcast and interactive media.[21] Consumers can now view sporting events on cell phones, for example. See Table 14.3 for the highest paid athletes in the world.

Athlete endorsers' responsibilities can range from using or wearing specific brands (e.g., Tiger Woods and *Nike* apparel) to offering actual testimonials on behalf of the brand (e.g., Payton Manning and *Sprint*). Despite the widespread use of athlete endorsers, their influence on advertising objectives remains controversial.[22] Some research suggests that sports celebrities may not connect to intended target markets.[23] Recent research, however, demonstrates that athlete endorsers positively influence adolescents'

TABLE 14.3 FORBES BEST-PAID ATHLETES[25]

Athlete	Sport	$ (millions)
Tiger Woods	Golf	$ 87.0
Michael Schumacher	Auto Racing	60.0
Oscar De La Hoya	Boxing	38.0
Michael Vick	Football	37.5
Shaquille O'Neal	Basketball	33.4
Michael Jordan	Basketball	33.0
David Beckham	Soccer	32.5
Kobe Bryant	Basketball	28.8
Lance Armstrong	Cycling	28.0
Valentino Rossi	Motorcycling	28.0
Alex Rodriquez	Baseball	27.5
Phil Mickelson	Golf	26.8
Andre Agassi	Tennis	26.2
Derek Jeter	Baseball	25.5
Manny Ramirez	Baseball	24.2
Jeff Gordon	Auto Racing	23.4
Walter Jones	Football	23.2
Ronaldo	Soccer	23.0
LeBron James	Basketball	22.9
Matt Hasselbeck	Football	22.8
Maria Sharapova	Tennis	18.2
Serena Williams	Tennis	12.7
Annika Sorenstam	Golf	7.3
Venus Williams	Tennis	6.5
Lindsay Davenport	Tennis	6.0

favorable world-of-mouth and brand loyalty. In other words, not only are athletes important to adolescents making brand choices, but teenagers also talk about the brands to their friends and peers. Regardless of whether athletes *desire* to be role models, research indicates that teenagers *consider* athletes as important role models—regardless of their public behavior.[24]

OBJECTIVE 5

Product Placement

What Is Product Placement?

The scene opens; it is an observational viewing gallery in a surgical suite. Two characters, Jerry and Kramer, sit in the front row, looking down on the operating table. As the operation begins, Kramer pulls out a box of candy. The dialogue proceeds:

> Jerry: What are you eating?
> Kramer: Junior Mints. Do you want one?
> Jerry: No
> Kramer: I can't see . . . Pssst . . .
> (Kramer motions to the nurse to move out of the way.)
> Jerry: Where'd you get those?
> Kramer: The machine. You want one? Here, take one.
> Jerry: I don't want any!

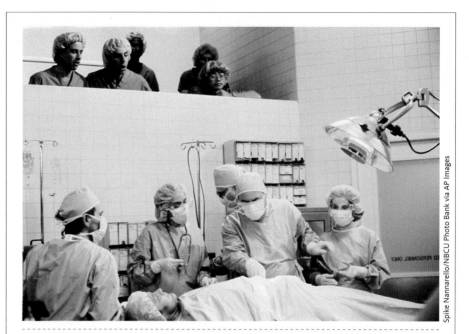

Product placement that is key to advancing the plot is called product integration. It is one of the most powerful forms of product placement.

Kramer: No, they're good!
Jerry: I don't want any!
Kramer: Just take one.
Jerry: No! Kramer, stop it!

As the two men struggle with the mint, it flies into the air toward the operating table. And so goes the famous "Junior Mint" scene on the popular show, "Seinfeld."[26] Would the scene have worked with a generic box of candy? Probably. But would it have been as funny or memorable? Probably not.

The classic Junior Mint television scene is the essence of great product placement. **Product placement** is the insertion of branded goods and services within the content of popular media, including television, movies, video games, books, and music. When done correctly, product placement adds a sense of continuity and realism to the context that a generic, blank "box of candy" cannot. On the flipside, if you have ever watched a television show or movie and felt like you were watching one really long commercial, you've probably been on the receiving end of poor product placement.

Product placement has been around since the beginning of movies and television, but has seen explosive growth as an alternative marketing method over the last few years. One of the earliest documented product placements was in 1951 for Gordon's Gin in the movie, "The African Queen."[27] Katherine Hepburn didn't drink the gin in the film but threw it overboard. Another classic example is the 1982 film, "E.T. The Extra-Terrestrial," which helped launch Reese's Pieces from Hershey Foods Corporation. While Hershey paid nothing for inclusion, the payoff for Reece's Pieces was significant, with sales for the candy shooting up 40 percent within a week of the movie's premier.[28] Interestingly, the producers originally wanted to use M&M's candy, but the company turned down the placement. More recently, BMW paid the producers of the movie "GoldenEye" to feature James Bond driving a BMW Z3 Roadster as

Spike Nannarello/NBCU Photo Bank via AP Images

MARKETING IN ACTION

The E.B. Horn Great Diamond Hunt

It was a bright morning in early fall, and a group of 400 eager people gathered at Boston Common to take part in a unique event—a day-long, city-wide treasure hunt for a $25,000 diamond provided by the E.B. Horn Company, a Boston jeweler. The lucky treasure hunters, working in teams of two, would spend the day following clever story-like clues to the elusive "lost diamond." By the end of the day, one lucky team would walk away with the gem.

The diamond hunt was a marketing event, designed to generate excitement and positive word-of-mouth, raise awareness for the jeweler, and increase sales during the upcoming Christmas holiday sales season. The campaign actually had started a few weeks earlier when 500 black velvet ring boxes were scattered around the city, on park benches, sidewalks, in restaurants, train stations, and

other public places. Inside the boxes were small pieces of paper reading, "Nope, it's not here." Next came a rotating billboard advertising the "GreatDiamondHunt.com" website mounted on a large panel truck that cruised around the city. And most bizarre, several mannequins were posed to look like they were searching for something in high-traffic locales around Boston, accompanied by signs that read, "Finders Keepers." The buzz campaign was also supported by more traditional online and radio spot advertising.[37]

Campaigns like the Great Diamond Hunt are designed to get people interested and talking about a brand, and are an alternative type of campaign that companies hope will cut through the clutter of traditional media today.

Courtesy of E.B. Horn.

http://www.greatdiamondhunt.com/home.html

---

part of a large promotional campaign introducing the product. Within a month of the movie opening, BMW had 9,000 orders for the car.[29]

While product placement is traditionally associated with movies and television, it is now present in all types of media. According to *Advertising Age* magazine, a few years ago, Seagram's brand gin was able to get a number of rap artists to talk about the brand, including Pety Pablo, whose "Freek-a-leek" was a hip-hop hit. Other brands often mentioned in popular music include Cadillac, Lexus, Versace, Porche, Gucci, and Cartier.[30] And, when product placement makes it into the lyrics of a song, the product itself is likely to be seen in the song's music video. Books are not immune to product placement either. Fay Weldon's book *The Bulgari Connection* featured the Bulgari Jewelry Company. Product placement is even appearing in more and more video games. Just like in movies, video game creators insert real products and brands into their cyberenvironments to lend realism and cohesiveness to the game. Going a step farther, *advergaming* is the practice of creating a whole game specifically designed around a product. For example, makers of Minute Maid juices, with Skyworks productions, created "Minute Maid Maj Jong," which combines brand messages and gaming.

Why Is Product Placement Growing?

In recent years, product placement has surged as companies search for new ways to reach consumers and as the costs of production for traditional advertising have risen. While product placement has become an essential tool for marketers, it is also an important revenue stream for media providers. Below are just some of the benefits of product placement.

ADDED REALISM   Product placements link fictional content to real life, making the story more believable. The benefit for the product is that consumers see it perform in real life situations (hopefully in ways that improve the perception of the brand).

Tom Cruise helped Ray Ban sunglasses sales skyrocket when he wore the glasses in the movie Risky Business.

©Warner Brothers/Everett Collection

REACH AND LONGEVITY   Product placement is extremely economical when you consider that television shows, movies, books, videos, and songs usually have a long shelf life and typically cost a fraction of traditional broadcast television advertising. A song may be heard by millions of people many times over months or even years. With DVD sales and syndication, movies and television shows can be watched for decades. Viewers still see Tom Cruise wearing Ray-Ban sunglasses in the movie, "Risky Business." Year after year, viewers watch Ralphie almost shoot out his eye with his longed-for Red Ryder BB Gun in "A Christmas Story." In addition, when a brand is featured in a show, it is definitely seen, but in a broadcast commercial, it can be skipped via the fast-forward button on the DVR.

INDIRECT ENDORSEMENTS   When an actor is seen in close proximity to a product or shown using a product in a dramatic scene or situation, an association between the character and/or the celebrity and the brand can be created in the consumer's mind, creating an indirect celebrity endorsement. Strategic product placement with the right characters or actors can convey ideas about the positioning of the brand. Research has shown that when consumers see celebrities endorsing a brand, they typically assume they like and use the brand "in real life."[31] Recall our earlier discussion of correspondent inferences.

COST REDUCTION Product placement can help reduce the costs of producing media because producers do not have to purchase set items and props, plus it can provide cash to support the creative process. For example, Mark Burnett, creator of CBS's "Survivor" helps finance the show this way.

OBJECTIVE 6

Types of Product Placement

All product placements are not created equal. They have varying degrees of impact on and interaction with the media. Typically, as the involvement of a brand with the editorial content increases, so does the value of placement within the media. Types of product placement include:

- **Visual Product Placement:** Visual placement entails placing the brand on screen within the setting or background of a program. While this is probably the most common form of product placement in movies, television, and other visual media, it is also the easiest to overlook, because there is little or no interaction between the actors and the product, and the product itself may not be integral to the story. Included in this category is a variant on product placement called *advertisement placement.* This occurs when an advertisement for a brand is placed in the media, rather than the brand itself. Examples include a television commercial playing in the background of a scene or an actor driving his car past a billboard in an action sequence.

- **Brand Interaction:** Brand interaction occurs when the characters talk about the product or brand or actually handle the product, i.e., they physically interact with it.

- **Brand Integration:** Brand integration occurs when the brand is woven into the thread of the story, becoming part of the plot or context, in a fashion similar to the famous Junior Mint scene in "Seinfeld."

- **Sponsorship and Branded Entertainment:** This type of product placement is the most intensive form of marriage between content and brand. In this type of placement, the brand is the sole sponsor of the content, has extensive editorial control of the content, and the editorial content or style typically matches closely the targeted audience of the brand.

Regardless of the type of product placement used, marketers must be creative to obtain the placement. The most straightforward way of placing a brand is for the marketer to pay a fee for the brand to appear in the show or program. According to a research firm PQ Media, estimated paid product placements for 2006 were $3.01 billion.[32] Ford Motor Co. and Coca-Cola Co. paid at least $30 million each for their sponsorship/product placement deals with

ETHICS

Is product placement a form of subliminal advertising? As has been already discussed in this book, *subliminal perception* is the unconscious perception of a stimulus. Many subliminal messages actually fall above the absolute threshold of physical perception, but are still consciously repressed by the viewer. Given this definition, does product placement fall within these boundaries? One might argue that this is indeed the case.

Many times, a person may not consciously notice a product or brand in the background of a television or movie scene. Even so, the brand may be noticed on some subconscious level. Other times, while the brand is noticed, it may be integrated so seamlessly into the action that viewers may simply not realize they are watching a type of advertisement. In addition, product placements are not overtly disclosed at the time the good or service is featured. Commercial Alert, a consumer advocacy group, has called for full disclosure of product placement arrangements both before and during television programs. In fact, the group claims that product placements are inherently deceptive and subliminal.[38]

On the flipside, product placements don't fall below the absolute threshold of perception; marketers want them to be seen and heard. Also, the appearance of a brand in itself does not call the consumer to action. In other words, there is no overt "sales pitch." The Federal Trade Commission has argued that this lack of overt adverting messages exempts product placement from full disclosure. Also, because some placements are unpaid, consumers cannot know which products are included for the sake of advertising and which are there to enhance the entertainment.

So, while most people would agree that product placement is some form of advertising, is it actually subliminal advertising? You decide.

Fox's "American Idol" reality show.[33] This investment has apparently paid off because the sponsors keep coming back year after year. In fact, the famous red Coca-Cola cups that are on the judges' table during the show are reported to be the most widely seen product placement on TV, according to an article in *Advertising Age.*[34] Although no industry standards exist regarding product placement cost and use, marketers usually have some "veto power" in decisions about how their brands are used.

Some companies do not like to pay for product placement, preferring instead to provide free merchandise to support the production of the show through a type of barter agreement. In exchange, the producers include the product. More than half of all product placements occur through this exchange method. For example, Apple Computer, Inc., does not pay for product placements, but Apple computers and iPods appear frequently in popular television shows, including CBS's "CSI: NY," NBC's "The Office," and Fox's "24."[35] In fact, in the early seasons of "24," the heroes in the show used Apple computers, while the villains used non-branded PCs.

Finally, some product placements just appear in some productions, with or without the brand's permission, because the producer or director feels the product enhances the quality of the production. For example, in an episode of HBO's "The Sopranos," a can of Raid bug killer was used in a violent scene without the permission of SC Johnson Company, the manufacturer. While some companies have tried to block some product placements by suing producers for trademark infringement, there are currently no specific laws that directly prohibit a director or producer from placing a product in a scene or context. Most disputes have been handled on a case-by-case basis. Given the rapid growth of this practice, however, more rigid regulation of product placement may be on the horizon.

Chapter Summary

In today's technology-driven, cluttered environment, companies cannot simply rely on traditional forms of marketing, such as advertising and face-to-face sales. In this chapter, we examined some contemporary strategies and unique ways marketers reach out to today's consumers, including word-of-mouth marketing, consumer generated advertising campaigns, celebrity and athlete endorsers, and product placements.

Word-of-mouth or buzz marketing is the execution of marketing tactics especially designed to generate positive word-of-mouth marketing messages and create a virus-like exponential spread of those positive messages throughout the population of interest. Marketers want to create and direct word-of-mouth because consumers see it as credible and authentic and because it is so easy to spread and sustain on the Internet. To help execute buzz marketing campaigns, companies often hire people to push the brand, either online or in person. When these people keep their activities clandestine, they are said to be engaging in stealth marketing.

Consumer generated advertising campaigns try to harness the benefits of traditional advertising and buzz marketing by encouraging the creation of advertisements by consumers themselves. These campaigns have the advantages of generating good advertisements in a relatively inexpensive way, engaging the customers in new, meaningful ways, and providing the company with valuable consumer insights.

Another contemporary strategy that has become standard in marketing, especially in the United States, is the use of celebrity and athlete endorsers. Consumers often think of brands in terms of the famous people who endorse them, and research has shown that celebrity endorsers can have positive persuasive effects. On the flipside, marketers must use care when using celebrity and athlete endorsers. Famous stars can overshadow a brand, and celebrity scandals can tarnish a brand's image.

Finally, product placement is the insertion of branded goods and services within the content of popular media, including television, movies, video games, books, and music. When done correctly, product placement adds a sense of continuity and realism to the story, while promoting the brand in subtle but meaningful ways.

Key Terms

word-of-mouth

organic word-of-mouth

buzz marketing

word-of-mouth marketing

viral marketing

stealth marketing

consumer generated marketing (advertising)

celebrity endorser

correspondent inference

product placement

visual product placement

brand interaction

brand integration

sponsorship and branded entertainment

Review and Discussion

1. Why is word-of-mouth so powerful?

2. Why is buzz marketing also referred to as "viral" marketing?

3. What is the distinction between buzz marketing and stealth marketing?

4. What are some of the potential ethical implications of doing a stealth marketing campaign?

5. What are some of the differences between traditional advertising and consumer generated advertising?

6. What are some of the benefits of a consumer generated advertising campaign? What are the risks?

7. Review the *Forbes Magazine* list of best-paid athletes presented in the text. Do you think they are worth the money they are paid for endorsements? Explain.

8. In what type of media is product placement found?

9. How do product placements add realism to the media in which they are placed?

10. Describe the differences between brand interaction product placement and brand integration product placement. Which is better? Why?

Short Application Exercises

1. Think back to your own experiences with word-of-mouth. Discuss one example of a time when you were influenced by word-of-mouth and one example of when you influenced someone else through word-of-mouth.

2. In buzz marketing, identifying and leveraging opinion leaders is very important. Choose a group that might be influenced by an opinion leader and put together a photo collage displaying at least five opinion leaders for that group. The collage should identify who the people are, why they are opinion leaders, and what products or brands each of them would most successfully endorse.

3. Think about one brand for which you would like to create a consumer generated advertisement. What would your ad say about the brand?

4. Watch one hour of television. Try to identify one example of each type of product placement in the program(s) you watch. Justify your example.

MANAGERIAL APPLICATION

Imagine that you have been hired by a company to "promote" their product via stealth marketing. You will most likely do this by pretending to be a "regular customer" yourself and by trying to influence other customers to show interest in or purchase the product.

Team up with a partner. Go to a mall or shopping area and choose a product to secretly promote. Choose a consumer or group of consumers as the object of this exercise. Then, using any kind of "stealth technique" you can think of, try to influence the consumer/consumers to purchase the product. You can be overt or subtle. It is up to you. Take your time; do not rush. You are successful if the person or group is persuaded in any way to take interest in the product—sampling it, examining it, or purchasing it. You should try this multiple times and see the various reactions you receive. For example, try it out on different demographic groups (e.g., older versus younger, like you versus different, etc.) with various approaches.

Next, develop a set of field notes, describing the experience. In these field notes, describe what you chose to do and the results of the exercise. After you have finished describing what took place, offer some analysis, explanation, and opinion of your actions and the subsequent results. Were you successful? Why or why not? Were your results surprising? Lastly, offer your opinion as to the ethical appropriateness of stealth marketing. Is this form of marketing okay? Should it be restricted or not allowed at all?

15

CONSUMER BEHAVIOR ONLINE

OBJECTIVES *After studying this chapter, you will be able to...*

1 | Explain the differences between online marketing and bricks-and-mortar marketing.

2 | Improve the design of a website.

3 | Define search goods, experience goods, and credence goods.

4 | Explain the implications of reduced search costs for consumer behavior.

5 | Explain the consumer advocacy paradigm.

YAHOO!

Yahoo! is currently battling Google for the number one spot for web search engines. However, in 2006, Yahoo!'s stock fell 36% and Google's ad sales and stock prices increased dramatically.[1] To compete more effectively against Google, Yahoo! announced in January, 2007, that Panama would be Yahoo!'s new advertising platform beginning in February, 2007. Panama gives advertisers more control by allowing them to change strategies and keywords to adapt to changing consumer preferences. Panama also rank orders ads in terms of relevance to a consumer's search rather than in terms of dollars. Yahoo! also underwent a major reorganization: 44 business units were reduced to just four. This streamlining redundancies and interdepartmental competition.

To compete against Google's YouTube, Yahoo! acquired Flickr, Answers, and Delicio .us. Although Yahoo! currently has more users than Google, Google is more profitable.

Nevertheless, Yahoo! attracts more users than AOL or Microsoft, and Yahoo!'s email is the largest in the world with 250 million users. Yahoo! is also ranked first or second in 17 different web categories. By carefully monitoring rapidly changing consumer behavior patterns on the web, Yahoo! may be able to compete more effectively against its number one competitor, Google.

AP Photo/Paul Sakuma

The Age of Interactivity

As the Yahoo! example illustrates, the Internet is changing the way firms do business. Manufacturers can now produce custom-made products and services more quickly and efficiently. Interactive shopping environments also enable marketers to learn more about satisfying consumers' diverse needs and wants more effectively. Consumers are learning that they can obtain a wide variety of products and services at a reasonable price. Moreover, the number of choices and amount of information available are increasing at a staggering pace. As the number of choice options increases, the potential for making better decisions increases. However, too much information can be overwhelming and confusing. Search engines like Yahoo! and Google attempt to help consumers use the large amount of information available on the web more effectively.

MARKETING IN ACTION
Blogs — A Double-edged Sword for Marketers

Weblogs, or for short, are frequently updated web journals that can be used to transmit cutting-edge information about products, services, politics, or just about anything. Although blogs have been around nearly as long as the web has, they became tremendously popular during the 2004 presidential election, and now there are over 35 million blogs worldwide covering a wide range of topics. Microsoft and many other companies have learned that blogs provide a tremendously useful tool for reaching consumers and for generating positive electronic word-of-mouth communications. Of course, blogs can also backfire. On December 1, 2004, Microsoft announced that it was planning on releasing a new software product called MSN Spaces that would enable consumers to easily create and maintain blogs.[21] This announcement lead to Boing Boing blog's co-editor Xeni Jardin to write a blog called "7 Dirty Blogs," in which she reported that MSN Spaces did not allow her to start a blog called "Pornography and the Law," but did allow her to start blogs entitled, "World of Poop," and "Smoking Crack: A How-To Guide for Teens." Microsoft learned the hard way that blogs are difficult to control and can lead to negative or positive electronic word-of-mouth.

Mazda learned the same lesson when it created a fake blog, allegedly created by 22-year-old Kid Halloween, showing a Mazda3 breakdancing, and a Mazda3 flying off a ramp like a skateboard. New blogs were quickly linked to the Mazda blog saying that the Mazda blog must be a fake because the videos were too slick to be made by a 22-year-old skateboarder. This led to a great deal of negative electronic word-of-mouth about Mazda.

porcorex/iStockphoto.com

Traditional mass marketing uses tools like television, radio, newspapers, and magazines to deliver a one-way message to consumers about product benefits. Internet marketing, however, uses interactive two-way communications between marketers and consumers with fast response times between communications and high levels of response contingency.[2] This means that one party's response depends on the other party's response, and this helps both parties get the information they need *when* they need it.

High levels of **interactivity** on the web enables **e-tailers** (electronic retailers) to provide exactly the type of information about products and services that individual consumers wish to receive. Interactivity also makes it easy for consumers to provide e-tailers with the information that they want—including credit card numbers, email addresses, shipping addresses, personal preferences, and purchase histories. E-tailers also try to make repeat purchase easy: With the click of a button a consumer can tell e-tailers to ship the requested items to the usual address and to bill a credit card which is already on file. Shopping becomes quick and easy. Consumers can shop from their homes for products from anywhere in the world without driving to traditional bricks-and-mortar retail stores, without struggling to find parking spots, and without waiting in lines.

In addition to making shopping easy, the web makes shopping fun, at least for some consumers. People are having the most fun when they are in a state of **flow**.[3] Flow is experienced when people perform an activity skillfully with little thought or effort. Golfers and other athletes often talk about being in the "zone," or performing extremely well without thinking. Birdies, touchdowns, baskets, and home runs just seem to come naturally, without a great deal of effort. Athletes sometimes say that golf balls, footballs, basketballs, or baseballs seem to pop right out at them when they're in a state of flow, and golf cups, end zones, baskets, and other targets look huge when they're in the "zone." Similarly, when consumers navigate through a well-designed website, shopping becomes automatic, effortless, and fun.

OBJECTIVE 2 — Features of a Well-Designed Website

Choice and Customization

The biggest difference between online stores (electronic stores on the Internet) and bricks-and-mortar stores (physical stores found in shopping plazas, shopping malls, etc.) is that online stores offer greater choice and greater customization.[4] Online stores have virtually unlimited inventory because they enable consumers to shop for products across stores, across state lines, and even across international borders. Online stores also permit greater customization because sellers can provide as much information as they wish, including product samples (e.g., music clips, video clips), comments from other customers, and comparisons to competitors' offerings.

In a recent study of 755 e-tailers from BizRate.com, it was found that online business success depends on brand name reputation, the type of products sold by the e-tailer, and the ease with which consumers could navigate the website.[5] Brand name reputation was perceived to be better if the e-tailer also had well-known

E-tailers benefit from having a well known bricks-and-mortar store with the same brand name.

bricks-and-mortar stores with the same brand name (e.g., JCPenney, Walmart, J. Crew), the e-tail sites were created by well-known manufacturers (e.g., Kodak, Casio), or if the e-tailer was well-known due to national advertising campaigns (e.g., amazon .com, pets.com).

OBJECTIVE 3

Information Search and Navigation

Some types of products are easier to shop for online than others. **Information search** refers to how much information consumers attempt to acquire. **Information search costs** refers to how difficult it is to acquire information in terms of time, money, or effort. Information search is greater and information search costs are lower in online environments than in offline, bricks-and-mortar environments. Furthermore, it is easier to obtain information and to evaluate the quality of **search goods**, relative to **experience goods** or **credence goods**.[6] The quality of search goods can be examined by simply examining a picture of it. The product might have a particularly effective design or appearance, or the brand name or the price of the product might be enough to convince consumers that the product is of high quality. The quality of experience goods, however, can only be determined by touching, feeling, or using the product. Sensory attributes like taste, smell, and touch determine the quality of experience goods. The quality of credence goods is even more difficulty to judge, because quality depends on years of experience and use. Attributes like reliability and durability determine the quality of credence goods. E-tailers are more successful if they primarily sell search goods, rather than experience goods or credence goods.

Some creative e-tailers, like landsend.com, have tried to make it easier to shop online for experience goods like clothes by providing detailed descriptions of experience and credence attributes, and by showing color pictures accompanied by information about stitching and construction materials. Landsend.com also uses a risk-free return policy to build trust and to assure consumers that its products are of high quality.

Navigation ease depends on ease of ordering, ease of payment, delivery methods, security, and the ease with which consumers can contact service representatives. Consumers prefer many different ordering methods (e.g., online, email, toll free phone, fax), many different payment methods (e.g., many different credit cards accepted, personal check, PayPal), and many different delivery methods (e.g., USPS, UPS, overnight shipping, two-day shipping).

Organization of Information

The design of a website also influences whether consumers are more likely to use a **compensatory decision making strategy** or a **non-compensatory decision making strategy**. When consumers use a compensatory strategy, they make trade-offs between attributes and this enables a good attribute to compensate for, or at least reduce concerns about, a bad attribute. When consumers use a non-compensatory strategy, they do not make trade-offs across attributes, and a bad attribute usually leads to the rejection of an alternative. Unfortunately, even an alternative that is very good overall can be rejected if that alternative has one bad attribute. Consumers often make better decisions if they use a compensatory strategy rather than a non-compensatory strategy, and consumers are more likely to use a compensatory strategy if a website is organized by options rather than by attributes.[7] When a website is organized by options, consumers are also likely to click on more options and consider a broader range of alternatives, and this also increases the quality of a decision. Consumers also click on more options when the

EYE ON INTERNATIONAL

INTERNET AIDS COUNTERFEIT BRANDS

In the 1990's, China and Taiwan were placed on the U.S. and the E.U. sanction list for their lack of trademark enforcement. According to the U.S. Patent and Trademark Office, 66% of the counterfeit products seized at U.S. borders come from China.[22] China produces counterfeit luxury watches, designer purses, scarves, computer chips, computer software, automobile parts, airplane parts, cosmetics, fertilizers, sunglasses, fragrances, prescription drugs, toys, and even automobiles. The Chinese Chery QQ Minicar is almost an exact copy of the Chevrolet Spark. New technology, including new manufacturing equipment and new computer software, has made pirating easy in China, and the Internet has made purchasing pirated brands easy.

Jason Kemplin/Getty Images

Famous brand names can be copied via rhyming, spelling similarity, and similar fonts or logos. For example, France's La Chemise Lacoste produces leisurewear and sportswear featuring Lacoste's famous crocodile logo. The Singapore company Crocodile uses a similar crocodile logo on their leisurewear and sportswear. Although Lacoste was founded in 1933 and Crocodile was founded in 1951, Crocodile sued Lacoste for trademark infringement in China and won its case. The Chinese court ruled that the Crocodile logo was original in terms of the shape and the expression of the crocodile.

---

attributes are negatively correlated, because negatively correlated attributes encourage consumers to attempt to make trade-offs between attributes. For example, e-tailers like HP provide laptop shoppers with a "customize and buy" option. Consumers click a series of options, beginning with components (processor, memory, hard-drive, graphics card, and display) and ending with accessories (e.g., mouse, keyboard, carrying case). Consumers can easily see the trade-offs between two, negatively correlated attributes such as processing speed and price. For instance, an Intel T6400 provides 2.0 GHz, whereas as a P8600 processor offers 2.4 GHz of speed for an additional $175. Thus, organizing the product by customized options encourages trade-offs and a compensatory strategy. In contrast, if HP organized its laptop offerings by attribute (e.g., by processor), consumers would be forced to evaluate one brand featuring an Intel T6400 processor, a second brand featuring a T6600, and so on. This presentation would discourage consumers from making trade-offs within each alternative and encourage noncompensatory decision-making. Consumers would tend look at each brand in isolation and reject those brands that failed to satisfy a specific criterion.

As noted earlier, e-tailers are more successful if they have bricks-and-mortar or offline stores as well as online stores (e.g., Sears.com and Sears). If an e-tailer does not have an offline store, managers should consider building an alliance or a partnership with an offline store. Research on online-offline brand alliances shows that such alliances encourage consumers to form assimilation effects between online and offline brands.[8] This means that as online brand quality increases, consumers' perceptions of the quality of offline brands also increase, and vice versa. Similarly, if online brand quality decreases, consumers' perceptions of the quality of offline brands decrease, and vice versa. Hence, if an alliance or a partnership is formed, it is important to choose a partner that is well known for selling high quality brands.

OBJECTIVE 4

The Implications of Reduced Search Costs for Information

Typically, consumers find it is easier to acquire information about products and services by using the click of a button on the Internet than by using phone calls and customer visits to several different bricks-and-mortar stores. Of course, so much information is available on the Internet that consumers can also become confused or overwhelmed. Consumers behave as limited information processors and are only able to consider about seven pieces of information at a time. One way consumers deal with this problem is by eliminating options that do not meet their requirements in the first stage of the decision making process, and then by evaluating the remaining options more carefully in the second stage of the decision making process. Consumers also have the option of using interactive decision aids (or smart agents or bots) that make it easier to eliminate options in the first stage and to evaluate options in the second stage.[9] A **recommendation agent** is an interactive decision aid that helps consumers to eliminate options by using information about their personal preferences or about their prior purchase histories. Amazon.com uses the latter approach. A **comparison matrix** is an interactive decision aid that helps consumers to evaluate options by providing a *Consumer Reports* style brand-by-attribute matrix that makes it easy for consumers to compare options. Research shows that both types of interactive decision aids improve the quality of consumers' decisions by helping them to manage large amounts of information more effectively.

Because it is easier to search for information in online environments than in offline environments, **search costs** are lower in online environments. Accordingly, consumers tend to search for more information in online environments. Consumers also search for more information when the purchase decision is important and consequential[10] or when they feel highly uncertain about which product or brand they should purchase.[11]

Purchase decisions are perceived as more consequential as involvement (personal relevance) or risk (the chance of negative outcomes) increases. Involvement and risk are often positively correlated. For example, involvement is higher for expensive products, like cars, because expensive products carry considerable financial risk. No one wants to pay thousands of dollars for a car to discover later it's a lemon. Involvement is also higher for publicly consumed products that carry social risks, like clothes. Consumers want to buy clothes that look sharp or stylish; they don't want to buy clothes that look ugly or nerdy. Involvement is also higher for products that carry physical risks, like lawn mowers, motorcycles, or pharmaceuticals. As involvement increases, it makes sense to gather a lot of information about many dealers, brands, and attributes before making a decision.

Prior knowledge also influences information search.[12] Novices, or consumers who are unfamiliar with a particular product category, tend to search for little information because they don't know how to interpret or how to use this information. For example, if you don't know anything about a complex product like plasma TVs, learning that a particular model has a resolution of 1080i doesn't help you to evaluate this product. Moderately knowledgeable consumers tend to search for a lot more information because they know how to interpret and how to use this information. Surprisingly, experts or highly knowledgeable consumers tend to search for relatively little information because they often feel confident that they already know everything they need to know to make an informed choice. Hence, there's an inverse-U shaped relationship between prior knowledge and search with the greatest amount of search occurring for moderately knowledgeable consumers.

Search costs are much higher in offline environments than in online environments. It takes planning, time, physical energy, and mental energy to visit many different offline stores and to compare many different brands on many different attributes. Consequently, consumers often search for relatively little information, even in a single offline store. For example, the typical grocery shopper spends only 12 seconds per decision, and many shoppers (41%) don't even bother to check the price of the products they purchased.[13] Comparing prices takes time and energy, even when brands are located right next to each other on the same shelf.

Conversely, search costs are much lower on the Internet. With the click of a button, consumers can scan the prices and features of hundreds of products quickly and easily by using interactive decision aids such as those provided by bizrate.com, botspot.com, bottomdollar.com, mysimon.com, pricescan.com, and other websites. When it is easy to compare prices for a product carried by many different retailers, cost transparency increases.[14] That is, a seller's costs become more obvious to buyers, and buyers can use this information to determine if a price is fair. Manufacturers and retailers are concerned about cost transparency because it decreases their ability to charge high prices and earn high margins. For example, when MCI and Sprint first started charging lower rates for long-distance phone calls, many consumers switched and AT&T was eventually forced to reduce its rates, also.

Cost transparency can potentially turn brands into commodities, subsequently reducing brand loyalty. Brokerage firms that rely more on an online presence (e.g., TD Ameritrade and E-trade) provide nearly the same products and services as traditional brokers (e.g., A. G. Edwards) for much lower fees. If a product or service is perceived as pretty much the same no matter who offers it, why not buy the least expensive option? Economists refer to this industry structure as perfect or "pure" competition because there is little to differentiate the brands and firms become "price takers," i.e., they must sell at the going rate. Brand loyalty can also diminish if consumers believe that a firm enjoys healthy profit margins, despite the presence of a sales promotion or price discount. For example, Procter & Gamble relied heavily on sales promotions in the 1980s and early 1990s, but in the mid-1990s, Procter & Gamble changed its policy to "efficient promotion" or no sales promotion. This change encouraged many consumers to switch to less expensive private label brands.

Of course, price information is not the only type of information available on the Internet. The Internet also offers vast amounts of information about product quality and product reliability (e.g., consumerreports.org, epinions.com). The Internet is dramatically reducing search costs for many different types of information.

Research on traditional advertising has shown that price advertising—or advertising that compares prices across brands—increases price sensitivity and encourages consumers to purchase the less expensive brand.[15] However, differentiating advertising—or advertising that compares specific features and benefits across brands—decreases price sensitivity and encourages consumers to purchase the higher quality brand.[16] Differentiating advertising also decreases the size of consumers' consideration sets.

Similar results have been found for Internet advertising.[17] In a highly influential experiment, mock web pages were created by systematically varying the design of web page similar to the real wine.com web page. Specifically, price comparability (high or low), quality comparability (high or low), and store comparability (high or low) were manipulated independently, and graduate students and university staff were randomly assigned to conditions. In high price comparability conditions, price information was presented on the first page and a tool that sorted wines by price was also provided. In low price comparability conditions, consumers had to click on a brand name to find its price and no sorting tool was provided. In high quality comparability conditions, wines could be sorted by grape (e.g., chardonnay, cabernet sauvignon) and detailed information about quality was provided (e.g., complexity, acidity, body, dryness). In low quality comparability conditions, consumers had to click on a brand name to obtain information about the grape and the quality of the wine. In high store comparability conditions, a split screen was used so that consumers could easily compare two stores (Dionysus and Jubilee). In low store comparability conditions, consumers could only visit one store at a time.

The results show that price sensitivity is lower when quality comparability is high rather than low. When it is easy to compare brands in terms of quality, the effects of price on choice decrease. Furthermore, when one store offered brands not offered by the other store, store comparability had no effect on price sensitivity. Store comparability influenced price sensitivity only when both stores offered the same brands. The results also demonstrate that consumers enjoy navigating through the website the most when all three search costs were low. Not surprisingly, consumers also made better decisions when all three search costs were low. These findings suggest that retailers should cooperate with smart agents and strive to reduce search costs for price, quality, and store information because this increases consumer satisfaction, which subsequently increases repeat purchase rates.

In a follow-up experiment, it was shown that using smart agents to reduce search costs for quality information can increase price sensitivity when price and quality are uncorrelated, especially when consumers are highly preoccupied with price.[18] Otherwise, search costs for quality information have opposite effects on price sensitivity and product differentiation, consistent with the results of the previous experiment. Furthermore, the follow-up experiment shows that these results generalize to several different product categories.

OBJECTIVE 5

The Consumer Advocacy Paradigm

The Internet has reduced consumers' information search costs, reduced transaction costs, increased the number of options available, and increased communication among consumers. As a result, the Internet has increased consumer power. According to Glen Urban, a former Dean of the MIT Sloan School of Management, the best way for firms to respond is to become consumer advocates.[19] Firms should improve product quality, improve customer service, improve privacy and security on the Internet, and provide honest and accurate information about their products and their competitors' products, and should do so even when competitors' products better serve consumers' wants and needs. For example, automobile insurance firms like Progressive provide competitors' rates even when some of the competitors have better rates. Similarly, Bankrate.com provides competitors' rates for different types of loans, mortgages, CDs, and other financial services even when some of the competitors have better rates. These companies try to help consumers and build trust even when this involves losing business in the short run. Helping consumers and building trust can benefit a company in the long run.

Firms like Progressive use the Internet to build trust with consumers.

The famous online auction site, eBay, enjoys billions of dollars worth of business every year. eBay builds trust by asking consumers to provide feedback about sellers and by presenting this feedback on their website. Reputable sellers receive 99% or higher levels of positive feedback and consumers learn to trust sellers with high levels of positive feedback. Furthermore, consumers are often willing to pay a little more for products sold by highly reputable sellers. eBay also provides excellent fraud protection, and fewer than 0.01% of the transactions performed on eBay are fraudulent. PayPal is used for making purchases on eBay, and PayPal helps protect against fraud by warning consumers about potentially suspicious sellers who changed their identification information recently by displaying a pair of sunglasses next to the seller. Consumers are also encouraged to communicate with sellers via email before buying and to report suspicious activities.

Approximately 25% of all products sold on the Internet are counterfeit, resulting in over $25 billion in lost revenues to the original firms.[23] Cybersquatting and typosquatting are also common on the Internet. Cybersquatting occurs when someone registers a domain name of another company's trademark and attempts to sell the domain name to the trademark owner. Typosquatting occurs when someone registers a domain name that is misspelled (e.g., silliconvalley.com) or that has typographical errors such as missing words (e.g., www.barnesnoble.com).

In the case of *Toronto-Dominion Bank v. Boris Karpachev* (2002), Karpachev invested in the bank's TD Waterhouse online brokerage service and lost approximately $35,000. Because he was angry about his loss, Karpachev registered 16 confusing domain names similar to TD Waterhouse (e.g., tdwoterhouse.com, dtwaterhouse.com) and wrote negative blogs about these companies on his sites. The Canadian court ordered Karpachev to delete his confusing domain names and to refrain from creating new domain names that could be confused with TD Waterhouse.

However, typosquatting is not always disallowed by the courts. The e-tailer Buy.com created several domain names similar to its competitors (e.g., 10percentoffamazon.com, 10percentoffreel.com, 10percentoffegg.com) that link consumers to Buy.com. Some of these sites have been discontinued, but some still exist (e.g., 10percentoffamazon.com).

Sportstock/iStockphoto.com

Travelers also love to use the Internet to search for information and to book flights on Expedia.com, Orbitz.com, and Travelocity.com. These companies have been driving travel agents out of business and saving consumers money by providing competitors' rates. Orbitz.com even provides information about how much consumers can save by changing their travel schedules slightly (e.g., leaving or returning a day earlier or later). Some consumers use these sites just to gather information. Consumers can book their flights on airlines' websites later, if they wish.

More and more consumers are using eTrade, TD Ameritrade, and Charles Schwab to buy stocks online. These companies have increased the amount of financial information and advice available to consumers and have reduced trading costs. Charles Schwab pays its brokers salaries rather than commissions to encourage brokers to help consumers as much as possible rather than simply trying to sell more stock. Commissions impede the development of consumer advocacy programs because commissions reward salespersons to sell as much as possible and to sell more expensive products and services even when consumers do not need these more expensive products and services.

Advanced Micro Devices (AMD) manufactures processors and flash drives and helps customers solve their connectivity problems. AMD recently created the AMDEdge online customer service program to help customers who want to build their own computer systems. AMDEdge provides technical tips, news, cutting edge information, and access to online forums where consumers facing a specific problem can interact with other consumers who have faced the same problem and have developed possible solutions to the problem.

Relationship marketing involves building stronger relationships with consumers by using information technology and improved business processes. The goal of relationship marketing is to build consumer trust and brand loyalty. L. L. Bean, Land's End, and Orvis use information technology to track consumers' purchase histories and this information is then used to send different customized catalogs to different consumers. These companies also collect demographic (e.g., age, gender, income) and psychographic (e.g., values and lifestyles) information from consumers to learn more about their wants and needs. The ideal relationship marketing program uses one-to-one marketing or individualized interactions with consumers, loyalty programs that promote repeat purchase with points or rewards for frequent transactions, and accurate and unbiased information, advice, and recommendations. For example, in 2004, a global auto manufacturer improved their relationship marketing program by (a) using individualized mailings based on consumers' ratings of safety, style, performance, and economy, (b) developing an Internet Auto Choice Advisor, which provided unbiased recommendations, (c) developing an Auto Show in Motion competitive test drive experience with no sales pressure, and (d) developing a community of 500 consumers who could discuss their concerns with other consumers similar to themselves and with product experts.

Many consumers do not trust large corporations because of accounting scandals (e.g., Enron, MCI-Worldcom, Tyco, Parmalat), insider trading charges (e.g., Ivan Boesky, Dennis Levine, Martin Siegal, Michael Milken), obstruction of justice charges (e.g., Martha Stewart), and other abuses of power. Because of the erosion of trust created by these problems, consumer advocacy is more important than ever. Nevertheless, consumer advocacy is not for all firms. Companies that sell commodities might not benefit from consumer advocacy programs because extreme price competition drives commodity industries. Monopolies also might not benefit from consumer advocacy programs because consumers have little power in monopolistic settings. Consumer advocacy is also not for firms facing uncontrollable quality problems. For example, airlines cannot control weather problems and air traffic control problems. Consumer advocacy is also not for firms with a short-term focus.

Chapter Summary

Search engines like Yahoo!, Google, MSN, Ask.com, and others help consumers to navigate through enormous amounts of information stored on the web. Reduced search costs have increased consumer power and have encouraged companies to adopt more consumer-friendly policies and services. The most successful websites are owned by companies with reputable brand names, sell goods and offer websites that are easy to evaluate, and have websites that are easy to navigate. High levels of interactivity provide two-way communication, fast response times between communications, and high levels of response contingency where the questions and answers of one party depend on the questions and answers of the other party. Interactivity helps consumers and retailers get the information they need when they need it.

Comparing prices and features of products offered by different offline or bricks-and-mortar stores is time consuming and difficult. Many consumers are unwilling to rearrange their schedules to visit many different stores to find the product that best meets their needs. Instead, consumers often settle for the first satisfactory product they encounter. In online environments, on the other hand, comparison shopping is quick and easy. With the click of a button, consumers can quickly access information about virtually any type of product or service that they might want. Interactive decision aids reduce search costs for price, search costs for quality, and search costs for e-tailers. Reduced search costs decrease decision effort and lead to better choices.

Reduced search costs also increase consumer power and encourage firms to develop consumer advocacy programs. This involves improving product quality, improving customer service, improving privacy and security on the Internet, and providing honest and accurate information about products and services. Some consumer advocacy programs provide information about competitors' products even when competitors' products better serve consumers' wants and needs than the firm's own products. Advocating for consumers builds trust and can benefit a firm in the long run.

Key Terms

blogs

interactivity

e-tailers

flow

information search

information search costs

search goods

experience goods

credence goods

compensatory decision
making strategy

non-compensatory decision
making strategy

recommendation agent

comparison matrix

search costs

relationship marketing

Review and Discussion

1. How will interactivity change the way consumers acquire, remember, and use product information?

2. What are the key differences between online and offline shopping environments?

3. What are the key features of a well-designed website?

4. What types of products are particularly easy to shop for on the web? What types of products have you shopped for on the web?

5. How do search costs influence amount of search?

6. What are the consequences of low search costs for price-related information?

7. What are the consequences of low search costs for quality-related information?

8. From a retailer's perspective, what are the advantages of having unlimited electronic shelf space?

9. What is the consumer advocacy paradigm? How could a company use this paradigm?

10. What future trends are likely to shape the way consumers use the web to shop?

Short Application Exercises

1. Visit a well-designed website, like amazon.com. How does the site make searching for information easy? What type of recommendation agent does the site use?

2. On a blank sheet of paper, draw a well-designed home web page that would make navigation easy for consumers.

3. Discuss your most favorite and least favorite web shopping experiences. What were the key factors that lead to these experiences?

4. Use a search engine to find information for a product that you have never shopped for and that you know little about. Although you know little about this product, could you use the web to learn a lot relatively quickly?

MANAGERIAL APPLICATION

Deanna Brown, President of Scripps Networks Interactive, says, "Being in tune with the consumer palette allows us to think smartly about what people are thinking about on a day-to-day, week-to-week basis." FoodNetwork.com has grown to 11.3 million users in 2009, and big events like the Super Bowl encourage many consumers to use FoodNetwork.com recipes and products for home entertaining. Walmart is one of FoodNetwork.com's largest clients, and Stephanie Prager, associate digital director for Walmart at MediaVest, says, "There's a challenge we've seen with other cable networks in that they might have a great program on-air, but their site is not as robust."

YOUR CHALLENGE:

1. Imagine that you are a manager at FoodNetwork.com and you've been asked to analyze your company's website. What are the most positive features of FoodNetwork.com's website?

2. How could you improve FoodNetwork.com's website?

3. Besides Walmart, what other new clients would you pursue and why?

4. Does FoodNetwork.com do a good job of serving as an advocate of consumers? How could consumer advocacy be improved at FoodNetwork.com?

CHAPTER

16

CONSUMER BEHAVIOR
AND BRANDING STRATEGY

OBJECTIVES *After studying this chapter, you will be able to...*

1 Develop new brand entry strategies and decrease new brand adoption rates.

2 Develop appropriate brand strategies for each stage of the product life cycle and develop marketing strategies for extending the product life cycle.

3 Develop a strong brand name.

4 Develop appropriate marketing strategies for strong brands and weaker brands.

5 Develop consumer acquisition and retention strategies for a new brand.

DISNEY

PRNewsFoto/Walt Disney Studios Home Entertainment/Newscom

Disney is one of the leading brands in the world, standing for excellence in children's entertainment. This brand includes famous cartoon characters (e.g., Mickey Mouse, Donald Duck), famous movies (e.g., *The Lion King*, *The Hunchback of Notre Dame*), and famous theme parks (e.g., Disneyland, Disney World, Tokyo Disneyland). In 1998, Disney's CEO, Michael Eisner, was one of the highest paid executives with a compensation package of $631 million.[1] However, even a formidable company like Disney can make blunders, such as the Euro Disney theme park near Paris, France. Disney spent $4.4 billion developing Euro Disney, and in its first few years of operation, attendance was reasonable. However, visitors spent very little after they entered the theme park. Eventually, Euro Disney had to lower

347

its prices for entrance to the theme park and its hotels, sell cheaper merchandise (e.g., t-shirts and crayons instead of jewelry), and train its employees to speak multiple languages and be responsive to people from many different cultures.

Because of its strong brand image, Disney may be able to recover its losses from Euro Disney. The Disney case is instructive because it highlights the importance of building a strong brand name worldwide, developing a coherent set of brand extensions (i.e., apply the brand name to many different products and services that appeal to children), and using a strong brand name to recover from bad decisions.

OBJECTIVE 1

Entry Strategy

Before managers can build a strong brand name for new products, they must develop appropriate entry strategies for bringing those products to market. The **diffusion of innovation**, or the rate a new product spreads or is adopted across the marketplace, differs among product categories. For example, diffusion was slow for black-and-white televisions when they were first introduced, but fast for color televisions when they hit the consumer marketplace. The reason for this is that diffusion is influenced by several factors, especially the relative advantage of the new product over the old product.[2] The advantages of black-and-white television over radio were not immediately obvious when black-and-white television was first introduced. However, after enjoying black-and-white television for decades, it was easy for consumers to imagine the relative advantages of color television over black-and-white.

Compatibility with consumers' beliefs, opinions, and lifestyles is another important factor. Wealthier consumers traveled and enjoyed active lifestyles; sitting home watching black-and-white television was incompatible with this way of life. This incompatibility slowed the diffusion of black-and-white TVs in the marketplace—because at the time, they were relatively expensive, i.e., only people with higher incomes were able to afford TVs. Complexity or user friendliness is another important factor. Black-and-white television was so novel when it was first introduced that consumers did not know how to use it. Incremental innovations, like color television, are often easier to use, so incremental innovations usually diffuse more quickly than totally new products.

Perceived risk also reduces the diffusion rate. This is true for financial risks (e.g., expensive products, like black-and-white television when it was first introduced), social risks (e.g., embarrassment at being unable to use the product successfully), and physical risk (e.g., risk of harm). Trialability, or the ease with which consumers can try or use the new product, increases the diffusion rate. Trialability tends to be higher for inexpensive products than for expensive products, but it can vary across the board; not all products can be taken for a test drive. It is very common to test drive a new automobile, and now, consumers can try out products like computers, mattresses, and even expensive rugs in their homes before finalizing purchases.

The typical diffusion curve is S-shaped; the proportion of potential adopters is low initially because it takes time for marketing programs to build awareness and stimulate trial. The adoption rate typically increases dramatically during the growth phase as a result of the "snowball" effect from word-of-mouth communications. The more consumers talk favorably about a new product to other consumers, the more these other consumers want to try the product. Eventually, however, the market becomes saturated, and the product is replaced by a new innovation. See Figure 16.1.

Although the diffusion rate is affected by several factors outside of marketing managers' control, they can influence the diffusion rate by identifying innovator consumers and targeting marketing programs toward them. Innovator consumers are usually venturesome, open-minded, and sensation-seeking. They are willing to try new things. They also tend to be highly educated and upwardly mobile. Innovator consumers also tend to be heavy users of a product category and active seekers of information via specialty magazines and the Internet. Focusing on innovator consumers helps firms increase initial sales and acceptance of a new product among other members of the channel of distribution, as well. This is especially important when a firm is new and has relatively little power in the channel of distribution.

Heavy promotion and advertising can be used to influence early adopters and to stimulate word-of-mouth. This is particularly important when a product is expected to have a relatively short life cycle as a result of rapidly changing technology (e.g., computers and other high-tech products). If the product is expected to have a relatively long life cycle and if a firm has asymmetrical power in the distribution channel, then a long-term market leadership strategy should be pursued, including segmentation, targeting, positioning, and protection from imitation. Usually only the largest and most powerful firms can pursue this strategy (e.g., Disney, Sony, Coca-Cola).

OBJECTIVE 2

Product Life Cycle Management

The diffusion curve has a powerful influence on the product life cycle, which also is typically S-shaped. However, the product life cycle curve is affected by several other factors as well, including repeat purchase rates, changes in consumer preferences, environmental changes, and other factors (see Figure 16.2).[3]

As the product life cycle curve indicates, during the introduction stage, managers need to focus on creating awareness and stimulating trial. Promotion and advertising

FIGURE 16.1 DIFFUSION CURVE

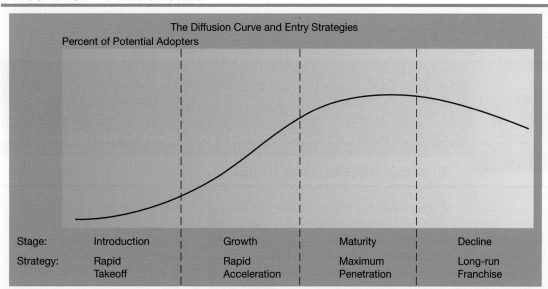

Source: Adapted from G.L. Urban and S.H. Star, (1991). *Advanced Marketing Strategy: Phenomena, analysis, and decisions,* p. 97. Reprinted by permission of Pearson Education, Inc., Upper Saddle River, NJ.

FIGURE 16.2   PRODUCT LIFE CYCLE CURVE

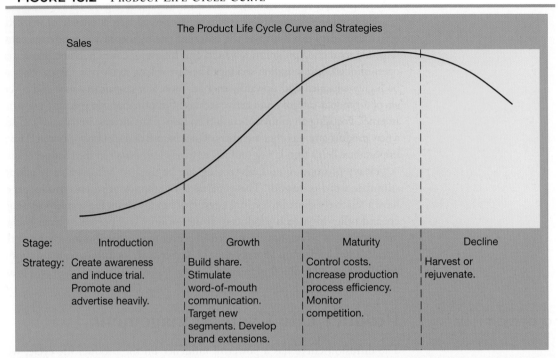

The Product Life Cycle Curve and Strategies

Stage:	Introduction	Growth	Maturity	Decline
Strategy:	Create awareness and induce trial. Promote and advertise heavily.	Build share. Stimulate word-of-mouth communication. Target new segments. Develop brand extensions.	Control costs. Increase production process efficiency. Monitor competition.	Harvest or rejuvenate.

Source: Adapted from G.L. Urban and S.H. Star, (1991). *Advanced Marketing Strategy: Phenomena, analysis, and decisions*, p. 94. Reprinted by permission of Pearson Education, Inc., Upper Saddle River, NJ.

are important tools for achieving these goals. During the growth stage, managers need to build market share by stimulating word-of-mouth communication. New market segments and brand extensions (i.e., variations on a theme) tend to appear during this stage. During the maturity stage, managers need to focus on reducing production and marketing costs. Competition intensity also increases during this stage. Finally, during the

EYE ON INTERNATIONAL

NEW CUSTOMERS AREN'T FREE

European cable companies served over 60 million consumers and earned more than 10 billion Euros in revenues by 2002.[13] The companies borrowed heavily to build networks and acquire new customers. The companies bet that many customers would adopt digital services. However, the lifetime value of the typical customer was much lower than the amount of money

peaceeye/iStockphoto.com

invested by these companies, and several of them went bankrupt, including Ish (a German company) and NTL (a U.S. company and Europe's fourth-largest operator). United Pan-Europe Communications, the third-largest operator, defaulted on its bond payments and was removed from one of the European stock exchanges.

decline stage, the product may be approaching obsolescence. If so, harvesting is appropriate; costs should be reduced to the bare minimum so future sales based on the reputation of the product yield high profits. Of course, harvesting shortens the product life cycle.

If the product is not yet obsolete, rejuvenation strategies can lengthen the product life cycle. One way to rejuvenate a product is to develop new uses for it. For example, Arm & Hammer baking soda can be used to deodorize refrigerators, freezers, sinks, carpets, and clothing. It can also be used as an ingredient in toothpastes, deodorant, and carpet fresheners. In other words, there are many uses of baking soda that do not involve baking. Similarly, DuPont continually develops new uses for its key product, nylon. Initially, nylon was used to make ropes and parachutes. Later, it was used in women's hosiery, clothing, tires, and carpets.

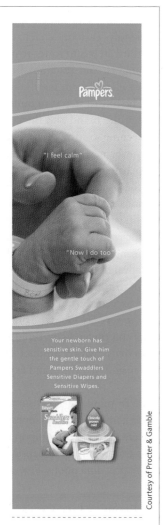

Pampers emphasizes benefits to the baby rather than benefits to the parent.

Courtesy of Procter & Gamble

Commodities, or generic products, can sometimes be rejuvenated via branding. Sunkist oranges seem better than ordinary oranges. Purdue chickens seem better than ordinary chickens, and Idaho potatoes are positioned as high quality. Advertising can also rejuvenate a product, under the right circumstances. In the past, it was considered distasteful to run television ads for hygiene-related products, such as feminine goods and deodorants. Now such ads are common, and Axe and Old Spice grooming products for men and Always feminine hygiene products (Procter & Gamble) have benefited greatly from advertising exposure. Effective advertising can even turn disadvantages into advantages. For example, "Avis is number two so they try harder." "With a name like Smucker's, it has to be good." Focusing on the correct advantages is also important. For example, Pampers disposable diapers originally sold poorly when advertising focused on benefits to the mother (i.e., convenience). Sales increased dramatically when advertising shifted its focus to benefits for the baby (i.e., helps keep baby drier and healthier).

Identifying new market segments or new potential users of a product can also rejuvenate a product. For example, Johnson & Johnson baby shampoo is not just for babies anymore. It's also mild and gentle enough for adults to use every day. Milk is not just for children anymore. It's healthy for adults, also. Lipton tea is not just for seniors; young people also enjoy Lipton tea. Another way to rejuvenate a product is to reduce its price, as Datril did to compete more effectively against Tylenol. Social trends should also be analyzed. Increasing concerns among consumers about health, pollution, and the environment have increased sales of organic produce, health foods, vitamins, and environmentally friendly products.

Sometimes unused by-products from a manufacturing process can be marketed to increase the profitability of a product in the decline stage. For example, kitty litter is made from disposable sawdust from lumberyards. Mesquite wood was once destroyed by Texas farmers, but now they sell it for grilling. Cat food and dog food are made from the unused by-products of food for people. Finally, developing a new channel of distribution can be used to rejuvenate a product, as Hanes did for L'eggs panty hose. Originally, panty hose, and women's hosiery in general, were available primarily in department stores. L'eggs became very successful when Hanes sold them through grocery stores, drugstores, and mass merchandisers, using a clever egg-shaped plastic package—which also protected the relatively delicate product from damage and simplified display in store aisles. Direct marketing and Internet sales can also lengthen a product's life cycle.

OBJECTIVE 3   Brand Equity Management

The brand name of a product is often its most important asset.[4] A strong brand name triggers many important associations stored in consumers' memories, and a strong brand name provides a promise of excellence. Strong brand names give consumers a

In 2007, 60 million cans of pet food from China were recalled because they were allegedly contaminated with melamine, a chemical used to make plastics and fertilizers. Also, in 2007, nine million toys from China were recalled because they were decorated with paint containing lead or included magnets that could be swallowed by small children. Some of the toys were well-known brands, including Barbie, Polly Pocket, and characters from the movie Cars.[14] Some of the toys were sold by Mattel and Fisher-Price. Is it ethical for Chinese companies to cut corners in order to make cheaper products? If this practice continues, how will it influence the image of products made in China? Could this image affect Chinese products that are not defective? Could this image influence the willingness of firms in the United States to do business with Chinese firms?

good reason for buying. They also increase trust, repeat purchase rates, and the willingness of consumers to pay more for one brand than for another. Of course, these effects lead to greater sales, profits, and power in the distribution channel for companies.

How can managers build strong brand names for their products? The first step is to establish a strong *brand identity* (who are you?). For example, Disney has a strong brand identity; consumers know that Disney stands for excellence in children's entertainment. The second step is to establish a strong *brand meaning* (what are you?). Disney performs well on this dimension, too. Consumers know that Disney creates family-friendly cartoon characters, movies, and theme parks. The third step is to foster strong *brand responses*, or feelings, thoughts, and reactions from consumers. For example, Disney elicits warm family feelings, thoughts, and reactions. The fourth step is to build a strong *brand relationship* between the brand and the consumer. Many consumers have become so strongly attached and committed to Disney that they immediately buy whatever new product Disney develops even if they know little about it and despite its expensive price.

Brand identity depends on the strength and the nature of the associations that come to mind whenever consumers encounter a brand. These associations can be linked to a product category, specific product attributes, specific product benefits, specific usage situations, or specific users of the product. When the associations are sufficiently strong, the relevant product category, attribute, benefit, usage situation, or user can prime or automatically activate thoughts about the brand. This leads to a significant advantage for strong brands.

Brand meaning depends on the strength and the nature of the image of the brand in terms of objective quality and performance. Does the brand exceed consumers' performance expectations? Is the brand reliable, durable, and easy to service? Does the brand satisfy consumers' utilitarian, aesthetic, and economic needs and preferences? Building brand meaning takes a long time, and just a single bad experience with a product can erode many years' worth of goodwill. So, managers need to ensure that the brand experience is consistently high in quality.

Brand responses are the feeling and judgments that come to mind when consumers think about a brand. Relevant feelings include warmth, fun, excitement, security, approval from others (won't the neighbors be impressed?), and self-esteem (I feel like an important person when I use this brand). Disney performs well on the warmth and fun dimensions, and BMW performs well on the approval from others and self-respect dimensions. Relevant

FIGURE 16.3 STRATEGIES FOR EXTENDING THE PRODUCT LIFE CYCLE

- Develop new uses
- Branding
- Advertise more heavily
- Identify new relative advantages
- Identify new users
- Reduce price
- Sell unused byproducts
- Develop new distribution channels

judgments include subjective quality, credibility, consideration, and superiority. To perform well on these dimensions, the brand must deliver a unique and consistently high-quality experience. Uniqueness is especially important. Many companies have tried to copy Disney but have failed because Disney's uniqueness is preemptive, i.e., it is difficult to copy.

Brand relationships take years to develop and can only occur after strong brand identities, brand meanings, and brand responses have been established. **Brand resonance** refers to a consumer's intense and actively loyal relationship with a brand. Brand resonance leads to high purchase frequencies and volumes, feelings of attachment, feelings of brand community or kinship with other users of the brand (e.g., anyone who uses my brand must be a good person), and active engagement, such as joining a fan club for the brand. See Figure 16.4.

Brand equity is the value that a brand accrues based on the goodwill attached to associations with the brand name. One simple and direct approach to measuring brand equity is to compare consumers' evaluation of a product with no brand name to their evaluation of the same product with a brand name attached.[5] This approach is especially useful in the early stages of market research when product concepts or ideas are tested for feasibility. For example, one group of consumers could be asked to evaluate a series of new product ideas (e.g., garden-vegetable flavored potato chips, Cajun-blackened steak frozen dinners, chunky peach cottage cheese, smoky bacon-flavored hotdogs, Italian spiced lunch meat, lemon mint soda). Another group could be asked to evaluate the same concepts with a brand name attached to each (e.g., Nabisco, Sealtest). If the same concepts are evaluated more favorably when a brand name is attached, the brand name adds value. Developing **brand extensions**, or different products with the same brand name (e.g., Coke Classic, Cherry Coke, Vanilla Coke, Coke Zero), is more problematic because the brand name becomes more variable and ambiguous. Consumers' perceptions as to why a company launches brand extensions are also important. Ideally, firms want consumers to assume that brand extensions

FIGURE 16.4 CUSTOMER-BASED BRAND EQUITY PYRAMID

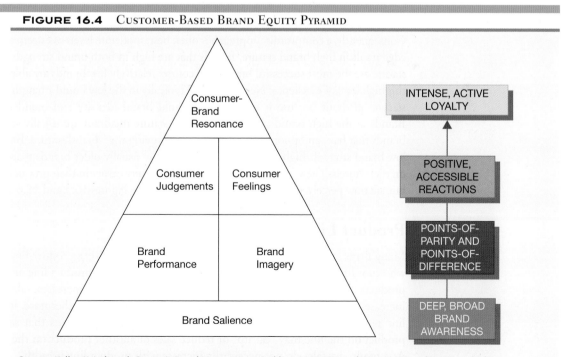

Source: Keller, K. L. (2003), *Strategic Brand Management: Building, Measuring and Managing Brand Equity*, 2nd ed., Prentice-Hall, Englewood Cliffs, NJ.

great coke taste zero sugar

IT'S
P⦿SSIBLE

Image courtesy of The Advertising Archives

Coke Zero is one of Coca-Cola's recent brand extensions.

were developed because they fit the unique skills of the manufacturer—and not because the manufacturer is simply copying competitors' products.

The **Young & Rubicam Brand Asset Valuator** uses a set of scales to measure differentiation (How unique is the brand?), relevance (How useful is the brand?), esteem (Is the brand the best?), and knowledge (Does the brand have a clear and consistent image?).[6] Multiplying differentiation scores by relevance scores provides a measure of brand strength. Usually, a high score on one dimension implies a low score on the other.

Consequently, a compromise approach is often best; moderate levels of differentiation and relevance lead to high brand strength.

Multiplying esteem scores by knowledge scores provides a measure of brand stature. Again, a high score on one of these dimensions implies a low score on the other. Consequently, a compromise approach is often best; moderate levels of esteem and knowledge result in high brand stature. Brands that are high in both brand strength and brand stature are the most successful brands. Of course, relatively few brands are able to achieve this high level of excellence. New brands are typically in the low brand strength/low brand stature quadrant because it takes time to build brand identity and brand reputation. Brands in the high brand strength/low brand stature quadrant are usually strong niche brands that have an opportunity to grow by improving their brand stature. Brands in the low brand strength/high brand stature quadrant are usually older brands that are resting on their laurels. These brands enjoyed high brand equity earlier in their product life cycles, but are now perceived as declining and unexciting. See Figures 16.5 and 16.6.

Product Line Management

Many firms are shifting from hiring brand managers to hiring product line managers who coordinate marketing and production activities across a product line or a family of products. As the number of products added to a product line increases, sales and costs increase. Managing the sales/costs trade-off can be difficult. Furthermore, if a product line is too large, product **cannibalization** may occur. This means that sales of one product on the line may "eat up" or reduce sales of another product on the same line. As a result, net sales do not necessarily increase with product line breadth.

However, research has shown that total market share increases with product line breadth.[7] For large Fortune 500 companies, however, product line breadth was not

FIGURE 16.5 YOUNG & RUBICAM POWER GRID

The Young & Rubicam Power Grid

Brand Stature
(Knowledge and Esteem)

Brand Strength (Differentiation and Relevance)		Low	High
	High	Dove Chocolates Teddy Grahams Snapple Swatch Molson Starbucks	Disney Sesame Street Doritos Sony Ocean Spray Kodak Mercedes-Benz Hallmark Coca-Cola
	Low	New dot-coms	Oldsmobile Bayer Wesson Ramada

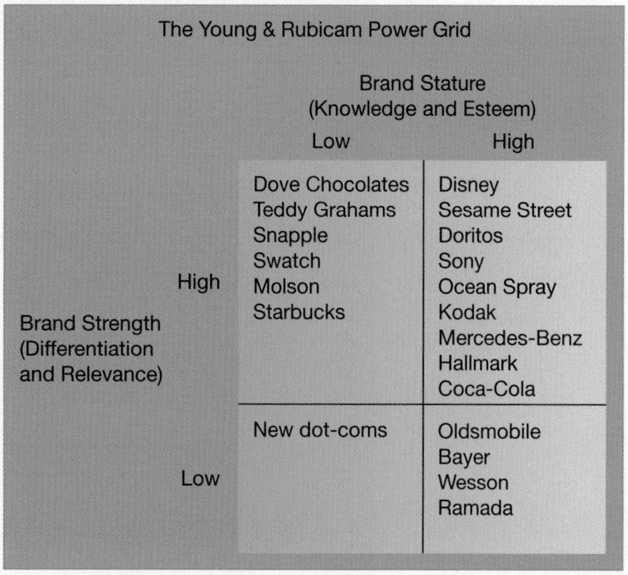

Source: From D.A. Aaker, *Building Strong Brands,* Fig. 10.3, p. 309. By David A. Aaker, (1996). Adapted with permission of The Free Press, a division of Simon & Schuster, Inc. All rights reserved

related to inventory costs and actually decreased manufacturing costs. As a result, many Fortune 500 companies have learned how to increase their product lines without increasing costs (although this study did not measure marketing costs) by incorporating cost-cutting procedures. Just-in-time computer-aided supply and ordering procedures reduce inventory costs. Flexible manufacturing and manufacturing-cell-group-based technologies reduce manufacturing costs. Offering a wide range of products that share a large number of common parts also reduces manufacturing costs, especially if the common parts are used during the early stages of the manufacturing process.

Although many Fortune 500 companies have learned to control manufacturing costs, smaller companies may be less able to do so. Also, the problems of marketing costs and product cannibalization remain. Cannibalization is problematic when one product takes significant market share away from another product within the same product line. For example, Miller Lite takes share away from Miller. Coke Zero takes share away from Diet Coke. Cannibalization is more likely to occur when consumers are brand loyal as opposed to attribute loyal. Consumers loyal to Miller Lite are likely to drink Miller when Miller Lite is unavailable. Consumers loyal to Coke Zero are likely to drink Diet Coke when Coke Zero is unavailable. On the other hand, consumers who are attribute loyal are less likely to create a cannibalization within a product line. Consumers loyal to light beer may switch to Bud Light when Miller Lite is unavailable. Similarly, consumers loyal to diet soft drinks may switch to Diet Pepsi when Diet Coke is unavailable. Thus, attribute loyalty can create brand-switching, which is worse than cannibalization.

One way to determine if consumers are brand loyal or attribute loyal is to show them a set of brands and ask them to indicate their first and second choices.[8] Brand-loyal consumers indicate first and second choices with the same brand name (e.g., Pepsi and Diet Pepsi). However, attribute-loyal consumers indicate first and second choices with the same attribute rather than with the same brand name (e.g., Pepsi and Coke or Diet Pepsi and Diet Coke).

FIGURE 16.6   YOUNG & RUBICAM POWER GRID

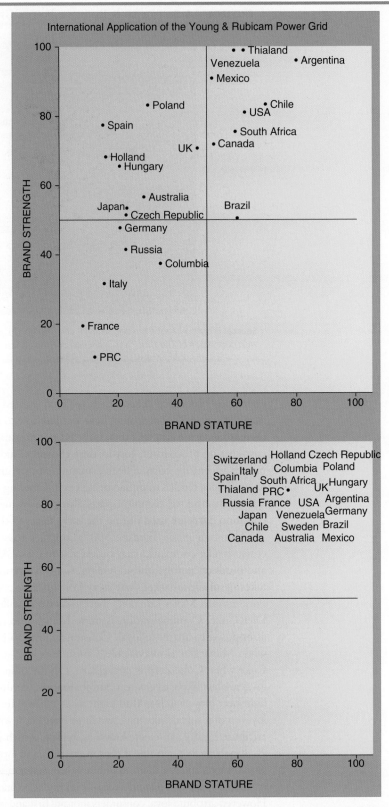

Source: Adapted from K.L. Keller, (1998). *Strategic Brand Management: Building, Measuring, and Managing Brand Equity*, p. 630–631. Reprinted by permission of Pearson Education, Inc., Upper Saddle River, NJ.

If the vast majority of their consumers are brand loyal, marketers should maintain a relatively narrow product line to avoid cannibalization. On the other hand, if the vast majority of their consumers are attribute loyal, it makes sense to consider increasing a product line so all relevant attributes are available under a particular brand name. The number of relevant attributes vary across product categories (e.g., diet versus non-diet, vanilla versus chocolate, decaf versus full strength, instant versus brewed, spicy versus non-spicy).

OBJECTIVE 4

Managing Market Leaders and Market Underdogs

Market leaders, or the strongest brands with the largest market shares in their product categories, are the easiest brands to manage because success breeds success. Market leaders have large marketing, production, and R&D budgets. Market leaders often have a large segment of loyal consumers, and a great deal of power in the channel of distribution. Inertia benefits the market leader, and any change in the marketplace is potentially threatening. Market leaders often try to prevent change.[9]

One way to prevent change is to encourage consumers to "stick with what works"; remind them that "you get what you pay for;" and emphasize that "we're always there when you need us." These types of claims discourage consumers from trying other brands because the status quo or current state of affairs seems safe and free of risk. Another way to prevent change is to increase ambiguity in the marketplace. Ambiguous information, or information that supports many different conclusions, is often interpreted as consistent with consumers' current conclusions. Of course, because most consumers buy the market leader, they have already concluded that the market leader is the best brand. Even when consumers try to be objective, they tend to interpret ambiguous evidence as consistent with their current beliefs. Known as the **confirmation bias**, this phenomenon occurs because people find it easier to identify and interpret information that supports their beliefs as opposed to information that fails to do so.

One way to increase ambiguity in the marketplace is to make it difficult to compare the prices of market leaders versus underdogs. This can be achieved through exclusive dealerships (e.g., many automobile dealers are allowed to sell only one brand), exclusive product displays (e.g., end-of-aisle displays in grocery stores), and confusing models (e.g., one dealer has model 505A and another has model 505B). Confusing model numbers, such as different numbers for products that are otherwise identical, increase ambiguity. Confusing brand names, such as the same appliances being sold under the Whirlpool name at H. H. Gregg stores and as Kenmore brand at Sears, also increase ambiguity.

Another way to increase ambiguity in the marketplace is to differentiate market leaders using irrelevant attributes. Budweiser beer is "beechwood aged"; Bud Lite offers "drinkability"; and Miller Genuine Draft is "cold filtered." These irrelevant attributes do not affect the taste of the beer, but they sound good to consumers who fall prey to confirmation bias. Similarly, Folger's coffee is "mountain grown," which is a meaningless attribute. Some powdered laundry detergents have blue specks in them that are supposed to give you whiter whites. The blue specks actually have no effect, but confirmation bias leads consumers to conclude that the blue specks increase the performance of the detergent.

Underdogs, or follower brands, need to do the opposite of market leaders. Market leaders promote the status quo, but underdogs need to disrupt it. Market leaders need to increase ambiguity in the marketplace, but underdogs need to decrease it. One way to disrupt the status quo is to encourage consumers to participate in blind taste tests and other evaluations that involve comparing underdogs to market leaders. Free samples; "try it, you'll like it" claims; websites that make it easy to compare prices; comparative ads; and side-by-side shelf placements with market leaders in grocery stores can potentially benefit underdogs.

Differentiating on irrelevant attributes creates ambiguity that benefits market leaders.

Encouraging consumers to challenge their current beliefs can also be helpful to underdog brands. For example, a Stove Top Stuffing television commercial asked a stay-at-home mom if she could predict her family's preferences for potatoes or stuffing. The stay-at-home mom predicted confidently that her husband, son, and daughters preferred potatoes. The narrator then asked the family which they preferred. Each family member responded, "Stuffing," much to the housewife's surprise. Surprise is a useful weapon for inducing people to challenge their beliefs. Unusual distribution channels, such as home parties (e.g., Tupperware, Mary Kay), and unusual educational approaches, such as cooking classes, wine tasting classes, and cosmetic clinics, can also disrupt the status quo, increase consumer learning, and benefit underdog brands.

Acquisition Versus Retention Strategies

OBJECTIVE 5

Managers need to think carefully about their **source of volume**, or from where future purchases of their products will come. As Figure 16.7 indicates, increased volume can come from **acquisition strategies** or **retention strategies**.[10] Acquisition strategies focus on attracting new customers, while retention strategies focus on keeping current ones. This distinction is important because acquisition strategies and retention strategies involve the use of different marketing activities. It is also difficult to forecast sales accurately without considering all sources of volume.

One way to acquire new customers is to stimulate demand for an entire category of products (e.g., green tea). Essentially, current non-users need to be educated about the benefits of a product category over the products they are currently using (e.g., green tea is healthier than coffee). However, consumer educational programs are very expensive because they require large promotion and advertising budgets. It may also be necessary to give away free samples of a product to encourage non-users to become users.

Another way to acquire new customers is to steal market share away from competitors. This approach is generally less expensive because competitors have already

FIGURE 16.7 ACQUISITION VS. RETENTION STRATEGIES

	Acquisition		Retention	
	Increase demand	**Steal share**	**Increase demand**	**Steal share**
Goal	Attract new category users	Attract new brand users	Increase consumption among current brand users	Increase consumption among multi-brand users
Product Strategy	Relative category advantage Satisfaction programs Search attributes Alignable differences	Relative brand advantage Satisfaction programs Search attributes Alignable differences	New uses Loyalty programs Experience attributes Nonalignable differences	New uses Loyalty programs Experience attributes Nonalignable differences
Promotion Strategy	Category advertising	Price advertising	Differentiation advertising	Differentiation advertising
Pricing Strategy	Trial pricing	Trial pricing	Continuity pricing	Continuity pricing
Place Strategy	Short channel	Short channel	Long channel	Long channel

absorbed the costs of consumer education and of convincing non-users to become users. Of course, one risk associated with this strategy is that competitors are likely to retaliate. Large competitors, such as Procter & Gamble and Coca-Cola, have the resources to retaliate severely. For example, Procter & Gamble's Ivory soap was the market leader for more than 100 years. When Lever 2000 launched a new soap that was very similar to Ivory, Procter & Gamble retaliated by offering deeply discounted, 11-pack bundles of Ivory soap that took buyers out of the market for several purchase cycles.

Retention strategies can also be used to build volume. One way to stimulate demand with current customers is to encourage them to use larger quantities or buy more frequently. Both goals can be achieved by selling the product in larger packages or by providing a price discount for larger packages. Typically, the more people buy, the more they consume. Anchoring can also be used to increase the number of packages that current customers purchase; claims emphasizing large numbers, such as "limit of 4 per household," "buy 12 for your freezer," or "101 uses," encourages consumers to buy larger quantities. Another way to stimulate demand is to encourage current customers to trade up. For example, satisfied customers who bought a relatively inexpensive cell phone in the past are likely to be interested in more feature-rich—and more expensive—cell phone models when it is time to purchase a new mobile phone.

Retention strategies can also be used to steal market share from competitors. For example, rather than eating the same brand of cereal every day, some consumers eat Kellogg's Corn Flakes on some days, Cheerios on others, and Kashi Good Friends on still others. Kellogg's could attempt to steal share by encouraging consumers to eat Kellogg's Corn Flakes more often and other brands less often. Of course, this strategy runs the risk of initiating competitive retaliation.

Acquisition and retention strategies influence all marketing activities by integrating each of the four Ps (product, promotion, price, place). For the acquisition/increase demand strategy, the product should be designed so it has a relative advantage over other product categories. In addition, it is useful to focus on search attributes because quality can be evaluated more readily for these as opposed to other types of attributes. It is also useful to focus on alignable attributes, or attributes that are directly comparable. For example, a car that gets 30 miles per gallon is better than another car that gets only 25 miles per gallon. The quality of alignable attributes is easy to evaluate. A similar approach should be used for the acquisition/steal share strategy, except the focus here is on individual brand differences, rather than on product category differences.

Patronage programs, such as frequent flyer rewards, are used to retain current customers.

PRNewsFoto/KeyCorp/AP Photo

For retention strategies, consumption among current users can be increased by developing new uses for the product, as Tums was able to do by promoting their product as a calcium supplement. Loyalty (patronage) programs that provide rewards for repeat purchases are also important. Examples include airline frequent flyer programs and hotel frequent user programs. Many grocery stores also provide points for purchases that accumulate and can be used for rewards. Satisfaction programs that provide excellent customer service for brands also facilitate retention. Retention strategies should also focus on experience attributes and nonalignable attributes. Current users are likely to overvalue their preferred brand's experience attributes because of confirmation bias. Also, nonalignable attributes seem unique, and current users are typically reluctant to give up a unique benefit of their preferred brand. For example, if one car brand offers rear motion detection systems and another offers heated steering wheels, it is difficult to compare these brands because these two attributes are not directly comparable.

Managers are free to choose from many different promotion and advertising strategies. For the acquisition/increase demand strategy, category advertising that highlights the benefits of an entire product category is likely to attract new users. For the acquisition/steal share strategy, price advertising is likely to convince users of other brands to switch, especially if the brands are similar in quality. For retention/increase demand and retention/steal share strategies, differentiating advertising that emphasizes the differences in quality among brands may be effective.

A large price discount on a single unit of a particular brand is referred to as **trial pricing**. The goal of trial pricing is to offer a price so low that it encourages potential new users to try the product. If they try the product and like it, they are likely to continue purchasing it even at a higher price. Trial pricing is useful for acquiring new users for a category or brand. Offering a lower price for multiple units of a product or **continuity pricing** encourages current users to continue using a brand. If they buy a large number of units at a discounted price, e.g., 11 bars of Ivory soap, these consumers will be committed to this particular brand for several purchase cycles. This is an excellent strategy for retaining current users.

Place strategies require careful planning of **channel length**, or the number of intermediaries (e.g., wholesalers, distributors, and retailers) needed to get the product from the manufacturer to the consumer. For example, Apple sells computers directly to consumers over the Internet and no intermediaries are used. This is a good example of a *short* channel. Intel, on the other hand, uses many different intermediaries to get the product to the consumer, which is an example of a *long* channel. In general, a short channel is useful for acquiring both new category users and new brand users because it is easier to educate new users when the manufacturer and the users communicate directly. A long channel is risky because consumers are more likely to encounter salespeople who may know little about the product. However, a long channel is useful for retaining existing customers. These customers are already familiar with the benefits of the product and, therefore, do not require education. On the other hand, long channels that use many different outlets (e.g., grocery stores, drug stores, Walmart, Target, etc.) facilitate product availability, which increases current users' convenience.

After identifying appropriate acquisition and retention strategies, managers need next to develop an STP—Segmentation, Targeting, and Positioning—strategy. Segmentation involves dividing the market into smaller subgroups of consumers with different needs. The premise of segmentation is that "not all consumers are alike." If consumers within a specific segment respond similarly to a brand, then the marketer is able to better satisfy their needs, rather than attempt to satisfy a broader and more diverse market with the same brand. Targeting involves choosing the appropriate segments to pursue. Marketers are advised to target segments that are easy to measure, sufficiently profitable, and accessible. Positioning involves communicating the differences and the relative advantages of one's products over competitors' offerings. Positioning should focus on the firm's unique key competencies or strengths that are lacking in other firms. Importantly, acquisition and retention strategies should drive STP strategies, rather than the other way around.

MARKETING IN ACTION
Managing Consumers as Investments

Consumers are important assets. Without consumers, there would be no profits. Many companies spend $100 million or more on consumer satisfaction programs. Is this too much or too little? What is the best way to measure the value of consumers in the long run?[12] Recent research shows that it is possible to estimate customer lifetime value (CLV) using a simple equation:

$$CLV = m \left(r \,/\, 1 + I - r \right)$$

where

m = margin or profit from a customer per quarter or year

r = retention rate

i = discount rate

C.J. Burton/Corbis

The retention rate or repurchase rate is a function of product quality, price, service, etc. For most companies, retention rates are between 60 and 90 percent. The discount rate is a function of the company's cost of capital, which depends on its risk and debt-equity structure. For most companies, discount rates are between 8 and 16 percent. This equation can be used to determine if a firm is spending too much or too little on marketing programs. It can also be used to value firms to determine if stock prices are too high or too low.

Chapter Summary

Product management involves monitoring and nurturing a product as it progresses through its life cycle. At first, managers must focus on building brand awareness. Later, promotion and advertising are used to stimulate growth. For mature products, it is important to reduce costs. Finally, during the decline phase, managers must decide whether to harvest the product or attempt to rejuvenate it.

Many managers view the reputation and image of a brand as its most important asset. Strong brand names help products through difficult times and provide unique opportunities during good times. Managers must also determine whether to reduce a product line to decrease brand cannibalization, or increase a product line through brand extensions to increase sales. In general, when consumers are brand loyal, the product line should be reduced to avoid cannibalization and diluting brand equity. When consumers are attribute loyal, firms should consider increasing their product lines to offer products that encompass all attributes under one brand name.

Acquisition strategies attempt to increase overall demand for a product category or to steal share from competing brands. Retention strategies attempt to increase consumption among current brand users or among multi-brand users. Acquisition and retention strategies influence all aspects of brand management, including product strategy, promotion strategy, pricing strategy, and place strategy.

Key Terms

entry strategy

diffusion of innovation

brand resonance

brand equity

brand extension

Young & Rubicam Brand Asset Valuator

cannibalization

confirmation bias

source of volume

acquisition

retention

brand loyalty

attribute loyalty

trial pricing

loyalty program

differentiation advertising

pricing strategy

place strategy

continuity pricing

channel length

Review and Discussion

1. Name and describe the four basic entry strategies that can influence the diffusion curve.

2. What type of entry strategy should be used to promote HDTV?

3. Think of a brand to which you are loyal. What experiences led to your brand loyalty in this case?

4. How can marketers extend the product life cycle of a worn-out product?

5. How does the Young & Rubicam Brand Asset Valuator help marketers?

6. What factors increase the likelihood of brand cannibalization?

7. How should marketers of a leading brand of coffee try to maintain their leadership position?

8. How should marketers of an underdog brand of furniture try to gain a stronger position in the marketplace?

9. What strategies should marketers use to acquire new customers?

10. What strategies should marketers use to retain old customers?

Short Application Exercises

1. Create a category advertisement, a price advertisement, and a differentiating advertisement.

2. Use the Young & Rubicam Brand Asset Valuator to evaluate the brand equity of Starbucks coffee.

3. Think of brand extensions that should be considered by KFC (fast-food restaurants), Panasonic (electronics), and Saturn (automobiles).

4. Think of strategies to increase ambiguity in the marketplace to help Disney retain its leadership position.

MANAGERIAL APPLICATION

One of the authors (FRK) had the pleasure of meeting Les Behrens, the owner of Behrens and Hitchcock, in 2008. Previously, Les Behrens had owned a restaurant, and Bob Hitchcock was an accountant. Both gave up these relatively secure jobs to make wine on top of Spring Mountain in Napa Valley. Many of their wines received high ratings from Robert Parker, the most influential wine critic of all time (he has been nicknamed the Emperor of Wine), and the label very quickly became a success. Hitchcock retired and left the partnership in 2005, and Behrens changed the name of the label to Erna Schein, after his mother. According to Parker, Erna Schein wines are "fun-filled, fruit-driven, amazingly delicious wines." [11] Annual, production is around 3,000 cases, which is quite small.

YOUR CHALLENGE:

1. What are the dangers of changing the brand name of an already successful brand?

2. What strategies can be taken to try to minimize these dangers?

3. What marketing strategies would you recommend to Mr. Behrens for acquiring new customers?

4. What marketing strategies would you recommend to Mr. Behrens for retaining old customers?

The part video is designed to expand and highlight the consumer behavior concepts in this part of the book. To view the videos, go to **http://www.cengage.com/international** and click on the student companion site link. After viewing the video, answer the following questions to test your knowledge on the part content and its application to the video case.

Online Marketing at Travelocity.com

Travelocity.com is the pioneer brand in the Internet travel business. This video case examines how the company re-energized its growth through the development of a new value proposition coupled with creative and innovative marketing tactics.

1. Think about what consumers want from online travel services providers. Develop five criteria that you think are key to satisfying customers. Compare and contrast Travelocity.com and two other online travel providers along the criteria you developed. Is Travelocity.com on the right track?

2. How could Travelocity.com take advantage the social influence heuristics discussed in Chapter 13 of the textbook? Develop a new promotional effort that leverages a social influence heuristic for Travelocity.com.

3. In the video case, Travelocity.com executives discussed the importance of co-branding with companies like Amazon.com and American Express. Develop a "piggyback" campaign for Travelocity.com that would reach you as a potential customer.

Managerial Decision Making

BIASES IN MANAGERIAL
DECISION MAKING

> **OBJECTIVES** *After studying this chapter, you will be able to . . .*

1 Understand biases resulting from attention- and memory-related constraints.

2 Understand biases relating to underprocessing.

3 Understand biases resulting from overprocessing.

SMART PEOPLE—DUMB DECISIONS

The onset of the recent global financial crisis may be rooted in some really dumb decisions by CEOs at key financial institutions such as Lehman Brothers and Merrill Lynch. Why do smart, experienced managers make really foolish decisions? Investing in the subprime mortgage market despite ominous signs that the real estate bubble was about to burst was definitely one of them. What could lead seemingly brilliant executives to make such lousy calls? Arrogance and greed are not the sole culprits. Sydney Finkelstein, of Dartmouth's Tuck School of Business and author of *Why Smart Executives Fail,* argues that managers' bad decisions are hard-wired. His book, *Think Again,* applies the complex and controversial world of neuroscience to management decision making.

Finkelstein identifies four internal biases that often lead to bad decisions: inappropriate prejudgments, inappropriate experience, self-interest, and attachments. The first two are particularly relevant to marketers. Prejudgment occurs when decision makers choose a course of action and ignore any advice or information that does not support that decision. Inappropriate experience can be summed up as "what worked before will work again," an approach that is far too common among marketing executives. It helps explain why marketers continue with the status quo in the face of ever-changing consumer needs in a global economy. For instance, Finkelstein implicates Yahoo!'s CEO as costing shareholders billions by stubbornly holding out for a better deal from suitor Microsoft, which subsequently walked away from the table. In that situation, the bias displayed by Yahoo!'s CEO was an attachment to the company he helped create.

Surprisingly, Finkelstein's advice for marketers coping with the current economic downturn is to act boldly. He implies that consumers are more willing to accept change during a crisis. This suggests that the recession is an opportunity to make hard choices that firms may have resisted heretofore.[1]

Effective managerial decision making begins with a clear understanding of consumer judgment and decision processes. After developing a clear understanding of these processes, a manager should scrutinize his or her own judgment and decision making. Although the typical manager is usually intelligent and well educated, his or her decisions are nevertheless susceptible to many common judgment and decision errors.[2] Biases affect decisions, as in the case of the recent financial crisis. This chapter describes and analyzes these biases, and Chapter 18 discusses de-biasing procedures for improving managerial judgment and decision making.

OBJECTIVE 1

Biases Resulting from Attention- and Memory-Related Constraints

Just as consumers attend to only a few things at a time, the attention spans of managers are also limited. Interestingly, consumers and managers alike are willing to acknowledge limitations in attention and memory, but are less willing to acknowledge limitations in judgment and decision making. This is ironic because attention- and memory-related constraints impart a strong influence on judgment and decision making. In fact, because attention and memory influence decision making, unbiased decision making is impossible when attention and memory are biased.

Salience and Vividness Effects

Because managers cannot attend to all available information relevant to a decision, they tend to focus on information that is interesting, attention-drawing, and easy to understand and process. For example, well-written and well-organized memos receive more attention than poorly written and poorly organized memos, regardless of the message content. At meetings, information presented in a colorful and interesting way receives more attention and weight than information presented in a dry or unappealing manner. Unfortunately, manner of presentation is unrelated to informational relevance. If highly relevant information is presented in a dry manner, it tends to be neglected. In contrast, if less relevant information is presented in an interesting manner, it tends to have a greater impact on a final decision.

Salient information stands out from its context or background. In the context of a sea of numbers, verbal information really sticks out. The same verbal information would not stand out, however, if an entire report or presentation were in the form of a narrative. In the context of a series of speakers wearing gray flannel suits, a presenter with a double-breasted aquamarine suit and multicolored tie really stands out. This same flashy presenter, however, would not stick out if all presenters were equally showy in their attire. In sum, salient information sticks out in one particular setting, but not in all possible settings.

Vivid information, on the other hand, always stands out regardless of the context or background in which it is presented.[3] Vivid information is emotionally interesting, concrete, and image-provoking and has immediate or direct implications for the decision maker.[4] Consumers' goals, hobbies, and interests determine what information is vivid to them personally. Of course, stimuli that are emotionally interesting to one individual may not be vivid to another. Thus, marketers must pay careful attention to their target markets.

Another factor that influences emotional impact and vividness is information concreteness. **Concrete information** pertains to only one particular object or issue, while abstract information is general and applies to a wide variety of objects or issues. Specific, concrete information has a much greater emotional impact than general, abstract information. A newspaper article about one poor victim's fight with cancer appears much more disturbing than an article about millions who die from cancer each year. Concrete information is also much easier to think about. It is easier to imagine the plight of one individual with cancer than the plight of millions with cancer. Emotional information has a greater impact on our decisions than abstract information. This is unfortunate in some situations. For example, one influential study showed that American voters tend to vote for the candidate who makes them feel good, even if they recognize intellectually that this candidate might make a very poor president and that the other candidate has much more to say about the issues.[5]

Information that has immediate and direct implications for the decision maker is more vivid and attention-drawing than information that has distant and indirect implications. For example, events occurring in one's own company, sales district, or market are much more vivid than events occurring in some other company, district, or market. Federal regulations, competitors' activities, and consumer preferences that affect an individual's company today are more vivid and attention-drawing than regulations, competitor's activities, and shifts in consumer preferences that will affect an individual's company sometime in the future. Similarly, short-term profits are more vivid and attention-drawing than long-term profits; consequently, many managers and investors tend to overemphasize short-term performance.

Finally, information obtained from firsthand experience is more vivid and compelling than secondhand information. Consumers and managers believe what they see and hear with their own eyes and ears more readily than what others have seen or heard. This practice is often wise because other people often simplify what they have seen and heard to tell a more comprehensible and informative story.[6] Moreover, people often exaggerate to tell a more entertaining story. It would be unwise to believe hearsay rumors that Osama bin Laden owns Snapple Beverages or that playing video games causes brain damage.[7] On the other hand, con artists and charlatans count on consumers to believe what they see and hear—otherwise their rigged demonstrations would be ineffective.

Regardless of whether information is salient or vivid, information that captures attention is likely to be stored in memory, retrieved, and have a disproportionate impact on subsequent judgments and decisions. Regrettably, salience and vividness are poor criteria for information usage because the extent to which information captures attention is often unrelated to the relevance and usefulness of that information. In other words, the most attention-drawing information is not always the most relevant.

Context Effects

Judgments pertaining to one piece of information, one object, or one particular issue are often influenced by other pieces of information, objects, or issues that happen to be present at the time of judgment. Unfortunately, these background factors often influence judgment even when they are irrelevant to the judgment task. In addition, judgments about the importance of an issue depend on other issues being considered. For example, after deciding when to hold a firm's annual picnic, deciding which print ad to run seems like a critical decision. However, after making a decision regarding the five-year strategic mission of a firm, the decision regarding a print ad seems relatively trivial. Thus, an issue can seem important or unimportant depending on the context in which it is judged.

The most common types of context effects are contrast, assimilation, and framing. A **contrast effect** is a shift in judgment *away* from a contextual reference point. Cold tap water seems warm after your hands have been exposed to the bitter cold of a midwinter's day. A $70 silk tie appears inexpensive after buying a $1,000 suit. A decision pertaining to a single product offered by a firm seems less important than a decision affecting all product offerings of a firm. Whenever two very different objects or issues are compared, judgments of the target are displaced away from the reference point.

Conversely, when two similar objects or issues are compared, judgments of the target are displaced *toward* the reference point. This type of context effect is known as an **assimilation effect**. For example, people who express opinions somewhat similar to ours are perceived to express identical opinions to our own. Consequently, we tend to agree too readily with similar others because we tend to perceive them as more similar to us than they actually are. In other words, perceived similarity tends to be greater than actual similarity, and this increases susceptibility to persuasion.

Framing effects represent shifts in judgment that occur when managers focus on different possible reference points.[8] For example, imagine that you are a hospital administrator preparing for an epidemic that, without medical intervention, is expected to kill 600 people in the local community. Your staff has developed two programs to combat the disease, and you can implement only one of these two programs. If Program A is adopted, 200 people will be *saved*. If Program B is adopted, there is a one-third probability that all 600 will be saved and a two-thirds probability that no one will be saved.

When the decision problem is framed or presented this way, most managers prefer Program A to Program B. Now consider the very same problem with a slight variation in wording. If Program A is adopted, 400 people will *die.* If Program B is adopted, there is a one-third probability that no one will die and a two-thirds probability that 600 will die. When the decision problem is framed this way, most managers prefer Program B over Program A. This is curious because the expected outcomes described by Programs A and B are identical in both scenarios. The only difference is that in the first scenario, outcomes are framed in terms of lives *saved*, but in the second scenario, outcomes are framed in terms of lives *lost.*

Why does something as trivial as the wording of a scenario produce such a large effect on decision making? Several empirical studies have shown that when outcomes are framed in terms of *gains*—such as lives saved, sales gained, or increased profits and market share—people are **risk-averse.**[9] That is, when people focus on gains and two alternative courses of action yield similar results in terms of expected utility, people prefer the sure thing over the riskier option. If a manager can *save* 200 lives for sure, then why should she take the risk of losing 600 lives? In contrast, when outcomes are described in terms of *losses*—such as lives lost, decreased sales, diminished profits, and market share—people behave in a **risk-seeking** manner.

Traditional economic theories suggest that the amount of "pain" experienced from losing $100 should be equivalent to the amount of "pleasure" experienced from winning $100, i.e., the respective positive and negative utilities should be symmetrical. However, recent research has shown that the amount of displeasure associated with losing $100 is greater than the amount of pleasure associated with winning $100.[10] In short, losses loom larger than gains and consequently create **loss aversion.** Furthermore, pleasure and displeasure increase as gains and losses increase, respectively, but displeasure increases at a much faster rate than pleasure. Consequently, decision makers are risk-averse when outcomes are framed in terms of gains and risk-seeking when outcomes are framed in terms of losses. Moreover, both gains and losses appear smaller as the distance between these relative outcomes and the reference point increases (**diminishing sensitivity**). For example, when zero serves as the reference point, the difference between $100 and $200 seems larger than the difference between $1,100 and $1,200. Similarly, the difference between a loss of $100 and a loss of $200 appears greater than the difference between a loss of $1,100 and a loss of $1,200.

Biased Assimilation

Managers' expectations frequently have a profound effect on the way they interpret events. When an event is ambiguous (i.e., when many possible interpretations exist), expectations guide interpretations. For example, imagine you are participating in a board meeting in which you offer some suggestions about an upcoming promotional campaign. Immediately after you offered these suggestions, one of your fellow participants aggressively voices several problems with your ideas. How would you interpret the behavior of this board member? Several interpretations are possible. First, he may be an aggressive individual by nature and has always behaved this way at board meetings. Second, he may have had a bad day and is in a foul mood. Third, there really are serious problems with your suggestions, and his concerns are valid. However, if you have known this person for a long time, you are likely to have well-defined expectations of his behavior based on prior experience and to use these expectations to interpret his behavior. For instance, if you expect this person to behave aggressively based on a personality trait, you interpret his behavior at this meeting simply as another of his typically aggressive displays and assume that there are no fundamental problems with your suggestions. This interpretation is known as **biased assimilation.**

Consider another scenario. In a classic example of biased assimilation, Lord and his colleagues presented "research evidence" on the effectiveness of capital punishment to subjects who already had strong opinions about the topic.[10] Attitude strength was operationalized in terms of the extremity of participants' ratings on standardized attitude scales. Half the subjects exhibited strong support for capital punishment, and half strongly opposed it. Both groups read descriptions of two studies, one supporting and one failing to support the deterrent efficacy of the death penalty. The descriptions contained detailed information about the procedures and the results of the studies. Although the results were held constant, two very different procedures that were counterbalanced across the two studies were described. For half the participants, Procedure A was paired with Study A, and Procedure B was paired with Study B. For the remaining participants, Procedure A was paired with Study B, and Procedure B was paired with Study A.

Although participants were exposed to mixed evidence, i.e., one study supported and one refuted the effectiveness of capital punishment, participants were even more confident about the validity of their initial beliefs after reading both studies. Regardless of whether Procedure A or B was used in the study that supported their initial beliefs, participants perceived the procedure as scientifically sound and viewed the study as providing important scientific evidence concerning the effectiveness of capital punishment (positive for those in support and negative for those against). Conversely, regardless of whether Procedure A or B was used in the study that contradicted their initial beliefs, subjects identified many fatal flaws in the procedure, and the study was perceived to be so poorly conducted that the results were virtually ignored.

Similarly, Lee, Acito, and Day (1987) showed MBA students two different ads and asked them to indicate which ad they thought would be more effective. After making their predictions, students received marketing research data that indicated that the ad they selected was ineffective and that the other ad was much more effective. Nevertheless, students persisted in believing that the ad they selected would actually be more effective over time. Their beliefs and expectations colored how they interpreted the research evidence and led them to ignore evidence that was inconsistent with their viewpoints.[11]

Pseudodiagnosticity

The appearance or illusion of **diagnosticity** (perceived relevance) is referred to as **pseudodiagnosticity**.[12] Managers exhibit the pseudodiagnosticity effect any time they treat nondiagnostic (irrelevant) information as if it were diagnostic (relevant). Marketers are especially likely to do this when they focus on one possible hypothesis, one possible interpretation of ambiguous evidence, or one possible categorization of a novel object to the exclusion of others. Focusing on only one possibility and ignoring other possibilities is known as **selective hypothesis testing**.[13] Selective or one-sided information search and interpretation often lead to the perception that there is strong support for a focal hypothesis or conclusion. This perception often leads to premature hypothesis confirmation, and managers come to the conclusion that they were right all along. Selective hypothesis testing causes weakly supportive evidence to appear strongly supportive, encouraging marketers to conclude that their preferred product concept, promotional campaign, distribution plan, or pricing strategy is a good one.

Information diagnosticity or relevance depends on the extent to which information supports one hypothesis over others. Unfortunately, managers often entertain only one hypothesis rather than many. Under these circumstances, the true diagnosticity or relevance of information cannot be established. Diagnosticity depends on the extent to which information implies one hypothesis over other possible hypotheses. For example, an executive for a prominent industrial firm was having lunch with a representative from a management consulting firm. The R&D division of the industrial firm had recently developed a new product, and the executive was looking for the right consulting firm to assist him in formulating an effective market entry strategy. The consultant provided data demonstrating that his firm enjoyed a 70 percent success rate with products similar to the one that the industrial firm had developed. The executive was so impressed that he hired the consultant.

Although it is true that a 70 percent success rate is impressive for a new product venture, this figure becomes considerably less awe-inspiring if other consulting firms also report a 70 percent success rate in this product category. It becomes even less impressive if the industrial firm has a record of 70 percent success rates without the assistance of consultation. Thus, although the 70 percent figure appears at first to be diagnostic, it is really not diagnostic if other courses of action produce the same outcome.

Obviously, the ability to separate relevant and irrelevant information is a very important managerial skill. Unfortunately, busy decision makers tend to focus on one hypothesis, one interpretation, one perspective, or one categorization much too intensely. Other possibilities do not draw their attention; consequently, other possibilities are easily overlooked. When this occurs, managers are susceptible to the pseudodiagnosticity effect.

Group Decision Making

Managers often make decisions in groups or committees because they believe that many heads are better than one. Presumably, multiple decision makers bring different information and perspectives to the table. In reality, however, most meetings are spent discussing information and issues already familiar to all present. Relatively little sharing of unique information takes place. This is known as the **common knowledge effect**.[14] In addition, group discussion often increases the extremity of the preferences shared by many individual group members. This is known as **group polarization**.[15] Early research suggested that group discussion increases learning about new information favoring a specific option, and as the amount of information favoring the option increases, the collective preference for this option increases.[16] However, more recent research demonstrates that negative arguments about unwanted options are much more persuasive than positive arguments about favored options.[17] As evaluations of unwanted options become less favorable during group discussion, evaluations of favored options become even more favorable.

Groupthink, or excessive conformity as the result of the illusion of group invincibility, is another danger of group decision making.[18] A powerful charismatic leader, insensitivity to information suggesting that the favored option might not be the best one, and extreme group polarization are common characteristics of groups suffering from groupthink. The best way to prevent groupthink is to frequently seek the opinion of impartial consultants who do not belong to the group and to encourage at least one group member to serve as a "devil's advocate," i.e., a person who provides strong counterarguments to the group's arguments. In addition, the leader should attempt to remain impartial and should avoid revealing his or her preferences too early in the group discussion.

Selective hypothesis testing tends to be even more extreme in group decision making than in individual decision making.[19] When only one option is considered, or when the group has a single favorite option, group members strongly prefer information consistent rather than inconsistent with the decision to choose this option. For example, managers evaluated a case study of an industrial firm that was considering investing $125 million in a developing country to relocate part of its production facility. Equally strong arguments for and against investment were presented in the case. After forming individual decisions for or against investment, the managers participated in a 10-minute discussion of the case in three-person groups. After reaching a preliminary decision, the groups were given the opportunity to obtain additional information relevant to the decision. The additional information was in the form of articles written by expert economists. Five of the articles favored the investment and five were against it. Although the groups were allowed to select all 10 articles, the groups selected more articles consistent, as opposed to inconsistent, with their preliminary decisions. This confirmation bias occurred in all groups but was more pronounced in unanimous groups. The reluctance to consider preference-inconsistent information increases group polarization and groupthink.

OBJECTIVE 2

Biases Resulting from Underprocessing

The previous section focused on judgmental biases resulting from limitations in managers' attentional and memory systems. People can attend to or recall only relatively small amounts of information at any one time. Unfortunately, people do not always attend to or recall the most diagnostic information. The previous section focused on what information is gathered or collected (because managers cannot focus on all available information at once); this section focuses on how information is used after it is gathered or collected. In particular, this section emphasizes managers' overreliance on cognitive heuristics, or strategies designed to simplify judgment and decision making. Simplifying strategies reduces the amount of cognitive effort required to reach a judgment or decision, which is called "underprocessing."[20]

Decision researchers Tversky and Kahneman[21] identified four key cognitive heuristics that people use to simplify judgment and decision making:

- Representativeness
- Availability
- Simulation
- Anchor-and-adjustment

The Representativeness Heuristic

Many decisions are based on beliefs about the likelihood of uncertain outcomes, such as the likelihood of a successful new product launch; the probability that a specific promotional program will be successful; the likelihood of arranging a satisfactory deal with suppliers; the probability that competitors will choose one course of action over another; and so on. How do managers estimate the probabilities of uncertain events? This is a difficult question to answer because decision makers are often unable to articulate exactly how they arrived at a particular prediction. Often, they say that their prediction is based simply on intuition, a hunch, or an educated guess. Nevertheless, Tversky and Kahneman were able to identify several key factors that influence intuitive prediction.

JUDGMENTS OF CATEGORY MEMBERSHIP   What is the probability that object A belongs in category B? What is the probability that process X caused outcome Y? The **representativeness heuristic** involves assessing the likelihood that A belongs to B on the basis of the extent to which A is *similar* to B. If A and B are highly similar, it seems likely that A belongs in B. If A and B are dissimilar, it appears unlikely that A belongs in B. If X and Y are highly similar, it seems probable that X caused Y. If X and Y are dissimilar, however, it appears unlikely that X caused Y. In other words, the representativeness heuristic involves judging probability on the basis of similarity.

For example, it is important to be able to predict whether consumers will categorize a new product as a fad or as an innovation capable of replacing a previous generation of products. If the new product is judged to be a fad, it will have a short life cycle (usually less than a year), and a satisfactory return on investment for such a product will be difficult to achieve. If the new product is viewed as a legitimate innovation, however, it will likely have a lengthy life cycle and require greater long-term investment. Using the representativeness heuristic, brand managers at Procter & Gamble categorized Pringles potato chips as a new innovation during the 1970s. Pringles appeared to be very similar to other successful innovations: It looked different from other products in the snack foods category; it was preferred over other brands in taste tests; and it had a long shelf life and complemented soft drinks and beer, and so on. After one year, however, market results indicated that Pringles was just a fad, and Procter & Gamble failed to recoup its extremely high initial investment in the product. Ironically, Pringles re-emerged as a dominant competitor in 1996 as a fat-free snack made with Olean.

CAUSAL JUDGMENTS   The representativeness heuristic influences causal judgments as well as judgments of category membership. It seems likely that process X caused outcome Y if X and Y are highly similar. Conversely, it appears unlikely that process X caused outcome Y if X and Y are dissimilar. For example, if process X is an expensive promotional campaign and outcome Y is large revenues, then X and Y resemble each other in the sense that both involve large amounts of money. So, on the basis of the representativeness heuristic, large causes are expected to produce large effects. However, although the representativeness heuristic often leads to accurate and useful predictions, whenever managers rely too heavily on a heuristic, they run the risk of overlooking something important. Imagine the difficulty Louis Pasteur had convincing people that invisible germs (a very small cause) produce disease, death, and epidemics (very large effects)!

Underprocessing leads managers to overlook things such as the prior probability or base rate of an outcome. A new product may have all the appearances of quality and success but it will still fail if the base rate or incidence of success in the product category is very low. Sample size is also neglected when managers rely too heavily on the representativeness heuristic. Extreme judgments are formed on the basis of a few observations, even though a large database is needed for accurate prediction. Misconceptions of chance are also likely when people rely heavily on the representativeness heuristic. After several new product failures, a marketer may believe that he or she is "due" for a success (the gambler's fallacy) because chance is expected to involve a mix of successes and failures (not just failures). Of course, this is true only in the very long run when an extremely large sample is examined and only if the marketer in question possesses at least average skills and judgment.

QUALITY OF INFORMATION Mangers also overlook the quality of the information they use as a basis for their decisions when they rely too heavily on the representativeness heuristic. Information quality is determined by two factors: reliability (repeatability) and validity (accuracy in measurement). If a competitor's prices for a given product offering remain fairly stable over time, and if a marketer learns that the competitor's current retail price is $25.99, this information is reliable and useful. On the other hand, if another competitor's prices fluctuate dramatically over time, and a marketer learns that this competitor's current retail price is $25.99, this information is unreliable and not particularly useful. Information validity refers to the extent to which information is associated with one and only one concept. For example, if a marketer learns for certain that a competitor's list price is $25.99, then this information can be valid and useful. However, if it is unclear whether the $25.99 represents the list price, a list price minus the retailer's discount, or a manufacturer's suggested retail price, then the $25.99 is not very informative. It would be much more useful to know the exact breakdown of prices.

NONREGRESSIVENESS Finally, intuitive judgments based on the representativeness heuristic tend to be nonregressive. That is, when managers rely too heavily on representativeness, they overlook the fact that extreme events tend to shift toward the mean (statistical average) on subsequent occasions. For example, when one employee performs extremely well on one occasion, her supervisors tend to expect too much from her in the future. The employee's performance on one occasion may have been artificially inflated because of many random events. Perhaps the employee was in a particularly good mood, slept well the night before, or stumbled on information that turned out to be extremely useful. Subsequently, the employee will not perform as well because she is unlikely to accrue so many fortuitous events. Conversely, when an employee performs extremely poorly on one occasion, this employee tends to perform more satisfactorily on subsequent occasions. Perhaps on the first occasion the employee was in a bad mood, lacked sleep, was unable to obtain the right information, and so on. Similarly, a product that breaks sales records in its first year because of favorable external conditions or chance factors typically performs less impressively in subsequent years. A product that performs poorly during its first year (because of external factors) typically performs better in subsequent years. Unfortunately, the second product is often withdrawn from the marketplace prior to regressing toward its mean performance. In sum, extremely good or bad performances tend to be artificially high or low as a result of exogenous events or unusual circumstances that are not likely to be repeated.

It is extremely difficult to learn the true relationship between events when random events are confused with nonrandom events. For example, Tversky and Kahneman (1974) found that Israeli Air Force pilots observed that trainees frequently performed better following a punishment and frequently performed worse after a reward was delivered. The officers concluded that punishment was effective but rewards were ineffective. However, they overlooked the fact that extremely bad or good performances are likely to be influenced heavily by chance factors. All trainees have their bad days and their good days; in the long run, people typically perform at their mean level of performance, rather than extremely good or extremely bad. Consequently, an extremely poor performance is likely to be followed by a more typical performance, which is better than an extremely poor performance (regression to the mean). An outstanding performance is likely to be followed by a more typical performance, which is worse than an outstanding performance. Because poor performances are punished and outstanding performances are rewarded, regression to the mean creates the illusion that punishment is effective and reward is ineffective. In reality, however, both are effective in raising trainees' mean performance levels over time.[22]

Similarly, Cox and Summers (1987) found that industrial buyers underestimate the influence of random factors on sales. Stores that experience extremely low sales in one sales period typically perform better in the next sales period. Stores that experience extremely high sales in one sales period typically perform worse in the next sales period. This is because extreme and atypical outcomes are likely to be followed by more moderate and typical outcomes. One of the main responsibilities of industrial buyers is to produce accurate sales forecasts to help store managers control inventory costs. When random fluctuations in sales are misinterpreted as meaningful, extreme predictions, overordering for successful stores, and underordering for unsuccessful stores result.[23]

The Availability Heuristic

Managers' predictions are also influenced by the **availability heuristic**. This heuristic involves searching memory for relevant examples of the event one is trying to predict and basing that prediction on the ease with which these examples come to mind. If examples come to mind quickly and easily, the event seems highly likely to occur. However, if examples do not come to mind readily, then the event seems highly unlikely to occur. For instance, suppose a homeowner is trying to predict the likelihood that an earthquake will damage his home. If he easily remembers earthquakes that occurred in the past, he will predict that future earthquakes are likely to occur. If he does not recall any earthquakes, he will predict that future earthquakes are unlikely. Of course, the cost of earthquake insurance will be much higher if earthquakes are expected in an area as opposed to their being unexpected.

However, memory for earthquakes is influenced by many factors besides objective frequency. Earthquakes are highly publicized by the media; consequently, earthquakes are very memorable. This makes earthquakes seem more likely to occur than is actually the case. Even in the San Francisco Bay Area of California, homes are more likely to be damaged by fire than by earthquakes. However, outside California, people are more likely to see San Francisco Bay Area earthquakes reported in the media than Bay Area fires. Moreover, events that occurred recently are much more memorable than events that occurred long ago, and events that occurred nearby are more memorable than events that occurred far away. Memory is influenced by many factors; consequently, basing predictions on memory can lead to highly erroneous predictions. It is better to base one's predictions on carefully recorded facts, which is why most insurance companies rely on actuarial data rather than on memory to price policies.

The Simulation Heuristic

Just as a single event that is easy to retrieve from memory seems very likely to occur again (the availability heuristic), a single event or sequence of events that is easy to imagine (or to simulate) also seems very likely to occur, according to the **simulation heuristic**. Simply imagining the occurrence of a hypothetical event increases the perceived likelihood of the event. Consumers who are asked to imagine using and enjoying cable television believe they are more likely to actually subscribe to cable television.[24]

Voters who are asked to imagine a particular political candidate winning an election believe that the candidate is actually more likely to win.[25] Sports fans who are asked to imagine one team winning believe that the team is actually more likely to win.[26] People who are asked to imagine contracting a disease believe that they are actually more likely to contract the disease.[27] Virtually any event seems more likely after one imagines its occurrence ("I can see that happening"). An event that is difficult to imagine, however, does not seem more likely after one attempts (and fails) to imagine its occurrence ("I can't see that happening").[28] Thus, imagining appears to make it so, even when what consumers imagine is not closely linked to reality.

In the same vein, imagining the occurrence of a complex sequence of events—a scenario—makes this sequence of events seem more likely. The finding that an imagined sequence of events seems more likely is known as the *scenario effect*.[29] When managers are asked how likely it is that a new product that sells very poorly in its first year will become the market leader by the end of its second year, most respond that this scenario is not likely. But consider a second scenario: How likely is it that a new product will sell poorly in its first year, be acquired by a larger firm with greater resources, be redesigned and marketed more effectively, and, finally, become the market leader by the end of its second year? The second scenario seems much more likely than the first, even though in reality, it is less probable.

The second scenario is more likely simply because it includes the first scenario, along with many other possible scenarios to turn the failing product around. The outcome, "becomes the market leader by the end of its second year," includes the sequence "will be acquired by a larger and more successful firm that redesigns the product, markets it more effectively, and turns it into the market leader by the end of its second year," and many other possible sequences as well. One specific sequence cannot be more likely than any one of many possible different specified and unspecified sequences.

Even if each of the individual events described in the second scenario is quite likely, the probability of their joint occurrence is surprisingly low. Suppose, for example, that the likelihood of each individual event in the sequence is 80 percent. That is, the probability of failure in the first year is 0.80, the probability of acquisition is 0.80, the probability of redesign is 0.80, the probability of developing a more effective marketing plan is 0.80, and the probability of becoming the market leader is 0.80. Subjectively, the likelihood of this particular scenario seems like it should be a little less than 0.80. Objectively, the likelihood of this particular scenario is $0.80 \times 0.80 \times 0.80 \times 0.80 \times 0.80 = 0.33$. Just as managers' imaginations make it seem that a single event is more likely to occur, their imaginations also make it seem that a complex sequence of events is more likely to occur. Managers recognize that imagination allows them to depart from reality, but they fail to realize how far these departures really are. This leads to poor predictions when they imagine the occurrence of a single event and even poorer predictions when they attempt to predict by imagining that a complex sequence of events will happen.

The Anchoring-and-Adjustment Heuristic

Probability estimates or predictions can be based on many different types of information, such as the degree of similarity between a causal factor and the target event (the representativeness heuristic), how easily examples of the target event can be retrieved from memory (the availability heuristic), and how easily the target event can be imagined to occur (the simulation heuristic). Often, however, a situation is so ambiguous that the manager does not know where to begin when attempting to make a prediction.

In these cases, even random anchors, or "starting points," can influence him or her. This phenomenon is known as the **anchoring-and-adjustment heuristic**.

For example, suppose a manager is interested in introducing a product popular in the United States to an international market. The manager is responsible for one specific international market, the African market. However, he or she recognizes that the product is inappropriate for all African nations and believes that the safest strategy is to introduce the product to only African nations belonging to the United Nations (UN). Most managers do not know how many or which African nations belong to the UN. However, if they are given an anchor, or a "starting point," they can usually guess whether the actual number is greater or smaller than the starting point. Tversky and Kahneman (1974) presented subjects with a spinning wheel with numbers ranging from 1 to 100; the wheel was rigged to stop at either a high (65) or a low (10) number. Although the subjects thought that the wheel was random, the high and low starting points had a profound effect on their estimates. In the high-starting-point (65) condition, subjects guessed that the actual percent was slightly lower, but their average estimate was that 45 percent of African nations belong to the UN. In the low-starting-point (10) condition, subjects guessed that the actual percent was somewhat higher, but their average estimate was only 25 percent. In both conditions, subjects' estimates were too close to the initial anchor. That is, their adjustments from the initial anchor were insufficient (underadjustment). Consequently, subjects in the high-starting-point condition overestimated the percent of African nations belonging to the UN, while subjects in the low-starting-point condition underestimated the percent of African nations belonging to the UN (the correct answer is 35 percent).[30]

Even expert decision makers are strongly influenced by anchors, or initial estimates. In an important study, expert real estate agents were asked to estimate the value of a house. Even though the agents spent several hours examining the same house, their final estimates were remarkably close to the anchor list price that was provided to them by the experimenter. The agents who randomly received a low list price seriously undervalued the house, while agents who were given a high list price significantly overvalued the house.[31]

Anchoring and adjustment is also involved in evaluating a risky decision, or a gamble. A gamble has two components: an outcome (e.g., the amount of money potentially available) and a probability (i.e., the likelihood of obtaining the outcome). For example, suppose Gamble A has an 11/36 probability of winning $16 and a 25/36 probability of losing $1.50, while Gamble B has a 35/36 probability of winning $4 and a 1/36 probability of losing $1 (the expected values of both gambles are about $3.85). When asked to indicate a "selling price" for each gamble (i.e., the amount of money they would charge others to play each gamble), most subjects focus on the outcomes and charge more for Gamble A because it has a greater outcome. However, when asked to indicate which gamble they themselves would prefer to play, most subjects anchor on the probabilities and choose Gamble B because the likelihood of winning is greater.[32] This is known as a **preference reversal**, because subjects prefer one gamble when they anchor on outcomes but another gamble when they anchor on probabilities.

This phenomenon is inconsistent with **subjective expected utility theory**, which suggests that preferences are stable and that people should always choose the gamble with the maximum expected utility.[33] Although managers do not like to think of their alternative courses of action as gambles, an option is always linked to an outcome that can be achieved with some probability of success—which is the definition of a gamble. For example, product managers must decide which new product concepts (or ideas) should be launched and which should be abandoned.

These decisions should be based on estimates of the probability of success for each new product concept and on estimates of profit potential if a particular new product concept is successful. In one study, subjects were asked to choose between pairs of new product concepts where one concept had a greater probability of success and the other concept had greater profit potential.[34] When subjects were asked to indicate which option of each pair of options should be launched, they preferred the options with the greater probability of success. By contrast, when subjects were asked to assign dollar values to each option of each pair of options, they preferred the options with the greater profit potential. This pattern of response suggests that managers anchor on probabilities when deciding whether to launch or abandon a new product concept. However, they anchor on profit potential when assessing the value of a new product concept. Focusing on different anchors in different situations leads to inconsistent preferences.

How serious is the problem of preference reversal? Consider the decision faced regularly by oil company executives. Any given drilling site has some probability of success and some level of profit potential if oil is found. Kerr (1979) found that oil companies paid more than $1 billion for the privilege of drilling in the Baltimore Canyon in the Atlantic Ocean, even though leading oil geochemists determined that the probability of finding oil there was extremely low. Kerr (1979) suggested that oil company executives focused on the extremely large size of potential trapping structures in the Baltimore Canyon (profit potential) and neglected the probabilities provided by the geochemists.[35] Ideally, of course, billion-dollar decisions should be based on *both* probabilities and potential.

OBJECTIVE 3

Biases Resulting from Overprocessing

Busy decision makers are often unmotivated or unable to consider each and every piece of information that appears relevant to a particular judgment or decision. Under these circumstances, a relatively small sample of information is considered and cognitive heuristics are used to simplify judgment and decision making. Of course, "underprocessing" leads to poor decisions when key pieces of information are overlooked or when the implications of information are not carefully considered. Ironically, "overprocessing" can also lead to poor decisions. When decision makers are motivated and able to consider large amounts of information very carefully, they may read too much into irrelevant information. When irrelevant information is overinterpreted, it may seem relevant. Consequently, overprocessing may result in overuse of irrelevant evidence.

Correspondence Bias

Managers are often unable to express their true opinions about a job-related topic because, in most firms, strong situational pressures exist that prevent managers from expressing them. Written and unwritten rules exert a powerful influence on managers. When situational constraints or norms (i.e., social rules) require people to behave a certain way, norm-consistent behaviors provide little or no information about personal dispositions (personality characteristics and personal opinions). Nevertheless, managers tend to overinterpret the behavior of other individuals and, consequently, tend to draw strong inferences based on weak evidence. This phenomenon is known as the **correspondence bias** because observable behaviors are perceived to correspond closely with unobservable dispositions (personality traits, personal opinions) even when the behaviors are actually influenced only by a situation.[36]

Consider the job interview, for example. Job applicants are not free to behave as they typically behave. Instead, most job applicants form impressions about the traits and characteristics required to perform a particular job effectively (e.g., salespeople are supposed to be gregarious; market researchers are supposed to be analytical; brand managers are supposed to be confident, etc.). Consequently, during the job interview, applicants tend to behave in a manner that implies that they possess these traits and characteristics. The interview situation imposes powerful constraints on the behavior of job applicants; consequently, normative behaviors are uninformative (of course, counternormative behaviors, such as showing up at the interview in dirty jeans, are very informative). Nonetheless, most interviewers believe that they can learn a lot about the dispositions of most interviewees on the basis of situation-constrained behaviors.

Situational constraints force brand managers to emit an air of confidence. This is necessary, of course, because their assistants work much harder if they believe their brands are likely to be successful (if success is impossible, why work hard?). However, executives who observe the confident behaviors of their brand managers are likely to infer that the brand managers really believe their brands will succeed. This inference is incorrect because their confident behavior is actually determined by the situation, not by the managers' beliefs. However, if an executive infers that a brand manager really believes a brand will succeed and the brand fails, the executive may conclude that the brand manager exhibited overconfidence and poor judgment. This conclusion is likely to influence the executive's performance evaluation of the brand manager.

Using Irrelevant Analogies

Often people we meet remind us of old acquaintances because their looks, speech, clothing, or mannerisms are similar. When this happens, we often infer that two people who appear to be similar on some irrelevant dimension are also likely to possess similar traits and characteristics.[37] For example, an interviewer may feel reluctant to hire a particular job candidate because the candidate is from the same hometown as a previous employee who was extremely unsuccessful. A brand manager may decide to launch a new product that performs poorly in pretest markets because it reminds him or her of another similarly packaged product that performed poorly in pretest markets but nevertheless turned out to be successful. An executive may decide to engage in a price war with an aggressive competitor because the competitor reminds him or her of a previous competitor with a similar corporate name that was driven out of business by a price war. Although focusing on similarities and reasoning by analogy can be useful analytic strategy, reasoning based on irrelevant analogies can lead to poor decisions.

The Perseverance Effect

Decision makers often continue to perceive a belief as true even when the basis for the belief is disproved. In the classic study on the **perseverance effect**, subjects received false feedback bearing on their performance on a judgment task.[38] Half the subjects were told they performed extremely well on the task (success condition), and half were told they performed extremely poorly (failure condition). Subjects were randomly assigned to success or failure conditions; consequently, performance feedback was unrelated to actual performance. Later, subjects were told that the feedback was false and that they were randomly assigned to experimental conditions. The results indicated that even though subjects recognized that the feedback was false, those who were randomly assigned to success condition continued to believe that they would perform well on this task in the future, and those who were randomly assigned to the failure condition continued to believe that they would perform poorly. Ross et al. (1975) suggest a that random feedback is uninformative and should be ignored. Nevertheless, people tend to overinterpret uninformative feedback and generate explanations for the feedback (e.g., "I'm the type of person who would do well on this type of judgment task"). Subsequently, if the feedback is eliminated but the explanations for the feedback are not eliminated, the explanations continue to provide support for the original belief. As a result, the belief is remarkably persistent even when the basis for the belief is removed.[38]

Unfortunately, the perseverance effect applies to any belief the decision maker may form, even erroneous ones. For example, a brand manager who worked with an ad agency to develop a novel advertising execution observed that sales increased dramatically after the ad was launched (success feedback). The brand manager concluded that this type of advertising execution is extremely effective. A good brand manager tries to understand why an ad is effective, and usually comes up with a number of reasons it was so successful. Of course, many factors influence sales, and advertising is just one factor. In this particular case, the increase in sales was actually indirectly caused by a distribution problem that affected a major competitor at the time the ad was launched; the ad itself was completely ineffective. Nevertheless, the brand manager continued to believe the ad execution was effective and planned to use this execution in future ad campaigns. Of course, by that time, he or she might have been fired for running ineffective ads in the face of skyrocketing media costs.

The Dilution Effect

The judgmental impact of diagnostic information is often diluted by the presence of nondiagnostic information.[39] This is known as the **dilution effect**. For example, subjects told that John had an extremely high grade point average (GPA) predicted that John would continue to earn extremely high grades in future courses. However, subjects told that John had an extremely high GPA, drove a Honda, wore plaid shirts, and used to work part-time as a draftsman predicted that John would earn moderately high grades in future courses.[40] In other words, irrelevant information (e.g., car driven, clothing style, prior work experience) reduces the effect of relevant information (e.g., extremely high GPA), and less extreme inferences are formed when irrelevant information is present (versus absent). Moreover, the dilution effect is even more pronounced when subjects expect to justify their predictions to others.[41] Although irrelevant information should have no effect on judgment, managers tend to overinterpret, read too much between the lines, and weigh irrelevant information too heavily in judgment, especially when they are likely to overprocess all available information (including irrelevant information) because they expect to justify their judgments and decisions to superiors.

Premature Cognitive Commitment

Irrelevant information also carries too much weight in judgment when it later becomes relevant.[42] For example, consumers are often exposed to ads for products that they would not consider purchasing. The information provided in these ads is likely to be accepted at face value, because consumers are unlikely to think extensively about irrelevant products. Consequently, even conclusions supported by weak arguments are likely to be encoded incidentally into long-term memory. Later, when consumers' attitudes, hobbies, needs, or interests change, prior beliefs are likely to be weighed heavily in judgment even if these were based originally on weak evidence. For instance, children are exposed to many automobile ads. Although they are not old enough to purchase an automobile, much of the information presented in the ads is likely to be accepted uncritically with little or no counterargument. Years later, when children grow up and need to decide which brand of automobile they should purchase, they may be influenced unduly by prior beliefs formed on the basis of weak evidence that was accepted uncritically. Of course, **premature cognitive commitment** is not limited to children. Anyone who pursues a new hobby or a new interest is susceptible to the effects of prior beliefs that were formed on the basis of information that was accepted uncritically with little thought or elaboration.

Overcorrection

The use of the anchoring-and-adjustment heuristic results in insufficient adjustment from an anchor or reference point. However, if managers recognize that an anchor can bias their judgments, they are likely to attempt to correct for the bias, and overadjustment, or **overcorrection**, can occur.[43] For example, suppose an interviewer happens to be in an especially good mood one day. If the interviewer fails to recognize that this good mood might cause him to form overly favorable first impressions of job candidates, the final evaluations of these candidates are likely to be adjusted insufficiently from the first impression anchor. As a result, the candidates will be judged too favorably (an assimilation effect). However, if an interviewer recognizes and attempts to correct for the biasing effects of positive mood on judgment, he is likely to overcorrect. As a result, the final evaluations are likely to be overadjusted, and the candidates will be judged too unfavorably (a contrast effect). Overcorrection occurs when managers overanalyze and overinterpret their decision-making processes.

Chapter Summary

Executives, managers, and decision makers are susceptible to a relatively lengthy list of judgmental biases. Some of these biases stem from attention and memory constraints. People are unable to attend to or remember all judgment-relevant information. Unfortunately, the risk of inaccurate judgment and suboptimal decision making exists whenever relevant information is overlooked or neglected. Underprocessing bias results when managers are unmotivated or unable to integrate judgment-relevant information in a systematic fashion. Under these circumstances, managers rely too heavily on cognitive heuristics, or shortcuts, that simplify judgment and decision making. By contrast, overprocessing bias results when managers overinterpret irrelevant information. Thus, judgmental accuracy is influenced jointly by the amount of processing effort a decision maker is likely to allocate to a judgment task and by the nature of the evidence available for judgment (e.g., the amount of relevant and irrelevant information present). Fortunately, decision researchers have extensively researched the psychological processes involved in judgment and decision making. One result of this deeper understanding is the development of debiasing procedures and decision aids that dramatically improve judgment and decision making.

Key Terms

salient information

vivid information

concrete information

contrast effect

assimilation effect

framing effects

risk-averse

risk-seeking

loss aversion

diminishing sensitivity

biased assimilation

diagnosticity

pseudodiagnosticity

selective hypothesis testing

group decision making

common knowledge effect

group polarization

groupthink

representativeness heuristic

availability heuristic

simulation heuristic

anchoring-and-adjustment heuristic

preference reversal

subjective expected utility theory

correspondence bias

perseverance effect

dilution effect

premature cognitive commitment

overcorrection

Review and Discussion

1. In what ways do salience and vividness affect managers' decisions? Are these good criteria for managerial decisions? Why or why not?

2. After a couple decides to get married, deciding where to eat dinner that night seems minor. What type of effect does this situation illustrate? Give three other examples illustrating this effect.

3. Imagine that your best friend is assigned an end-of-term project that includes a written report as well as an oral presentation. Without naming names, predict how you think your friend would handle the project. Would he or she begin early? Do a lot of research? Wait until the last minute to begin the project? Ask the instructor for an extension? Do as little work as possible? Try an innovative approach? Ask friends for help? On what information did you base your prediction? What type of bias effect does this exercise illustrate?

4. Name and describe briefly the four key cognitive heuristics that people use to simplify judgment making.

5. How might managers in industries like financial services, insurance, and healthcare use the availability heuristic to make decisions?

6. How might the simulation heuristic help or hinder the success of a new product?

7. What do you think is the single most common reason that managers engage in underprocessing?

8. Why do personal interviews sometimes provide unreliable information?

9. Describe an instance in which you made a decision based on an irrelevant analogy.

10. How might premature cognitive commitment come into play when a person is promoted from a staff position to a managerial position?

STRATEGIES FOR IMPROVING MANAGERIAL DECISION MAKING

OBJECTIVES   *After studying this chapter, you will be able to . . .*

1 | Understand decision frame management.

2 | Define epistemic unfreezing.

3 | Determine how to increase predictive accuracy via defining the base rate, assessing the reliability and validity of

information, distinguishing between convergence and redundancy, resisting scenario thinking, and avoiding overconfidence.

4 | Define judgment updating and revision.

LEVI STRAUSS & CO.

It's hard to imagine a world without jeans—straight leg, boot cut, flared, stretch. Levi's have been with us for more than 130 years, ever since German-born dry goods wholesaler Levi Strauss was approached by a Nevada tailor named Jacob Davis. Davis had an idea for work pants with pockets reinforced by metal rivets, but he needed $68 to file a patent for the idea. Strauss came up with the money, and together, the two produced the first pair of "waist-high overalls."

Since then, millions of pairs of jeans have left the Levi's factory, involving thousands of managerial decisions. Some of those decisions have involved product development—for instance, the creation of entire product lines such as women's wear and Dockers. Some have involved social responsibility, as when Levi's discovered that two of its sewing contractors in Bangladesh were using child labor: Levi's chose to remove the children from the factories but continued to pay their wages as long as they attended school. Some have involved the entire structure of the company, as was the case recently when top managers announced sweeping changes that included requiring employees to resign and reapply for jobs.

Many of Levi's decisions have been in response to customer preferences and complaints. Prior to reengineering, Thomas M. Kasten, Levi's vice president and member of the company's U.S. Leadership Team, listened to customers tell him, "We trust many of your competitors implicitly. We sample their deliveries. We open all Levi's deliveries. Your lead times are the worst. If you weren't Levi's, you'd be gone." Clearly, change was necessary. The multibillion-dollar company was a leader in its field, but it had become overconfident. Well known for its attention to ethics, its humane treatment of workers, and its brand name, Levi's was failing terribly at satisfying its channel members.

So management embarked on an incredibly ambitious effort to reengineer the company—but perhaps, it was too ambitious. The cost of the program topped $850 million; employees were thrown into a state of chaos about their job security; and the timeline for completion of these changes extended much longer than intended by its planners. Goals were unclear, yet the money flowed because the company had enjoyed such solid success for so long. Board member Warren Hellman recalls, "[We had the atmosphere of] 'Well, we've got a lot of cash, the business is doing wonderfully, we can spend our way through this thing.' We were too casual at the outset." Eventually, Thomas Kasten admitted, "It became clear to us that what we were trying to achieve was not doable."

The results were traumatic, including a leveraged buyout and a round of layoffs. But Levi's is still in business. In 2008, Levi's generated more than $4.4 billion in net revenue, a one percent increase over 2007. Few people doubt that Levi's will be around for another 100 years.[1]

As you read this chapter, consider carefully the consequences that managers face when they try to make predictions about outcomes without using systematic strategies.

OBJECTIVE 1 # Decision Frame Management

Managers and consumers are susceptible to a wide variety of judgment and decision-making biases and errors. Busy decision makers tend to consider a small amount of information but often fail to consider the quality of that information or the strength of readily available evidence. Managers with tight deadlines tend to use heuristics that cause them to overlook important pieces of information (underprocessing). Conversely, managers allocating large amounts of time and effort to important business decisions tend to use too much information and to overinterpret and overweigh irrelevant or tangentially relevant data (overprocessing). Fortunately, scientific research has increased our understanding of these problems and has led to the development of debiasing techniques to help managers make better judgments and decisions.

The first step in decision making is to consider how a decision problem should be framed or interpreted, a process known as **decision frame management**. What are the costs and benefits associated with each option? Decision makers sometimes consider only one option and as a result, run into trouble right from the start. Statistically, the more options considered, the greater is the chance of finding an optimal solution. Focusing narrowly on only one or two options often leads managers to overlook many important alternatives. Moreover, as research on the framing effect has shown, once the options have been identified, managers tend to focus mainly on costs (losses) *or* benefits (gains). Ideally, managers should weigh costs and benefits equally because the asymmetric treatment of costs and benefits often leads to regretful decisions. This occurs because focusing mainly on costs leads decision makers to behave in a risk-seeking manner, preferring options that offer a chance of avoiding losses even if that chance is fairly slim. Conversely, focusing mainly on benefits leads decision makers to act risk-averse, accepting options that virtually guarantee a good outcome, even though riskier options may provide even better outcomes. If decision makers focus mainly on costs initially, they are likely to choose a risky option. If they later focus on benefits, they may wish they had chosen a less risky option and regret their earlier decision. Preference reversals are much less likely to occur when decision makers routinely treat costs and benefits as equally important.

A classic case of decision frame mismanagement occurred in the early 1970s when the U.S. automobile industry exhibited frame blindness while the Japanese automobile industry developed innovative new solutions to old production problems.[2] The U.S. automobile industry continued to use an operations research frame or perspective, but the Japanese automobile industry was open to new frames and new perspectives. The operations research perspective suggests that the best way to control product costs is to produce many units of the same component (or set of components) before resetting the plant equipment to produce a different component. So, thousands of units would be produced before the equipment was re-tooled to make different types of components.

In Japan, instead of blindly accepting this assumption, engineers developed a way to reset plant equipment in a matter of minutes (rather than hours). This innovation allowed the Japanese to offer a greater variety of automobile models while still controlling costs and quality. This led to the downturn of the once seemingly invincible U.S. automobile industry. Thirty years later, the U.S. automotive industry again suffered from decision frame mismanagement. Facing substantial increases in gasoline prices starting in 2003, consumers purchased fewer and fewer vehicles with poor fuel economy such as pickup trucks and sport utility vehicles (SUVs). Because of these larger vehicles' relatively higher profit margins, they were the focus of the American auto industry at the time. As consumers searched for more fuel-efficient models, sales of U.S. trucks and SUVs decreased, and consumers purchased larger numbers of smaller, fuel-efficient vehicles from foreign automakers.

Frames, perspectives, and assumptions should be questioned frequently, and decision makers should be willing to consider a wide range of frames, perspectives, and options. Moreover, managers should carefully consider the costs *and* benefits of each decision option and avoid focusing too heavily on costs *or* benefits separately. Focusing too heavily on one or the other can lead to decisions that managers later regret when they consider it from a different perspective.

OBJECTIVE 2

Epistemic Unfreezing

Decision makers must frequently make a difficult trade-off between decision speed and decision accuracy. Some problems demand immediate action. Other problems do not, which affords managers the opportunity to think about the problem more carefully for a longer period of time. Quick decisions run the risk of serving as mere "band-aids," or temporary and partial solutions to a problem. Long periods of deliberation usually result in better decisions. How do managers make this difficult trade-off between speed and accuracy (or quality) of a decision? Recent research based on Kruglanski's[3] **theory of lay epistemology** (or theory of everyday knowledge formation and use) suggests that individuals differ in how they exhibit the **need for cognitive closure** and that situations differ in the extent to which they elicit this need. The need for cognitive closure is a desire for definite knowledge—any knowledge, rather than confusion or ambiguity. As the need for cognitive closure increases, people consider fewer alternatives; consider smaller amounts of information about each alternative; make snap conclusions that have obvious and immediate implications for action; are insensitive to evidence inconsistent with these conclusions; and exhibit high levels of confidence in their conclusions, decisions, and actions.

In short, the need for cognitive closure promotes **epistemic seizing** and **epistemic freezing**. *Seizing* refers to the tendency to attain closure quickly, even if this means oversimplifying an issue or failing to carefully consider all its ramifications. *Freezing* refers to the tendency to maintain closure as long as possible, even if this means being closed-minded or unwilling to consider alternatives. People differ in their need for closure; some are strongly motivated to reach conclusions quickly at the risk of overlooking important qualifiers and limiting conditions; others are willing to deliberate carefully for a long period of time at the risk of appearing to be indecisive or lack confidence. Situations also differ in the extent to which they increase or decrease the need for closure. Deadlines and time pressures increase the motivation to attain closure quickly. Concerns about accuracy and the long-term consequences of one's actions decrease the motivation to attain closure quickly.

Many firms try to hire decisive and confident people. Moreover, deadlines and severe time pressures are part of everyday life in the business environment. For example, Procter & Gamble and a number of other firms have a rule that all memos must be limited to one page. This rule forces managers to oversimplify issues, sweep complexities and ambiguities under a rug, and focus on a single clear course of action. It also forces managers to be "one-armed" psychologists and economists, i.e., only one possible scenario is offered, and managers are not allowed to waver by saying, "On the other hand. . . ." Of course, the dangers of oversimplifying and jumping to conclusions include overlooking important information (including information inconsistent with a conclusion); overlooking important alternative courses of action (opportunity costs); and failing to develop contingency plans and safety measures to guard against potentially bad decisions.

Fortunately, many firms also require their managers to justify and explain their judgments and decisions to their superiors. This sort of accountability works in one of two ways: First, it can pressure managers to adopt the perspective of a senior executive when his or her perspective is known. Second, it can motivate managers to think in more integratively complex ways about an issue when the senior officer's perspective is unknown.[4] Simply adopting the perspective of the senior executive is potentially dangerous if this perspective is biased or limited in some way. A safer strategy is for the senior executive to hide his or her personal preferences and biases in order to force managers to think in more integratively complex ways. **Integrative complexity** means considering a wider range of options and the implications of greater amounts of information pertaining to each option. For example, marketing managers should not consider just one positioning strategy; they should consider many (e.g., positioning by attributes/benefits, price, use, user; repositioning). They should not consider just one segmentation strategy; they should consider many (e.g., segmentation by geography, demography, psychographics, or behaviors). Marketers should consider many different new product concepts or ideas, many different pricing strategies, many different promotion and advertising strategies, and many different distribution strategies. Unseizing, unfreezing, and considering a wider range of possibilities generally improve managerial judgment and decision making.

OBJECTIVE 3

Increasing Predictive Accuracy

A critically important element of any decision is predicting what will happen if one option is selected instead of another. Unfortunately, extensive research shows that people are not very good at predicting the future.[5] Frequently, predictions are overly optimistic. For example, British Columbia agreed to join Canada in 1871 on the condition that the Canadian government would complete production of the transcontinental railroad by 1881.[6] This project was not completed until 1885. In 1969, the mayor of Montreal predicted that the 1976 Olympics in that city would feature a new state-of-the-art stadium with the first retractable roof. The mayor also predicted that the entire Olympic exhibition would cost $120 million and "can no more have a deficit than a man can have a baby."[7] The stadium was actually completed in 1989, 13 years *after* the Montreal Olympics, and the roof alone cost $120 million. More recently, it was predicted that the Eurotunnel, connecting Paris and London, would be completed in 1993 at a cost of about $7 billion; it was actually completed more than a year later at a cost of more than $15 billion. Another example of overoptimistic prediction is the Sydney, Australia, Opera House, a landmark building that was supposed to be completed in 1963 at a cost of $7 million; a scaled-down version opened in 1973 at a cost of $102 million.[8]

The overconfident belief that a project will proceed smoothly as planned is known as the **planning fallacy**.[9] The planning fallacy occurs in major projects, such as those just mentioned, and in more mundane, everyday projects as well. How often have you taken books and schoolwork home over a weekend or holiday, expecting to get a lot of work done, only to find that when the next working day rolls around, you accomplished nothing at all? Don't feel too bad. Professors do this, too.

Why do people fall prey to the planning fallacy so easily? First, people tend to neglect **base rates**, or previous rates of occurrence.[6] The length of time and the costs of completing similar projects in the past provide useful guides for projecting completion times and costs of current projects, but this information often is dismissed. Even when people consider base rates, they often discount them as irrelevant by inferring that unusual, unforeseen flukes caused plans to go awry. In addition, people tend to imagine themselves working hard on a project. They tend to overestimate the likelihood of an imagined sequence of events (scenario thinking). Scenarios tend to be optimistic generally and may be even more optimistic when the decision maker is trying to please a supervisor or a client. Together, neglecting base rates, discounting relevant past experiences, and scenario thinking all can lead to unrealistic predictions that result in planning disasters.

What's the Base Rate?

One of the most important pieces of information for accurate prediction is the **base rate**, or prior incidence of the to-be-predicted event. Events that have occurred frequently in the past are likely to occur again in the future. Events that have occurred infrequently in the past are less likely to recur. Sometimes, however, representativeness, or similarity, seems like a more appropriate cue for prediction. New products that are similar to other successful products seem likely to succeed, even when the base rate for new-product success generally is very low. New ads that are similar to other successful ads seem likely to succeed, even when the base rate of success for a particular advertising strategy is very low. Focusing on similarities and neglecting important base rates can lead to very poor predictions, especially when managers focus on salient but trivial similarities.

One reason people sometimes ignore or underuse base-rate information is because a base rate is a statistic (specifically, a percent) based on a distribution of scores. People not trained in statistics have difficulty thinking in terms of distributions and find it much easier to approach each decision problem as a unique and isolated case.[10] Treating each new problem as unique and isolated encourages people to ignore the past, even when the past is highly relevant.

Fortunately, people do not always neglect base rates. They use base-rate information when it is consistent with case-specific information (i.e., when both types of information imply the same conclusion).[11] People also use base-rate information when its causal relevance is apparent[12] and when they think about several different decision problems with differing base rates at the same time.[13] Nevertheless, decision makers can often improve their decisions by paying closer attention to base rates and thinking more carefully about the implications of this information.

Assessing the Reliability and Validity of Information

Managers frequently try to use whatever information is available for solving a decision problem, even when the relevance or usefulness of this information is limited. Consequently, they tend to use differing types and amounts of information for different alternatives and weigh or use this information inconsistently across alternatives and situations. Moreover, managers tend to be insensitive as to the quality or usefulness of the available information.

Usefulness is determined by the reliability or stability of the information and by its validity or specificity. **Unreliable information** varies because of poor measurement, even when the target does not change (e.g., unreliable economic indicators shift even when the economy does not change). **Invalid information** confounds measures of the target with measures of nontargets (e.g., invalid economic indicators measure changes in the economy that are linked to other irrelevant external changes). Managers do not routinely consider the reliability and validity of the information available to them. Instead, they tend to use whatever information is readily available; neglect important omissions (missing pieces of information) and limitations of evidence; and treat presented information as if it were complete and highly relevant.[14]

Unsystematic and inconsistent information use can lead to poor decisions. Ideally, decision options should be evaluated systematically on the same dimensions, and importance weights for each dimension should be held constant across alternatives and situations.

LINEAR MODELS Fortunately, decision aids exist to help managers be more systematic and consistent when evaluating different decision options. One important decision aid is a **linear model**,[15] which is an equation that contains a list of the most important attributes for evaluating and comparing decision options. Each option is evaluated on each attribute, and each attribute is rated for its importance. This evaluation and rating task forces managers to judge all options on all attributes, and the individual attribute importance weights remain constant across alternatives. Thus, a linear model forces managers to be systematic and consistent. Moreover, if a linear model is relatively complete (i.e., all important attributes are included in the model), it reduces the chances of overlooking important omissions (missing pieces of information) and increases sensitivity to limitations of evidence.

For example, suppose that a personnel director for a large firm needs to evaluate 100 job applicants to determine which candidates should be hired. The director could simply interview each candidate and hire the ones he or she likes best. This is a poor decision strategy, however, because interviews provide only a very small and unrepresentative sample of a candidate's behavior and capabilities. The sample is small because very little information can be conveyed in a one-hour interview. The sample is unrepresentative because people behave differently in interview situations than in normal, everyday workplace situations.

A better strategy would be to use a linear model. (See Table 18.1.) A file of information is collected for each candidate, including attributes such as the candidate's university degree (e.g., B.B.A. or M.B.A.), quality of the candidate's university (e.g., Stanford, MIT, and Ivy League schools would be rated very high; unaccredited schools would be rated very low), quality of the candidate's letters of recommendation, quality of interviews with the candidate, the candidate's GPA, number of science, math, and writing courses completed, and number of years of work experience. Each candidate is evaluated on each of these attributes, and each attribute is weighted by degree of importance. Evaluations are made on a scale of 0 (very poor) to 100 (outstanding), and importance ratings are made by allocating 100 points across the attributes (more points indicate greater importance). Extremely important attributes, such as the quality of the candidate's resume would receive a large number of points; less important attributes, such as quality of interviews, would receive a much smaller number of points. This example represents **subjective linear model**, because all inputs (evaluations and importance weights) are subjective judgments provided by the director or a committee. The model, however, is systematic because all candidates are compared on all attributes; it is consistent because the attribute importance weights do not change across candidates. The model is used by multiplying the importance weight of an attribute by a candidate's rating for that attribute. This is done for each attribute and the products are added to yield a single overall score for each candidate. The candidates with the top 10 overall scores are hired. So, in order to use a subjective linear model, a decision maker needs to know only how to multiply and add.

Using a subjective linear model is also sometimes referred to as **bootstrapping**, because the model helps the decision maker pick himself up by his own "bootstraps." All inputs to the model are based on the decision maker's subjective judgments, and these inputs are integrated or combined mechanically (through multiplication and addition). (See Table 18.2.)

In some situations, it is possible to use inputs based solely on objective data (rather than subjective judgments). Such models are known as **objective linear models** or **actuarial models**. Insurance firms, for example, base nearly all their decisions on actuarial data. They keep careful records of automobile theft and accident rates for different

TABLE 18.1   A SUBJECTIVE LINEAR MODEL

(a) Summary Sheet of Applicant Information

Applicant	Personal Essay	Selectivity of Undergraduate Institution	Undergraduate Major	College Grade Point Average	Work Experience	GMAT Verbal	GMAT Quantitative
1	Poor	Highest	Science	2.50	10	98%	60%
2	Excellent	Above Average	Business	3.82	0	70%	80%
3	Average	Below Average	Other	2.96	15	90%	80%
.	.	.	.	.	.	.	.
.	.	.	.	.	.	.	.
117	Weak	Least	Business	3.10	100	98%	99%
118	Strong	Above Average	Other	3.44	60	68%	67%
119	Excellent	Highest	Science	2.16	5	85%	25%
120	Strong	Not Very	Business	3.96	12	30%	58%

(b) Rescaled Table for Subjective Linear Model

Applicant	Essay	Selectivity	Major	GPA	Work Experience	GMAT Verbal	GMAT Quantitative	Overall Score*
1	0	100	100	25	10	98	60	59.1
2	100	60	50	91	0	70	80	67.8
3	50	40	0	48	15	90	80	49.0
.	.	.	.	.	.	.	.	.
.	.	.	.	.	.	.	.	.
117	25	0	50	55	100	98	99	59.7
118	75	60	0	72	60	68	67	60.0
119	100	100	100	8	5	85	25	51.0
120	75	20	50	98	12	30	58	54.0
Weights used	5%	20%	10%	25%	10%	10%	20%	

*The overall score was obtained by multiplying the weights shown in the last row with each attribute score and summing these product terms across attributes to arrive at a weighted average.

Source: From J.E. Russo and P.J.H. Schoemaker, *Decision Traps: The Ten Barriers to Brilliant Decision-making and How to Overcome Them*, 1989. Adapted with permission of The Free Press, a division of Simon & Schuster, Inc. All rights reserved[2]

groups of potential automobile insurance clients; fire, theft, earthquake, and flood rates are determined for different groups of potential home insurance clients; and base rates are calculated for fatalities caused by different medical conditions for different groups of potential life insurance clients. Base rates for each relevant event are broken down for each segment to inform insurance salespeople how much to charge each prospective customer. Banks, for example, use base rate data to determine credit limits for credit cards or loans to potential clients. (See Table 18.3.)

TABLE 18.2 LINEAR MODELS IMPROVE PREDICTION

	Degree of Correlation with the True Outcomes		
Types of Judgments Experts Had to Make	Intuitive Prediction	"Bootstrapped" Model	Objective Model
Academic Performance of Graduate Students	0.19	0.25	0.54
Life Expectancy of Cancer Patients	-0.01	0.13	0.35
Changes in Stock Prices	0.23	0.29	0.80
Mental Illness Using Personality Tests	0.28	0.31	0.46
Grades and Attitudes in Psychology Course	0.48	0.56	0.62
Business Failures Using Financial Ratios	0.5	0.53	0.67
Student's Ratings of Teaching Effectiveness	0.35	0.56	0.91
Performance of Life Insurance Salesman	0.13	0.14	0.43
IQ Scores Using Rorschach Tests	0.47	0.51	0.54
Mean (across many studies)	0.33	0.39	0.64

Prediction is least accurate for intuition, more accurate with bootstrapping, and most accurate with objective linear models.

Source: From J.E. Russo and P.J.H. Schoemaker, *Decision Traps: The Ten Barriers to Brilliant Decision-making and How to Overcome Them*, 1989. Adapted with permission of The Free Press, a division of Simon & Schuster, Inc. All rights reserved.[2]

Linear models are useful anytime a large number of alternatives (e.g., different job candidates, different ads, different product concepts, different potential clients) need to be compared on a large number of attributes. The models ensure that all alternatives are compared on all attributes and that the data are used consistently. Unfortunately, many managers are reluctant to use linear models because they think it dehumanizes the decision process or because they believe they can integrate large amounts of complex information in their heads more effectively than a computer. This is a fallacy. The research evidence is unambiguous: Subjective linear models consistently outperform unaided human judgments, and objective linear models consistently outperform subjective linear models.[15]

Busy decision makers need decision aids. Managers often think that they use large amounts of information and that they integrate complex configurations of information in ways that cannot be simulated with a computer. However, even when people think that they are using large amounts of data and processing them it in complex ways, they are usually using small amounts of information and processing it in a simple manner.[15]

THE FAULT TREE   A **fault tree** is a decision aid that consists of branches, or general categories, of common problems in a system. Each branch is broken down further into specific examples of a general category of problems. Fault trees are used for troubleshooting or identifying causes of problems in many different industries; examples include restaurant management, hospital administration, nuclear power plant administration, and NASA space shuttle launch management.[16] A well-designed fault tree helps managers identify causes for problems in a system faster than would be possible if they had to think of common causes on their own. For example, imagine that a manager is concerned about a restaurant suffering from declining profits. A restaurant fault tree suggests that this problem may stem primarily from one or two possibilities:

TABLE 18.3   CREDIT SCORING SYSTEM OF MAJOR RETAIL CHAIN

Zip Code		Unemployed	33
Zip Codes A	60	All other	46
Zip Codes B	48	Not answered	47
Zip Codes C	41		
Zip Codes D	37	Time at Present Address	
Not answered	53	Less than 6 months	39
		6 months–1 year 5 months	30
Bank Reference		1 year 6 months–3 years 5 months	27
Checking only	0	3 years 6 months–7 years 5 months	30
Savings only	0	7 years 6 months–12 years 5 months	39
Checking and savings	15	12 years 6 months or longer	50
Bank name or loan only	0	Not answered	36
No bank reference	7		
Not answered	7	Time at Employer	
		Less than 6 months	31
Type of Housing		6 months–5 years 5 months	24
Owns/buying	44	5 years 6 months–8 years 5 months	26
Rents	35	8 years 6 months–15 years 5 months	31
All other	31	15 years 6 months or longer	39
Not answered	39	Homemakers	39
		Retired	31
Occupation		Unemployed	29
Clergy	46	Not answered	29
Creative	41		
Driver	33	Finance Company Reference	
Executive	62	Yes	0
Guard	46	Other references only	25
Homemaker	50	No	25
Labor	33	Not answered	15
Manager	46		
Military enlisted	46	Other Department Store/Oil Car/Major Credit Card	
Military officer	62	Department store only	12
Office staff	46	Oil card only	12
Outside	33	Major credit card only	17
Production	41	Department store and oil card	17
Professional	62	Department store and credit card	31
Retired	62	Major credit card and oil card	31
Sales	46	All three	31
Semiprofessional	50	Other references only	0
Service	41	No credit	0
Student	46	Not answered	12
Teacher	41		

Source: From J.E. Russo and P.J.H. Schoemaker, *Decision Traps: The Ten Barriers to Brilliant Decision-making and How to Overcome Them,* 1989.[2]

decreasing revenues or increasing costs.[17] The decreasing revenues branch is broken down into two more branches: decreasing number of customers and decreasing average check sizes. These branches are broken down further into numerous examples of causes for each problem. This fault tree is quite comprehensive and provides lists of many common problems that a manager might otherwise overlook. Moreover, managers can usually identify the source of a problem more quickly when they have these lists of problems at their fingertips.

Distinguishing Between Convergence and Redundancy

To be useful, information (such as sales data, consumer preference data, consumer satisfaction data, etc.) must be measured reliably and validly. However, large data sets are likely to contain intercorrelated, or redundant, subsets of data. For example, suppose that market pretest data for a new product concept show that consumers have favorable beliefs, attitudes, and preferences about the new product, along with intentions to purchase it. That is, several pieces of information point to the same conclusion—it is a good product. However, different pieces of information may point to the same conclusion for one of two different reasons: **convergence** or **redundancy**. Several independent or unrelated pieces of information converging on the same conclusion provide strong evidence for the conclusion. However, several correlated pieces of information suggesting the same conclusion provide relatively weak support for the conclusion. Unfortunately, a large amount of supporting evidence is often interpreted as strong support even when the individual pieces of information are highly correlated or redundant. Moreover, people are generally inaccurate when estimating the degree of correlation among these pieces of information.[18]

Fortunately, however, the degree of correlation between two or more variables can be estimated accurately and easily using statistical measures of association (e.g., the Pearson correlation coefficient, the Spearman rank-order test; the chi-square test for association), which are widely available on many different statistical software packages (e.g., SPSS, SAS). Managers should routinely examine correlation matrices to determine if a set of variables provides convergent or redundant support for a conclusion. If such data are convergent or redundant, then they provide only weak support for the conclusion.

Resisting Scenario Thinking

It is easier to think in terms of scenarios than in terms of probabilities and statistics. Moreover, a growing body of research evidence suggests that information is represented in memory in the form of scenarios, narratives, or stories and that people naturally and spontaneously think in terms of scenarios.[19] Unfortunately, scenario thinking can lead to erroneous likelihood judgments and poor predictions. A target event seems much more likely to occur when a story or sequence of events leading to the target event is presented, rather than not presented. Of course, the presence or absence of a story does not influence that actual likelihood of the target event— that probability remains the same. However, a story makes an event easy to imagine, and easy-to-imagine events are perceived as highly probable. This is true even when many different scenarios can lead to the same target events, which is usually the case. Statistically, the general likelihood of an event occurring through some unspecified sequence of events must be higher than the likelihood of the event occurring through just one specific sequence of events. Subjectively, however, the latter probability seems higher because of the operation of the simulation (or imagination) heuristic.

Some management consultants, managers, and salespeople are master storytellers. They can make an event seem inevitable. The best defense against good storytellers is to try to generate your own story or set of stories leading to very different conclusions. People are seduced too easily into focusing on only one possible story or outcome. Merely thinking about many different possible stories and outcomes helps managers to formulate more informed opinions and judgments.

Avoiding Overconfidence

Research on confidence suggests that people tend to be overconfident in many different settings.[20] Overconfidence is dangerous because confident managers believe that they do not need to develop contingency plans or safety measures to protect themselves against surprises; also, confidence influences how resources (e.g., budgets, time, and effort) are allocated.[21] For example, overconfidence on the part of the railroad industry in the 1920s led railway executives to ignore airplanes. Overconfidence on the part of U.S. automobile manufacturers in the early 1970s led them to ignore the growing Japanese automobile industry. Shortly before the *Challenger* disaster in 1986, NASA officials stated that the odds of failure were 1 in 100,000 launches (or 1 in 300 years), and two months before the Chernobyl nuclear power plant disaster, also in 1986, Ukraine's minister of power and electrification stated that "the odds of a meltdown are one in 10,000 years."[22]

What factors influence confidence? Set size or the amount of information available for judgment often influences confidence. Typically, people become more confident as the amount of information available for judgment increases, even when the accuracy of the information does not increase.[23] Confidence also increases as insensitivity to omissions (missing information) increases[24] and as need for cognitive closure increases.[25] The pseudodiagnosticity effect also contributes to overconfidence, because people tend to focus on how well the evidence supports the target conclusion and to neglect how well the evidence supports other conclusions.[26] Moreover, confidence tends to be greatest when people are least sensitive to base-rate information and, therefore, least accurate.[27]

Calibration refers to the degree to which confidence matches accuracy. Thus, when people are asked to provide an interval or range around their answers such that they are 90 percent confident that the correct answer lies within this stated interval, the correct answer should actually lie within the interval in 90 percent of the cases (e.g., in 9 out of 10 questions or 90 out of 100 questions). Instead, the typical finding is that people's confidence intervals are too small, and the correct answer actually lies within the intervals in far fewer than 90 percent of the cases.[20] Calibration tends to decrease as accuracy decreases, and overconfidence tends to be greatest when people focus too heavily on one possibility (e.g., one alternative, one conclusion, one answer). The best way to reduce overconfidence is to think about many different possibilities (e.g., many different alternatives, many different conclusions, and many different answers). Considering multiple possibilities not only decreases overconfidence; it also increases accuracy.[28]

OBJECTIVE 4

Judgment Updating and Revision

Managerial judgment often involves forming an initial judgment, first impression, or anchor. Frequently, managers realize that their anchor is not quite right, so they adjust their judgment toward a more accurate position. Typically, however, the adjustment is insufficient (underadjustment). That is, the final judgment tends to be too close to the initial judgment.[29] So, how should people adjust their judgments?

Once again, probability and statistical theory provide the answer. According to **Bayes' theorem**, amount of adjustment depends on the diagnosticity (or relevance) of the information brought to bear after forming the initial opinion. More formally, Bayes' theorem states that:

$$P(H|D) = \frac{p(D|H)}{p(D|H')} \times \frac{p(H)}{p(H')}$$

That is, the probability of a hypothesis being true, given the data, is known as a *posterior probability*. The conditional probability, $p(D|H)$ divided by the conditional probability of $p(D|H')$, is known as the *likelihood ratio,* and this serves as a measure of diagnosticity, or relevance (i.e., the extent to which the data support one hypothesis H rather than other hypotheses H'). The simple probabilities $p(H)$ and $p(H')$ are referred to as base rates, or *prior probabilities* (i.e., probabilities prior to the collection of new data). The prior probability that a hypothesis, or conclusion, is correct can also be interpreted as the prior judgment, or anchor. As the likelihood ratio increases, adjustment should increase. If the likelihood ratio is equal to 1 (the numerator and the denominator are equal), no adjustment should be performed (the posterior probability equals the ratio of the prior probabilities) because the new data are uninformative. Basically, the more informative the data, the more a manager should adjust his or her initial judgment, given the data.

Bayes' theorem can be rewritten as:

$$P(H/D) = \frac{p(D|H)p(H)}{p(D|H)p(H) + p(D|H')p(H')}$$

Why is this important? Imagine that a manager of a leading pharmaceutical company must decide whether a new drug is safe enough to market. The drug was designed to reduce blood clots, but some doctors believe the drug may cause a rare form of cancer in some patients. The U.S. Food and Drug Administration requires clinical tests involving human subjects before a new drug is approved, so the drug is currently being tested on a small sample of patients. One patient develops a tumor, but the doctor running the study is initially unconcerned because the prior probability, or base rate, of this type of cancer is only 1 percent, $p(H) = 0.01$. To be safe, the doctor orders a test. The test returns a positive result, so the doctor must adjust her judgment. Research has shown that the test is 80 percent reliable, i.e., there is an 80 percent chance of a positive test, given cancer, $p(D|H) = 0.80$, and the test has a false positive rate of 10 percent (i.e., there is a 10 percent chance of a positive test given no cancer, $p(D|H') = 0.10$. So, the doctor adjusts her estimate of the likelihood of cancer for this patient to about 70 percent. Is this estimate appropriate?

Plugging the numbers into Bayes' formula yields

$$p(Cancer|Positive\ Test) = \frac{(0.80)(0.01)}{(0.80)(0.01)+(0.01)(0.99)} = 0.075$$

That is, there is only a 7.5 percent chance that the patient has cancer, given the positive test, $p(D|H) = 0.0748$. This surprises most people (including most doctors) because they tend to focus on the 80 percent figure and adjust insufficiently down from 80 percent. The actual answer (7.5 percent) is much lower because the base rate is very low (1 percent) and because the test is not perfect—there is an 80 percent chance of true positive tests and a 10 percent chance of false positive tests. Moreover, most people, including experts, tend to commit the **confusion of the inverse fallacy.**[30] That is, people tend to confuse $p(H|D)$ with $p(D|H)$. These two conditional probabilities are not at all equivalent. In this example, $p(H|D) = 0.075$ *and* $p(D|H) = 0.80$. Moreover, in most cases $p(H|D)$ does not equal $p(D|H)$.

You probably found the logic underlying Bayes' theorem difficult to follow. This is because intuition does not follow the rules of Bayes' theorem. This is yet another example of how intuition can lead decision makers astray. This book is full of examples of how intuition can lead to poor decision making. The use of Bayes' theorem can improve decision making by

- Increasing attention paid to base rates
- Reducing pseudodiagnostic thinking (i.e., the tendency to focus on hits and to ignore false alarms)
- Eliminating the confusion of the inverse fallacy
- Helping managers to adjust initial estimates appropriately in light of new information

Prediction should be based only on the base rate when no relevant information is available. Adjustment should increase as the relevance of the new information increases. Relevance increases as the percentage of hits (i.e., correct predictions) increases and as the percentage of false alarms (i.e., predicted hits that turn out to be misses) decreases. Bayes' theorem integrates a large amount of information in an appropriate manner that usually cannot be duplicated by intuitive judgment, even if made by experts.[31]

Chapter Summary

Managers should not consider only one positioning strategy, but rather many different alternatives (e.g., positioning by attributes/benefits, price, use, and user; repositioning). Similarly, managers should not consider only one segmentation strategy but rather many alternatives (e.g., segmenting by geography, demography, psychographics, or behavior). Managers should also consider many different new product concepts or ideas, many different pricing strategies, many different promotion and advertising strategies, and many different distribution strategies. Epistemic freezing, or focusing too heavily on one option or alternative, often leads to poor decisions. Even very busy and time-pressured individuals need to consider a wide range of options to reach good decisions. Managers should also use decision aids (such as linear models, fault trees, and Bayes' theorem) to improve their judgment and decision making by helping them to be more systematic, consistent, and careful in their thinking. Many managers prefer to base their decisions on feelings or hunches rather than models. However, relying too heavily on feelings, hunches, and stories (scenarios) causes managers to fall into the intuition trap.

I hope that this book will help you to be more scientific, systematic, and consistent in your thinking and reasoning. Being more analytic and less intuitive should help you to develop more effective and rewarding solutions to the difficult managerial judgment and decision-making challenges that lie ahead.

Key Terms

decision frame management	epistemic seizing	planning fallacy
theory of lay epistemology	epistemic freezing	base rate
need for cognitive closure	integrative complexity	unreliable information

invalid information	objective linear model	redundancy
linear model	actuarial model	calibration
subjective linear model	fault tree	Bayes' theorem
bootstrapping	convergence	confusion of the inverse fallacy

Review and Discussion

1. Why do managers sometimes focus on only one frame in decision making? How can using multiple frames lead to better managerial decisions?

2. What five things begin to occur as the need for cognitive closure increases?

3. Some researchers believe that the need for closure may increase with age and experience. How might this hypothesis affect managerial decisions?

4. Describe a situation in which you engaged in planning fallacy. What was your thinking process? What was the outcome?

5. What is the difference between unreliable information and invalid information? Give an example of each.

6. How might a subjective linear model help a restaurant owner decide the best location for a new restaurant?

7. How might convergence and redundancy in data affect the success of a new product?

8. Describe an instance in which you either used scenario thinking to influence someone to make a decision in your favor or were influenced by scenario thinking to make a decision?

9. What factors influence confidence in one's decisions? Why is overconfidence dangerous for managers?

10. Why is Bayes' theorem a good tool for managers to use in adjusting original judgments?

Chapter 1

1 Agrell, S. (2004, May 8). Her field of scholarship is reality TV: "The whole dynamic of humiliation is central to reality TV," says communication professor Alison Hearn. "There's a certain car-wreck mentality." *Saturday Post*, p. SP7. Frankel, J. (2004, April 20). Networks pile it on with more reality TV. *Capital Times (Madison, WI)*, p. 1B. Johnson, A. (2004, April 4). Speakers reveal reality hooks. *Daily Illini* [Online]. Available: www.uwire.com.

2 Recent television ratings news. (2009, June 6). *Reality TV World* [Online]. Available: www.RealityTVWorld.com.

3 There's no sign that reality TV is about to die. (2003, December 6). *Canberra Times (Federal Capital Press of Australia Pty. Limited)*, p. B3.

4 Johnson, A. (2004, April 4). Speakers reveal reality hooks. *Daily Illini* [Online]. Available: www.uwire.com.

5 Aoki, N. (2004, March 23). Where reality TV, commerce meet. *The Boston Globe*, p. A1.

6 Aoki, N. (2004, March 23). Where reality TV, commerce meet. *The Boston Globe*, p. A1.

7 Gunelius, S. (2008, January 18). Ford, Coke and AT&T pay more to sponsor American Idol. *Brandcurve*, [Online]. Available: http://www.bizzia.com/brandcurve/ford-coke-att-pay-more-to-sponsor-american-idol.

8 Definition adapted from, Kerin, R. A., Berkowitz, E. N., Hartley, S. W., & Rudelius, W. (2003). *Marketing* (3rd ed.). New York: McGraw-Hill, p. 150.

9 Zeithaml, V. A. (1988). Consumer perceptions of price, quality, and value: A means-end model and synthesis of evidence. *Journal of Marketing, 52 (July)*, 2–22, p. 14.

10 Chairman's address: 2002 annual meeting of Procter & Gamble shareholders. (2002, October 23). *Procter & Gamble Management Speeches and Perspectives* [Online]. Available: www.pg.com.

11 Keiningham, T., & Vavra, T. (2001). *The customer delight principle*. New York: McGraw-Hill.

12 Obrec, L. (1999, December). Marketing, motives and Dr. Freud. *Detroiter Magazine* [Online]. Available: www.moline-consulting.com.

13 Dichter, E. (1960). *A strategy of desire*. Garden City, NY: Doubleday. Dichter, E. (1964). *Handbook of consumer motivations*. New York: McGraw-Hill.

14 Durgee, J. F. (1991). Interpreting Dichter's interpretations: An analysis of consumption symbolism in the handbook of consumer motivations. In H. Hartvig-Larsen, D. G. Mick, and C. Alstead (Eds.), *Marketing and semiotics: Selected papers from the Copenhagen symposium* (as cited in Solomon, M. R. (2002). *Consumer behavior* (5th ed.). Upper Saddle River, NJ: Prentice Hall.).

15 Blackwell, R. D., & Miniard, P. W. (2003). *Consumer behavior* (9th ed.). New York: South-Western, p. 20. Dichter, E. (1964). *Handbook of consumer motivations*. New York: McGraw-Hill.

16 Kardes, F. R. (2002). *Consumer behavior and managerial decision making* (2nd ed.). Upper Saddle River, NJ: Pearson Education/Prentice Hall.

17 Clancy, K. J., & Krieg, P. C. (2003). Surviving Innovation. *Marketing Management, March/April*, 14–20.

18 Cronley, M. L., Houghton, D. C., Goddard, P., & Kardes, F. R. (1998). Endorsing products for the money: The role of the correspondence bias in celebrity advertising. *Advances in Consumer Research*, 26, 627–631. McCracken, G. (1989). Who is the celebrity endorser? Cultural foundations of the endorsement process. *Journal of Consumer Research*, 16 (December), 310–321.

19 Rosenthal, R., & Rosnow, R. L. (1991). *Essentials of behavioral research: Methods and data analysis* (2nd ed.). New York: McGraw-Hill.

20 Assmus, G., Farley, J. U., & Lehmann, D. R. (1984). How advertising affects sales: Meta-analyses of econometric results. *Journal of Marketing Research, 21*, 65–74.

21 Kardes, F. R. (2002). *Consumer behavior and managerial decision making* (2nd ed.). Upper Saddle River, NJ: Pearson Education/Prentice Hall.

22 Geary, S. P. (Producer). (1999). *Sell and spin: A history or advertising* [Film]. (Available from A&E Home Video, A&E Television Network, Cat. No AAE-17607).

23 Mcfarland, J. (2001, September 24). The consumer anthropologist. *Harvard Business School: Working Knowledge* [Online]. Available: www.hbswk.hbs.edu. Wellner, A. S. (2002, October 1). The test drive—ethnographic research and marketing research. *Amercian Demographics* [Online]. Available: www.findarticles.com.

24 For more information, visit the company website at *www.harris.com*.

25 Irving, J. (1972). *Victims of groupthink*. Boston: Houghton Mifflin. Irving, J. (1982). *Groupthink: Psychological studies of policy decisions and fiascos* (2nd ed.). Boston: Houghton Mifflin.

26 Malhotra, N.K., Peterson, M., & Kleiser, S.B. (1999). Marketing research: A state-of-the-art review and directions for the twenty-first century. *Journal of the Academy of Marketing Science, 27 (2)*, 160–184.

27 Chairman's address: 2002 annual meeting of Procter & Gamble shareholders. (2002, October 23). *Procter & Gamble Management Speeches and Perspectives* [Online]. Available: www.pg.com.

28 Johnson, B. A., and Nunes, P. F. (2002, December 12). Bah, humbug!: Study shows retailers pay the price for poor customer contact and lack of innovation. *CRMGuru.com* [Online], p. 2. Available: www.crmguru.com.

29 All of the sources for this article: Chairman's address: 2002 annual meeting of Procter & Gamble shareholders. (2002, October 23). *Procter & Gamble Management Speeches and Perspectives* [Online]. Available: www.pg.com. Crest Whitestrips the most recommended OTC tooth whitener by US pharmacists (2003, January 20). *Procter & Gamble Press Release Archive* [Online]. Available: www .pg.com. Giving an innovative product extra bite (2001). *Procter & Gamble 2001 Annual Report—Stories from our Brands* [Online]. Available: www.pg.com. Johnson, B. A., and Nunes, P. F. (2002, December 12). Bah, humbug!: Study shows retailers pay the price for poor customer contact and lack of innovation. *CRMGuru.com* [Online], p. 2. Available: www.crmguru.com.

30 Inner beauty (2004, June 1). L'Oréal Active Cosmetics [Online]. Available: www.loreal.com.

31 Sources for the entire article include: A year of strong growth (2004, June 1). *L'Oréal Annual Report for 2003* [Online], pp. 48–50. Available: www.loreal.com. Inner beauty (2004, June 1). *L'Oréal Active Cosmetics* [Online]. Available: www .loreal.com. Morthished, C. (2003, April 3). L'Oréal: The perpetual beauty machine (2004, June 6). *Times Online* [Online]. Available: www.timesonline.co.uk. Nutracosmetics: A timely market enjoying obvious growth (2004) *Cosmeeting* [Online]. Available: www.cosmeeting.com.

32 Sources for the entire article include: Rigging a promotion cost Coca-Cola big bucks and trigger grand-jury investigation (2003, August 13). *By No Other—Business Law Lessons and Stories: Embarrassments and Bad Career Moves* [Online]. Available: bynoother.com. Day, S. (2003, August 13). Coke to pay Burger King $21 million over rigged test. *The New York Times* [Online]. Available: www .nytimes.com. Howard, T. (2003, June 4). Burger King, Coke may face off in frozen Coke suit. *USA Today* [Online]. Available: www.usatoday.com. Howard, T. (2003, August 1). Burger King, Coke deal may reach $20M. *USA Today* [Online]. Available: www.usatoday.com.

Chapter 2

1 Source for Eye on International: Mordin, C. (2005, May). Connecting with consumers. *4Cs Overview* [Online]. Available: www.4cs.yr.com.

2 Aaker, D. A. (1998). *Strategic Market Management* (5th ed.). New York: Wiley and Sons, Inc.

3 For more information, visit the company's website at *www.pepsi.com.*

4 Geary, S. P. (Producer) (1999). *Sell and Spin: A History of Advertising* [Film]. (Available from A&E Home Video, A&E Television Network, Cat. No AAE-17607).

5 Crow, J. J. (2005). Factors Influencing Product Customization. *International Journal of Internet Marketing and Advertising*, (April). Crow, J. J., & Shenteau J. (2005). Online product customization. In C. P. Haugtvedt, K. Machleit, R. Yalch (Eds.), *Online Consumer Psychology: Understanding and Influencing Behavior in the Virtual World*. Mahwah, NJ: Lawrence Erlbaum Associates, in press.

6 For more information, visit the company's website at *www.bmw.com.*

7 Japan: A nation of coffee lovers (2003, August 12). *Euromonitor* [Online]. Available: www.euromonitor.com.

9 Edmondson, B. (1999). The Dawn of the Mega City. *Marketing Tools,* 64.

9 Claritas Products and Services: Segmentation Analysis (2005, May 1) [Online]. Available: www.claritas.com.

10 Understanding U.S. consumers (2003). *VALS™ Program SRI Consulting Business Intelligence.*

11 Reis, A., & Trout, J. (1981). *Positioning: The Battle for Your Mind.* New York: McGraw-Hill.

12 Kardes, F. R., & Gurumurthy, K. (1992). "Order of entry effects on consumer memory and judgment: An information integration perspective." *Journal of Marketing Research, 29,* 343–357. Kardes, F. R., Gurumurthy, K., Chandrashekaran, M., & Dornoff, R. J. (1993). "Brand retrieval, consideration set composition, consumer choice, and the pioneering advantage." *Journal of Consumer Research, 20,* 62–75.

13 Carpenter, G. S., & Nakamoto, K. (1989). "Consumer preference formation and pioneering advantage." *Journal of Marketing Research, 26,* 285–298.

14 Carpenter, G. S., & Nakamoto, K. (1989). "Consumer preference formation and pioneering advantage." *Journal of Marketing Research, 26,* 285–298.

15 Reis, A., & Trout, J. (1994). *The 22 Immutable Laws of Marketing.* New York: Harper Business.

16 Reis, A., & Trout, J. (1994). *The 22 Immutable Laws of Marketing.* New York: Harper Business.

17 Reis, A., & Trout, J. (1994). *The 22 Immutable Laws of Marketing.* New York: Harper Business.

18 Reis, A. (2005), The battle over positioning still rages to this day. *Advertising Age, April, 31,* 88.

19 Reis, A. (2005), The battle over positioning still rages to this day. *Advertising Age, April, 31,* 88.

20 Cronley, M. L., Posavac, S. S., Meyer, T., Kardes, F. R., & Kellaris, J. J. (2005). A selective hypothesis testing perspective on price-quality inference and inference-based choice. *Journal of Consumer Psychology, 15 (2),* 159–169. Kardes, F. R., Cronley, M. L., Kellaris, J. J., & Posavac, S. S. (2004). The role of selective information processing in price-quality inference. *Journal of Consumer Research, 31 (2),* 368–374. See also, Kardes, F. R., Posavac, S. S., and Cronley, M. L. (2004). Consumer inference: A review of processes, bases, and judgment contexts. *Journal of Consumer Psychology, 14 (3),* 230–256.

21 Reis, A., & Trout, J. (1981). *Positioning: The battle for your mind.* New York: McGraw-Hill.

22 Sangiacomo, M. (2004, November 3). Jungle Jim's Exotic Journey. *Cleveland Plain Dealer* [Online]. Available: www.junglejims.com.

23 Hartinger, Debby. Jungle Jim's International Market (personal communication, August 11, 2009). Bianco, A. (2005, April 18). The Wizard of Odd. *BusinessWeek,* 82-83.

24 All information for this section taken from: Schumann, D. W. (1999, February 19). The transmission of prejudice: What do our marketing strategies really reinforce? *Presidential address presented to the membership of the Society for Consumer Psychology.*

Chapter 3

1 Associated Press (2007, August 17). Reported in *The Wall Street Journal* [Online]. Available: http://online.wsj.com/article/SB118737017784201124.html.

2 Assael, H. (1998). *Consumer Behavior and Marketing Action.* Cincinnati, OH: South-Western Publishing.

3 Laurent, G. and Kapferer, J-N. (1985). Measuring Consumer Involvement Profiles, *Journal of Marketing Research,* 22:41–53.

4 Dowling, G. R., and Staelin, R. (1994). A Model of Perceived Risk and Risk-handling Activity. *Journal of Consumer Research,* 21:119–134.

5 Cacioppo, J. T., Petty, R. E., and Kao, C. F. (1986). Central and Peripheral Routes to Persuasion: An Individual Difference Perspective. *Journal of Personality and Social Psychology,* 51:1032–1043.

6 Batra, R., and Ray, M. L. (1986). Situational Effects of Advertising Repetition: The Moderating Influence of Motivation, Ability, and Opportunity to Respond. *Journal of Consumer Research,* 12:432–445.

7 Robertson, T. S. (1976). Low-commitment Consumer Behavior. *Journal of Advertising Research,* 16:19–27.

8 Venkatesan, M. (1973). Cognitive Consistency and Novelty Seeking. In S. Ward and T. S. Robertson (eds.), *Consumer Behavior: Theoretical Sources,* (354–384). Englewood Cliffs, NJ: Prentice Hall.

9 Van Triip, H. C. M., Hoyer, W. D., and Inman, J. J. (1996). Why Switch? Product Category-level of Explanations for True Variety-seeking Behavior. *Journal of Marketing Research,* 33:281–292.

10 Holbrook, M. B. (1984). Situation-specific Ideal Points and Usage of Multiple Dissimilar Brands. In J. N. Sheth (ed.), *Research in Marketing,* vol. 7, 93–131. Greenwich, CT: JAI Press.

11 McReynolds, P. (1971). The Nature and Assessment of Intrinsic Motivation. In P. McReynolds (ed.), *Advances in Psychological Assessment,* vol. 2, (157–177). Palo Alto, CA: Science and Behavior Books.

12 McAlister, L., and Pessemier, E. A. (1982). Variety Seeking Behavior: An Interdisciplinary Review. *Journal of Consumer Research,* 9:311–322.

13 Sheth, J. N., and Raju, P. S. (1974). Sequential and Cyclical Nature of Information Processing Models in Repetitive Choice Behavior. In S. Ward and P. Wright (eds.), *Advances in Consumer Research,* vol. 1,(348–358).

14 Zuckerman, M. (1979). *Sensation Seeking: Beyond the Optimal Level of Arousal.* Hillsdale, NJ: Lawrence Erlbaum Associates.

15 Ratner, R. K., Kahn, B. E., and Kahneman, D. (1999). Choosing Less-preferred Experiences for the Sake of Variety. *Journal of Consumer Research,* 26:1–15.

16 Kahn, B. E., and Isen, A. M. (1993). The Influence of Positive Affect on Variety Seeking among Safe, Enjoyable Products. *Journal of Consumer Research,* 20:257–270.

17 Simonson, I. (1990). The Effect of Purchase Quantity and Timing on Variety Seeking Behavior. *Journal of Marketing Research,* 27:150–162.

18 Choi, J., Kim, B. K., Choi, I., and Yi, Y. (2006). Variety-seeking Tendency in Choice for Others: Interpersonal and Intrapersonal Causes. *Journal of Consumer Research,* 32:590–595.

19 Howard, J. A. and Sheth, J. N. (1969). *The Theory of Buyer Behavior.* New York: Wiley.

20 Leuba, C. (1955). Toward Some Integration of Learning Theories: The Concept of Optimal Stimulation. *Psychological Reports,* 1:27–33.

21 Menon, S., and Kahn, B. (1995). The Impact of Context on Variety Seeking in Product Choices. *Journal of Consumer Research,* 22:285–295.

22 Sutherland, M. and Sylvester, A. K. (2000). *Advertising and the Mind of the Consumer,* 2nd ed. St. Leonards NSW, Australia: Allen & Unwin.

23 Myers, J. H., and Alpert, M. (1968). Determinant Buying Attitudes: Meaning and Measurement. *Journal of Marketing,* 32:13–20.

24 Guiltinan, J. P., Paul, G.W., and Madden, T. J. (1997). *Marketing Management: Strategies and Programs*, 6th ed. New York: The McGraw-Hill Companies, Inc.

25 Dewy, J. (1910). *How We Think*. Boston, MA: D. C. Health; Brim, O. G. Jr., Glass, D. C., Lavin, D. E., and Goodman, N. (1963). Personality and Decision Processes. *The American Journal of Sociology*, 69:96.

26 Engel, J. Blackwell, R. D., and Miniard, P. W. (1995). *Consumer Behavior*, 8th ed. Hinsdale, IL: Dryden Press.

27 We credit James G. Clawson with popularizing the "want-got gap" model while teaching organizational behavior at the University of Virginia's Darden School of Business.

28 Bruner, G. C. II (1986). Problem Recognition Styles and Search Patterns: An Empirical Investigation. *Journal of Retailing*, 62:281–297.

29 Bruner, G. C. and Pamazal, R. J. (1988). Problem Recognition: The Crucial First Stage of the Consumer Decision Process. *Journal of Consumer Marketing*, 5:53–63.

30 Rossiter, J. R., Percy, L., and Donovan, R. J. (1991). A Better Advertising Planning Grid. *Journal of Advertising Research*, 31:11–21.

31 Rossiter, J. R., and Percy, L. (1997). *Advertising Communications and Promotion Management*. New York: The McGraw-Hill Companies, Inc.

32 Gundlach, G. T., Block, L. G., and Wilkie, W. L. (2007). *Explorations of Marketing in Society*. Mason, OH: Thomson Higher Education.

33 Pollay, R. W. and Banwari, M. (1993). Here's the Beef: Factors, Determinants, and Segments in Consumer Criticism of Advertising. *Journal of Marketing*, 57:99–114.

34 Wilkie, W. L., and Moore, E. S. (2007). Marketing's Contributions to Society. In G. T. Gundlach, L. G. Block, and W. L. Wilkie (eds.) *Explorations of Marketing in Society*, 2–39. Mason, OH: Thomson Higher Education.

35 Punj, G. N., and Staelin, R. (1983). A Model of Consumer Information Search for New Automobiles. *Journal of Consumer Research*, 9:366–380.

36 Bettman, J. R. (1979). Memory Factors in Consumer Choice: A Review. *Journal of Marketing*, 43:37–53.

37 Bloch, P. H., Sherrell, D. L., and Ridgeway, N. M. (1986). Consumer Search: An Extended Framework. *Journal of Consumer Research*, 13:119–126.

38 Houston, M. J., and Rothschild, M. L. (1978). Conceptual and Methodological Perspectives on Involvement. In S. C. Jain (ed.), *Educator's proceedings*, 184–187. Chicago, IL: American Marketing Association

39 Celsi, R. L., and Olson, J. C. (1988). The Role of Involvement in Attention and Comprehension Processes. *Journal of Consumer Research*, 15:210–224.

40 Clarke, K. and Belk, R. (1979). The Effects of Product Involvement and Task Definition on Anticipated Consumer Effort. In W. L. Wilkie (ed.). *Advances in Consumer Research*, vol. 6, 313–318. Ann Arbor, MI: Association for Consumer Research.

41 Dellaert, B. G. C. (1998). Investigating Consumers' Tendency to Combine Multiple Shopping Purposes and Destinations. *Journal of Marketing Research*, 35:177–189.

42 Ratchford, B.T., Lee, M-S, and Talukdar, D. (2003). The Impact of the Internet on Information Search for Automobiles. *Journal of Marketing Research*, 40:193–209.

43 Weenig, M. W. H., and Maarleveld, M. (2002). The Impact of Time Constraint of Information Search Strategies in Complex Choice Tasks. *Journal of Economic Psychology*, 23:689–702.

44 Machleit, K. A., Eroglu, S. A., and Mantel, S. P. (2000). Perceived Retail Crowding and Shopping Satisfaction. *Journal of Consumer Psychology*, 9:29–42.

45 Gladwell, M. (2002). *The Tipping Point: How Little Things Can Make a Big Difference*. New York: Back Bay Books.

46 Klein, M. (1998). He Shops, She Shops. *American Demographics*, 20:83–95.

47 Bettman, J. R., and Park, C. W. (1986). Effects of Prior Knowledge and Experience and Phase of the Choice Process on Consumer Decision Processes: A Protocol Analysis. *Journal of Consumer Research*, 7:234–248.

48 McGuire, W. J. (1968). Personality and Susceptibility to Social Influences. In E. F. Borgatta and W. W. Lambert (eds.), *Handbook of Personality Theory and Research*, (1130–1187). Chicago, IL: Rand McNally; McGuire, W. J. (1972). Attitude Change: The Information-processing Paradigm. In C. G. McClintock (ed.), *Experimental Social Psychology*, (108–141). New York: Holt, Rinehart & Winston; McGuire, W. J. (1976). Some Internal Psychological Factors Influencing Consumer Choice. *Journal of Consumer Research*, 2:302–319.

49 Hirschman, E. C. and Wallendorf, M. R. (1982). Motive Underlying Marketing Formation Acquisition and Transfer. *Journal of Advertising*, 11:25–31.

50 Hirschman, E. C. (1980). Innovativeness, Novelty Seeking, and Consumer Creativity. *Journal of Consumer Research*, 7:283–295.

51 Fleischmann, G. (1981). Sources for Product Ideas: A Proactive View on the Consumer. In K. B. Monroe (ed.), *Advances in Consumer Research*, vol. 8, (386–390). Ann Arbor, MI: Association for Consumer Research.

52 Bellenger, D. N. and Korgoankar, P. (1980). Profiling the Recreational Shopper. *Journal of Retailing*, 58:58–81.

53 Simon, H. A. (1982). *Models of Bounded Rationality*. Cambridge, MA: MIT Press.

54 Davies, A., and Cline T. W. (2005). A Consumer Behavior Approach to Modeling Monopolistic Competition. *Journal of Economic Psychology*, 26:797–826.

55 Kahneman, D. (1973). *Attention and Effort*. Englewood Cliffs, NJ: Prentice Hall; Beatty, S.E. and Smith, S. M. (1987). External Search Effort: An Investigation across Several Product Categories, *Journal of Consumer Research*, 14:83–95; Brucks, M. (1985). The Effect of Product Class Knowledge on Information Search Behavior. *Journal of Consumer Research*, 12:1–6.

56 Simonson, I. (1989). Choice Based on Reason. The Case of Attraction and Compromise Effects. *Journal of Consumer Research*, 16:158–174.

57 Bettman, J. R. (1979). *An Information Processing Theory of Consumer Choice*. Reading, MA: Addison-Wesley; Kardes, F. R., Kalyanaram, G. Chandrashekaran, M., and Dornoff, R. J. (1993). Brand Retrieval, Consideration Set Composition, Consumer Choice, and the Pioneering Advantage. *Journal of Consumer Research*, 20:62–75.

58 Dhar, R., and Glazer, R. (1996). Similarity in Context: Cognitive Representation and Violation Preference and Perceptual Invariance in Consumer Choice. *Organization Behavior and Human Decision Processes*, 67:280–293; Nosofsky, R. M. (1987). Attention and Learning Processes in Identification and Categorization of Integral Stimuli. *Journal of Experimental Psychology: Learning, Memory, and Cognition*, 13:87–108.

59 Pinsky, J., and Slade, M. E. (1998). Contracting in Space: An Application of Spatial Statistics to Discrete Choice Models. *Journal of Econometrics*, 85:125–154.

60 Baumeister, R. E. (1982). Self-esteem, Self-preservation, and Future Interaction: A Dilemma of Reputation. *Journal of Personality*, 50:29–45.

61 Hall, C. S., and Lindzey, G. (1978). *Theories of Personality*. New York: Wiley.

62 Festinger, L. (1957). *A Theory of Cognitive Dissonance*. Evanston, IL: Row, Peterson & Company.

63 Bell, D. E. (1982). Regret in Decision Making under Uncertainty. *Operations Research*, 30:961–981.

64 Tse, D. K., Nicosia, F. M, and Wilton, P. C. (1990). Consumer Satisfaction as a Process. *Psychology & Marketing*, 7:177–193.

65 Seiders, K., Voss, G., Grewal, D., and Godfrey, A. L. (2005). Do Satisfied Customers Buy More? Examining Moderating Influences in a Retail Context. *Journal of Marketing*, 69:26–43.

66 Homburg, C. Koschate, N., and Hoyer, W. D. (2005). Do Satisfied Customers Really Pay More? A Study of the Relationship between Customer Satisfaction and Willingness to Pay. *Journal of Marketing*, 69:84–96.

67 Chandrashekaran, M., Rotte, K., Tax, S. S., and Grewal, R. (2007). Satisfaction Strength and Customer Loyalty. *Journal of Marketing Research*, 44:153–163.

68 Brehm, J. W. (1956). Postdecision Changes in the Desirability of Alternatives. *Journal of Abnormal and Social Psychology* 52:384–389.

69 Oliver, R. L. (1980). A Cognitive Model of the Antecedents and Consequences of Satisfaction Decisions. *Journal of Marketing Research*, 17:460–469; Oliver, R. L. (1981). Measurement and Evaluation of Satisfaction Process in Retail Settings. *Journal of Retailing*, 57:25–48; Oliver, R. L., and DeSarbo, W. S. (1988). Response Determinants in Satisfaction Judgments. *Journal of Consumer Research*, 14:495–507.

70 Spencer, J. (2007, August 6). In China, Lenovo Sets Sights on Rural Market. *The Wall Street Journal* [Online] Available: http://online.wsj.com/article/SB118634998647088589.html.

71 Farooq, S. F. (2007, August 10). Economic Superpower in Crisis. *United News of Bangladesh*. Reported in *Manufacturing Business Technology*. [Online]. Available: http://www.mbtmag.com/articleXml/LN653394652.html.

72 Parker, E. (2007, July 12). Made in China. *The Wall Street Journal* [Online] Available: http://online.wsj.com/article/SB118420252485564055.html.

Chapter 4

1 4.7% of TV sets Sold in the US are US-made. (2003, December 3). *ITFacts* [Online]. Available: www.itfacts.biz.

2 All Brands in Television (TV). (2004, November 4). *BizRate Shopping Search* [Online]. Available: www.Bizrate.com.

3 Dhar, R. (1997). Consumer Preference for a No-choice Option. *Journal of Consumer Research*, 24:211–231.

4 Miller, G. A. (1956). The Magical Number Seven, Plus or Minus Two: Some Limits on Our Capacity for Processing Information. *Psychological Review*, 63:8–97. Russo, J. E. (1977). The Value of Unit Price Information. *Journal of Marketing Research*, 14l:193–201.

5 Alba, J. W., and Chattopadhyay, A. (1985). Effects of Context and Part-category Cues on Recall of Competing Brands. *Journal of Marketing Research*, 22:340–349. Alba, J. W., and Chattopadhyay, A. (1986). Salience Effects on Brand Recall. *Journal of Marketing Research*, 23:363–369.

6 Nedungadi, P. (1990). Recall and Consumer Consideration Sets: Influencing Choice without Altering Evaluations. *Journal of Consumer Research*, 17:263–276.

7 Huber, J., Payne, J. W., and Puto, C. (1982). Adding Asymmetrically Dominated Alternatives: Violations of Regularity and the Similarity Hypothesis. *Journal of Consumer Research*, 9:90–98. Huber, J., and Puto, C. (1983). Market Boundaries and Product Choice: Illustrating Attraction and Substitution Effects. *Journal of Consumer Research*, 10:31–44. Simonson, I., and Tversky, A. (1992).

Choice in Context: Trade-off Contrast and Extremeness Aversion. *Journal of Marketing Research*, 29:281–295.

8 Simonson, I. (1989). Choice Based on Reasons: The Case of Attraction and Compromise Effects. *Journal of Consumer Research*, 16:158–174; Simonson, I., and Tversky, A. (1992). Choice in Context: Trade-off Contrast and Extremeness Aversion. *Journal of Marketing Research,* 29:281–295.

9 Kardes, F. R. (2002). *Consumer Behavior and Managerial Decision Making*, 2nd ed. Upper Saddle River, NJ: Pearson Education/Prentice Hall.

10 For a discussion of stimulus-based, memory-based, and mixed choice, see Lynch, J. G., and Srull, T. K. (1982). Memory and Attentional Factors in Consumer Choice: Concepts and Research Methods. *Journal of Consumer Research*, 9:18–37.

11 Biehal, G. J., and Chakravarti, D. (1983). Information Accessibility as a Moderator of Consumer Choice. *Journal of Consumer Research*, 10:1–14.

12 Alba, J. W., Marmorstein, H., and Chattopadhyay, A. (1992). Transitions in Preference over Time: The Effects of Memory on Message Persuasiveness. *Journal of Marketing Research,* 29:406–416.

13 Kardes, F. R. (1986). Effects of Initial Product Judgments on Subsequent Memory-based Judgments. *Journal of Consumer Research*, 13:1–11.

14 Fazio, R. H. (1990). Multiple Processes by Which Attitudes Guide Behavior: The MODE Model as an Integrative Framework. In M. P. Zanna (ed.), *Advances in Experimental Social Psychology*, (75–109). New York: Academic Press; Sanbonmatsu, D. M., and Fazio, R. H. (1990). The Role of Attitudes in Memory-based Decision Making. *Journal of Personality and Social Psychology*, 59:614–622.

15 Chaiken, S., and Trope, Y. (eds.) (1999). *Dual-process Theories in Social Psychology*. New York: Guilford.

16 Stec, A. M., and Bernstein, D. A. (1999). The Scope of Psychology: More Than Meets The Eye. In Stec, A. M. and Bernstein, D. A. (eds.), *Psychology: Fields of Application*, (1–16). Boston, MA: Houghton Mifflin Company.

17 Kardes, F. R., Posavac, S. S., and Cronley, M. L. (2004). Consumer Inference: A Review of Processes, Bases, and Judgment Contexts, *Journal of Consumer Psychology*, 14:3, 230–256; Kardes, F. R., Cronley, M. L., Kellaris, J. J., and Posavac, S. S. (2004). The Role of Selective Information Processing in Price-quality Inference, *Journal of Consumer Research*, 31:2, 368–374; Lichtenstein, D. R., and Burton, S. (1989). The Relationship between Perceived and Objective Price-quality. *Journal of Marketing Research*, 26:429–443.

18 Tversky, A., and Kahneman, D. (1974). Judgment under Uncertainty: Heuristics and Biases. *Science,*

185:1124–1131; Gilovich, T., Griffin, D., and Kahneman, D. (2002). Heuristics and Biases: *The Psychology of Intuitive Judgment*. Cambridge, UK: Cambridge University Press.

19 Tversky, A., and Kahneman, D. (1974). Judgment under Uncertainty: Heuristics and Biases. *Science,* 185:1124–1131; Gilovich, T., Griffin, D., and Kahneman, D. (2002). *Heuristics and Biases: The Psychology of Intuitive Judgment*. Cambridge, UK: Cambridge University Press.

20 Gilovich, T., Vallone, R., and Tversky, A. (1985). The Hot Hand in Basketball: On the Misperception of Random Sequences. *Cognitive Psychology*, 17:295–314.

21 Tversky, A., and Kahneman, D. (1974). Judgment under Uncertainty: *Heuristics and Biases. Science*, 185:1124–1131; Gilovich, T., Griffin, D., and Kahneman, D. (2002). *Heuristics and Biases: The Psychology of Intuitive Judgment*. Cambridge, UK: Cambridge University Press.

22 Plous, S. (1993). *The Psychology of Judgment and Decision Making*. New York: McGraw-Hill.

23 Schwarz, N. (1998). Accessible Content and Accessibility Experiences: The Interplay of Declarative and Experiential Information in Judgment. *Personality and Social Psychology Review*, 2:87–99.

24 Schwarz, N. (1998). Accessible Content and Accessibility Experiences: The Interplay of Declarative and Experiential Information in Judgment. *Personality and Social Psychology Review*, 2:87–99.

25 Schwarz, N. (1998). Accessible Content and Accessibility Experiences: The Interplay of Declarative and Experiential Information in Judgment. *Personality and Social Psychology Review*, 2:87–99.

26 Kahneman, D., and Tversky, A. (1984). Choice, Values, and Frames. *American Psychologist*, 39:341–350.

27 Sherman, S. J., Cialdini, R. B., Schwartzman, D. F., and Reynolds, K. D. (1985). Imagining Can Heighten or Lower the Perceived Likelihood of Contracting a Disease: The Mediating Effect of Ease of Imagery. *Personality and Social Psychology Bulletin*, 11:118–127.

28 Tversky, A., and Kahneman, D. (1974). Judgment under Uncertainty: Heuristics and Biases. *Science*, 185:1124–1131; Gilovich, T., Griffin, D., and Kahneman, D. (2002). *Heuristics and Biases: The Psychology of Intuitive Judgment*. Cambridge, UK: Cambridge University Press.

29 Northcraft, G. B., and Neale, M. A. (1987). Experts, Amateurs, and Real Estate: An Anchoring and Adjustment Perspective on Property Pricing Decisions. *Organizational Behavior and Human Decision Processes*, 39:84–97.

30 Wansink, B., Kent, R. J., and Hoch, S. J. (1998). An Anchoring and Adjustment Model of Purchase Quantity Decisions. *Journal of Marketing Research*, 35:71–81.

31 Payne, J. W., Bettman, J. R., and Johnson, E. J. (1993). *The Adaptive Decision Maker*. Cambridge, UK: Cambridge University Press.

32 Payne, J. W., Bettman, J. R., and Johnson, E. J. (1993). *The Adaptive Decision Maker*. Cambridge, UK: Cambridge University Press; Tversky, A. (1972). Elimination by Aspects: A Theory of Choice. *Psychological Review*, 79:281–299.

33 Payne, J. W., Bettman, J. R., and Johnson, E. J. (1993). *The Adaptive Decision Maker*. Cambridge, UK: Cambridge University Press; Tversky, A. (1969). Intransitivity of Preferences. *Psychological Review*, 76:31–48.

34 Payne, J. W., Bettman, J. R., and Johnson, E. J. (1993). *The Adaptive Decision Maker*. Cambridge, UK: Cambridge University Press.

35 Shafir, E., Osherson, D. N., & Tversky, A. (1993). Reason-based Choice. *Cognition*, 49, 11–36.

36 Ardichvili, A., and Kuchinke, K. P. (2002). Leadership Style and Cultural Values among Managers and Subordinates: A Comparative Study of Four Countries of the Former Soviet Union, Germany, and the US. *Human Resources Development International*, 5:1, 99–117; DuPraw, M. E., and Axner, M. (2005, January 11). Working on Common Cross-cultural Communication Challenges. *A More Perfect Union* [Online]. Available: www.wwcd.org; Guss, C. D. (2002). Decision Making in Individualistic and Collectivistic Cultures. In W. J. Lonner, D. L. Dinnel, S. A. Hayes, and D. N. Sattler (eds.), *Online Readings in Psychology and Culture*, ch. 3. Center for Cross-Cultural Research, Western Washington University, Bellingham, Washington, [Online]. Available: www.wwu.edu; Schramm-Nielsen, J. (2001). Cultural Dimensions of Decision Making: Denmark and France Compared. *Journal of Managerial Psychology*, 16:6, 404–423.

37 Ardichvili, A., and Kuchinke, K. P. (2002). Leadership Style and Cultural Values among Managers and Subordinates: A Comparative Study of Four Countries of the Former Soviet Union, Germany, and the US. *Human Resources Development International*, 5:1, 99–117.

38 Morrison, T. C. (2002, Spring). How a Seemingly Innocuous Slogan Led to the Pizza Wars. *IP on Trial* [Online]. Available: www.pbwt.com.

39 Gindy, D. M. (2001, June 26). Dual between Pizza Hut and Papa John's Comes to an End. *Los Angeles Daily Journal* [Online]. Available: www.gindylaw.com.

40 Milloy, S. (2000, January 22). Pepperoni, Cheese and Whining; Pizza Hut Targets the Competition. *Cato.org* [Online]. Available: www.cato.org; Harshaw, R. (2004, October 15). Do You Really Believe That? *Rising Media* [Online]. Available: www.risingmedia.com.

41 Harshaw, R. (2004, October 15). Do You Really Believe That? *Rising Media* [Online]. Available: www.risingmedia.com.

Chapter 5

1 von Neumann, J., and Morgenstern, O. (1947). *Theory of Games and Economic Behavior*. Princeton, NJ: Princeton University Press.

2 Kahneman, D., and Tversky, A. (1979). Prospect Theory: An Analysis of Decision under Risk. *Econometrica*, 47:263–291; Tversky, A., and Kahneman, D. (1981). The Framing of Decisions and the Psychology of Choice. *Science*, 211:453–458.

3 Kahneman, D., and Tversky, A. (1984). Choices, Values, and Frames. *American Psychologist*, 39:341–350.

4 Thaler, R. H. (1985). Mental Accounting and Consumer Choice. *Marketing Science*, 4:199–214.

5 Dhar, R. (1997). Consumer Preference for a No-Choice Option. *Journal of Consumer Research*, 24:215–231; Dhar, R., and Nowlis, S. M. (1999). The Effect of Time Pressure on Consumer Choice Deferral. *Journal of Consumer Research*, 25:369–384.

6 Thaler, R. H. (1985). Mental Accounting and Consumer Choice. *Marketing Science*, 4:199–214.

7 Soman, D., & Gourville, J. (2001). Transaction Decoupling: How Price Bundling Affects the Decision to Consume. *Journal of Marketing Research*, 38:30–44.

8 Gourville, J. (1998). Pennies-a-Day: The Effect of Temporal Reframing on Transaction Evaluation. *Journal of Consumer Research*, 24:395–408.

9 Grether, D. M., and Plott, C. R. (1979). Economic Theory and the Preference Reversal Phenomenon. *American Economic Review*, 69:623–638; Lichtenstein, S., and Slovic, P. (1971). Reversal of Preferences between Bids and Choices in Gambling Decisions. *Journal of Experimental Psychology*, 89:46–55.

10 Tversky, A., Sattah, S., and Slovic, P. (1988). Contingent Weighting in Judgment and Choice. *Psychological Review*, 95:371–384.

11 Nowlis, S. M., and Simonson, I. (1997). Attribute-Task Compatibility as a Determinant of Consumer Preference Reversals. *Journal of Marketing Research*, 34:205–218.

12 Hsee, C. K. (1996). The Evaluability Hypothesis: An Explanation of Preference Reversals Between Joint and Separate Evaluations of Alternatives. *Organizational Behavior and Human Decision Processes*, 46:247–257; Hsee, C. K., and LeClerc, F. (1998). Will Products Look More Attractive When Evaluated Jointly or When Evaluated Separately? *Journal of Consumer Research*, 25:175–186; Hsee, C. K, Loewenstein, G. R., Blount, S., and Bazerman, M. H. (1999). Preference Reversals Between Joint and Separate Evaluation of Options: A

Review and Theoretical Analysis. *Psychological Bulletin*, 125:576–590.

13 Sanbonmatsu, D. M., Posavac, S. S., Kardes, F. R., and Mantel, S. P. (1998). Selective Hypothesis Testing. *Psychonomic Bulletin & Review*, 5:197–220.

14 Shafir, E. (1993). Choosing Versus Rejecting: Why Some Options Are Both Better and Worse Than Others. *Memory & Cognition*, 21:546–556.

15 Ofir, C., & Simonson, I. (2001). In Search of Negative Customer Feedback: The Effect of Expecting to Evaluate on Satisfaction Evaluations. *Journal of Marketing Research*, 38:170–182.

16 Posavac, S. S., Kardes, F. R., Sanbonmatsu, D. M., and Fitzsimons, G. J. (2005). Blissful Insularity: When Brands Are Judged in Isolation from Competitors. *Marketing Letters*, 16:87–97; Posavac, S. S., Sanbonmatsu, D. M., Kardes, F. R., and Fitzsimons, G. J. (2004). The Brand Positivity Effect: When Evaluation Confers Preference. *Journal of Consumer Research*, 31:643–651.

17 Cronley, M. L., Posavac, S. S., Meyer, T., Kardes, F. R., and Kellaris, J. J. (2005). A Selective Hypothesis Testing Perspective on Price-Quality Inference and Inference-Based Choice. *Journal of Consumer Psychology*, 15:159–169; Kardes, F. R., Cronley, M. L., Kellaris, J. J., and Posavac, S. S. (2004). The Role of Selective Information Processing in Price-Quality Inference. *Journal of Consumer Research*, 31:368–374.

18 Neff, J. (2009). Private Label Winning Battle of Brands; Marketers Face Moment of Truth as Retailers' Lines Soar to Historic Sales High. *Advertising Age*, February 3, 1.

19 Yates, J. F., Lee, J. W., and Bush, J. G. (1997). General Knowledge Overconfidence: Cross-National Variations, Response Style, and "Reality." *Organizational Behavior and Human Decision Processes*, 70:87–94.

20 Kerr, R. A. (1979). Petroleum Explorations: Discouragement about the Atlantic Outer Continental Shelf Deepens. *Science*, 1069–1072.

Chapter 6

1 Harrods introduces scent marketing (2009, March 19). UTalkMarketing.com News [Online]. Available: http://www.utalkmarketing.com; see also http://www.brandsenseagency.com.

2 Statistics on U.S. media gathered from the following sources (2007, July): http://www.global computing.com; http://radio.about.com; http://www.naa.org; http://www.magazine.org. Shenk, D. (1997). *Surviving the information glut*. New York: Harper Edge.

3 Nielsen report Americans watch TV at record levels (2005, September 29). *Nielson Media Research* [Online]. Available: http://www.neilsonmedia.com. The source: Newspapers

by the numbers (2006). *Newspaper Association of America* [Online]. Available: http://www.naa.org. Almost three-quarters of all U.S. adults—An estimated 163 million—Go online (2005, May 12). *Harris Interactive Online* [Online]. Available: http://www.harrisinteractive.com. AT&T survey reveals that guys still gab more—barely (2007, June 12). *AT&T Newsroom* [Online]. Available: http://www.att.com/gen/press-room.

4 Howard, T. (2003). Pay the same, get less as package volume falls. *USA Today, March 17*, 3b. Winter, G. (2001). What keeps a bottom line healthy? Weight loss. *New York Times, Jan. 2*, 1.

5 Howard, T. (2003). Pay the same, get less as package volume falls. *USA Today, March 17*, 3b.

6 Parmar, A. (2004). Marketers ask: Hues on first? *Marketing News, Feb. 5*, 8, 10.

7 Hesseldahl, A. (2000). Ten o' clock tech: Colorful computers here to stay. *Forbes.com* [Online], 1. Available: www.forbes.com.

8 Parmar, A. (2004). Marketers ask: Hues on first? *Marketing News, Feb 5*, 8, 10. See also *www.apple.com*.

9 Based on anecdotal evidence collected by two of this book's authors over five years.

10 Zanot, E. J., Pincus, J. D., and Lamp, E. J. (1983). Public perceptions of submliminal advertising. *Journal of Advertising, 12*, 37–45. Pratkanis, A. R., Eskenazi, J., and Greenwald, A. G. (1994). What you expect is what you believe (but not necessarily what you get): A test of the effectiveness of subliminal self-help audiotapes. *Journal of Applied Social Psychology, 15 (3)*, 251–276.

11 Pratkanis, A. R., Eskenazi, J., and Greenwald, A. G. (1994). What you expect is what you believe (but not necessarily what you get): A test of the effectiveness of subliminal self-help audiotapes. *Journal of Applied Social Psychology, 15 (3)*, 251–276. Haberstroh, J. (1994). *Ice cube sex*. Notre Dame: Cross Roads Books. Rogers, S. (1993). How a publicity blitz created the myth of subliminal advertising. *Public Relations Quarterly*, 12–17.

12 Key, W. B. (1973). *Subliminal seduction*. Englewood Cliffs, NJ: Signet. Key, W. B. (1976). *Media sexploitation*. Englewood Cliffs, NJ: Signet. Key, W. B. (1980). *The clam-plate orgy*. Englewood Cliffs, NJ: Signet.

13 Miller, G. A. (1956). The magical number seven, plus or minus two: Some limits on our capacity for processing information. *Psychological Review, 63*, 81–97.

14 Newell, A. and Simon, H. A. (1972). *Human Problem Solving*. Englewood Cliffs, NJ: Prentice-Hall.

15 Alba, J. W. and Hutchinson, J. W. (1987). Dimensions of consumer expertise. *Journal of Consumer Research, 13*, 411–454.

16 Kahneman, D. (1973). *Attention and Effort*. Englewood Cliffs, NJ: Prentice-Hall.

17 Pavelchak, M. A., Antil, J. H., and Munch, J. M. (1988). The Super Bowl: An investigation into the relationship among program context, emotional experience, and ad recall. *Journal of Consumer Research, 15,* 360–367.

18 Kahneman, D. (1973). *Attention and Effort.* Englewood Cliffs, NJ: Prentice-Hall.

19 Greenwald, A. G. and Leavitt, C. (1984). Audience involvement in advertising: Four levels. *Journal of Consumer Research, 11,* 581–592. Nisbett, R. E. and Ross, L. (1980). *Human inference: Strategies and shortcomings of social judgment.* Englewood Cliffs, NJ: Prentice-Hall.

20 Pisani, J. (2006, August 1). Ad placement gets extreme. *BusinessWeek* [Online]. Available: BusinessWeek.com.

21 Haugtvedt, C. P., Schumann, D. W., Schneier, W. L., and Warren, W. L. (1994). Advertising repetition and variation strategies: Implications for understanding attitude strength. *Journal of Consumer Research, 21,* 176–189. Schumann, D. W., Petty, R. E., and Clemons, D. S. (1990). Predicting the effectiveness of different strategies of advertising variation: A test of the repetition-variation hypotheses. *Journal of Consumer Research, 17,* 192–202. Unnava, R. H. and Burnkrant, R. E. (1991). An imagery-processing view of the role of pictures in print advertisements. *Journal of Marketing Research, 28,* 226–231.

22 Kisielius, J., and Sternthal, B. (1984). Detecting and explaining vividness effects in attitudinal judgments. *Journal of Marketing Research, 21,* 54–64. Kisielius, J. and Sternthal, B. (1986). Examining the vividness controversy: An availability-valence interpretation. *Journal of Consumer Research, 12,* 418–431. Taylor, S. E. and Thompson, S. C. (1982). Stalking the elusive' vividness' effect.' *Psychological Review, 89,* 155–181.

23 Nisbett, R. E. and Ross, L. (1980). *Human inference: Strategies and shortcomings of social judgment.* Englewood Cliffs, NJ: Prentice-Hall, 45.

24 MacKenzie, S. B. (1986). The role of attention in mediating the effect of advertising on attribute importance. *Journal of Consumer Research, 13,* 174–195.

25 Herr, P. M., Kardes, F. R., and Kim, J. (1991). Effects of word-of-mouth and product-attribute information on persuasion: An accessibility-diagnosticity perspective. *Journal of Consumer Research, 17,* 454–462.

Chapter 7

1 Gilovich, T. (1991). *How We Know What Isn't So: The Fallibility of Human Reason in Everyday Life.* New York: Free Press.

2 Wyer, R. S. (2004). *Social Comprehension and Judgment: The Role of Situation Models, Narratives, and Implicit Theories.* Mahwah, NJ: Erlbaum; Wyer, R. S. and Srull, T. K. (1989). *Memory and Cognition in Its Social Context.* Hillsdale, NJ: Erlbaum.

3 Darby, M. R. and Karni, E. (1973). Free competition and the optimal amount of fraud. *Journal of Law and Economics,* 16, 66–86; Wright, A. and Lynch, J. G. (1995). Communication effects of advertising versus direct experience when both search and experience attributes are present. *Journal of Consumer Research,* 21, 708–718.

4 Fishbein, M. and Ajzen, I. (1975). *Belief, Attitude, Intention, and Behavior: An Introduction to Theory and Research.* Reading, MA: Addison-Wesley.

5 Kardes, F. R., Posavac, S. S., and Cronley, M. L. (2004). Consumer inference: A review of processes, bases, and judgment contexts. *Journal of Consumer Psychology,* 14, 230–256.

6 Kardes, F. R., Cronley, M. L., Kellaris, J. J., and Posavac, S. S. (2004). The role of selective information processing in price-quality inference. *Journal of Consumer Research,* 31, 368–374; Cronley, M. L., Posavac, S. S., Meyer, T., Kardes, F. R. and Kellaris, J. J. (2005). A selective hypothesis testing perspective on price-quality inference and inference-based choice. *Journal of Consumer Psychology,* 15, 159–169.

7 Sanbonmatsu, D. M., Kardes, F. R., and Sansone, C. (1991). Remembering less and inferring more: The effects of the timing of judgment on inferences about unknown attributes. *Journal of Personality and Social Psychology,* 61, 546–554.

8 Sujan, M. (1985). Consumer knowledge: Effects on evaluation processes mediating consumer judgments. *Journal of Consumer Research,* 12, 31–46; Sujan, M. and Dekleva, C. (1987). Product categorization and inference making: Some implications for comparative advertising. *Journal of Consumer Research,* 14, 372–378.

9 Albarracin, D., Johnson, B. T. and Zanna, M. P. (Eds.) (2005). *The Handbook of Attitudes.* Mahwah, NJ: Erlbaum.

10 Fazio, R. H. (1989). On the Power and Functionality of Attitudes: The Role of Attitude Accessibility. In A. R. Pratkanis, S. J. Breckler, and A. G. Greenwald (eds.), *Attitude Structure and Function,* 153–179. Hillsdale, NJ: Erlbaum; Kruglanski, A. W. and Stroebe, W. (2005). The Influence of Beliefs and Goals on Attitudes: Issues of Structure, Function, and Dynamics. In D. Albarracin, B. T. Johnson, and M. P. Zanna (eds.), *The Handbook of Attitudes,* 323–368. Mahwah, NJ: Erlbaum.

11 Zanna, M. P. and Rempel, J. K. (1988). Attitudes: A New Look at an Old Concept. In D. Bar-Tal and A. W. Kruglanski (eds.), *The Social Psychology of Knowledge,* 315–334. Cambridge, UK: Cambridge University Press.

12 Kardes, F. R., Kim, J. and Lim, J. S. (1994). Moderating effects of prior knowledge on the perceived diagnosticity of beliefs derived from implicit versus explicit product claims. *Journal of Business Research,* 29, 219–224.

13 Clore, G. L. and Schnall, S. (2005). The Influence of Affect on Attitude. In D. Albarracin, B. T. Johnson, and M. P. Zanna (eds.), *The Handbook of Attitudes, 437–489.* Mahwah, NJ: Erlbaum; Kruglanski, A. W. and Stroebe, W. (2005). The Influence of Beliefs and Goals on Attitudes: Issues of Structure, Function, and Dynamics. In D. Albarracin, B. T. Johnson, and M. P. Zanna (eds.), *The Handbook of Attitudes, 323–368.* Mahwah, NJ: Erlbaum.

14 Chaiken, S. and Trope, Y. (eds.) (1999). *Dual-process Theories in Social Psychology.* New York: Guilford; Albarracin, D., Johnson, B. T., and Zanna, M. P. (eds.), *The Handbook of Attitudes.* Mahwah, NJ: Erlbaum; Zaichowsky, J. (1985). Measuring the involvement construct, *Journal of Consumer Research,* 12, 341–352.

15 Chaiken, S. and Trope, Y. (eds.) (1999). *Dual-process Theories in Social Psychology.* New York: Guilford.

16 Fishbein, M. and Ajzen, I. (1975). *Belief, Attitude, Intention, and Behavior: An Introduction to Theory and Research.* Reading, MA: Addison-Wesley.

17 Anderson, N. H. (1981). *Foundations of Information Integration Theory.* New York: Academic Press; Anderson, N. H. (1982). *Methods of Information Integration Theory.* New York: Academic Press; Lynch, J. G. (1985). Uniqueness issues in the decompositional modeling of multiattribute overall evaluations: An information integration perspective. *Journal of Marketing Research,* 22, 1–19.

18 Petty, R. E., Cacioppo, J. T., and Schumann, D. (1983). Central and peripheral routes to advertising effectiveness: The moderating role of involvement. *Journal of Consumer Research,* 10, 135–146; Petty, R. E. and Wegener, D. T. (1999). The Elaboration Likelihood Model: Current Status and Controversies. In Chaiken, S. and Trope, Y. (eds.). *Dual-process Theories in Social Psychology,* 41–72. New York: Guilford.

19 Chen, S. and Chaiken, S. (1999). The Heuristic/Systematic Model in Its Broader Context. In Chaiken, S. and Trope, Y. (eds.). *Dual-process Theories in Social Psychology,* 73–96. New York: Guilford; Maheswaran, D., Mackie, D. M., and Chaiken, S. (1992). Brand name as a heuristic cue: The effects of task importance and expectancy confirmation on consumer judgments. *Journal of Consumer Psychology,* 1, 317–336.

20 Albarracin, D., Johnson, B. T., and Zanna, M. P. (eds.) (2005). *The Handbook of Attitudes.* Mahwah, NJ: Erlbaum.

21 Wyer, R. S. and Albarracin, D. (2005). Belief Formation, Organization, and Change: Cognitive and Motivational Influences. In Albarracin, D., Johnson, B. T., and Zanna, M. P. (eds.) (2005). *The Handbook of Attitudes, 273–322.* Mahwah, NJ: Erlbaum.

22 Kruglanski, A. W. and Orehek, E. (2007). Partitioning the domain of social inference: Dual mode and systems models and their alternatives. *Annual Review of Psychology,* 58, 291–316.

23 Villanueva, J., Yoo, S. and Hanssens, D. (2008). The impact or marketing-induced versus word-of-mouth customer acquisition on customer equity growth. *Journal of Marketing Research,* 45, 48–59.

24 Gupta, S. and Lehmann, D. R. (2005). *Managing Customers as Investments: The Strategic Value of Customers in the Long Run.* Upper Saddle River, NJ: Wharton School Publishing, a division of Pearson Education.

25 Hempel, J. (2006). Selling a cause? Better make it pop. *BusinessWeek,* 3972, 75.

Chapter 8

1 Holbrook, M. B. (1993). Nostalgia and Consumption Preferences: Some Emerging Patterns of Consumer Tastes. *Journal of Consumer Research,* 20:245–256.

2 Brendl, C. M., Markman, A. B., and Messner, C. (2003). Devaluation of goal-unrelated choice options. *Journal of Consumer Research,* 29:463–473. Markman, A. B., and Brendl, C. M. (2005). Goals, policies, preferences, and actions. In Kardes, F. R., Herr, P. M., and Nantel, J. (eds.), *Applying Social Cognition to Consumer-Focused Strategy,* 183–199. Mahwah, NJ: Lawrence Erlbaum Associates.

3 Hull, C. L. (1943). *Principles of Behavior.* New York: Appleton-Century-Crofts.

4 Maslow, A. H. (1970). Motivation and Personality. New York: Harper.

5 Ryan, R. M., and Deci, E. L. (2000). Self-Determination Theory and the Facilitation of Intrinsic Motivation, Social Development, and Well-Being. *American Psychologist,* 55:68–78.

6 Cialdini, R. B., Trost, M. R., and Newsom, J. T. (1995). Preference for Consistency: The Development of a Valid Measure and the Discovery of Surprising Behavioral Implications. *Journal of Personality and Social Psychology,* 69:318–328.

7 Katz, D. (1960). The Functional Approach to the Study of Attitudes. *Public Opinion Quarterly,* 24:163–204; Petty, R. E., and Wegener, D. T. (1998). Matching versus Mismatching Attitude Functions: Implications for Scrutiny of Persuasive Messages. *Personality and Social Psychology Bulletin,* 24:227–240; Smith, M. B., Bruner, J. S., and White, R. W. (1956). Opinions and Personality. New York: Wiley.

8 Higgins, E. T. (1998). Promotion and Prevention: Regulatory Focus as a Motivational Principle. In Zanna, M. P. (ed.), Advances in Experimental Social Psychology. San Diego, CA: Academic Press; Higgins, E. T. (2002). How Self-Regulation Creates Distinct Values: The Case of Promotion and Prevention Decision Making. *Journal of Consumer Psychology,* 12:177–192.

9 Kardes, F. R. (2005). The Psychology of Advertising. In Brock, T. C., and Green, M. C. (eds.), Persuasion:

Psychological Insights and Perspectives. Thousand Oaks, CA: Sage Publications; Kardes, F. R., and Cronley, M. L. (2000). The Role of Approach/Avoidance Asymmetries in Motivated Belief Formation and Change. In Ratneshwar, S., Mick, D. G., and Huffman, C. (eds.), The Why of Consumption: Contemporary Perspectives on Consumer Motives, Goals, and Desires. London: Routledge.

10 Fazio, R. H., Herr, P. M., and Powell, M. C. (1992). On the Development and Strength of Category-Brand Associations in Memory: The Case of Mystery Ads. *Journal of Consumer Psychology*, 1:1–13.

11 Heider, F. (1958). *The Psychology of Interpersonal Relations.* New York: Wiley.

12 Festinger, C. (1957). A *Theory of Cognitive Dissonance.* Evanston, IL: Row and Peterson.

13 Brehm, J. W. (1956). Post-Decision Changes in Desirability of Alternatives. *Journal of Abnormal and Social Psychology*, 52:384–389.

14 Isen, A. M. (2001). An Influence of Positive Affect on Decision Making in Complex Situations: Theoretical Issues with Practical Implications. *Journal of Consumer Psychology*, 11:75–86; Isen, A. M. (2008). Positive Affect and Decision Processes: Some Recent Theoretical Developments with Practical Implications. In C. P. Haugtedt, P. M. Herr, and F. R. Kardes (eds.), Handbook of Consumer Psychology, 273–296. New York: Psychology Press.

15 Cohen, J. B., Pham, M. T., and Andrade, E. B. (2008). The Nature and Role of Affect in Consumer Behavior. In C. P. Haugtedt, P. M. Herr, and F. R. Kardes (eds.), Handbook of Consumer Psychology, 297–348. New York: Psychology Press; Pham, M. (1998). Representativeness, Relevance and the Use of Feelings in Decision Making. *Journal of Consumer Research*, 25:144–159; Schwarz, N., and Clore, G. L. (2007). Feelings and Phenomenal Experiences. In A. W. Kruglanski, and E. T. Higgins (eds.), Social Psychology: Handbook of Basic Principles, 385–407. New York: Guilford.

16 Yeung, C. W. M., and Wyer, R. S. (2004). Affect, Appraisal, and Consumer Judgment. *Journal of Consumer Research*, 31:412–424.

17 Adaval, R. (2001). Sometimes It Just Feels Right: The Differential Weighting of Affect-Consistent and Affect-Inconsistent Product Information. *Journal of Consumer Research,* 28:1–17.

18 Watson, D., and Tellegen, A. (1985). Toward a Consensual Structure of Mood. *Psychological Bulletin*, 98:219–235.

19 Schwarz, N., and Clore, G. L. (2007). Feelings and Phenomenal Experiences. In A. W. Kruglanski, and E. T. Higgins (eds.), Social Psychology: Handbook of Basic Principles, 385–407. New York: Guilford.

20 Schacter, S., and Singer, J. E. (1962). Cognitive, Social, and Physiological Determinants of Emotional State. *Psychological Review*, 69:379–399.

21 Mandler, G. (1982). The Structure of Value: Accounting for Taste. In M. S. Clark, & S. T. Fiske (eds.), Affect and Cognition: The 17th Annual Carnegie Symposium on Cognition. Hillsdale, NJ: Erlbaum; Meyers-Levy, J., and Tybout, A. M. (1989). Schema Congruity as a Basis for Product Evaluation. *Journal of Consumer Research*, 16:39–54. Stayman, D. M., Alden, D. L., and Smith, K. H. (1992). Some Effects of Schematic Processing on Consumer Expectations and Disconfirmation Judgments. *Journal of Consumer Research*, 19:240–255.

22 Zillmann, D. (1978). Attribution and Misattribution of Excitatory Reactions. In J. H. Harvey, W. Ickes, and R. F. Kidd (eds.), New Directions in Attribution Research, vol. 2. Hillsdale, NJ: Erlbaum.

23 Kardes, F. R., Cronley, M. L., and Posavac, S. S. (2005). Using Implementation Intentions to Increase New Product Consumption: A Field Experiment. In F. R. Kardes, P. M. Herr, and J. Nantel (eds.), Applying Social Cognition to Consumer-Focused Strategy, 219–233. Mahwah, NJ: Erlbaum.

24 Aaker, J. L., and Lee, A. Y. (2001). "I" Seek Pleasures and "We" Avoid Pains: The Role of Self-Regulatory Goals in Information Processing and Persuasion. *Journal of Consumer Research*, 28:33–49.

Chapter 9

1 West, P. M., Brown, C. L., and Hoch, S. J. (1996). Consumption Vocabulary and Preference Formation. *Journal of Consumer Research*, 23:120–135.

2 Mackintosh, N. J. (1974). *The Psychology of Animal Learning.* London: Academic Press.

3 Gorn, G. J. (1982). The Effects of Music in Advertising on Choice Behavior: A Classical Conditioning Approach. *Journal of Marketing*, 46:94–101; Kim, J., Allen, C. T., and Kardes, F. R. (1996). An Investigation of the Mediational Mechanisms Underlying Attitudinal Conditioning. *Journal of Marketing Research*, 33:318–328; McSweeney, F. K., and Bierley, C. (1984). Recent Developments in Classical Conditioning. *Journal of Consumer Research*, 11:619–631; Shimp, T. A., Stuart, E. W., and Engle, R. W. (1991). A Program of Classical Conditioning Experiments Testing Variations in the Conditioned Stimulus and Contents. *Journal of Consumer Research*, 18:1–12.

4 Cacioppo, J. T., Marshall-Goodell, B. S., Tassinary, L. G., and Petty, R. E. (1992). Rudimentary Determinants of Attitudes: Classical Conditioning Is More Effective When Prior Knowledge about the Attitude Stimulus Is Low Than High. *Journal of Experimental Social Psychology*, 28:207–233.

5 van Osselaer, S. M. J., and Janiszewski, C. (2001). Two Ways of Learning Brand Associations. *Journal of Consumer Research*, 28:202–223.

6 van Osselaer, S. M. J., and Alba, J. W. (2000). Consumer Learning and Brand Equity. *Journal of Consumer Research*, 27:1–16.

7 van Osselaer, S. M. J., and Alba, J. W. (2003). Locus of Equity and Brand Extension. *Journal of Consumer Research*, 29:539–550.

8 Feinburg, R. A. (1986). Credit Cards as Spending Facilitating Stimuli. *Journal of Consumer Research*, 13:348–356.

9 Nord, W. R., and Peter, J. P. (1980). A Behavior Modification Perspective on Marketing. *Journal of Marketing*, 41:36–47; Skinner, B. F. (1969). *Contingencies of Reinforcement: A Theoretical Analysis*. New York: Appleton-Century-Crofts.

10 Alba, J. W., and Hutchinson, J. W. (1987). Dimensions of Consumer Expertise. *Journal of Consumer Research*, 13:411–454.

11 Bransford, J. D., and Johnson, M. K. (1972). Contextual Prerequisites for Understanding: Some Investigations of Comprehension and Recall. *Journal of Verbal Learning and Verbal Behavior*, 11:717–726.

12 Bransford, J. D., and Johnson, M. K. (1972). Contextual Prerequisites for Understanding: Some Investigations of Comprehension and Recall. *Journal of Verbal Learning and Verbal Behavior*, 11:717–726.

13 Harris, R. J. (1977). Comprehension of Pragmatic Implications in Advertising. *Journal of Applied Psychology*, 62:603–609; Harris, R. J., and Monaco, G. E. (1978). Psychology of Pragmatic Implications in Advertising: Information Processing between the Lines. *Journal of Experimental Psychology: General*, 107:1–22.

14 Preston, I. L. (1977). The FTC's Handling of Puffery and Other Selling Claims Made "By Implication." *Journal of Business Research*, 5:155–181.

15 Mazis, M. B., and Adkinson, J. E. (1976). An Experimental Evaluation of a Proposed Corrective Advertising Remedy. *Journal of Marketing Research*, 13:178–183. Mazursky, D. and Schul, Y. (1988). The Effects of Advertisement Encoding on the Failure to Discount Information: Implications for the Sleeper Effect. *Journal of Consumer Research*, 15:24–36; Schul, Y., and Mazursky, D. (1990). Conditions Facilitating Successful Discounting in Consumer Decision Making. *Journal of Consumer Research*, 16:442–451; Wilkie, W., McNeill, D., and Mazis, M. (1984). Marketing's "Scarlet Letter": The Theory and Practice of Corrective Advertising. *Journal of Marketing*, 48:11–31.

16 Gilbert (1991). How Mental Systems Believe. *American Psychologist*, 46:107–119.

17 Anderson, J. R. (1983). *The Architecture of Cognition*. Cambridge, MA: Harvard University Press; Atkinson, R. C., and Shiffrin, R. M. (1968). Human Memory: A Proposed System and Its Control Processes. In K. W. Spence, and J. T. Spence (eds.), *Advances in the Psychology of Learning and Motivation Research and Theory*, vol. 2. New York: Academic Press.

18 Schacter, D. L. (1999). The Seven Sins of Memory: Insights from Psychology and Cognitive Neuroscience. *American Psychologist*, 54:182–203.

19 Craik, F. I. M., and Lockhart, R. S. (1972). Levels of Processing: A Framework for Memory Research. *Journal of Verbal Learning and Verbal Behavior*, 11:671–684; Craik, F. I. M., and Tulving, E. (1975). Depth of Processing and the Retention of Words in Episodic Memory. *Journal of Experimental Psychology: General*, 104:268–294.

20 Slamecka, N. J., and Graf, P. (1978). The Generation Effect: Delineation of a Phenomenon. *Journal of Experimental Psychology: Learning, Memory, and Cognition*, 4:592–604.

21 Brown, A. S. (1991). A Review of the Tip-of-the-Tongue Experience. *Psychological Bulletin*, 109:204–223; Schacter, D. L. (1999). The Seven Sins of Memory: Insights from Psychology and Cognitive Neuroscience. *American Psychologist*, 54:182–203.

22 Bahrick, H. P., Bahrick, L. E., Bahrick, A. S., and Bahrick, P. E. (1993). Maintenance of Foreign Language and the Spacing Effect. *Psychological Science*, 4:316–321; Bahrick, H. P., Bahrick, H. P., and Hall, L. K. (1991). Lifetime Maintenance of High School Mathematics Content. *Journal of Experimental Psychology: General*, 104:54–75.

23 Nelson, T. O. (1971). Savings and Forgetting from Long-Term Memory. *Journal of Verbal Learning and Verbal Behavior*, 10:568–576; Nelson, T. O. (1978). Detecting Small Amounts of Information in Memory: Savings for Nonrecognized Items. *Journal of Experimental Psychology: Human Learning and Memory*, 4:453–468.

24 Anderson, J. R. (1983). *The Architecture of Cognition*. Cambridge, MA: Harvard University Press; Tybout, A. M., Calder, B. J., and Sternthal, B. (1981). Using Information Processing Theory to Design Marketing Strategies. *Journal of Marketing Research*, 18:73–79.

25 Aaker D. A. (1996). *Building Strong Brands*. New York: Free Press; Burke, R. R., and Srull, T. K. (1988). Competitive Interference and Consumer Memory for Advertising. *Journal of Consumer Research*, 15:55–68.

26 Tulving, E. (1983). *Elements of Episodic Memory*. Oxford, England: Oxford University Press; Keller, K. L. (1987). Memory in Advertising: The Effect of Advertising Memory Cues on Brand Evaluations. *Journal of Consumer Research*, 14:316–333.

27 Johnson, M. K., and Rahe, C. L. (1981). Reality Monitoring. *Psychological Review*, 88:67–85; Johnson, M. K., Hastroudi, S., and Lindsay, D. S. (1993). Source

Monitoring. *Psychological Bulletin*, 114:3–28; Pham, M. T., and Johar, G. V. (1997). Contingent Processes of Source Identification. *Journal of Consumer Research*, 24:249–265.

28 Jacoby, L. L., Kelley, C. M., and Dywan, J. (1989). Memory Attributions. In H. L. Roediger and F. I. M. Craik (eds.), *Varieties of Memory and Consciousness: Essays in Honor of Endel Tulving*, 391–422. Hillsdale, NJ: Lawrence Erlbaum Associates; Schwarz, N. (2004). Metacognitive experiences in consumer judgment and decision making. *Journal of Consumer Psychology*, 14:332–348.

29 Hawkins, S. A., and Hoch, S. J. (1992). Low-Involvement Learning: Memory Without Evaluation. *Journal of Consumer Research*, 19:212–225; Hawkins, S. A., Hoch, S. J., and Meyers-Levy, J. (2001). Low-Involvement Learning: Repetition and Coherence in Familiarity and Belief. *Journal of Consumer Psychology*, 11:1–12; Law, S., Hawkins, S. A., and Craik, F. I. M. (1998). Repetition-Induced Belief in the Elderly: Rehabilitating Age-Related Memory Deficits. *Journal of Consumer Research*, 25:91–107; Skurnik, I., Yoon, C., Park, D. C., and Schwarz, N. (2005). How Warnings about False Claims Become Recommendations. *Journal of Consumer Research*, 31:713–724.

30 Roediger, H. L. III. (1996). Memory Illusions. *Journal of Memory and Language*, 35:76–100; Roediger, H. L. III. (1995). Creating False Memories: Remembering Words Not Presented in Lists. *Journal of Experimental Psychology: Learning, Memory, and Cognition*, 21:803–818.

31 Braun, K. (1999). Postexperience Advertising Effects on Consumer Memory. *Journal of Consumer Research*, 25:319–334; Loftus, E. F. (1993). The Reality of Repressed Memories. *American Psychologist*, 48:518–537.

32 Ha, Y., and Hoch, S. J. (1989). Ambiguity, Processing Strategy, and Advertising-Evidence Interactions. *Journal of Consumer Research*, 16:354–360; Hoch, S. J., and Ha, Y. (1986). Consumer Learning: Advertising and the Ambiguity of Product Experience. *Journal of Consumer Research*, 13:221–233.

33 Alba, J. W., and Hasher, L. (1983). Is Memory Schematic? *Psychological Bulletin*, 93:203–231; Alba, J. W., and Hutchinson, J. W. (1987). Dimensions of Consumer Expertise. *Journal of Consumer Research*, 13:411–454; Hoch, S. J., and Deighton, J. (1989). Managing What Consumers Learn from Experience. *Journal of Marketing*, 53:1–20; Sanbonmatsu, D. M., Posavac, S. S., Kardes, F. R., and Mantel, S. P. (1998). Selective Hypothesis Testing. *Psychonomic Bulletin & Review*, 5:197–220.

34 Kardes, F. R., Chandrashekaran, M., and Kellaris, J. J. (2002). Preference Construction and Reconstruction. In R. Zwick, and A. Rapoport (eds.), *Experimental Business Research*, 301–327. Boston, MA: Kluwer.

35 Kellaris, J. J. (2008). Music and Consumers. In C. P. Haugtvedt, P. M. Herr, and F. R. Kardes (eds.), *Handbook of Consumer Psychology*, 837–856. Psychology Press: New York.

36 Greenwald, A. G., Spangenberg, E. R., Pratkanis, A. R., and Eskanazi, J. (1991). Double-Blind Tests of Subliminal Self-Help Audiotapes. *Psychological Science*, 2:119–122.

37 Harris, R. J. (1977). Comprehension of Pragmatic Implications in Advertising. *Journal of Applied Psychology*, 62:603–608; Harris, R. J. & Monaco, G. E. (1978). Psychology of Pragmatic Implications in Advertising: Information Processing Between the Lines. *Journal of Experimental Psychology: General*, 107:1–22; Preston, I. L. (1977). The FTC's Handling of Puffery and Other Selling Claims Made "By Implication." *Journal of Business Research*, 5:155–181.

Chapter 10

1 North, A. C., Hargreaves, D. J., and McKendrick, J. (1997). In-Store Music Affects Product Choice. *Nature*, 390:132.

2 Bargh, J. (2002). Losing Consciousness: Automatic Influences on Consumer Judgment, Behavior, and Motivation. *Journal of Consumer Research*, 29:280–285.

3 Nisbett, R. E., and Wilson, T. D. (1977). Telling More Than We Can Know: Verbal Reports on Mental Processes. *Psychological Review*, 84:231–259.

4 Gilbert, D., Gill, M. J., and Wilson, T. D. (2002). The Future Is Now: Temporal Correction in Affective Forecasting. *Organizational Behavior and Human Decision Processes*, 88:430–444.

5 Fazio, R. H., Sanbonmatsu, D. M., Powell, M. C., and Kardes, F. R. (1986). On the Automatic Activation of Attitudes. *Journal of Personality and Social Psychology*, 50:229–238.

6 Damasio, A. (1994). *Descartes' Error: Emotion, Reason, and the Human Brain*. New York: Grosset/Putnam.

7 Ambady, N., Krabbenhoft, M. A., and Hogan, D. (2006). The 30-Sec Sale: Using Thin-Slice Judgments to Evaluate Sales Effectiveness. *Journal of Consumer Psychology*, 16:4–13.

8 Wilson, T. D., and Schooler, J. W. (1991). Thinking Too Much: Introspection Can Reduce the Quality of Preferences and Decisions. *Journal of Personality and Social Psychology*, 60:181–192.

9 Wilson, T. D., Lisle, D. J., Schooler, J. W., Hodges, S. D., Klaaren, K. J., and LaFleur, S. J. (1993). Introspecting About Reasons Can Reduce Post-Choice Satisfaction. *Personality and Social Psychology Bulletin*, 19:331–339.

10 McMackin, J., and Slovic, P. (2000). When Does Explicit Justification Impair Decision Making? *Journal of Applied Cognitive Psychology*, 14:527–541.

11 Kardes, F. R. (2006). When Should Consumers and Managers Trust Their Intuition? *Journal of Consumer Psychology*, 16:20–24.

12 Wyer, R. S. (2008). The Role of Knowledge Accessibility in Cognition and Behavior: Implications for Consumer Information Processing, 31–76. In C. P. Haugtvedt, P. M. Herr, and F. R. Kardes (eds.), *Handbook of Consumer Psychology*. Mahwah, NJ: Lawrence Erlbaum Associates.

13 Herr, P. M. (1989). Priming Price: Prior Knowledge and Context Effects. *Journal of Consumer Research*, 16:67–75.

14 Yi, Y. (1990). The Effects of Contextual Priming in Print Advertisements. *Journal of Consumer Research*, 17:215–222.

15 Shrum, L. J., Wyer, R. S., and O'Guinn, T. C. (1998). The Effects of Television Consumption on Social Perceptions: The Use of Priming Procedures to Investigate Psychological Processes. *Journal of Consumer Research*, 24:447–458.

16 Dijksterhuis, A., Smith, P. K., van Baaren, R. B., and Wigboldus, D. H. J. (2005). The Unconscious Consumer: Effects of Environment on Consumer Behavior. *Journal of Consumer Psychology*, 15:193–202.

17 Johnston, L. (2002). Behavioral Mimicry and Stigmatization. *Social Cognition*, 20:18–35.

18 Bargh, J. A., Chen, M., and Burrows, L. (1996). The Automaticity of Social Behavior: Direct Effects of Trait Concept and Stereotype Activation on Action. *Journal of Personality and Social Psychology*, 71:230–244.

19 Dijksterhuis, A., and van Knippenberg, A. (1998). The Relation Between Perception and Behavior or How to Win a Game of Trivial Pursuit. *Journal of Personality and Social Psychology*, 74:865–877.

20 Shen, H. (2008). Procedural Priming and Consumer Judgments: Effects on the Impact of Positively and Negatively Valenced Information. *Journal of Consumer Research*, 34:727–737.

21 Dhar, R., Huber, J., and Khan, U. (2007). The Shopping Momentum Effect. *Journal of Marketing Research*, 44:370–378.

22 Xu, A. J., and Wyer, R. S. (2007). The Effect of Mindsets on Consumer Decision Strategies. *Journal of Consumer Research*, 34:556–566.

23 Xu, A. J., and Wyer, R. S. (2008). The Comparative Mindset: From Animal Comparisons to Increased Purchase Intentions. *Psychological Science*, 19:859–864.

24 Hirt, E. R., Kardes, F. R., and Markman, K. D. (2004). Activating a Mental Simulation Mindset through Generation of Alternatives: Implications for Debiasing in Related and Unrelated Domains. *Journal of Experimental Social Psychology*, 40:374–383.

25 Greenwald, A. G., McGhee, D. C., and Schwarz, J. (1998). Measuring Individual Differences in Implicit Social Cognition: The Implicit Association Test. *Journal of Personality and Social Psychology*, 74:1464–1480; Maison, D., Greenwald, A. G., and Bruin, R. H. (2004). Predictive Validity of the Implicit Association Test in Studies of Brands, Consumer Attitudes, and Behavior. *Journal of Consumer Psychology*, 14:405–415.

26 Brunel, F. F., Tietje, B. C., and Greenwald, A. G. (2004). Is the Implicit Association Test a Valid and Valuable Measure of Implicit Consumer Cognition? *Journal of Consumer Psychology*, 14:385–404.

27 Schwarz, N. (2004). Metacognitive Experiences in Consumer Judgment and Decision Making. *Journal of Consumer Psychology*, 14:332–348.

28 Hawkins, S. A., and Hoch, S. J. (1992). Low-Involvement Learning: Memory Without Evaluation. *Journal of Consumer Research*, 19:212–225; Hawkins, S. A., Hoch, S. J., and Meyers-Levy, J. (2001). Low-Involvement Learning: Repetition and Coherence in Familiarity and Belief. *Journal of Consumer Psychology*, 11:1–12; Law, S., Hawkins, S. A., and Craik, F. I. M. (1998). Repetition-Induced Belief in the Elderly: Rehabilitating Age-Related Memory Deficits. *Journal of Consumer Research*, 25:91–107; Skurnik, I., Yoon, C., Park, D. C., and Schwarz, N. (2005). How Warnings about False Claims Become Recommendations. *Journal of Consumer Research*, 31:713–724.

29 Richter, T., Schroeder, S., and Wohrmann, B. (2009). You Don't Have to Believe Everything You Read: Background Knowledge Permits Fast and Efficient Validation of Information. *Journal of Personality and Social Psychology*, 96:538–558.

30 Strahan, E. J., Spencer, S. J., and Zanna, M. P. (2002). Subliminal Priming and Persuasion: Striking While the Iron Is Hot. *Journal of Experimental Social Psychology*, 38:556–568.

31 Shiv, B., Carmon, Z., and Ariely, D. (2005). Placebo Effects of Marketing Actions: Consumers May Get What They Pay For. *Journal of Marketing Research*, 37:383–393.

32 Kardes, F. R. (2005). The Psychology of Advertising. In T. C. Brock & M. C. Green (eds.), *Persuasion: Psychological Insights and Perspectives*, 281–303. Thousand Oaks, CA: Sage Publications.

33 Gilbert, D. T., Tafarodi, R. W., and Malone, P. S. (1993). You Can't Not Believe Everything You Read. *Journal of Personality and Social Psychology*, 65:221–233.

Chapter 11

1 Freling, T. H. and Forbes, L. P. (2005). An Empirical Analysis of the Brand Personality Effect. *Journal of Product & Brand Management*, 14:404–413.

2 Crab, N. (2007, April 20). Transforming Trousers. *The Wall Street Journal* [Online]. Available: http://online.wsj.com/article/SB117703659888376491.html

3 Rosenberg, M. (1979). *Conceiving the Self.* New York: Basic Books, Inc.

4 Gordon, C. (1968). Self-conceptions: Configurations of Content. In C. Gordon and K. J. Gergen (eds.), *The Self in Social Interaction, I: Classic and Contemporary Perspectives*, 115–136. New York: Wiley.

5 Michener, H. A., and DeLamater, J. D. (1994). *Social Psychology* (3rd ed.). Fort Worth, TX: Harcourt Brace & Company.

6 Richins, M. L. (1991). Social Comparison and the Idealized Images of Advertising, *Journal of Consumer Research*, 19:303–316; Richins, M. L. (1995). Materialism, Desire, and Discontent. Contributions of Idealized Advertising Images and Social Comparison. In R. P. Hill (ed.), *Marketing and Consumer Research in the Public Interest*, 109–132. London: Sage Publications.

7 Lockwood, P., and Kuna, Z. (1997). Superstars and Me: Predicting the Impact of Role Models on the Self. *Journal of Personality and Social Psychology*, 73:91–103.

8 Kiran, K., Zinkhan, G. M. and Lum, A. B. (1997). Brand Personality and Self-concept: A Replication and Extension. *AMA Summer 1997 Conference*, 165–171.

9 Sirgy, M. J. (1980). Self-Concept in Relation to Product Preferences and Purchase Intentions. In V. V. Bellur (ed.), *Developments in Marketing Science*, 3, 350–355. Marquette, MI: Academy of Marketing Science; Sirgy, M. J. (1982). Self-Concept in Consumer Behavior: A Critical Review. *Journal of Consumer Research*, 9:287–300.

10 Sirgy, M. J. (1987). The Moderating Role of Response Mode in Consumer Self-esteem/Self-consistency Effects. *AMA Winter Educator's Conference*, 5–55.

11 Zinkhan, G. M., and Hong, J. W. (1991). Self Concept and Advertising Effectiveness: A Conceptual Model of Congruency, Conspicuousness, and Response Mode. *Advances in Consumer Research*, 18:348–354.

12 Belk, R. W. (1988). Possessions and the Extended Self. *Journal of Consumer Research*, 15:139–168.

13 James, W. (1890). *The Principles of Psychology* vol. 1., New York: Henry Holt.

14 McClelland, D. (1951). *Personality*. New York: Holt, Rinehart, & Winston.

15 Ellis, L. (1985). On the Rudiments of Possessions and Property. *Social Science Information*, 24:113–143.

16 Rosenblatt, P. C., Walsh, R, P., and Jackson, D. Q. (1976). Grief and Mourning in Cross-cultural Perspective. New Haven, CT: *Human Relations Area Files*.

17 McLeod, B. (1984). In the Wake of Disaster. *Psychology Today*, 18:54–57.

18 Niederland, W. G., and Sholevar, B. (1981). The Creative Process—A Psychoanalytic Discussion. *The Arts in Psychotherapy*, 8:71–101.

19 Sherry, J. F., and McGrath, M. A. (1989). Unpacking the Holiday Presence: A Comparative Ethnography of Two Gift Stores. In E. C. Hirschman (ed.), *Interpretive Consumer Research*, 148–167. Provo, UT: Association for Consumer Research.

20 Ahuvia, A. C. (2005). Beyond the Extended Self: Loved Objects and Consumers' Identity Narratives. *Journal of Consumer Research*, 32:171–184.

21 Snyder, M. (1974). The Self-monitoring of Expressive Behavior. *Journal of Personality and Social Psychology*, 30:526–537.

22 Snyder, M., and Tanke, E. D. (1976). Behavior and Attitude: Some People Are More Consistent Than Others. *Journal of Personality*, 44:501–517.

23 Graeff, T. R. (1996). Image Congruence Effects on Product Evaluations: The Role of Self-monitoring and Public/Private Consumption. *Psychology & Marketing*, 13:481–499.

24 Becherer, R. C., and Richard, L. M. (1978). Self-monitoring as a Moderating Variable in Consumer Behavior. *Journal of Consumer Research*, 5:159–162.

25 Mischel, W. (1968). *Personality and Assessment.* New York: John Wiley & Sons.

26 Markus, H., and Kunda, Z. (1986). Stability and Malleability of the Self-concept. *Journal of Personality and Social Psychology*, 51:858–866.

27 Aaker, J. (1999). The Malleable Self: The Role of Self-expression in Persuasion. *Journal of Marketing Research*, 36:45–47.

28 Snyder, M. (1987). *Public Appearances, Private Realities: The Psychology of Self-monitoring.* New York: W. H. Freeman.

29 Tetlock, P., and Manstead, A. S. (1985). Impression Management versus Intrapsychic Explanations in Social Psychology: A Useful Dichotomy? *Psychological Review*, 92:59–77.

30 Stone, G. P. (1962). Appearances and the Self. In A. Rose (ed.), *Human Behavior and Social Processes*, 86–118. Boston, MA: Houghton Mifflin.

31 Von Baeyer, C. L., Sherk, D. L., and Zanna, M. P. (1981). Impression Management in the Job Interview: When the Female Applicant Meets the Male (Chauvinist) Interviewer. *Personality and Social Psychology Bulletin*, 7:45–51.

32 Schlenker, B. R., and Leary, M. (1982). Audiences' Reactions to Self-enhancing, Self-denigrating, and Accurate Self-presentations. *Journal of Experimental Social Psychology*, 18:89–104.

33 Baumeister, R. F., Hutton, D. G., and Tice, D. M. (1989). Cognitive Processes during Deliberate Self-presentations: How Self-presenters Alter and Misinterpret the Behavior

of Their Interaction Partners. *Journal of Experimental Social Psychology*, 25:59–78; Frey, D. (1978). Reactions to Success and Failure in Public and Private Conditions. *Journal of Experimental Social Psychology*, 14:172–179.

34 Harlow, R. E., and Cantor, N. (1994). Social Pursuit of Academics: Side Effects and Spillover of Strategic Reassurance Seeking. *Journal of Personality and Social Psychology*, 66:386–397.

35 Jones, E. E., and Wortman, C. (1973). *Ingratiation: An Attributional Approach*. Morristown, NJ: General Learning Press.

36 Tice, D. M., Butler, J. L., Muraven, M. B., and Stillwell, A. M. (1995). When Modesty Prevails: Differential Favorability of Self-presentation to Friends and Strangers. *Journal of Personality and Social Psychology*, 69:1120–1138.

37 Schlenker, B. R. (1975). Self-presentation: Managing the Impression of Consistency When Reality Interferes with Self-enhancement. *Journal of Personality and Social Psychology*, 32:1030–1037.

38 Byrne, D. (1971). *The Attraction Paradigm*. New York: Academic Press.

39 Cline, T. W., Mertens, D. P., Vowels, N. S., and Davies, A. (2009). All Ingratiation Is Not Equal: A Two Dimensional Model of Consumer Ingratiation, *Society for Consumer Psychology 2009 Winter Conference*.

40 Hunter, C. H. (1984). Aligning Actions: Types and Social Distribution. *Symbolic Interactions*, 7:155–164.

41 Hewitt, J. P., and Stokes, R. (1975). Disclaimers. *American Sociological Review*, 40:1–11.

42 Riordan, C. A., Marlin, N. A., and Kellogg, R. T. (1983). The Effectiveness of Accounts Following Transgression. *Social Psychology Quarterly*, 46:213–219.

43 Blumstein, P. W. (1974). The Honoring of Accounts. *American Sociological Review*, 39:551–566.

44 Referred to as the "father of psychoanalysis," Sigmund Freud (1856–1939) popularized such notions as the unconscious, defense mechanisms, dream symbolism, psychosexual development, and Freudian slips. Freud maintained that a person's personality is developed based on a fundamental, internal conflict between physical gratification and appropriate social behavior. Freud's work is preserved in the 24-volume *The Standard Edition of the Complete Psychological Works of Sigmund Freud*. (2001). London: Hogarth Press.

45 Horney, K. (1950). *Neurosis and Human Growth*. New York: Norton; Jung, C. G. (1959). The Archetypes and the Collective Unconscious. In H. Read, M. Fordham, and G. Adler (eds.), *Collected Works*, vol. 9, part 1. Princeton, NJ: Princeton University Press.

46 Cattell, R. B. (1957). *Personality and Motivation: Structure and Measurement*. New York: Harcourt, Brace & World.

47 Goldberg, L. R. (1992). The Development of Markers for the Big Five-Factor Structure. *Psychological Assessment*, 4:26–42.

48 Wiggins, J. S. (1996). *The Five-Factor Model of Personality*. New York: Guilford Press.

49 Mowen, J. C. (1999). Understanding Compulsive Buying among College Students: A Hierarchical Approach, *Journal of Consumer Psychology*, 8:407–430.

50 Faber, R. J., and O'Guinn, T. C. (1988). Compulsive Consumption and Credit Abuse. *Journal of Consumer Policy*, 11:97–109.

51 Harris, E. G., and Mowen, J. C. (2001). The Influence of Cardinal-, Central-, and Surface-level Personality Traits on Consumers' Bargaining and Complaint Behaviors. *Psychology & Marketing*, 18:1155–1185.

52 Schoen, H., and Schumann, S. (2007). Personality Traits, Partisan Attitudes, and Voting Behavior: Evidence from Germany. *Political Psychology*, 28:471–498.

53 Hopwood, C. J., Morey, L. C., Skodol, A. E., Stout, R. L., Yen, S., Ansell, E. B., Grilo, C. M., and McGlashan, T. H. (2007). Five-Factor Model Personality Traits Associated with Alcohol-Related Diagnoses in a Clinical Sample. *Journal of Studies on Alcohol & Drugs* 68:455–460.

54 Aaker, J. L. Dimensions of Brand Personality. *Journal of Marketing Research*, 35:347–356.

55 Park, B. (1986). A Method for Studying the Development of Impressions of Real People. *Journal of Personality and Social Psychology*, 51:907–917.

56 McCracken, G. (1989). Who Is the Celebrity Endorser? Cultural Foundations of the Endorsement Process. *Journal of Consumer Research*, 16:310–321.

57 Batra, R., Lehmann, D. R., and Singh, D. (1993). The Brand Personality Component of Brand Goodwill: Some Antecedents and Consequences. In D. A. Aaker and A. Biel (eds.), *Brand Equity and Advertising*, 83–96. Hillsdale, NJ: Lawrence Erlbaum Associates.

58 Keller, K. (1993). Conceptualizing, Measuring, and Managing Customer-based Brand Equity. *Journal of Marketing*, 57:1–22.

59 Gecko-mania Sweeps Country. [Online]. Available: http://www.geico.com/about/background/geicoWordSponsor.htm. Retrieved July 27, 2007.

60 M&M Characters Are US Favourites. [Online]. Available: http://www.bandt.com.au/news/89/0c027889.asp. Retrieved September 23, 2004.

61 *Forbes*, June 17, 1996.

62 Ogilvy, D. (1983). *Confessions of an Advertising Man*. New York: Dell.

63 Fennis, B. M., Pruyn, A. T., and Maasland, M. (2005). Revisiting the Malleable Self: Brand Effects on Consumer Self-perceptions of Personality. *Advances in Consumer Research*, 32:371–377.

64 Rotter, J. B. (1966). Generalized Expectancies for Internal versus External Control of Reinforcement. *Psychological Monographs*, 80, (1, Whole No. 609).

65 Sherman, S. J. (1973). Internal-external Control and Its Relationship to Attitude Change under Different Social Influence Techniques. *Journal of Personality and Social Psychology*, 26:23–29.

66 Cacioppo, J. T., and Petty, R. E. (1982). The Need for Cognition. *Journal of Personality and Social Psychology*, 42:116–131.

67 Haugtvedt, C. P., Petty, R. E., and Cacioppo, J. T. (1992). Need for Cognition and Advertising: Understanding the Role of Personality Variables in Consumer Behavior. *Journal of Consumer Psychology*, 1:239–260.

68 Tuten, T. L., and Bosnjak, M. (2001). Understanding Differences in Web Usage: The Role of Need for Cognition and the Five-Factor Model of Personality. *Social Behavior and Personality*, 29:391–398.

69 Venkatraman, M. P., Marlino, D., Kardes, F., and Sklar, K. B. (1990). The Interactive Effects of Message Appeal and Individual Differences on Information Processing and Persuasion. *Psychology & Marketing*, 7:85–96.

70 Carnaghi, A., Cadinu, M., Castelli, L., Kiesner, J., and Bragantini, C. (2007). The Best Way to Tell You to Use a Condom: The Interplay between Message Format and Individuals' Level of Need for Cognition. *AIDS Care*, 19:432–440.

71 Cacioppo, J. T., Petty, R., Feinstein, J., and Jarvis, B. (1996). Dispositional Differences in Cognitive Motivation: The Life and Times of Individuals Varying in Need for Cognition. *Psychological Bulletin*, 119:197–253.

72 Cline, T. W., Machleit, K., and Kellaris, J. J. (1999). Is There a Need for Levity? In K.A. Machleit and M. Campbell (eds.), *Proceedings of the Society for Consumer Psychology 1998 Winter Conference*. Austin, TX: American Psychological Association.

73 Cline, T. W., Altsech, M. B., and Kellaris, J. J. (2003). When Does Humor Enhance or Inhibit Ad Responses? The Moderating Role of Need for Humor, *Journal of Advertising*, 32:31–46.

74 Kellaris, J. J., and Cline, T. W. (2007). Humor and Ad Memorability: On the Contributions of Humor Expectancy, Relevancy, and Need for Humor. *Psychology & Marketing*, 24:497–509.

75 Kruglanski, Q. W., and Webster, D. M. (1996). Motivated Closing of the Mind: "Seizing" and "Freezing." *Psychological Review*, 103:263–283.

76 Cronley, M. L., Posavac, S. S., Meyer, T., Kardes, F. R., and Kellaris, J. J. (2005). A Selective Hypothesis Testing Perspective on Price-Quality Inference and Inference-based Choice. *Journal of Consumer Psychology*, 15:159–169.

77 Zhang, S., Kardes, F., and Cronley, M. (2002). Comparative Advertising: Effects of Structural Alignability on Target Brand Evaluations. *Journal of Consumer Psychology*, 12:303–311.

78 Ask, K., and Granhag, P. A. (2005). Motivational Sources of Confirmation Bias in Criminal Investigations: The Need for Cognitive Closure. *Journal of Investigative Psychology and Offender Profiling*, 2:43–63.

79 Army Insight (2001, Spring) [Online]. Available: http://www.blackprwire.com/clients/Army/index.html.

80 Burns, Robert (2006, October 9). Army Launching "Army Strong" Campaign. *Boston.com National News* [Online]. Available: http://www.boston.com/news/nation/washington/articles/2006/10/09/army_launching_army_strong_ad_campaign/.

81 Rochelle, C. (2001, January 10). Army Retires "Be All You Can Be" Jingle. *CNN.com U.S. News*. Available: http://archives.cnn.com/2001/US/01/10/new.army/index.html.

82 Chan, P. Y. L., Saunders, J, Taylor, G. and Souchon, A. (2003). Brand Personality Perceptions: Regional or Country Specific? In D. Turley and S. Brown (eds.), *European Advances in Consumer Research*, 6:300–307.

83 Rothenberg, R. (2007, March 5). Dove Effort Gives Package-goods Marketers Lessons for the Future. *Advertising Age* [Online]. Available: http://adage.com/columns/article?article_id=115370&search_phrase=%2Bdove+%2Breal+%2Bbeauty.

84 Clegg, Alicia (2005, April 18). Dove Gets Real. *Brandchannel.com* [Online]. Available: http://www.brandchannel.com/features_effect.asp?pf_id=259#more.

85 Howard, Theresa (2005, August 28). Dove Ads Enlist All Shapes, Styles, and Sizes. *USAToday.com* [Online]. Available: http://www.usatoday.com/money/advertising/adtrack/2005-08-28-track-dove_x.htm.

86 Howard, Theresa (2006, November 11). Dove Ad Gets Serious for Super Bowl. *USAToday.com* [Online]. Available: http://www.usatoday.com/money/industries/retail/2006-01-11-dove-usat_x.htm.

87 Clegg, Alicia (2005, April 18). Dove Gets Real. *Brandchannel.com* [Online]. Available: http://www.brandchannel.com/features_effect.asp?pf_id=259#more.

Chapter 12

1 Francis X. Rocca, "Italians Cheat to Win," *The Wall Street Journal*, June 28, 2007.

2 Tylor, E. B. (1871). *Primitive culture*. New York: Brentano's.

3 Hofstede, G. (2001), *Culture's Consequences*, 2nd ed. Thousand Oaks, CA: Sage Publications.

4 McCracken, G. (1986). Culture and Consumption: A Theoretical Account of the Structure and Movement of the Cultural Meaning of Consumer Goods. *Journal of Consumer Research*, 13:71–84.

5 Dittmar, H, Long, K., and Meek, R. (2004). Buying on the Internet: Gender Differences in Online and Conventional Buying Motivations. *Sex Roles: A Journal of Research*, 50:423–444.

6 Rogers, S., and Harris, M. A. (2003). Gender and E-commerce: An Exploratory Study. *Journal of Advertising Research*, 43:322–329.

7 Barthes, J. (1983). *The Fashion System*. New York: Hill and Wang.

8 McCracken, G. (1985). The Trickle-down Theory Rehabilitated. In M. Solomon (ed.), *The Psychology of Fashion*, (39–54). Lexington, MA: Lexington Books.

9 Levi-Strauss, C. (1966). *The Savage Mind*. Chicago, IL: University of Chicago Press.

10 Blumberg, P. (1974). The Decline and Fall of the Status Symbol: Some Thoughts on Status in Post-industrial Society. *Social Problems* 21:480–498.

11 Rook, D. W. (1985). The Ritual Dimension of Consumer Behavior. *Journal of Consumer Research*, 12:251–264.

12 Giesler, M., and Pohlmann, M. (2003). The Anthropology of File Sharing: Consuming Napster as a Gift. In P. Keller and D. Rook (eds.), *Advances in Consumer Research*, vol. 30. Provo, UT: Association for Consumer Research.

13 Green, R. and Alden, D. (1988). Functional Equivalence in Cross-cultural Consumer Behavior: Gift Giving in Japan and the United States. *Psychology & Marketing*, 5:155–168.

14 Rook, D. and Levy, S. (1983). Psychological Themes in Consumer Grooming Rituals. In R. Bagozzi and A. Tybout (eds.), *Advances in Consumer Research*, vol. 10, (329–333). Provo, UT: Association for Consumer Research.

15 Faber, R. J., O'Guinn, T. C., and McCarty, J. A. (1987). Ethnicity, Acculturation, and the Importance of Product Attributes. *Psychology & Marketing*, Summer, 121–134.

16 Carol, J. (1956). *Language, Thought and Reality: Selected Writings of Benjamin Lee Whorf*. Cambridge, MA: MIT Press.

17 Steinmetz, G. and Quintanilla, C. (April 10, 1988). Tough Target: Whirlpool Expected Easy Going in Europe, and It Got a Big Shock. *The Wall Street Journal*, A1, A6.

18 Usunier, J. (1993). *International Marketing: A Cultural Approach*. Englewood Cliffs, NJ: Prentice Hall International (UK) Limited.

19 Ekman, P., and Friesen, W. V. (1975). *Unmasking the Face*. Englewood Cliffs, NJ: Prentice Hall.

20 Hall, E. (1959). *The Silent Language*. New York: Doubleday.

21 Kellaris, J. (2003). Dissecting Earworms: Further Evidence on the 'Song-stuck-in-your head' Phenomenon, presentation to Society for Consumer Psychology, Feb. 22, 2003.

22 Cuneo, A. (2007, March 16). AT&T sues NASCAR over Logo: Wants to Rebrand Cingular Car in Nextel-sponsored Racing Series. *Advertising Age*. Available at: http://adage.com/abstract.php?article_id=115626.

23 Jackson, J. (1965). Structural Characteristics of Norms. In I. D. Steiner and M. Fishbein (eds.). *Current Studies in Social Psychology*. New York: Holt, Rinehart and Winston, Inc.

24 Hofstede, G., and Bond, M. H. (1988). The Confucius Connection: From Cultural Roots to Economic Growth. *Organizational Dynamics*, Spring, 5.

25 Han, S-P., and Shavitt, S. (1994). Persuasion and Culture: Advertising Appeals in Individualistic and Collectivistic Societies. *Journal of Experimental Social Psychology*, 30:326–350.

26 Gutman, J., and Reynolds, T. J. (1979). An Investigation of the Levels of Cognitive Abstraction Utilized by Consumers in Product Differentiation. In J. Eighmey (ed.), *Attitude Research under the Sun*, (125–150). Chicago, IL: American Marketing Association.

27 Alternatively, vegetarianism could serve as a functional benefit for consumers who have improved their health through this diet.

28 Henry, W. (1976). Cultural Values Do Correlate with Consumer Behavior. *Journal of Marketing Research*, 13:121–127.

29 Rosenberg, M. J. (1957). *Occupations and Values*. Glencoe, IL: The Free Press.

30 Becker, B. W. and Conner, P. E. (1981). Personal Values of the Heavy User of Mass Media. *Journal of Advertising Research*, 21:37–43.

31 Rokeach, M. J. (1979). *The Nature of Human Values*. New York: Free Press.

32 Pollay, R. W. (1983). Measuring the Cultural Values Manifest in Advertising. *Current Issues and Research in Advertising*, 6:71–92.

33 Peter, J. P., and Olson, J. C. (2008), *Consumer Behavior & Marketing Strategy*, 8th ed. New York: McGraw-Hill/Irwin.

34 Kamakura, W. A. and Mazzon, J. A. (1991). Value Segmentation: A Model for the Measurement of Values and Value Systems. *Journal of Consumer Research*, 18:208–218.

35 Kahle, L. R. (1983). *Social Values and Social Change*. New York: Praeger.

36 Kahle, L. R., Beatty, S. E., and Homer, P. (1986). Alternative Measurement Approaches to Consumer Values: The List of Values (LOV) and Values and Life Style (VALS). *The Journal of Consumer Research*, 13:405–409.

37 Beatty, S. E., Kahle, L. R., Homer, P. and Misra, S. (1985). Alternative Measurement Approaches to Consumer Values: The List of Values and the Rokeach Value Survey. *Psychology & Marketing*, 2:181–200.

38 Kahle, L. R., & Kennedy, P. (1988). Using the List of Values (LOV) to Understand Consumers. *Journal of Consumer Marketing*, 2:49–56; Kahle, L., Poulos, B., and Sukhdial, A. Changes in Social Values in the United States during the Past Decade. *Journal of Advertising Research*, 28:35–41.

39 Corfman, K. P., Lehmann, D. R., and Narayanan, S. (1991). Values, Utility, and Ownership: Modeling the Relationships for Consumer Durables. *Journal of Retailing*, 67:184–204.

40 Pareles, Jon (1993, March 22). Review/Pop; A Party Based on the Grid of Rap. *The New York Times* [Online]. Available: http://query.nytimes.com/gst/fullpage.html?res=9F0CE4DD103BF931A15750C0A965958260.

41 The mid-1990s hip-hop style of wearing sagging pants without a belt originated in prison, where new inmates are immediately stripped of their belts as a safety precaution, i.e., the belts cannot be used as weapons or substitutes for a noose. This particular hip-hop trend reemerged in the 2000s, except this time, youth began wearing baggy denim below their waistlines, often exposing their underwear. When the Virginia State House of Representatives passed House Bill No. 1981 (February 8, 2005) establishing a $50 penalty for any person who exposes his below-waist undergarments in a lewd or indecent manner, the hip-hop culture adjusted. This time, trendsetters used belts and long T-shirts to avoid the fine; the jeans were still worn below the belt.

42 [Online]. Available: http://www.pakwheels.com/forumreply_az_TopicID!74106~ForumID!28~pw.html

43 Keegan, W. and Green M. (2005). *Global Marketing*, 4th ed. Upper Saddle River, NJ: Pearson Prentice Hall.

Chapter 13

1 Cialdini, R.B. (2007). *Influence: The Psychology of Persuasion*. New York: HarperCollins.

2 Langer, E. J. (1978). Rethinking the Role of Thought in Social Interaction. In J. H. Harvey, W. I. Ickers, and R. F. Kidd (eds.), *New Directions in Attribution Research*, vol. 2, (35–38). Hillsdale, NJ: Lawrence Erlbaum Associates.

3 Langer, E.J., Blank, A., and Chanowitz, B. (1978). The Mindlessness of Ostensibly Thoughtful Action: The Role of 'Placebic' Information in Interpersonal Interaction. *Journal of Personality and Social Psychology*, 36:635–642.

4 Dawes, R. M. (1994). *House of Cards: Psychology and Psychotherapy Built on Myth*. New York: Free Press.

5 Obermiller, C. (2004). Improving Telephone Fundraising by Use of Self-prophecy. X Forum of International Association of Jesuit Business Schools, Bilbao Spain.

6 Cialdini, R.B. (2007). *Influence: The Psychology of Persuasion*. New York: HarperCollins.

7 Freedman, J., and Fraser, S. (1966). Compliance without Pressure: The Foot-in-the-door Technique. *Journal of Personality and Social Psychology*, 4:195–202.

8 Bem, D. J. (1972). Self-perception Theory. In L. Berkowitz (ed.), *Advances in Experimental Social Psychology*, 1:199–218.

9 Cialdini, R. B., Cacioppo, J. T., Bassett, R., and Miller, J. A. (1978). Low-ball Procedures for Producing Compliance: Commitment Then Cost. *Journal of Personality and Social Psychology*, 36:463–476.

10 Gouilloux, F., and Weber, F. (1989). The Lure: A New Compliance Procedure. *Journal of Social Psychology*, 129:741–749.

11 Cialdini, R. B., Vincent, J. E., Lewis, S. K., Catalan, J., Wheeler, D., and Darby, B. L. (1975). Reciprocal Concessions Procedure for Inducing Compliance: The Door-in-the-face Technique. *Journal of Personality and Social Psychology*, 31:206–215.

12 Cann, A., Sherman, S. J., and Elkes, R. (1975). Effects of Initial Request Size and Timing of a Second Request on Compliance: The Foot-in-the-door and Door-in-the-face. *Journal of Personality and Social Psychology*, 32:774–782.

13 Burger, J. M. (1986). Increasing Compliance by Improving the Deal: The That's-not-all Technique. *Journal of Personality and Social Psychology*, 51:277–283.

14 Comer, J. M., Kardes, F. R., and Sullivan, A. K. (1992). Multiple Deescalating Requests, Statistical Information, and Compliance: A Field Experiment. *Journal of Applied Social Psychology*, 22:1199–1207.

15 Cialdini, R. B., and Schroeder, D. A. (1976). Increasing Compliance by Legitimizing Paltry Contributions: When Even a Penny Helps. *Journal of Personality and Social Psychology*, 34:599–604.

16 Reingen, P. H. (1978). On Inducing Compliance with Requests. *Journal of Consumer Research*, 5:96–102.

17 Brockner, J., Guzzi, B., Kane, J., Levine, E., and Shaplen, K. (1984). Organizing Fundraising: Further Evidence on the Effect of Legitimizing Small Donations. *Journal of Consumer Research*, 11:611–614.

18 Johnson, A. (2007, February 27). Honus Wagner Card Sells for $2.35 Million. *ABC News* [Online]. Available: http://abcnews.go.com/US/wireStory?id=2907128.

19 Research Triangle Institute (1994). Past and Future Directions of the D.A.R.E. Program: An Evaluation Review. Supported under Award # 91-DD-CX-K053 from the National Institute of Justice, Office of Justice Programs, U.S. Department of Justice.

20 Worchel, S. Arnold, S. E. and Baker, M. (1975). The Effect of Censorship on Attitude Change: The Influence of Censor and Communicator Characteristics. *Journal of Applied Social Psychology,* 5:222–239.

21 Nosanchuk, T.A., and Lightstone, J. (1974). Canned Laughter and Public and Private Conformity. *Journal of Personality and Social Psychology,* 29:153–156.

22 Kruglanski, A. W., and Mayseless, O. (1990). Classic and Current Social Comparison Research: Expanding the Perspective. *Psychological Bulletin,* 108:195–208.

23 Reingen, P. H. (1982). Test of List Procedure for Inducing Compliance with a Request to Donate Money. *Journal of Applied Psychology,* 67:110–118.

24 Rosenthal, A. M. (1969). *Thirty-eight Witnesses.* New York: Free Press.

25 Latane, B. and Rodin, J. (1969). A Lady in Distress: Inhibiting Effects of Friends and Strangers on Bystander Intervention. *Journal of Experimental Social Psychology,* 5:189–202.

26 Bandura, A. and Menlove, F. L. (1968). Factors Determining Vicarious Extinction of Avoidance Behavior through Symbolic Modeling. *Journal of Personality and Social Psychology,* 8:99–108.

27 Asch, S. (1948). The Doctrine of Suggestion, Prestige, and Imitation in Social Psychology. *Psychological Review,* 55:250–276.

28 Bearden, W. O. and Roase, R. L. (1990). Attention to Social Comparison Information: An Individual Difference Factor Affecting Consumer Conformity. *Journal of Consumer Research,* 16:461–471.

29 Han, S. and Shavitt, S. (1994). Persuasion and Culture: Advertising Appeals in Individualistic and Collectivistic Societies. *Journal of Experimental Social Psychology,* 30:326–350.

30 Cialdini, R. B., Wosinska, W., Barrett, D. W., Butner, J., and Gornik-Durose, M. (1999). Compliance with a Request in Two Cultures: The Differential Influence of Social Proof and Commitment/Consistency on Collectivists and Individualists. *Personality and Social Psychology Bulletin,* 25:1242–1253.

31 Cialdini, R. (1996). Activating and Aligning Two Kinds of Norms in Persuasive Communications. *Journal of Interpretation Research,* 1:3–10.

32 Milgram, S., Bickman, L., and Berkowitz, O. (1969). Note on the Drawing Power of Crowds of Different Size. *Journal of Personality and Social Psychology,* 13:79–82.

33 Cialdini, R.B. (1993). *Influence: Science and Practice.* New York: HarperCollins.

34 Deutsch, M. and Gerard, H. B. (1955). A Study of Normative and Informational Social Influences upon Individual Judgment. *Journal of Abnormal and Social Psychology,* 51:629–636.

35 Gladwell, M. (2002). *The Tipping Point.* New York: Back Bay Books.

36 Smoking by Students Declines (2008, September 8). *Inside Higher Ed* [Online]. Available: http://www .insidehighered.com/news/2008/09/08/smoking.

37 Harmon-Jones, E., and Allen, J. J. B. (2001). The Role of Affect in the Mere Exposure Effect: Evidence from Psychophysiological and Individual Differences Approaches. *Personality and Social Psychology Bulletin,* 27:889–898.

38 Eagly A. H., Ashmore, R. D., Makhijani, M. G., and Longo, L. C. (1991). What Is Beautiful is Good, But…: A Meta-analytic Review of Research on the Physical Attractiveness Stereotype. *Psychological Bulletin,* 110:109–128.

39 Mack, D. and Rainey, D. (1990). Female Applicants' Grooming and Personnel Selection. *Journal of Social Behavior and Personality,* 5:399–407.

40 Hamermesh, D. S., and Biddle, J. E. (1994). Beauty and the Labor Market. *American Economic Review,* 84:1174–1194.

41 Kurtzburg, R. L., H. Safar, and N. Cavior (1968). Surgical and Social Rehabilitation of Adult Offenders. *Proceedings of the 76th Annual Convention of the American Psychological Association,* 3:649–650.

42 Benson, P. L., Karabenic, S. A., and Lerner, R. M. (1976). Pretty Pleases: The Effects of Physical Attractiveness, Race, and Sex on Receiving Help. *Journal of Experimental Social Psychology,* 12:409–415.

43 Efran, M. and Patterson, E. (1974). Voters Vote Beautiful: The Effect of Physical Appearance on National Debate. *Canadian Journal of Behavioral Science,* 6:352–356.

44 American Society of Plastic Surgeons (ASPS), cited in Clayton V. (2007, May, 11). Way to Go, Grad! Here's a Check for a New Nose. Is Cosmetic Surgery an Appropriate Commencement Gift for Teens? *MSNBC* [Online]. Available: http://www.msnbc.msn.com/ id/17932515/.

45 Byrne, D. (1971). *The Attraction Paradigm.* New York: Academic Press.

46 Rosenbaum, M. E. (1986). The Repulsion Hypothesis: On the Nondevelopment of Relationships. *Journal of Personality and Social Psychology,* 51:1156–1166.

47 Emswiller, T., Deaux, K., and Willits, J. (1971). Similarity, Sex, and Requests for Small Favors. *Journal of Applied Social Psychology,* 1:284–291.

48 LaFrance, M. (1985). Postural Mirroring and Intergroup Relations. *Personality and Social Psychology Bulletin,* 11:207–217.

49 Drachman, D., deCarufel, A., and Insko, C. A. (1978). The Extra Credit Effect in Interpersonal Attraction, *Journal of Experimental Social Psychology,* 14:458–465.

50 Howard, D. J., Gengler, C., and Jain, A. (1995). What's in a Name? A Complimentary Means of Persuasion. *Journal of Consumer Research,* 22:200–211.

51 Howard, D. J. (1990). The Influence of Verbal Responses to Common Greetings on Compliance Behavior: The Foot-in-the-mouth Effect. *Journal of Abnormal and Social Psychology,* 20:1185–1196.

52 Jones, E. E., & Wortman, C. (1973). *Ingratiation: An Attributional Approach.* Morristown, NJ: General Learning Press.

53 Shari, C. (1997). The Fine Art of Ingratiation. *Industry Week,* 246:41.

54 Hirt, E. R., Zillmann, D., Erickson, G. A., and Kennedy, C. (1992). Costs and Benefits of Allegiance: Changes in Fans' Self-ascribed Competencies after Team Victory versus Defeat. *Journal of Personality and Social Psychology,* 63:724–738.

55 Tesser, A., and Rosen, S. (1975). The Reluctance to Transmit Bad News. In L. Berkowitz (ed.), *Advances in Experimental Social Psychology,* vol. 8, 193–232. New York: Academic Press.

56 Kardes, F., and Kimble, C. E. (1984). Strategic Self-presentation as a Function of Message Valence and the Prospect of Future Interaction. *Representative Research in Social Psychology,* 14:2–11.

57 Milgram, S. (1963). Behavioral Study of Obedience. *Journal of Abnormal and Social Psychology,* 67:371–378.

58 Meeus, W. H. J., and Raaijmakers, Q. Q. W. (1986). Administrative Obedience: Carrying Out Orders to Use Psychological-Administrative Violence. *European Journal of Social Psychology,* 16:311–324.

59 Fowler, Geoffery A., Steinberg, Brian, and Patrick, Aaron O. Mac and PC's Overseas Adventures, *The Wall Street Journal,* March 1, 2007.

60 Moraski, Lauren. Happy Graduation! Enjoy Your New Nose: Plastic Surgeons See More Teens Getting Work Done at Milestones Like Graduation, ABC News Internet Ventures, May 19, 2007. Available: http://abcnews.go.com/Health/Story?id=3190279&page=1.

Chapter 14

1 Fowler, G. (2007, May 15). In China, Sports Stars Face Hurdles in the Race for Ad Riches. *The Wall Street Journal* [Online] Available: http://archives.cnn.com/2001/US/01/10/new.army/index.html.

2 Based on one of the authors' anecdotal research.

3 Garfield, B. (2005, April 4). The Chaos Scenario. *Advertising Age,* 1:57–59.

4 Garfield, B. (2005, April 4). The Chaos Scenario. *Advertising Age,* 1:57–59.

5 Kaikati, A. M., and Kaikati, J. G. (2004). Stealth Marketing: How to Reach Consumers Surreptitiously. *California Management Review,* 46 (4):6–22.

6 Walker, R. (2004, December 4). The Hidden (in Plain Sight) Persuaders. *New York Times Magazine,* vol. 154, 68–75.

7 Gladwell, M. (2000). *The Tipping Point.* New York: Little, Brown and Company.

8 Khermouch, G. and Green, J. (2001, July 30). Buzz-z-z Marketing. *BusinessWeek,* Issue 3743, 50–56.

9 For information on BzzAgent: www.bzzagent.com. See also: Walker, R. (2004, December 4). The Hidden (in Plain Sight) Persuaders. *New York Times Magazine,* vol. 154, 68–131.

10 For information on Vocalpoint and TremorTeen: www.tremorteam.com.

11 Kaikati, A. M., and Kaikati, J. G. (2004). Stealth Marketing: How to Reach Consumers Surreptitiously. *California Management Review,* 46 (4):6–22.

12 Kaikati, A. M., and Kaikati, J. G. (2004). Stealth Marketing: How to Reach Consumers Surreptitiously. *California Management Review,* 46 (4):6–22.

13 For more information on the campaign, see: www.fritolay.com.

14 Friedman, H. H. and Friedman, L. (1979). Endorser Effectiveness by Product Type. *Journal of Advertising Research,* 19:63–71.

15 Petty, R. E., Cacioppo, J. T., and Schumann, D. (1983). Central and Peripheral Routes to Advertising Effectiveness: The Moderating Role of Involvement. *Journal of Consumer Research,* 10:135–146.

16 Freiden, J. B. (1984). Advertising Spokesperson Effects: An Examination of Endorser Type and Gender on Two Audiences. *Journal of Advertising Research,* 24:33–41.

17 Agrawal, J., and Kamakura, W. A. (1995). The Economic Worth of Celebrity Endorsers: An Event Study Analysis. *Journal of Marketing,* 59:56–62.

18 Dipayan, B. Abhijit, B., and Das, N. (2006). The Differential Effects of Celebrity and Expert Endorsements on Consumer Risk Perceptions. *Journal of Advertising,* 35:17–31.

19 Atkin, C., and Block, M. (1983). Effectiveness of Celebrity Endorsers. *Journal of Advertising Research,* 23:57–61.

20 Goldman, L., Burke, M., and Blakeley, K. (2007, June 14). The Celebrity 100. *Forbes.com* [Online]. Available: http://www.forbes.com/2007/06/14/best-paid-celebrities-07celebrities_cz_lg_0614celeb_land.html.

21 Jones, M. J., and Schumann, D. W. (2000). The Strategic Use of Celebrity Athlete Endorsers in *Sports Illustrated:* An Historic Perspective. *Sports Marketing Quarterly,* 9:65–76.

22 Miciak, A. R., and Shaklin, W. L. (1994). Choosing Celebrity Endorsers. *Marketing Management,* 3:51–58.

23 Sukhdial, A. S., Aiken, D., and Kahle, L. (2002). Are You Old School? A Scale for Measuring Sports Fans' Old-school Orientation. *Journal of Advertising Research,* 42:71–81.

24 Bush, A. J., Martin, C. A., and Bush, V. D. (2004). Sports Celebrity Influence on Behavioral Intentions of Generation Y. *Journal of Advertising Research,* 44:108–118.

25 Rose, L. (2006, March 22). The World's Best Paid Athletes. *Forbes.com* [Online]. Available: http://www .forbes.com/business/2006/03/22/woods-sharapova -nike_cx_lr_0322athletes_2.html.

26 Script taken from: http://www.seinfeldscripts.com.

27 Duffy, J. (2005, March 30). Well Placed. *BBC News Magazine* [Online]. Available: http://www.news.bbc .co.uk/1/hi/magazine/4391955.stm.

28 A Look at Some of the Biggest Hits in Film and TV Product Placement (2005, April 28). *Hollywood Reporter* [Online]. Available: www.hollywoodreporter.com.

29 A Look at Some of the Biggest Hits in Film and TV Product Placement (2005, April 28). *Hollywood Reporter* [Online]. Available: www.hollywoodreporter.com.

30 Graser, M. (2005, March 28). McDonald's on Lookout to Be Big Mac Daddy. *Advertising Age,* 76(13):123.

31 Cronley, M. L., Houghton, D. C., Goddard, P., and Kardes, F. R. (1999). Endorsing Products for the Money: The Role of the Correspondence Bias in Celebrity Advertising. *Advances in Consumer Research,* vol. 26, 627–631.

32 Edwards, J. (2006, August 17). PQ Media Releases New Numbers. *Brandweek* [Online]. Available: www.brandweek.com.

33 Atkinson, C. (2007, January 8). "Idol" Juggernaut Passes $2.5 bil and Hits the Gas. *Advertising Age,* 78(2):1–29, 2p.

34 Atkinson, C. (2007, January 8). "Idol" Juggernaut Passes $2.5 bil and Hits the Gas. *Advertising Age,* 78(2):1–29, 2p.

35 Goo, S. K. (2006, April 15). Apple Gets a Big Slice of the Product-placement Pie. *WashingtonPost.com* [Online], D01. Available: www.washingtonpost.com.

36 All information for the Marketing In Action box was drawn from the following sources: Rose, F. (2006, December). In a Risky Experiment, Chevrolet Asked Web Users to Make Their Own Video Spots for the Tahoe. A Case Study in Customer Generated Advertising, *Wired* [Online], issue 14.12. Available: www.wired.com; Donaton, S. (2006). How to Thrive in the New World of User-created Content: Let Go. *Advertising Age,* 77(18): 38; see also: www.YouTube.com.

37 Sources for E.B. Diamond Hunt include: Van Der Pool, L. (2006, October 27). Bling Buzz Campaign: Jeweler Launches Treasure Hunt. *Boston Business Journal* [Online]. Available: www.boston.bizjournals. com/boston/stories/2006/10/30. See also: http://www .greatdiamondhunt.com/home.html.

38 For information on Commercial Alert, see: http://www .commercialalert.org/issues/culture/product-placement.

Chapter 15

1 Caplan, J. (2007). How Yahoo! aims to reboot. *Time,* 169 (7), 52–53.

2 Alba, J., Lynch, J., Weitz, B., Janiszewski, C., Lutz, R., Sawyer, A., & Wood, S. (1997). Interactive Home Shopping: Consumer, Retailer, and Manufacturer Incentives to Participate in Electronic Marketplaces. *Journal of Marketing,* 61, 38–53.

3 Csikszentmihalyi, M. (1990). *Flow: The Psychology of Optimal Experience.* New York: Harper & Row.

4 Bellman, S., Johnson, E. J., Lohse, G. L., & Mandel, N. (2006). Designing Marketplaces of the Artificial with Consumers in Mind: Four Approaches to Understanding Consumer Behavior in Electronic Environments. *Journal of Interactive Marketing,* 20, 21–33.

5 Weathers, D., & Makienko, I. (2006). Assessing the Relationships Between E-Tail Success and Product and Website Factors. *Journal of Interactive Marketing,* 20, 41–54.

6 Darby, M. R., & Karni, E. (1973). Free Competition and the Optimal Amount of Fraud. *Journal of Law and Economics,* 16, 66–86; Nelson, P. (1970). Information and Consumer Behavior. *Journal of Political Economy,* 78, 311–329; Nelson, P. (1974). Advertising as Information. *Journal of Political Economy,* 81, 729–754; Wright, A., & Lynch, J. G. (1995). Communication Effects of Advertising Versus Direct Experience When Both Search and Experience Attributes Are Present. *Journal of Consumer Research,* 21, 708–718.

7 Fasolo, B., McClelland, G. H., & Lange, K. A. (2005). The Effect of Site Design and Interattribute Correlations on Interactive Web-Based Decisions. In C. P. Haugtvedt, K. A. Machleit, & R. F. Yalch (Eds.), Online consumer psychology: Understanding and influencing consumer behavior in the virtual world (pp. 325–342). Mahwah, NJ: Erlbaum.

8 Levin, A. M., Levin, I. P., & Heath, C. E. (2005). Finding the Best Ways to Combine Online and Offline Shopping Features. In C. P. Haugtvedt, K. A. Machleit, & R. F. Yalch (Eds.), *Online Consumer Psychology: Understanding and Influencing Consumer Behavior in the Virtual World* (pp. 401–417). Mahwah, NJ: Erlbaum.

9 Haubl, G., & Trifts, V. (2005). Consumer Decision Making in Online Shopping Environments: The Effects of Interactive Decision Aids. *Marketing Science*, 19, 4–21; Murray, K. B., & Haubl, G. (2005). Processes of Preference Construction in Agent-Assisted Online Shopping. In C. P. Haugtvedt, K. A. Machleit, & R. F. Yalch (Eds.), Online consumer psychology: Understanding and influencing consumer behavior in the virtual world (pp. 265–283). Mahwah, NJ: Erlbaum.

10 Beatty, S. & Smith, S. (1987). External Search Effort: An Investigation Across Several Product Categories. *Journal of Consumer Research*, 14, 83–95.

11 Urbany, J. E., Dickson, P. R., & Wilkie, W. L. (1989). Buyer Uncertainty and Information Search. *Journal of Consumer Research*, 16, 208–215.

12 Johnson, E. J., & Russo, J. E. (1984). Product Familiarity and Learning New Information. *Journal of Consumer Research*, 11, 542–550.

13 Dickson, P. R., & Sawyer, A. G. (1990). The Price Knowledge and Search of Supermarket Shoppers. *Journal of Marketing*, 54, 42–53.

14 Sinha, I. (2000). Cost Transparency: The Net's Real Threat to Prices and Brands. *Harvard Business Review*, 43–50.

15 Popkowski-Leszczyc, P. T. L., & Rao, R. C. (1990). An Empirical Analysis of National and Local Advertising Effects on Price Elasticity. *Marketing Letters*, 1, 149–160.

16 Mitra, A., & Lynch, J. G. (1995). Toward a Reconciliation of Market Power and Information Theories of Advertising Effects on Price Elasticity. *Journal of Consumer Research*, 21, 644–659; Mitra, A., & Lynch, J. G. (1996). Advertising Effects on Consumer Welfare: Prices Paid and Liking for Brands Selected. *Marketing Letters*, 7, 19–29.

17 Lynch, J. G., & Ariely, D. (2000). Wine Online: Search Costs Affect Competition on Price, Quality, and Distribution. *Marketing Science*, 19, 83–103.

18 Diehl, K., Kornish, L. J., & Lynch, J. G. (2003). Smart Agents: When Lower Search Costs for Quality Information Increase Price Sensitivity. *Journal of Consumer Research*, 30, 56–71.

19 Urban, G. (2005). *Don't Just Relate–Advocate: A Blue Print for Profit in the Era of Customer Power*. Upper Saddle River, NJ: Wharton School Publishing.

20 Hampp, A. (2009). Food Network Seeing Huge Growth from Web Offerings. *Advertising Age*, March 2, p. 8.

21 Wright, J. (2006). *Blog Marketing: The Revolutionary New Way to Increase Sales, Build Your Brand, and Get Exceptional Results*. New York: McGraw-Hill; Kirkpatrick, D. (2005). Why There's No Escaping the Blog. *Fortune*, January 10, 2005.

22 Zaichowsky, J. L. (2006). *The Psychology Behind Trademark Infringement and Counterfeiting*. Mahwah, NJ: Erlbaum.

23 Zaichowsky, J. L. (2006). *The Psychology Behind Trademark Infringement and Counterfeiting*. Mahwah, NJ: Erlbaum.

Chapter 16

1 Hartley, R. F. (2001). *Marketing Mistakes and Successes*. New York: John Wiley & Sons.

2 Rogers, E. M. (1983). *Diffusion of Innovations*. New York: Free Press.

3 Urban, G. L., and Star, S. H. (1991). *Advanced Marketing Strategy: Phenomena, Analysis, and Decisions*. Englewood Cliffs, NJ: Prentice Hall.

4 Aaker, D. A. (1991). *Managing Brand Equity*. New York: Free Press; Aaker, D. A. (1996). *Building Strong Brands*. New York: Free Press; Keller, K. L. (2007). *Strategic Brand Management: Building, Measuring, and Managing Brand Equity*, 3rd ed. Upper Saddle River, NJ: Prentice Hall.

5 Kardes, F. R., and Allen, C. T. (1991). Perceived Variability and Inferences about Brand Extensions. *Advances in Consumer Research*, 18:392–398.

6 Keller, K. L. (2007). *Strategic Brand Management: Building, Measuring, and Managing Brand Equity*, 3rd ed. Upper Saddle River, NJ: Prentice Hall.

7 Kekre, S., and Srinivasan, K. (1990). Broader Product Line: A Necessity to Achieve Success? *Management Science*, 36:1216–1231.

8 Urban, G. L., Johnson, P. L., and Hauser, J. R. (1984). Testing Competitive Market Structures. *Marketing Science*, 3:83–112.

9 Hoch, S. J., and Deighton, J. (1989). Managing What Consumers Learn From Experience. *Journal of Marketing*, 53:1–20.

10 Nordhielm, C. L. (2006). *Marketing Management: The Big Picture*. New York: John Wiley & Sons.

11 Parker, R. M. (2008). *Parker's Wine Buyer's Guide*, 7th ed. New York: Simon & Schuster, 1121.

12 Gupta, S., and Lehmann, D. R. (2005). *Managing Customers as Investments: The Strategic Value of Customers in the Long Run*. Upper Saddle River, NJ: Wharton School Publishing (division of Pearson Education).

13 Gupta, S., and Lehmann, D. R. (2005). *Managing Customers as Investments: The Strategic Value of Customers in the Long Run*. Upper Saddle River, NJ: Wharton School Publishing (division of Pearson Education).

14 usatoday.com (04/02/2007).

15 msnbc.msn.com (08/14/2007).

Chapter 17

1   Boyle, M. (2008, November 14). Bad Management: Why Managers Make Poor Decisions. *BusinessWeek* [Online]. Available: http://www.businessweek.com/managing/content/nov2008/ca20081114_461475.htm.

2   Bazerman, M. H. (1990). *Judgment in Managerial Decision Making*. New York: Wiley. Russo, J.E., and Shoemaker, P. J. H. (1989). *Decision Traps: The Ten Barriers to Brilliant Decision Making and How to Overcome Them*. New York: Simon & Schuster.

3   Nisbett, R. E., and Ross, L. (1980). *Human Inference: Strategies and Shortcomings of Social Judgment*. Englewood Cliffs, NJ: Prentice-Hall.

4   Taylor, S. E. and Thompson, S. C. (1982). Stalking the Elusive "Vividness" Effect. *Psychological Review,* 89:155–181.

5   Ableson, R. P., Kinder, D.R., Peters, M.D., and Fiske, S. T. (1982). Affective and Semantic Components in Political Person Perception. *Journal of Personality and Social Psychology,* 42:619–630.

6   Gilovich, T. (1987). Secondhand Information and Social Judgment. *Journal of Experimental Psychology,* 23:59–74.

7   Gilovich, T. (1991). *How We Know What Isn't So: The Fallibility of Human Reason in Everyday Life*. New York: Free Press.

8   Kahneman, D. and Tversky, A. (1984). Choice, Values, and Frames. *American Psychologist,* 39:314–350; Tversky, A. and Kahneman, D. (1981). The Framing of Decisions and the Psychology of Choice. *Science,* 211:453–458.

9   Linville, P.W., and Fisher, G. W. (1991). Preferences for Separating or Combining Events. *Journal of Personality and Social Psychology,* 60:5–23; Puto, C. (1987). The Framing of Buying Decisions. *Journal of Consumer Research,* 3:301–315; Qualls, W. J., and Puto, C. (1989). Organizational Climate and Decision Framing: An Integrated Approach to Analyzing Industrial Buying Decisions. *Journal of Marketing Research,* 26:179–192; Thaler, R. (1985). Mental Accounting and Consumer Choice. *Marketing Science,* 4:199–214.

10 Lord, C. G., Ross, L., and Leppter, M. R. (1979). Biased Assimilation and Attitude Polarization: The Effects of Prior Theories on Subsequently Considered Evidence. *Journal of Personality and Social Psychology,* 37: 2098–2109.

11 Lee, H., Acito, F., and Day, R. L. (1987). Evaluation and Use of Marketing Research Decision Makers: A Behavioral Simulation. *Journal of Marketing Research*, 24:187–196.

12 Fischhoff, B. and Beyth-Marom, R. (1983). Hypothesis Evaluation from a Bayesian Perspective. *Psychological Review,* 90:239–260; Herr, P. M., Kardes, F. R., and Kim, J. (1991). Effects of Word-of-mouth and Product-attribute Information on Persuasion: An Accessibility-diagnosticity Perspective. *Journal of Consumer Research,* 17:454–462; Hoch, S. J., and Deighton, J. (1989). Managing What Consumers Learn from Experience. *Journal of Marketing,* 53:1–20.

13 Kardes, F. R., and Cronley, M. L. (2000). Managerial Decision Making. In S. B. Dahiya, (ed.), *The Current State of Business Disciplines*, vol. 6, 2921–2934. Rohtak, India: Spellbound Publications; Sanbonmatsu, D. M., Posavac, S. S., Kardes, F. R., and Mantel, S. P. (1998). Selective Hypothesis Testing. *Psychonomic Bulletin & Review*, 5:197–220.

14 Gigone, D., and Hastie, R. (1993). The Common Knowledge Effect: Information Sharing and Group Judgment. *Journal of Personality and Social Psychology,* 61:181–194. Gigone, D., and Hastie, R. (1997). Proper Analysis of the Accuracy of Group Judgments. *Psychological Bulletin,* 121:149–167.

15 Chandrashekaran, M., Walker, B. A., Ward, J. C., and Reingen, P. H. (1996). Modeling Individual Preference Evolution and Choice in a Dynamic Group Setting. *Journal of Marketing Research,* 33:211–223; Ward, J. C., and Reingen, P. H. (1990). Sociocognitive Analysis of Group Decision Making among Consumers. *Journal of Consumer Research,* 17:245–262.

16 Vinokur, A. Y., and Burnstein, E. (1974). Effects of Partially Shared Persuasive Arguments on Group Induced Shifts: A Group-problem-solving Approach. *Journal of Personality and Social Psychology,* 29:305–315.

17 Chandrashekaran, M., Walker, B. A., Ward, J. C., and Reingen, P. H. (1996). Modeling Individual Preference Evolution and Choice in a Dynamic Group Setting. *Journal of Marketing Research,* 33:211–223.

18 Janis, I. L. (1982). *Groupthink*. Boston: Houghton Mifflin.

19 Schulz-Hardt, S., Fre, D., Luthgens, C., and Moscovici, S. (2000). Conditions Facilitating Successful Discounting in Consumer Decision Making. *Journal of Personality and Social Psychology*, 78:655–669.

20 Gilbert, D. T., and Krull, D. S. (1988). Seeing Less and Knowing More: The Benefits of Perceptual Ignorance. *Journal of Personality and Social Psychology,* 54:193–202.

21 Tversky, A., and Kahneman, D. (1974). Judgment under Uncertainty: Heuristics and Biases. *Science,* 185:1124–1131.

22 Tversky, A., and Kahneman, D. (1994). Judgment under Uncertainty: Heuristics and Biases. *Science,* 185:1124–1131.

23 Cox, A. D., and Summers, J. O. (1987). Heuristics and Biases in the Intuitive Projection of Retail Sales. *Journal of Marketing Research,* 24:290–297.

24 Gregory, W. L., Cialdini, R. B., and Carpenter, K. M. (1982). Self-relevant Scenarios as Mediators of Likelihood Estimates and Compliance: Does Imagining Make It So? *Journal of Personality and Social Psychology,* 43:89–99.

25 Carroll, J. S. (1978). The Effect of Imagining an Event on Expectations for the Event: An Interpretation in Terms of the Availability Heuristic. *Journal of Experimental Social Psychology,* 14:88–96.

26 Hirt, E. R., and Sherman, S. J. (1985). The Role of Prior Knowledge in Explaining Hypothetical Events. *Journal of Experimental Social Psychology,* 21:519–543; Sherman, S. J., Zehner, K. S., Johnson, J., and Hirt, E. R. (1983). Social Explanation: The Role of Timing, Set, and Recall on Subjective Likelihood Estimates. *Journal of Personality and Social Psychology,* 44:1127–1143.

27 Sherman, S. J., Cialdini, R. B., Schwartzman, D. F., and Reynolds, K. D. (1985). Imagining Can Heighten or Lower the Perceived Likelihood of Contracting a Disease: The Mediating Effect of Ease of Imagery. *Personality and Social Psychology Bulletin,* 11:118–127.

28 Anderson, C. A. (1983). Abstract and Concrete Data in the Perseverance of Social Theories: When Weak Data Lead to Unshakable Beliefs. *Journal of Experimental Social Psychology,* 19:93–108; Anderson, C. A., and Godfrey, S. S. (1987). Thoughts about Actions: The Effects of Specificity and Availability of Imagined Behavioral Scripts on Expectations about Oneself and Others. *Social Cognition,* 5:238–258; Anderson, C.A., Lepper, M. R., and Ross, L. (1980). Perseverance of Social Theories: The Role of Explanation in the Persistence of Discredited Information. *Journal of Personality and Social Psychology,* 39:1037–1049; Sherman, S. J., and Cory, E. (1984). Cognitive Heuristics. In R. S. Wyer and T. K. Srull (eds.), *Handbook of Social Cognition,* vol. 2, 189–286. Hillsdale, NJ: Lawrence Erlbaum Associates.

29 Dawes, R. M., (1988). *Rational Choice in an Uncertain World.* San Diego: Harcourt Brace Jovanovich.

30 Tversky, A., and Kahneman, D. (1974). Judgment under Uncertainty: Heuristics and Biases. *Science,* 185:1124–1131.

31 Northcraft, G. B., and Neale, M. A. (1987). Experts, Amateurs, and Real Estate: An Anchoring and Adjustment Perspective on Property Pricing Decisions. *Organizational Behavior and Human Decision Processes,* 39:84–97.

32 Slovic, P., and Lichtenstein, S. (1983). Preference Reversals: A Broader Perspective. *American Economic Review,* 73:596–605; Tversky, A., Slovic, P., and Kahneman, D. (1990). The Determinants of Preference Reversal. *American Economic Review,* 80:204–217.

33 Slovic, P. (1995). The Construction of Preference. *American Psychologist,* 50:364–371.

34 Mown, J. C., and Gentry, J. W. (1980). Investigation of the Preference-reversal Phenomenon in a New Product Introduction Task. *Journal of Applied Psychology,* 65:715–722.

35 Kerr, R. A. (1979). Petroleum Exploration: Discouragement about the Atlantic Outer Continental Shelf Deepens. *Science,* vol. 204, 1069–1072.

36 Jones, E. E., and Davis, K. (1965). From Acts to Dispositions: The Attribution Process in Person Perception. In L. Berkowitz (ed.), *Advances in Experimental Social Psychology,* vol. 2, 219–266. New York: Academic Press; Gilbert, D. T., and Jones, E. E. (1986). Perceiver-induced Constraint: Interpretations of Self-generated Reality. *Journal of Personality and Social Psychology,* 50:269–280; Gilbert, D. T., Jones, E. E., and Pelham, B. W. (1987). Influence and Inference: What the Active Perceiver Overlooks. *Journal of Personality and Social Psychology,* 52:861–870; Gilbert, D. T., and Krull, D. S. (1988). Seeing Less and Knowing More: The Benefits of Perceptual Ignorance. *Journal of Personality and Social Psychology,* 54:193–202; Gilbert, D. T., and Malone, P. S. (1995). The Correspondence Bias. *Psychological Bulletin,* 117:21–38.

37 Gilovich, T. (1981). Seeing the Past in the Present: The Effect of Associations to Familiar Events on Judgments and Decisions. *Journal of Personality and Social Psychology,* 40:797–808.

38 Ross, L., Lepper, M. R., and Hubbard, M. (1975). Perseverance in Self-perception and Social Perception: Biased Attribution Processes in the Debriefing Paradigm. *Journal of Personality and Social Psychology,* 35:485–494.

39 Nisbett, R. E., Zukier, H., and Lemley, R. E. (1981). The Dilution Effect: Nondiagnostic Information Weakens the Implications of Diagnostic Information. *Cognitive Psychology,* 13:248–277.

40 Zukier, H. (1982). The Role of the Correlation and the Dispersion of Predictor Variables in the Use of Nondiagnostic Information. *Journal of Personality and Social Psychology,* 43:1163–1175.

41 Tetlock, P. E., and Boettger, R. (1989). Accountability: A Social Magnifier of the Dilution Effect. *Journal of Personality and Social Psychology,* 57:388–398.

42 Chanowitz, B., and Langer, E. J. (1981). Premature Cognitive Commitment. *Journal of Personality and Social Psychology,* 41:1051–1063.

43 Petty, R. E., and Wegener, D. T. (1993). Flexible Correction Processes in Social Judgment: Correcting for Context-induced Contrast. *Journal of Experimental Social Psychology,* 29:137–165; Wegener, D. T., and Petty, R. E. (1995). Flexible Correction Processes in Social Judgment: The Role of Naïve Theories in Corrections for Perceived Bias. *Journal of Personality and Social Psychology,* 68:36–51.

Chapter 18

1 Stratford, S. (1997, May 12). Levi's. *Fortune,* 104–116; Sheff, D. (1997). Levi's Changes Everything. *The Greatest Hits,* 1:24–31.

2 Russo, J. E., and Schoemaker, P. J. H. (1989). *Decision Traps: The Ten Barriers to Brilliant Decision Making and How to Overcome Them.* New York: Simon & Schuster.

3 Kruglanski, A.W. (1989). *Lay Epistemics and Human Knowledge: Cognitive and Motivational Bases.* New York: Plenum Press; Kruglanski, A. W. (1990). Lay Epistemic Theory in Social Cognitive Psychology. *Psychological Inquiry,* 1:181–197; Kruglanski, A. W., and Webster, D. M. (1996). Motivated Closing of the Mind: 'Seizing' and 'Freezing.' *Psychological Review,* 103:263–283.

4 Kruglanski, A.W. (1989). *Lay Epistemics and Human Knowledge: Cognitive and Motivational Bases.* New York: Plenum Press; Kruglanski, A. W. (1990). Lay Epistemic Theory in Social Cognitive Psychology. *Psychological Inquiry,* 1:181–197; Kruglanski, A. W., and Webster, D. M. (1996). Motivated Closing of the Mind: 'Seizing' and 'Freezing.' *Psychological Review,* 103:263–283; Tetlock, P. E. (1992). The Impact of Accountability on Judgment and Choice: Toward a Social Contingency Model. In M. P. Zanna (ed.), *Advances in Experimental Social Psychology,* 331–376. New York: Academic Press.

5 Kahneman, D., Slovic, P., and Tversky, A. (1982). *Judgment under Uncertainty: Heuristics and Biases.* Cambridge, UK: Cambridge University Press; Nisbett, R. E., and Ross, L. (1980). *Human Inference: Strategies and Shortcomings of Social Judgment.* Englewood Cliffs, NJ: Prentice-Hall.

6 Buehler, R., Griffin, D., and Ross, M. (1994). Exploring the 'Planning Fallacy': Why People Underestimate Their Completion Times. *Journal of Personality and Social Psychology,* 67:366–381.

7 Colombo, J. R. (1987). *New Canadian Quotations.* Edmonton, Alberta: Hurtig.

8 Hall, P. (1980). *Great Planning Disasters.* London: Weidenfeld & Nicolson.

9 Buehler, R., Griffin, D., and Ross, M. (1994). Exploring the 'Planning Fallacy': Why People Underestimate Their Completion Times. *Journal of Personality and Social Psychology, 67,* 366–381; Kahneman, D., and Tversky, A. (1979). Intuitive Prediction: Biases and Corrective Procedures. *TIMS Studies in Management Science,* 12:313, 327.

10 Kahneman, D., and Lovallo, D. (1993). Timid Choices and Bold Forecasts: A Cognitive Perspective on Risk Taking. *Management Science,* 39:17–31.

11 Lynch, J. G., and Ofir, C. (1989). Effects of Cue Consistency and Value on Base-rate Utilization. *Journal of Personality and Social Psychology,* 56:170–181.

12 Ajzen, I. (1977). Intuitive Theories of Events and the Effects of Base-rate Information on Prediction. *Journal of Personality and Social Psychology,* 35:303–314.

13 Fischhoff, B., Slovic, P., and Lichtenstein, S. (1979). Subjective Sensitivity Analysis. *Organizational Behavior and Human Decision Processes,* 23:339–359.

14 Sanbonmatsu, D. M., Kardes, F. R., and Herr, P. M. (1992). The Role of Prior Knowledge and Missing Information in Multiattribute Evaluation. *Organizational Behavior and Human Decision Processes,* 51:76–91; Sanbonmatsu, D. M., Kardes, F. R., and Sansone, C. (1991). Remembering Less and Inferring More: The Effects of the Timing of Judgment on Inferences about Unknown Attributes. *Journal of Personality and Social Psychology,* 61:546–554; Sanbonmatsu, D. M., Kardes, F. R., Posavac, S. S., and Stasney, R. (1997). The Subjective Beliefs Underlying Probability over Estimation. *Journal of Experimental Social Psychology,* 33:276–295.

15 Dawes, R. M. (1988). *Rational Choice in an Uncertain World.* San Diego: Harcourt Brace Jovanovich; Dawes, R. M. (1994). *House of Cards: Psychology and Psychotherapy Built on Myth.* New York: Free Press; Russo, J. E., and Schoemaker, P. J. H. (1989). *Decision Traps: The Ten Barriers to Brilliant Decision Making and How to Overcome Them.* New York: Simon & Schuster.

16 Dube-Rioux, L., and Russo, J. E. (1988). An Availability Bias in Professional Judgment. *Journal of Behavioral Decision Making,* 1:223–227; Fischhoff, B., Slovic, P., and Lichtenstein, S. (1978). Fault Trees: Sensitivity of Estimated Failure Probabilities to Problem Representation. *Journal of Experimental Psychology: Human Perception and Performance,* 4:330–344; Hirt, E. R., and Castellan, N. J. (1988). Probability and Category Redefinition in the Fault Tree Paradigm. *Journal of Experimental Psychology: Human Perception and Performance,* 14:122–131. Russo, J. E., and Kolzow, K. J. (1994). Where Is the Fault in Fault Trees? *Journal of Experimental Psychology: Human Perception and Performance,* 20:17–32.

17 Dube-Rioux, L., and Russo, J. E. (1988). An Availability Bias in Professional Judgment. *Journal of Behavioral Decision Making,* 1:223–227.

18 Broniarczyk S. M., and Alba, J. W. (1994a). The Role of Consumers' Intuitions in Inference Making. *Journal of Consumer Research,* 18:325–345; Broniarczyk S. M., and Alba, J. W. (1994b). Theory versus Data in Prediction and Correlation Tasks. *Organizational Behavior and Human Decision Processes,* 57:117–139.

19 Adaval, R., and Wyer, R. S. (1998). The Role of Narratives in Consumer Information Processing. *Journal of Consumer Psychology,* 7:207–246; Pennington, N., and Hastie, R. (1986). Evidence Evaluation in Complex Decision Making. *Journal of Personality and Social Psychology,* 51:242–258; Pennington, N., and Hastie, R. (1988). Explanation-based Decision Making: Effects of Memory Structure on Judgment. *Journal Experimental Psychology: Learning, Memory, and Cognition,* 14:521–533; Pennington, N., and Hastie, R. (1993). Reasoning in Explanation-based Decision Making. *Cognition,* 49:123–163; Schank, R. C., and Abelson, R. P. (1995). Knowledge and Memory: The Real Story. In R. S. Wyer (ed.), *Advances in Social*

Cognition, vol. 8, 1–86. Hillsdale, NJ: Lawrence Erlbaum Associates.

20 Lichtenstein, S., Fischhoff, B., and Phillips, L. D. (1982). Calibration of Probabilities: The State of the Art to 1980. In D. Kahneman, P. Slovic, and A. Tversky (eds.), *Judgment under Uncertainty: Heuristics and Biases.* Cambridge, UK: Cambridge University Press.

21 Dunning, D., Griffin, D. W., Milojkovic, J. D, and Ross, L. (1990). The Overconfidence Effect in Social Prediction. *Journal of Personality and Social Psychology,* 58:568–581. Griffin, D. W., Dunning, D., and Ross, L. (1990). The Role of Construal Processes in Overconfident Predictions about the Self and Others. *Journal of Personality and Social Psychology,* 59:1128–1139; Vallone, R. P., Griffin, D., Lin, S., and Ross, L. (1990). Overconfident Prediction of Future Actions and Outcomes by Self and Others. *Journal of Personality and Social Psychology,* 58:582–592.

22 Plous, S. (1993). *The Psychology of Judgment and Decision Making.* New York: McGraw-Hill, 217.

23 Fischhoff, B., Slovic, P., and Lichtenstein, S. (1977). Knowing with Certainty: The Appropriateness of Extreme Confidence. *Journal of Experimental Psychology: Human Perception and Performance,* 3:552–564; Koriat, A., Lichtenstein, S., and Fischoff, B. (1980). Reasons for Confidence. *Journal of Experimental Psychology: Human Learning and Memory,* 6:107–118; Oskamp, S., (1965). Overconfidence in Case-study Judgments. *Journal of Consulting Psychology,* 29:261–265.

24 Sanbonmatsu, D. M., Kardes, F. R., and Herr, P. M. (1992). The Role of Prior Knowledge and Missing Information in Multiattribute Evaluation. *Organizational Behavior and Human Decision Processes,* 51:76–91. Sanbonmatsu, D. M., Kardes, F. R., and Sansone, C. (1991). Remembering Less and Inferring More: The Effects of the Timing of Judgment on Inferences about Unknown Attributes. *Journal of Personality and Social Psychology,* 61:546–554.

25 Kruglanski, A.W. (1989). *Lay Epistemics and Human Knowledge: Cognitive and Motivational Bases.* New York: Plenum Press; Kruglanski, A. W., and Webster, D. M. (1996). Motivated Closing of the Mind: 'Seizing' and 'Freezing.' *Psychological Review,* 103:263–283. Kruglanski, A. W., and Mayesless, O. (1987). Motivational Effects in the Social Comparison of Opinions. *Journal of Personality and Social Psychology,* 53:834–842.

26 Kruglanski, A.W., and Mayseless, O. (1988). Contextual Effects in Hypothesis Testing: The Role of Competing Alternatives and Epistemic Motivations. *Social Cognition,* 6:1–20.

27 Dunning, D., Griffin, D. W., Milojkovic, J. D., and Ross, L. (1990). The Overconfidence Effect in Social Prediction. *Journal of Personality and Social Psychology,* 58:568–581:Vallone, R. P., Griffin, D., Lin, S., and Ross, L. (1990). Overconfident Prediction of Future Actions and Outcomes by Self and Others. *Journal of Personality and Social Psychology,* 58:582–592.

28 Griffin, D. W., Dunning, D., and Ross, L. (1990). The Role of Construal Processes in Overconfident Predictions about the Self and Others. *Journal of Personality and Social Psychology,* 59:1128–1139; Hirt, E. R., and Markman, K. D. (1995). Multiple Explanations: A Consider-and-alternative Strategy for Debiasing Judgments. *Journal of Personality and Social Psychology,* 69:1069–1086; Hoch, S. J. (1984). Availability and Interference in Predictive Judgment. *Journal of Experimental Psychology: Learning, Memory, and Cognition,* 10:649–662; Hoch, S. J. (1985). Counterfactual Reasoning and Accuracy in Predicting Personal Events. *Journal of Experimental Psychology: Learning, Memory, and Cognition,* 11:719–731; Lord, C. G., Lepper, M. R., and Preston, E. (1984). Considering the Opposite: A Corrective Strategy for Social Judgment. *Journal of Personality and Social Psychology,* 47:1231–1243. Sanbonmatsu, D. M., Kardes, F. R., Posavac, S. S., and Stasney, R. (1997). The Subjective Beliefs Underlying Probability over Estimation. *Journal of Experimental Social Psychology,* 33:276–295.

29 Tversky, A., and Kahneman, D. (1974). Judgment under Uncertainty: Heuristics and Biases. *Science,* 185:1124–1131.

30 Dawes, R. M. (1988). *Rational Choice in an Uncertain World.* San Diego: Harcourt Brace Jovanovich.

31 Dawes, R. M. (1988). *Rational Choice in an Uncertain World.* San Diego: Harcourt Brace Jovanovich. Dawes, R. M. (1994). *House of Cards: Psychology and Psychotherapy Built on Myth.* New York: Free Press.

Glossary

absent-mindedness forgetting as a result of shallow or superficial processing of information during encoding or retrieval (205)

absolute threshold minimum level of stimuli needed for an individual to experience a sensation (144)

accessibility easy to retrieve (205)

accounts *excuses* and *justifications.* The former reduce or deny one's responsibility for inappropriate actions; the latter acknowledge responsibility but rationalize the behavior as appropriate, given the circumstances (239)

acculturation the process when people in one culture adapt to meanings in another culture (268)

acquisition strategies that focus on attracting new customers, while retention strategies focus on keeping current ones (364)

actual public-concept embodies others' true perceptions of a consumer (231)

actual self-concept represents how consumers in fact perceive themselves (230)

actuarial models in some situations, it is possible to use inputs based solely on objective data. Insurance firms base nearly all their decisions on actuarial data (389)

adaptation process of becoming desensitized to sensual stimuli (69)

adaptive unconscious the unconscious mind trained to perform routine mental activities (215)

additive-difference heuristic comparing two brands at a time, one attribute at a time, and subtract the evaluative differences (114)

adjustment function the hedonic (or pleasure/pain) appeals which are useful for changing attitudes (185)

advertising wear-out when an advertisement is overexposed, it loses the ability to attract attention and interest (147)

affect confirmation model the affect or mood that influence how consumers use product attribute information (191)

affect transfer a special case of classical conditioning, occurs when the positive affect (or feelings) created by an unconditioned stimulus becomes associated with a conditioned stimulus (309)

affirmation of the consequent the backwards logic or confusion of the inverse (299)

aligning activities consist of comments that attempt to realign our behavior with norms (239)

anchoring-and-adjustment heuristic making predictions based on a first impression or an initial judgment (or anchor) and then shift (adjust or fine-tune) this judgment upward or downward depending on the implications of the imagined possibilities (112, 377)

appearance management the decisions regarding how consumers control their physical appearances and surroundings (237)

applied research examines variables within a specific context of interest to a marketer (20)

approach a movement towards a desired object or outcome (182)

arousal a state of physical wakefulness or alertness, also influences consumers' attention (151)

arousal triggers the physical changes in the body; nonspecific with respect to emotion (181)

assimilation effect participants who completed the puzzle with expensive brand names rated the ambiguous automobile as expensive (219, 368)

associative interference the interference which is commonly observed in advertising and in which the new associations compete with and block old associations (207)

attention focusing on one or more environmental stimuli while potentially ignoring others (142)

attitude-based choice overall evaluations and general impressions of brands in the consideration set based on a combination of everything (103)

attitude function theory A theory that describes four major types of attitudes such as, knowledge function, value-expressive function, ego-defensive function, and adjustment function. These attitudes help consumers to make decisions, to interact, to feel good about themselves, to enjoy pleasure rather pain more quickly, respectively (185)

attitudes evaluative judgments, or ratings of how good or bad, favorable or unfavorable, or pleasant or unpleasant consumers find a particular person (e.g., salesperson, spokesperson), place (e.g., retail outlet, website, vacation site), thing (e.g., product, package, advertisement), or issue (e.g., political platform, economic theory) (164)

attraction effect a target brand seems more attractive when it is compared to inferior brands and less attractive when compared to superior brands (100)

attribute loyalty consumers who indicate first and second choices with the same attribute rather than with the same brand name (361)

attribute-based choices comparing the specific attributes or features of each brand and selecting the one that performs best on key attributes (103)

attributes the basic characteristics of goods and services (279)

authority principle the principle that uses titles, clothes (such as uniforms), or expensive possessions that convey status to impress and influence others (309)

automatic information processing the mental processes that occur without awareness or intention, but nevertheless influence judgments, feelings, goals, and behaviors (214)

automaticity principle the cornerstone of all influence techniques, where it asserts that people often think mindlessly and as a result, behave automatically, without fully evaluating the consequences of a request (288)

availability heuristic making predictions based on how easily they can retrieve information from memory (110, 375)

avoidance a movement away from an undesired object or outcome (185)

backward conditioning the conditioned stimulus (the advertised brand) is presented after the unconditioned stimulus (e.g., likable music, people, places, or things) (199)

bait-and-switch a special case of the low-ball technique (293)

balance theory the theory that focuses on the degree of consistency among three elements such as *p*—the person, *o*—the other person, and *x*—a stimulus (188)

base rates previous rates of occurrence (387)

basic research looks for general relationships between variables, regardless of the specific situation (19)

Bayes' theorem amount of adjustment depends on the diagnosticity (or relevance) of the information brought to bear after forming the initial opinion (395)

because heuristic processing small requests mindlessly by people (289)

behavioral compliance a situation where someone actually carries out that request (288)

behavioral science applies the scientific method, relying on systematic, rigorous procedures to explain, control, and predict consumer behavior (15)

behavior-based segmentation groups consumers based on their preference for a particular product attribute or benefit, usage occasion, user status, rate of product usage, and loyalty status (46)

beliefs nonevaluative judgments or ratings about product attributes and benefits (161)

benefits the second stage in a means-end chain and embody consumers' perceptions about the outcomes or *consequences* provided by the attributes (279)

biased assimilation When an event is ambiguous (i.e., when many possible interpretations exist), expectations guide interpretations (370)

bipolar adjective scales (165)

blocking the first predictive stimulus blocks or prevents learning for other predictive stimuli encountered later (200)

blogs frequently updated Web journals that can be used to transmit cutting-edge information about products, services, politics, or just about anything (335)

bootstrapping the model helps the decision maker pick himself up by his own ìbootstraps (389)

bounded rationality the idea that consumers can only make rational decisions within the limits of time and cognitive capability (81)

brand anthropomorphism both human form and human traits to non-humans (246)

brand chaos a condition brought on by the proliferation of brands that offer few distinctive attributes or benefits (78)

brand equity the value that a brand accrues based on the goodwill attached to associations with the brand name (359)

brand extension different products with the same brand name (e.g., Cherry Coke) (359)

brand images comprises all the thoughts and feelings consumers have about a particular brand (243)

brand integration occurs when the brand is woven into the thread of the story, becoming part of the plot or context, in a fashion similar to the famous Junior Mint scene in "Seinfeld" (329)

brand interaction occurs when the characters talk about the product or brand or actually handle the product, i.e., they physically interact with it (329)

brand jingles short, catchy tunes—with or without words—that represent a brand or organization (273)

brand laziness a consumer's natural inertial movement toward a product or service based on familiarity and convenience, rather than a fundamental commitment to the brand (66)

brand logos a variety of forms, including colors, shapes, words, and other images (273)

brand loyalty consumers who indicate first and second choices with the same brand name rather than within the same attribute (361)

brand loyalty intrinsic commitment to a brand based on the benefits or values it provides consumers (66)

brand personality the set of human characteristics associated with a brand. Brand personality comprises the human side of a brand's image (243)

brand personification giving non-humans human-like traits (246)

brand positivity effect consumers form unrealistically favorable evaluations of moderately favorable brands when they form singular evaluations, but not when they form comparative evaluations (131)

brand resonance a consumer's intense and actively loyal relationship with a brand (359)

brand variance a consumer's awareness of uncertainty as to a brand's attributes (85)

buzz marketing buzz marketing is a general term, encompassing any campaign designed at generating word-of-mouth (318)

calibration refers to the degree to which confidence matches accuracy (394)

cancellation a game show in which you need to win in stage one in order to advance to stage two, stage one should cancel out, or be ignored, if it is identical for two different gambling games (121)

cannibalization occurs when consumers are brand loyal as opposed to attribute loyal (361)

cannibalization occurs when products offered by the same firm are so similar that they compete among themselves, thus creating a case of *oversegmentation* (37)

causal relationship between two variables means that the variables are correlated and that one variable influences the other, but not vice versa (21)

celebrity endorser an individual who enjoys public recognition and uses this recognition on behalf of a consumer product by appearing in an advertisement or engaging in some other marketing tactic (322)

central route when involvement is high, and when the ability to think about a marketing claim is high, consumers are likely to follow the central route to persuasion by focusing on information most central to or important for forming an accurate attitude (172)

channel length number of intermediaries (e.g., wholesalers, distributors, and retailers) needed to get the product from the manufacturer to the consumer (367)

choice deferral the reluctance to make any decision even though the decision could benefit both parties (126)

classical conditioning a learning theory centered on creating associations between meaningful objects or ideas (199)

closure tendency for a person to perceive an incomplete picture as complete, either consciously or subconsciously (154)

cluster frontier the best possible combination of attributes observed within a cluster, or the ideal combination of attributes.

cluster size the number of brands the consumer places in the cluster (85)

cluster variance the degree to which brands within a single cluster are dissimilar from each other (85)

cognitive capacity ability to pay attention to and think about information is limited (143)

cognitive dissonance theory a theory that suggests consumers shift their attitudes to increase behavior-attitude consistency (189)

cognitive personality variables the personality traits that describe an individual's mental responses to objects (247)

commitment and consistency principle inconsistencies often invite interpretations of personality flaws or, in extreme cases, mental illness (290)

commitment theory the purpose of obtaining an initial commitment is to impart resistance to change (293)

common knowledge effect discussing information and issues already familiar to all present (371)

comparative evaluation comparing two or more products concurrently by the consumers (128)

comparison matrix an interactive decision aid that helps consumers to evaluate options by providing a *Consumer Reports* style brand-by-attribute matrix that makes it easy for consumers to compare options (339)

compatibility principle the principle in which different measurement techniques highlight different aspects of the choice options (128)

compensatory decision making strategy making trade-offs between attributes and this enables a good attribute to compensate for, or at least reduce concerns about, a bad attribute (337)

compensatory process the process which the consumers select a single brand from among the brands in the considered cluster (86)

comprehension ability to interpret and assign meaning to the new information by relating it to knowledge already stored in memory (143)

compromise effect the increased probability of buying a compromise brand, is especially likely to occur when consumers are concerned about making a bad decision (100)

compulsive buying the drive to consume uncontrollably and to buy in order to avoid problems (241)

Concrete information pertains to only one particular object or issue (367)

conditioned response the response evoked the original unconditioned stimulus (199)

conditioned stimulus the other object that paired with the meaningful object used in unconditioned stimulus (199)

confirmation bias occurs when people find it easier to identify and interpret information that supports their beliefs as opposed to information that fails to do so (363)

confusion of the inverse fallacy people tend to confuse $p(H|D)$ with $p(D|H)$ (395)

conjunctive heuristic setting a minimum value for all relevant attributes and select the first brand that meets this value for each attribute (114)

consideration set the group of brands that consumers think about buying when they need to make a purchase (98)

consumer behavior entails all consumer activities associated with the purchase, use, and disposal of goods and services, including the consumer's emotional, mental, and behavioral responses that precede, determine, or follow these activities (8)

consumer generated marketing (advertising) the creation of advertising or other marketing content by the customer (320)

consumer preference heterogeneity the extent to which tastes and preferences differ among consumers (35)

continuity pricing a lower price offered for multiple units of a product or encouraging current users to continue using a brand (366)

continuous reinforcement the reinforcement occurs every time the desired response occurs (202)

contrast effect participants who were primed with inexpensive brands rated the moderately priced target (with a clearly visible brand name) as expensive, while participants who were primed with expensive brands rated the target as inexpensive (219, 368)

conventions the norms that deal less with right or wrong or tradition, but rather with what is more or less "correct" (276)

convergence several independent or unrelated pieces of information converging on the same conclusion provide strong evidence for the conclusion (393)

core benefit proposition relies on a single attribute or benefit that differentiates the brand from competitors' offerings (51)

correlated when a statistically testable and significant relationship exists between two variables (20)

correspondence bias observable behaviors perceived to correspond closely with unobservable dispositions (personality traits, personal opinions) even when the behaviors are actually influenced only by a situation (378)

correspondent inference the assumption that a person's behavior is a reflection of their beliefs and underlying dispositions, rather than the result of some situational variable (323)

credence attributes a special case of experience attributes, are attributes that can be judged or rated only after *extended* use (162)

credence goods goods which is even more difficulty to judge, because quality depends on years of experience and use (337)

crescive norms implicit and learned only through interacting with other members of a culture (275)

cultural categories help organize a society by dividing the world into specific and distinct segments of time, space, nature, and people (262)

cultural principles the *ideas* that help guide the construction of cultural categories (263)

cultural translation the difficulties and problems related to the spirit of the language (270)

cultural values a collective set of beliefs about what is important, useful, and desirable (261)

culturally constituted world the place where all consumer experiences are shaped by the intangible beliefs and values of society (262)

culture the patterns of meaning acquired by members of society expressed in their knowledge, beliefs, art, laws, morals, customs, and habits (261)

customer delight goes a step beyond customer perceived value, suggesting customer benefits that not only meet, but also exceed expectations in unanticipated ways (13)

customer perceived value consumer's overall assessment of the utility of a product based on perceptions of what is received and what is given (13)

customs the overt behaviors that have been passed down from one generation to the next (275)

decision frame management the first step in decision making is to consider how a decision problem should be framed or interpreted (385)

demographic characteristics popular demographic characteristics that include age, gender, income, education, occupation, social class, marital status, household size, family life cycle, and culture or ethnicity (37)

descriptive beliefs are based on direct experience with a product or what we see with our own eyes or hear with our own ears (162)

descriptive norms involve perceptions of which behaviors are common or popular, i.e., what is everyone doing? (303)

determinant attributes characteristics of a product that are most likely to affect the buyer's final choice (69)

devaluation effect when consumers are extremely hungry, they rate non-food products as less desirable (182)

diagnosticity perceived relevance (370)

differentiation advertising emphasizing the differences in quality among brands (366)

diffusion of innovation the rate a new product spreads or is adopted across the marketplace, differs among product categories (354)

diffusion of responsibility the peculiar inaction where people look for cues from other group members. If no one quickly steps forward to act, then the likelihood of anyone acting decreases and a snowball of pluralistic ignorance ensues (301)

dilution effect the judgmental impact of diagnostic information is often diluted by the presence of nondiagnostic information (380)

diminishing sensitivity the outcomes having weaker effects on people as distance from the reference point increases (123, 369)

disclaimers verbal assertions, made in advance, to offset the potential negative effects of a behavior (239)

discrepancy-interruption theory discrepancies or surprises and interruptions or unexpected events that prevent us from pursuing a goal that we are currently trying to achieve also increase arousal and emotion (193)

disjunctive heuristic setting an acceptable value, rather than a minimum value, for all relevant attributes and select the first brand that meets this value on one particular attribute—which is not necessarily the most important attribute (114)

divestment rituals the ritual in which consumers who believe cultural meaning can be transferred from products to people (267)

dominate better choices than alternatives with lower expected values (121)

door-in-the-face technique following up a large, unreasonable request with a smaller, more sensible request usually improves behavioral compliance (294)

drive the tension that influences the urgency with which actions are taken to return to the desired goal-state (104)

drive theory one of the earliest theories of motivation that deals with several basic physiological needs of people, such as food, water, air, etc (182)

dual-process models of attitude formation assume that consumers think a great deal when involvement is high but they don't think much when involvement is low (168)

ego-defensive function the function in which authority and fear appeals are useful for changing attitudes (185)

elaboration likelihood model a high involvement route in which consumers think a lot (i.e., the central route of the elaboration likelihood model and the systematic route of the heuristic/systematic model) (168)

elimination-by-aspects heuristic rejecting all brands that do not have a key feature they want (113)

emotion a person's affect—feelings and moods—plus arousal (180)

enacted norms explicitly and formally prescribe acceptable behaviors (275)

encoding the attention, comprehension, and the transference of information from short-term memory to long-term memory (205)

encoding-specificity principle memory is context dependent (207)

enculturation referred by anthropologists in learning about one's own culture (268)

endowment effect the tendency to view a product as more valuable if one owns it than if one does not own it (125)

enduring involvement a consumer's long-term and continuous interest in a brand or product category (77)

entry strategy developing appropriate strategies for bringing new products to market (354)

epistemic freezing refers to the tendency to maintain closure as long as possible, even if this means being closed-minded or unwilling to consider alternatives (386)

epistemic seizing refers to the tendency to attain closure quickly, even if this means oversimplifying an issue or failing to carefully consider all its ramifications (386)

e-tailers electronic retailers (335)

evaluative-cognitive consistency strong attitudes tend to be highly accessible from memory, maintained with high confidence, held with little uncertainty, and highly correlated with beliefs (164)

even-a-penny technique the legitimization of trivial contributions (a penny, a dollar, one minute of your time) (298)

exchange rituals the ritual that involve one person or a group of people purchasing and presenting consumer products to another (266)

excitation transfer theory the theory that rests upon four key principles of emotion (193)

expectancy disconfirmation model the model in which consumers form expectations about product performance prior to purchasing a brand (92)

expectancy-value models suggest that attitudes toward a product depend on consumers' subjective evaluation of the product's attributes multiplied by the expectancy that the product possesses each attribute (168)

expected utility theory the theory in which the alternatives can be ranked from worst to best (121)

experience attributes are attributes that can be judged or rated only by using a product (162)

experience goods goods determined only by touching, feeling, or using the product (337)

experiments manipulate variables in a controlled setting to determine their relationship to one another (26)

explicit attitudes attitudes that consumers express consciously (222)

explicit memory searching for information stored in memory (217)

extended self the relationship between a consumer's self-concepts and his/her possessions (233)

extensive problem solving a deliberate and systematic effort from consumers, where they generally do not have well-established criteria to evaluate brands or may be unfamiliar with the product category (64)

external search search which involves personal sources (e.g., friends and relatives), market sources such as advertisements and brochures, public sources (e.g., *Consumer Reports*), and product trial, i.e., examining or testing the product on a limited basis (77)

external uncertainty causing consumer's perceived brand universe to differ from the true brand universe (83)

extinction the absence of a reward which decreases the probability of a response (202)

fault tree a decision aid that consists of branches, or general categories, of common problems in a system (391)

figure-and-ground principle from a perception perspective, when a stimulus is salient, it is figural or focal, and everything else fades into the background. This is known as the figure-ground principle of perception (152)

Five-Factor Model the most popular multiple trait theory taxonomies (241)

flattery excessive compliments or praise designed to make someone feel good about her/himself (239)

flow an activity performed by people skillfully with little thought or effort (335)

focus group consists of 6 to 12 current or potential customers run by a facilitator who monitors and guides the group discussion (25)

foot-in-the-door technique making a small request followed by a larger one (290)

forward conditioning the conditioning occurs when the conditioned stimulus is presented before the unconditioned stimulus (199)

frames perspectives that guide the decision making process (121)

Framing effects represent shifts in judgment that occur when managers focus on different possible reference points (368)

frequency of good and bad features heuristic consumers form a simple attitude toward each brand alternative by counting the number of good and bad product features and choosing the brand with the greatest difference between good product features and bad product features (114)

geo-demographic segmentation combines geography and demographic segmentation bases (39)

geographic based segmentation marketers split the market based on physical location of potential customers (37)

goal a state of tension created that energizes a person to reduce or eliminate the need, returning to a preferred state (181)

grooming rituals the ritual allowing consumers to extract cultural meaning from perishable possessions through repeated use (267)

group decision making managers often make decisions in groups or committees because they believe that many heads are better than one (371)

group polarization group discussion often increases the extremity of the preferences shared by many individual group members (371)

grouping tendency to arrange stimuli together to form well-organized units (155)

groupthink excessive conformity as the result of the illusion of group invincibility (371)

hedonic products the products consumers use to enjoy positive experiences (191)

heuristic processing mental shortcuts that help consumers simplify their decision-making tasks (105)

heuristic/systematic model a low involvement route in which consumers think very little (i.e., the peripheral route of the elaboration likelihood model and the heuristic route of the heuristic/systematic model) (168)

heuristics enables consumers to make decisions quickly and easily (105)

heuristics people often use simple heuristics when evaluating the requests of others, sometimes automatically (288)

ideal public-concept represents how consumers would like others to see them (231)

ideal self-concept describes how consumers would like to be (231)

Implicit Association Test a new procedure for measuring sensitive beliefs, including those held without awareness or intention (221)

implicit attitudes more favorable for sneakers endorsed by white spokespersons than for sneakers endorsed by black spokespersons (222)

implicit memory the memory is used as a tool without awareness or intention (218)

impression management the process of creating desirable images of ourselves for others (237)

impulse buying purchases made without prior planning (80)

in-depth interview a one-on-one interview of at least one hour in length, but sometimes considerably longer (25)

individual consumers purchase goods and services to satisfy their own personal needs and wants or to satisfy the need and wants of others (8)

inferential beliefs are beliefs that go beyond the information given (163)

influence or choice heuristics the choice which affects consumers' decisions directly (e.g., lexicographic, additive-difference, conjunctive, disjunctive, frequency of good-bad features) (106)

information integration theory type of expectancy-value model that explains how beliefs are combined to influence attitudes (168)

information search consumers attempting for information to acquire (337)

information search costs acquire information in terms of time, money, or effort (337)

informational beliefs are based on indirect experience or on what other people tell us (162)

ingratiation one of the tactics people use to get others to like them (238)

injunctive norms perceptions of which behaviors are accepted or rejected by society (303)

instrumental product products that consumers use to solve a problem (191)

instrumental values represent preferred modes of behavior. They are actions or "instruments" that provide positive value for consumers (280)

integrative complexity considering a wider range of options and the implications of greater amounts of information pertaining to each option (387)

interactivity providing exactly the type of information about products and services that individual consumers wish to receive (335)

intermediate problem solving involves limited information search and deliberation (63)

internal search the deliberate retrieval of information which is common with low involvement decisions that comprise much of consumers' day-to-day activities (77)

internal uncertainty uncertainty about the consumer him/-herself—cause a consumer's perceived utility function to differ from his/her true utility function: absolute utility error and relative utility error (83)

interpretivism (or *postmodernism*) alternative research approach to behavioral science that relies less on scientific and technological methodology (17)

intrinsic variety seeking consumer seeking variety for the inherent pleasure of change and the positive stimulation it brings (68)

intuition knowing or understanding without purposeful thinking (217)

invalid information information which confounds measures of the target with measures of nontargets (388)

invariance principle preferences should remain the same no matter how preferences are measured or no matter how decision alternatives are described (121)

involvement the personal relevance and importance of an issue or situation (166)

judgments the evaluation of information in the decision making process (161)

just noticeable difference (j.n.d.) amount of incremental change required for a person to detect a difference between two similar stimuli, also called the *differential threshold* (145)

knowledge function the information and facts which are useful for changing attitudes (185)

lexicographic heuristicvcomparing all brands on one *key* attribute, such as price, size, weight, reliability, durability, calories, sugar, etc., and choose the brand that performs the best on that single attribute, while generally ignoring the other attributes (113)

Likert scales also called agree/disagree scales. Marketers ask consumers to indicate how much they agree or disagree with several statements about a product's attributes (165)

liking principle complying with the requests of those whom we like (306)

linear model an equation that contains a list of the most important attributes for evaluating and comparing decision options (389)

List of Values (LOV) the process developed at the University of Michigan Survey Research Center to identify nine consumer value segments and link them to value-related consumer behavior (282)

list technique a list of supporters or donors to a prospect (301)

locus of control the extent to which an individual possesses internal or external reinforcement beliefs (247)

loss aversion the losses have a bigger impact on people, relative to equivalent gains (123, 369)

loved objects a special subset of all possessions that comprise the extended self, play a central role in our knowledge of who we are as people (235)

low-ball technique trying to get an initial commitment, and then changing the deal (292)

loyalty program programs that provide rewards for repeat purchases (366)

majority fallacy the tendency wherein because it is logical to assume that size of the potential market segment is positively correlated to profit, it is often easy for a company to focus exclusively on large average segments, where the majority of customer preferences lie, and neglect smaller less typical segments (36)

malleable self a multifaceted self-concept that includes a *good self, bad self, not-me self, desired self, ideal self, ought-to-be self* (236)

market mavens people who search, accumulate, and share product knowledge with others (78)

market segmentation the process of dividing the large and diverse mass market into subsets of consumers who share common needs, characteristics, or behaviors, and then targeting one or more of those segments with a distinct marketing mix (32)

marketing concept idea that firms should discover and satisfy customer needs and wants in an efficient and profitable manner, while benefiting the long-term interests of society (13)

marketing research is a systematic process of planning, collecting, analyzing, and interpreting data and information relevant to marketing problems and consumer behavior (18)

Maslow's hierarchy of needs the highest level of self-actualization, which is the state of mind of people who feel that they have reached their full potential after their physiological needs, safety and security needs, social needs are met, however, in theory, only few people have reached this ultimate level (182)

memory-based choice consumers' retrieval of brand and information from memory (102)

Miller's rule according to famous Harvard psychologist George Miller (1956), people are able to consider approximately five to nine (seven plus/minus two) units of information at one time (150)

mindset priming effect the cognitive activity performed during the first session tends to be performed again in the second, even if the products considered during the two sessions are completely different (221)

misattribution distortion as a result of confusion (209)

mixed choice the choice where consumers can see some brands but must remember others (102)

MODE model Motivation and Opportunity to deliberate are key DEterminants of the processes that influence consumer choice (104)

mood-as-information model mood is often treated like any other piece of information and is integrated along with other information when consumers form an overall evaluation of a product (191)

moré a custom with strong moral implications (275)

motivation a driving force that moves or incites us to act and is the underlying basis of all behavior (180)

multiple-deescalating-requests technique the technique that involves more than two requests (298)

MUM effect the tendency to keep mum about unpleasant messages (309)

need a fundamental physical or psychological state of felt deprivation (72)

needs desires that arise when a consumer's current state does not match the consumer's preferred state (181)

need for cognition measures an individual's natural tendency to engage in and enjoy effortful cognitive activities (247)

need for cognitive closure describes a consumer's desire for definite knowledge of any kind to reduce confusion or ambiguity (249, 386)

need for humor an individual's tendency to crave, seek out, and enjoy humor, a construct more motivationally driven than sense of humor (248)

negative reinforcement the absence of punishment which increases the probability of a response (202)

non-compensatory decision making strategy not making trade-offs across attributes, and a bad attribute usually leads to the rejection of an alternative (337)

non-compensatory process a simple, although error-prone, way to make a decision in which the person does not consider trade-offs (85)

objective linear models in some situations, it is possible to use inputs based solely on objective data (389)

ongoing search the search involves external search activities independent of solving an immediate purchase problem (77)

operant conditioning the conditioning in which the stimulus follows the response (202)

opinion conformity expressing insincere agreement on important issues (239)

opinion leaders the individuals who, by virtue of birth, beauty, talent, or accomplishment, are held in high esteem and provide cultural meaning to those of lesser standing (264)

opportunities a consumer's ideal and actual states simultaneously move in opposite directions (75)

opportunity costs hidden or unseen costs, including non-monetary costs such as the lost time and pleasure associated with choosing one course of action over another (125)

organic word-of-mouth word-of-mouth that occurs naturally (318)

organizational consumers purchase goods and services in order to produce other goods or services, resell them to other organizations or to individual consumers, and help manage and run their organization (9)

overcorrection occurs when managers overanalyze and over-interpret their decision-making processes (381)

parity products brands that possess functionally equivalent attributes, making one brand a satisfactory substitute for most others (69)

partial reinforcement the reinforcement occurs only some of the times the desired response occurs (202)

part-list cuing the names of just some brands when consumers are trying to recall as many brands as possible (99)

perceived brand universe prohibitively costly to gather complete and fully accurate information about all existing brands and their attributes, what is in a consumer's head is not the true brand universe (83)

perceived product-market patterned organization of brands in a consumer's mind (84)

perceived risk the possibility of negative outcomes where consumers are more likely to demonstrate higher levels of involvement (64)

perceived utility function a consumer believes his/her reaction will be to a brand with certain attributes, differs from his/her true utility function (83)

perception a process of receiving, selecting, and interpreting environmental stimuli involving the five senses (141)

peripheral route when consumers are unable to think about a marketing claim, they focus on peripheral cues or superficial information that makes it easy to form an opinion without much thought (172)

perseverance effect decision makers often continue to perceive a belief as true even when the basis for the belief is disproved (379)

persistence the inability to forget what one wants to forget (210)

personal qualities modes of interpersonal behavior that distinguish people from one another, such as sense of humor or friendliness (229)

personality a set of unique psychological characteristics that influence how a person responds to his or her environment, including cognitive, affective, and behavioral tendencies (240)

personality traits consumers' tendencies to respond in a certain way across similar situations (241)

persuasion heuristics influencing consumers' beliefs and attitudes (105)

phenomenal absolutism erroneous assumption that everyone else perceives the world as we do (142)

place strategy careful planning of channel length, or the number of intermediaries (367)

placebo effect the pricing information influences consumers' expectations, which then influence behavior without awareness and without intention (216)

planning fallacy the overconfident belief that a project will proceed smoothly as planned (387)

positioning the process of communicating with our target market(s) through the use of marketing mix variables—a specific product, price, distribution channel, and promotional appeal—in such a way as to help consumers differentiate a product from competitors and understand how a particular product best satisfies their needs (33)

positive affect simple feelings that have powerful and complex effects on behavior (191)

positive reinforcement presenting of a reward that increases the probability of a response (202)

possession rituals the ritual that occur when consumers discuss, compare, reflect upon, and display their belongings (266)

prediction heuristics used to form likelihood judgments (e.g., representativeness, availability, simulation, and anchoring-and-adjustment) (106)

pre-exposure effect the effect of using unconditioned stimuli that are ineffective because they were previously encountered alone without pairing (200)

preference reversal a reversal that people prefer option A over option B at one point in time but can prefer option B over option A at another point in time (122, 377)

premature cognitive commitment the effects of prior beliefs that were formed on the basis of information that was accepted uncritically with little thought or elaboration (381)

premium pricing pricing the brand at the high end of product category's price range (51)

prepurchase search Once a problem is recognized, consumers often gather information to inform their purchasedecisions if a problem is recognized (77)

price bundling the process used by some firms to aggregate losses (126)

price-quality heuristic belief of the consumers that if the price increases, quality also increases (131)

primary data new data collected specifically for the research purpose at hand (22)

priming effect a strong association that leads consumers to think about a brand name, like McDonald's and they start thinking about associations to the brand (207)

proactive interference the information learned earlier blocks memory for information learned later (207)

problem solving the type of decision combines high involvement with high levels of information processing (69)

procedural priming effects the effect that occurs when situations are linked to cognitive or motor processes via "if X, then Y" linkages, where X refers to a specific situation and Y refers to a cognitive or behavioral activity (220)

product placement the insertion of branded goods and services within the content of popular media, including television, movies, video games, books, and music (326)

projective techniques are an unstructured, indirect form of questioning that encourages respondents to project their underlying beliefs, attitudes, feelings, and motivations in an apparently unrelated or ambiguous scenario (26)

pseudodiagnosticity the appearance or illusion of diagnosticity (370)

psychographics the measurement of lifestyle, often combined with measures of attitudes, beliefs, and personalities (41)

punishment the negative reinforcement (202)

qualitative research methods descriptive, non-empirical data are collected that describe an individual consumer's subjective experience with the product or service (17)

quantitative research methods methods that involve the collection of empirical data on which sophisticated statistical analyses can be preformed and generalization can be made (15)

reciprocity principle someone does you a favor, you feel obligated to return it in kind (293)

recommendation agent an interactive decision aid that helps consumers to eliminate options by using information about their personal preferences or about their prior purchase histories (339)

redundancy several correlated pieces of information suggesting the same conclusion provide relatively weak support for the conclusion (393)

reference dependence prospect theory that suggests, all outcomes are evaluated with respect to a neutral reference point, and that preferences change as reference points change (123)

regulatory focus theory consumers regulate or control their behavior by using either a promotion focus or a prevention focus (185)

relationship marketing building stronger relationships with consumers by using information technology and improved business processes (343)

repositioning attempts to change the way consumers perceive a brand, either their own brand or a competitor's (52)

representativeness heuristic predictions based on perceived similarities between a specific target and a general category (108, 373)

retention strategies strategy that increases consumption among current brand users or among multi-brand users (364)

retrieval the transference of information from long-term memory to short-term memory (205)

retroactive interference the information learned later blocks memory for information learned earlier (207)

return potential model the model that describes norms on two dimensions. The *behavioral dimension* specifies the amount of behavior regulated by the norm, and the *evaluation dimension* shows the cultural response to that behavior (276)

risk aversion the choice problem in terms of positive outcomes, such as lives saved or money gained, people typically prefer the sure thing (122, 369)

risk seeking a choice in terms of negative outcomes, such as deaths or money lost, people typically prefer the risky alternative (122, 369)

risky decision making decision making under uncertainty (119)

Rokeach Value Survey (VALS) the study that researchers have begun to use value models in consumer behavior studies since instrumental and terminal values can help predict consumer attitudes and behaviors towards brands (281)

role identities the numerous *positions* that people occupy in society such as student, friend, son or daughter, and consumer (229)

routine choice carried out automatically, with little conscious effort. As such, it involves no information search or deliberation (63)

sales-cost trade-off this trade-off recognizes that, as market segmentation increases, sales increase because a firm's offerings align more closely to consumers' preferences (36)

Salient information sticks out in one particular setting, but not in all possible settings (367)

salient stimuli draw consumers' attention involuntarily (152)

scarcity principle people often want what they cannot have (299)

search attributes are attributes that can be judged or rated simply by examining a product without necessarily buying it (162)

search costs searching information in online environments than in offline environments, are lower in online environments (339)

search goods obtaining information and to evaluate the quality of goods (337)

secondary data data that already exist and is readily accessible (22)

selective hypothesis testing focusing on only one possibility and ignoring other possibilities (370)

selective thinking interpretation of ambiguous information as supportive and to integrate information so a preferred brand is cast in a favorable light (129)

self-concept one's awareness and perceptions about him/herself (278)

self-concept the beliefs and attitudes we hold about ourselves and it is complicated and multidimensional (229)

self-conceptions any one of these self-concept that includes a *good self, bad self, not-me self, desired self, ideal self, ought-to-be self* (236)

self-determination theory when intrinsic motivation is high, the autonomy, belongingness, and competence (the ABCs of self-determination) are high (184)

self-esteem the overall evaluative component of a person's self-concept (230)

self-evaluations describe idiosyncratic parts of the self—concept that are not so clear-cut (229)

self-monitoring the extent to which consumers use situational cues to guide their social behavior (236)

self-perception theory complying with a small request leads people to label themselves as helpful, good citizens or as reasonable people (291)

self-presentation involves either *self-enhancement* or *self-deprecation* (238)

self-schemas the cognitive structures that help us make sense of who we are (232)

semantic differential scale beliefs about attributes and overall attitudes can be measured on these scales, also called bipolar adjective scales (165)

sensation body's first and immediate response to a stimulus (142)

shaping the reinforcement of successive approximations of the desired response (202)

short-term memory part of memory where small bits of information are stored for short periods of time (150)

simulation heuristic making predictions based on how easily an event or a sequence of events can be imagined or visualized (112, 375)

singular evaluation a process in which consumers often evaluate products one at a time (128)

situational involvement a consumer's relatively temporary and context-dependent interest in a product or category (77)

social validation principle the perceived validity (or correctness) of an idea increases as the number of people supporting the idea increases (301)

sponsorship and branded entertainment the most intensive form of marriage between content and brand. In this type of placement, the brand is the sole sponsor of the content, has extensive editorial control of the content, and the editorial content or style typically matches closely the targeted audience of the brand (329)

stealth marketing a buzz marketing campaign that specifically relies on spreading word-of-mouth in a covert or clandestine manner (318)

stimulus-based choice the choice where consumers can directly and physically observe all relevant brands in the consideration set and their brand attributes (102)

subcultures smaller groups of a larger culture that share some cultural values with society overall and yet demonstrate unique cultural values and patterns of behavior within the individual subgroup (261)

subjective expected utility theory suggests that preferences are stable and that people should always choose the gamble with the maximum expected utility (377)

subjective linear model all inputs (evaluations and importance weights) are subjective judgments provided by the director or a committee (389)

subliminal advertising messages that are processed below the threshold of consciousness (148)

subliminal perception unconscious awareness of a stimulus (148)

sunk cost effect the effect resulting from insensitivity to opportunity costs because as the amount of time or money invested in a product or a service increases, people are more reluctant to give up the product or service (125)

survey a set of structured questions to which a person is asked to respond (24)

systematic processing the process in which consumers think carefully about decisions, using all relevant information and considering all implications (105)

target market simply the segment(s) toward which a firm's marketing efforts are directed (32)

that's-not-all technique the technique starts high and builds in a downward fashion, i.e., the initial deal is changed into an even better deal *before* the consumer has an opportunity to reject the first offer (296)

theory of cognitive itch properties of music may be analogous to biochemical agents, such as histamines, which cause an itch on the skin (273)

theory of lay epistemology the formation and use of everyday knowledge, suggests that individuals differ in the degree to which they make the important trade-off between speed and accuracy (249, 386)

theory of reasoned action one specific type of expectancy-value model that explains how beliefs are combined to influence attitudes and how social norms or rules and attitudes influence behavior (168)

thin-slice inferences the particularly useful skill that people have learned automatically (217)

traits tendencies to behave a certain way across similar situations (229)

transience forgetting over time (205)

transitive if a consumer prefers A over B, and B over C, then she should prefer A over C (121)

trial pricing a large price discount on a single unit of a particular brand (366)

true brand universe the set of all brands that exist along with measures of each of their attributes (83)

true utility function the *actual* satisfaction s/he will obtain from consuming a brand, i.e., another objective reality (83)

truth effect as familiarity increases, a brand name seems more famous, liking for the brand increases, judgments about the brand are held with greater confidence, and product claims seem more likely to be true (222)

uncertainty-reduction process the consumer decision process, given incomplete information (82)

unconditioned response a consumer's automatic or unlearned response to a stimulus (199)

unconditioned stimulus the meaningful object that helps to learn the results in Pavlovian conditioning (199)

unreliable information varies because of poor measurement, even when the target does not change (388)

valuation effect an effect produced by consumers when they are extremely hungry as they rate food products more desirable (182)

value-expressive function the image appeals which are useful for changing attitudes (185)

variety seeking the desire to choose new alternatives over more familiar ones (67)

verbal compliance a situation where someone says "yes" to a specific request (288)

viral marketing usually involves the Internet to facilitate the spread of word-of-mouth and spark buzz (318)

visual product placement placing the brand on screen within the setting or background of a program (329)

vivid information always stands out regardless of the context or background in which it is presented (367)

vivid stimuli like salient stimuli, draw attention automatically and involuntarily (155)

want-got gap a *discrepancy* exists between what the consumer wants the situation to be and what the situation really is (71)

wants *need satisfiers* that are shaped by a consumer's personality, experiences, and culture—including marketing (74)

Weber's law the greater or stronger the initial stimulus was, the greater was the amount of change required for it to be noticed (145)

word-of-mouth marketing the execution of marketing tactics specially designed to generate positive word-of-mouth marketing messages and create a virus-like exponential spread of those messages throughout the population of interest (318)

word-of-mouth the act of one consumer talking to another about a brand, and it can happen face-to-face and indirectly via phone, mail, or the Internet (317)

Young & Rubicam Brand Asset Valuator set of scales to measure differentiation, relevance, esteem, and knowledge (359)

Zanna and Rempel's a theory suggesting that attitudes can be based on cognition (beliefs), affect (feelings, moods, and emotions), or behavior (164)

Name Index

Subject Index

Product/Company Index

DIGITAL BUSINESS AND E-COMMERCE MANAGEMENT